Selbstbezogene Kognitionen, sprachliche Kompetenzen
und Professionalisierung von Lehrkräften

Prof. Dr. Jens Möller

Jan Retelsdorf, Friederike Zimmermann,
Anna Südkamp und Olaf Köller (Hrsg.)

Im Blickpunkt pädagogisch-psychologischer Forschung

Selbstbezogene Kognitionen, sprachliche Kompetenzen und Professionalisierung von Lehrkräften

FESTSCHRIFT FÜR JENS MÖLLER

Waxmann 2017
Münster · New York

Bibliografische Informationen der Deutschen Nationalbibliothek
Die Deutsche Nationalbibliothek verzeichnet diese Publikation in der Deutschen Nationalbibliografie; detaillierte bibliografische Daten sind im Internet über http://dnb.dnb.de abrufbar.

Print-ISBN 978-3-8309-3680-0

Steinfurter Straße 555, 48159 Münster

www.waxmann.com
info@waxmann.com

Umschlaggestaltung: Karin Vierk

Satz: Sonja Taut, Karin Vierk
(IPN · Leibniz Institut für die Pädagogik der Naturwissenschaften und Mathematik)

Druck: Hubert & Co., Göttingen
Gedruckt auf alterungsbeständigem Papier, säurefrei gemäß ISO 9706

FSC www.fsc.org MIX Papier aus verantwortungsvollen Quellen FSC® C016439

Printed in Germany

Inhalt

Sprachliche Kompetenzen

Vorwort

Das vorliegende Buch haben wir anlässlich des 60. Geburtstags von Jens Möller am 10. November 2017 zusammengestellt. Daher möchten wir mit einigen Anmerkungen zu seiner Person beginnen.

Jens Möller begann seine akademische Laufbahn 1978 mit dem Studium der Psychologie an der Christian-Albrechts-Universität zu Kiel (CAU). Im Anschluss war er ab 1986 in verschiedenen Funktionen eben dort am Institut für Psychologie tätig. In dieser Zeit wurde er 1991 mit einer Arbeit zum Thema „Attributionen in Massenmedien: Zum Einfluss nationaler Gruppenzugehörigkeit, Gruppengröße und Geschlecht auf spontane Ursachenzuschreibungen" promoviert, bevor er sich 1996 habilitierte. Die Habilitationsschrift trug den Titel „Auslösende Bedingungen leistungsbezogener Attributionen. Paradigma – Forschungsstand – empirische Studien." Im Jahr 1999 folgte er einem Ruf der Universität Bielefeld, wo er bis 2003 eine Professur für Psychologie in der Arbeitseinheit Lernen und Kognition inne hatte. Von dort kehrte er nach Kiel zurück, wo er seit 2003 Leiter der Arbeitseinheit Psychologie für Pädagogen ist. Seine Professur war bis 2016 am Institut für Psychologie verortet. Seit Januar 2017 befindet sich seine Arbeitseinheit an dem von Jens Möller mitgegründeten Institut für Pädagogisch-Psychologische Lehr- und Lernforschung. Zu den Meilensteinen seiner akademischen Tätigkeiten gehören seine zweijährige Funktion als Sprecher der Fachgruppe Pädagogische Psychologie in der Deutschen Gesellschaft für Psychologie (DGPs) und der Vorsitz der DGPs-Kommission Psychologie in den Lehramtsstudiengängen (2006 bis 2010). Zudem war er für drei Jahre bis 2010 geschäftsführender Herausgeber der Zeitschrift für Pädagogische Psychologie und Mitglied im Editorial Board renommierter Fachzeitschriften wie dem Journal of Educational Psychology (2007 bis 2009) oder dem Review of Educational Research (2014 bis 2016). Schließlich ist er seit 2012 Mitglied des Fachkollegiums Psychologie der Deutschen Forschungsgemeinschaft und seit 2014 externer Gutachter des Senatsausschusses Wettbewerb der Leibniz-Gemeinschaft.

Neben diesen Tätigkeiten liegt Jens Möller die Förderung junger Wissenschaftlerinnen und Wissenschaftler besonders am Herzen. So bietet er seinen Mitarbeiterinnen und Mitarbeitern nicht nur den notwendigen Raum für die eigenständige Entwicklung von Forschungsideen, sondern steht ihnen auch mit seiner fachlichen Expertise zur Seite und hat bei Fragen rund um die Wissenschaft und manchmal auch darüber hinaus eine offene Tür und ein offenes Ohr. Auch Nachwuchswissenschaftlerinnen und Nachwuchswissenschaftler außerhalb seiner Abteilung profitieren von seinem Fachwissen, etwa auf Konferenzen, in Workshops oder durch Mentorenschaften. Nicht nur der Nachwuchs, auch fortgeschrittene Wissenschaftlerinnen und Wissenschaftler national wie international kooperieren gern und häufig auch über die Grenzen verschiedener Disziplinen hinweg mit Jens Möller. Schließlich ist es ihm neben seinem Engagement in der Forschung auch ein Anliegen, dass die Erkenntnisse pädagogisch-psychologischer Forschung zur Anwendung kommen. Hier sind seine Kooperationen mit dem Institut für Qualitätsentwicklung an Schulen Schleswig-Holstein und sein nachhaltiges Interesse an der Ausbildung künftiger Lehrerinnen und Lehrer hervorzuheben. Beispielhaft für beides seien der Master-Weiterbildungsstudiengang „Schulmanagement und Qualitätsentwicklung", den er mitgegründet hat und zu dessen Leitungsteam er gehört, sowie seine langjährige Beteiligung an der schleswig-holsteinischen Sommeruniversität für Lehrkräfte genannt.

In seiner Forschung widmete und widmet Jens Möller sich einer breiten Palette an Themen, die sich in zahlreichen qualitativ hochwertigen Publikationen sowie der Einwerbung von Fördergeldern renommierter Drittmittelgeber niederschlägt (z. B. Deutsche Forschungsgemeinschaft, Bundesministerium für Bildung und Forschung, Stiftung Mercator). Für die vorliegende Festschrift haben wir aus dieser Vielfalt drei inhaltliche Bereiche herausgegriffen, die unserer Meinung nach die aktuelle Forschung von Jens Möller gut repräsentieren: Selbstbezogene Kognitionen, sprachliche Kompetenzen und die Professionalisierung von Lehrkräften. Zu jedem dieser Forschungsfelder haben wir Arbeiten aktueller und früherer Weggefährtinnen und Weggefährten von Jens Möller zusammengetragen. Manchen von ihnen hat er als studentischen Mitarbeiterinnen und Mitarbeitern oder in der Promotionszeit die Tür zur Wissenschaft geöffnet, andere hat er kollegial begleitet. Jens Möllers überaus freundliche und konstruktiv-unterstützende Art hat sich auch bei der Erstellung dieser Festschrift widergespiegelt. So haben alle Autorinnen und Autoren ihre Beteiligung ohne großes Zögern zugesagt und die Fertigstellung ihrer Beiträge mit hohem Engagement verfolgt. Auch dies zeigt die hohe Wertschätzung, die Jens Möller von „seinem" wissenschaftlichen Nachwuchs und seinen Kolleginnen und Kollegen entgegengebracht wird.

Wir freuen uns, dass es gelungen ist, sowohl die inhaltliche als auch die methodische Vielfalt widerzuspiegeln, die sich in den Arbeiten von Jens Möller zeigt. So besteht dieser Band aus theoretischen bzw. Überblicksbeiträgen, Studien mit querschnittlichen wie auch prospektiven Designs sowie aus experimentellen Arbeiten, die Jens Möller stets besonders wichtig sind. Im Forschungsfeld zu selbstbezogenen Kognitionen geht es zunächst um das Internal/External-Frame-of-Reference-Modell (I/E-Modell) sowie um dimensionale Vergleiche. Eröffnet wird dieser Teil durch eine Überblicksarbeit zur Theorie Dimensionaler Vergleiche, die von Jens Möller entscheidend mitgestaltet wurde (Marsh, Dicke, Seaton, Parker, Guo & Craven). Es folgen zwei empirische Originalarbeiten, die sich mit der Moderation der Vergleichsprozesse im I/E Modell (Zimmermann, Becherer & O. Köller) sowie Determinanten und Konsequenzen akademischer Selbstkonzepte (Pohlmann & Streblow) befassen. Der nachfolgende Beitrag untersucht Fragen zur unterschiedlichen Wichtigkeit sozialer, temporaler und dimensionaler Vergleiche bei allgemeinen und akademischen Selbstbeschreibungen (Helm, Müller-Kalthoff & Nagy). Schließlich wird in zwei theoretischen Beiträgen die Anwendung der Theorie Dimensionaler Vergleiche auf Agency und Communion als fundamentale Dimensionen sozialer Urteilsbildung erörtert (Abele) und ein Plädoyer für den stärkeren Einbezug des sozialen Selbst in die Forschung zu Zusammenhängen von Selbst und lernrelevanten Outcomes gehalten (Hannover & Zander). Ergänzt werden die Artikel zu diesem Forschungsfeld durch einen Beitrag zu den Auswirkungen von Self-Affirmation auf Effekte von Stereotype Threat (M. Köller & Nagy). Der zweite Teil bündelt Forschungsarbeiten zu sprachlichen Kompetenzen. Dieser Bereich wird durch zwei Beiträge zu Lesefähigkeit und Lesemotivation eröffnet. Zunächst wird die Relevanz elterlichen Vorlesens für die Lesemotivation und das Leseverstehen im Grundschulalter untersucht (Stutz & Schiefele). Der zweite Beitrag befasst sich mit indirekten Effekten des Leseselbstkonzepts über Lesegewohnheiten auf die Leseleistung von Schülerinnen und Schülern (Retelsdorf & Schmidt). Es folgen drei Artikel zum Fremdsprachenerwerb im Fach Englisch. Zunächst steht der Vergleich von Rechtsschreibstrategien immersiv und monolingual unterrichteter Kinder im Vordergrund (Fleckenstein, Reble & Hohenstein), der ein Beitrag zur Beschreibung des Englischunterrichts aus Perspektive der Schülerinnen und Schüler in der gymnasialen Oberstufe folgt (Keller, Krüger, Leucht & O. Köller). Abschließend wird untersucht inwieweit die Ziele gymnasialen Fremdsprachenlernens von Abiturientinnen und Abiturienten erreicht werden (O. Köller, Leucht, Fleckenstein & Baumert). Im dritten und letzten Teil dieses Buchs sind Beiträge zur Professionalisierung von Lehrkräften versammelt. Dieser Abschnitt wird durch einen Beitrag zur Frage nach Typen von Lehramtsstudierenden hinsichtlich ihrer Studienwahlmotivation eröffnet (Streblow & Pohlmann). Als zweites folgt ein Artikel, in dem unterschiedliche Ausprägungen von Eigenstereotypen von Lehramtsstudierenden und deren Erleben von Stereotype Threat untersucht werden (Ihme). Der dritte Artikel untersucht Zusammenhänge von Urteilsgenauigkeit und Urteilssicherheit ebenfalls im Lehramtsstudium (Kaiser & Südkamp). Es folgt ein Beitrag zur Vorhersage des Wohlbefindens von Lehrkräften durch globale Persönlichkeitseigenschaften (Roloff, Klusmann, Lüdtke & Trautwein) und schließlich ein Artikel, der sich mit dem Zusammenhang des Wissens von Lehrkräften und dem von Schülerinnen und Schülern befasst (Kleickmann, Steffensky & Wendt).

Unser Dank gilt allen Autorinnen und Autoren für die zumeist pünktliche Lieferung der Beiträge, die durchweg unkomplizierte Zusammenarbeit und ihre Diskretion bei der Zusammenstellung dieses Jubiläumsbandes. Zudem danken wir den anonymen Gutachterinnen und Gutachtern, die in einem doppelt-blinden Begutachtungsverfahren zur Qualität der Texte beigetragen haben (siehe Verzeichnis der Gutachterinnen und Gutachter). Für die Unterstützung bei der Gestaltung und dem Satz des Buchs danken wir Karin Vierk und Sonja Taut vom Leibniz-Institut für die Pädagogik der Naturwissenschaften und Mathematik in Kiel (IPN) sowie Annika Siegenthaler ebenfalls vom IPN und Ole Gries von der CAU für die Unterstützung beim Korrekturlesen der Beiträge. Schließlich danken wir dem Waxmann Verlag in Münster und hier insbesondere Beate Plugge für die Unterstützung beim Lektorat und bei der finalen Druckabwicklung.

Dortmund und Kiel im Juli 2017,

Jan Retelsdorf, Friederike Zimmermann, Anna Südkamp und Olaf Köller

Dimensional Comparison Theory: Something Old, Something New, Something Borrowed, Something Blue

HERBERT W. MARSH, THERESA DICKE, MARJORIE SEATON, PHILIP D. PARKER, JIESI GUO, AND RHONDA CRAVEN

ABSTRACT: Every once in a while two mindsets with common interests, mutual respect, and dedication meet, engage in a partnership, and commit to something big. The reader might now be inclined to think of a romantic relationship, might imagine a wedding with cake, or even happy children, as a result of such an encounter. And indeed, in this chapter we are referring to something comparable; at least in part (and without a cake). This chapter deals with the development of Dimensional Comparison Theory (DCT), an extension of the I/E model that posits that self-evaluations are based on dimensional comparisons (e.g., accomplishments in different domains), as a result of continuing research collaboration by Möller and Marsh (2013). Here we illustrate new predictions, theoretical insights, and methodology associated with the I/E model and its extension into DCT considering multiple academic domains (e.g., foreign language, history, biology, and math), showing significant contrast effects for far comparisons and significantly smaller contrast or assimilation effects for near domains. Viewing DCT, as the result of a successful marriage (or partnership) of research we encourage the reader to find something old, something new, something borrowed, and something blue within this chapter.

Keywords: Dimensional Comparison Theory, self-concept, academic achievement, Frame-of-Reference, assimilation and contrast

Dimensional Comparison Theory – Drum forsche, wer sich wissenschaftlich bindet

ZUSAMMENFASSUNG: Wenn zwei Gesinnungen mit gemeinsamen Interessen, gegenseitigem Respekt und Hingabe aufeinander treffen, kommt es vor, dass diese sich dazu entschließen, gemeinsam etwas Großes zu beginnen. Der Leser mag nun an eine romantische Beziehung denken, sich Hochzeitstorte und vielleicht sogar Kinder als Ergebnis einer solchen Begegnung vorstellen. Und in der Tat geht es in diesem Kapitel um etwas Vergleichbares, zumindest beinahe (und ohne Kuchen). Es geht um die Entwicklung der Dimensional Comparison Theorie (DCT) – eine Erweiterung des I/E-Models, welches besagt, dass Bewertungen des Selbst auf dimensionalen Vergleichen beruhen (z.B. Leistung in verschiedenen Domänen) – als Ergebnis der andauernden Zusammenarbeit von Möller und Marsh (2013). Es werden neue theoretische und methodische Erkenntnisse bezüglich DCT, welche verschiedene akademische Domänen (z.B. Fremdsprachen, Geschichte, und Physik) berücksichtigt, vorgestellt. Es zeigen sich signifikante Kontrasteffekte für weiter entfernte Domänen, aber signifikant kleinere Kontrasteffekte oder sogar Assimilationseffekte für ähnliche Domänen. Da wir DCT als Ergebnis einer erfolgreichen Forschungsehe (oder -partnerschaft) betrachten, wird der Leser dazu eingeladen, in diesem Kapitel etwas Altes, Neues, Gebrauchtes sowie Blaues zu finden.

Schlüsselwörter: Dimensional Comparison Theory, Selbstkonzept, Akademische Leistung, Bezugsrahmen, Assimilation und Kontraste

Introduction

Self-concept, the perception of oneself (Marsh, 2007), is one of the *old*est constructs in psychology and the social sciences more generally (Marsh, Lüdtke et al., 2015; Möller, Pohlmann, Köller, & Marsh, 2009). It is a critical component in the positive psychology revolution, which focusses on how healthy, normal, and exceptional individuals can get the most from life (e.g., Marsh, 2007; Marsh & Craven, 2006; Seligman & Csikszentmihalyi, 2000). Thus, self-concept plays a major role in enabling humans to thrive and ensure wellbeing as it is not only an important outcome itself (i.e. positive self-concept), but also a mediator for many other important and desirable psychological and behavioral outcomes (Marsh, 2007). In this chapter we begin with an overview of self-concept research underpinning and supporting the Internal/External Frame of Reference (I/E) model and its extension generalization to Dimensional Comparison Theory (DCT). We then review the relation of DCT to other major self-concept theories (e.g., fish little pond effect, BFLPE; reciprocal effects model, REM) and discussion of policy and practical implications.

In research on self-concept it is important to take into account the multidimesional hierarchical structure of self-concept, as proposed by Shavelson, Hubner, and Stanton (1976). According to Shavelson et al. (1976), self-concept consists of an overarching global factor, which can then be broken down into academic self-concept (ASC) and non-academic self-concepts such as physical, emotional, or social self-concept. These higher order self-concept factors can then, in turn, be broken down into lower level self-concept factors. In particular, ASC consists of self-concept factors of various academic sub-domains, such as math, English (or other languages), and science.

However, Marsh and Shavelson (1985) subsequently revised the hierarchical structure of the ASC. They found that despite the routinely observed high correlations between math and verbal achievements (typically .5 to .8, see Marsh, 2007), the math and verbal self-concept factors were nearly uncorrelated. Hence, in the revised model Marsh & Shavelson proposed two higher order ASCs: verbal academic self-concept (VSC) and math academic self-concept (MSC). These factors could then be considered opposite poles on a continuum of numerous subject-specific ASCs ordered along this line (see Figure 1). Within this continuum, based on the aforementioned correlations, subjects such as physics and math are considered to be close to the math domain, while native and foreign languages are closer to the verbal domain. These interesting findings have provoked the question as to why ASCs should show a very much different pattern than academic achievement itself. The I/E model was developed to explain these near-zero correlations (Marsh, 1986, 1990a) and is the theoretical base of Dimensional Comparison Theory (DCT).

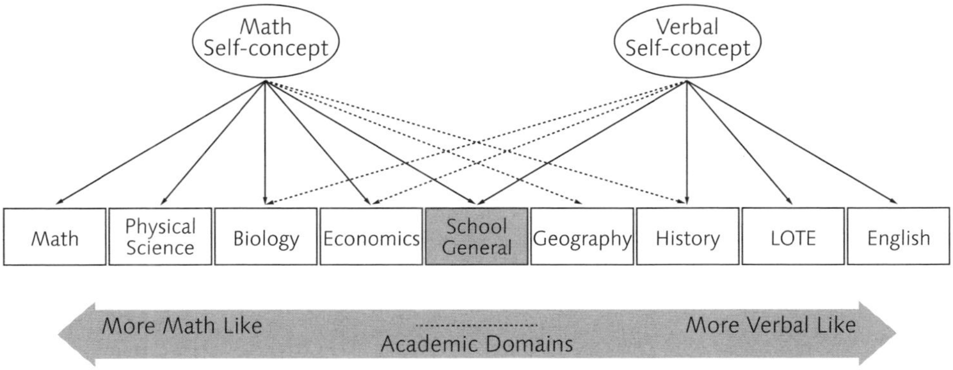

Figure 1. The Marsh/Shavelson revised academic self-concept model, which includes a wider variety of specific academic facets. LOTE: Language other than English (in reference to English-speaking students).

1 Something Old: The Internal/External Frame of Reference (I/E) Model

According to the I/E model many people think of themselves as mostly math or mostly verbal persons, even though individuals who are good at one also tend to be good at the other (see Marsh, 1986, 1990a). The I/E model posits that ASC in a particular school subject is jointly formed in relation to two different frames of reference: (1) an external (social comparison) reference in which students compare their self-perceived performances in a particular school subject with the perceived performances of other students in the same school subject; and (2) an internal (dimensional, ipsative comparison) reference in which students compare their own performances in the particular school subject with their own performances in other school subjects. Hence, students may have a favorable MSC if math is their best subject, even if they are not particularly good at math relative to other students. Methodologically speaking, the model on the one hand postulates positive regression effects of achievement on ASC within each domain (good verbal skills lead to higher VSC and good math skills lead to higher MSC; see Figure 2) based on external comparison processes (Marsh, Möller et al., 2015). Due to internal comparison processes, on the other hand, the model also postulates negative marginal effects of achievement on ASCs across domains (good math skills lead to lower VSCs once the positive effects of good verbal skills are controlled for, and better verbal skills lead to lower MSCs once the positive effects of good math skills are controlled for; see Figure 2). Thus, two students with the same ability in English will report different VSCs depending on their achievement in math i.e., the student with the better math skills will report lower VSC (Marsh, 1990a).

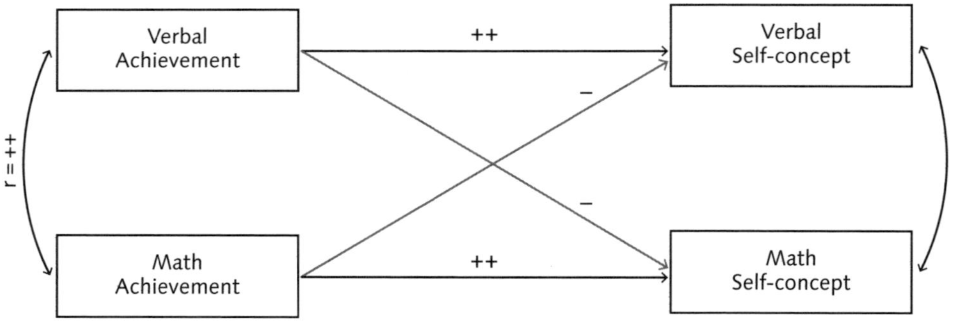

Figure 2. The 'Classic' Internal/External Frame of Reference (I/E) Model. According to predictions from the I/E model, the horizontal paths from achievement to self-concept in the matching domains (content area) are predicted to be substantial and positive (++), whereas the cross paths from achievement in one domain area to self-concept in a non-matching domain (in grey) are predicted to be negative (–).

1.1 Empirical research on the I/E model

A growing body of research, using various approaches, has shown consistent support for the I/E model assumptions (Marsh, 1986, 1990a, 2007; Möller & Marsh, 2013). For example, cross-cultural comparisons have validated the model in more than 35 countries including many non-English speaking Western, Asian, and Islamic countries (Marsh, Abduljabbar et al., 2015; Marsh & Hau, 2004). Indeed, Marsh and Hau (2004; also see Marsh, Hau, Artelt, Baumert, & Peschar, 2006) demonstrated that support for the predictions of the I/E model generalized over large, nationally representative samples of 15-year-olds from each of 26 countries.

Longitudinally, Marsh, Kong, and Hau (2001) replicated the model over a five year period in line with similar findings by Marsh and Köller (2004; see also Möller, Retelsdorf, Köller, & Marsh, 2011). Other studies have found the I/E model to be useful for predicting academic choices over a long-term (Nagy, Trautwein, Baumert, Köller, & Garrett, 2006; Parker, Marsh, Ciarrochi, Marshall, & Abduljabbar, 2014; Parker et al., 2012). For example, math achievement and MSC positively predicted choosing math related advanced courses and entry into university majors in math and the physical sciences, but negatively predicted verbal related advanced courses and entry into university majors of the humanities (Parker et al., 2012).

The model has also been validated using introspective diary studies and experimental designs. For example, in two diary studies, Möller and Husemann (2006) confirmed that students spontaneously carry out dimensional comparisons in everyday life, with contrast effects from one domain to self-evaluations and emotions in the other. Experimentally, Möller and Köller (2001) and Pohlmann and Möller (2006, 2009) showed how manipulated feedback on either verbal or math achievement in one subject area had an inverse effect on ASC in a different area.

Meta-analyses have also provided support for the model. Möller, Pohlmann et al. (2009) conducted a meta-analysis of 69 datasets (n = 125,308). They only included studies that simultaneously evaluated the effects of math and verbal achievements on MSC and VSC. Results revealed a high correlation of math and verbal achievements (.67), but nearly uncorrelated MSCs and VSCs (.10) across all studies. Path coefficients from achievement to ASC in the matching domains were positive (.61 for math, .49 for verbal) but negative from math achievement to VSC (–.21) and verbal achievement to MSC (–.27). Support for the I/E predictions generalized across age group, gender, and country.

1.2 Generalized I/E Model

While the origins of the I/E model are based on the relation between academic achievement and ASC, researchers have found that it can be extended to other variables as well (see Möller, Müller-Kalthoff, Helm, Nagy, & Marsh, 2016). Arens and Möller (2016) found evidence of I/E-like effects for the relation of students' achievement (grades) and students' perceptions of the learning environment (student-teacher relations and instructional quality). Based on the TIMSS (2007) data Marsh, Abduljabbar et al. (2015) showed support for I/E predictions generalized to intrinsic motivation. Goetz, Frenzel, Hall, and Pekrun (2008) also found support for the I/E model in relation to both ASC and enjoyment but showed that achievement/enjoyment relations were mediated by ASC. This finding is in line with Schurtz, Pfost, Nagengast, and Artelt (2014) who demonstrated the same pattern of results for subject interest. Utilizing expectancy/value theory (EVT; Guo, Marsh, Parker, Morin, & Dicke, 2017, Wigfield & Eccles, 2002), Dietrich, Dicke, Kracke, and Noack (2015) examined the effects of teacher support on students' intrinsic value and effort with regard to math and German language. They demonstrated that teacher support in math was negatively related to students' intrinsic value and effort in German and vice versa.

The model has also been extended by examining ASC as perceived by others. Although previous reviews (e.g., Marsh et al., 2014; Marsh, Möller et al., 2015) suggested that the I/E model may not apply to perceptions by others, recent research by van Zanden et al. (2017) suggests that this conclusion might be premature. Van Zanden et al. assessed student ASCs and achievements in the math and verbal domains achievements, but also assessed matching parent perceptions of the student's ASC. Van Zanden et al. showed that support for the I/E model based on student responses generalized to parents' perceptions of their child's ASCs.

2 Something New, Something Borrowed: Assimilation, Contrast and Dimensional Comparison Theory

So far we have reviewed the I/E model. But what is *new* about DCT and why is it so important? Historically, I/E research has focused on the math and verbal domains (Marsh, Möller et al., 2015), but the I/E model is truly based on a continuum of academic domains that vary between the end-points of mathematical and verbal subjects (Figure 1; see also Marsh & Yeung, 2001). Now, for an elegant elaboration of our title theme we will cautiously say that DCT *borrows*, but actually we mean extends, the core assumptions of the I/E model, applying them to this continuum (Möller & Marsh, 2013; Marsh, Lütdke et al., 2015) and also positioning this model more broadly into frame of reference research. Two frequently posited frames of references are temporal and social comparisons (Möller, 2005; Möller et al., 2009; Möller et al., 2011); self-perceptions are based in part on comparisons of one's own accomplishments and skills with one's own past performances (temporal) as well as with others' performances in one's immediate and relevant context (social). Particularly in educational settings, however, a growing body of research based on the I/E model (Marsh, 1986) demonstrates that self-perceptions may also be the result of internal comparisons, in which accomplishments in one school subject can serve as a frame of reference for another school subject—hereafter referred to as "dimensional" comparisons. Acknowledging the importance of this long understudied frame of reference perspective, in 2013 Möller and Marsh proposed Dimensional Comparison Theory (DCT) as an extension of the already established I/E theory.

DCT expands and theoretically explains (Möller et al., 2016) the I/E model to include a wider variety of academic domains. As a result cross-paths involve "near" and "far" comparisons in relation to how similar or dissimilar different school subjects are to each other. While far comparisons should provoke contrast effects (negative effects of academic achievement in one subject on ASC in the other), near comparisons will result in diminishing contrast effects or assimilation effects (positive effects of academic achievement in one subject on ASC in the other; Möller & Marsh, 2013; Marsh, Lüdtke et al., 2015). A possible explanation for these processes is that students believe achievement in far subjects to require different sets of competencies and thus, to be uncorrelated, or even negatively correlated (e.g., English and math; Jansen, Schroeders, Lüdtke, & Marsh, 2015; Möller & Marsh, 2013), despite their actual empirical high positive dependency. For near comparisons students most likely consider the subjects to be more similar and complementary such that accomplishments in one subject are closely related to accomplishments in related subjects, e.g., math and physics (Jansen et al., 2015; Möller & Marsh, 2013; Möller, Streblow, Pohlmann, & Köller, 2006). A recent study by Helm, Müller-Kalthoff, Nagy, and Möller (2016) experimentally investigated the causal effect of perceived subject similarity on domain-specific ASCs and indeed found that induced lower perceived subject similarity led to stronger ASC differences than did higher perceived similarity, even for subjects that were assumed to be near (e.g., math and physics).

3 Empirical Research on DCT

Empirically, results on contrast and assimilation effects are in part still inconsistent. Having already provided much evidence for the contrast effects of math and verbal with regard to the I/E model we now focus on results including several near and far comparisons of subjects over and beyond math and verbal.

3.1 DCT studies focusing on the academic context

Focusing on the math end of the continuum, Möller et al. (2006) found that math achievement had a positive effect on physics self-concepts. Further, Parker, Marsh, Lüdtke, and Trautwein (2013) found science achievement to positively predict MSC, even after controlling for science achievement. A study by Jansen et al. (2015), however including biology, physics, and chemistry as separate science subjects as well as math and German shed light on these seemingly contradictory findings. They found small assimilation effects between math achievement and physics and chemistry self-concept, as well as among all sciences included in their study. Moreover, Jansen et al. (2015) found contrast effects between achievement in German and physics and chemistry self-concept, but more importantly between achievement in math and biology self-concept. Thus, they deduced that in studies using mixed science subjects these contrasting effects (that they find to be stronger than the assimilation effects) of math achievement and the biology component could overshadow the assimilation effects of the other science components (Jansen et al., 2015).

For the verbal domains some studies (e.g., Marsh & Yeung, 2001; Marsh et al., 2001) have found negative (i.e., contrast) effects between subjects of the verbal domain (e.g., Xu et al., 2013). More recent studies, based on stronger statistical methodology than previously used in I/E research (e.g., Marsh et al., 2014), however, have shown that for standardized test results there were positive predictions (i.e., assimilation effects) of Dutch and English achievement on self-concept in English and self-concept in Dutch respectively and negative (contrast) effects of math achievement on both language self-concepts. For class marks they found a similar pattern, although the near comparisons were not positive. However, as a test of the differences of near and far comparisons showed, in both cases the far comparisons were significantly more negative than the near comparisons. Similarly, Ehm,

Lindberg, and Hasselhorn (2014) found such assimilation effects between writing achievement and reading self-concept, while math achievement and reading self-concept were negatively related as were reading achievement and MSC, again indicating contrast effects.

In one of the most comprehensive DCT investigations (comprised of two studies) so far, Marsh, Lüdtke et al. (2015) supported DCT predictions in relation to domains spanning the academic continuum (Figure 3; German, English, history, biology, physics, and math). Although they only found actual positive (assimilation) effects for near comparisons in their second study, both studies showed significant differences between near and far comparisons of all subjects. Overall, there has been consistent support for diminishing contrast effects for increasingly "near" academic domains, but support for the shift in direction from contrast to assimilation has been mixed.

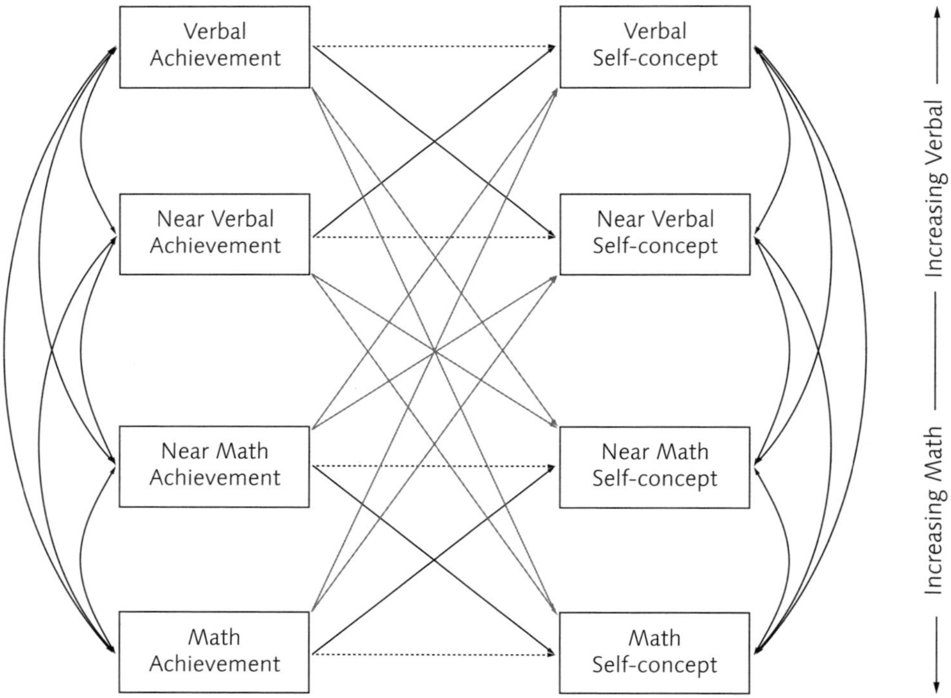

Figure 3. Extending the I/E model to include the verbal domain, one or more verbally-related domains, the math domain, and one or more math-related domains. Far cross paths (in grey; any of the math domains to any of the verbal domains) are again predicted to be negative. However, the near cross paths (in black; relating the different verbal domains to each other, or the different math domains to each other) are predicted to be significantly less negative, non-significant, or even positive (assimilation).

3.2 DCT studies beyond achievement and ASC

DCT research has focused on achievement and ASC, but has been extended to include other variables. While staying within the realm of academia, Guo, et al. (2017) focused on four science subjects (biology, physics, chemistry, and earth science) and utilized EVT in a similar manner as the aforementioned Dietrich et al. (2015) study. They showed positive relationships of achievement and ASC for near (physics with chemistry) domains and negative relationships for far domains (physics with biology and chemistry with biology). Cross-paths between earth science and the other science domains were slightly positive or non-significant. The pattern was the same for intrinsic value (Guo et al., 2017). Further, when predicting aspirations through motivational beliefs, paths between physics and biology were significantly negative. Again, the pattern of results was found for ASC and intrinsic value but not utility value. However, the majority of these cross-paths involving ASC, intrinsic value, and utility value were non-significant or slightly positive (see also Guo, Parker, Marsh, & Morin, 2015).

3.3 DCT outside of the realm of academia

Much of the research reviewed thus far has focused on the effects of dimensional comparisons within academic domains. For validating the theory it is important to also use standards of other domains. This research, however, is still scarce (Möller & Marsh, 2013), although there are exceptions (e.g., Möller & Husemann, 2006; Möller & Savyon, 2003; Möller & Weber, 2001). Focusing on the general nature of dimensional comparisons, conducting several diary studies, Möller and colleagues found that participants (adults aged 65–92 years) who were asked to compare self-evaluations on three dimensions (mental flexibility and memory, physical fitness and health, coping with problems) preferred dimensional over social and temporal comparisons, as these resulted in more positive self-evaluations (Möller & Weber, 2001). This is not surprising as other studies revealed that people also tend to prefer upward dimensional comparisons which are related to a positive affective state (Möller & Husemann, 2006). Further, these studies showed that most dimensional comparisons are based on domains from the same context, most frequently from academic categories, followed by personal relationships.

In a study of self-concepts in relation to intelligence (ASC) and honesty, Möller and Savyon (2003) demonstrated that rating oneself as more honest than intelligent depended on the level of ASC. Thus, only students with low ASC believed themselves to be more honest than intelligent. In their second study they experimentally manipulated feedback on an academic task, showing that participants who had received negative feedback (failure) rated themselves as significantly more honest than participants who had reviewed positive feedback (success). Möller and Savyon concluded that following failure, participants tended to overestimate their honesty more strongly than following success.

4 Extensions of DCT Studies: Integration with other ASC Models

As demonstrated, the development of ASC is undoubtedly closely linked to dimensional comparison processes. Hence, other theoretical models dealing with ASC and achievement, such as the reciprocal effects model (REM) and the big-fish-little-pond effect (BFLPE), although traditionally focusing on a single domain of ASC have started integrating a dimensional perspective.

4.1 Reciprocal Effects Model (REM) and DCT

The reciprocal effects model was first introduced by Marsh (1990b; see also Marsh & Craven, 2006). Their goal was to find a satisfactory answer as to whether academic achievement was a predictor or cause of ASC. Based on theoretical and empirical evidence Marsh and Craven (2006) proposed a dynamic REM, in which both ASC and achievement are causes and effects of each other (Figure 4). REM posits that both sets of paths are statistically significant, but the linkages from prior ASC to subsequent achievement are particularly important. There now exists substantial support for the generalizability of the findings over age, nationality, attendance at academically selective and non-selective schools, and different measures of ASC and achievement (Marsh & Craven, 2006; Seaton, Marsh, Parker, Craven, & Yeung, 2015; see also Retelsdorf, Köller, & Möller, 2014). Expanding this model to incorporate more than one academic domain, Marsh and Yeung (1997,

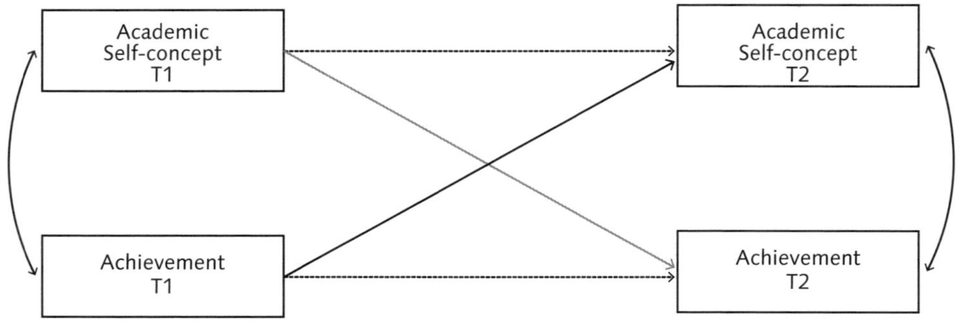

Figure 4. Prototypical reciprocal-effects model. In this model, academic self-concept and achievement are collected in two successive waves (T1 and T2). Within each wave, academic self-concept and achievement are assumed to be correlated. Paths connecting the same variable on multiple occasions reflect stability (dashed). The solid black line reflects effects of prior achievement on subsequent self-concept, whereas the grey lines reflect the effects of prior self-concept on subsequent achievement.

1998; see also Marsh, 1989) developed early support for what was subsequently called the Reciprocal Internal/External frame of reference model (RI/EM; e.g., Marsh & Köller 2004; Möller et al., 2011). In particular, Möller et al. (2011) not only found good support for both models considered separately but also found positive longitudinal effects for their integration: positive effects of grades and ASCs on subsequent grades and ASCs within matching domains (consistent with the REM); negative effects of grades on subsequent ASCs across non-matching domains (consistent with dimensional comparison processes of DCT); and negative effects of ASCs in one domain on grades in a non-matching domain (new to the integration of DCT and REMs, but consistent with the logic of DCT). Recently, Möller, Zimmermann, and Köller (2014) replicated this pattern of results with test scores rather than school grades.

4.2 Big-Fish-Little-Pond Effect (BFLPE) and DCT

Another important ASC model, namely the Big-Fish-Little-Pond Effect (BFLPE; Marsh, 1984; Marsh & Parker, 1984; see also review by Marsh et al., 2008) is also based on a frame of reference effect, but emphasizes a social comparison perspective integrating a variety of different theoretical models (e.g., relative deprivation theory, social comparison theory, psychophysical judgment, and social judgment). In the BFLPE model, students are hypothesized to compare their abilities with the abilities of their classmates and to use this social comparison impression as one basis for forming their own ASC. The model hypothesizes that individual ability is positively related to ASC (the brighter I am the higher my ASC) but school-average ability has a negative effect on ASC (the brighter my classmates, the lower my ASC). Extensive support for the BFLPE generalizes across student groups, subject domains, ASC instruments and cultures (see review by Marsh, 2007; Marsh et al., 2008). However, again nearly all of the research on the BFLPE to date is based on a single domain of ASC: typically MSC, VSC, or global ASC. Based on early research by Marsh (1990a), recent studies (e.g., Parker et al., 2013; Pinxten et al., 2015) have tried to fill this gap, by applying BFLPE models to several academic domains simultaneously, thereby combing social and dimensional comparisons. Taking into account the assumptions of the BFLPE and dimensional comparison theory, Marsh posited compensatory effects: (a) school-average ability in math should have a negative effect on MSC (the BFLPE) but a small positive effect on VSC; and (b) school-average verbal ability should have a negative effect on VSC (BFLPE) but a small positive effect on MSC. Empirical support for this hypothesis is limited, in part because school-average abilities in different school subjects is so highly correlated (e.g., $r > .95$) that they cannot be discriminated. However, evolving statistical methodology has demonstrated stronger evidence for such effects for students of German themed (magnet) schools (Parker et al., 2013) as well as Dutch elementary students (Pinxten et al., 2015).

5 Policy and Practice Implications

In addition to social and temporal comparisons, dimensional comparisons seem to play a significant role in self-evaluation, particularly ASC. In juxtaposition to temporal and social comparisons, dimensional comparisons evoke an apparently paradoxical effect on ASC: bright students might have an average or below-average ASC in their weakest school subjects, despite their good achievement, but even poor students may have an average or above-average ASC in their best school subject, despite their below average performance in this subject. Both of these effects are paradoxical when only taking the comparison to other students into account. Considering however, the comparison of the student's performance to his or her own performance, but in a different domain, explains these effects (see also Marsh, Möller et al., 2015). Teachers might wrongly assume that students' academic emotions, interest, and motivation to learn, which are influenced by ASC, generalize across school subjects. Thus, knowledge of the apparent domain specificity of ASC formations is thus, of major importance as it will enable teachers to have a better understanding of their students and provide more appropriate, credible feedback, particularly for less able students. Additionally, awareness of dimensional comparisons is important for the students themselves. As research has shown that ASC and achievement have a reciprocal relationship, ASC also influences later achievement. Thus, low ASC in one domain, due to dimensional comparisons with a stronger domain, might lead to even lower performance in the former and higher performance in the latter domain and consequently, an even stronger pronunciation of achievement differences in these domains. In addition, the aforementioned influence of ASC on students' academic emotions, interest, and also aspirations could lead to career choices made on wrong assumptions of one's own abilities. An important point for researchers is clearly that results of studies including near and far comparisons, as proposed by DCT, suggest that comparisons depend on what domains are presented in a particular design. Thus, when presenting two specific domains to students, irrespective of which domains are presented, there is an implicit demand that they contrast responses to these domains in a manner consistent with the classic I/E model (i.e., contrast for non-matching domain) but perhaps not as consistent with the more nuanced predictions based on DCT.

6 Something Blue

Overall, this stream of research demonstrates the pressing need to expanding research horizons and *blue*-sky thinking, building on solid theoretical and empirical groundwork. Möller and Marsh (2013) have made an important step in this direction with formulating dimensional comparisons as an innovative and new theory, based on the established I/E model. Now, research needs to test and validate dimensional comparison theory, by developing novel research questions and utilizing state of the art methods for testing these. This kind of research is based on fruitful and engaged research collaborations such as the one of Möller, Marsh, and colleagues. It is an honor being a part of this and we are looking forward to all future ideas, projects, and an ongoing research partnership, for better and for worse.

References

Arens, A. K., & Möller, J. (2016). Dimensional comparisons in students' perceptions of the learning environment. *Learning and Instruction, 42*, 22–30.

Dietrich, J., Dicke, A. L., Kracke, B., & Noack, P. (2015). Teacher support and its influence on students' intrinsic value and effort: Dimensional comparison effects across subjects. *Learning and Instruction, 39*, 45–54.

Ehm, J. H., Lindberg, S., & Hasselhorn, M. (2014). Reading, writing, and math self-concept in elementary school children: Influence of dimensional comparison processes. *European Journal of Psychology of Education, 29*, 277–294.

Goetz, T., Frenzel, C. A., Hall, N. C., & Pekrun, R. (2008). Antecedents of academic emotions: Testing the internal/external frame of reference model for academic enjoyment. *Contemporary Educational Psychology, 33*, 9–33.

Guo, J., Marsh, H. W., Parker, P. D. Morin, A. J., & Dicke, T. (2017). Extending expectancy-value theory predictions of achievement and aspirations in science: Internal comparison processes and expectancy-by-value interactions. *Learning and Instruction, 49*, 81–91.

Guo, J., Nagengast, B., Marsh, H. W., Kelava, A., Gaspard, H., Brandt, H., ... Trautwein, U. (2016). Probing the Unique Contributions of Self-Concept, Task Values, and Their Interactions Using Multiple Value Facets and Multiple Academic Outcomes. AERA Open, 2, 1–20.

Guo, J., Parker, P. D., Marsh, H. W., & Morin, A. J. (2015). Achievement, motivation, and educational choices: A longitudinal study of expectancy and value using a multiplicative perspective. *Developmental Psychology, 51*, 1163–1176.

Helm, F., Müller-Kalthoff, H., Nagy, N. & Möller, J. (2016). Dimensional comparison theory: Perceived subject similarity impacts on students' self-concepts. *AERA Open, 2*(2), 1–9.

Jansen, M., Schroeders, U., Lüdtke, O., & Marsh, H. W. (2015). Contrast and assimilation effects of dimensional comparisons in five subjects: An extension of the I/E model. *Journal of Educational Psychology, 107*, 1086–1101.

Marsh, H. W. (1984). Self-concept: The application of a frame of reference model to explain paradoxical results. *Australian Journal of Education, 28*, 165–181.

Marsh, H. W. (1986). Verbal and math self-concepts: An internal/external frame of reference model. *American Educational Research Journal, 23*, 129–149.

Marsh, H. W. (1989). Sex differences in the development of verbal and mathematics constructs: The high school and beyond study. *American Educational Research Journal, 26*, 191–225.

Marsh, H. W. (1990a). The influences of internal and external frames of reference on the formation of English and math self-concepts. *Journal of Educational Psychology*, *82*, 107–116.

Marsh, H.W. (1990b). The causal ordering of academic self-concept and academic achievement: A multiwave, longitudinal panel analysis. *Journal of Educational Psychology, 82*, 646–656.

Marsh, H. W. (2007). *Self-concept theory, measurement and research into practice: The role of self-concept in Educational Psychology*. Leicester, UK: British Psychological Society.

Marsh, H. W., Abduljabbar, A. S., Parker, P. D., Morin, A. J., Abdelfattah, F., Nagengast, B., ... Abu-Hilal, M. M. (2015). The internal/external frame of reference model of self-concept and achievement relations age-cohort and cross-cultural differences. *American Educational Research Journal, 52*, 168–202.

Marsh, H. W., & Craven, R. G. (2006). Reciprocal effects of self-concept and performance from a multidimensional perspective: Beyond seductive pleasure and unidimensional perspectives. *Perspectives on Psychological Science*, *1*, 133–163.

Marsh, H. W. & Hau, K. T. (2004). Explaining paradoxical relations between academic self-concepts and achievements: Cross-cultural generalizability of the internal-external frame of reference predictions across 26 countries. *Journal of Educational Psychology, 96*, 56–67.

Marsh, H. W., Hau, K. T., Artelt, C., Baumert, J., & Peschar, J. L. (2006). OECD's brief self-report measure of educational psychology's most useful affective constructs: Cross-cultural, psychometric comparisons across 25 countries. *International Journal of Testing, 6*, 311–360.

Marsh, H. W., & Köller, O. (2004). Unification of theoretical models of academic self-concept/achievement relations: Reunification of East and West German school systems after the fall of the Berlin Wall. *Contemporary Educational Psychology, 29*, 264–282.

Marsh, H. W., Kong, C. K., & Hau, K. (2001). Extension of the internal/external frame of reference model of self-concept formation: Importance of native and nonnative languages for Chinese students. *Journal of Educational Psychology, 93*, 543–553.

Marsh, H. W., Kuyper, H., Seaton, M., Parker, P. D., Morin, A. J., Möller, J., & Abduljabbar, A. S. (2014). Dimensional comparison theory: An extension of the internal/external frame of reference effect on academic self-concept formation. *Contemporary Educational Psychology, 39*, 326–341.

Marsh, H. W., Lüdtke, O., Nagengast, B., Trautwein, U., Abduljabbar, A. S., Abdelfattah, F., & Jansen, M. (2015). Dimensional comparison theory: Paradoxical relations between self-beliefs and achievements in multiple domains. *Learning and Instruction*, *35*, 16–32.

Marsh, H. W., Möller, J., Parker, P. D., Xu, M. K., Nagengast, B., & Pekrun, R. (2015). Academic internal/external frame of reference model. In J. D. Wright (Ed.), *International Encyclopedia of the Social & Behavioural Sciences* (2nd ed., pp. 425–432). Oxford, UK: Elsevier.

Marsh, H. W., & Parker, J. (1984). Determinants of student self-concept: Is it better to be a relatively large fish in a small pond even if you don't learn to swim as well? *Journal of Personality and Social Psychology*, *47*, 213–231.

Marsh, H. W., Seaton, M., Trautwein, U., Lüdtke, O., Hau, K. T., O'Mara, A. J., & Craven, R. G. (2008). The big-fish-little-pond-effect stands up to critical scrutiny: Implications for theory, methodology, and future research. *Educational Psychology Review, 20*, 319–350.

Marsh, H. W., & Shavelson, R. (1985) Self-concept: Its multifaceted, hierarchical structure. *Educational Psychologist, 20*, 107–125.

Marsh, H. W., & Yeung, A. S. (1997). Causal effects of academic self-concept on academic achievement: Structural equation models of longitudinal data. *Journal of Educational Psychology, 89*, 41–54.

Marsh, H. W., & Yeung, A. S. (1998). Longitudinal structural equation models of academic self-concept and achievement: Gender differences in the development of math and English constructs. *American Educational Research Journal, 35*, 705–738.

Marsh, H. W., & Yeung, A. S. (2001). An extension of the internal/external frame of reference model: A response to Bong (1998). *Multivariate Behavioral Research, 36*, 389–420.

Möller, J. (2005). "Paradoxical" effects of praise and criticism: Social, dimensional, and temporal comparisons. *British Journal of Educational Psychology, 75*, 275–295.

Möller, J., & Husemann, N. (2006). Internal comparisons in everyday life. *Journal of Educational Psychology, 98*, 342–353.

Möller, J., & Köller, O. (2001). Dimensional comparisons: An experimental approach to the internal/external frame of reference model. *Journal of Educational Psychology, 93*, 826–835.

Möller, J., & Marsh, H. W. (2013). Dimensional comparison theory. *Psychological Review, 120*, 544–560.

Möller, J., Müller-Kalthoff, H., Helm, F., Nagy, N., & Marsh, H. W. (2016). The generalized internal/external frame of reference model: An extension to Dimensional Comparison Theory. *Frontline Learning Research, 4(2)*, 1–11.

Möller, J., Pohlmann, B., Köller, O., & Marsh, H. W. (2009). A meta-analytic path analysis of the internal/external frame of reference model of academic achievement and academic self-concept. *Review of Educational Research, 79*, 1129–1167.

Möller, J., Retelsdorf, J., Köller, O., & Marsh, H. W. (2011). The reciprocal I/E model: An integration of models of relations between academic achievement and self-concept. *American Educational Research Journal, 48*, 1315–1346.

Möller, J., & Savyon, K. (2003). Not very smart thus moral: Dimensional comparisons between academic self-concept and honesty. *Social Psychology of Education, 6*, 95–106.

Möller, J., Streblow, L., Pohlmann, B., & Köller, O. (2006). An extension to the internal/external frame of reference model to two verbal and numerical domains. *European Journal of Psychology of Education, 21*, 467–487.

Möller, J., & Weber, F. (2001). Dimensionale, soziale, und temporale Vergleiche von alten Menschen: Selbstbewertungen, Virulenz, und Präferenz [Dimensional, social, and temporal comparisons in old age: Self-evaluation, virulence, and preference]. *Zeitschrift für Entwicklungspsychologie und Pädagogische Psychologie, 33*, 178 –186.

Möller, J., Zimmermann, F., & Köller, O. (2014). The reciprocal internal/external frame of reference model using grades and test scores. *British Journal of Educational Psychology, 84*, 591–611.

Nagy, G., Trautwein, U., Baumert, J., Köller, O., & Garrett, J. (2006). Gender and course selection in upper secondary education: Effects of academic self-concept and intrinsic value. *Educational Research and Evaluation, 12*, 323–345.

Parker, P. D., Marsh, H. W., Ciarrochi, J., Marshall, S., & Abduljabbar, A. S. (2014). Juxtaposing math self-efficacy and self-concept as predictors of long-term achievement outcomes. *Educational Psychology, 34*, 29–48.

Parker, P. D., Marsh, H. W., Lüdtke, O., & Trautwein, U. (2013). Differential school contextual effects for math and English: Integrating the Big-Fish-Little-Pond Effect and the internal/external frame of reference. *Learning and Instruction, 23*, 78–89.

Parker, P. D., Schoon, I., Tsai, Y., Nagy, G., Trautwein, U., & Eccles, J. (2012). Achievement, agency, gender, and socioeconomic background as predictors of postschool choices: A multi-context study. *Developmental Psychology, 48*, 1629–1642.

Pinxten, M., Wouters, S., Preckel, F., Niepel, C., De Fraine, B., & Verschueren, K. (2015). The formation of academic self-concept in elementary education: A unifying model for external and internal comparisons. *Contemporary Educational Psychology, 41*, 124–132.

Pohlmann, B., & Möller, J. (2006). Vergleichseffekte auf kognitive, affektive und motivationale Variablen [Comparison effects on cognitive, affective, and motivational variables]. *Zeitschrift für Entwicklungspsychologie und Pädagogische Psychologie, 38*, 79–87.

Pohlmann, B., & Möller, J. (2009). On the benefits of dimensional comparisons. *Journal of Educational Psychology, 101*, 248–258.

Retelsdorf, J., Köller, O., & Möller, J. (2014). Reading achievement and reading self-concept testing the reciprocal effects model. *Learning and Instruction, 29*, 21–30.

Schurtz, I. M., Pfost, M., Nagengast, B., & Artelt, C. (2014). Impact of social and dimensional comparisons on student's mathematical and English subject-interest at the beginning of secondary school. *Learning and Instruction, 34*, 32–41.

Seaton, M., Marsh, H. W., Parker, P., Craven, R. G., & Yeung, A. (2015). The Reciprocal Effects Model revisited: Extending its reach to academically selective students. *Gifted Child Quarterly, 59*, 143–156.

Seligman, M. E. P., & Csikszentmihalyi, M. (2000). Positive psychology: An introduction. *American Psychologist, 55*, 5–14.

Shavelson, R. J., Hubner, J. J., & Stanton, G. C. (1976). Self-concept: Validation of construct interpretations. *Review of Educational Research, 46*, 407–444.

Van Zanden, B., Marsh, H. W., Seaton, M., Parker, P. D., Guo, J., & Duineveld, J. J. (2017). How well do parents know their adolescent children? Parent inferences of student self-concepts reflect dimensional comparison processes. *Learning and Instruction, 47*, 25–32.

Wigfield, A., & Eccles, J. S. (2002). The development of competence beliefs and values from childhood through adolescence. In A. Wigfield & J. S. Eccles (Eds.), *Development of achievement motivation* (pp. 92–120). San Diego, CA: Academic Press.

Xu, M. K., Marsh, H. W., Hau, K.-T., Ho, I. T., Morin, A. J. S., & Abduljabbar, A. S. (2013). The internal/external frame of reference of academic self-concept: Extension to a foreign language and the role of language of instruction. *Journal of Educational Psychology, 105*, 489–503.

Autorinnen und Autoren

PROFESSOR HERB W. MARSH
Institute for Positive Psychology and Education, Australian Catholic University.

DR. THERESA DICKE
Institute for Positive Psychology and Education, Australian Catholic University.

DR. MARJORIE SEATON
Institute for Positive Psychology and Education, Australian Catholic University.

DR. PHILIP D. PARKER
Institute for Positive Psychology and Education, Australian Catholic University.

DR. JIESI GUO
Institute for Positive Psychology and Education, Australian Catholic University.

PROFESSOR RHONDA CRAVEN
Institute for Positive Psychology and Education, Australian Catholic University.

CONTACT
Herb W. Marsh, Institute for Positive Psychology and Education,
Australian Catholic University, Strathfield Campus, Locked Bag 2002, Strathfield,
NSW 2135, Australia.
E-Mail: *Herb.Marsh@acu.edu.au*

Wenn die diagnostische Kompetenz von Lehrkräften bezweifelt wird: Eine Replikation der Moderation von Effekten der Noten auf das Selbstkonzept im I/E-Modell

FRIEDERIKE ZIMMERMANN, JULIA BECHERER UND OLAF KÖLLER

ZUSAMMENFASSUNG: Die im *Internal/External Frame of Reference*-Modell (I/E-Modell) postulierten Effekte von Leistungen auf Selbstkonzepte eigener Fähigkeiten wurden vielfach empirisch gestützt. Potenzielle Moderatoren für Effekte innerhalb des I/E-Modells wurden hingegen bisher nur wenig beforscht. Diese Studie untersucht, ob es von der schülerseitig wahrgenommenen diagnostischen Kompetenz von Lehrkräften abhängt, inwieweit Noten zur Bildung von Fähigkeitsselbstkonzepten herangezogen werden. An $N = 5628$ Schülerinnen und Schülern der siebten Jahrgangsstufe wurden Jahresnoten und Fähigkeitsselbstkonzepte in Mathematik und Englisch erhoben sowie Einschätzungen der Kompetenz der Lehrkräfte dieser Fächer, Leistungen zu diagnostizieren. Das um latente Interaktionen ergänzte I/E-Modell wurde mittels Strukturgleichungsmodellierung analysiert. Die Ergebnisse stützen grundlegend das I/E-Modell. Der signifikante Effekt einer latenten Interaktion zeigt: Je geringer die Schülerinnen und Schüler die Kompetenz ihrer Mathematiklehrkraft einschätzten, desto stärker war der negative Effekt der Englischnote auf das Mathematikselbstkonzept ausgeprägt. Damit werden erste vorliegende Befunde zur Moderation im I/E-Modell mit den Domänen Mathematik und Deutsch konzeptuell repliziert.

Schlüsselwörter: Akademisches Selbstkonzept, dimensionale Vergleiche, wahrgenommene diagnostische Kompetenz im Leistungsbereich

When students doubt their teachers' diagnostic competence: A replication of moderation in the Internal/External Frame of Reference Model

ABSTRACT: Self-concept formation from academic achievements as theorized in the internal/external frame of reference model (I/E model) is widely supported. Evidence regarding moderation of the postulated effects is scarce. We investigated whether it depends on the students' perceptions of teachers' diagnostic competence to what extent teacher assigned grades are utilized for self-concept formation. We drew on $N = 5628$ 7th graders and assessed their report card grades and self-concepts in mathematics and English as well as their perceptions of teachers' competence to judge achievements in these subjects. Structural equation modelling was used to analyse the I/E model augmented with latent interactions. Results support the I/E model. A significant interaction effect shows that the lower students perceived their teachers' diagnostic competence in mathematics, the stronger the path from the English grade to the mathematics self-concept. The results conceptually replicate findings from a previous study using mathematics and German as domains in the I/E model.

Keywords: academic self-concept; dimensional comparison; perceived accuracy of teachers' judgments

Einleitung

Das *Internal/External Frame of Reference*-Modell (I/E-Modell; Marsh, 1986) bietet einen theoretisch und empirisch bewährten Zugang zu der Frage, wie domänenspezifische Selbstkonzepte gebildet werden (z. B. Möller, Pohlmann, Köller & Marsh, 2009). In dem Modell werden innerhalb von Domänen soziale Vergleichsprozesse angenommen, wonach Selbstkonzepte über die eigenen Fähigkeiten in einem Fach aus der Einordnung der eigenen Leistung im Vergleich zu den Leistungen anderer in diesem Fach gespeist werden. Zwischen kontrastierenden Domänen, wie etwa Mathematik und Deutsch, werden dimensionale Vergleichsprozesse angenommen, bei denen der Vergleich der Leistungen zu Kontrastierungen eigener Stärken und Schwächen beiträgt, was sich in Überhöhungen bzw. Abwertungen der Selbstkonzepte niederschlägt. Das I/E-Modell leistet damit auch einen Beitrag zur Erklärung des faszinierenden Effekts, dass Leistungen zwischen kontrastierenden Bereichen, wie etwa Mathematik und verbaler Domäne, zwar hoch miteinander korreliert sind, die entsprechenden Selbstkonzepte hingegen nicht. Während die positiven Effekte zwischen Leistung und Selbstkonzept innerhalb von Domänen sowie die negativen Kontrasteffekte zwischen den Domänen empirisch erhebliche Stützung erfuhren, finden sich nur wenige Hinweise auf Bedingungen, die diese Phänomene beeinflussen, also moderieren, können (z. B. Möller, Streblow & Pohlmann, 2006). Eine Kandidatin für Moderationseffekte im I/E-Modell ist die von den Schülerinnen und Schülern wahrgenommene Kompetenz ihrer Lehrkräfte, Leistungen zu diagnostizieren. In dieser Studie streben wir danach, erste vorliegende Befunde für Moderationen im I/E-Modell mit den Domänen Mathematik und Deutsch zu replizieren (vgl. Zimmermann, Möller & Köller, 2017). Für eine mögliche Generalisierung der Effekte verwenden wir in der vorliegenden Studie für die verbale Domäne des Selbstkonzepts eigener Fähigkeit nicht die Muttersprache Deutsch, sondern die Fremdsprache Englisch.

1 Theoretischer Hintergrund

1.1 Das *Internal/External Frame of Reference*-Modell (I/E-Modell)

Im I/E-Modell werden die Einflüsse von Leistungen in verschiedenen Schulfächern auf entsprechende Fähigkeitsüberzeugungen von Schülerinnen und Schülern durch soziale und dimensionale Vergleiche begründet (Marsh, 1986). Schülerinnen und Schüler vollziehen soziale Vergleiche, indem sie ihre eigenen Leistungen mit den Leistungen ihrer Mitschülerinnen und Mitschüler vergleichen (externaler Referenzrahmen). Sieht sich eine Schülerin oder ein Schüler im Vergleich zu den Mitschülerinnen und Mitschülern beispielsweise als überdurchschnittlich gut in Mathematik, wird die Überzeugung eigener mathematischer Fähigkeiten wahrscheinlich ebenfalls überdurchschnittlich gut ausfallen. Schülerinnen und Schüler vollziehen dimensionale Vergleiche, indem sie ihre Leistungen in einem Bereich mit ihren Leistungen in einem anderen Bereich vergleichen (internaler Referenzrahmen). Wenn die Leistungen einer Schülerin oder eines Schülers in Mathematik beispielsweise besser ausfallen als in Deutsch, wird die individuelle Stärke in Mathematik gegenüber der individuellen Schwäche in Deutsch kontrastiert, was zu einer Überhöhung des Fähigkeitsselbstkonzepts in Mathematik und einer relativen Abwertung des Fähigkeitsselbstkonzepts in Deutsch beiträgt. Anhand der gleichzeitigen Berücksichtigung dieser zwei gegenläufigen Prozesse erklärt das I/E-Modell den zunächst paradox wirkenden Befund, dass die Leistungen in der mathematischen und der verbalen Domäne zwar moderat bis hoch positiv korreliert, die zugehörigen Fähigkeitsselbstkonzepte jedoch nahezu unkorreliert sind.

In einer Metaanalyse mit 69 Studien zum I/E-Modell konnten Möller et al. (2009) zeigen, dass die durchschnittliche Korrelation zwischen mathematischen und verbalen Leistungen positiv und hoch ausfiel ($r = .67$), die jeweiligen Selbstkonzepte hingegen paradoxerweise nur gering korrelierten ($r = .10$). Bezüglich sozialer Vergleiche zeigten sich deutliche Effekte der mathematischen ($\beta = .61$) und verbalen Leistungen ($\beta = .49$) auf die jeweiligen Selbstkonzepte. Für die Annahme dimensionaler Vergleiche sprechen die jeweils negativen Effekte mathematischer Leistungen auf das verbale Selbstkonzept ($\beta = -.21$) und der verbalen Leistungen auf das mathematische Selbstkonzept ($\beta = -.27$). Des Weiteren werden diese Befunde durch längsschnittliche, experimentelle sowie Tagebuchstudien gestützt (Marsh et al., 2014; Möller & Husemann, 2006; Möller & Köller, 2001; Pohlmann & Möller, 2009; Strickhouser & Zell, 2015).

1.2 Moderatoren im I/E-Modell

Mögliche Moderatoren innerhalb des I/E-Modells wurden bisher selten untersucht und dementsprechend wenig ist bisher darüber bekannt, unter welchen Bedingungen Schülerinnen und Schüler das Feedback über die eigenen Leistungen überhaupt zur Einschätzung ihrer Fähigkeiten heranziehen. In der bereits angeführten Metaanalyse von Möller et al. (2009) wurden Alter, Geschlecht, Land des Wohnsitzes, Art der Erfassung von Schulleistungen und selbstbezogenen Kognitionen sowie Stichprobengröße und Publikationsjahr als potenzielle Moderatoren einbezogen. Die Art der Erfassung von Schulleistungen (Fachnoten oder standardisierte Leistungstests) und von selbstbezogenen Kognitionen (Selbstkonzept oder Selbstwirksamkeit) moderierte die Effekte des externalen Referenzrahmens innerhalb der Domänen. Bezüglich der Effekte des internalen Referenzrahmens zwischen den Domänen erwies sich lediglich die Stichprobengröße als Moderator des Effekts von der Leistung in Mathematik auf das verbale Selbstkonzept.

Bisher beschäftigten sich nur wenige Studien direkt mit der Untersuchung moderierender Variablen im I/E-Modell. Für die kontrastierenden dimensionalen Vergleiche verweisen erste Untersuchungen auf die Bedeutung der wahrgenommenen Ähnlichkeit der untersuchten Fächer bzw. der Leistungen in den Fächern sowie auf die Bedeutung der Überzeugung, inwieweit mathematische und verbale Begabung einander ausschließen (Helm, Müller-Kalthoff, Nagy & Möller, 2016; Möller, Pohlmann, Streblow & Kauffmann, 2002; Möller et al., 2006; Skaalvik & Rankin, 1992). In einer aktuellen Arbeit (Helm & Möller, 2017) wurde mit der Gleichzeitigkeit bzw. Ungleichzeitigkeit der Erhebung der Selbstkonzepte in der mathematischen und verbalen Domäne ein methodischer Aspekt als Moderator in den Blick genommen. Dabei zeigte sich, dass der Kontrasteffekt der Mathematik-Note auf das Deutsch-Selbstkonzept nur bei gleichzeitiger Abfrage der mathematischen und verbalen Domäne auftrat, was nahelegt, dass dimensionale Vergleiche in dieser Richtung dadurch erst angeregt werden.

In einer anderen aktuellen Studie wurde untersucht, ob die von Schülerinnen und Schülern wahrgenommene diagnostische Kompetenz ihrer Lehrkräfte hinsichtlich der Beurteilung von Leistungen eine moderierende Rolle der im I/E-Modell postulierten Effekte einnimmt (Zimmermann et al., 2017). Diese Annahme erscheint plausibel. Sowohl den sozialen als auch den dimensionalen Vergleichen wird zugrunde gelegt, dass Menschen dazu bestrebt sind, ihre eigenen Fähigkeiten einzuschätzen (Festinger, 1954; Möller & Marsh, 2013). Auch wenn die Motivationen dafür sehr unterschiedlich ausfallen können, wie etwa die eigenen Stärken und Schwächen genau zu kennen (z. B. Mead, 1934), die eigene Selbstsicht konsistent zu stützen, sich selbst durch sozialen Abwärtsvergleich aufzuwerten (Tesser, 1988) oder die eigenen Leistungen tatsächlich zu verbessern, indem von fähigeren Personen gelernt wird (Dijkstra, Kuyper, van der Werf, Buunk & van der Zee, 2008) – die herangezogenen Informationsquellen sollten dafür jeweils als geeignet wahrgenommen werden. In früheren Arbeiten wurden dazu Bedingungen formuliert, von denen etwa die Ergebnisse sozialer Vergleiche abhängen können. Im Forschungsteam um Tesser (1988) konnte beispielsweise gezeigt werden, dass die empfundene Relevanz einer Dimension, auf der verglichen wird, und die wahrgenommene Ähnlichkeit zur Vergleichsperson das Auftreten sozialer Vergleiche moderieren (siehe auch Dijkstra et al., 2008). Ob Informationen, die Vergleichsprozessen zugrunde gelegt werden, als relevant und passend wahrgenommen werden, könnte auch von der empfundenen Glaubwürdigkeit der Informationsquelle abhängen. Um zu aussagekräftigen, bedeutsamen Schlussfolgerungen über das eigene Selbstbild zu kommen, sollte die Informationsbasis möglichst verlässlich sein. Die Verlässlichkeit von Informationen über Leistungen als Quelle fähigkeitsbezogener Selbstkonzepte in der Schule wird beispielsweise repräsentiert durch die von Schülerinnen und Schülern wahrgenommene diagnostische Kompetenz der Lehrkräfte hinsichtlich ihrer Leistungsbeurteilungen (Zimmermann et al., 2017). Die subjektive Sicht der Schülerinnen und Schüler auf die Kompetenz ihrer Lehrkräfte, Leistungen zu diagnostizieren, ist entscheidend für die schülerseitige Aufnahme und Verarbeitung dieser Informationen, beispielsweise beim Heranziehen zur Einschätzung der eigenen Fähigkeiten. Auch wenn Lehrkräfte die Leistungen ihrer Schülerinnen und Schüler im Mittel sehr gut beurteilen können (Südkamp, Kaiser & Möller, 2012), ist die messbare Urteilsgenauigkeit für die aktuelle Fragestellung vermutlich weniger ausschlaggebend. Vielmehr sollte die wahrgenommene Kompetenz zur Leistungsbeurteilung bedeutend dafür sein, inwieweit Schülerinnen und Schüler Lehrkrafturteile bezüglich ihrer Leistungen als Informationsquelle für ihre Selbstkonzepte nutzen.

Die Studie von Zimmermann et al. (2017) weist empirisch darauf hin, dass der wahrgenommenen diagnostischen Kompetenz eine solche moderierende Rolle zukommt. In beiden untersuchten Stichproben, bestehend aus Schülerinnen und Schülern der siebten Klasse, zeigte sich übereinstimmend, dass bei gering wahrgenommener diagnostischer Kompetenz der Mathematiklehrkraft, die Fachnote in Deutsch verstärkt zur Beurteilung des Selbstkonzeptes in Mathematik herangezogen wurde. Des Weiteren weisen die Ergebnisse in einer Stichprobe auch darauf hin, dass, bei gering wahrgenommener diagnostischer Kompetenz der Deutschlehrkraft die Fachnote in Mathematik verstärkt zur Bildung des Selbstkonzeptes in Deutsch herangezogen wird. Ein Interaktionseffekt innerhalb einer Domäne besagte, dass die Deutschnote bei hoher wahrgenommener diagnostischer Kompetenz der Deutschlehrkraft größere Effekte auf das Selbstkonzept in Deutsch hatte. Zusammenfassend weist die Studie erstmals darauf hin, dass der wahrgenommenen diagnostischen Kompetenz eine moderierende Rolle der im I/E-Modell postulierten Effekte zukommt. Die vorliegende Studie soll dies nun erneut prüfen, wobei eine konzeptuelle Erweiterung dahingehend vollzogen wird, dass für die verbale Domäne statt der Muttersprache Deutsch die Fremdsprache Englisch untersucht wird.

1.3 Die vorliegende Studie

Mit der vorliegenden Arbeit möchten wir zu einem tieferen Verständnis der im I/E-Modell beschriebenen Prozesse beitragen, indem in den Blick genommen wird, ob die postulierten Effekte sozialer und dimensionaler Vergleiche in Abhängigkeit der wahrgenommenen diagnostischen Kompetenz der Lehrkräfte variieren. Damit untersuchen wir im I/E-Modell die identische und auf gleiche Weise operationalisierte Moderatorvariable wie in der vorgestellten früheren Arbeit (Zimmermann et al., 2017). Über den dort beschriebenen direkten Replikationsversuch an zwei unabhängigen Stichproben hinausgehend, beginnen wir in der vorliegenden Studie damit, Variablen im I/E-Modell auch konzeptuell zu variieren. Diese Studie soll somit einen weiteren Beitrag liefern, falsch-positiven Befunden vorzubeugen und zusätzlich zu prüfen, ob der Gültigkeitsbereich der Befunde ausgedehnt werden kann (Murayama, Pekrun & Fiedler, 2014; Schmidt, 2009; Ulrich et al., 2016). Hier soll zunächst ein erster Schritt zur konzeptuellen Replikation getan werden, indem für die verbale Domäne des Fähigkeitsselbstkonzepts nicht die Muttersprache Deutsch, sondern die Fremdsprache Englisch verwendet wird. Beide Domänen liegen nahe beisammen auf dem Kontinuum des akademischen Selbstkonzepts von der Mathematik-Subdimension, die typisch für das mathematische Fähigkeitsselbstkonzept ist, bis hin zur muttersprachlichen Subdimension, die typisch für das verbale Selbstkonzept ist (Marsh, Byrne & Shavelson, 1988). Mit dem Nutzen der Domäne Englisch als fremdsprachliche Subdimension des verbalen Selbstkonzepts wurde die häufigste erste Fremdsprache von Schülerinnen und Schüler in Deutschland gewählt, die eine hohe Ähnlichkeit zur Domäne Deutsch aufweist (vgl. Helm et al., 2016), was für eine konzeptuelle Replikation der Befunde vielversprechend erscheint.

Grundlegend erwarten wir, dass die das I/E-Modell konstituierenden positiven Effekte von Leistungen auf Selbstkonzepte innerhalb von Domänen und negativen Effekte von Leistungen auf Selbstkonzepte in der jeweils kontrastierenden Domäne gestützt werden. Da die Befundlage zur Moderation von Effekten im I/E-Modell insgesamt noch nicht sehr weit fortgeschritten ist, testen wir alle theoretisch plausiblen Interaktionen der Noten im I/E-Modell mit den wahrgenommenen diagnostischen Kompetenzen der Lehrkräfte in beiden Fächern. Für die Pfade des externalen Referenzrahmens ist dabei anzunehmen, dass sich die durch die Lehrkraft gegebene Note stärker auf das Selbstkonzept im gleichen Fach auswirken sollte, je höher die diagnostische Kompetenz der Lehrkraft in diesem Fach eingeschätzt wird. Für die Pfade des internalen Referenzrahmens postulieren wir, dass die Note in einem Fach stärker in das Selbstkonzept in der kontrastierenden Domäne einfließt, wenn die diagnostische Kompetenz der Lehrkraft für Leistungen in der kontrastierenden Domäne gering eingeschätzt wird. In Anlehnung an die Befunde von Zimmermann et al. (2017) erwarten wir dabei im Wesentlichen, die über beide Teilstudien robuste Moderation des Kreuzpfads von Leistung in der verbalen Domäne auf das Mathematik-Selbstkonzept replizieren zu können: Je geringer Schülerinnen und Schüler die Kompetenz ihrer Lehrkräfte einschätzen, ihre Leistung in Mathematik beurteilen zu können, desto stärker sollten sie ihre Note in Englisch für die Beurteilung der eigenen Fähigkeiten in Mathematik heranziehen.

2 Methode

2.1 Stichprobe

Die Daten der vorliegenden Arbeit entstammen dem Projekt „Bildungsverläufe und psychosoziale Entwicklung im Jugendalter“ (BIJU; Baumert, Gruehn, Heyn, Köller, & Schnabel, 1997). Es handelt sich bei BIJU um eine umfangreiche Studie, die zwei Kohorten verschiedener Jahrgangsstufen zeitlich versetzt längsschnittlich verfolgte und um einen jahrgangsübergreifenden Querschnitt ergänzte. Die Studie wurde in den vier Bundesländern Nordrhein-Westfalen, Mecklenburg-Vorpommern, Sachsen-Anhalt und Berlin durchgeführt. Für den vorliegenden Beitrag wurden Daten der ersten Längsschnittkohorte aus der siebten Jahrgangsstufe verwendet, da hier Daten in den untersuchten Variablen, insbesondere zur wahrgenommenen diagnostischen Kompetenz in den Fächern Mathematik und Englisch, erhoben wurden. Um den erheblichen Anteil an fehlenden Werten zu reduzieren, wurden ausschließlich Daten von Schülerinnen und Schülern verwendet, für die mindestens eine der beiden Jahresnoten vorlag. Die $N = 5628$ Schülerinnen und Schüler (54 % weiblich, durchschnittlich 13.7 Jahre alt, $SD = 0.6$) des verwendeten Datensatzes entstammten 169 Schulen, welche die gesamte Bandbreite des gegliederten Schulsystems abdecken.

2.2 Maße

2.2.1 Leistungen in Mathematik und Englisch

Für die Leistungen in den Fächern Mathematik und Englisch wurden die Noten in Mathematik (MNOTE) und Englisch (ENOTE) am Ende der sechsten Klasse verwendet. Um die Interpretation zu erleichtern, wurden die Noten rekodiert, so dass höhere Werte der 6-stufigen Skala höheren Leistungen entsprechen von *ungenügend* (1) bis *sehr gut* (6).

2.2.2 Wahrgenommene diagnostische Kompetenz der Lehrkräfte in Mathematik und Englisch

In der siebten Klasse schätzten die Schülerinnen und Schüler getrennt für die Fächer Mathematik und Englisch ihre Lehrkräfte hinsichtlich ihrer Kompetenz, Leistungen im jeweiligen Fach zu diagnostizieren ein. Dazu wurde die 5-Item-Skala *Diagnostische Kompetenz im Leistungsbereich* genutzt, die teilweise unter Rückgriff auf frühere Items im BIJU-Projekt entwickelt wurde (Baumert et al., 1997; Fend & Specht, 1986). Beispielitems lauten: „Unser Mathematiklehrer [Englischlehrer] …" „… weiß genau, was jeder von uns leistet", „… weiß sofort, was jemand nicht verstanden hat", „merkt sofort, wenn ein Schüler im Unterricht nicht mitkommt". Das Antwortformat war 4-stufig auf einer Skala von *trifft voll und ganz zu* (1) bis *trifft überhaupt nicht zu* (4). Um die Interpretation zu erleichtern wurden die Items rekodiert, so dass höhere Werte einer höheren wahrgenommenen diagnostischen Kompetenz entsprechen. Die Reliabilitäten waren gut: Sowohl die wahrgenommene diagnostische Kompetenz der Lehrkraft in Mathematik (DKM) als auch in Englisch (DKE) wies ein Cronbachs Alpha von .86 auf.

2.2.3 Selbstkonzept eigener Fähigkeiten in Mathematik und Englisch

Ebenfalls gaben die Schülerinnen und Schüler in der siebten Klasse Auskunft über ihre domänenspezifischen Selbstkonzepte, die mit jeweils fünf Items erfasst wurden (Jopt, 1978). Beispielitems lauten: „Mathematik [Englisch] liegt mir nicht besonders", „Kein Mensch kann alles. Für Mathematik [Englisch] habe ich einfach keine Begabung". Das Antwortformat war 4-stufig auf einer Skala von *trifft voll und ganz zu* (1) bis *trifft überhaupt nicht zu* (4). Um die Interpretation zu erleichtern, wurden die Items rekodiert, so dass höhere Werte höheren Selbstkonzepten entsprechen. Die Reliabilitäten der Skalen zum Mathematikselbstkonzept (MSK, Cronbachs Alpha = .91) und zum Englischselbstkonzept (ESK, Cronbachs Alpha = .89) waren gut.

2.3 Statistische Analysen

Um das I/E-Modell inklusive Moderatoren zu prüfen, wurde ein Strukturgleichungsmodell in *Mplus* Version 7.4 gerechnet (Muthén & Muthén, 2015). Es wurde ein robuster Maximum-Likelihood-Schätzer (MLR) verwendet. Mit fehlenden Werten wurde modellbasiert mittels Full Information Maximum Likelihood (FIML) Verfahren umgegangen (Allison, 2003; Graham, 2009). Die Standardfehler wurden adjustiert für die geschachtelte Datenstruktur von Schülerinnen und Schülern mit Schulen als Clustervariable und der *Mplus* Option <type is complex> (Hox, 2002).

Alle Konstrukte, die mit mehreren Items erfasst wurden, gingen als latente Faktoren in die Analyse ein. Für gleich formulierte Items zwischen den beiden Domänen Mathematik und Englisch wurden Korrelationen zugelassen (Marsh, 1990). Für die Moderation der Pfade innerhalb und zwischen den Domänen im I/E-Modell wurden latente Interaktionen nach dem sogenannten *unconstrained approach* gebildet, bei dem keine einschränkenden Vorgaben für die Schätzung der Faktorladungen der Interaktionsterme gemacht werden und keine Vorannahmen zur Normalverteilung der Variablen bestehen (Marsh, Wen & Hau, 2004). Dazu wurden Produktterme zwischen den zentrierten Indikatoren der in die jeweilige Interaktion eingehenden Variablen (bzw. den zentrierten manifest erfassten Noten) gebildet. Die Produkte wurden schließlich als Indikatoren der latenten Interaktionsfaktoren verwendet. Alle weiteren Spezifikationen des *unconstrained approach* wurden übernommen (Marsh et al., 2004; Steinmetz, Davidov & Schmidt, 2011). Die latenten Interaktionen wurden gemeinsam mit den in sie eingehenden Komponenten als Prädiktoren modelliert. Korrelationen wurden zugelassen sowohl zwischen den latenten und manifesten exogenen Variablen als auch zwischen den Residuen latenter abhängiger Variablen im Modell. Abbildung 1 bietet eine Veranschaulichung des spezifizierten Modells.

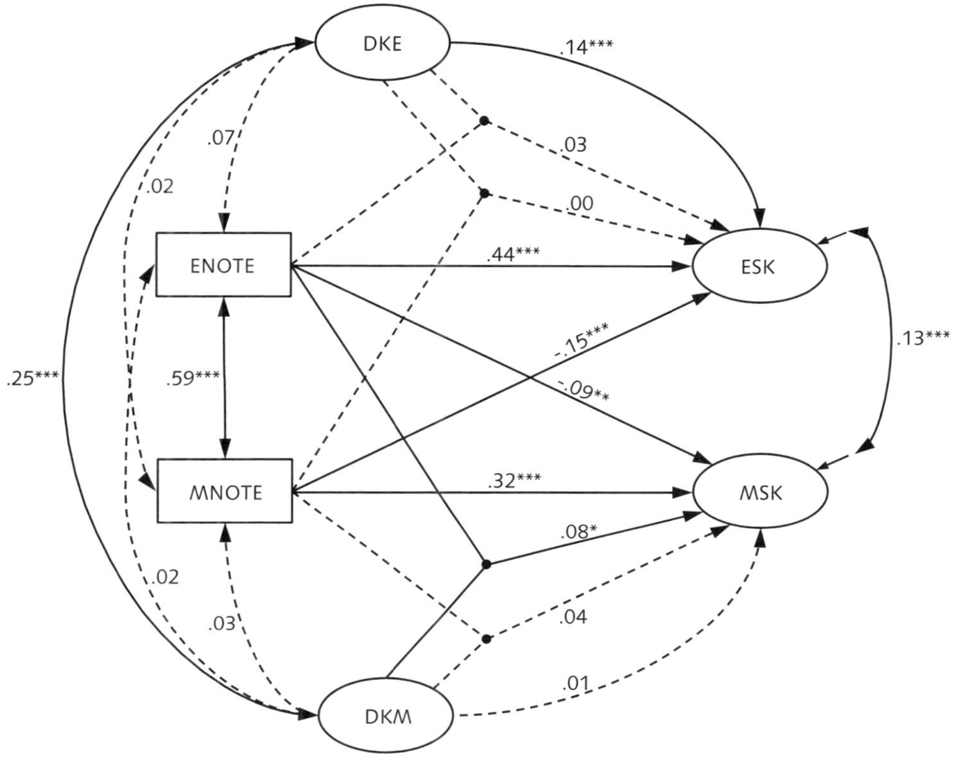

Abbildung 1. Ergebnisse für das I/E-Modell inklusive der potenziell moderierenden Effekte durch die wahrgenommenen diagnostischen Kompetenzen der Lehrkräfte in den beiden Fächern. Rekodierte Noten in Mathematik (MNOTE) und Englisch (ENOTE), Mathematikselbstkonzept (MSK), Englischselbstkonzept (ESK), wahrgenommene diagnostische Kompetenz in Mathematik (DKM) und in Englisch (DKE). Standardisierte Pfadkoeffizienten; gestrichelte Pfade sind nicht signifikant.
* $p \leq .05$. ** $p \leq .01$. *** $p \leq .001$.

3 Ergebnisse

3.1 Deskriptive Statistiken und Korrelationen

Für deskriptive Statistiken und Korrelationen zwischen den verwendeten Variablen siehe Tabelle 1. Wie erwartet waren die Noten in Mathematik und in Englisch positiv miteinander korreliert, ebenso wie Noten und Selbstkonzepte innerhalb einer Domäne. Die Wahrnehmung der diagnostischen Kompetenz der Lehrkraft in Mathematik war nicht mit der Mathematiknote, diejenige für die Lehrkraft in Englisch nur schwach mit der Englischnote, korreliert. Während die wahrgenommene diagnostische Kompetenz der Lehrkraft in Englisch schwach mit dem Englischselbstkonzept korreliert war, bestand kein Zusammenhang zwischen der wahrgenommenen diagnostischen Kompetenz der Lehrkraft in Mathematik mit dem

Mathematikselbstkonzept. Die durch die Schülerinnen und Schüler wahrgenommenen diagnostischen Kompetenzen der Mathematik- und der Englischlehrkraft korrelierten gering miteinander.

Tabelle 1. Deskriptive Statistiken und manifeste Korrelationen der verwendeten Variablen

	M	*SD*	1	2	3	4	5
1. MNOTE[a]	4.49	1.04	–				
2. ENOTE[a]	4.32	1.11	.60***	–			
3. MSK	2.80	0.77	.24***	.06**	–		
4. ESK	3.06	0.72	.07**	.32***	.12***	–	
5. DKM	2.80	0.64	.03	.02	.02	.08**	–
6. DKE	2.84	0.63	.02	.06*	-.09**	.13***	.24***

Anmerkungen. MNOTE = rekodierte Note in Mathematik, ENOTE = rekodierte Note in Englisch, MSK = Mathematikselbstkonzept, ESK = Englischselbstkonzept, DKM = wahrgenommene diagnostische Kompetenz in Mathematik, DKE = wahrgenommene diagnostische Kompetenz in Englisch. 4-stufige Skalen von 1 bis 4, insofern nicht anders angegeben.
[a]auf einer Skala von 1 bis 6. * $p \leq .05$. ** $p \leq .01$. *** $p \leq .001$.

3.2 Strukturgleichungsanalyse für das I/E-Modell inklusive Moderatoren

Das aufgestellte theoretische I/E-Modell inklusive der postulierten Interaktionen wies eine akzeptable Anpassungsgüte an die Daten auf: $\chi^2(684) = 2984.96$, CFI = .91, TLI = .90, RMSEA = .02, SRMR = .04. Die Vorhersagen des I/E-Modells wurden vollständig gestützt. Innerhalb jeder Domäne führten positive Pfade von den Noten zu den domänenspezifischen Selbstkonzepten entsprechend der Annahme sozialer Vergleichsprozesse. Zwischen den Domänen führten jeweils negative Pfade von der Note in einem Fach zum Selbstkonzept im kontrastierenden Fach entsprechend der Annahme zugrunde liegender dimensionaler Vergleichsprozesse. Während die Leistungen in Mathematik und Englisch hoch miteinander korreliert waren, bestand ein nur kleiner Zusammenhang zwischen den Selbstkonzepten in diesen Fächern.

Von den vier theoretisch postulierten Interaktionseffekten war einer signifikant. Der negative Kreuzpfad der Englischnote auf das Mathematikselbstkonzept variierte in Abhängigkeit von der wahrgenommenen diagnostischen Kompetenz der Lehrkraft in Mathematik. Zur Veranschaulichung dieses Interaktionseffekts zeigt Abbildung 2 die Simple-slopes der Regression der Englischnote auf das Mathematikselbstkonzept auf verschiedenen Niveaus des Moderators. Der negative Kreuzpfad war stärker, je geringer die wahrgenommene diagnostische Kompetenz der Lehrkraft in Mathematik war. Der negative Einfluss der Englischnote auf das Mathematikselbstkonzept der Schülerinnen und Schüler wurde geringer, je höher sie die Kompetenz ihrer Lehrkraft einschätzten, ihre Leistungen in Mathematik beurteilen zu können.

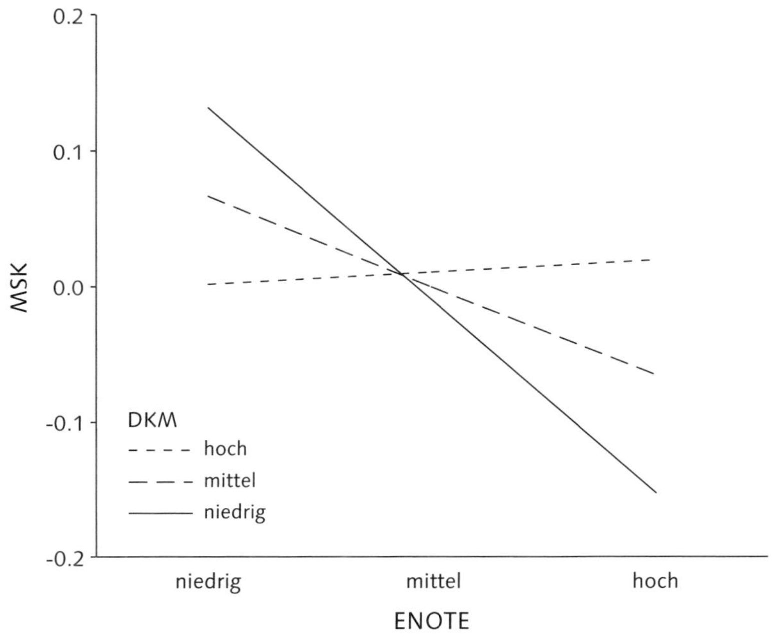

Abbildung 2. Moderation des Effekts zwischen den Domänen auf das Mathematikselbstkonzept (MSK). Simple-slopes für den Einfluss der Englischleistung (rekodierte Englischnote, ENOTE) auf MSK für verschiedene Niveaus der wahrgenommenen diagnostischen Kompetenz der Lehrkraft hinsichtlich Schülerleistungen in Mathematik (DKM); hoch = *M* + 1 *SD*, mittel = *M*, niedrig = *M* – 1 SD (Cohen, Cohen, West & Aiken, 2003). Basierend auf zentrierten Daten; Einheiten der y-Achse in Standardabweichungen.

4 Diskussion

Die Effekte von Leistungen innerhalb und zwischen verschiedenen Domänen auf die entsprechenden Fähigkeitsselbstkonzepte im I/E-Modell wurden bereits vielfach repliziert (Möller et al., 2009). Ziel der vorliegenden Studie war die konzeptuelle Replikation einer früheren Studie zur Untersuchung von Bedingungen unter denen Schülerinnen und Schüler das Feedback über ihre Leistungen in das Selbstbild ihrer eigenen Fähigkeiten übernehmen (Zimmermann et al., 2017). Hierfür wurden die von den Schülerinnen und Schülern wahrgenommenen Kompetenzen ihrer Lehrkräfte, fachliche Leistungen zu diagnostizieren, als potenzielle Moderatoren der Effekte im I/E-Modell mit den Domänen Mathematik und Englisch in die Analysen einbezogen.

Die grundlegenden Annahmen des I/E-Modells konnten erneut repliziert werden. Es traten sowohl Effekte der Fachnoten auf die Selbstkonzepte im selben Fach auf, was für die Annahme sozialer Vergleiche spricht, als auch Effekte der Fachnoten auf die Selbstkonzepte im jeweils anderen Fach, was für die Annahme dimensionaler Vergleiche spricht (Marsh, 1986). Die Höhe der gefundenen Effekte fällt jedoch teilweise etwas geringer aus, als anhand metaanalytischer Befunde zu erwarten gewesen wäre (Möller et al., 2009).

Bezüglich der Moderation durch die wahrgenommene diagnostische Kompetenz zeigte sich eine signifikante Interaktion hinsichtlich der diagnostischen Kompetenz der Mathematiklehrkraft: Je geringer diese wahrgenommen wurde, umso stärker wurde der verzerrende Kontrasteffekt der Englischnote auf das mathematische Selbstkonzept. Schülerinnen und Schüler scheinen bei mangelndem Vertrauen in die diagnostische Kompetenz ihrer Mathematiklehrkraft stärker auf Alternativen zur Mathematiknote, nämlich dimensionale Vergleiche mit Leistungen in der verbalen Domäne zurückzugreifen, um ihr mathematisches Selbstkonzept zu bilden, als wenn sie ihrer Mathematiklehrkraft eine hohe diagnostische Kompetenz zuschreiben. Dafür sprechen auch die Befunde in zwei anderen Stichproben einer ähnlichen Studie (Zimmermann et al., 2017).

Hinsichtlich der Effekte von Leistungen auf Selbstkonzepte innerhalb der Domänen ergaben sich in dieser Studie keine Hinweise auf eine Moderation durch die wahrgenommene diagnostische Kompetenz der Lehrkräfte in den untersuchten Fächern Mathematik und Englisch als Fremdsprache. Dies geht einher mit den Ergebnissen vorheriger Untersuchungen, in denen keine signifikanten oder inkonsistente Befunde bezüglich Moderationen der Effekte innerhalb von Mathematik und der muttersprachlichen verbalen Domäne berichtet wurden (Möller et al., 2002; Möller et al., 2006; Skaalvik & Rankin, 1992; Steinmayr & Spinath, 2015; Zimmermann et al., 2017). Dennoch bleibt unklar, warum eher dimensionale als soziale Vergleiche moderiert werden. Es erscheint vorstellbar, dass durch die in der Schule stets verfügbaren Informationen über eigene Leistungsstände im Vergleich zu anderen, beispielsweise durch die unmittelbaren Rückmeldungen von Klausurergebnissen und mündlichen Leistungen im Klassenraum, soziale Vergleichsprozesse innerhalb eines Schulfachs bei den Schülerinnen und Schülern regelmäßig direkt angestoßen und geradezu automatisiert werden. Solche unmittelbar ablaufenden Vergleichsprozesse innerhalb eines Fachs, denen man sich möglicherweise nur schwer entziehen kann, lassen eventuell weniger Spielraum für Bedingungen, unter denen das Ergebnis des sozialen Vergleichs weniger stark in das Selbstkonzept eingeht.

Die im Rahmen dieser Studie untersuchten Schülerinnen und Schüler schätzten die diagnostischen Kompetenzen ihrer Lehrkräfte im Mittel recht hoch ein und diese Einschätzung wird auch durch metaanalytische Befunde zur Urteilsgenauigkeit von Lehrkräften gestützt (Hoge & Coladarci, 1989; Südkamp et al., 2012). Dennoch gibt es auch substanzielle Varianz sowohl in der diagnostischen Kompetenz der Lehrkräfte, wie Schülerinnen und Schüler sie sehen, als auch in der Urteilsgenauigkeit der Lehrkräfte, was auf Verbesserungspotenziale hinweist. Zum einen ist eine hohe Kompetenz zur Beurteilung von Leistungsständen entscheidend für die Gestaltung und Optimierung eines adaptiven Unterrichts, der hinreichend an die Lernausgangslagen der Schülerinnen und Schüler angepasst wird (Hattie, 2009; Schrader & Helmke, 1987). Zum anderen haben die von Lehrkräften vergebenen Leistungsurteile in Form von Noten eine große Bedeutung für die weitere akademische Laufbahn. Eine hohe diagnostische Kompetenz und entsprechende Wahrnehmung durch die Schülerinnen und Schüler könnte zudem die Entwicklung realistischer, weniger durch Kontrastierungen dimensionaler Vergleiche verzerrter Selbstkonzepte unterstützen, was aufgrund der Implikationen hinsichtlich Interesse, schulbezogenem Verhalten und Leistungen als ein wichtiges schulisches Ziel angesehen werden kann (z. B. Eccles, 1983; Eccles & Wigfield, 2002; Valentine, DuBois & Cooper, 2004). Auch können sich Unterschätzungen nicht nur ungünstig auf das Selbstkonzept der Schülerinnen und Schüler, sondern auch auf deren Emotionen und Verhalten auswirken (z. B. Urhahne, Chao, Florineth, Luttenberger & Paechter, 2011; Zimmermann, Schütte, Taskinen & Köller, 2013). Entsprechend wird die Vermittlung diagnostischer Kompetenzen in den Standards für die Lehrerbildung im Bereich Bildungswissenschaften gefordert und sollte zentral in der Lehramtsausbildung thematisiert werden (KMK, 2004).

Interessant erscheint auch das Ergebnis der vorliegenden Studie, dass eine hohe wahrgenommene Kompetenz der Lehrkraft, Englischleistungen zu diagnostizieren, in direktem Zusammenhang mit dem Englischselbstkonzept stand. Möglicherweise spiegelt sich darin eine höhere Adaptivität des Unterrichts an die besser diagnostizierten Lernausgangslagen wider, die über passendere Kompetenzrückmeldungen an die Schülerinnen und Schüler zu mehr Lernzuwachs und darüber auch zu höheren Selbstkonzepten in dieser Domäne beitragen könnte. In der Studie von Zimmermann et al. (2017) zeigte sich ein analoger Effekt in der mathematischen Domäne. Noch erscheinen Interpretationen dieser Zusammenhänge aber verfrüht. Aufgrund des korrelativen Designs kann nicht ausgeschlossen werden, dass Schülerinnen und Schüler mit besserem Englisch- (bzw. Mathematik-)selbstkonzept dazu tendieren, die diagnostische Kompetenz der Lehrkräfte in Englisch (bzw. Mathematik) besser zu beurteilen. Von den durch die Lehrkräfte vergebenen Noten scheint die Einschätzung der diagnostischen Kompetenz in den entsprechenden Fächern durch die Schülerinnen und Schüler hingegen weitestgehend unabhängig zu sein.

Im Rahmen dieser Studie konnten erste Befunde zur Moderation der Effekte im I/E-Modell durch die wahrgenommene diagnostische Kompetenz der Lehrkraft repliziert werden. Robust in den zwei früheren Stichproben (Zimmermann et al., 2017) sowie in dieser Stichprobe wurde gefunden, dass bei niedriger wahrgenommener diagnostischer Kompetenz der Mathematiklehrkraft eigene verbale Leistungen stärker kontrastierend für die Einschätzung des Fähigkeitsselbstkonzepts in Mathematik herangezogen werden. Einschränkend ist anzumerken, dass in der vorliegenden Studie lediglich dieser eine Interaktionseffekt signifikant war. Zudem fielen die Pfade des I/E-Modells im Vergleich zu metaanalytischen Befunden teilweise geringer aus (Möller et al., 2009), was für die Möglichkeit stichprobenspezifischer Effekte sprechen könnte. Dass die Ergebnisse dieser Studie jedoch mit den existierenden Ergebnissen in den früheren Stichproben vereinbar sind, spricht gegen diese Annahme. Hinsichtlich der insgesamt bescheiden ausfallenden Interaktionseffekte bleibt fraglich, inwieweit die schülerseitig wahrgenommene diagnostische Kompetenz von Lehrkräften substanziell zur Auffindung von Bedingungen beiträgt, unter denen die Effekte des externalen und des internalen Referenzrahmens im I/E-Modell variieren. Die praktische Relevanz der robust aufgefundenen Moderation erscheint gering. Nichtsdestotrotz gibt diese Studie vielversprechende theoretische Einblicke und wertvolle Anstöße für die zukünftige Forschung, sich dem interessanten Thema der Bedingungen zu widmen, unter denen die Effekte sozialer und dimensionaler Vergleiche auf das schulische Selbstkonzept wirken. Zukünftige Studien könnten weitere potenzielle Moderatoren in den Blick nehmen und die bisher zu diesem Zweck untersuchten Variablen wie die wahrgenommene Ähnlichkeit der untersuchten Fächer bzw. der Leistungen, die Spezifität der Begabungsüberzeugung oder die Intelligenz der Schülerinnen und Schüler weiter ergänzen (Helm et al., 2016; Möller, et al., 2002; Skaalvik & Rankin, 1992, Steinmayr & Spinath, 2015).

Literatur

Allison, P. D. (2003). Missing data techniques for structural equation modeling. *Journal of Abnormal Psychology, 112*, 545–557.

Baumert, J., Gruehn, S., Heyn, S., Köller, O. & Schnabel, K. (1997). *Bildungsverläufe und psychosoziale Entwicklung im Jugendalter (BIJU). Dokumentation, Band 1. Skalen Längsschnitt I, Welle 1–4.* Berlin: Max-Planck-Institut für Bildungsforschung.

Cohen, J., Cohen, P., West, S. G. & Aiken, L. S. (2003). *Applied multiple regression/correlation analysis for the behavioral sciences* (3rd ed.). Mahwah, NJ: Lawrence Erlbaum Associates.

Dijkstra, P., Kuyper, H., van der Werf, G., Buunk, A. P. & van der Zee, Y. G. (2008). Social comparison in the classroom: A review. *Review of Educational Research, 78*, 828–879.

Eccles, J. S. (1983). Expectancies, values, and academic behaviors. In J. T. Spence (Ed.), *Achievement and achievement motives* (pp. 75–146). San Francisco, CA: Freeman.

Eccles, J. S. & Wigfield, A. (2002). Motivational beliefs, values, and goals. *Annual Review of Psychology, 53*, 109–132.

Fend, H. & Specht, W. (Hrsg.). (1986). *Erziehungsumwelten*. Bericht aus dem Projekt „Entwicklung im Jugendalter". Konstanz: Universität, Sozialwissenschaftliche Fakultät.

Festinger, L. (1954). A theory of social comparison processes. *Human Relations, 7*, 117–140.

Graham, J. W. (2009). Missing data analysis: Making it work in the real world. *Annual Review of Psychology, 60*, 549–576.

Hattie, J. (2009). *Visible learning. A synthesis of over 800 meta-analyses relating to achievement*. London: Routledge.

Helm, F. & Möller, J. (2017). Der Einfluss von Erhebungsbedingungen auf Kontrasteffekte dimensionaler Vergleiche. *Psychologie in Erziehung und Unterricht, 64*, 24–34.

Helm, F., Mueller-Kalthoff, H., Nagy, N. & Möller, J. (2016). Dimensional comparison theory. Perceived subject similarity impacts on students' self-concepts. *AERA Open, 2*.

Hoge, R. D. & Coladarci, T. (1989). Teacher-based judgments of academic achievement: A review of literature. *Review of Educational Research, 59*, 297–313.

Hox, J. (2002). *Multilevel analysis. Techniques and applications*. Mahwah, NJ: Lawrence Erlbaum Associates.

Jopt, U. J. (1978). *Selbstkonzept und Ursachenerklärung in der Schule*. Bochum: Kamp.

Kultusministerkonferenz. (2004). *Standards für die Lehrerbildung: Bildungswissenschaften*. Bonn: KMK.

Marsh, H. W. (1986). Verbal and math self-concepts: An internal/external frame of reference model. *American Educational Research Journal, 23*, 129–149.

Marsh, H. W. (1990). Influences of internal and external frames of reference on the formation of math and English self-concepts. *Journal of Educational Psychology, 82*, 107–116.

Marsh, H. W., Byrne, B. M. & Shavelson, R. J. (1988). A multifaceted academic self-concept: Its hierarchical structure and its relation to academic achievement. *Journal of Educational Psychology, 80*, 366–380.

Marsh, H. W., Kuyper, H., Seaton, M., Parker, P. D., Morin, A. J. S., Möller, J. & Abduljabbar, A. S. (2014). Dimensional comparison theory: An extension of the internal/external frame of reference effect on academic self-concept formation. *Contemporary Educational Psychology, 39*, 326–341.

Marsh, H. W., Wen, Z. & Hau, K.-T. (2004). Structural equation models of latent interactions: Evaluation of alternative estimation strategies and indicator construction. *Psychological Methods, 9*, 275–300.

Mead, G. H. (1934). *Mind, self, and society*. Chicago, IL: University of Chicago Press.

Möller, J. & Husemann, N. (2006). Internal comparisons in everyday life. *Journal of Educational Psychology, 98*, 342–353.

Möller, J. & Köller, O. (2001). Dimensional comparisons: An experimental approach to the internal/external frame of reference model. *Journal of Educational Psychology, 93*, 826–835.

Möller, J. & Marsh, H. W. (2013). Dimensional comparison theory. *Psychological Review, 120*, 544–560.

Möller, J., Pohlmann, B., Köller, O. & Marsh, H. W. (2009). A meta-analytic path analysis of the internal/external frame of reference model of academic achievement and academic self-concept. *Review of Educational Research, 79*, 1129–1167.

Möller, J., Pohlmann, B., Streblow, L. & Kauffmann, J. (2002). Die Spezifität von Begabungsüberzeugungen als Determinante des verbalen und mathematischen Begabungsselbstkonzepts. *Zeitschrift für Pädagogische Psychologie, 16*, 87–97.

Möller, J., Streblow, L. & Pohlmann, B. (2006). The belief in a negative interdependence of math and verbal abilities as determinant of academic self-concepts. *British Journal of Educational Psychology, 76*, 57–70.

Murayama, K., Pekrun, R. & Fiedler, K. (2014). Research practices that can prevent an inflation of false-positive rates. *Personality and Social Psychology Review, 18*, 107–118.

Muthén, L. K. & Muthén, B. O. (2015). *Mplus* [Computer software]. Los Angeles, CA: Authors.

Pohlmann, B. & Möller, J. (2009). On the benefit of dimensional comparisons. *Journal of Educational Psychology, 101*, 248–258.

Schmidt, S. (2009). Shall we really do it again? The powerful concept of replication is neglected in the social sciences. *Review of General Psychology, 13*, 90–100.

Schrader, F.-W. & Helmke, A. (1987). Diagnostische Kompetenz von Lehrern: Komponenten und Wirkungen. *Empirische Pädagogik, 1*, 27–52.

Skaalvik, E. M. & Rankin, R. J. (1992). Math and verbal achievement and self-concepts: Testing the internal/external frame of reference model. *The Journal of Early Adolescence, 12*, 267–279.

Steinmayr, R. & Spinath, B. (2015). Intelligence as a potential moderator in the internal/external frame of reference model.

Journal for Educational Research Online, 7, 198–218.

Steinmetz, H., Davidov, E. & Schmidt, P. (2011). Three approaches to estimate latent interaction effects: Intention and perceived behavioral control in the Theory of Planned Behavior. *Methodological Innovations Online, 6*, 95–110.

Strickhouser, J. E. & Zell, E. (2015). Self-evaluative effects of dimensional and social comparison. *Journal of Experimental Social Psychology, 59*, 60–66.

Südkamp, A., Kaiser, J. & Möller, J. (2012). Accuracy of teachers' judgments of students' academic achievement: A meta-analysis. *Journal of Educational Psychology, 104*, 743–762.

Tesser, A. (1988). Toward a self-evaluation maintenance model of social behavior. *Advances in Experimental Social Psychology, 27*, 181–227.

Ulrich, R., Erdfelder, E., Deutsch, R., Strauß, B., Brüggemann, A., Hannover, B., Tuschen-Caffier, B., Kirschbaum, C., Blickle, G., Möller, J. & Rief, W. (2016). Inflation von falsch-positiven Befunden in der psychologischen Forschung. *Psychologische Rundschau, 67*, 163–174.

Urhahne, D., Chao, S.-H., Florineth, M. L., Luttenberger, S. & Paechter, M. (2011). Academic self-concept, learning motivation, and test anxiety of the underestimated student. *British Journal of Educational Psychology, 81*, 161–177.

Valentine, J. C., DuBois, D. L. & Cooper, H. (2004). The relation between self-beliefs and academic achievement: A meta-analytic review. *Educational Psychologist, 39*, 111–133.

Zimmermann, F., Möller, J. & Köller, O. (2017). When students doubt their teachers' diagnostic competence: Moderation in the internal/external frame of reference model. *Journal of Educational Psychology*. Advance online publication.

Zimmermann, F., Schütte, K., Taskinen, P. & Köller, O. (2013). Reciprocal effects between adolescent externalizing problems and measures of achievement. *Journal of Educational Psychology, 105*, 747–761.

Autorinnen und Autoren

PROF. DR. FRIEDERIKE ZIMMERMANN
Institut für Pädagogisch-Psychologische Lehr- und Lernforschung, Christian-Albrechts-Universität zu Kiel.

JULIA BECHERER
Institut für Pädagogisch-Psychologische Lehr- und Lernforschung, Christian-Albrechts Universität zu Kiel.

PROF. DR. OLAF KÖLLER
Erziehungswissenschaft, IPN · Leibniz-Institut für die Pädagogik der Naturwissenschaften und Mathematik, Kiel.

KONTAKT
Friederike Zimmermann, Institut für Pädagogisch-Psychologische Lehr- und Lernforschung, Christian-Albrechts-Universität zu Kiel, Olshausenstraße 75, 24118 Kiel.
E-Mail: *fzimmermann@ipl.uni-kiel.de*

Vorhersage von Kurswahl und Leistung in der gymnasialen Oberstufe: Fächerübergreifende Zusammenhänge

BRITTA POHLMANN UND LILIAN STREBLOW

ZUSAMMENFASSUNG: Die vorliegende Studie untersucht den komplexen Zusammenhang zwischen motivationalen Einstellungen und Leistungen in den Fächern Mathematik und Englisch. Als theoretische Basis dienen das das Erwartungs-Wert-Modell und das Reciprocal Internal/External Frame of Reference Model. Eine Stichprobe von *N* = 2.391 Schülerinnen und Schülern bearbeitete zu Beginn und am Ende der gymnasialen Oberstufe Fachleistungstests und Fragebögen, anhand derer standardisierte Testergebnisse und Noten sowie Selbstkonzept, Aufgabenwert und Kurswahl in den Fächern Mathematik und Englisch erfasst wurden. Innerhalb der Domänen konnten positive Effekte von den Leistungen auf die motivationalen Überzeugungen (Selbstkonzept und Aufgabenwert) und von den motivationalen Überzeugungen auf das nachfolgende Leistungsverhalten (Kurswahl und Testergebnis) nachgewiesen werden. Zwischen den Domänen ergaben sich negative Effekte von den Leistungen auf das Selbstkonzept und den Aufgabenwert in der nicht korrespondierenden Domäne. Reziproke negative Effekte von den motivationalen Variablen auf die nachfolgende Leistung blieben größtenteils aus. Die Ergebnisse werden vor dem Hintergrund bildungstheoretischer Ziele der gymnasialen Oberstufe diskutiert.

Schlüsselwörter: Erwartungs-Wert-Modell, reciprocal internal/external frame of reference model, Leistung, Selbstkonzept, Kurswahl

Predicting course selection and achievement in the upper secondary school: relationships across domains

ABSTRACT: The present study investigated the complex relationship between motivational beliefs and performances in mathematics and English. As theoretical framework, the expectancy-value model and the reciprocal internal/external frame of reference model were used. A sample of *N* = 2.391 students worked on achievement tests and questionnaires at the beginning and the end of upper secondary school. Thereby, test scores and grades as well as self-concepts and task values and course choices in mathematics and English were assessed. Within the domains positive effects from academic achievements on motivational beliefs (self-concept and task value) and from motivational beliefs on subsequent performances (course selection and test score) could be demonstrated. Across the domains negative effects of achievement on self-concept and task value in the non-corresponding domain were found. Reciprocal negative effects of motivational beliefs on subsequent performance largely failed to appear. The results are discussed in the light of educational aims of the upper stage at high school.

Keywords: expectancy-value model, reciprocal internal/external frame of reference model, achievement, self-concept, course selection

Einleitung

Motivationale Überzeugungen wie Selbstkonzept und Fachinteresse gelten als bedeutsame Einflussfaktoren für schulische Leistungsentwicklungen und Bildungserträge. Positive Selbstkonzepte und höhere Interessen begünstigen das Lernen und führen zur Wahl anspruchsvoller Kurse und Aufgaben und zu besseren Leistungsergebnissen (z. B. Köller, Baumert & Schnabel, 2001; Marsh & Yeung, 1997; Marsh & Martin, 2011; Valentine, DuBois & Cooper, 2004). Zur Entwicklung ihrer fachbezogenen Erfolgserwartungen und Einstellungen nutzen Personen Informationen über ihre bisherigen Leistungen.

1 Theoretischer Hintergrund

1.1 Vorhersage von Kurswahlen und Leistungsverhalten

Einen theoretischen Ansatz zur Beschreibung des Zusammenhangs von motivationalen Überzeugungen und Leistungsverhalten bietet das Erwartungs-Wert-Modell (EW-Modell) von Eccles und Kollegen (Eccles et al., 1983; Wigfield & Eccles, 2000). Demnach wird leistungsbezogenes Verhalten wie die Wahl bestimmter Aufgaben oder Kurse durch die Erfolgserwartung und den subjektiven Wert der Aufgabe bestimmt. Die Erfolgserwartung ist als Annahme einer Person definiert, wie gut sie in einer bevorstehenden Aufgabe abschneiden wird (Eccles, Wigfield & Schiefele, 1998) Frühere Arbeiten zum EW-Modell differenzieren zwischen Erfolgserwartung und Selbstkonzept. Die Erfolgserwartung speist sich aus dem Selbstkonzept und der wahrgenommenen Schwierigkeit einer Aufgabe, wobei das Selbstkonzept der erklärungsmächtigere Prädiktor zu sein scheint. Empirische Studien zeigten eine hohe Korrelation zwischen der Erfolgserwartung und dem Selbstkonzept einer Person, so dass diese beiden Komponenten zu einem Konstrukt zusammenfielen. In der vorliegenden Studie wird nicht zwischen diesen beiden Komponenten unterschieden, sondern das Selbstkonzept als alleiniger Prädiktor zur Abbildung der Erfolgskomponente verwendet.

Der Aufgabenwert spaltet sich nach Eccles und Kollegen in vier Komponenten: eine intrinsische Komponente, eine Wichtigkeitskomponente, eine Nützlichkeitskomponente und Kosten (Eccles et al., 1998). Die Wichtigkeit beschreibt die Bedeutung für eine Person, in einer Aufgabe erfolgreich zu sein. Die affektive oder emotionale Komponente spiegelt die Freude an der Ausübung einer Tätigkeit wieder, die Nützlichkeit das Ausmaß, in dem die Aufgabe für das Erreichen persönlicher Ziele relevant ist. Die Kosten beziehen sich auf die erforderliche Anstrengung und den Zeitaufwand für die Bewältigung der Aufgabe sowie die negativen Konsequenzen eines möglichen Misserfolgs. In der vorliegenden Studie wurden zur Erfassung des Aufgabenwerts die intrinsische Komponente, die Wichtigkeits- und die Nützlichkeitskomponente einbezogen.

Erfolgserwartung und Aufgabenwert werden durch individuelle Ziele bestimmt, die wiederum durch die wahrgenommenen Einstellungen und Erwartungen wichtiger Bezugspersonen und durch frühere Leistungserfahrungen beeinflusst werden (Eccles & Wigfield, 2002). Empirische Studien bestätigen die im EW-Modell postulierten Zusammenhänge. Einflüsse motivationaler Überzeugungen wurden sowohl für Kurs- und Berufswahlen als auch für späteres Leistungsverhalten nachgewiesen (z. B. Guo, Marsh, Parker, Morin & Yeung, 2015; Köller, Trautwein, Lüdtke & Baumert, 2006; Nagy, Trautwein, Baumert, Köller & Garrett, 2006).

1.2 Entwicklung fachspezifischer Selbstkonzepte infolge sozialer und dimensionaler Vergleiche

Das EW-Modell beschreibt die Ausbildung aufgaben- oder fachbezogener Selbstkonzepte als Ergebnis der Interpretation vergangener Leistungsresultate und damit einhergehender Erfolgs- und Misserfolgserfahrungen. Dabei werden insbesondere soziale und dimensionale Vergleichsinformationen herangezogen (im Überblick Möller & Köller, 2004). Beim sozialen Vergleich stellen Personen ihre Leistungen den Leistungen anderer gegenüber. Wenn sie in einem Bereich besser abschneiden als ihre Vergleichspersonen, führt das zu einem sozialen Abwärtsvergleich und zur Entwicklung eines höheren Selbstkonzepts; wenn sie schlechter abschneiden entsprechend zu einem Aufwärtsvergleich und einem niedrigen Selbstkonzept. Beim dimensionalen Vergleich (Möller & Marsh, 2013) wird die eigene Leistung in einem Bereich mit der eigenen Leistung in einem anderen Bereich verglichen. Hier führt die vergleichsweise bessere Leistung in einem Bereich (dimensionaler Abwärtsvergleich) zu einem höheren Selbstkonzept in diesem Bereich und gleichzeitig zu einem niedrigeren Selbstkonzept in der Vergleichsdomäne (dimensionaler Aufwärtsvergleich).

Marsh (1986) beschreibt den Zusammenhang zwischen Leistung und Selbstkonzept in zwei Domänen in seinem Internal/External Frame of Reference Model (I/E-Modell). Sowohl feldanalytische (z. B. Marsh & Hau, 2004) als auch experimentelle Studien (Möller & Köller, 2001; Pohlmann & Möller, 2009) lieferten Unterstützung für das Modell, indem positive Effekte von der Leistung auf das Selbstkonzept innerhalb der Domänen und negative Effekte von der Leistung auf das Selbstkonzept zwischen den Domänen nachgewiesen wurden. Dieser Zusammenhang wurde sowohl mit verschiedenen Leistungsindikatoren (Testergebnisse vs. Noten) als auch für unterschiedliche Altersgruppen (Schülerinnen und Schüler der Primarstufe, der Sekundarstufe I und der Sekundarstufe II) belegt (Möller, Pohlmann, Köller & Marsh, 2009). In Studien zum EW-Modell wurden Effekte internaler und externaler Vergleiche nicht für das Selbstkonzept, sondern auch für den Aufgabenwert beobachtet (Nagy et al., 2008; Guo, Parker, Marsh & Morin, 2015).

1.3 Reziproke Zusammenhänge zwischen Leistung und Selbstkonzept

Das Reciprocal Internal/External Frame of Reference Model (RI/EM; Möller, Retelsdorf, Köller und Marsh (2011) erweitert das I/E-Modell, indem es das Reciprocal Effects Model (REM; Marsh & Craven, 2006; Valentine et al., 2004) integriert und parallel die Einflüsse von Leistung auf Selbstkonzept und von Selbstkonzept auf Leistung in zwei Domänen in den Blick nimmt. Sowohl Möller et al. (2011) als auch Niepel, Brunner und Preckel (2014) fanden empirische Unterstützung für das RI/EM. In Übereinstimmung mit dem REM zeigten sich innerhalb der Domänen sowohl positive Effekte von der Leistung auf das Selbstkonzept als auch vom Selbstkonzept auf die Leistung. Das I/E-Modell wurde durch die Kontrasteffekte zwischen den Domänen von der Leistung auf das Selbstkonzept bestätigt. Umgekehrt ergaben sich vom Selbstkonzept in einem Bereich auf die Leistung im anderen Bereich schwache negative Effekte. Bei einer weiteren Überprüfung des RI/EM (Möller, Zimmermann & Köller, 2014) konnten diese negativen Effekte zwischen den Domänen vom Selbstkonzept auf die Leistung jedoch nicht nachgewiesen werden.

2 Ziel der Untersuchung

Die vorliegende Studie untersucht das Zusammenspiel von motivationaler Überzeugungen und Leistungsindikatoren in der gymnasialen Oberstufe. Dabei werden die Einflüsse innerhalb und zwischen den Fächern Mathematik und Englisch betrachtet. Die Studie kombiniert das EW-Modell und das RI/EM und leitet daraus Annahmen über die komplexen Wirkmechanismen innerhalb und zwischen den Domänen ab.

Dem EW-Modell zufolge erwarten wir innerhalb der beiden Fächer Mathematik und Englisch jeweils positive Effekte von der Ausgangsleistung zu Beginn der Sekundarstufe II auf das fachspezifische Selbstkonzept und den Aufgabenwert. Als Prädiktoren werden dabei Testergebnisse und Noten einbezogen. Die Noten stellen Leistungsrückmeldungen dar, über die die Effekte der Testergebnisse auf die Selbstkonzepte vermittelt sein sollten. Ausgangsleistung, Selbstkonzept und Aufgabenwert beeinflussen wiederum die nachfolgenden Bildungsergebnisse. Als Indikatoren für die Bildungsergebnisse werden die Kurswahl und die Leistungsergebnisse am Ende der Oberstufe betrachtet.

Zwischen den beiden Domänen erwarten wir – wie im RI/EM postuliert – negative reziproke Effekte. So sollten sich a) negative Effekte von den Leistungen auf die motivationalen Einstellungen und b) negative Effekte von den motivationalen Einstellungen auf das nachfolgende Leistungsverhalten im nichtkorrespondierenden Fach ergeben. Die postulierten Effekte zwischen den verschiedenen Konstrukten sind in Abbildung 1 dargestellt.

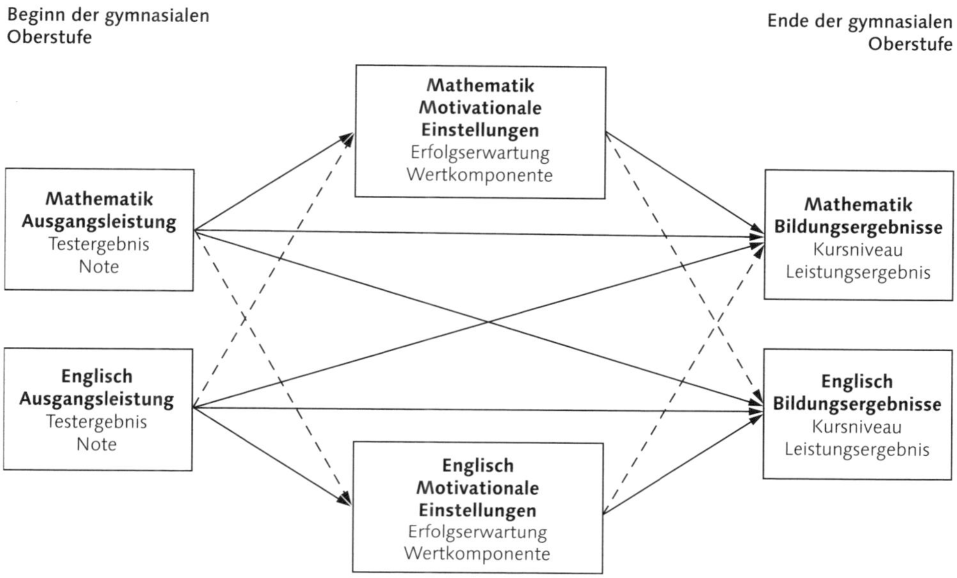

Abbildung 1. Hypothetisches Modell. Erwartete positive Effekte sind mit einer durchgezogenen Linie gekennzeichnet, erwartete negative Effekte mit einer gestrichelten Linie.

Zusammenfassend werden mit der vorliegenden Untersuchung folgende Hypothesen untersucht:

1. Auf die motivationalen Einstellungen (Selbstkonzept und Aufgabenwert) in den Fächern Mathematik und Englisch zeigen sich positive Effekte von den Leistungen im korrespondierenden Fach und negative Effekten von den Leistungen im nichtkorrespondierenden Fach. Die Effekte der Testleistungen sind dabei zum Teil über die Notenrückmeldungen vermittelt.

2. Bei Kontrolle der Ausgangsleistungen zeigen sich positive Effekte von den motivationalen Einstellungen auf das nachfolgende Leistungsverhalten (Kurswahl und Testleistung) im korrespondierenden Fach und negative Effekte auf das Leistungsverhalten im nichtkorrespondierenden Fach.

3 Methode

Zur Untersuchung der Fragestellungen wurde ein längsschnittliches Design mit zwei Messzeitpunkten gewählt. Beim ersten Messzeitpunkt wurde die Testleistung, die Zeugnisnote, das Selbstkonzept und der Aufgabenwert in den Fächern Mathematik und Englisch erfasst. Beim zweiten Messzeitpunkt wurde erneut die Testleistung erhoben und das gewählte Kursniveau in den beiden Fächern erfragt.

3.1 Stichprobe

Zu Beginn und am Ende der Studienstufe der gymnasialen Oberstufe wurden $N = 2.391$ Schülerinnen und Schüler (54,6 % weiblich) aus 23 Hamburger Schulen (15 Gymnasien und 8 Stadtteilschulen) untersucht. An den Gymnasien umfasst die Studienstufe die Jahrgangsstufen 11 und 12, an den Stadtteilschulen die Jahrgangsstufen 12 und 13. Die beteiligten Schulen stellten eine geschichtete Zufallsstichprobe für das Bundesland Hamburg dar, die Auswahl erfolgte nach sozioökonomischen und regionalen Kriterien. Die Testung zu Beginn der Studienstufe fand im Herbst 2010 statt, die Testung am Ende der Studienstufe im Frühjahr 2012. Zu beiden Messzeitpunkten erfolgte die Datenerhebung im Kursverband durch geschulte Testleiterinnen und Testleiter. Neben Leistungstests in den Fächern Mathematik und Englisch wurden Fragebögen eingesetzt, mit denen Hintergrundmerkmale, Noten und motivationale Variablen erhoben wurden.

3.2 Instrumente

Testleistungen. Zur Erfassung der Mathematik- und der Englischleistungen wurden Untertests aus der standardisierten Testbatterie Hamburger Schulleistungstests für zehnte und elfte Klassen – SL-HAM 10/11 (Behörde für Schule, Jugend und Berufsbildung, Amt für Schule, Hamburg, 2000) eingesetzt. Der Mathematiktest enthält Multiple-Choice-Aufgaben zur Erfassung der mathematischen Grundbildung und zeigte in beiden Erhebungen zufrieden stellende Reliabilitäten (> .75). In Englisch wurde ein C-Test (Cloze-Test) eingesetzt, der das allgemeine Sprachverständnis misst und sich als hoch reliabel erwies (> .85). Die Berechnung der Testwerte erfolgte auf Basis der Item Response Theory mit Hilfe der Software ConQuest (Wu, Adams & Wilson, 1998). Zum Messzeitpunkt 1 wurden die Testwerte auf eine Skala mit dem Mittelwert von $M = 500$ und der Standardabweichung von $SD = 100$ transformiert, zum zweiten Messzeitpunkt wurden die Testwerte an den Parametern von Messzeitpunkt 1 standardisiert, so dass die Werte zu beiden Erhebungen auf einer gemeinsamen Metrik liegen.

Noten. In den Fragebögen wurden die Schülerinnen und Schüler nach ihren letzten Zeugnisnoten in den Fächern Mathematik und Englisch gefragt. Die Noten wurden auf der sechsstufigen Notenskala (1 = sehr gut bis 6 = ungenügend) angegeben. Zur leichteren Interpretierbarkeit der Ergebnisse wurden die Noten umkodiert, so dass höhere Werte jeweils bessere Leistungen bedeuten.

Fachspezifisches Selbstkonzept. Das Selbstkonzept in den Fächern Mathematik und Englisch wurden jeweils anhand von vier Items aus dem Self Description Questionnaire (SDQ III; Marsh, 1992) erhoben (Itembeispiel: „Ich war in Mathematik [Englisch] immer gut"). Vorgegeben wurde jeweils ein vierstufiges Antwortformat. Die Reliabilitäten der Skala waren für beide Fächer sehr hoch (> .85).

Fachspezifische Wertkomponente. Zur Operationalisierung des Aufgabenwerts wurde die von Eccles et al. (1998) beschriebene intrinsische Komponente, die Wichtigkeitskomponente und die Nützlichkeitskomponente berücksichtigt. Die intrinsische Komponente wurde anhand von vier Items (Itembeispiel: „Ich hätte gern mehr Mathematik [Englisch]-Stunden"), erfasst; die Wichtigkeitskomponente anhand von drei Items (Itembeispiel: „Mathematik [Englisch] gehört für mich persönlich zu den wichtigsten Fächern"), und die Nützlichkeitskomponente anhand von drei Items (Itembeispiel: „Eine gute Note in Mathematik [Englisch] kann mir später sehr nutzen."). Diese drei Subskalen wiesen für beide Fächer gute Reliabilitäten auf (> .78).

Kurswahl. Nach der gültigen Ausbildungs- und Prüfungsordnung zum Erwerb der allgemeinen Hochschulreife müssen alle Schülerinnen und Schüler in Hamburg die Fächer Deutsch, Mathematik und eine spätestens ab Jahrgangsstufe 8 unterrichtete Fremdsprache (so genannte Kernfächer) bis zum Ende der Studienstufe belegen. Der Unterricht wird auf grundlegendem oder erhöhtem Anforderungsniveau erteilt. Die Schülerinnen und Schüler wählen mindestens zwei Kernfächer auf erhöhtem Niveau. Im Fragebogen gaben die Schülerinnen und Schüler an, welches Anforderungsniveau sie in den Fächern Mathematik und Englisch gewählt haben.

3.3 Statistische Analysen

Zur Prüfung der postulierten Zusammenhänge zwischen den untersuchten Konstrukten wurden Strukturgleichungsmodelle mit der Statistiksoftware Mplus 7.4 (Muthén & Muthén, 2015) gerechnet. Die motivationalen Konstrukte „Selbstkonzept" und „Aufgabenwert" gingen dabei als latente Faktoren in die Analysen ein. Als Schätzmethode wurde der „maximum likelihood estimator with robust standard errors" verwendet. Wie für das Feld der empirischen Bildungsforschung typisch, weist der zugrunde liegende Datensatz eine geschachtelte Struktur auf, da Schülerinnen und Schüler verschiedenen Schulen zugeordnet sind. Um der geschachtelten Datenstruktur Rechnung zu tragen, wurde die Option TYPE = COMPLEX in Mplus genutzt. Ließe man diese Struktur unberücksichtigt, könnte dies zu inkorrekten Standardfehlern der Regressionskoeffizienten und Verzerrungen bei der Signifikanzprüfung führen (Hox, 2002).

Üblicherweise liegen bei Längsschnittstudien nicht für alle Teilnehmerinnen und Teilnehmer vollständige Datensätze vor. Ein Ausschluss aller Personen mit fehlenden oder ungültigen Werten würde die Stichprobengröße erheblich einschränken und könnte zu verzerrten Parameterschätzungen führen. Aus diesem Grund wurde dem Problem der fehlenden Werte durch das Verfahren der multiplen imputation (Allison, 2001) begegnet. Für die Schätzungen wurden neben den in der vorliegenden Studie berücksichtigten Variablen weitere Hintergrundmerkmale wie Geschlecht, Migrationshintergrund und das kulturelle Kapital berücksichtigt.

Tabelle 1. Mittelwerte (*M*), Standardabweichungen (*SD*) und Interkorrelationen der berücksichtigten Variablen

	M	*SD*	(1)	(2)	(3)	(4)	(5)	(6)	(7)	(8)	(9)	(10)	(11)	(12)
MTL (1)	500.00	100.00												
ETL (2)	500.00	100.00	.34**											
MN (3)	4.25	.97	.39**	.11**										
EN (4)	4.43	.86	.09**	.36**	.25**									
MSK (5)	2.69	.76	.42**	.01	.60**	.00								
ESK (6)	3.13	.74	.02	.43**	–.09**	.51**	–.16**							
MW (7)	2.57	.69	.30**	–.06**	.44**	–.06**	.66**	–.20**						
EW (8)	3.07	.53	–.08**	.27**	–.09**	.39**	–.19**	.61**	–.06**					
MKURS (9)	.37	.48	.30**	–.12**	.50**	–.11**	.49**	–.29**	.46**	–.26**				
EKURS (10)	.78	.42	–.11**	.27**	–.24**	.26**	–.28**	.41**	–.26**	.32**	–.58**			
MTL T2 (11)	520.54	109.56	.64**	.33**	.37**	.11**	.39**	.03	.28**	–.07**	.27**	–.08**		
ETL T2 (12)	546.52	99.45	.31**	.68**	.15**	.36**	.06**	.38**	–.03	.23**	–.08**	.22**	.37**	

Anmerkung. MTL = Mathematik-Testleistung, ETL = Englisch-Testleistung, MN = Mathematiknote, EN = Englischnote, MSK = Mathematikselbstkonzept, ESK = Englischselbstkonzept, MW = Mathematik-Wert, EW = Englisch-Wert, MKURS = Kurswahl Mathematik, EKURS = Kurswahl Englisch; T2 = Ende der Oberstufe; KURS: 1 = erhöhtes Niveau, 0 = grundlegendes Niveau; * $p < .05$, ** $p < .01$.

4 Ergebnisse

4.1 Deskriptive Befunde und bivariate Zusammenhänge

In Tabelle 1 sind Mittelwerte, Standardabweichungen und Interkorrelationen der berücksichtigen Variablen ausgewiesen.

Im Fach Mathematik zeigt sich über den Erhebungszeitraum von etwa anderthalb Jahren ein Kompetenzzuwachs in Höhe von $d = .21$, im Fach Englisch ein Zuwachs von $d = .47$. Der verhältnismäßig geringere Zuwachs in Mathematik ist zum Teil darauf zurückzuführen, dass der Test die mathematische Grundbildung erfasst, die Unterrichtsinhalte in der Studienstufe sich aber vornehmlich auf die voruniversitäre Mathematik konzentrieren. Darüber hinaus wählten im Fach Mathematik deutlich weniger Schülerinnen und Schüler (37,0 %) einen Kurs auf erhöhtem Anforderungsniveau als im Fach Englisch (77,6 %). Entsprechend gaben die befragten Schülerinnen und Schüler für das Fach Englisch höhere Selbstkonzepte und höhere Interessen an als für Fach Mathematik.

Innerhalb der beiden Domänen zeigen sich durchgängig signifikant positive Interkorrelationen zwischen den berücksichtigen Variablen. Zwischen den Domänen ergaben sich bei den Leistungsindikatoren positive Interkorrelationen, bei den motivationalen Variablen dagegen Korrelationen um null oder negative Korrelationen. Dieses Muster entspricht den domänenübergreifenden Zusammenhängen zwischen Leistung und Selbstkonzept, die typischerweise in den Studien zum I/E-Modell gefunden werden.

4.2 Effekte auf motivationale Überzeugungen

Vorhersage der Erfolgserwartung

Zunächst werden die Effekte der Ausgangleistungen auf die fachspezifischen Selbstkonzepte untersucht (siehe Tabelle 2). Als Kriteriumsvariablen werden das Selbstkonzept in Mathematik und das Selbstkonzept in Englisch gleichzeitig im Modell aufgenommen. Als Prädiktoren dienen die Testergebnisse und die Noten in den beiden Fächern. Gemäß den Annahmen des I/E-Modells ergeben sich für die fachspezifischen Selbstkonzepte starke positive Effekte von den Leistung in der korrespondierenden Domäne und negative Effekte von den Leistungen in der nichtkorrespondierenden Domäne. Von den Testleistungen zeigen sich dabei neben den direkten Effekten auch indirekte Effekte, die über die Noten vermittelt sind.

Vorhersage der Wertkomponente

Zur Vorhersage der Wertkomponenten wird ein analoges Modell gerechnet (Tabelle 3). Die Kriteriumsvariablen bilden die Wertkomponenten für Mathematik und Englisch,

Tabelle 2. Direkte, indirekte und totale Effekte zur Vorhersage der Selbstkonzepte in Mathematik und Englisch; standardisierte Regressionskoeffizienten und Standardfehler (in Klammern)

	Selbstkonzept Mathematik			Selbstkonzept Englisch		
	Direkt	Indirekt	Total	Direkt	Indirekt	Total
MTL	.27** (.02)	.22** (.02)	.49** (.03)	-.05* (.02)	-.06** (.01)	-.12** (.02)
ETL	-.02 (.03)	-.06** (.01)	-.08** (.03)	.35** (.02)	.15** (.01)	.50** (.02)
MN	.55** (.02)	-	-	-.16** (.02)	-	-
EN	-.16** (.02)	-	-	.40** (.02)	-	-
R^2		.46			.35	

Anmerkung. MTL = Mathematik-Testleistung, ETL = Englisch-Testleistung, MN = Mathematiknote, EN = Englischnote; * $p < .05$, ** $p < .01$; R^2 = Anteil aufgeklärter Varianz auf Individualebene.

als Prädiktoren gingen die Testleistungen und Noten der beiden Fächer ein. Auch für den Aufgabenwert können die erwarteten positiven Effekte sozialer Vergleiche und negativen Effekte dimensionaler Vergleiche von beiden Leistungsindikatoren nachgewiesen werden. Die Effekte der Testleistungen sind dabei wiederum zum Teil über die Noten vermittelt.

Tabelle 3. Direkte, indirekte und totale Effekte zur Vorhersage der Wertkomponenten in Mathematik und Englisch; standardisierte Regressionskoeffizienten und Standardfehler (in Klammern)

	Wert Mathematik			Wert Englisch		
	Direkt	Indirekt	Total	Direkt	Indirekt	Total
MTL	.23** (.02)	.16** (.02)	.39**(.03)	-.11** (.02)	-.04** (.01)	-.15** (.02)
ETL	-.08** (.02)	-.06** (.01)	-.13** (.02)	.25** (.02)	.12** (.01)	.37** (.02)
MN	.41** (.03)	-	-	-.11** (.02)	-	-
EN	-.15** (.02)	-	-	.32** (.03)	-	-
R^2		.27			.20	

Anmerkung. MTL = Mathematik-Testleistung, ETL = Englisch-Testleistung, MN = Mathematiknote, EN = Englischnote; * $p < .05$, ** $p < .01$; R^2 = Anteil aufgeklärter Varianz auf Individualebene.

4.3 Effekte auf Bildungsergebnisse

Vorhersage der Kurswahlen in Mathematik und Englisch

In Tabelle 4 sind die Modelle zur Vorhersage des gewählten Kursniveaus dargestellt. Da es sich bei der Kurswahl um eine dichotome Variable (0 = grundlegendes Anforderungsniveau, 1 = erhöhtes Anforderungsniveau) handelt, wurden logistische Regressionsanalysen gerechnet. Die Effektgrößen werden als odds ratios (*OR*) berichtet. Alle Prädiktorvariablen wurden vor den Analysen z-standardisiert. Die resultierenden odds ratios geben somit an, wie sich die relative Wahrscheinlichkeit der Wahl eines anspruchsvolleren Kurses bei einem Anstieg der Prädiktorvariablen um eine Standardabweichung verändert. Die Analysen ergeben positive Effekte von den Leistungsindikatoren (Testleistung und Note) auf das Kursniveau in der korrespondierenden Domäne und negative Effekte auf das Kursniveau in der nichtkorrespondierenden Domäne. Bei einer um eine Standardabweichung besseren Mathematiknote steigt die Wahl eines anspruchsvolleren Mathematikkurses um mehr als das 1,5-Fache. Eine bessere Englischleistung reduziert hingegen die Wahrscheinlichkeit eines höheren Kursniveaus in Mathematik. Entsprechende Effekte zeigen sich für die

Tabelle 4. Direkte, indirekte und totale Effekte zur Vorhersage der Kurswahlen in Mathematik und Englisch; odds ratios

	Kurswahl Mathematik			Kurswahl Englisch		
	Direkt	Indirekt	Total	Direkt	Indirekt	Total
MTL	1.15**	1.38**	1.59**	0.92**	0.80**	0.74**
ETL	0.82**	0.88**	0.73**	1.29**	1.20**	1.56**
MN	1.55**	1.17**	1.82**	0.78**	0.87**	0.68**
EN	0.84**	0.93**	0.78**	1.28**	1.10**	1.41**
MSK	1.19*			0.80**		
ESK	0.97			1.11*		
MW	1.14*			1.03		
EW	0.96			1.07		
R^2		.55			.41	

Anmerkung. MTL = Mathematik-Testleistung, ETL = Englisch-Testleistung, MN = Mathematiknote, EN = Englischnote; MSK = Mathematik-Selbstkonzept; ESK = Englisch-Selbstkonzept; MW = Mathematik-Wert; EW =Englisch-Wert; * $p < .05$, ** $p < .01$; R^2 = Anteil aufgeklärter Varianz auf Individualebene.

Kurswahl im Fach Englisch. Die Wahrscheinlichkeit eines anspruchsvolleren Englischkurses steigt mit besseren Englischleistungen und sinkt mit besseren Mathematikleistungen. Insgesamt scheinen die Mathematiknoten für die Kurswahl stärkere Prädiktoren zu sein als die Englischnoten.

Zusätzlich ergeben sich signifikante Effekte von den motivationalen Variablen auf die Kurswahl im korrespondierenden Fach. Hier konnten positive Effekte sowohl vom Selbstkonzept als auch vom Aufgabenwert auf das gewählte Kursniveau in Mathematik beobachtet werden. Für die Kurswahl im Fach Englisch zeigt sich ein bedeutsamer Effekt vom Selbstkonzept, der Effekt von dem Aufgabenwert wurde nicht signifikant. Die erwarteten negativen Effekte zwischen den Fächern ließen sich größtenteils nicht finden. Es ergab sich lediglich ein signifikanter negativer Effekt vom Selbstkonzept in Mathematik auf die Kurswahl in Englisch. Bei gleichen Leistungen reduziert damit ein höheres Mathematikselbstkonzept die Wahrscheinlichkeit für die Wahl eines höheren Kursniveaus in Englisch.

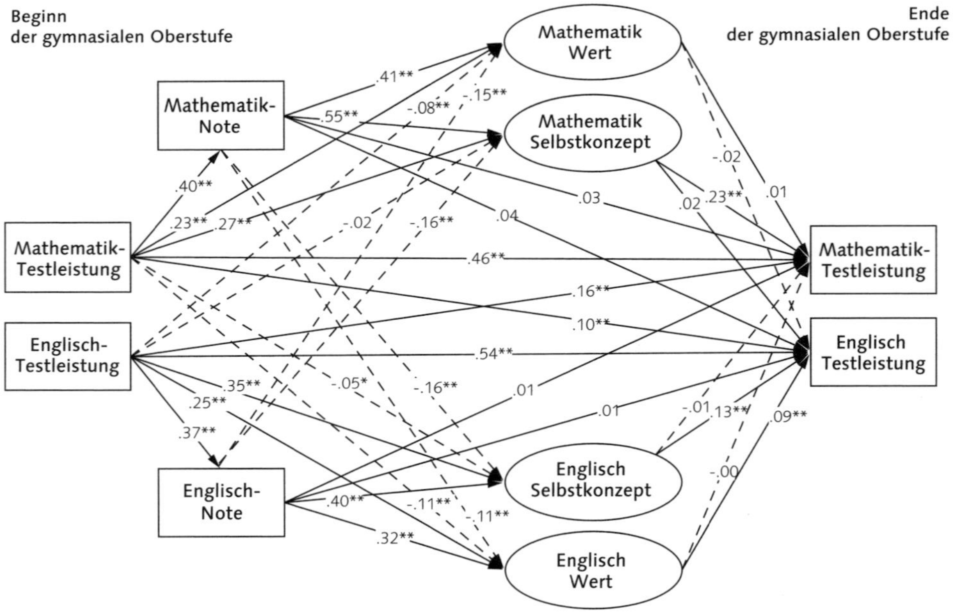

Abbildung 2. Modell zur Vorhersage der Testleistungen am Ende der Oberstufe; standardisierte Regressionskoeffizienten. Positive Effekte sind mit einer durchgezogenen Linie gekennzeichnet, negative Effekte mit einer gestrichelten Linie; * $p < .05$, ** $p < .01$.

4.4 Effekte auf die Leistungen am Ende der Oberstufe

Schließlich wurden Regressionsanalysen zur Vorhersage der am Ende der Studienstufe erzielten Testleistungen in Mathematik und Englisch durchgeführt. Sämtliche Pfadkoeffizienten sind in Abbildung 2 dargestellt. Erwartungsgemäß stellen die Testleistungen zu Beginn der Studienstufe in beiden Fächern die erklärungsmächtigsten Prädiktoren dar. Die Testleistungen im anderen Fach haben zusätzlich einen positiven Einfluss. Das bedeutet, dass sich eine gute Leistung in Englisch (Mathematik) günstig auf die Lernentwicklung in Mathematik (Englisch) auswirkt. Entsprechend dem REM zeigen sich bei Kontrolle der Ausgangsleistung in beiden Fächern positive Effekte des Selbstkonzepts auf die nachfolgende Leistung im jeweiligen Fach. Zusätzliche ergibt sich im Fach Englisch ein positiver Effekt der Wertzuschreibung auf die Leistungsentwicklung. Die im RI/EM angenommenen negativen Effekte der motivationalen Variablen in einem Fach auf die Leistung im anderen Fach konnten in der vorliegenden Studie nicht bestätigt werden.

5 Diskussion

Die vorliegende Studie untersucht den komplexen Wirkzusammenhang zwischen motivationalen Überzeugungen und Leistungen innerhalb und zwischen den Fächern Mathematik und Englisch. Unsere Hypothesen konnten dabei in weiten Teilen bestätigt werden. In Übereinstimmung mit den Befunden bisheriger Untersuchungen (z.B. Guo, Marsh, Morin, Parker & Kaur, 2015; Köller et al., 2001; Marsh & Yeung, 1997) zeigten sich innerhalb der Domänen positive Effekte von den Leistungen auf motivationale Einstellungen, die wiederum das nachfolgende Leistungsverhalten vorhersagen. Diese Zusammenhänge konnten sowohl für die Kurswahl als auch für die Testergebnisse am Ende der gymnasialen Oberstufe nachgewiesen werden. Zwischen den Domänen ergaben sich negative Effekte von den Leistungsindikatoren auf die motivationalen Variablen in der nichtkorrespondierenden Domäne. Entgegen den Befunden von Möller et al. (2011) und Niepel et al. (2014) ließen sich hingegen – wie auch in der Replikationsstudie von Möller et al. (2014) – keine negativen Effekte von den motivationalen Überzeugungen auf das das nachfolgende Leistungsverhalten beobachten. Es zeigte sich lediglich ein negativer Effekt vom Mathematikselbstkonzept auf die Kurswahl in Englisch.

Grenzen der Studie

Das in dieser Studie gewählte längsschnittliche Design ist die Methode der Wahl, um Leistungsverhalten im schulischen Kontext vorherzusagen. Die Längsschnittstudie beschränkt sich allerdings auf zwei Messzeitpunkte, wobei zum ersten Erhebungszeitpunkt Ausgangsleistung, Selbstkonzept und Aufgabenwert parallel erfasst wurden. Um die im EW-Modell angenommenen Wirkrichtungen und vermittelnden Einflüsse differenzierter zu analysieren, wären weitere Messzeitpunkte erforderlich, zu denen die verschiedenen Merkmale wiederholt erhoben und damit kontrolliert werden könnten. Darüber hinaus wird mit den einbezogenen Variablen nur ein Teil des komplexen EW-Modells abgebildet, die Zusammenhänge mit weiteren individuellen Merkmalen und Kontextfaktoren bleiben dabei unberücksichtigt. Auch wurde die Interaktion zwischen der Erwartungs- und der Wertkomponenten in der vorliegenden Studie nicht untersucht. Bei der Interpretation der Ergebnisse ist des Weiteren zu beachten, dass die Kurswahlen in Mathematik und Englisch aufgrund der Belegauflagen nicht unabhängig voneinander sind. Da mindestens zwei der drei Kernfächer Deutsch, Mathematik und Englisch in der Oberstufe auf erhöhtem Anforderungsniveau gewählt werden müssen, bedingt die Wahl eines Kurses auf grundlegendem Niveau in einem Fach die Wahl eines Kurses auf erhöhtem Niveau im anderen Fach. Diese Rahmenvorgabe trägt vermutlich zur Verstärkung der Kontrasteffekte auf die Kurswahl bei.

Praktische Implikationen und Ausblick

Die Befunde machen deutlich, dass Schülerinnen und Schüler sowohl soziale als auch dimensionale Vergleiche zur Entwicklung und Ausdifferenzierung ihrer Selbstkonzepte und Interessen vornehmen. Dieses Phänomen steht in Einklang mit den Zielen und der damit verbundenen Ausgestaltung der gymnasialen Oberstufe (Kultusministerkonferenz, 2006), wonach individuelle Schwerpunktsetzungen durch Kurs- und Profilwahlen ermöglicht und unterstützt werden. In Vorbereitung auf die anstehende Studien- oder Berufswahl erscheint es sinnvoll, Interessen weiter auszubilden und das persönliche Engagement auf bestimmte Bereiche zu konzentrieren. Baltes (1997) beschreibt diese Entwicklung als Prozess der Selektion und Optimierung. Parallel dazu soll der Unterricht in der gymnasialen Oberstufe eine profunde Allgemeinbildung und vertiefte Kenntnisse in allen Kernfächern (Deutsch, Mathematik und eine Fremdsprache) vermitteln (Kampa, Leucht & Köller, 2016). Der fachlichen Isolierung soll entgegengewirkt und fächerübergreifendes und fächerverbindendes Lernen gefördert werden. In der vorliegenden Studie erzielten Schülerinnen und Schüler mit besseren Englischleistungen auch günstigere Kompetenzentwicklungen im Fach Mathematik und umgekehrt. Negative Effekte von den motivationalen Überzeugungen auf die Leistungsentwicklung im jeweils anderen Fach wurden hingegen nicht beobachtet. Die Ergebnisse sprechen demnach insgesamt dafür, dass zentrale Ziele der Oberstufe erreicht werden. Zu klären bleibt, ob die positiven fächerübergreifenden Leistungseffekte auf die Gestaltung der Lerngelegenheiten zurückzuführen sind oder vielmehr auf zugrunde liegende Drittvariable wie die kognitiven Grundfähigkeit, eine hohe Leistungsmotivation oder erfolgreiche Lernstrategien.

In Übereinstimmungen mit den Befunden von Nagy et al. (2008) wird die Kurswahl in Mathematik durch die berücksichtigen Variablen besser erklärt als die

Kurswahl in Englisch. Bemerkenswert ist, dass sich die Noten im Fach Mathematik für die Kurswahl in Englisch als ähnlich stärke Prädiktoren erweisen wie die Noten im Fach Englisch selbst. Umgekehrt zeigen sich für die Kurswahl in Mathematik deutlich größere Einflüsse von der Mathematik- im Vergleich zur Englischleistung. Demnach scheinen Schülerinnen und Schüler die Wahl ihrer Fächerkombination in besonderem Maße von ihrer Mathematiknote abhängig zu machen. Bei besseren Leistungen in Mathematik wird ein Mathematikkurs auf erhöhtem Niveau gewählt, bei schwächeren Mathematikleistungen fällt die Entscheidung im Sinne einer Negativauswahl gegen einen anspruchsvolleren Mathematikkurs und damit für einen anspruchsvolleren Englischkurs aus. Köller et al. (2006) weisen darauf hin, dass die Leistungsunterschiede im Fach Mathematik für Schülerinnen und Schüler besonders transparent sind und die Leistungsergebnisse daher besonders gut für soziale Vergleiche genutzt werden können. Für die zukünftige Erfolgs- und Wirksamkeitserwartung sind jedoch nicht nur die Leistungsresultate, sondern auch die damit verbundenen Attributionsprozesse (Möller & Jerusalem, 1997) relevant, die sich wiederum zwischen den Fächern unterscheiden können. Um die Entscheidungsprozesse näher zu untersuchen, wären Folgestudien notwendig, in denen die Kurswahlmotive (siehe dazu auch Abel, 2002) fachspezifisch erfasst und hinsichtlich ihrer unterschiedlichen Relevanz analysiert werden. Die differenzierte Betrachtung wert- und gefühlsbezogener Valenzüberzeugungen kann weitere Hinweise zur Erklärung von Kurs- und Studienwahlen liefern.

Zusammenfassend bleibt festzuhalten, dass sich die Verknüpfung des EW-Modells und des RI/EM als fruchtbarer Ansatz zur Erklärung fachbezogener Einstellungen und zukünftigen Leistungsverhaltens erweist. Die Analyse der Zusammenhänge in jüngeren Altersstufen kann zusätzliche Beiträge zur Beschreibung frühzeitiger Entwicklungen bei der Ausdifferenzierung von Selbstkonzepten liefern und Unterschiede zwischen den Fächern nachzeichnen. Durch die Berücksichtigung weiterer individueller Merkmale und Kontextfaktoren sowie durch die Erweiterung auf andere Fächer und Fachbereiche können zusätzliche Erkenntnisse für die Interessen- und Leistungsentwicklung gewonnen werden.

Literatur

Abel, J. (2002). Kurswahlen aus Interesse? Wahlmotive in der gymnasialen Oberstufe und Studienwahl. *Die Deutsche Schule, 94*, 192-203.

Allison, P. D. (2001). *Missing Data. Sage university papers series on quantitative applications in the social sciences, 07–136.* Thousand Oaks, CA: Sage.

Baltes, P. B. (1997). On the incomplete architecture of human ontogeny: Selection, optimization, and compensation as foundation of developmental theory. *American Psychologist, 52*, 366-380

Behörde für Schule, Jugend und Berufsbildung, Amt für Schule, Hamburg (Hrsg.) (2000). *Hamburger Schulleistungstest für zehnte und elfte Klassen – SL-HAM 10/11.* Hamburg.

Eccles, J. S., Adler, T. F., Futterman, R., Goff, S. B., Kaczala, C. M., Meece, J. L. & Midgley, C. (1983). Expectancies, values, and academic behaviors. In J. T. Spence (Ed.), *Achievement and achievement motivation* (pp. 75–146). San Francisco, CA: W. H. Freeman.

Eccles, J. S. & Wigfield, A. (2002). Motivational beliefs, values, and goals. *Annual Review of Psychology, 53*, 109–132.

Eccles, J. S., Wigfield, A. & Schiefele, U. (1998). Motivation to succeed. In W. Damon & N. Eisenberg (Eds.), *Handbook of Child Development* (5th ed., Vol. 3, pp. 1017–1095). New York: Wiley.

Guo, J., Marsh, H. W., Parker, P. D., Morin, A. J. & Yeung, A. S. (2015). Expectancy-value in mathematics, gender and socioeconomic background as predictors of achievement and aspirations: A multicohort study. *Learning and Individual Differences, 37*, 161–168.

Guo, J., Parker, P. D., Marsh, H. W. & Morin, A. J. (2015). Achievement, motivation, and educational choices: A longitudinal study of expectancy and value using a multiplicative perspective. *Developmental Psychology, 51*, 1163.

Guo, J., Marsh, H. W., Morin, A. J., Parker, P. D. & Kaur, G. (2015). Directionality of the Associations of High School Expectancy-Value, Aspirations, and Attainment A Longitudinal Study. *American Educational Research Journal, 52*, 371–402.

Hox, J. J. (2002). *Multilevel analysis: Techniques and applications.* Mahwah, NJ: Lawrece Erlbaum Associates.

Kampa, N., Leucht, M. & Köller, O. (2016). Mathematische Kompetenzen in unterschiedlichen Profilen der gymnasialen Oberstufe. In J. Kramer, M. Neumann & U. Trautwein (Hrsg.), *Abitur und Matura im Wandel. Historische Entwicklungslinien, aktuelle Reformen und ihre Effekte* (S. 161–187). Wiesbaden: Springer VS.

Köller, O., Baumert, J. & Schnabel, K. U. (2001). Does interest matter? The relationship between academic interest and achievement in mathematics. *Journal for Research in Mathematics Education, 32*, 448–470.

Köller, O., Trautwein, U., Lüdtke, O. & Baumert, J. (2006). Zum Zusammenspiel von schulischer Leistung, Selbstkonzept und Interesse in der gymnasialen Oberstufe. *Zeitschrift für Pädagogische Psychologie, 20*, 27–39.

Kultusministerkonferenz (2006). Vereinbarung zur Gestaltung der gymnasialen Oberstufe in der Sekundarstufe II. (Beschluss der Kultusministerkonferenz vom 07.07.1972 i.d.F. vom 02.06.2006). Zugriff am 30.09.2016. Verfügbar unter: http://www.kmk.org/fileadmin/Dateien/pdf/PresseUndAktuelles/1999/Vereinb-z-Gestalt-d-gymOb-i-d-SekII.pdf.

Marsh, H. W. (1986). Verbal and math self-concepts: An Internal/External Frame of Reference Model. *American Educational Research Journal, 23*, 129–149.

Marsh, H. W. (1992). *Self-Description Questionnaire (SDQ) III: A theoretical and empirical basis for the measurement of multiple dimensions of late adolescent self-concept - An interim test manual and a research monograph*. Macarthur, New South Wales, Australia: University of Western Sydney, Faculty of Education.

Marsh, H. W. & Craven, R. G. (2006). Reciprocal effects of self-concept and performance from a multidimensional perspective: Beyond seductive pleasure and unidimensional perspectives. *Perspectives on Psychological Science, 1*, 133–163.

Marsh, H. W. & Hau, K.-T. (2004). Explaining paradoxical relations between academic self-concepts and achievements: Cross-cultural generalizability of the Internal/External Frame of Reference predictions across 26 countries. *Journal of Educational Psychology, 96*, 56–67.

Marsh, H. W. & Martin, A. J. (2011). Academic self-concept and academic achievement: Relations and causal ordering. *British Journal of Educational Psychology, 81*, 59–77.

Marsh, H. & Yeung, A. S. (1997). Coursework selection: Relations to academic self-concept and achievement. *American Educational Research Journal, 34*, 691–720.

Möller, J. & Jerusalem, M. (1997). Attributionsforschung in der Schule. *Zeitschrift für Pädagogische Psychologie, 11*, 151–166.

Möller, J. & Köller, O. (2001). Dimensional comparisons: An experimental approach to the internal/external frame of reference model. *Journal of Educational Psychology, 93*, 826–835.

Möller, J. & Köller, O. (2004). Die Genese akademischer Selbstkonzepte: Effekte dimensionaler und sozialer Vergleiche. *Psychologische Rundschau, 55*, 19–27.

Möller, J. & Marsh, H. W. (2013). Dimensional comparison theory. *Psychological Review, 120*, 544–560.

Möller, J., Pohlmann, B., Köller, O. & Marsh, H. W. (2009). A metaanalytic path analysis of the internal/external frame of reference model of academic achievement and academic self-concept. *Review of Educational Research, 79*, 1129–1167.

Möller, J., Retelsdorf, J., Köller, O. & Marsh, H. W. (2011). The reciprocal I/E model: An integration of models of relations between academic achievement and self-concept. *American Educational Research Journal, 48*, 1315–1346.

Möller, J., Zimmermann, F., Köller, O. & Marsh, H. W. (2014). The reciprocal internal/external frame of reference model using grades and test scores. *British Journal of Educational Psychology, 84*, 591–611.

Muthén, L. K. & Muthén, B. (2015). *Mplus version 7.4 [Computer software]*. Los Angeles, CA: Muthén & Muthén.

Nagy, G., Garrett, J. L., Trautwein, U., Cortina, K. S., Baumert, J. & Eccles, J. (2008). Gendered high school course selection as a precursor of gendered careers: The mediating role of self-concept and intrinsic value. In H. M. G. Watt & J. S. Eccles (Eds.), *Explaining gendered occupational outcomes: Examining individual and social explanations through school and beyond* (pp. 115-143). Washington DC: APA books.

Nagy, G., Trautwein, U., Köller, O., Baumert, J. & Garrett, J. (2006). Gender and course selection in upper secondary education: Effects of academic self-concept and intrinsic value. *Educational Research and Evaluation, 12*, 323–345.

Niepel, C., Brunner, M. & Preckel, F. (2014). The longitudinal interplay of students' academic self-concepts and achievements within and across domains: Replicating and extending the reciprocal internal/external frame of reference model. *Journal of Educational Psychology, 106*, 1170–1191.

Pohlmann, B. & Möller, J. (2009). On the benefit of dimensional comparisons. *Journal of Educational Psychology, 101*, 248–258.

Valentine, J. C., DuBois, D. L. & Cooper, H. (2004). The relation between self-beliefs and academic achievement: A meta-analytic review. *Educational Psychologist, 39*, 111–133.

Wigfield, A. & Eccles, J. S. (2000). Expectancy-Value Theory of achievement motivation. *Contemporary Educational Psychology, 25*, 68–81.

Wu, M. L., Adams, R. J. & Wilson, M. (1998). *ConQuest: Generalized item response modeling software [Computer software]*. Melbourne: Australian Council for Educational Research.

Autorinnen

DR. BRITTA POHLMANN
Institut für Bildungsmonitoring und Qualitätsentwicklung, Hamburg.

DR. LILIAN STREBLOW
Bielefeld School of Education, Universität Bielefeld.

KONTAKT
Britta Pohlmann, Institut für Bildungsmonitoring und Qualitätsentwicklung,
Beltgens Garten 25, 20537 Hamburg.
E-Mail: *britta.pohlmann@ifbq.hamburg.de*

Ein dritter Vergleichsprozess: Dimensionale Vergleiche in Selbstberichten

FRIEDERIKE HELM, HANNO MÜLLER-KALTHOFF UND NICOLE NAGY

ZUSAMMENFASSUNG: Die Theorie dimensionaler Vergleiche (DCT; Möller & Marsh, 2013) postuliert dimensionale Vergleiche als einen relevanten Vergleichsprozess in der Evaluation eigener Merkmale. Die Effekte dimensionaler Vergleiche konnten bisher vor allem im Leistungskontext gezeigt werden, im Kontext von persönlichen Selbstbeschreibungen dominiert in der Literatur bisher die Betonung der Wichtigkeit sozialer Vergleiche. Aufbauend auf einer Studie von Wilson und Ross (2000) wurden 96 Personen gebeten, sich allgemein oder in Bezug auf ihr akademisches Selbstbild zu beschreiben. Die Selbstberichte wurden hinsichtlich vorgenommener dimensionaler, temporaler und sozialer Vergleiche kodiert. Es zeigte sich, dass in der Gesamtstichprobe dimensionale, soziale und temporale Vergleiche gleich häufig zur Selbstbeschreibung genutzt wurden. Soziale Vergleiche traten in der Bedingung ‚akademisches Selbstbild' signifikant häufiger auf als in der Bedingung ‚allgemeines Selbstbild'. Tiefergehende Analysen zu dimensionalen Vergleichen zeigten, dass am häufigsten Eigenschaften und Fähigkeiten dimensional verglichen werden und, konform mit Annahmen der DCT, der Vergleich überwiegend innerhalb einer Merkmalskategorie stattfindet. Implikationen für die DCT werden diskutiert.

Schlüsselwörter: Theorie dimensionaler Vergleiche, dimensionale Vergleiche, Selbstbeschreibungen, soziale Vergleiche, temporale Vergleiche

A third comparison process: Dimensional comparisons in open self-descriptions

ABSTRACT: The dimensional comparison theory (DCT; Möller & Marsh, 2013) assumes dimensional comparisons to constitute a relevant comparison process in the evaluation of a person's attributes. Effects of dimensional comparisons so far have been shown mostly in achievement-related contexts, whereas in the context of personal self-descriptions, the importance of social comparisons is emphasized. On the basis of research by Wilson and Ross (2000) 96 persons were asked to describe themselves either with regard to their attributes in general or with regard to their academic attributes. Self-descriptions were coded regarding dimensional, social and temporal comparisons. It showed that dimensional, social and temporal comparisons were used equally frequently for self-description in the whole sample. Social comparisons were more frequent in the academic self-description than in the general self-description. Deeper analyses regarding dimensional comparisons showed that most frequently personal attributes and abilities were compared and, in line with DCT's predictions, dimensional comparisons mostly were drawn between attributes ascribable to the same context. Implications for DCT are discussed.

Keywords: dimensional comparison theory, dimensional comparisons, self-descriptions, social comparisons, temporal comparisons

Einleitung

Die beiden traditionell als determinierende Faktoren der Genese von Selbsteinschätzungen untersuchten Vergleichsprozesse sind soziale (Festinger, 1954) und temporale Vergleiche (Albert, 1977). Soziale Vergleiche bezeichnen den Vergleich eigener Leistungen oder Eigenschaften mit den Leistungen oder Eigenschaften anderer Personen und werden nach Festinger (1954) als zentral für die Einschätzung der Eigenschaften der eigenen Person empfunden. Unter temporalen Vergleichen werden Vergleiche eigener Leistungen oder Eigenschaften mit eigenen Leistungen oder Eigenschaften zu einem anderen (meist früheren) Zeitpunkt verstanden, es handelt sich also um intrapersonale Vergleiche. Ihre Funktion ist es Albert (1977) zufolge, Personen zu ermöglichen, ein über die Zeit hinweg kohärentes Selbstbild zu entwickeln, in das aber auch wahrgenommene Veränderungen integriert werden.

Diesen beiden Vergleichsprozessen stellen Möller und Marsh (2013) einen weiteren intrapersonalen Vergleichsprozess zur Seite, die dimensionalen Vergleiche. Diese bezeichnen Vergleiche eigener Fähigkeiten oder Eigenschaften in zwei verschiedenen Lebensbereichen (Möller & Marsh, 2013; Möller, Müller-Kalthoff, Helm, Nagy & Marsh, 2016). Sie sind in jüngerer Zeit vermehrt in den Fokus der Forschung zur Genese bereichsspezifischer Selbsteinschätzungen gerückt. In der vorliegenden Studie wird angesichts des zunehmenden Forschungsinteresses an dimensionalen Vergleichen untersucht, ob dimensionale Vergleiche, wie von Möller und Marsh (2013) angenommen, eine zentrale Rolle in der Beschreibung von Selbsteinschätzungen spielen. Dafür wird das Vorkommen dimensionaler, sozialer und temporaler Vergleiche in offenen Selbstbeschreibungen analysiert. Die Theorie dimensionaler Vergleiche (Möller & Marsh, 2013) macht zudem Annahmen darüber, in welchen Kontexten und welchen Bereichen dimensionale Vergleiche vermehrt auftreten. Die Überprüfung einiger dieser Annahmen ist ebenfalls Gegenstand der vorliegenden Arbeit.

1 Theoretischer und empirischer Hintergrund

1.1 Internal/External Frame of Reference Model (I/E-Modell; Marsh, 1986)

Die Forschung zu dimensionalen Vergleichen nahm ihren Ausgangspunkt mit der Formulierung des *Internal/External Frame of Reference*-Modells (I/E-Modell; Marsh, 1986). Das Modell beschreibt den pfadanalytischen Befund, dass die Fähigkeitsselbsteinschätzungen (Selbstkonzepte) von Schülerinnen und Schülern im verbalen und mathematischen Bereich geringer korrelieren als die Fachleistungen sowie dass positive Effekte der Fachleistungen auf das jeweils korrespondierende Selbstkonzept und negative Effekte der Fachleistungen auf das Selbstkonzept im jeweils anderen Bereich zu verzeichnen sind (z. B. Möller, Pohlmann, Köller & Marsh, 2009; siehe Abbildung 1). Marsh (1986) liefert eine mögliche Erklärung für dieses Zusammenhangsmuster: Es werden zum einen externale (soziale) Vergleiche vollzogen, indem eigene Leistungen in einer Domäne mit den Leistungen von Mitschülerinnen und Mitschülern in dieser Domäne verglichen werden. Zum anderen wird ein internaler Referenzrahmen zur Beurteilung eigener Leistungen angewendet, indem eigene Leistungen in einer Domäne (der mathematisch-naturwissenschaftlichen oder der verbalen) mit eigenen Leistungen in einer anderen Domäne verglichen werden. Marsh (1986) definiert demnach internale Vergleiche (später als dimensionale Vergleiche bezeichnet; Möller & Köller, 1998; Möller & Köller, 2001a; Möller & Marsh, 2013) als Vergleiche der eigenen Leistung oder Fähigkeit in einer Domäne mit der eigenen Leistung oder Fähigkeit in einer anderen Domäne. Effekte dimensionaler Vergleiche auf bereichsspezifische Selbsteinschätzungen wurden in pfadanalytischen (z. B. Köller, Klemmert, Möller & Baumert, 1999; Möller & Köller, 2001b; Marsh et al., 2014; Marsh et al., 2015; Möller et al., 2009), experimentellen (Möller & Köller, 2001a; Möller & Savyon, 2003; Pohlmann & Möller, 2009; Strickhouser & Zell, 2015) und introspektiven Studien (Möller & Husemann, 2006) nachgewiesen. Dimensionale Vergleiche sind damit ein inzwischen gut belegter Vergleichsprozess. In den folgenden beiden Abschnitten werden Annahmen und Befunde zu dimensionalen Vergleichen dargelegt, welche die Fragestellungen der vorliegenden Arbeit begründen.

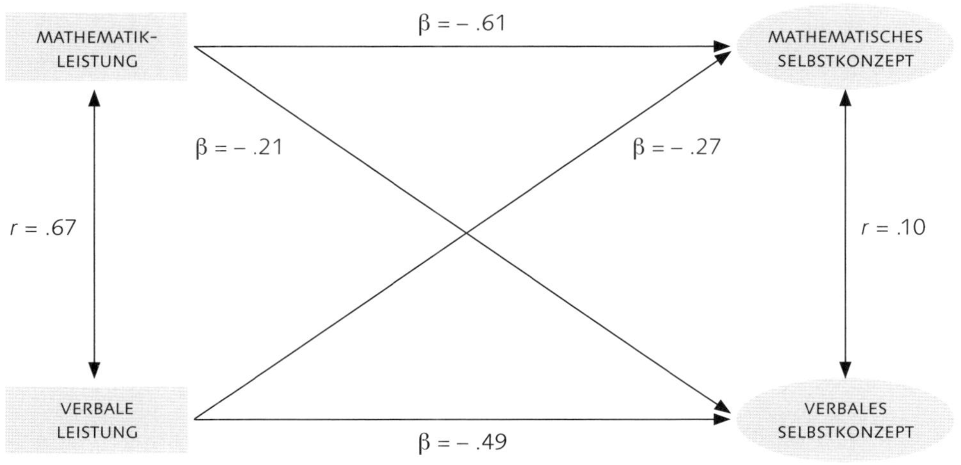

Abbildung 1. Befunde der Metaanalyse von Möller et al. (2009).

1.2 Zentrale Annahmen der Theorie dimensionaler Vergleiche (Möller & Marsh, 2013)

Für die vorliegende Arbeit sind zum einen Annahmen der Theorie dimensionaler Vergleiche zentral, die sich auf Bereiche, zwischen denen dimensionale Vergleiche durchgeführt werden, beziehen. Mit Blick auf Bereiche dimensionaler Vergleiche legen Möller und Marsh (2013) ein im Gegensatz zum I/E-Modell erweitertes Verständnis dimensionaler Vergleiche dar, das sich aufgrund theoretischer Annahmen und einzelner Forschungsarbeiten (z. B. Möller & Husemann, 2006; Möller & Weber, 2001) seit der Formulierung des I/E-Modells herauskristallisiert hat: Dimensionale Vergleiche werden nach dem Verständnis der Theorie dimensionaler Vergleiche auch zwischen unterschiedlichen nichtakademischen Leistungen, Fähigkeiten oder Eigenschaften vorgenommen (Möller & Marsh, 2013; Möller et al., 2016) und können sich auch auf andere Variablen außer auf Selbsteinschätzungen auswirken, wie auf Motivation oder Verhalten (Möller et al., 2016). Die Arbeit von Möller und Husemann (2006) dokumentiert dieses erweiterte Verständnis dimensionaler Vergleiche: In zwei Tagebuchstudien hielten Studierende (Studie 1) sowie Schülerinnen und Schüler (Studie 2) die von ihnen im Alltag angestellten dimensionalen Vergleiche über einen Zeitraum von zwei Wochen fest. Es zeigte sich, dass dimensionale Vergleiche im Alltag vollzogen werden und sich auch auf nichtakademische Bereiche beziehen, wie auf soziale Beziehungen, Persönlichkeitseigenschaften, sportliche Fähigkeiten oder gesundheitliche Aspekte. Ein Drittel der durchgeführten dimensionalen Vergleiche fand innerhalb der akademischen Domäne statt, ebenfalls häufig wurden dimensionale Vergleiche zwischen Beziehungen zu Familienmitgliedern und Freunden durchgeführt. Die Theorie dimensionaler Vergleiche nimmt dementsprechend an, dass Personen dimensionale Vergleiche überwiegend zwischen Bereichen durchführen, die demselben Kontext angehören, so dem akademischen Kontext im Falle des Vergleichs von Schul- oder Studienfächern oder dem sozialen Kontext im Falle des Vergleichs verschiedener familiärer oder freundschaftlicher Beziehungen (Möller et al., 2015).

Zum anderen werden in der Theorie dimensionaler Vergleiche Annahmen über Motivationen für dimensionale Vergleiche und Situationen, in denen Personen dimensionale Vergleiche durchführen, gemacht. Für die vorliegende Arbeit ist die Annahme zentral, dass externe Gegebenheiten zu dimensionalen Vergleichen führen können, wie beispielsweise häufige (simultane) Leistungsrückmeldungen zu verschiedenen Schul- oder Studienfächern (Möller & Marsh, 2013).

1.3 Bedeutsamkeit dimensionaler Vergleiche

Es stellt sich die Frage, ob dimensionalen Vergleichen für die Bildung von Selbsteinschätzungen generell eine ähnlich wichtige Rolle wie den traditionell untersuchten Vergleichsarten sozialer und temporaler Vergleiche zukommt. Möller und Marsh (2013) bezeichnen dimensionale Vergleiche als einen zentralen Vergleichsprozess neben sozialen und temporalen Vergleichen. Die Annahme, dass dimensionale Vergleiche im Alltag eine Bedeutung besitzen, wird durch die Tagebuchstudien von Möller und Husemann (2006) unterstrichen. In diesen Studien wurde allerdings nicht die relative Bedeutsamkeit dimensionaler Vergleiche im Vergleich zu der Bedeutsamkeit sozialer und temporaler Vergleiche analysiert. Diese kann auf verschiedene Arten betrachtet werden: Personen können direkt zu der Bedeutsamkeit aller drei Vergleichsprozesse befragt werden; es können die Effekte dimensionaler, sozialer und temporaler Vergleiche auf Selbsteinschätzungen simultan analysiert werden; oder es kann untersucht werden, wie häufig dimensionale, soziale und temporale Vergleiche verwendet werden, um sich einen Eindruck über eigene Eigenschaften zu bilden.

Eine direkte Befragung zur Bedeutsamkeit dimensionaler, sozialer und temporaler Vergleiche nahmen Möller und Weber (2001) an einer Stichprobe älterer Menschen vor. Sie erfassten die subjektive Bedeutsamkeit dimensionaler Vergleiche für das Alltagsdenken sowie die geäußerte Präferenz für dimensionale, temporale und soziale Vergleiche im Alltag. Dimensionalen und temporalen Vergleichen wurde eine höhere Bedeutsamkeit für das Alltagsdenken zugesprochen als sozialen Vergleichen und dimensionale Vergleichsinformation gegenüber temporaler und sozialer Vergleichsinformation präferiert. Möller und Weber (2001) merken allerdings zu Recht an, dass die Ergebnisse nicht ohne weiteres auf jüngere Populationen übertragen werden können: Für ältere Menschen ist soziale Vergleichsinformation möglicherweise aufgrund abnehmender Sozialkontakte im Alter weniger verfügbar (siehe auch Suls & Mullen, 1982), und temporale Vergleiche führen möglicherweise vor Augen, dass sich eigene Fähigkeiten in vielen Bereichen verschlechtert haben (siehe auch Filipp & Buch-Bartos, 1994).

Effekte sozialer, temporaler und dimensionaler Vergleiche auf die Fähigkeitsselbsteinschätzungen von Grundschülerinnen und -schülern wurden von Dickhäuser und Galfe (2004) untersucht. Sie erfassten die mathematische Fähigkeitsselbsteinschätzung vor und nach Rückgabe einer Mathematikarbeit und ließen die Schülerinnen und Schüler Angaben zu Vergleichsprozessen machen. Ausschließlich der soziale Vergleich zeigte einen Effekt auf die mathematische Selbsteinschätzung. Studien jedoch, die lediglich die Effekte sozialer und dimensionaler Vergleiche oder sozialer und temporaler Vergleiche auf Selbsteinschätzungen simultan erfassen, finden Effekte für jeweils beide Vergleichsarten, wobei die Effekte sozialer Vergleiche zumeist die Effekte dimensionaler und temporaler Vergleiche übersteigen (Butler, 2000; Möller et al., 2009; Strickhouser & Zell, 2015; Zell & Alicke, 2009, 2010): In der Studie von Strickhouser und Zell (2015) beispielsweise zeigte sich ein großer Effekt sozialer Vergleiche ($\eta_p^2 = .53$), wohingegen der Effekt dimensionaler Vergleiche mittelhoch ausfiel ($\eta_p^2 = .26$).

Die auf direkter Befragung zur Bedeutsamkeit der drei Vergleichsarten und auf der Untersuchung der Stärke der Effekte der drei Vergleichsarten basierende Befundlage ist dementsprechend heterogen und spricht zudem für Unterschiede der relativen Bedeutsamkeit dimensionaler Vergleiche zwischen verschiedenen Altersgruppen.

Bislang existieren keine Studien, die untersuchen, wie häufig Personen dimensionale Vergleiche tatsächlich anwenden, wenn sie sich einen Eindruck über sich selbst bilden und zudem soziale und temporale Vergleiche berücksichtigt werden. Wilson und Ross (2000) stellten eine solche Analyse für soziale und temporale Vergleiche an: Sie untersuchten die relative Häufigkeit sozialer und temporaler Vergleiche in offenen Selbstbeschreibungen von Studierenden. Es zeigte sich, dass mindestens ebenso viele temporale wie soziale Vergleiche verwendet wurden sowie dass temporale Vergleiche von den jungen Erwachsenen eher verwendet wurden, um sich durch die Feststellung von Verbesserungen in bestimmten Fähigkeitsbereichen möglichst positiv zu beschreiben, während soziale Vergleiche eher vollzogen wurden, wenn es um eine akkurate Beschreibung eigener Eigenschaften und Fähigkeiten ging.

2 Ableitung der Fragestellungen

Angesichts der insgesamt heterogenen Befundlage zur relativen Bedeutsamkeit dimensionaler Vergleiche sowie der Forschungslücke mit Blick auf die sich in Häufigkeiten widerspiegelnde Bedeutung dimensionaler Vergleiche fokussiert die vorliegende Studie die Häufigkeit dimensionaler, sozialer und temporaler Vergleiche in offenen Selbstbeschreibungen. Die Methode der Selbstbeschreibung wird gewählt, um Selbsteinschätzungen in Bezug auf unterschiedliche Bereiche zu erfassen, die aufgrund dimensionaler, sozialer und temporaler Vergleiche entstehen. Eine vergleichbar hohe Anzahl dimensionaler wie sozialer und temporaler Vergleiche könnte die Bedeutung dimensionaler Vergleiche für die Ausbildung von Selbstbildern im Alltag unterstreichen: Im Gegensatz zu den Tagebuchstudien von Möller und Husemann (2006) werden in der vorliegenden Studie alle drei Vergleichsarten für die Teilnehmerinnen und Teilnehmer explizit thematisiert, so dass die Häufigkeiten ihrer Nennungen in den Selbstberichten verglichen werden können. Ausgehend von den Befunden von Wilson und Ross (2000) sowie von der Annahme der Theorie dimensionaler Vergleiche wird erwartet, dass soziale und temporale Vergleiche gleich häufig angestellt werden und dass dimensionale Vergleiche als dritter zentraler Vergleichsprozess ebenso häufig wie soziale und temporale Vergleiche angestellt werden (Hypothese 1).

Mit Bezug auf dimensionale Vergleiche werden zudem zwei Bedingungen untersucht, zwischen denen Unterschiede in der Häufigkeit der Vergleiche vermutet werden: Es werden allgemeine Selbstbeschreibungen mit Selbstbeschreibungen im Hinblick auf akademische Eigenschaften und Fähigkeiten verglichen. So kann untersucht werden, ob dimensionale Vergleiche, wie in der Theorie dimensionaler Vergleiche angenommen, tatsächlich gehäuft in akademischen Kontexten vorgenommen werden: Vergleiche zwischen verschiedenen Fähigkeiten sollten angesichts der häufigen Leistungsrückmeldungen im Studium des Öfteren nahegelegt werden (Möller & Marsh, 2013). Daher wird angenommen, dass sich in der Selbstbeschreibung mit Blick auf akademische Eigenschaften und Fähigkeiten mehr dimensionale Vergleiche als in der allgemeinen Selbstbeschreibung finden lassen (Hypothese 2).

Zum anderen wird die Annahme der Theorie dimensionaler Vergleiche überprüft, dass dimensionale Vergleiche eher innerhalb als zwischen Kontexten stattfinden. Erwartet wird, dass überwiegend dimensionale Vergleiche zwischen Eigenschaften und Fähigkeiten, die sich auf denselben Kontext beziehen, vorgenommen werden (Hypothese 3).

3 Methode

3.1 Stichprobe

An der Befragung nahmen $N = 94$ Lehramtsstudierende verschiedener Fächer teil ($M_{\text{Alter}} = 23.57$, $SD = 3.55$; 66 % weiblich). Die Befragung wurde in ausgewählten Kursen durchgeführt, die Teilnahme war freiwillig. Die Studierenden wurden randomisiert den beiden Bedingungen „allgemeine Selbstbeschreibung" ($n = 45$) und „akademische Selbstbeschreibung" ($n = 49$) zugeteilt.

3.2 Vorgehen

Anhand einer schriftlichen Instruktion (weitgehend identisch mit der bei Wilson und Ross (2000) verwendeten Instruktion) wurden die Studierenden dazu aufgefordert, sich selbst in ihren eigenen Worten zu beschreiben. Soziale, temporale und dimensionale Vergleiche wurden erwähnt und die Studierenden gebeten, so viele Vergleiche wie möglich aufzuschreiben. Es wurde jedoch darauf hingewiesen, dass es keine Verpflichtung gebe, sich nach den gegebenen Anregungen zu richten, und dass auch weitere wichtige Informationen in die Selbstbeschreibungen aufgenommen werden sollten. Entsprechend der jeweiligen Versuchsbedingung lautete die Instruktion:

> *Wir möchten Sie nun bitten, sich selbst zu beschreiben / sich in Bezug auf Ihr akademisches Selbstbild zu beschreiben.*
>
> *Beschreiben Sie zum Beispiel, wie Sie sich gesellschaftlich, akademisch und als Freund oder Freundin oder Familienmitglied sehen / Beschreiben Sie zum Beispiel Ihre akademischen Fähigkeiten und Eigenschaften, Ihr Bild von sich als Student oder Studentin etc. Sie können besondere Fähigkeiten und Eigenschaften nennen, die Sie kennzeichnen. Dazu können Sie sich im Vergleich zu anderen Menschen beschreiben oder im Vergleich dazu, wie Sie früher waren beziehungsweise in der Zukunft vermutlich sein werden. Sie können auch diejenigen Ihrer (akademischen) Eigenschaften beschreiben, die sich von Ihren anderen Eigenschaften abheben oder Ihnen ähneln. Bitte nennen Sie so viele Vergleiche, wie Ihnen einfallen, z. B. können Sie Ihre Stärken und Schwächen oder Ihre Rolle in verschiedenen Lebensbereichen / akademischen Bereichen vergleichen.*

Sie können jede dieser Anregungen gern aufgreifen oder ignorieren. Bitte ergänzen Sie Ihre Beschreibung auch durch alle anderen Informationen, die Ihnen einfallen und die wichtig sind, um ein klares Bild von Ihnen zu bekommen.

Nach Beendigung der Selbstbeschreibung wurden die Studierenden gebeten, jede zusammenhängende Aussage (Sinneinheit) zu unterstreichen, um für dimensionale Vergleiche eindeutig feststellen zu können, welche Bereiche jeweils miteinander verglichen wurden.

3.2.1 Kodierschema der Art der Vergleiche

Die in den Selbstbeschreibungen enthaltenen Vergleiche wurden von zwei unabhängigen Raterinnen nach einem vorher festgelegten Kodierschema als soziale, temporale oder dimensionale Vergleiche kodiert. Soziale Vergleiche waren definiert als *„jede Aussage, in der eine Person einen Aspekt ihres Selbst mit einer anderen Person oder einer anderen Gruppe vergleicht"*. Temporale Vergleiche mit der eigenen Person in der Vergangenheit/Zukunft waren definiert als *„jede Aussage, in der eine Person einen Aspekt ihres Selbst mit dem gleichen oder einem anderen Aspekt ihres Selbst in der Vergangenheit/Zukunft vergleicht"*. Dimensionale Vergleiche waren definiert als *„jede Aussage, in der eine Person einen oder mehrere Aspekte ihres Selbst mit einem anderen oder mehreren anderen Aspekten des Selbst vergleicht"*. Beispiele für die von den Probandinnen und Probanden verwendeten Formulierungen sind in Tabelle 1 aufgeführt. Zwei geschulte Mitarbeiterinnen kodierten die Gesamtzahl der Selbstbeschreibungen. Die Übereinstimmung der Raterinnen für die Identifikation aller drei Vergleichsarten war hoch (Cohens Kappa = .75). Bei fehlender Übereinstimmung wurde durch Diskussion eine Übereinstimmung erzielt.

Tabelle 1. Beispiele dimensionaler, temporaler und sozialer Vergleiche

Vergleichsstandard	Beispiel
Sozial	*Im Vergleich zum Durchschnitt der Lehramtsstudent/innen halte ich mich für etwas weniger kreativ, was beispielsweise Methoden oder Einstiege angeht.*
Temporal	*Früher war ich viel zurückhaltender, ist deutlich besser geworden und wird immer besser.*
Dimensional	*Ich habe Stärken im formal-logischen Bereich und im kritischen, schlussfolgernden Denken, bin insgesamt fleißig und zuverlässig, gleichzeitig habe ich Schwächen im zwischenmenschlichen Bereich, im sozialen Kontext usw.*

3.2.2 Inhaltliches Kodierschema

Um feststellen zu können, welche übergeordneten Bereiche miteinander verglichen wurden, wurden die in den Vergleichen enthaltenen Merkmale anhand eines an Wilson und Ross (2000) angelehnten Schemas kodiert. Das Kodierschema enthielt vier Oberkategorien, denen jeweils verschiedene Unterkategorien zugeordnet wurden: Eigenschaften (Offenheit, Extraversion, emotionale Stabilität, Verträglichkeit, Gewissenhaftigkeit, Aussehen), Fähigkeiten/Leistungen (akademische Fähigkeiten, sportliche Fähigkeiten, soziale Fähigkeiten, künstlerische Fähigkeiten), Einstellungen/Ziele (Einstellungen, Werte, Ziele, Hobbies), Beziehungen (Familie, Freunde, Fremde, Öffentlichkeit, Beruf, Kommilitoninnen und Kommilitonen). Die inhaltliche Kodierung der Vergleiche wurde von zwei geschulten Mitarbeiterinnen vorgenommen, die Interrater-Übereinstimmung war hoch (Cohens Kappa = .86).

4 Ergebnisse

4.1 Hypothese 1: Anzahl dimensionaler, sozialer und temporaler Vergleiche

Zur Überprüfung von Hypothese 1 wurde analysiert, ob es Unterschiede zwischen den pro Person vorgenommenen durchschnittlichen Anzahlen dimensionaler, sozialer und temporaler Vergleiche gibt. Tabelle 2 zeigt die durchschnittlichen Anzahlen der Vergleiche pro Person und deren Standardabweichungen. Zudem sind die mittleren Anzahlen genannter Vergleiche in den beiden Bedingungen „generelle Selbstbeschreibung" und „akademische Selbstbeschreibung" aufgeführt.

Tabelle 2. Mittelwerte und Standardabweichungen der Anzahl dimensionaler, sozialer und temporaler Vergleiche pro Person

	Dimensional *M (SD)*	Sozial *M (SD)*	Temporal *M (SD)*
Gesamt	0.86 *(0.82)*	0.64 *(1.45)*	0.74 *(0.89)*
Allgemeine Selbstbeschreibung	0.87 *(0.83)*	0.30 *(0.59)*	0.74 *(0.77)*
Akademische Selbstbeschreibung	0.86 *(0.81)*	0.94 *(1.89)*	0.74 *(0.99)*

Um die Unterschiede in den mittleren Anzahlen dimensionaler, sozialer und temporaler Vergleiche inferenzstatistisch abzuklären, wurden die mittleren Anzahlen der Vergleiche anhand einer Varianzanalyse mit Messwiederholung mit dem Vergleichstyp als Messwiederholungsfaktor analysiert. Es zeigten sich keine signifikanten Unterschiede für die Gesamtstichprobe ($F(2, 186) = 1.23$, *ns*), soziale, temporale und dimensionale Vergleiche wurden demnach in der Gesamtstichprobe im Mittel gleich häufig vorgenommen und Hypothese 1 kann bestätigt werden.

4.2 Hypothese 2: Anzahl dimensionaler Vergleiche in der allgemeinen und der akademischen Selbstbeschreibung

Zur Beantwortung der Fragestellung, ob unter der Bedingung „akademische Selbstbeschreibung" eine höhere Anzahl dimensionaler Vergleiche genannt wurde als unter der „allgemeinen Selbstbeschreibung", wurde ein *t*-Test für unabhängige Stichproben durchgeführt. Es zeigte sich kein Unterschied in der Anzahl dimensionaler Vergleiche zwischen akademischer und allgemeiner Selbstbeschreibung ($t(94) = 0.06$, *ns*). Hypothese 2 konnte damit nicht bestätigt werden.

Zusätzlich wurde explorativ analysiert, ob es für temporale und soziale Vergleiche einen Unterschied zwischen der allgemeinen und der akademischen Selbstbeschreibung gibt und ob sich außerdem die Anzahlen dimensionaler, sozialer und temporaler Vergleiche in Abhängigkeit von den Bedingungen voneinander unterscheiden. Zur Beantwortung dieser Fragestellung wurde eine Varianzanalyse mit Messwiederholung (Messwiederholungsfaktor: Vergleichstyp; Zwischensubjektfaktor: Bedingung der Selbstbeschreibung) durchgeführt. Es zeigte sich kein signifikanter Haupteffekt der Bedingung ($F(2, 184) = 1.41$, *ns*). Auch nach Einbeziehung sozialer und temporaler Vergleiche zeigt sich also kein Unterschied in der Anzahl gemachter Vergleiche zwischen allgemeiner und akademischer Selbstbeschreibung. Der für die Beantwortung der Fragestellung zentrale Effekt der Interaktion zwischen Vergleichstyp und Bedingung fiel signifikant aus ($F(2, 184) = 3.27, p < .05$). Nachfolgend durchgeführte Paarvergleiche mit einer Alpha-Adjustierung nach Bonferroni zeigten, dass in der akademischen Selbstbeschreibung mehr soziale Vergleiche angestellt wurden als in der allgemeinen Selbstbeschreibung ($t(94) = 2.19$, $p < .05$, $d = 0.45$). Für die mittlere Anzahl temporaler Vergleiche ($t(94) = 0.01$, *ns*) ließen sich keine signifikanten Unterschiede zwischen den beiden Bedingungen feststellen.

4.3 Hypothese 3: Analyse der dimensionalen Vergleiche in Bezug auf die verglichenen Bereiche

Die inhaltliche Kodierung der angestellten dimensionalen Vergleiche zeigte, dass 42.9 % der angestellten dimensionalen Vergleiche ausgehend vom Bereich „Persönlichkeit und Aussehen", 35.2 % ausgehend vom Bereich „Fähigkeiten", 4.4 % ausgehend vom Bereich „Einstellungen" und 17.6 % der Vergleiche ausgehend vom Bereich „Beziehungen" durchgeführt wurden. Damit überwiegen insgesamt Vergleiche, die von Persönlichkeitseigenschaften und dem körperlichen Erscheinungsbild ausgehen, gefolgt von Vergleichen ausgehend von Fähigkeiten. Die Fragestellung, ob dimensionale Vergleiche eher zwischen oder eher innerhalb von Kontexten vollzogen werden, wird in Tabelle 3 beleuchtet. Es ist dargestellt, welcher prozentuale Anteil der Vergleiche, die von den jeweiligen Ausgangsbereichen ausgingen, auf den jeweiligen Vergleichsbereich entfällt.

Tabelle 3. Dimensionale Vergleiche: Prozentuale Anteile gewählter Vergleichsbereiche für die verschiedenen Ausgangsbereiche

Ausgangsbereich	Vergleichsbereich			
	Persönlichkeit und Aussehen	Fähigkeiten	Einstellungen	Beziehungen
Persönlichkeit und Aussehen	88.1	9.5	2.4	0
Fähigkeiten	11.8	82.3	2.9	3
Einstellungen	0	25	75	0
Beziehungen	11.8	0	0	88.2

Diese Zahlen zeigen, dass überwiegend Vergleichsbereiche gewählt werden, die aus demselben Kontext stammen wie der Ausgangsbereich (siehe Zellen auf der Tabellendiagonale).

Zudem wurde analysiert, welche Bereiche überwiegend in sozialen und temporalen Vergleichen thematisiert wurden. Soziale Vergleiche fanden mit 54.4 % der Vergleiche am häufigsten im Bereich „Fähigkeiten" statt, 33.8 % lassen sich dem Bereich „Persönlichkeit und Aussehen" zuordnen, 7.4 % beziehen sich auf den Bereich „Einstellungen", und 4.4 % der sozialen Vergleiche sind den „Beziehungen" zuzuordnen. Temporale Vergleiche wurden mit 60.3 % der Vergleiche überwiegend im Bereich „Persönlichkeit und Aussehen" vorgenommen, 30.1 % fanden im Bereich „Fähigkeiten" statt, 2.7 % bezogen sich auf den Bereich „Einstellungen", und 6.8 % fanden im Bereich „Beziehungen" statt.

5 Diskussion

Die vorliegende Studie untersuchte das Auftreten dimensionaler Vergleiche in Selbstbeschreibungen mit drei Fragestellungen:

Fragestellung 1 beschäftigte sich mit der Frage, ob dimensionale Vergleiche in Selbstbeschreibungen ähnlich häufig wie soziale und temporale Vergleiche genannt werden. Im Einklang mit der Annahme zeigte die entsprechende Analyse, dass dimensionale Vergleiche ebenso häufig wie soziale und temporale Vergleiche genannt wurden, dass also ausgehend von den Häufigkeiten von einer ebenso großen Relevanz dimensionaler wie sozialer und temporaler Vergleiche für die Selbsteinschätzung und -beschreibung ausgegangen werden kann. Die vorliegende Studie ist die erste Arbeit, welche die Häufigkeit dimensionaler Vergleiche gemeinsam mit der Häufigkeit sozialer und temporaler Vergleiche in Selbstbeschreibungen untersucht. Sie konnte die Ergebnisse von Wilson und Ross (2000) bestätigen, dass temporale Vergleiche mindestens ebenso häufig wie soziale Vergleiche angestellt werden. Die vorliegende Studie spricht für die Annahme der Theorie dimensionaler Vergleiche, dass dimensionale Vergleiche einer der drei für die Entstehung von Selbsteinschätzungen zentralen Vergleichsprozesse und in ihrer Relevanz für die Selbstbeurteilung von Eigenschaften und Fähigkeiten den sozialen und temporalen Vergleichen nicht nachgestellt sind. Zukünftig könnte dies mit Blick auf Effekte dimensionaler, sozialer und temporaler Vergleiche auf nichtakademische Selbsteinschätzungen untersucht werden. Ebenfalls stehen weitere Studien aus, die direkte Befragungen zur Bedeutsamkeit dimensionaler Vergleiche durchführen.

Die zweite Fragestellung beschäftigte sich mit der Anzahl dimensionaler Vergleiche in der allgemeinen und der akademischen Selbstbeschreibung. Aufgrund der Annahme der Theorie dimensionaler Vergleiche, dass dimensionale Vergleiche gehäuft bei Leistungsrückmeldungen für verschiedene Fächer stattfinden, wurde erwartet, dass in der akademischen Selbstbeschreibung mehr dimensionale Vergleiche auftreten sollten als in der allgemeinen Selbstbeschreibung. Dies war nicht der Fall: Die Beschreibung der eigenen akademischen Fähigkeiten und Eigenschaften enthielt genauso viele dimensionale Vergleiche wie die allgemeine Beschreibung. Der Grund für dieses Ergebnis ist fraglich; Lehramtsstudierende erhalten regelmäßige Leistungsrückmeldungen in ihren Fächern und weisen zudem unterscheidbare Selbsteinschätzungen für die drei Bereiche des Fachwissens, des pädagogischen Wissens und des fachdidaktischen Wissens auf (Paulick, Großschedl, Harms & Möller, 2016). Zwischen den zu diesen Bereichen gehörigen Fächern könnten, wie zwischen dem mathematischen und dem verbalen Bereich im Schulkontext, dimensionale Vergleiche auftreten. Ein Grund dafür, dass in der akademischen Selbstbeschreibung dimensionale Vergleiche nicht häufiger genannt wurden, könnte sein, dass ein Teil der Vergleiche unbewusst verläuft und auch durch die Instruktion nicht bewusstgemacht werden konnte: Möller und Marsh (2013) nehmen an, dass dimensionale Vergleiche häufig dann unbewusst verlaufen, wenn die Situation einen bestimmten Vergleichsbereich für die Einschätzung der eigenen Fähigkeit in einem Bereich nahelegt. So lege beispielsweise die Zeugnisrückgabe in der Schule einen Vergleich der verschiedenen Fachnoten nahe, der dann in vielen Fällen automatisiert und unbewusst verlaufe. Dies ist natürlich auch für Studierende ein möglicher Mechanismus, der bei der Rückmeldung von Leistungen in verschiedenen Studienfächern auftreten könnte. Zukünftige Studien könnten beispielsweise anhand von Tagebuchstudien wie der von Möller und Husemann (2006) versuchen, stattfindende Vergleichsprozesse im akademischen Bereich durch Introspektion besser zugänglich zu machen.

Die Studierenden unserer Stichprobe wendeten in der akademischen Selbstbeschreibung im Vergleich zur allgemeinen Selbstbeschreibung vermehrt soziale Vergleiche an, die sich bei Wilson und Ross (2000) verstärkt nach Anregung des Motivs einer akkuraten Selbstbeschreibung zeigten. Dieses Motiv könnte also bei den

Studierenden in der akademischen Selbstbeschreibung im Vordergrund gestanden haben; Annahmen zu Motivationen für soziale, temporale und dimensionale Vergleiche sollten aber in künftigen Studien explizit überprüft werden, indem Personen dazu befragt werden, in welchen Situationen sie aus welchen Gründen bestimmte Vergleiche anstellen.

Die zur Überprüfung der dritten Fragestellung vorgenommene inhaltliche Auswertung der dimensional verglichenen Bereiche zeigte, dass ein Großteil der Vergleiche sich auf Persönlichkeitseigenschaften, das physische Erscheinungsbild und auf Fähigkeiten bezog. Zudem wurden dimensionale Vergleiche wie angenommen überwiegend innerhalb einer Kategorie durchgeführt. Dieses Ergebnis stützt die Annahme der Theorie dimensionaler Vergleiche, dass verglichene Eigenschaften zumeist aus Bereichen stammen, die einem übergeordneten Kontext zugeordnet werden können. Die ergänzenden Analysen zeigten, dass soziale Vergleiche zu einem überwiegenden Teil zwischen Fähigkeiten, gefolgt von Persönlichkeitseigenschaften und dem physischen Erscheinungsbild, erfolgten. Der überwiegende Vergleich von Fähigkeiten mag erklären, warum soziale Vergleiche häufiger in der akademischen Selbstbeschreibung als in der allgemeinen Selbstbeschreibung genannt wurden. Temporale Vergleiche wurden (wie dimensionale Vergleiche) überwiegend zwischen Persönlichkeitseigenschaften, dem physischen Erscheinungsbild und schließlich Fähigkeiten vorgenommen. Die beiden internalen Vergleichsprozesse zeigen also ein vergleichbares Muster. Beide Prozesse beziehen sich überwiegend auf Eigenschaften (die Persönlichkeit oder das Aussehen betreffend), vor allem im Falle dimensionaler Vergleiche werden aber ebenfalls häufig Fähigkeiten miteinander verglichen. Dies deutet darauf hin, dass die Annahme von Möller und Marsh (2013), dimensionale Vergleiche würden unter anderem aufgrund einer Motivation der Selbstverbesserung, der Übertragung von Lösungsstrategien und Fähigkeiten in einem Bereich auf einen anderen Bereich, durchgeführt, tatsächlich eine wichtige Rolle spielen könnte. Im Falle sozialer Vergleiche deutet das Überwiegen des Vergleichens von Fähigkeiten noch stärker auf die Motivation der Selbstverbesserung hin, die möglicherweise zu häufigen Vergleichen mit Personen mit überlegenen Fähigkeiten führt. In weiteren Studien sollte überprüft werden, ob das jeweilige Überwiegen der verglichenen Bereiche für dimensionale, temporale und soziale Vergleiche eine generelle Systematik darstellt und ob es sich bei den angestellten Vergleichen jeweils überwiegend um Vergleiche mit als positiver oder als negativer gesehenen Eigenschaften und Fähigkeiten handelt.

Eine Stärke der vorliegenden Studie liegt in der gleichzeitigen Untersuchung der Häufigkeit aller drei Vergleichsprozesse in offenen Selbstbeschreibungen, wodurch es für die Studierenden keine Beschränkung auf die Protokollierung dimensionaler Vergleiche wie in der Studie von Möller und Husemann (2006) gab. Dadurch lassen sich aus der vorliegenden Untersuchung Schlüsse über die Relevanz dimensionaler Vergleichsprozesse im Vergleich zu sozialen und temporalen Vergleichsprozessen ziehen.

Eine Limitation der vorliegenden Studie ist die Tatsache, dass in der Instruktion zur freien Selbstbeschreibung die möglichen Vergleichsprozesse explizit genannt wurden. Dieses Vorgehen könnte suggestiv eine Nennung von Vergleichen bewirkt haben, welche sonst nicht genannt worden wären. Die explizite Nennung wurde gewählt, da die Probandinnen und Probanden angeregt werden sollten, tatsächlich alle Vergleichsprozesse zu nennen, die im Alltag möglicherweise stattfinden, aber selten explizit erwähnt werden. Dies könnte bei Vergleichen mit unbewusstem Verlauf der Fall sein, wie von Möller und Marsh (2013) für viele Vergleiche im Schulkontext angenommen. Um außerdem die Nennung weiterer möglicher Vergleichsprozesse zu ermöglichen, wurde in der Instruktion auch darauf hingewiesen, dass die genannten Anregungen gern ignoriert werden könnten sowie die Selbstbeschreibungen auch durch alle weiteren Informationen, die wichtig seien, ergänzt werden sollten. Auf der anderen Seite ist nicht auszuschließen, dass Vergleiche, die zwar angestellt wurden, aber dem Bewusstsein auch nach dem Hinweis durch die Instruktion nicht zugänglich waren, nicht genannt wurden.

Eine weitere Limitation ist die Beschränkung auf eine studentische Stichprobe, und hier auf Lehramtsstudierende. Mit der Befragung von Studierenden können die Ergebnisse nur eingeschränkt auf andere Populationen übertragen werden. Die Ergebnisse der Studie von Möller und Weber (2001) beispielsweise sprechen für die Population älterer Menschen insgesamt für eine größere Relevanz dimensionaler als temporaler und sozialer Vergleiche. Diese Beschränkung erfolgte aus dem Grund, dass sich die Befragung thematisch gut in Veranstaltungen der pädagogischen Psychologie für Lehramtsstudierende einbetten ließ. Die Studierenden sollten unter anderem durch die Befragung zur Selbstreflexion über die Verwendung verschiedener Vergleichsrahmen bei der Einschätzung eigener Fähigkeiten und Eigenschaften angeregt werden. Die Fragestellungen der vorliegenden Studie sollten jedoch noch einmal an anderen als studentischen Stichproben überprüft werden.

Zusammenfassend unterstreicht die vorliegende Studie die Bedeutung dimensionaler Vergleichsprozesse für Selbstbeschreibungen und gibt zudem Hinweise auf die Bereiche, zwischen denen bevorzugt dimensionale Vergleiche vorgenommen werden. Die Relevanz dimensionaler Vergleiche sowie ihre psychologischen Mechanismen und Folgen sollten in introspektiven und experimentellen Studien weiterhin untersucht werden.

Literatur

Albert, S. (1977). Temporal comparison theory. *Psychological Review, 84*, 485–503.

Butler, R. (2000). Making judgments about ability: The role of implicit theories of ability in moderating inferences from temporal and social comparison information. *Journal of Personality and Social Psychology, 78*, 965–978.

Dickhäuser, O. & Galfe, E. (2004). Besser als..., schlechter als.... *Zeitschrift für Entwicklungspsychologie und Pädagogische Psychologie, 36*, 1–9.

Festinger, L. (1954). A theory of social comparison processes. *Human Relations, 7*, 117–140.

Filipp, S.-H. & Buch-Bartos, K. (1994). Vergleichsprozesse und Lebenszufriedenheit im Alter: Ergebnisse einer Pilotstudie. *Zeitschrift für Entwicklungspsychologie und Pädagogische Psychologie, 26,* 22–34.

Köller, O., Klemmert, H., Möller, J. & Baumert, J. (1999). Eine längsschnittliche Überprüfung des Modells des internal/external frame of reference. *Zeitschrift für Pädagogische Psychologie, 13,* 128–134.

Marsh, H. W. (1986). Verbal and math self-concepts: An internal/external frame of reference model. *American Educational Research Journal, 23,* 129–149.

Marsh, H. W., Abduljabbar, A. S., Parker, P. D., Morin, A. J. S., Abdelfattah, F. & Nagengast, B. (2014). The Big-Fish-Little-Pond Effect in Mathematics: A cross-cultural comparison of U.S. and Saudi Arabian TIMSS responses. *Journal of Cross-Cultural Psychology, 45,* 777–804.

Marsh, H. W., Lüdtke, O., Nagengast, B., Trautwein, U., Abduljabbar, A. S., Abdelfattah, F. & Jansen, M. (2015). Dimensional comparison theory: Paradoxical relations between self-beliefs and achievements in multiple domains. *Learning and Instruction, 35,* 16–32.

Möller, J. & Husemann, N. (2006). Internal comparisons in everyday life. *Journal of Educational Psychology, 98,* 342–353.

Möller, J. & Köller, O. (1998). Dimensionale und soziale Vergleiche nach schulischen Leistungen. *Zeitschrift für Entwicklungspsychologie und Pädagogische Psychologie, 30,* 118–127.

Möller, J. & Köller, O. (2001a). Dimensional comparisons: An experimental approach to the internal/external frame of reference model. *Journal of Educational Psychology, 93,* 826–835.

Möller, J. & Köller, O. (2001b). Frame of reference effects following the announcement of exam results. *Contemporary Educational Psychology, 26,* 277–287.

Möller, J. & Marsh, H. W. (2013). Dimensional comparison theory. *Psychological Review, 120,* 544–560.

Möller, J., Müller-Kalthoff, H., Helm, F., Nagy, N. & Marsh, H. W. (2016). The generalized internal/external frame of reference model: An extension to dimensional comparison theory. *Frontline Learning Research, 4,* 1–11.

Möller, J., Pohlmann, B., Köller, O. & Marsh, H. W. (2009). A Meta-analytic path analysis of the internal/external frame of reference model of academic achievement and academic self-concept. *Review of Educational Research, 79,* 1129–1167.

Möller, J. & Savyon, K. (2003). Not very smart, thus moral: Dimensional comparisons between academic self-concept and honesty. *Social Psychology of Education, 6,* 95–106.

Möller, J. & Weber, F. (2001). Dimensionale, soziale und temporale Vergleiche von alten Menschen: Selbstbewertungen, Virulenz und Präferenz. *Zeitschrift für Entwicklungspsychologie und Pädagogische Psychologie, 33,* 178–186.

Paulick, I., Großschedl, J., Harms, U. & Möller, J. (2016). Preservice teachers' professional knowledge and its relation to academic self-concept. *Journal of Teacher Education, 67,* 173–182.

Pohlmann, B., & Möller, J. (2009). On the benefit of dimensional comparisons. *Journal of Educational Psychology, 101,* 248–258.

Skaalvik, E. M. & Skaalvik, S. (2002). Internal and external frames of reference for academic self-concept. *Educational Psychologist, 37,* 233–244.

Strickhouser, J. E. & Zell, E. (2015). Self-evaluative effects of dimensional and social comparison. *Journal of Experimental Social Psychology, 59,* 60–66.

Suls, J. & Mullen, B. (1982). From the cradle to the grave: Comparison and self-evaluation across the life-span. In J. Suls (Ed.), *Psychological perspectives on the self* (pp. 97–128). Hillsdale, NJ: Erlbaum.

Wilson, A. E. & Ross, M. (2000). The frequency of temporal-self and social comparisons in people's personal appraisals. *Journal of Personality and Social Psychology*, *78*, 928–942.

Zell, E. & Alicke, M. D. (2009). Self-evaluative effects of temporal and social comparison. *Journal of Experimental Social Psychology*, *45*, 223–227.

Zell, E. & Alicke, M. D. (2010). Comparisons over time: Temporal trajectories, social comparison, and self-evaluation. *European Journal of Social Psychology*, *40*, 375–382.

Autorinnen und Autoren

DR. FRIEDERIKE HELM
Institut für pädagogisch-psychologische Lehr- und Lernforschung, Christian-Albrechts-Universität zu Kiel.

DR. HANNO MÜLLER-KALTHOFF
Institut für pädagogisch-psychologische Lehr- und Lernforschung, Christian-Albrechts-Universität zu Kiel.

DR. NICOLE NAGY
Institut für pädagogisch-psychologische Lehr- und Lernforschung, Christian-Albrechts-Universität zu Kiel.

KONTAKT
Friederike Helm, Institut für pädagogisch-psychologische Lehr- und Lernforschung, Christian-Albrechts-Universität zu Kiel, Olshausenstraße 75, 24118 Kiel.
E-Mail: *fhelm@ipl.uni-kiel.de*

Anwendung der Theorie dimensionaler Vergleiche auf die fundamentalen Dimensionen der sozialen Wahrnehmung, Agency und Communion

ANDREA E. ABELE

ZUSAMMENFASSUNG: Die Theorie dimensionaler Vergleiche beschäftigt sich mit den Auswirkungen von Feedback auf einer Dimension des (Fähigkeits-)Selbstkonzepts auf eine andere Dimension. Für den Leistungskontext gibt es viele Belege für Kontrasteffekte dimensionaler Vergleiche. Vergleichsprozesse spielen jedoch nicht nur im Leistungskontext, sondern in allen Lebenslagen eine wichtige Rolle. Die Theorie der „Fundamentalen Dimensionen der sozialen Urteilsbildung" hat gezeigt, dass sich Inhalte, hinsichtlich derer Menschen sich selbst einschätzen und andere einschätzen, auf zwei fundamentale Dimensionen zurückführen lassen, diejenige von „agency" (Verfolgung eigener Ziele, „getting ahead") und diejenige von „communion" (Betonung der Beziehungen zu anderen, „getting along"). Im Beitrag wird die Theorie dimensionaler Vergleiche auf diese fundamentalen Dimensionen angewandt und es wird gezeigt, welche Befunde es bisher zur Wirkung des Vergleichs zwischen beiden Dimensionen gibt. Hierbei findet man, dass verschiedene Formen von Kontrasteffekten insbesondere bei der Beurteilung anderer Personen auftreten, während die Befunde für die Selbstbewertung uneindeutig sind. Einige neue Fragestellungen werden aus der Zusammenschau von diesen Theorien unterschiedlicher psychologischer Provenienz (Pädagogische Psychologie, Sozialpsychologie) entwickelt.

Schlüsselwörter: Dimensionale Vergleiche, Agency, Communion, Selbstwahrnehmung, Fremdwahrnehmung, Perspektivenmodell, Kompensationseffekte

Dimensional comparison theory applied to the fundamental dimensions of social judgment, agency and communionn

ABSTRACT: The theory of dimensional comparisons studies the impact of performance feedback in one ability domain on the self-concept in a different ability domain. Quite a few studies revealed contrast effects resulting from such dimensional comparisons. The framework of the fundamental dimensions of social judgment has shown that the content of self-judgments and judgments of others can be traced back to two fundamental dimensions, i. e., the dimension of "agency" (pursuing own goals, "getting ahead") and the dimension of "communion" (being connected to others, "getting along"). The present paper discusses an application of the theory of dimensional comparisons to these fundamental dimensions, and it discusses findings pertaining to the effects of comparisons between agency and communion. There are different types of contrast effects, especially with respect to judgments of other persons. Findings on self-judgments are inconclusive yet. Bringing together these theories and findings from different fields of psychology (educational psychology and social psychology) leads to a number of new and challenging research questions.

Keywords: dimensional comparisons, agency, communion, self-perception, person perception, dual-perspective model, compensation effects

Einleitung

Vergleichsprozesse spielen in allen Lebenslagen eine bedeutsame Rolle (vgl. Festinger, 1954): Wenn man wissen möchte, wie erfolgreich die eigene Berufskarriere ist, dann gibt es dafür keinen klaren objektiven Maßstab, aber es gibt verschiedene Vergleichsmöglichkeiten, die bei der Einschätzung helfen: Man vergleicht sich beispielsweise mit anderen, die im gleichen Berufsfeld arbeiten, dies ist ein externer, sozialer Vergleich (z. B. Abele, Hagmaier & Spurk, 2016); man vergleicht den gegenwärtigen Karrierestand mit demjenigen vor einer gewissen Zeit, dies ist ein temporaler Vergleich (z. B. Albert, 1977); oder man vergleicht den eigenen beruflichen Karrierestand mit einem anderen wichtigen Lebensbereich, z. B. dem Erfolg bei eigenen freizeitsportlichen Aktivitäten, dies ist ein interner, auf verschiedene Lebensbereiche bezogener Vergleich, der auch als dimensionaler Vergleich bezeichnet wird (Möller & Marsh, 2013).

In der Psychologie beschäftigt sich eine ganze Reihe von Theorien mit solchen Vergleichsprozessen und deren Auswirkungen auf Urteilsbildungsprozesse. Auffällig ist hierbei, dass es relativ wenig Überschneidung zwischen z. B. der pädagogisch-psychologischen und der sozialpsychologischen Erforschung von Vergleichsprozessen gibt. Im vorliegenden Beitrag stelle ich eine solche Verbindung her, indem ich die im pädagogisch-psychologischen Kontext entstandene Theorie dimensionaler Vergleiche (Möller & Marsh, 2013) mit der im sozialpsychologischen Kontext entstandenen Theorie der „Big Two" bzw. „fundamentalen Dimensionen der sozialen Urteilsbildung", nämlich Agency und Communion (Abele & Wojciszke, 2014; Bakan, 1966; Paulhus & Trappnell, 2008), verbinde und Hypothesen der Theorie dimensionaler Vergleiche auf diese fundamentalen Dimensionen anwende. Nach einer kurzen Einführung der Theorie dimensionaler Vergleiche beschreibe ich die fundamentalen Dimensionen der sozialen Urteilsbildung und diskutiere empirische Studien, die sich mit Fragestellungen beschäftigt haben, die zum Kontext dimensionaler Vergleiche in Bezug gesetzt werden können. Abschließend wird der potenzielle erkenntnistheoretische „Mehrwert" einer Zusammenschau von Theorien unterschiedlicher psychologischer Provenienz (Pädagogische Psychologie, Sozialpsychologie) am konkreten Beispiel erläutert.

1 Die Theorie dimensionaler Vergleiche

In der Pädagogischen Psychologie beschäftigt man sich u. a. mit der Ausbildung bereichsspezifischer Selbstkonzepte, z. B. dem Selbstkonzept hinsichtlich mathematischer oder sprachlicher Fähigkeiten. Die oben genannten sozialen, externen und auf die eigene Person bezogenen internen Vergleiche spielen hier eine wichtige Rolle. Sowohl externe („ich habe in Mathematik eine Eins geschrieben, mein Sitznachbar eine Vier – ich bin wohl besser in Mathematik als mein Sitznachbar") als auch interne, dimensionale Vergleiche („ich habe in Mathematik eine Eins geschrieben, in Deutsch eine Vier – ich bin wohl in Mathematik besser als in Deutsch") finden statt (vgl. Marsh, 1986). Die aus dem Modell interner/externer Vergleiche weiterentwickelte Theorie dimensionaler Vergleiche (Möller & Marsh, 2013) erklärt z. B., dass infolge des gleichzeitigen Auftretens externer („sozialer") und interner („dimensionaler") Vergleiche z. B. Selbstkonzepte in Mathematik und Deutsch unkorreliert sind – obwohl sie z. B. im Lehrerurteil positiv korrelieren; oder dass eine positive Leistungsrückmeldung in einem Fach („hurra, endlich einmal eine Eins in Deutsch") zu einer Verschlechterung des Selbstkonzepts in einem anderen Fach („eine Eins in Deutsch – offensichtlich bin ich in Mathe doch nicht so viel besser als in Deutsch") führt. Viele Studien belegen diese Effekte (vgl. Metaanalyse von Möller, Pohlmann, Köller & Marsh, 2009). Die Theorie beansprucht, nicht nur für den pädagogischen Kontext relevant zu sein, sondern auch für andere Bereiche des Selbstkonzepts.

2 Fundamentale Dimensionen der sozialen Urteilsbildung: Das Agency/Communion-Modell

Selbstwahrnehmung und Selbstkonzept beziehen sich natürlich nicht nur auf die eigene Leistung, sondern auf viele Bereiche. Man kann sich selbst als „freundlich und hilfsbereit" wahrnehmen oder als „skrupellos und durchsetzungsfähig", als „kompetent und zuverlässig" oder als „einfühlsam und sensibel", um nur ein paar Beispiele zu nennen. Interessanterweise lassen sich Selbstwahrnehmungen solcher Eigenschaften, aber auch Selbstwahrnehmungen eigener Verhaltensweisen genauso wie Beschreibungen anderer Personen und sozialer Gruppen in zwei Hauptinhaltsklassen einordnen. Diese beiden Inhaltsklassen sind zwar von verschiedenen Autorinnen und Autoren unterschiedlich bezeichnet worden (agency/communion; competence/warmth; instrumentality/expressiveness; Abele & Wojciszke, 2007; Bakan, 1966; Cuddy, Fiske & Glick, 2008; Fiske, Cuddy & Glick, 2007; Judd, James-Hawkins, Yzerbyt & Kashima, 2005; Paulhus & Trappnell, 2008; Peeters, 2008), inhaltlich sind sie jedoch vergleichbar (vgl. Abele & Wojciszke, 2014): Agentische Inhalte beziehen sich auf die Verfolgung eigener Ziele: Beispiele sind Kompetenz, Selbstsicherheit, Entscheidungsfreude, Durchsetzungsfähigkeit, aber auch Skrupellosigkeit. Hogan (1983) hat diese Gruppe von Eigenschaften/Verhaltensweisen mit dem Begriff „getting ahead" zusammengefasst, also Vorwärtskommen, Vorankommen. Kommunale Inhalte beziehen sich auf die Pflege von Gemeinschaft sowie auf soziales Verhalten. Beispiele sind Hilfsbereitschaft, Freundlichkeit, Zuverlässigkeit oder Empfindsamkeit. Diese Gruppe von Eigenschaften hat Hogan (1983) als „getting along" zusammengefasst, also miteinander auskommen bzw. sich verstehen.

Aus einer ontologischen Perspektive reflektieren Agency (A) und Communion (C) die Dualität der menschlichen Existenz (Bakan, 1966) sowie die basalen Herausforderungen, mit denen sich Personen konfrontiert sehen: einerseits Kompetenz und Status zu erwerben sowie andererseits anerkannt und eingebunden zu sein (Ybarra et al., 2008; vgl. auch Hogan, 1983). A und C sind insofern interessante Konstrukte für die Anwendung der Theorie dimensionaler Vergleiche, als dass sie grundlegende Dimensionen sowohl für die Selbstwahrnehmung bzw. das Selbstkonzept als auch – das spielt in der Theorie dimensionaler Vergleiche weniger eine Rolle – für die Fremdwahrnehmung/Gruppenwahrnehmung sind.

3 Dimensionale Vergleiche bei Agency und Communion

Man kann sich leicht vorstellen, dass Personen dimensionale Vergleiche bezüglich A und C vornehmen (z. B. „ich bin zwar nicht der Durchsetzungsstärkste, aber ich bin äußerst beliebt") bzw. dass positive Rückmeldungen bezüglich eines Bereichs negative Effekte auf den jeweils anderen haben (z. B. „schon wieder eine Eins in Mathematik, jetzt halten mich die Mitschüler für noch unsympathischer" [positive Kompetenz, d. h. A, versus negative soziale Fertigkeiten, d. h. C]), doch gibt es erst sehr wenige einschlägige Studien.

Möller und Savyon (2003) ließen ihre Versuchspersonen eine Aufgabe bearbeiten, gaben ihnen anschließend manipuliertes Feedback (Kompetenz: A hoch versus niedrig) und erfassten das Selbstkonzept hinsichtlich kommunaler Eigenschaften (Hilfsbereitschaft, Moralität). In Übereinstimmung mit der Vorhersage war nach negativer Leistungsrückmeldung die Selbsteinschätzung hinsichtlich kommunaler Eigenschaften höher als nach positiver Leistungsrückmeldung. Bei einer neuen Studie von Helm, Abele, Müller-Kalthoff & Möller (2017) zeigte sich ebenfalls, dass agentisches Feedback zu Unterschieden in der Selbstwahrnehmung kommunaler Eigenschaften führte. Bei einer anderen Studie wurde kommunales Feedback manipuliert und es zeigte sich, dass die Selbstwahrnehmung agentischer Eigenschaften dadurch beeinflusst wurde.

Bei einer Studie mit ähnlichem Aufbau (manipulierte positive versus negative Leistungsrückmeldung) und sowohl vorher Messung von A und C als auch nachher Messung beider Konstrukte (Abele, Rupprecht & Wojciszke, 2008) fanden wir, dass A nach positiver Leistungsrückmeldung anstieg und nach negativer Rückmeldung geringer wurde. Allerdings fanden wir keinen dimensionalen Vergleichseffekt, d. h., C wurde durch die Manipulation nicht beeinflusst. Nach den bisherigen Befunden gab es also dimensionale Vergleichseffekte, wenn nur die Dimension erfasst wird, auf der keine Rückmeldung erfolgt war (vgl. Helm et al., 2017; Möller & Savyon, 2003).

Sie traten nicht auf, wenn beide Dimensionen erfasst wurden (vgl. Abele, Rupprecht et al., 2008). Möglicherweise ist der Aufforderungscharakter, eigene agentische Eigenschaften nach negativer kommunaler Rückmeldung höher zu bewerten bzw. eigene kommunale Eigenschaften nach negativer agentischer Rückmeldung höher zu bewerten, stärker, wenn nur die jeweils nicht manipulierte Eigenschaft erfasst wird und schwächer, wenn sowohl eigene agentische Eigenschaften als auch eigene kommunale Eigenschaften (und dies in zufälliger Reihenfolge) erfasst werden. Dies muss jedoch in weiterer Forschung untersucht werden.

Neben diesen wenigen Studien zu A/C, die für die Theorie dimensionaler Vergleiche direkt relevant sind, gibt es weitere Arbeiten zu den „Big Two", die ebenfalls für dimensionale Vergleiche interessant sind.

Die Theorie dimensionaler Vergleiche sagt z. B. vorher, dass Selbstkonzepte mathematischer versus sprachlicher Fertigkeiten generell unkorreliert sind, während Einschätzungen die andere über die Person abgeben (z. B. Lehrerratings) positiv korrelieren. Studien zu den „Big Two" erbrachten ebenfalls, dass Selbsteinschätzungen hinsichtlich A und C – insbesondere dann, wenn standardisierte Messinstrumente verwendet wurden – weniger korrelieren als Fremdeinschätzungen (Abele, 2003; Abele, Bruckmüller & Wojciszke, 2014; Abele & Spurk, 2011; Wojciszke & Abele, 2008).

In der Theorie dimensionaler Vergleiche wird vorhergesagt, dass negative Rückmeldung in einem Leistungsbereich zu positiverer Selbstwahrnehmung in einem kontrastierenden anderen Leistungsbereich führen. Diese Effekte sind gut belegt (Möller & Marsh, 2013). Die bisherigen Befunde hinsichtlich Rückmeldung zu A und C sind uneindeutig (s.o.).

Die Theorie dimensionaler Vergleiche beschäftigt sich mit Selbstwahrnehmung, die Forschung zu A und C auch mit Fremdwahrnehmung. Bei letzterer gibt es einige interessante Befunde, die sich im Sinne dimensionaler Vergleiche interpretieren lassen.

In einer Serie von Studien ließen wir zwei Personen miteinander sprechen und manipulierten dabei die Körperhaltung eines der Interaktionspartner. Diese war einmal ausgreifend und „Macht" symbolisierend, beim anderen Mal eher in sich gekauert, Unterwürfigkeit symbolisierend. Im Anschluss an das Gespräch sollten sich die Gesprächspartner selbst hinsichtlich gezeigter A und C einschätzen und auch ihren Gesprächspartner anhand der gleichen Eigenschaften beurteilen. Es zeigte sich bei der Fremdeinschätzung, dass die Macht signalisierende Person hinsichtlich A höher, aber hinsichtlich C niedriger eingeschätzt wurde als die Person, die keine Macht signalisierte (Abele, Meier & Wildner, 2012). Bei der Selbsteinschätzung gab es geringere Unterschiede je nach Machtposition.

Wojciszke (1994, 1997) ließ seine Versuchspersonen hinsichtlich A und C ambivalente Verhaltensweisen anderer Personen beurteilen, beispielsweise, „X hilft seinem Freund beim Reifenwechsel". Dies ist sowohl ein agentisches Verhalten, da X Reifen wechseln kann, als auch ein kommunaler Verhalten, da X hilfsbereit ist. Der Autor fand negative Korrelationen zwischen den A und C Beurteilungen, d. h., Personen, die als agentischer beurteilt wurden, wurden als weniger kommunal bewertet. Und umgekehrt wurden Personen, die kommunaler bewertet wurden, als weniger agentisch wahrgenommen.

Judd et al. (2005) prägten für die negative A – C-Korrelation bei der Beurteilung von Gruppen den Begriff des „Kompensationseffekts": Wenn Gruppen paarweise beurteilt werden und die eine Gruppe positiver auf der A-Dimension beurteilt wird, dann wird die andere Gruppe auf der C-Dimension positiver bewertet. Gleiches gilt, wenn die eine Gruppe auf der C-Dimension positivere Werte erhält, dann bekommt die andere Gruppe auf der A-Dimension positivere Bewertungen. Beispielsweise werden „Franzosen" als agentischer beurteilt als die französisch sprechenden „Belgier", letztere aber als kommunaler als „die Franzosen" (Yzerbyt, Provost & Corneille, 2005). „Griechen" werden als warmherziger beurteilt als „Deutsche", „Deutsche" dagegen als kompetenter als „Griechen" (Carlsson, Björklund & Bäckström, 2012). Judd und Kollegen (2005) vermuteten ursprünglich, dass solche Kompensationseffekte auf ein Gerechtigkeitsmotiv im Sinne von „wenn ich X schon auf der einen Dimension negativer beurteile als Y, dann muss ich X wenigstens auf der anderen Dimension positiver beurteilen als Y" zurückzuführen seien. Abele und Mayer (2014) haben jedoch keinen Beleg gefunden, dass ein Gerechtigkeitsmotiv für diesen Effekt eine Rolle spielt. Sie induzierten bei der Hälfte ihrer Versuchspersonen das Gerechtigkeitsmotiv, bei der anderen Hälfte nicht. Die Effekte auf die Beurteilung von „Griechen" versus „Deutschen" waren die gleichen. Möglicherweise kommt der Kompensationseffekt weniger durch motivationale Mechanismen zustande, sondern vielmehr durch dimensionale Vergleiche.

Ein weiterer Forschungsbereich, der im vorliegenden Kontext interessant ist, sind Studien zum sogenannten Innuendo-Effekt (Kervyn, Yzerbyt, Judd & Nunes, 2009). Dieser Effekt, im Deutschen etwa als „Anspielung" übersetzbar, bezieht sich darauf, dass aus der Art und Weise, wie eine andere Person oder Gruppe beschrieben wird, etwas abgeleitet werden kann, was über das tatsächlich Gesagte hinausgeht. Kervyn, Bergsieker und Fiske (2012) haben diesen Innuendo-Effekt beispielsweise dadurch demonstriert, dass klar positive Information auf einer Dimension (z. B. A) und fehlende Information auf der anderen Dimension (hier: C) dazu führt, dass man die Stimulusperson auf der fehlenden Dimension eher negativ wahrnimmt. Hierbei könnte eine ungeschriebene Regel lauten, dass man dann, wenn man nichts Positives zu sagen hat, lieber gar nichts sagt. Der Innuendo Effekt ist in Kontexten, in denen man erwartet, zu dieser Dimension etwas zu erfahren (z. B. A im Arbeitskontext), stärker als in Kontexten, in denen man weniger erwartet, zu dieser Dimension etwas zu erfahren (z. B. A im Freundschaftskontext). Innuendo Effekte können damit erklärt werden, dass man implizit erwartet, bei der Beschreibung anderer Personen Informationen über beide Bereiche, A und C, zu bekommen. Wenn dies nicht der Fall ist, nimmt man an, dass der nicht genannte Bereich negativer ausgeprägt ist als der genannte. Der genannte Kontexteffekt könnte damit erklärt werden, dass die Erwartung, für bestimmte Kontexte auch bestimmte Eigenschaftsinformationen zu bekommen, unterschiedlich hoch ist. Je höher die Erwartung, desto stärker der Innuendo Effekt, wenn die Erwartung nicht erfüllt wurde.

Der Vollständigkeit halber muss erwähnt werden, dass es auch positive Korrelationen zwischen A und C gibt. Wenn man z. B. Eigenschaftsbegriffe danach beurteilen lässt, wie sehr sie A- bzw. C-Inhalte repräsentieren, dann finden sich positive Korrelationen zwischen den beiden Einschätzungen (Polnisch: Abele & Wojciszke, 2007; Italienisch: Suitner & Maass, 2008; Deutsch: Abele, Uchronski, Suitner & Wojciszke, 2008). Interessanterweise werden diese Korrelationen jedoch negativ, wenn man die Valenzbeurteilung herausrechnet, d. h. wie positiv bzw. wie negativ ein bestimmter Eigenschaftsbegriff bewertet wird. Dies lässt vermuten, dass positive Korrelationen von A und C bei der Beurteilung von Eigenschaftsbegriffen auf geteilte Valenz, aber nicht auf geteilten Inhalt zurückzuführen sind.

Zusammenfassend gibt es also im Bereich der „Big Two"-Forschung einige Befunde, die zu den Annahmen der Theorie dimensionaler Vergleiche passen. Während durch dimensionale Vergleiche hervorgerufene Kontrasteffekte im Leistungskontext für Selbsteinschätzungen gut belegt sind, zeigen sich Kontrasteffekte im Kontext von A und C Bewertungen dagegen deutlicher für Fremdeinschätzungen.

Hierfür gibt es verschiedene Gründe: Zum einen sind Informationen zu A und C weniger eindeutig als Leistungsrückmeldungen zu z. B. Mathematik oder Deutsch. Wie wir oben gesehen haben, kann ein und dieselbe Verhaltensinformation unterschiedlich bewertet werden und es besteht insofern mehr Spielraum bei der Interpretation. Dieser Interpretationsspielraum ist bei der Bewertung eigenen Verhaltens bzw. eigener Eigenschaften noch größer als wenn fremdes Verhalten beurteilt wird.

Dass diese Effekte bei der Fremdbeurteilung stärker sind als bei der Selbstbeurteilung könnte auch damit zusammenhängen, dass die Akteursperspektive (Selbstbeurteilung) generell eine andere ist als die Beobachterperspektive (Fremdbeurteilung). Wie in der „Zwei-Perspektiven-Theorie" (Abele & Wojciszke, 2014) erläutert, ist die Akteursperspektive stärker mit einer agentischen Sichtweise („man möchte seine Ziele erreichen"; getting ahead) verknüpft, während die Beobachterperspektive stärker mit einer kommunalen Perspektive („man möchte mit dem Interaktionspartner gut auskommen"; getting along) verknüpft ist. Akteure sind in der Lage, variabel zu handeln und den Eindruck, den sie erwecken möchten, zu steuern (Holoien & Fiske, 2012). Sie können ihr eigenes Verhalten je nach Zielorientierung unterschiedlich interpretieren. Dies könnte dazu führen, dass die Korrelation zwischen der Selbsteinschätzung von A und C über verschiedene Situationen hinweg niedrig ist. Beobachtende sind bei ihrer Beurteilung stärker auf das Verhalten per se angewiesen.

Zum jetzigen Wissensstand sind die Befunde zu Selbst- versus Fremdbeurteilungen hinsichtlich A und C dahingehend zusammenzufassen,

- dass Selbstbeurteilungen hinsichtlich A und C weniger korrelieren als Fremdbeurteilungen; dieser Befund ist mit der Theorie dimensionaler Vergleiche insofern kompatibel, da Fähigkeitsselbstkonzepte in Mathematik und Deutsch unkorreliert sind, Lehrereinschätzungen dagegen positiv korrelieren;

-

- dass positive Rückmeldungen zu z. B. A nicht unbedingt zu einer negativen Veränderung von Selbsteinschätzungen zu C führen, während positive Leistungsrückmeldungen zu einem Bereich negativere Selbsteinschätzungen zum anderen Bereich nach sich ziehen;
- dass positive Korrelationen zwischen A und C auf gemeinsame Variation mit Valenz zurückzuführen sind; dieser Befund entspricht dem Ergebnis, dass z. B. Lehrerurteile zu den Leistungen von Schülerinnen und Schülern in verschiedenen Fächern positiv korrelieren;
- dass bei der Fremdeinschätzung Kompensations- und Innuendo-Effekte auftreten können; dies ist für die Theorie dimensionaler Vergleiche weniger relevant, da hier ja in erster Linie die Selbstperspektive zählt.

Aus diesen Gemeinsamkeiten und Unterschieden zwischen beiden Ansätzen ergeben sich einige neue Forschungsperspektiven in beiden Bereichen. Zum Beispiel sollte genauer untersucht werden, unter welchen Bedingungen die Selbstwahrnehmung in A oder C dimensionalen Vergleichen folgt und unter welchen Bedingungen dies nicht der Fall ist. Es könnte untersucht werden, inwiefern Fähigkeitsselbstkonzepte klarer und eindeutiger sind, d. h. konkreter an bestimmte Verhaltensweisen und Resultate geknüpft, als Selbstkonzepte hinsichtlich A und C, sowie, ob unterschiedliche Eindeutigkeit zu unterschiedlichen Vorhersagen hinsichtlich dimensionaler Vergleiche führen kann. Als drittes Beispiel könnte sich die Forschung zur Theorie dimensionaler Vergleiche auch vermehrt mit Fremdbeurteilungen beschäftigen.

Literatur

Abele, A. E. (2003). The dynamics of masculine-agentic and feminine-communal traits: Findings from a prospective study. *Journal of Personality and Social Psychology, 85*, 768–776.

Abele, A. E., Bruckmüller, S. & Wojciszke, B. (2014). You are so kind – and I am kind *and* smart: Actor – Observer differences in the interpretation of on-going behavior. *Polish Psychological Bulletin, 45*, 394–401.

Abele, A. E., Hagmaier, T. & Spurk, D. (2016). Does career success make you happy? The mediating role of multiple subjective success evaluations. *Journal of Happiness Studies, 17*, 1615–1633.

Abele, A. E. & Mayer, A. (2014). *Nimmt das Gerechtigkeitsmotiv Einfluss auf den Kompensationseffekt bei der Stereotypisierung von Angehörigen verschiedener europäischer Nationalitäten?* Unveröffentlichtes Manuskript, Universität Erlangen.

Abele, A. E., Meier, I. & Wildner, B. (2012). *Influence of power and of embodied cues of power on self- and other-perception.* Unveröffentlichtes Manuskript, Universität Erlangen.

Abele, A. E., Rupprecht, T. & Wojciszke, B. (2008). The influence of success and failure experiences on agency. *European Journal of Social Psychology, 38*, 436–448.

Abele, A. E. & Spurk, D. (2011). The dual impact of gender and the influence of timing of parenthood on men's and women's career development: Longitudinal findings. *International Journal of Behavioral Development, 35*, 225–232.

Abele, A. E., Uchronski, M., Suitner, C. & Wojciszke, B. (2008). Towards an operationalization of the fundamental dimensions of agency and communion: Trait content ratings in five countries considering valence and frequency of word occurrence. *European Journal of Social Psychology, 38*, 1202–1217.

Abele, A. E. & Wojciszke, B. (2007). Agency and communion from the perspective of self versus others. *Journal of Personality and Social Psychology, 93*, 751–763.

Abele, A. E. & Wojciszke, B. (2014). Communal and agentic content. A dual perspective model. *Advances in Experimental Social Psychology, 50*, 195–255.

Albert, S. (1977). Temporal comparison theory. *Psychological Review, 84*, 485–503.

Bakan, D. (1966). *The duality of human existence. An essay on psychology and religion.* Chicago, IL: Rand Mcnally.

Carlsson, R., Björklund, F. & Bäckström, M. (2012). Mixed discriminatory judgments of individuals' warmth and competence-related abilities. *Social Psychology, 43*, 160–167.

Cuddy, A. J. C., Fiske, S. T. & Glick, P. (2008). Warmth and competence as universal dimensions of social perception: The stereotype content model and the BIAS Map. *Advances in Experimental Social Psychology, 40*, 61–149.

Festinger, L. (1954). A theory of social comparison processes. *Human Relations*, 117–140.

Fiske, S. T., Cuddy, A. J. C. & Glick, P. (2007). Universal dimensions of social cognition: Warmth and competence. *Trends in Cognitive Sciences, 11*, 77–83.

Helm, F., Abele, A. E., Müller-Kalthoff, H. & Möller, J. (2017). Applying dimensional comparison theory to the fundamental dimensions of social judgment – Agency and communion. *Learning and Individual Differences 54*, 116–125.

Hogan, R. (1983). A socioanalytic theory of personality. In M. Page (Ed.), *Nebraska Symposium on Motivation* (pp. 336–355). Lincoln, NE: University of Nebraska Press.

Holoien, D. S. & Fiske, S. T. (2012). Downplaying positive impressions: Compensation between warmth and competence in impression management. *Journal of Experimental Social Psychology, 49*, 33–41.

Judd, C. M., James-Hawkins, L., Yzerbyt, V. & Kashima, Y. (2005). Fundamental dimensions of social judgment: Understanding the relations between judgments of competence and warmth. *Journal of Personality and Social Psychology, 89*, 899–913.

Kervyn, N., Bergsieker, H. B. & Fiske, S. T. (2012). The innuendo effect: Hearing the positive but inferring the negative. *Journal of Experimental Social Psychology, 48*, 77–85.

Kervyn, N., Yzerbyt, V., Judd, C. & Nunes, A. (2009). A question of compensation: The social life of the fundamental dimensions of social perception. *Journal of Personality and Social Psychology, 96*, 828–842.

Marsh, H. W. (1986). Verbal and math self-concepts: An internal/external frame of reference model. *American Educational Research Journal, 23*, 129–149.

Möller, J. & Marsh, H. W. (2013). Dimensional comparison theory. *Psychological Review, 120,* 544–560.

Möller, J., Pohlmann, B., Köller, O. & Marsh, H. W. (2009). A meta-analytic path analysis of the internal/external frame of reference model of academic achievement and academic self-concept. *Review of Educational Research, 79,* 1129–1167.

Möller, J. & Savyon, K. (2003). Not very smart, thus moral: Dimensional comparisons between academic self-concept and honesty. *Social Psychology of Education, 6,* 95–106.

Paulhus, D. L. & Trapnell, P. D. (2008). Self-presentation of personality: An agency-communion framework. In O. P. John, R. W. Robins & L. A. Pervin (Eds.). *Handbook of personality: Theory and research* (3rd ed., pp. 492–517). New York, NY: Guilford Press.

Peeters, G. (2008). The evaluative face of a descriptive model: Communion and agency in Peabody's tetradic model of trait organization. *European Journal of Social Psychology, 38,* 1066–1072.

Suitner, C. & Maass, A. (2008). The role of valence in the perception of agency and communion. *European Journal of Social Psychology, 38,* 1073–1082.

Wojciszke, B. (1994). Multiple meanings of behavior: Construing actions in terms of competence or morality. *Journal of Personality and Social Psychology, 67,* 222–232.

Wojciszke, B. (1997). Parallels between competence- versus morality-related traits and individualistic versus collectivistic values. *European Journal of Social Psychology, 27,* 245–256.

Wojciszke, B. & Abele, A. E. (2008). The primacy of communion over agency and its reversals in evaluations. *European Journal of Social Psychology, 38,* 1139–1147.

Ybarra, O., Chan, E., Park, H., Burnstein, E., Monin, B. & Stanik, C. (2008). Life's recurring challenges and the fundamental dimensions: An integration and its implications for cultural differences and similarities. *European Journal of Social Psychology, 38,* 1083–1092.

Yzerbyt, V. Y., Provost, V. & Corneille, O. (2005). Not competent but warm ... really? Compensatory stereotypes in the French-speaking world. *Group Processes and Intergroup Relations, 8,* 291–308.

Autorin

PROF. DR. ANDREA E. ABELE
Lehrstuhl Sozialpsychologie, Senior Fellow of Psychology,
Universität Erlangen-Nürnberg.

KONTAKT
Andrea E. Abele, Lehrstuhl Sozialpsychologie, Universität Erlangen-Nürnberg,
Bismarckstr. 6, 91054 Erlangen.
E-Mail: E-Mail: *andrea.abele-brehm@fau.de*

Einflüsse des personalen und des sozialen Selbst auf Motivation, lernrelevantes Verhalten und Bildungserträge

BETTINA HANNOVER UND LYSANN ZANDER

ZUSAMMENFASSUNG: Unser Wissen über die Zusammenhänge zwischen dem Selbst von Kindern und Jugendlichen und ihrer schulischen Entwicklung ist deutlich geprägt durch die Forschung zum Selbstkonzept eigener Fähigkeit, zu der Jens Möller maßgeblich beigetragen hat. In diesem Beitrag plädieren wir dafür, neben diesem Aspekt des personalen Selbst bei der Untersuchung von Zusammenhängen zwischen dem Selbst auf der einen Seite und Motivation, lernrelevantem Verhalten und Bildungserträgen auf der anderen Seite stärker auch Aspekte des sozialen Selbst, nämlich des Wissens über eigene Gruppenzugehörigkeiten und den mit ihnen zusammenhängenden Bewertungen, zu berücksichtigen. In einer ersten Näherung versuchen wir, verschiedene einschlägige Theorien darzustellen und herauszuarbeiten, über welche Mechanismen personales und soziales Selbst Einfluss auf die schulische Entwicklung von Kindern und Jugendlichen nehmen können.

Schlüsselwörter: Fähigkeitsselbstkonzept, soziales Selbst, schulische Motivation, lernrelevantes Verhalten

Collective identities: Why we should give them more serious attention when predicting students' academic development

ABSTRACT: Research on the interrelation of self and scholastic attainments has been notably shaped by the influential works on the self-concept of ability, including the contributions of Jens Möller. In this chapter we propose that taking into account social aspects of the self, i. e., individuals' knowledge and evaluation of their group memberships, in their impact on motivation, learning relevant behaviors and educational outcomes more systematically will deepen our understanding of the interrelation between self and academic development. In a first approximation, we describe relevant theories and carve out mechanisms through which personal and social self unfold their influence on students' scholastic development.

Keywords: academic self-concept, social self, academic motivation, learning relevant behaviors

Einleitung

Das Selbst (synonym auch: Selbstkonzept) ist definiert als das Wissen und die Theorien, die Menschen im Laufe ihres Lebens als erkennende Subjekte über sich selbst generieren und in ihrem Gedächtnis repräsentieren (z. B. Markus, 1977). Die Inhalte des Selbst beziehen sich einerseits auf Merkmale, die die Person als Individuum auszeichnen (z. B. Fähigkeiten, Werte, Persönlichkeitseigenschaften, soziale Eingebundenheit, Emotionen, körperliche Erscheinung; im Folgenden *personales Selbst*), und andererseits auf ihre Zugehörigkeiten in verschiedenen sozialen Gruppen und die damit verbundenen Bewertungen (z. B. Geschlecht, Ethnie, Zugehörigkeit zu einem bestimmten Leistungskurs in der Schule; im Folgenden *soziales Selbst*).

Die pädagogische Psychologie hat sich vorzugsweise mit Aspekten des personalen Selbst in seiner Bedeutung für die schulische Entwicklung von Kindern und Jugendlichen beschäftigt, und zwar insbesondere mit dem Selbstkonzept eigener Fähigkeiten. Unser Aufsatz ist ein Plädoyer dafür, systematischer, als dies in der Vergangenheit geschehen ist, auch das soziale Selbst in seinen Auswirkungen auf die akademische Entwicklung von Schülerinnen und Schülern zu berücksichtigen. Das soziale Selbst ist in der Vergangenheit typischerweise in sozialpsychologischen Arbeiten in den Blick genommen worden, in denen Intergruppenprozesse oder der Einfluss von Stereotypen im Mittelpunkt des Interesses stehen. Mit diesem Aufsatz möchten wir einen Versuch machen, die teilweise unverbunden, nebeneinander bestehenden Forschungstraditionen der Untersuchung des Selbstkonzeptes eigener Fähigkeit in der pädagogischen Psychologie und der Untersuchung des sozialen Selbst in der Sozialpsychologie auf die schulische Entwicklung zu beziehen und Mechanismen zu beschreiben, über die personales und soziales Selbst Motivation, lernrelevantes Verhalten und Bildungserträge beeinflussen können. Zu diesem Zweck haben wir Theorien des Selbst daraufhin geprüft, ob sie relevante Aussagen zur schulischen Entwicklung treffen. In Abbildung 1 versuchen wir dann darzustellen, wie personale und soziale Selbstaspekte vermittelt über unterschiedliche – im Folgenden näher beschriebene – Mechanismen (Zukunftsentwürfe des Selbst, Selektion / Passung, Exklusion / Inklusion) Einfluss auf Motivation, lernrelevantes Verhalten und Bildungserträge nehmen können.

1 Personales Selbst

In ihrem in der pädagogischen Psychologie sehr einflussreichen Strukturmodell haben Shavelson, Hubner und Stanton (1976) das Selbst in domänenspezifische akademische, soziale, emotionale und körperbezogene Selbstkonzepte differenziert – sämtlich Aspekte des personalen Selbst. Am häufigsten ist das Selbstkonzept eigener Fähigkeiten in seinen Auswirkungen auf Motivation und Lernen untersucht worden, nämlich der Teil des personalen Selbst, der auf eigene Fähigkeiten und Leistungen in akademischen Kontexten bezogen ist. Denn das Selbstkonzept eigener Fähigkeit,

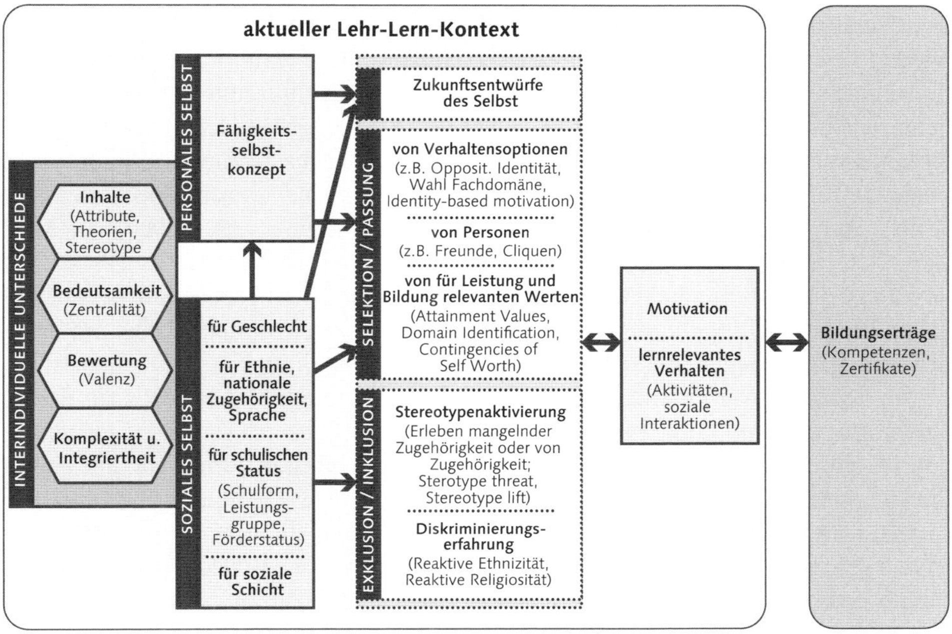

Abbildung 1. Personales und soziales Selbst, Bildungserträge und vermittelnde Mechanismen.

nicht aber nicht-akademische Komponenten des personalen Selbstkonzepts, haben sich als prädiktiv für schulische Erträge (z. B. Noten, Leistung, Kurswahlen, Motivation) erwiesen (Marsh & Craven, 2006; Marsh & Martin, 2011). So fanden Marsh, Trautwein, Lüdtke, Köller und Baumert (2006) unter Verwendung des auf dem Strukturmodell von Shavelson et al. (1976) beruhenden Self-Description-Questionnaire III (Marsh & O'Neill, 1984), dass bei den von ihnen in ihrem letzten Schuljahr untersuchten Jugendlichen Fähigkeitsselbstkonzepte im mathematischen und sprachlichen Bereich substanziell mit verschiedenen Maßen akademischer Kompetenz in den jeweiligen disziplinären Bereichen zusammenhingen und das Fähigkeitsselbstkonzept eigener Problemlösekompetenzen moderat mit den Maßen akademischer Kompetenz zusammenhing, während die nichtakademischen Selbstkonzepte (physical appearance, physical ability, popularity with same and opposite sex, relation with parents, honesty/trustworthiness, religion/spritual values, emotional stability, global self-esteem) mit den Maßen akademischer Kompetenz im Wesentlichen unkorreliert waren (bis auf schwach negative Zusammenhänge mit dem Selbstkonzept der eigenen Beliebtheit beim anderen Geschlecht und schwach positive Zusammenhänge mit dem Selbstkonzept der Beziehung zu den Eltern). Für die Vorhersage der schulischen Entwicklung ist also aus den verschiedenen Aspekten des personalen Selbst das Fähigkeitsselbstkonzept entscheidend, entsprechend ist es in Abbildung 1 besonders hervorgehoben.

Psychologisch sind die positiven Zusammenhänge zwischen akademischen Aspekten des personalen Selbst und schulischen Erträgen damit zu erklären, dass eine positive Selbsteinschätzung der eigenen Fähigkeit wie eine optimistische Erwartung wirkt: Es befördert anspruchsvolle Zielsetzungen und Investition von Anstrengung und Beharren, wenn Schwierigkeiten oder Fehlschläge auftreten und hat dadurch einen leistungssteigernden Effekt (z. B. Eccles, 2011). Positive Leistungsergebnisse wirken ihrerseits begünstigend auf das Fähigkeitsselbstkonzept zurück. Dieser wechselseitige kausale Zusammenhang zwischen Fähigkeitsselbstkonzept und Leistungen ist in vielen Studien gezeigt worden (z. B. Marsh & Craven, 2006; Marsh & Martin, 2011). Beispielsweise maßen Retelsdorf, Köller und Möller (2014) lesebezogene Fähigkeitskonzepte und Lesekompetenzen in einer Stichprobe von über 1500 Sekundarstufenschülerinnen und -schülern zu Beginn der fünften Klasse, am Ende der sechsten, zu Beginn der achten und am Ende der neunten Klasse. Die Ergebnisse zeigen deutliche Auswirkungen des individuellen Lesekompetenzniveaus auf das zu einem späteren Zeitpunkt gemessene Fähigkeitsselbstkonzept. Darüber hinaus fanden Retelsdorf et al. (2014) vom ersten zum zweiten Messzeitpunkt begünstigende Effekte eines positiven Fähigkeitsselbstkonzepts auf die Lesekompetenz.

Um herauszufinden, wie optimistische Fähigkeitsselbstkonzepte im Kontext der Schule gefördert werden können, ist untersucht worden, von welchen anderen Faktoren sie neben tatsächlichen Leistungen abhängen. Während in den Grundschuljahren Kinder ihre Leistungen deutlich überschätzen, werden ihre Fähigkeitsselbstkonzepte zunehmend realistisch (z. B. Arens et al., 2016). Diese Veränderungen hängen unter anderem damit zusammen, dass Kinder erst in dieser Entwicklungsphase die kognitive Fähigkeit entwickeln, sich selbst im sozialen Vergleich mit anderen einzuschätzen (Ruble, 1994). Das Leistungsniveau der Personen, mit denen die eigenen Leistungen verglichen werden, stellt einen wichtigen Einflussfaktor dar: Das Fähigkeitsselbstkonzept ist umso negativer ausgeprägt, je schwächer die Leistungen relevanter Vergleichspersonen sind und umgekehrt; der sog. *Big Fish Little Pond*-Effekt (vgl. Marsh & Hau, 2003).

Jens Möller hat in seiner *Dimensional Comparison Theory* (Möller & Marsh, 2013) einen weiteren Einflussfaktor auf das Fähigkeitsselbstkonzept beschrieben, nämlich Vergleiche, die eine Person über ihre Kompetenzen in verschiedenen Domänen hinweg vornimmt (z. B. „Wie gut bin ich in Mathematik verglichen mit Englisch?"). Möller und Marsh (2013) präsentieren Evidenz aus introspektiven, pfadanalytischen und experimentellen Studien, die belegen, dass dimensionale Vergleiche das Fähigkeitsselbstkonzept in der Domäne schwächen, in der die Person vergleichsweise schlechter ist, und in der Domäne stärken, in der die Person vergleichsweise besser ist. Dieser Effekt dimensionaler Vergleiche ergibt in Verbindung mit den Auswirkungen sozialer Vergleiche, dass gute Leistungen einen positiven Effekt auf das Selbstkonzept eigener Fähigkeit in der jeweiligen Domäne haben, gleichzeitig aber einen negativen Effekt auf das Fähigkeitsselbstkonzept in anderen Domänen (Möller, Müller-Kalthoff, Helm, Nagy & Marsh, 2015; Möller, Retelsdorf, Köller & Marsh, 2011; für eine Studie mit Stichproben verschiedener Altersgruppen, Nationalitäten und fachlicher Domänen siehe z. B. Marsh et al., 2015).

2 Soziales Selbst

Neben dem personalen Selbst umfasst das Selbstkonzept soziales Selbstwissen. Tajfel (1978) definierte das soziale Selbst als "that part of an individual's self-concept which derives from his knowledge of his membership of a social group (or groups) together with the value and emotional significance attached to that membership" (S. 63)[1]. Soziales Selbstwissen kann sowohl auf stabile (z. B. Ethnie) als auch auf erworbene, veränderbare Gruppenzugehörigkeiten (z. B. Zugehörigkeit zu einer Schulform) bezogen sein. Den Wert eines sozialen Selbst leitet die Person aus dem Wissen ab, wie die jeweilige eigene Gruppe (*Ingroup*) relativ zu anderen relevanten Gruppen, zu denen sie selbst nicht gehört (*Outgroups*), im sozialen Wettbewerb abschneidet (Tajfel & Turner, 1986). Wird die eigene Gruppe als von der Outgroup positiv distinkt wahrgenommen, erlebt und bewertet die Person ihr entsprechendes soziales Selbst als positiv.

Grundlage für jedes soziale Selbst ist eine Selbstkategorisierung als Mitglied der Ingroup, in Abgrenzung von der jeweiligen Outgroup (Tajfel & Turner, 1986). Dafür muss die Person ein Verständnis haben, welche Merkmale die Ingroup – im Unterschied zu Outgroups – auszeichnen. Mit der Selbstkategorisierung entsteht ein Bestreben herauszufinden, was es sozial bedeutet, Mitglied der jeweiligen Ingroup zu sein; entsprechend sucht die Person ihre Umwelt nach relevanten Informationen ab. Das resultierende soziale Selbstwissen besteht aus mit der jeweiligen Gruppe verbundenen Theorien oder Ideologien, aus Attributen, die gemäß Stereotypen die jeweilige Gruppe charakterisieren und die gleichzeitig als charakteristisch für die eigene Person gehalten werden, und aus Bewertungen und affektiven Bedeutungen, die sich aus der Wahrnehmung ergeben, wie die Ingroup im sozialen Wettbewerb mit anderen Gruppen abschneidet (für einen Überblick siehe z. B. Bennett & Sani, 2004; Ruble et al., 2004).

Entwicklungspsychologisch betrachtet gehört die Selbstkategorisierung nach Geschlecht zu den ersten sozialen Selbsten; sie ensteht im Alter von 2 bis 3 Jahren (z. B. Fagot & Leinbach, 1985). Im Alter von ca. 10 Jahren entwickeln sich soziale Selbste als Mitglied bestimmter ethnischer, nationaler oder kultureller Gruppen (für einen Überblick siehe Ruble et al., 2004) und im Alter von ca. 11 Jahren beginnend bilden sich soziale Selbste als Mitglied einer bestimmten sozialen Schicht heraus (z. B. Andersen et al., 2008; Vereecken & Vandegehuchte, 2003).

---

1 Im Rahmen der sozialen Identitätstheorie (Tajfel & Turner, 1986) wird von personalen und sozialen Identitäten (statt Selbsten) gesprochen, um hervorzuheben, dass in Abhängigkeit der Situation für Menschen unterschiedliche Aspekte ihres Selbst identitätsrelevant werden, sie also durch unterschiedliche Aspekte ihres personalen oder sozialen Selbst in ihrem Denken, Fühlen und Handeln gesteuert werden. Für eine Darstellung der teilweise synonymen und teilweise differentiellen Verwendung der Begriffe „Selbst" und „Identität" in der Literatur siehe z. B. Oyserman, Elmore & Smith (2012).

3 Situationale Aktivierung personaler und sozialer Selbstaspekte

In Abhängigkeit des aktuellen Lehr-Lern-Kontextes (siehe Abbildung 1) werden entweder personales Selbst oder unterschiedliche Aspekte des sozialen Selbst mental zugänglich und zum Arbeitsselbst oder *Working Self* (Hannover, 1997; Markus & Kunda, 1986). So zeigt sich empirisch beispielsweise, dass das soziale Selbst als Mädchen oder Junge im Klassenzimmer psychologisch salient wird, wenn soziale Vergleiche zwischen den Geschlechtsgruppen statt Vergleiche zwischen Individuen betont werden, wenn der Anteil an Mädchen und Jungen deutlich unbalanciert ist oder wenn die Lernenden mit geschlechtsstereotypisierten (vs. egalitären) Überzeugungen anderer (z. B. der Lehrperson oder der Peers) konfrontiert werden (Bigler & Liben, 2007; Hannover, 2000).

Entsprechend sollten von den zahlreichen möglichen sozialen Selbsten diejenigen für die akademische Entwicklung besonders bedeutsam sein, die auf im Kontext der Schule unterscheidbare soziale Gruppen bezogen sind. Typischerweise dürften in der Schule Gruppenzugehörigkeiten in Bezug auf Geschlecht (für einen Überblick siehe z. B. Kessels, Heyder, Latsch & Hannover, 2014), ethnische oder kulturelle Zugehörigkeit (z. B. Hannover et al., 2013; Zander & Hannover, 2013), Leistungsstatus (besuchte Schulform: z. B. Knigge & Hannover, 2011; sonderpädagogischer Förderstatus: z. B. Nusser & Wolter, 2016; Spörer et al., 2015) und soziale Herkunft eine Rolle für das soziale Selbst der Kinder und Jugendlichen spielen (siehe Abbildung 1).

4 Interindividuelle Unterschiede in personalen und sozialen Selbsten

Wie Abbildung 1 zeigt, gilt sowohl für das personale als auch das soziale Selbst, dass Menschen sich bzgl. der in ihnen repräsentierten Inhalte (bestehend aus Attributen, Theorien, Stereotypen) voneinander unterscheiden können. Weiter unterscheiden sich Personen in der Bedeutsamkeit oder Relevanz, die sie verschiedenen Selbstaspekten zuweisen (vgl. Abbildung 1). Markus (1977) hat Aspekte, die die Person als besonders zentral für ihre Selbstdefinition erachtet und deshalb extensiv elaboriert, als Selbstschemata bezeichnet. In solchen Domänen werden einschlägige Informationen auf der Grundlage des Selbstschemas, d. h. konzeptgesteuert, verarbeitet: sie werden besonders wahrscheinlich wahrgenommen, besonders schnell und auf eine Weise interpretiert, dass sie das bestehende Selbstschema bestätigen. Schließlich unterscheiden sich Menschen in der Bewertung oder Valenz ihrer personalen und sozialen Selbste (vgl. Abbildung 1). Der globale Selbstwert ist definiert als die Gesamtheit der evaluativen Konnotationen, die die Inhalte des Selbst haben (Marsh, 1986). Entsprechend können Menschen in verschiedenen Domänen Selbste mit unterschiedlichen Valenzen haben, z. B. ein positiv valentes personales Selbst in Bezug auf die eigene physische Attraktivität, ein negatives Fähigkeitsselbstkonzept in Mathematik, ein positiv valentes soziales Selbst in Bezug auf die Zugehörigkeit zur Gruppe der Italienerinnen und Italiener und ein negativ valentes soziales Selbst in

Bezug auf die Zugehörigkeit zur Integrierten Sekundarschule. Die Valenz sozialer Selbste zerfällt dabei jeweils in zwei Teilaspekte: die Bewertung, die die jeweilige Gruppe nach Meinung der Person in der Gesellschaft erfährt (*public regard*) und die Bewertung, die die Person selbst mit ihrer Gruppenmitgliedschaft verbindet (*private regard*; Luhtanen & Crocker, 1992). Schließlich bestehen interindividuelle Unterschiede im Hinblick auf die Komplexität (Linville, 1985) und Integriertheit verschiedener Selbstkonzepte (z. B. Benet-Martínez & Haritatos, 2005), also in der Anzahl unterschiedlicher Selbste, die zur Beschreibung und Organisation selbstbezogenen Wissens zur Verfügung stehen, sowie in dem Ausmaß, in dem sich diese verschiedenen Selbste unterscheiden bzw. miteinander kompatibel sind (vgl. Abbildung 1).

5 Mechanismen, über die personales und soziales Selbst die schulische Entwicklung beeinflussen können

Wenn wir im Folgenden von Mechanismen sprechen, über die das Selbst die schulische Entwicklung beeinflussen kann, so gehen wir von folgenden empirisch gut belegten Vorannahmen aus. Wie in der sozialkognitiven Forschung über Selbstschemata vielfach gezeigt wurde, haben diejenigen Inhalte des personalen und sozialen Selbst besonders wahrscheinlich einen Einfluss, die für die Person eine hohe Bedeutsamkeit oder Zentralität haben (vgl. Abbildung 1; z. B. Crane & Markus, 1982; Cross & Markus, 1994; Oyserman, Kemmelmeier, Fryberg, Brosh & Hart-Johnson, 2003). Dabei ist die Bedeutsamkeit, die eine Person einem bestimmten Selbstaspekt zumisst, nicht nur von idiosynkratischen Bedingungskonstellationen abhängig. So haben beispielsweise solche sozialen Selbste für Menschen eine höhere Bedeutsamkeit, die auf Gruppen bezogen sind, die (im jeweiligen Kontext) numerisch unterrepräsentiert, die in ihrem sozialen Status bedroht sind oder die eine optimale Distinktheit (in dem Konflikt zwischen dem Streben nach Einzigartigkeit und Ähnlichkeit mit anderen) gewähren (z. B. Brewer, 1991; Crocker & Garcia, 2006; Deaux, 1993; McGuire & Padawer-Singer, 1976). Ein Beispiel ist, dass die Zugehörigkeit zu einer bestimmten Ethnie für Schülerinnen und Schüler mit Migrationshintergrund eine höhere Bedeutsamkeit hat als für Angehörige der ethnischen Majorität; mit der Folge, dass das entsprechende soziale Selbst auch wahrscheinlicher Einfluss auf Motivation, Lernverhalten und schlussendlich Bildungserträge nimmt, als dies bei Mitgliedern der ethnischen Majorität der Fall ist (Walton & Carr, 2012; für einen Überblick siehe z. B. Berry, Phinney, Sam & Vedder, 2006). Ein anderes Beispiel ist, dass das auf Geschlecht bezogene soziale Selbst im Mittel für Mädchen und Frauen bedeutsamer für die Definition ihrer Person ist, als dies bei Jungen und Männern der Fall ist – der Grund hierfür ist der relativ geringere soziale Status des weiblichen Geschlechts (für einen Überblick siehe z. B. Hannover, Wolter, Drewes & Kleiber, 2014).

Eine zweite Vorannahme ist, dass Menschen nach einem positiven Selbstwert streben (Baumeister & Leary, 1995; Leary, 2012). Ein positiver Selbstwert ist begleitet von Gefühlen wie Sicherheit und Zufriedenheit, ein negativer Selbstwert geht mit dem Erleben von Angst und Bedrohung oder von Trauer und Hoffnungslosigkeit einher (Baumeister & Leary, 1995). Weiter streben Menschen nach Autonomie, sozialer Eingebundenheit und persönlicher Kompetenz (Deci & Ryan, 1985; Ryan & Deci, 2000). Schulische Motivation und engagiertes Lernverhalten sind also auch davon bestimmt, inwieweit die Lehr-Lern-Situation positiv erlebt wird und die Befriedigung dieser menschlichen Grundbedürfnisse ermöglicht (z. B. Assor, Vansteenkiste & Kaplan, 2009; Church et al., 2013).

Schließlich nehmen wir an, dass soziale Selbste auch Einfluss auf das personale Selbst haben (vgl. Pfeil in Abbildung 1). Ein prominentes Beispiel sind Einflüsse, die von mit bestimmten sozialen Selbsten verbundenen Stereotypen auf das Fähigkeitsselbstkonzept in unterschiedlichen fachlichen Domänen ausgehen (z. B. Klieme et al., 2010; Schiepe-Tiska & Schmidtner, 2013).

5.1 Zukunftsentwürfe des Selbst

Einen Mechanismus, über den einerseits das personale Selbst und andererseits soziale Selbstaspekte, die auf erworbene, veränderbare Gruppenzugehörigkeiten bezogen sind (z. B. Schulformzugehörigkeit), die schulische Entwicklung beeinflussen können, stellen mentale Entwürfe des Selbst in der Zukunft, sog. *possible selves* (Cross & Markus, 1994; Markus & Nurius, 1986; Markus & Ruvolo, 1989) dar (vgl. Abbildung 1). Sie sind relevant für Motivation und lernrelevantes Verhalten, weil sie auf die eigene Person bezogene Ziele, Hoffnungen und Befürchtungen repräsentieren und deshalb als Standards für die Selbstbewertung dienen. Werden sie in einem Lehr-Lern-Kontext aktiviert, so motivieren sie auf die Erreichung erhoffter Zukunftsentwürfe oder auf die Vermeidung befürchteter Zukunftsentwürfe gerichtete Handlungen (Oyserman, Brickman & Rhodes, 2007; Oyserman, Bybee & Terry, 2006). Sie stellen damit eine konzeptuelle Verbindung zwischen Selbstwissen und exekutiven Funktionen des Selbst dar.

5.2 Selektion und Passung

Für soziale Selbste möchten wir die von uns identifizierten einschlägigen Theorien zwei Mechanismen zuordnen, über die sie Einfluss auf die schulische Entwicklung einer Person nehmen können: 1) Selektion und Passung und 2) Exklusion und Inklusion (vgl. Abbildung 1). „Selektion und Passung" beschreiben Theorien, nach denen Menschen stärker intrinsisch motiviert handeln und entsprechend auch wahrscheinlicher erfolgreich sind, wenn sie die jeweilige Aktivität als kongruent mit ihrem Selbst erleben, als wenn sie keine Relevanz für ihr Selbst oder gar eine Inkongruenz erkennen. Dieser Gedanke geht bereits auf Waterman (1990) zurück, der in Erweiterung der Identitätstheorie von Marcia (1966) postuliert hat, dass Menschen die Aufgabe haben, ihr „wahres Selbst" zu finden, indem sie sich für personal expressive – statt instrumentelle – Verhaltensoptionen entscheiden (*personal expressiveness*). Personal expressive Aktivitäten geben dem Individuum das Gefühl, sein wahres Selbst auszudrücken und ermöglichen es auch Außenstehenden zu erkennen, wer oder wie die Person wirklich ist – ein Gefühl, das klar von dem Erleben hedonischer Freude abgegrenzt werden kann (Waterman, 1990).

Waterman (1990) geht davon aus, dass Personen mit hoher personaler Expressivität stark intrinsisch motiviert handeln, da sie sich Selbstaspekten verpflichten, mit denen sie ihre Potenziale am besten zur Wirkung bringen können. Modernere Theorien, die in unserem Ordnungsversuch dem Mechanismus „Selektion und Passung" (vgl. Abbildung 1) zugeordnet werden können, verzichten hingegen auf die Annahme, dass Menschen ein „wahres Selbst" haben – und machen die Frage zum Untersuchungsgegenstand, wovon es abhängig ist, welche Verhaltensoptionen Menschen in einer gegebenen Situation als selbstkongruent erleben (Passung) und entsprechend besonders wahrscheinlich wählen (Selektion). Dabei wird deutlich, dass solche als selbstkongruent erlebten Wahlen keineswegs immer günstige Auswirkungen auf Motivation, Lernverhalten und Bildungserträge haben müssen.

Dies wird in dem Ansatz der *Oppositional Identity* (vgl. Abbildung 1) deutlich (Ogbu, 2004). Ogbu (2004) argumentiert, dass afrikanisch-stämmige amerikanische Jugendliche in der Schule unter Umständen nicht nach guten Noten oder Abschlüssen streben, weil sie ein solches Verhalten als *„acting White"* wahrnehmen würden. Die Selbstkategorisierung der Gruppe der afrikanisch-stämmigen Amerikanerinnen und Amerikaner ist nach Ogbu (2004) auch heute noch von der leidvollen Geschichte dieser Bevölkerungsgruppe geprägt. Mit ihrer Versklavung wurden sie gezwungen, ihre afrikanische Kultur aufzugeben, durften sich aber auch nicht wie Weiße verhalten – z. B. waren Lesen oder Schreiben bei schwerer Strafe verboten. Vielmehr mussten sie sich so verhalten, wie Schwarze (in der Rolle des Sklaven) es den stereotypen Vorstellungen der Weißen nach tun. Die kollektive Erfahrung von Unterdrückung und Ausbeutung führte laut Ogbu (2004) zur Herausbildung eines neuen schwarzen sozialen Selbst, das durch Abgrenzung von den Verhaltensweisen geprägt ist, die Weiße von Schwarzen erwarten, und das sich gleichzeitig von dem ursprünglichen mit der ethnischen Herkunftsidentität verbundenen sozialen Selbst unterscheidet. Mit dieser *Oppositional Identity* befreiten sie sich von der *„burden of acting White"*. Manifestationen seien Ausdrucksweisen, durch die ein deutlicher Unterschied zu Weißen markiert wird, wie z. B. der schwarze Englisch-Dialekt, bestimmte Arten, sich zu bewegen und zu gestikulieren oder bestimmte kulturelle und religiöse Praktiken. Auch nach der Abschaffung der Sklaverei und der formalen Gleichstellung von Schwarzen und Weißen in Amerika machten afrikanisch-stämmige Menschen die Erfahrung, dass sie in Situationen, in denen Weiße nach wie vor die kontrollierende Majorität sind – wie z. B. in Institutionen formaler Bildung – wie Weiße sprechen und sich verhalten müssten, wenn sie als gleichberechtigte Personen anerkannt werden wollten. Würde Erfolg in Bildungsinstitutionen „as an assimilation, a one way acculturation or a subtractive process, that takes away their Black identity" (a.a.O., S. 20) interpretiert, könne sich dies über lernabträgliches Verhalten auf Bildungserträge ungünstig auswirken.

Hannover und Kessels (z. B. Hannover & Kessels, 2004; Kessels et al., 2014) haben in ihren Arbeiten in allgemeinerer Form die Mechanismen von „Selektion und Passung" beschrieben, die zwischen sozialen Selbsten auf der einen Seite und schulischen Erträgen auf der anderen Seite vermitteln: Warum erlangen bestimmte Verhaltensoptionen bestimmte soziale Bedeutungen, werden also in einer Gruppe von Personen übereinstimmend als Ausdruck bestimmter sozialer Selbste interpretiert? In ihrem *Interessen-als-Identitätsregulation-Modell* betonen sie die wechselseitigen Wirkprozesse, in denen das Bestreben, das eigene Selbst zu veranschaulichen, zur Wahl bestimmter Kontexte, Aktivitäten, Entscheidungsoptionen oder Interaktionspartnerinnen und -partner führt (vgl. Abbildung 1), die ihrerseits dann zu einer Rückversicherung dieses Selbstaspektes für die Person und einer Zuschreibung dieses Selbst durch andere führt, die diese Darstellungen wahrnehmen (wie Peers oder Lehrpersonen). Bezogen auf die Schule sind beispielsweise bestimmte Aktivitäten (Experimentieren im Physikunterricht, absichtsvoll den Unterricht stören) oder Verhaltensoptionen (Wahl eines Musik-Leistungskurses, Schulabsentismus) mit stereotypen Annahmen darüber verbunden, welche Merkmale prototypische Personen haben, die die betreffende Aktivität zeigen oder Verhaltensoption wählen. So kann das soziale Selbst als Mädchen besser durch die Wahl eines Englisch- als eines Mathematikleistungskurses veranschaulicht werden, da Geschlechterstereotypen zufolge Englisch, nicht aber Mathematik, zum Mädchensein gehört (vgl. Hannover & Kessels, 2004). Umgekehrt kann es für Jungen selbstbedrohlich sein, sich in der Schule anzustrengen, wenn sie Schule als „weiblich" kategorisieren (Heyder & Kessels, 2013), wenn sie als weniger erfolgreich als Mädchen in der Schule stereotypisiert werden (Latsch & Hannover, 2014) und wenn sie sich in der Schule helfen lassen, weil Hilfesuchen als inkompatibel mit bestimmten maskulinen Personeigenschaften gilt (Kessels & Steinmayr, 2013). Entsprechend wählen Mädchen und Jungen unterschiedliche Fachdomänen und Verhaltensoptionen; fachspezifische Kompetenzunterschiede und Geschlechtsdisparitäten in der Bildungsbeteiligung sind die Folge (für einen Überblick siehe Kessels et al., 2014).

Auch die *Identity-Based-Motivation-Theory* von Oyserman (2015) kann dem Mechanismus „Selektion und Passung" zugeordnet werden (vgl. Abbildung 1). Identität wird hier als gleichbedeutend mit selbstgesetzten Zielen interpretiert. Ausgangspunkt ist wiederum die Annahme, dass Menschen besonders motiviert sind, sich auf eine Weise zu verhalten, die als kongruent mit ihrer Identität, d. h. mit selbstgesetzten Zielen, erlebt wird. Ob Menschen ihr Verhalten dann aber auch an ihren Zielen ausrichten, ist davon abhängig, (1) welcher Selbstaspekt in einem gegebenen Kontext aktiviert wird (z. B. ich als Schüler, der Abitur macht vs. ich als Mitglied der Clique der Jungs, die rauchen) und ob der aktivierte Selbstaspekt relevant für die Entscheidung zwischen situational gegebenen Verhaltensoptionen ist (z. B. ob der Schüler sich freiwillig für eine Zusatzaufgabe meldet). Die Erreichung eines selbstgesetzten Ziels (z. B. das Abitur schaffen) ist also daran gebunden, inwieweit es (und nicht andere) im Schulkontext aktiviert wird und Verhaltensoptionen bestehen, die für das Streben nach diesem Ziel als relevant erlebt werden.

Schließlich kann die Wahl von Peers (Freundschaften, Cliquen) im Klassenzimmer als Ausdruck des Mechanismus „Selektion und Passung" interpretiert werden (vgl. Abbildung 1). Homophilie, nämlich die Tendenz, vorzugsweise mit anderen zu interagieren, mit denen soziale Gruppenzugehörigkeiten geteilt werden (z.B. Geschlecht, Ethnie), kann Ausdruck einer hohen situationalen Salienz der entsprechenden Merkmale sein, die dann dazu führt, dass Verhaltensoptionen – in diesem Fall, mit welchen Peers man im Unterricht oder nach der Schule zusammen ist – in Übereinstimmung mit diesem sozialen Selbstaspekt gewählt werden (vgl. Brechwald & Prinstein, 2011; Hafen, Laursen, Burk, Kerr & Stattin, 2011). Im Ergebnis sind Interaktionen zwischen Peers gleichen Geschlechts (z.B. Martin, Fabes & Hanish, 2014) oder gleicher ethnischer Herkunft (z.B. Vermeij, van Duijn & Baerveldt, 2009) typischerweise deutlich häufiger als Interaktionen über diese „Gruppengrenzen" hinweg. Dies führt wiederum dazu, dass der Einfluss des jeweiligen sozialen Selbst auf die weitere schulische Entwicklung der Person verstärkt wird. Wenn beispielsweise eine kleine Gruppe der Schülerinnen und Schüler einer Klasse eine von der Unterrichtssprache abweichende gemeinsame Erstsprache hat, so kann es sein, dass ein auf die Erstsprache bezogenes soziales Selbst psychologisch salient wird. Im Ergebnis kommunizieren diese Schülerinnen und Schüler besonders oft untereinander, so dass sie weniger wahrscheinlich ein vergleichbar hohes Kompetenzniveau in beiden Sprachen erlangen, als wenn das auf die Erstsprache bezogene soziale Selbst eine weniger hervorgehobene Bedeutung hat (z.B. in bilingual immersiven Klassenzimmern; vgl. Zander, Hannover, Steglich & Baumert, 2017).

Eine weitere Variante, über die durch den „Selektion und Passung"-Mechanismus ein Zusammenhang zwischen sozialen Selbsten und schulischen Erträgen erzeugt wird, wird in Theorien beschrieben, in denen es um für Leistung und Bildung relevante Werte geht (vgl. Abbildung 1). Werte sind abstrakte Konzepte oder Glaubenssätze, die wünschenswerte und moralisch als gut befundene Zustände beschreiben und handlungsleitende Prinzipien für die Person darstellen (Schwartz, 1992). Für Leistung und Bildung relevante Werte sind *achievement values* im Ansatz von Schwartz (1992), der insgesamt zehn universale Werte unterscheidet. Weiter zu nennen sind *attainment values* (vgl. Abbildung 1), die (gemeinsam mit *intrinsic values, utility values* und *costs*) die *subjective task values* in Eccles' *Expectancy-value model of achievement-related choices* bilden (z.B. Eccles, 2005). Attainment values sind hoch ausgeprägt, "when individuals view engaging in the task as central to their own sense of themselves (i.e., their core social and personal identities), because such tasks provide the opportunity for the individual to express or confirm important aspects of the self" (Eccles, 2005, S. 109). Werte stellen auch die Grundlage der Konstrukte *domain identification* oder *domain importance* dar (Osborne & Jones, 2011), die darüber definiert sind, dass eine Person eine inhaltliche Domäne als zentral oder wichtig für die Definition ihres Selbst erachtet, und für das Konstrukt *domain disidentification* (Steele, 1997) (vgl. Abbildung 1). Steele (1997) postuliert, dass die wiederholte Konfrontation mit auf ein soziales Selbst bezogenen negativen Stereotypen zu domain disidentification führen kann, nämlich dass die Person ihr Selbst loslöst von Erfahrungen in diesem Bereich; Beispiele können die Abwahl von Kursen oder Schulabsentismus sein (Steele, 1997). Schließlich ist der *Contingencies-of-self-worth*-Ansatz (Crocker, Luhtanen & Sommers, 2004) zu nennen; in diesem Fall geht es um den Selbst-„Wert" (vgl. Abbildung 1). Selbstwert-Kontingenzen stellen diejenigen Domänen des Selbst dar, von denen eine Person ihren Selbstwert abhängig macht. "Contingencies of self-worth are the domains in which people invest their self-esteem – the areas in which they believe success means they are wonderful or worthwhile, and failure means they are worthless" (a.a.O., S. 135). Dass Schülerinnen und Schüler ihren Selbstwert kontingent zu akademischen Leistungen machen, begünstigt schulischen Erfolg (z. B. Wolfgramm, Rau, Zander-Musić, Neuhaus & Hannover, 2010); umgekehrt kann es sich ungünstig auf die schulische Entwicklung auswirken, wenn ein Lernender seinen Selbstwert ausschließlich von außerschulischen Domänen abhängig macht (z. B. von seinem personalen Selbst als beliebt beim anderen Geschlecht, Marsh et al., 2006; vgl. auch Crocker et al., 2004).

Wir ordnen diese Theorien dem Mechanismus „Selektion und Passung" zu, da sie sämtlich beschreiben, dass Menschen die Bedeutsamkeit ihrer Werte so anpassen, dass sie ein positives Selbstbild und eine kohärente Identität bewahren (siehe auch das *Self-Evaluation Maintenance*-Modell von Tesser, 1988): Das Selbst bedrohende Erfahrungen in einer Domäne (z. B. schlechte Leistungsergebnisse, mangelnde soziale Unterstützung im Klassenzimmer) führen dazu, dass die Person den Wert dieser Domäne als weniger wichtig für ihre Selbstdefinition erachtet – oft damit verbunden, dass eine alternative Domäne eine entsprechende Aufwertung erfährt. So fand beispielsweise Osborne (1997), dass eine über die Zeit abnehmende Identifikation mit der akademischen Domäne einherging mit einer zunehmend starken Identifikation mit Peerbeziehungen und sportlichen Aktivitäten. Wolfgramm et al. (2014) fanden bei Schülerinnen und Schülern mit Migrationshintergrund in Deutschland und der Schweiz, dass Angst vor Zurückweisung aufgrund der eigenen ethnischen Zugehörigkeit schlechtere Ergebnisse in einem Lesekompetenztest vorhersagte, wobei dieser Zusammenhang teilweise darüber vermittelt war, dass die Schülerinnen und Schüler ihren Selbstwert stärker zu dem auf ihre kulturelle Herkunftsgruppe bezogenen sozialen Selbst kontingent machten (z. B. „My self-esteem is based on my membership in the cultural group I belong to") und sich stärker in ihre Herkunftsgruppe zurückzogen – sichtbar in einer geringeren Zahl von Freundinnen und Freunden aus der Majoritätskultur. Zander und Wolter (2016) zeigten vom Selbst abhängige Variationen in der *domain identification*: Jugendliche, die ihrem auf ihr Geschlecht bezogenen sozialen Selbst eine hohe Bedeutsamkeit beimaßen (hohe Zentralität), gaben fachspezifische Aspirationen an, die in Übereinstimmung mit Geschlechtsstereotypen waren: Mädchen erachteten gute Leistungen in Deutsch als wichtiger als gute Leistungen in Mathematik; Jungen waren gute Leistungen in Mathematik wichtiger als in Deutsch. Jugendliche, die ihrem auf ihr Geschlecht bezogenen sozialen Selbst eine geringe Bedeutsamkeit beimaßen, richteten ihre relativen fachlichen Aspirationen hingegen am jeweiligen Kontext aus (nämlich daran, ob relativ mehr Mädchen oder mehr Jungen in der Klasse waren).

Boehnke und Mitarbeitende haben darauf verwiesen, dass die Notwendigkeit, Werte anzupassen oder selektiv zur Anwendung zu bringen, für die Person mit psychologischen Kosten einhergeht. Sie verdeutlichen dies am Beispiel Jugendlicher mit einer Migrationsgeschichte, die mit unterschiedlichen kulturellen Wertesystemen konfrontiert sind. In der Folge können sie mehrere auf ihre kulturellen Zugehörigkeiten bezogenen Selbste haben, die mit einer unterschiedlichen Priorisierung von Werten assoziiert sind, so dass je nach Kontext verschiedene Werte für sie handlungsleitend werden. Daniel, Boehnke und Knafo-Noam (2016) fanden in einer Untersuchung israelischer Jugendlicher, dass in dem Maße, wie sie ihre Werte kontextualisierten (*Value-Differentiation*; z. B. stark divergierende Werte auf die Fragen hin: „As an Israeli, it is important to me to be successful" vs. "As an Arab, it is important to me to be successful"), sie Einbußen in ihrem Selbstwert zeigten. Die Ergebnisse der Studie von Daniel, Benish-Weisman, Boehnke und Knafo (2014) zeigen weitergehend, dass eine starke Value-Differentiation mit Separationsstrategien einherging, während Assimilations- und Integrationsstrategien bei Jugendlichen vorherrschten, die die mit ihren verschiedenen kulturellen Identitäten zusammenhängenden Werte als ähnlich erlebten.

Ein anderes Beispiel für psychologische Kosten, die sich ergeben können, wenn Menschen ihre Werte nicht stimmig mit ihrem Selbst anpassen oder selektieren können, zeigt die Studie von Boehnke (2008). Thema ist hier der Wertekonflikt, dem sich Jugendliche mit sehr starken schulischen Leistungen ausgesetzt sehen können: Sie laufen in ihrer Peergruppe Gefahr, als „Streber" sozial abgewertet und exkludiert zu werden. Bei einem Vergleich Jugendlicher aus Deutschland, Kanada und Israel fand Boehnke (2008) zunächst, dass *achievement values* (Schwartz, 1992) von den Jugendlichen aus Deutschland am wenigsten und von denen aus Israel am stärksten bejaht wurden. Daraus ergab sich erwartungsgemäß, dass in der Mathematik sehr leistungsstarke Jugendliche sich insbesondere in Deutschland von sozialer Exklusion bedroht sahen. Weiter zeigte sich nur für Deutschland ein klarer Zusammenhang zwischen Leistungsstärke in der Mathematik und Angst vor sozialer Zurückweisung durch die Peers und hier insbesondere für Mädchen. Dieser Wertekonflikt kann sich ungünstig auf die Entfaltung der schulischen Potenziale leistungsstarker Jugendlicher auswirken: Für diese Teilgruppe zeigten sich negative Zusammenhänge zwischen ihren standardisiert gemessenen Mathematikkompetenzen und ihren Mathematiknoten – während dieser Zusammenhang in den Gruppen mittelstarker und leistungsschwacher Jugendlicher positiv war (Boehnke, 2008). Es scheint, die leistungsstarken Jugendlichen versuchen, die Werte-Inkompatibilität dadurch zu lösen, dass sie ihr Leistungspotential zurückhalten auf Dimensionen, die neben ihrer tatsächlichen Mathematikleistung für die Benotung durch die Lehrkraft eine Rolle spielen (z. B. mündliche Beteiligung) und entsprechend gemessen an ihrer tatsächlichen Leistung zu schlecht benotet werden.

5.3 Exklusion vs. Inklusion

Ein zweiter Mechanismus, über den das soziale Selbst Einfluss auf Motivation und lernrelevantes Verhalten nehmen kann, stellt die erlebte (bzw. tatsächliche) „Exklusion und Inklusion" in der Lehr-Lern-Situation dar (vgl. Abbildung 1). Exklusion und Inklusion sind dabei auf das jeweilige soziale Selbst bezogen: Fühlt die Person sich aufgrund oder in Bezug auf diese Gruppenzugehörigkeit zum akademischen Kontext zugehörig oder nicht zugehörig? Das Erleben, exkludiert zu sein, hat ungünstige und das Erleben von Inklusion in den akademischen Kontext günstige Auswirkungen auf Motivation und lernrelevantes Verhalten (für einen Überblick siehe z. B. Walton & Brady, in Druck; Wentzel, Russell & Baker, 2014). Während einige der durch „Exklusion und Inklusion" ausgelösten Reaktionen mit denen identisch sind, die bereits im Kontext des „Selektion und Passung"-Mechanismus zur Sprache kamen, unterscheiden sich beide Mechanismen dadurch, dass bei „Selektion und Passung" das Individuum eher Akteur ist und sich die Umwelt zur Erhöhung der Passung mit der eigenen Identität gestaltet, während bei „Exklusion und Inklusion" eher tatsächliche bzw. antizipierte Reaktionen der anderen ursächlich sind. „Selektion und Passung" beschreiben also stärker innerpsychische Modi, während der „Exklusion vs. Inklusion"-Mechanismus vergleichsweise stärker Reaktionen des Individuums auf äußere (situationale und chronische) Einflüsse bezeichnet.

Zum Exklusionserleben können negative leistungsbezogene Stereotype führen, die auf das soziale Selbst einer Person bezogen sind. So haben Walton und Mitarbeitende in einem umfangreichen Forschungsprogramm gezeigt, dass Mitglieder sozialer Gruppen, die von solchen Stereotypen betroffen sind (z. B. ethnische Minoritäten: Walton & Carr, 2012; Frauen in MINT: Walton, Logel, Peach, Spencer & Zanna, 2015), immer dann, wenn sie in einer Lehr-Lern-Situation Schwierigkeiten erleben, sie darauf attribuieren, dass sie nicht in dieses Setting gehören (für einen Überblick siehe Walton & Brady, in Druck). Negative leistungsbezogene Stereotype signalisierten Betroffenen in Lehr-Lern-Situationen, dass sie nicht als Individuen, sondern als Mitglieder der stereotypisierten Gruppe wahrgenommen werden und dass sie zum akademischen Kontext möglicherweise nicht dazugehören. Entsprechend seien Betroffene besonders aufmerksam gegenüber Hinweisen darauf, dass sie nicht sozial eingebunden oder nicht zugehörig sind. Wenn sie solche Hinweise finden, würden ihr Zugehörigkeitserleben, ihre Motivation und Leistung beeinträchtigt (Walton & Carr, 2012). Okonofua, Walton und Eberhardt (2016) argumentieren am Beispiel der in den USA sehr viel häufiger gegen Schülerinnen und Schülern aus ethnischen Minoritätsgruppen verhängten disziplinarischen Maßnahmen, dass diese auf eine ungünstige Dynamik zwischen Lehrkräften und Lernenden zurückgehen. Verhält sich eine Schülerin oder ein Schüler aus einer solchen Gruppe uneindeutig (zeigt z. B. ein Verhalten, das entweder als Ausdruck fachlichen Desinteresses oder aber als Ausdruck mangelnden Respekts gegenüber der Lehrkraft interpretiert werden kann), so wird es von der Lehrkraft auf der Grundlage des negativen Stereotyps besonders wahrscheinlich als absichtsvoll gegen sie gerichtetes Verhalten interpretiert und entsprechend häufiger und härter bestraft. Der betroffene Lernende interpretiert das Verhalten der Lehrkraft als stereotypbasiertes unfaires Verhalten und als Zeichen dafür, dass er nicht dazugehört. Das Erleben, nicht zur eigenen Klasse oder Schule dazu zu gehören, macht weiteres und noch gesteigertes abweichendes Verhalten wahrscheinlich.

Walton, Spencer und Erman (2013) argumentieren, dass viele akademische Settings und vor allem solche, in denen Leistungen getestet werden, so gestaltet sind, dass durch sie negative leistungsbezogene Stereotype aktiviert werden (z.B. weil Mitglieder negativ stereotypisierter Gruppen unter Lehrkräften oder Prüfungsberechtigten unterrepräsentiert sind) und entsprechend zu Exklusionserleben bei Lernenden führen, deren soziales Selbst auf eine der stereotypisierten Gruppen bezogen ist. Werden in einer Lehr-Lern-Situation negative leistungsbezogene Stereotype aktiviert, so sind Schülerinnen und Schüler, die zu der betreffenden Gruppe gehören, nicht nur von mangelndem Zugehörigkeitserleben, sondern auch von der Vorstellung bedroht, das Stereotyp mit ihren Leistungen selbst zu bestätigen (*stereotype threat*, Steele, 1997; vgl. Abbildung 1). Stereotypenbedrohung führt bei ansonsten gleichen Leistungsvoraussetzungen zu Leistungseinbußen. So fanden beispielsweise Appel, Weber und Kronberger (2015) in einer Metaanalyse zu Konsequenzen der Aktivierung negativer, auf die Gruppe Zugewanderter in den USA oder Europa bezogene Stereotypen Leistungsbeeinträchtigungen mittlerer Effektstärke. Dies galt auch für die für Deutschland identifizierten Studien, die sämtlich türkische Migrantinnen und Migranten untersucht haben. Personen können von der situationalen Aktivierung eines Stereotyps jedoch auch profitieren, also sogar gesteigerte Inklusion erleben, nämlich dann, wenn sie zur nach dem jeweiligen Stereotyp überlegenen Gruppe gehören (*stereotype lift*). Und es kann dazu kommen, dass Personen sich genau entgegen den mit dem aktivierten Stereotyp assoziierten Vorhersagen verhalten (*stereotype reactance*). Allerdings ist bisher ungeklärt, welche genauen Voraussetzungen für eine solche Reaktion gegeben sein müssen (Javadian & Zoogah, 2014), außer dass sich die Person über den Einfluss des Stereotyps auf ihr persönliches Erleben bewusst sein muss (Kray, Thompson & Galinsky, 2001).

Weiter haben wir dem „Exklusion vs. Inklusion"-Mechanismus Erklärungsansätze zugeordnet, die sogenannte reaktive Identitäten (also Exklusion) als Folge von Diskriminierungserfahrungen vorhersagen (vgl. Abbildung 1). Ausgangspunkt für diese theoretischen Ansätze ist beispielsweise das Phänomen, dass Bildungserträge und Arbeitsmarktbeteiligung Zugewanderter im Vergleich zu Mitgliedern der Majoritätskultur nicht unbedingt mit der Aufenthaltsdauer zunehmen, sondern insbesondere sozioökonomisch benachteiligte Zuwanderergruppen häufig ein Muster *segmentierter Assimiliation* zeigen. Dies bedeutet, dass sie in ihrer Herkunftsgruppe verbleiben, Kontakte zu Mitgliedern der Mehrheitsgesellschaft meiden, die Lebenspraxis ihrer kulturellen Gruppe unverändert fortsetzen und sich stark über ihre ethnische, nicht aber ihre nationale Zugehörigkeit identifizieren (auch: *Segregation*; Berry et al., 2006). Dies kann zur Folge haben, dass Disparitäten in Bildungserträgen oder Arbeitsmarktbeteiligung über die Einwanderergenerationen hinweg erhalten bleiben oder sich sogar verstärken (für einen Überblick siehe z.B. Diehl & Schnell, 2006).

In einer qualitativen Interviewstudie befragte Çelik (2015) 20 türkischstämmige männliche Jugendliche, die aus der Schule in Deutschland ohne Abschluss ausgeschieden waren und sich folglich im Übergangssystem (z.B. Berufsvorbereitungsjahr) befanden. Çelik fand, dass keiner der Befragten deutsche Freunde hatte, sich als Deutscher oder als hybrid deutsch-türkisch identifizierte, sondern alle Befragten eine starke pro-türkische Identität beschrieben und sich sämtlich für den türkischen statt den deutschen Reisepass entschieden (zum Zeitpunkt der Untersuchung war eine Entscheidung zwingend). Wenn solche Muster segmentierter Assimilation in Deutschland insbesondere bei Schülerinnen und Schülern mit türkischem Hintergrund gefunden werden (z.B. Segeritz, Walter & Stanat, 2010; Walter, 2014), so ist eine mögliche Erklärung, dass eine verstärkte Identifikation mit der eigenen Herkunftsgruppe eine Reaktion auf negative Einstellungen darstellt, die gegenüber Migrantengruppen mit überwiegend muslimischer Glaubenszugehörigkeit seit den Terroranschlägen in New York im Jahre 2001 zunehmend verbreitet sind (z.B. Shaw, 2012).

Reaktive Identitäten zeigen sich nicht nur in einer zunehmenden Bedeutung, die dem jeweiligen ethnischen sozialen Selbst beigemessen wird, sondern können sich dann, wenn die Herkunftskultur mit starker Religiosität verbunden ist, auch in reaktiver Religiosität (vgl. Abbildung 1) zeigen, verbunden mit einer intensivierten religiösen Praxis. So ist für verschiedene Länder gezeigt worden, dass die Religiosität bei Muslimen mit Migrationshintergrund stärker ausgeprägt ist als bei Muslimen in den jeweiligen Herkunftsländern und dass sie in der ersten Generation (die selbst gewandert ist) schwächer ausgeprägt ist als in den in der Aufnahmekultur geborenen Nachfolgegenerationen (z.B. Brettfeld & Wetzels, 2007; Maliepaard, Gijsberts & Phalet, 2015). Ein weiterer Beleg für reaktive Religiosität ist, dass religiöse Orientierungen, Einstellungen und Verhaltensroutinen über Migrantengenerationen hinweg in Abhängigkeit der Herkunftskultur in unterschiedlich starkem Ausmaß weitergegeben werden. Diehl und König (2013) fanden beispielsweise, dass sowohl polnisch-stämmige als auch türkisch-stämmige Zugewanderte nach ihrer Übersiedlung nach Deutschland zunächst einen Rückgang vor allem öffentlicher religiöser Praktiken, weniger hingegen privater religiöser Praktiken, zeigten, und dass dies bei polnischen, nicht aber türkischen Zugewanderten mit einer Zunahme der sozialen Vernetzung in die Aufnahmegesellschaft hinein verbunden war. Weiter zeigte sich, dass türkische, nicht aber polnische Zugewanderte, nach kurzer Zeit wieder zu ihren ursprünglichen religiösen Praktiken zurückkehrten.

Reaktive Religiosität (also Exklusion) kann sich ungünstig auf schulische Erträge auswirken, wenn die deutsche Schule von Angehörigen religiöser Minoritäten mit den beiden großen christlichen Glaubensgemeinschaften, der katholischen oder der protestantischen Kirche, nicht aber ihrer eigenen Religion assoziiert wird. An deutschen allgemeinbildenden Schulen ist laut Artikel 7 Absatz 3 des Grundgesetzes der Religionsunterricht konfessionell ausgerichtet und bekenntnisgebunden, d.h., die Glaubenssätze der jeweiligen Religion werden hier als Wahrheiten vermittelt. Gleichwohl inzwischen in einigen Bundesländern bekenntnisorientierter Unterricht auch für Schülerinnen und Schüler syrisch-orthodoxer, orthodoxer, jüdischer, islamischer und alevitischer Religionszugehörigkeit angeboten wird (für eine detaillierte Darstellung vgl. Sachverständigenrat, 2016, S. 105 ff.), kann reaktive Religiosität zu dem Erleben führen, dass die deutsche Schule inkompatibel mit der eigenen religiösen Identität ist. Eine geringe Bedeutsamkeit und negative Bewertung, die der Identität als Mitglied der Schule in Deutschland zugemessen wird, mangelndes schulisches Engagement und nur wenige Kontakte zu Peers mit anderer (oder keiner) Religionszugehörigkeit können die Folge sein.

Während reaktive Ethnizität oder Religiosität bedeuten, dass dem auf die eigene ethnische oder religiöse Gruppe bezogenen sozialen Selbst eine starke Bedeutsamkeit beigemessen wird, ist mit oppositioneller Identität (siehe bei Selektion / Passung in Abbildung 1) gemeint, dass in Folge der erlebten Geringschätzung durch die dominante kulturelle Gruppe auch das eigene ethnische soziale Selbst zurückgewiesen und durch ein neues, oppositionelles soziales Selbst ersetzt wird (vgl. Osborne & Jones, 2011). In ihren Interviews fand Çelik (2015) auch Formen oppositioneller sozialer Selbste, die sich in einer Ablehnung von Autoritäten wie Lehrkräften oder der Polizei in Deutschland und in Verhaltensweisen äußerten, die die Jugendlichen als „cool" erlebten: „The interviewees' appropriation of such attitudes cannot be interpreted as maintaining their ethnic culture. Rather, it refers to a subculture where 'coolness' and ethnic pride bestow empowerment among peers, even though it comes at the expense of academic achievement" (a.a.O., S. 1655 f.). Entscheidender Mechanismus dürfte hier die Schaffung alternativer Quellen zur Befriedigung des Bedürfnisses nach sozialer Zugehörigkeit (Baumeister & Leary, 1995; Deci & Ryan, 1985) sein, die weder in der Gruppe der ethnischen Herkunftskultur noch in der Aufnahmekultur gefunden werden. Reaktive Identitäten können also in oppositionelle Identitäten übergehen. Wir haben beide Formen sozialer Selbste dem Inklusion-Exklusion-Mechanismus zugeordnet, sie sind jedoch von entsprechenden Selektions- und Passungsprozessen – sowohl in Bezug auf die Auswahl von Aktivitäten als auch bestimmter Personengruppen – begleitet (vgl. Abbildung 1).

Während Exklusion über bedrohtes Zugehörigkeitserleben und die Aktivierung negativer leistungsbezogener Stereotype oder durch die Beförderung reaktiver sozialer Identitäten ungünstige Auswirkungen auf Motivation und lernrelevantes Verhalten erwarten lässt, gilt umgekehrt, dass das Erleben von Inklusion eine Ressource darstellt, die sich positiv auf Bildungserträge auswirkt. Inklusion befriedigt das menschliche Bedürfnis nach sozialer Eingebundenheit: Regelmäßige, vielfältige und positiv erlebte Sozialkontakte sind Voraussetzung für emotionales Wohlbefinden und einen positiven Selbstwert (Baumeister & Leary, 1995). Entsprechend hat das Erleben von Zugehörigkeit zur Schule oder zur eigenen Schulklasse günstige Auswirkungen: Es fördert Motivation, lernrelevantes Verhalten und Leistungsergebnisse, die ihrerseits wiederum das Zugehörigkeitserleben stärken (für einen Überblick siehe Hannover & Zander, 2016; Walton & Brady, in Druck; Wentzel et al., 2014).

Dies ist auch die Hoffnung, die sich mit der neuen Praxis der inklusiven Beschulung von Kindern und Jugendlichen mit und ohne Förderbedarf verbindet. Hier ist die Idee, dass die Selbstkategorisierung als Person mit Beeinträchtigungen im inklusiven Klassenzimmer abgeschwächt oder sogar gänzlich verhindert werden kann. Mögliche negative Folgen einer auf den eigenen Förderstatus bezogenen sozialen Identität (z. B. Homophilie, Stereotypenbedrohung) sollen so ausbleiben und gleichzeitig die Ressourcen erweitert werden, auf die Kinder und Jugendliche in der Schulklasse zugreifen können (z. B. akademische Hilfe, die Peers ohne Förderstatus gewähren können). Während inzwischen erste Evidenz dafür vorliegt, dass Schülerinnen und Schüler mit Förderbedarf in ihren akademischen Kompetenzen von inklusiver Beschulung profitieren (Kocaj, Kuhl, Kroth, Pant & Stanat, 2014), gibt es bisher noch kaum Befunde betreffend die emotionalen und sozialen Erträge für diese Gruppe von Kindern und Jugendlichen (z. B. Huber & Wilbert, 2012; Nusser & Wolter, 2016).

6 Ausblick

In diesem Aufsatz haben wir ausgehend von einer Würdigung der Arbeiten, die den Einfluss des Fähigkeitsselbstkonzepts als eines Aspekts des personalen Selbst auf die schulische Entwicklung zeigen, dafür plädiert, noch systematischer als bisher geschehen auch soziale Selbste in ihrem Einfluss auf Motivation und lernrelevantes Verhalten zu untersuchen. In den USA sind soziale Selbste bisher vor allem zur Beschreibung der besonderen Situation von Schülerinnen und Schülern ethnischer Minoritäten betrachtet worden. Weitere soziale Selbste, die in der Schule eine Rolle spielen, wurden nur vergleichsweise selten betrachtet. Für Deutschland liegen noch weniger einschlägige Arbeiten vor; hier dominieren bei der Untersuchung bestimmter marginalisierter sozialer Gruppen bis heute eher qualitative Arbeiten. Wir hoffen, durch unseren Systematisierungsversuch Impulse für zukünftige Forschung zum Zusammenhang zwischen personalem und sozialem Selbst auf der einen Seite und der schulischen Entwicklung von Kindern und Jugendlichen auf der anderen Seite gegeben zu haben.

Literatur

Andersen, A., Krølner, R., Currie, C., Dallago, L., Due, P., Richter, M., Örkényi, Á. & Holstein, B. (2008). High agreement on family affluence between children's and parents' reports: International study of 11-year-old children. *Journal of Epidemiology and Community Health, 62*, 1092–1094.

Appel, M., Weber, S. & Kronberger (2015). The influence of stereotype threat on immigrants: Review and meta-analysis. *Frontiers in Psychology, 6: 900.*

Arens, A. K., Marsh, H. W., Craven, R. G., Yeung, A. S., Randhawa, E. & Hasselhorn, M. (2016). Math self-concept in preschool children: Structure, achievement relations, and generalizability across gender. *Early Childhood Research Quarterly, 36*, 391–403.

Assor, A., Vansteenkiste, M. & Kaplan, A. (2009). Identified versus introjected-approach and introjected-avoidance motivations in school and in sports: The limited benefits of self-worth strivings. *Journal of Educational Psychology, 101*, 482–497.

Baumeister, R. F. & Leary, M. R. (1995). The need to belong: Desire for interpersonal attachments as a fundamental human motivation. *Psychological Bulletin, 117*, 497–529.

Benet-Martínez, V. & Haritatos, J. (2005). Bicultural identity integration (BII): Components and psychosocial antecedents. *Journal of Personality, 73*, 1015–1050.

Bennett, M. & Sani, F. (Hrsg.). (2004). *The development of the social self.* New York, NY: Psychology Press.

Berry, J., Phinney, J., Sam, D. & Vedder, P. (2006). *Immigrant youth in cultural transition: Acculturation, identity, and adaptation across national contexts.* Mahwah, NJ: Lawrence Erlbaum Associates.

Bigler, R. & Liben, L. (2007). Developmental intergroup theory explaining and reducing children's social stereotyping and prejudice. *Current Directions in Psychological Science, 16*, 162–166.

Boehnke, K. (2008). Peer pressure: A cause of scholastic underachievement? A cross-cultural study of mathematical achievement among German, Canadian, and Israeli middle school students. *Social Psychology of Education, 11*, 149–160.

Brechwald, W. & Prinstein, M. (2011). Beyond homophily: A decade of advances in understanding peer influence processes. *Journal of Research on Adolescence, 21*, 166–179.

Brettfeld, K. & Wetzels, P. (2007). *Muslime in Deutschland. Integration, Integrationsbarrieren, Religion und Einstellungen zu Demokratie, Rechtsstaat und politisch-religiös motivierter Gewalt. Gutachten im Auftrag des Bundesministeriums des Innern.* Universität Hamburg: Fakultät für Rechtswissenschaft, Institut für Kriminalwissenschaften, Abteilung Kriminologie.

Brewer, M. B. (1991). The social self: On being the same and different at the same time. *Personality and Social Psychology Bulletin, 17*, 475–482.

Çelik, C. (2015). 'Having a German passport will not make me German': Reactive ethnicity and oppositional identity among disadvantaged male Turkish second-generation youth in Germany. *Ethnic and Racial Studies, 38*, 1646–1662.

Church, A. T., Katigbak, M. S., Locke, K. D., Zhang, H., Shen, J., de Jesús Vargas-Flores, J. & Mastor, K. A. (2013). Need satisfaction and well-being testing self-determination theory in eight cultures. *Journal of Cross-Cultural Psychology, 44*, 507–534.

Crane, M. & Markus, H. (1982). Gender identity: The benefits of a self-schema approach. *Journal of Personality and Social Psychology, 43*, 1195–1197.

Crocker, J. & Garcia, J. A. (2006). Stigma and the social basis of the self: A synthesis. In S. Levin & C. van Laar (Eds.), *Stigma and group inequality: Social psychological perspectives* (pp. 287–308). Mahwah, NJ: Lawrence Erlbaum Associates.

Crocker, J., Luhtanen, J. & Sommers, S. (2004). Contingencies of self-worth: Progress and prospects. *European Review of Social Psychology, 15*, 133–181.

Cross, S. E. & Markus, H. R. (1994). Self-schemas, possible selves, and competent performance. *Journal of Educational Psychology, 86*, 423–438.

Daniel, E., Benish-Weisman, M., Boehnke, K. & Knafo, A. (2014). Personal and culture-dependent values as part of minority adolescent identity. In R. Silbereisen,

P. Titzmann & Y. Shavit (Eds.), *The challenges of diaspora migration. Interdisciplinary perspectives on Israel and Germany* (pp. 103–126). Farnham, UK: Ashgate Publishing

Daniel, E., Boehnke, K. & Knafo-Noam, A. (2016). Value-differentiation and self-esteem among majority and immigrant youth. *Journal of Moral Education, 45*, 338–353.

Deaux, K. (1993). Reconstructing social identity. *Personality and Social Psychology Bulletin, 19*, 4–12.

Deci, E. L. & Ryan, R. M. (1985). *Intrinsic motivation and self-determination in human behavior*. New York, NY: Plenum.

Diehl, C. & König, M. (2013). Zwischen Säkularisierung und religiöser Reorganisation – Eine Analyse der Religiosität türkischer und polnischer Neuzuwanderer in Deutschland. *Kölner Zeitschrift für Soziologie & Sozialpsychologie, 65*, 235–258.

Diehl, C. & Schnell, R. (2006). "Reactive ethnicity" or "assimilation"? Statements, arguments, and first empirical evidence for labor migrants in Germany. *International Migration Review, 40*, 786–816.

Eccles, J. (2005). Subjective task value and the Eccles et al. model of achievement-related choices. In A. J. Elliot & C. S. Dweck (Eds.), *Handbook of competence and motivation* (pp. 105–121). London: Guilford Press.

Eccles, J. (2011). Gendered educational and occupational choices: Applying the Eccles et al. model of achievement-related choices. *International Journal of Behavioral Development, 35*, 195–201.

Fagot, B. I. & Leinbach, M. D. (1985). Gender identity: Some thoughts on an old concept. *Journal of the American Academy of Child Psychiatry, 24*, 684–688.

Hafen, C., Laursen, B., Burk, W., Kerr, M. & Stattin, H. (2011). Homophily in stable and unstable adolescent friendships: Similarity breeds constancy. *Personality and Individual Differences, 51*, 607–612.

Hannover, B. (1997). *Das dynamische Selbst. Zur Kontextabhängigkeit selbstbezogenen Wissens.* Bern: Huber.

Hannover, B. (2000). Development of the self in gendered contexts. In T. Eckes & H. Trautner (Eds.), *The developmental social psychology of gender* (pp. 177–206). Hillsdale, NJ: Lawrence Erlbaum Associates.

Hannover, B. & Kessels, U. (2004). Why German school students don't like math and sciences. A self-to-prototype matching approach. *Learning and Instruction, 14*, 51–67.

Hannover, B., Morf, C., Neuhaus, J., Rau, M., Wolfgramm, C. & Zander-Musić, L. (2013). How immigrant adolescents' self-views in school and family context relate to academic success in Germany. *Journal of Applied Social Psychology, 43*, 175–189.

Hannover, B., Wolter, I., Drewes, J. & Kleiber, D. (2014). Geschlechtsidentität: Selbstwahrnehmung von Geschlecht. In D. Lück & W. Cornelißen (Hrsg.), *Geschlechterunterschiede und Geschlechterunterscheidungen in Europa* (S. 143–160). Stuttgart: Lucius & Lucius.

Hannover, B. & Zander, L. (2016). Die Bedeutung der Peers für die individuelle schulische Entwicklung. In J. Möller, M. Köller & T. Riecke-Baulecke (Hrsg.), *Basiswissen Lehrerbildung. Schule und Unterricht. Lehren und Lernen* (S. 91–105). Seelze: Klett-Kallmeyer.

Heyder, A. & Kessels, U. (2013). Is school feminine? Implicit gender stereotyping of school as a predictor of academic achievement. *Sex Roles, 69*, 605–617.

Huber, C. & Wilbert, J. (2012). Soziale Ausgrenzung von Schülern mit sonderpädagogischem Förderbedarf und niedrigen Schulleistungen im gemeinsamen Unterricht. *Empirische Sonderpädagogik, 4*, 147–165.

Javadian, G. & Zoogah, D. (2014). Toward a comprehensive understanding of stereotype vulnerability and stereotype reactance in organizational settings: The contribution of relative deprivation theory. *Industrial and Organizational Psychology: Perspectives on Science and Practice, 7*, 403–408.

Kessels, U., Heyder, A., Latsch, M. & Hannover, B. (2014). How gender differences in academic engagement are related to students' gender identity. *Educational Research, 56*, 220–229.

Kessels, U. & Steinmayr, R. (2013). Macho-man in school: Toward the role of gender role self-concepts and help seeking in school performance. *Learning and Individual Differences, 23*, 234–240.

Klieme, E., Artelt, C., Hartig, J., Jude, N., Köller, O., Prenzel, M., Schnider, W. & Stanat, P. (Hrsg.). (2010). *PISA 2009: Bilanz nach einem Jahrzehnt.* Münster: Waxmann.

Knigge, M. & Hannover, B. (2011). Collective school type identity: Predicting students' motivation beyond academic self-concept. *International Journal of Psychology, 46*, 191–205.

Kocaj, A., Kuhl, P., Kroth, A., Pant, H. A. & Stanat, P. (2014). Wo lernen Kinder mit sonderpädagogischem Förderbedarf besser? Ein Vergleich schulischer Kompetenzen zwischen Regel- und Förderschulen in der Primarstufe. *Kölner Zeitschrift für Soziologie und Sozialpsychologie, 66*, 165–191.

Kray, L., Thompson, L. & Galinsky, A. (2001). Battle of the sexes: Gender stereotype confirmation and reactance in negotiations. *Journal of Personality and Social Psychology, 80*, 942–958.

Latsch, M. & Hannover, B. (2014). Smart girls, dumb boys!? How the discourse on "failing boys" impacts performances and motivational goal orientation in German school students. *Social Psychology, 45*, 112–126.

Leary, M. R. (2012). Sociometer theory. In P. M. van Lange, A. W. Kruglanski & E. T. Higgins (Eds.), *Handbook of theories of social psychology*, (Vol. 2, pp. 151–59). Thousand Oaks, CA: Sage.

Linville, P. (1985). Self-complexity and affective extremity: Don't put all your eggs in one cognitive basket. *Social Cognition, 3*, 94–120.

Luhtanen, R. & Crocker, J. (1992). A collective self-esteem scale: Self-evaluation of one's social identity. *Personality and Social Psychology Bulletin, 3*, 302–318.

Maliepaard, M., Gijsberts, M. & Phalet, K. (2015). Islamic gatherings: Experiences of discrimination and religious affirmation across established and new immigrant communities. *Ethnic and Racial Studies, 38*, 2635–2651.

Marcia, J. (1966). Development and validation of ego identity status. *Journal of Personality and Social Psychology, 3*, 551–558.

Markus, H. (1977). Self-schemata and processing information about the self. *Journal of Personality and Social Psychology, 35*, 63–78.

Markus, H. & Kunda, Z. (1986). Stability and malleability of the self-concept. *Journal of Personality and Social Psychology, 51*, 858–866.

Markus, H. & Nurius, P. (1986). Possible selves. *American Psychologist, 41*, 954–969.

Markus, H. & Ruvolo, A. (1989). Possible selves: Personalized representations of goals. In L. A. Pervin (Ed.), *Goal concepts in personality and social psychology* (pp. 211–241). Hillsdale, NJ: Lawrence Erlbaum Associates.

Marsh, H. (1986). Global self-esteem: Its relation to specific facets of self-concept and their importance. *Journal of Personality and Social Psychology*, *51*, 1224–1236.

Marsh, H., Abduljabbar, A., Parker, P., Morin, A., Abdelfattah, F., Nagengast, B., Möller, J. & Abu-Hilal, M. (2015). The internal/external frame of reference model of self-concept and achievement relations: Age-cohort and cross-cultural differences. *American Educational Research Journal*, *52*, 168–202.

Marsh, H. & Craven, R. (2006). Reciprocal effects of self-concept and performance from a multidimensional perspective: Beyond seductive pleasure and unidimensional perspectives. *Perspectives on Psychological Science*, *1*, 133–163.

Marsh, H. & Hau, K. (2003). Big fish little pond effect on academic self-concept: A crosscultural (26 country) test of the negative effects of academically selective schools. *American Psychologist*, *58*, 364–376.

Marsh, H. & Martin, A. (2011). Academic self-concept and academic achievement: Relations and causal ordering. *British Journal of Educational Psychology*, *81*, 59–77.

Marsh, H. & O'Neill, R. (1984). Self Description Questionnaire III: The construct validity of multidimensional self-concept ratings by late adolescents. *Journal of Educational Measurement*, *21*, 153–174.

Marsh, H., Trautwein, U., Lüdtke, O., Köller, O. & Baumert, J. (2006). Integration of multidimensional self-concept and core personality constructs: Construct validation and relations to well-being and achievement. *Journal of Personality*, *74*, 403–456.

Martin, C. L., Fabes, R. A. & Hanish, L. D. (2014). Gendered-peer relationships in educational contexts. *Advances in Child Development and Behavior*, *47*, 151–187.

McGuire, W. J. & Padawer-Singer, A. (1976). Trait salience in the spontaneous self-concept. *Journal of Personality and Social Psychology*, *33*, 743–754.

Möller, J. & Marsh, H. (2013). Dimensional comparison theory. *Psychological Review*, *120*, 544–560.

Möller, J., Müller-Kalthoff, H., Helm, F., Nagy, N. & Marsh, H. W. (2015). The generalized internal/external frame of reference model: An extension to dimensional comparison theory. *Frontline Learning Research*, *3*, 37–47.

Möller, J., Retelsdorf, J., Köller, O. & Marsh, H. W. (2011). The reciprocal internal/external frame of reference model: An integration of models of relations between academic achievement and self-concept. *American Educational Research Journal*, *48*, 1315–1346.

Nusser, L. & Wolter, I. (2016). There's plenty more fish in the sea. Das akademische Selbstkonzept von Schülerinnen und Schülern mit sonderpädagogischem Förderbedarf. Lernen in integrativen und segregierten Schulsettings. *Empirische Pädagogik*, *30*, 130-143.

Ogbu, J. (2004). Collective identity and the burden of "acting White" in Black history, community, and education. *The Urban Review*, *36*, 1–35.

Okonofua, J., Walton, G. & Eberhardt, J. (2016). A vicious cycle: A social–psychological account of extreme racial disparities in school discipline. *Perspectives on Psychological Science, 11*, 381–398.

Osborne, J. (1997). Race and academic disidentification. *Journal of Educational Psychology, 89*, 728–735.

Osborne, J. & Jones, B. (2011). Identification with academics and motivation to achieve in school: How the structure of the self influences academic outcomes. *Educational Psychological Review, 23*, 131–158.

Oyserman, D. (2015). *Pathways to success through identity-based motivation.* Oxford: University Press.

Oyserman, D., Brickman, D. & Rhodes, M. (2007). School success, possible selves, and parent school involvement. *Family Relations: An Interdisciplinary Journal of Applied Family Studies*, *56*, 479–489.

Oyserman, D., Bybee, D. & Terry, K. (2006). Possible selves and academic outcomes: How and when possible selves impel action. *Journal of Personality and Social Psychology*, *91*, 188–204.

Oyserman, D., Elmore, K. & Smith, G. (2012). Self, self-concept, and identity. In M. Leary & J. Tangney (Eds.), *Handbook of self and identity,* (2nd ed., pp. 69–104). New York, NY: Guilford Press.

Oyserman, D., Kemmelmeier, M., Fryberg, S., Brosh, H. & Hart-Johnson, T. (2003). Racial-ethnic self-schemas. *Social Psychology Quarterly*, *66*, 333–347.

Retelsdorf, J., Köller, O. & Möller, J. (2014). Reading achievement and reading self-concept—Testing the reciprocal effects model. *Learning and Instruction*, *29,* 21–30.

Ruble, D. N. (1994). A phase model of transitions: Cognitive and motivational consequences. In M. P. Zanna (Ed.), *Advances in experimental social psychology,* (Vol. 26, pp. 163–214). San Diego, CA, US: Academic Press.

Ruble, D. N., Alvarez, J. M., Bachman, M., Cameron, J. A., Fuligni, A. J., García Coll, C. & Rhee, E. (2004). The development of a sense of "we": The emergence and implications of children's collective identity. In M. Bennett & F. Sani (Eds.), *The development of the social self* (pp. 29–76). New York, NY: Psychology Press.

Ryan, R. M. & Deci, E. L. (2000). Self-determination theory and the facilitation of intrinsic motivation, social development, and well-being. *American Psychologist, 55*, 68–78.

Sachverständigenrat deutscher Stiftungen für Integration und Migration (2016). *Viele Götter, ein Staat: Religiöse Vielfalt und Teilhabe im Einwanderungsland. Jahresgutachten 2016 mit Integrationsbarometer.* Berlin: SVR GmbH.

Schiepe-Tiska, A. & Schmidtner, S. (2013). Mathematikbezogene emotionale und motivationale Orientierungen, Einstellungen und Verhaltensweisen von Jugendlichen in PISA 2012. In M. Prenzel, C. Sälzer, E. Klieme & O. Köller (Hrsg.), *PISA 2012. Fortschritte und Herausforderungen in Deutschland* (S. 99–122). Münster: Waxmann.

Schwartz, S. (1992). Universals in the content and structure of values: Theoretical advances and empirical test in 20 countries. *Advances in Experimental Social Psychology, 25,* 1–65.

Segeritz, M., Walter, O. & Stanat P. (2010). Muster des schulischen Erfolgs von jugendlichen Migranten in Deutschland: Evidenz für segmentierte Assimilation? *Kölner Zeitschrift für Soziologie und Sozialpsychologie, 62,*113–138.

Shavelson, R. Hubner, J. & Stanton, G. (1976). Self concept: Validation of construct interpretations. *Review of Educational Research, 46*, 407–441.

Shaw, I. (2012). Stereotypical representations of Muslims and Islam following the 7/7 London terror attacks: Implications for intercultural communication and terrorism prevention. *International Communication Gazette, 74*, 509–524.

Spörer, N., Maaz, K., Vock., M., Schründer-Lenzen, A., Luka, T., Bosse, S., Vogel, J. & Jäntsch, C. (2015). Lernen in der inklusiven Grundschule: Zusammenhänge zwischen fachlichen Kompetenzen, Sozialklima und Facetten des Selbstkonzepts. *Unterrichtswissenschaft, 43*, 22–35.

Steele, C. (1997). A threat in the air: How stereotypes shape intellectual identity and performance. *American Psychologist, 52*, 613–629.

Tajfel, H. (1978). *Differentiation between social groups: Studies in the social psychology of intergroup relations.* London: Academic Press.

Tajfel, H. & Turner, J. C. (1986). The social identity theory of inter-group behavior. In S. Worchel and L. W. Austin (Eds.), *Psychology of intergroup relations.* Chicago, IL: Nelson-Hall.

Tesser, A. (1988). Toward a self-evaluation maintenance model of social behavior. In L. L. Berkowitz (Ed.), *Advances in experimental social psychology*, (Vol. 21, pp. 181–228). San Diego, CA: Academic Press.

Vereecken, C. & Vandegehuchte, A. (2003). Measurement of parental occupation: Agreement between parents and their children. *Archives Public Health, 61*, 141–149.

Vermeij, L., van Duijn, M.A. & Baerveldt, C. (2009). Ethnic segregation in context: Social discrimination among native Dutch pupils and their ethnic minority classmates. *Social Networks, 31*, 230–239.

Walter, O. (2014). Immigrant optimism in Deutschland? Die Überprüfung einer Hypothese anhand der mathematikbezogenen Motivation und realistischen Bildungsaspiration von Schülerinnen und Schülern mit Migrationshintergrund. *Empirische Pädagogik, 28*, 36–53.

Walton, G. & Brady, S. (in Druck). The many questions of belonging. In A. Elliot, C. Dweck & D. Yeager. *Handbook of competence and motivation: theory and application* (2nd ed.) New York, NY: The Guilford Press.

Walton, G. & Carr, P. (2012). Do I belong? How negative intellectual stereotypes undermine people's sense of social belonging in school and how to fix it. In M. Inzlicht & T. Schmader (Eds.), *Stereotype threat: Theory, processes, and application* (pp. 89–106). New York, NY: Oxford University Press.

Walton, G., Logel, C., Peach, J., Spencer, S. & Zanna, M. P. (2015). Two brief interventions to mitigate a "chilly climate" transform women's experience, relationships, and achievement in engineering. *Journal of Educational Psychology, 107*, 468–485.

Walton, G., Spencer, S. & Erman, S. (2013). Affirmative meritocracy. *Social Issues and Policy Review, 7*, 1–35.

Waterman, A. S. (1990). Personal expressiveness: Philosophical and psychological foundations. *Journal of Mind and Behavior, 11*, 47–73.

Wentzel, K., Russell, S. & Baker, S. (2014). Peer relationships and positive adjustment at school. In M. Furlong, R. Gilman, E. Huebner & E. Scott (Eds.), *Handbook of positive psychology in schools* (2nd ed., pp. 260–277). New York, NY: Routledge.

Wolfgramm, C., Morf, C. & Hannover, B. (2014). Ethnically-based rejection sensitivity and academic achievement: The danger of retracting into one's heritage culture. *European Journal of Social Psychology, 44*, 313–326.

Wolfgramm, C., Rau, M., Zander-Musić, L., Neuhaus, J. & Hannover, B. (2010). Zum Zusammenhang zwischen kollektivem Selbstwert und der Motivation, Deutsch zu lernen: Eine Untersuchung von Schülerinnen und Schülern mit Migrationshintergrund in Deutschland und der Schweiz. In C. Allemann-Ghionda, P. Stanat, K. Göbel & C. Röhner (Hrsg.), *Migration, Identität, Sprache und Bildungserfolg. 55. Beiheft der Zeitschrift für Pädagogik* (S. 59–77). Weinheim: Beltz.

Zander, L. & Hannover, B. (2013). Die Bedeutung der Identifikation mit der Herkunftskultur und mit der Aufnahmekultur Deutschland für die soziale Integration Jugendlicher mit Migrationshintergrund in ihrer Schulklasse. *Zeitschrift für Entwicklungspsychologie und Pädagogische Psychologie, 45*, 142–160.

Zander, L., Hannover, B., Steglich, C. & Baumert, J. (2017). Soziale Eingebundenheit in immersiven und monolingualen Klassenzimmern. Ein Index zur Messung sprachbezogener Inklusion. In J. Möller, F. Hohenstein, J. Fleckenstein & J. Baumert (Hrsg.), *Zweisprachigkeit in einer multiethnischen Gesellschaft – Was leistet die Staatliche Europaschule Berlin?* (S. 285–303). Münster: Waxmann.

Zander, L. & Wolter, I. (2016). Deutsch oder Mathe? Wie die Zusammensetzung der Schulklasse und die Bedeutsamkeit des eigenen Geschlechts geschlechtstypische Aspirationen von Jugendlichen bestimmen. *Zeitschrift für Entwicklungspsychologie und Pädagogische Psychologie, 48*, 59–68.

Autorinnen

PROF. DR. BETTINA HANNOVER
Arbeitsbereich Schul- und Unterrichtsforschung, Freie Universität Berlin.

DR. LYSANN ZANDER
Arbeitsbereich Schul- und Unterrichtsforschung, Freie Universität Berlin.

KONTAKT
Bettina Hannover, Arbeitsbereich Schul- und Unterrichtsforschung,
Freie Universität Berlin, Habelschwerdter Allee 45, 14195 Berlin.
E-Mail: *bettina.hannover@fu-berlin.de*

Self-Affirmation in der Schule: Eine Intervention zur Leistungssteigerung von Schülerinnen und Schülern aus nichttraditionellen Familien

MICHAELA KÖLLER UND NICOLE NAGY

ZUSAMMENFASSUNG: Self-Affirmation-Interventionen, bei denen Personen typischerweise über für sie bedeutsame Werte schreiben (z. B. Beziehung zur Familie, unabhängig sein), konnten bei Mitgliedern stereotypisierter Gruppen, z. B. afroamerikanischen Schülerinnen und Schülern in den USA oder Mädchen im Fach Mathematik die negativen Folgen von stereotyper Bedrohung für die Leistungsfähigkeit mindern (Cohen & Sherman, 2014). Diese Studie wendet sich der bisher noch nicht untersuchten Gruppe der Kinder von Alleinerziehenden und aus Stieffamilien zu (hier als Kinder aus nichttraditionellen Familien bezeichnet, NTF), welche schlechtere schulische Leistungen zeigen als Kinder aus traditionellen Familien mit zwei leiblichen Eltern (TF). Insgesamt 614 Schülerinnen und Schüler (127 aus NTF) wurden randomisiert einer Self-Affirmation-Bedingung oder den Kontrollgruppen zugewiesen. Nach einer Aktivierung des Stereotyps „Kind aus NTF" bearbeiteten alle Kinder einen kognitiven Fähigkeitstest. Es zeigte sich ein Haupteffekt der Self-Affirmation, nicht jedoch der angenommene Interaktionseffekt. Entgegen der Erwartungen profitierten nicht nur vom Stereotyp NTF bedrohte Schülerinnen und Schüler von der Self-Affirmation-Intervention, sondern die Leistungen aller Kinder in der Self-Affirmation-Bedingung lagen signifikant über den Leistungen in den Kontrollgruppen. Es lässt sich resümieren, dass Self-Affirmation eine Intervention mit geringem Aufwand ist, welche vielen Schülerinnen und Schülern kurzfristige Vorteile und keinen Nachteil hinsichtlich der Leistungsperformanz gebracht hat.

Schlüsselwörter: Kinder aus nichttraditionellen Familien, Stereotype-Threat, Self-Affirmation-Intervention

Self-affirmation interventions at school: Improving performance of students from non-traditional families

ABSTRACT: In self-affirmation interventions people typically write about core personal values such as the relationship to their family or being independent. Numerous studies have demonstrated that these interventions can reduce the negative effects of stereotypical threats on performance for members of stereotyped groups. Although they belong to a stereotyped group, there have been no studies so far that investigate the effectiveness of a self-affirmation intervention for children of one-parent families or step-families (hereby referred to as children from non-traditional families). These children show a lower performance at school in comparison to children of traditional families, living with two biological parents. In a field experiment, 614 students (127 of one-parent families and step-families) were randomly assigned to either the self-affirmation, the non-affirmation condition, or to a control group. After activating the stereotype "child of a non-traditional" family, all students worked on a cognitive ability test. Results suggest a marked efficacy of the self-affirmation intervention. The achievement of students of one-parent families and step-families in the affirmation-condition was significantly better than the achievement of these children in the control-group and the non-affirmation group. Contrary to expectations, children who live with both biological parents equally profited from the self-affirmation. Altogether the study demonstrates that self-affirmation is a very effective intervention when it comes to increased performance.

Keywords: children from non-traditional families, stereotype-threat, self-affirmation intervention

Einleitung

Studien zeigen, dass Schülerinnen und Schüler und Studentinnen und Studenten, die einer stigmatisierten sozialen Gruppe angehören, größere Schwierigkeiten und schlechtere Leistungen in zahlreichen Unterrichts- bzw. Studienfächern zeigen als nicht-stereotypisierte Personen, obwohl sie aufgrund ihrer Fähigkeiten bessere Leistungen erbringen könnten (z. B. Aronson, Fried & Good, 2002; Harackiewicz et al., 2014). Allein die Erwartung, als intellektuell weniger leistungsfähig oder auf Basis anderer Maßstäbe als der erbrachten Leistung beurteilt zu werden, kann dazu führen, dass Schülerinnen und Schüler sowie Studentinnen und Studenten den Schul- oder Hochschulkontext trotz gleicher umgebender Bedingungen als bedrohlich erleben und unterdurchschnittliche Leistungen erzielen (Cohen & Sherman, 2014). Dieser Effekt des sogenannten *Stereotype Threat* wurde in vielen Studien mit unterschiedlichen Methoden und Gruppen gezeigt (z. B. Steele, 1997; Stone, Lynch, Sjomeling & Darley, 1999; Stone & McWhinnie, 2008). Daraus ergab sich die Frage, welche Möglichkeiten es gibt, diesem „threat in the air" (Steele, 1997) entgegenzuwirken. Cohen und Mitarbeiterinnen und Mitarbeiter (Cohen, Garcia, Apfel & Master, 2006) entwickelten eine sogenannte Self-Affirmation Intervention, die die durch Stereotype Threat bedrohte Selbstintegrität wiederherstellen soll (Harackiewicz et al., 2014). Die Intervention besteht darin, dass eine Person über selbstrelevante Werte oder Fähigkeiten reflektiert. Diese Form der Selbstbestätigung erinnert Menschen daran, wer sie sind und was ihnen wichtig ist. Der Fokus der Aufmerksamkeit soll dadurch auf nicht-bedrohte Aspekte des Selbst gerichtet werden, was zu einer Stressreduzierung führen und den Zugang zu den kognitiven Ressourcen freimachen kann (Cohen & Sherman, 2014). Die Self-Affirmation-Intervention wurde bereits bei stereotypisierten Gruppen erfolgreich eingesetzt, z. B. bei afroamerikanischen Schülerinnen und Schülern in den USA, bei Frauen in Mathematik oder bei Collegestudentinnen und Collegestudenten der ersten Generation (Doyle & Voyer, 2016; Harackiewicz et al., 2014).

In dieser Studie soll die bisher nicht berücksichtigte Gruppe der Kinder aus nichttraditionellen Familien (NTF) untersucht werden. Der Terminus nichttraditionelle Familie umfasst Kinder Alleinerziehender und aus Stieffamilien. Amato und Keith (1991) konnten zeigen, dass es in Bezug auf Leistung und Wohlbefinden keinen Unterschied macht, ob Kinder in Stieffamilien oder mit einem Elternteil leben. Dies betrifft bei 13.1 Millionen minderjährigen Kindern in Deutschland rund 3.2 Millionen Kinder (Statistisches Bundesamt, 2011). Dass Kinder aus NTF zu einer stereotypisierten Gruppe gehören könnten, zeigen u.a. die Studien von Sander, Endepohls-Ulpe und Gollia (2005) sowie Ghysens (2009). Lehrkräfte beurteilen diese Kinder im Hinblick auf ihr schulisches Anpassungs- und Leistungsverhalten und die elterliche Unterstützung signifikant ungünstiger als Kinder aus TF. Ebenso zeigen Kinder aus NTF schlechtere schulische Leistungen (Babalis, Tsoli, Nikolopoulos & Maniatis, 2014), absolvieren insgesamt mehr Schuljahre und brechen die Schule öfter ab als ihre Altersgenossen aus TF (Painter & Levine, 2000). Diese Leistungskluft zwischen Kindern mit unterschiedlichem Familienstatus könnte ein Hinweis auf Stereotype Threat sein, denn in ihrer Metaanalyse über den Zusammenhang von Familienstruktur und Stereotypisierung kamen Valiquette-Tessier, Vandette und Gosselin (2016) zu dem Schluss: "Married parents also appear to remain the parental type that is the most positively stereotyped and against which other types are compared" (S. 162).

In der aktuellen Studie sollen daher mit einem randomisierten Kontrollgruppendesign die Effekte einer Self-Affirmation-Intervention auf das Leistungsverhalten von Kindern aus NTF untersucht werden. Im Folgenden werden kurz die Unterschiede zwischen Kindern aus NTF und TF sowie deren mögliche Ursachen dargestellt.

1 Kinder aus nichttraditionellen Familien

Kinder aus NTF zeigen gegenüber Kindern aus TF unter Kontrolle von Alter, Geschlecht und Schulklasse z.B. schlechtere Leistungen in Mathematik und Naturwissenschaften (Schneider, Atteberry & Owens, 2006), in ihrer sprachlichen Leistung (Carlson & Corcoran, 2001; Manning & Lamb, 2003) sowie in kognitiven Fähigkeitstests und sie absolvieren mehr Schuljahre (Mandara & Murray, 2006; Sigle-Rushton & McLanahan, 2004). In ihrer Metaanalyse untersuchten Amato und Keith (1991) Unterschiede zwischen Kindern aus TF und Scheidungsfamilien inklusive Patchwork-Familien im Hinblick auf Leistung und Wohlbefinden. Insgesamt wurden über 81.000 Personen untersucht. Im Vergleich zu Erwachsenen, deren Eltern verheiratet geblieben waren, berichteten die Erwachsenen mit geschiedenen Eltern über eine Vielzahl negativer Auswirkungen, u.a. auf die psychische und physische Gesundheit, die Stabilität der eigenen Ehe und den sozioökonomischen Status. Amato und Keith resümierten „Die Behauptung, eine elterliche Scheidung habe nur geringe Langzeitauswirkungen für die Entwicklung eines Kindes, widerspricht der einschlägigen Forschung" (1991, S. 54). Diese Studie von 1991 bildete die Grundlage für den Vergleich eine Dekade später (Amato, 2001). Entgegen der Erwartung blieben die Differenzen zu Ungunsten der Scheidungskinder in allen untersuchten Variablen bestehen. Neben den Langzeitfolgen zeigten Studien auch kurzfristige negative Konsequenzen. So fand z. B. Arkes (2015), dass die elterliche Scheidung Leseverstehen und Leseleistung beeinträchtigt.

Insgesamt zeigt die Befundlage, dass zwischen Kindern aus TF und NTF sowohl Leistungs- als auch Unterschiede im physischen und psychischen Wohlbefinden sowie hinsichtlich ökonomischer Variablen bestehen. Worauf sind diese Unterschiede zurückzuführen? Nach Lillard und Gerner (1999) sind zu einem großen Teil die zusätzlichen wirtschaftlichen Ressourcen zweier Elternteile für den Unterschied verantwortlich. Van Laar und Sidanius (2001) argumentieren, Kinder aus NTF hätten einen geringeren sozialen Status und erführen auf Grund dessen stärkere Diskriminierungen als Kinder aus TF, die sich dann u.a. in schlechterer schulischer Leistung und geringerem Wohlbefinden niederschlüge. Sander et al. (2005) fanden, dass Lehrerinnen und Lehrer Scheidungskinder signifikant schlechter u.a. hinsichtlich Leistung, Mitarbeit, Motivation und Konzentration beurteilten als Kinder aus TF. Sie resümieren, dass „Lehrer offensichtlich anhand ihrer Informationen über den familiären Hintergrund von Kindern spezifische [stereotype] Erwartungen ausbilden" (Sander et al., 2005, S. 273).

2 Negative Stereotypisierung und Self-Affirmation

Welche Folgen können negative Stereotypisierungen haben? Menschen streben danach, ihre Selbstintegrität aufrecht zu erhalten, die u.a. grundlegend ist für die Motivation (Martens, Johns, Greenberg & Schimel, 2006) und die die Basis für Leistungsfähigkeit und Lebensfreude darstellt (Steele, 1988). Sie kann durch Stereotype Threat bedroht werden (Sherman & Hartson, 2011). Stereotype Threat bezeichnet ein Bedrohungsgefühl, das aus der Befürchtung entsteht, entsprechend eines negativen Stereotyps der eigenen Gruppe bewertet zu werden bzw. durch das eigene Verhalten die negativen Stereotype hinsichtlich der Gruppe unbeabsichtigt zu bestätigen (Steele & Aronson, 1995). Stereotype Threat wiederum kann dazu führen, dass Menschen schlechter abschneiden, als es ihrer Fähigkeit entspricht (Steele, 1997). Häufig reagieren Menschen auf solche Bedrohungen mit Rationalisierung und Selbstrechtfertigung oder Verzerrungen der Realität (Fein & Spencer, 1997; Sherman & Cohen, 2002; Sherman & Hartson, 2011; Silverman, Logel & Cohen, 2013). Dazu gehören z. B. Leugnung und Ablehnung der bedrohlichen Information, Infragestellung der Validität eines Leistungstests oder die Abwertung der Anderen, um sich selbst zu bestätigen (Cohen & Sherman, 2014). Diese defensiven Strategien sind kurzfristig effektiv, um den Selbstwert wiederherzustellen, langfristig können sie Lernen, persönliches Wachstum und Erfolg unterminieren (Legault, Al-Khindi & Inzlicht, 2012). Studien konnten zeigen, dass die Leistung verschiedener stereotypisierter Gruppen – Frauen, Männer, Kinder aus Familien mit niedrigem sozioökonomischen Status, verschiedene ethnische Gruppen und Lehramtsstudierende – in zahlreichen Domänen – Mathematik, Sport (z. B. Stone et al., 1999), kognitiven Fähigkeitstests (Ihme & Möller, 2015) durch negative Stereotype beeinflusst wird.

Bedrohungen der Integrität können aber auch adaptiv bewältigt werden, indem Personen einen anderen als den bedrohten Aspekt des Selbst als Ressource für den eigenen Selbstwert bekräftigen. Steele und Liu (1983) entwickelten dazu die Self-Affirmation-Intervention, bei der die Person über für sie relevante Werte oder Fähigkeiten reflektiert. Wenn Individuen mit einem Bereich ihres Selbst zufrieden sind, tolerieren sie eine Bedrohung ihrer Selbstintegrität in einem anderen Bereich und haben wieder Zugriff auf ihre mentalen Ressourcen (Cohen & Sherman, 2014).

In einer Studie von Sherman et al. (2013) konnten die Effekte einer Self-Affirmation-Intervention bei latein- und afroamerikanischen Jugendlichen nachgewiesen werden. Hypothesenkonform führte die Self-Affirmation-Intervention kurzfristig zu einer Leistungssteigerung in Klassenarbeiten und langfristig zu einer Verbesserung des Notendurchschnitts über die gesamte Schulzeit. Dabei näherte sich die Leistung der latein- und afroamerikanischen Jugendlichen der Leistung der europäisch-amerikanischen Schülerinnen und Schüler an, blieb jedoch weiterhin unter deren Leistung. In der Kontrollgruppe und bei den europäischen Amerikanerinnen und Amerikaner waren keine Leistungsverbesserungen festzustellen.

Im Rahmen eines Experiments gingen Martens, Johns, Greenberg und Schimel (2006) der Frage nach, inwieweit eine Self-Affirmation-Intervention Frauen dabei unterstützen kann, dem negativen Stereotyp „Frauen sind in Mathematik unterlegen" zu begegnen. Randomisiert legten sie den Probandinnen und Probanden (77 Frauen und 70 Männer) unterschiedliche Instruktionen eines zu bearbeitenden Mathematiktests vor (Stereotype-Threat-Bedingung „Test misst die mathematische Intelligenz", Kontrollbedingung „Pilotstudie zur allgemeinen Eindrucksbildung der Items"). Anschließend nahmen die Teilnehmerinnen und Teilnehmer an einer Self-Affirmation oder einer Non-Affirmation-Intervention teil. Eine Non-Affirmation-Intervention bedeutet, dass die Person sich mit den für sie am wenigsten bedeutsamen Werten auseinandersetzt, die damit nicht bestimmender Teil ihrer Selbstintegrität sind. Nach den Interventionen bearbeiteten alle Teilnehmerinnen und Teilnehmer einen Mathematiktest. Hypothesenkonform zeigten Frauen in der Self-Affirmation-Bedingung bessere Testleistungen als in der Non-Affirmation Bedingung. Bei den Männern zeigten sich keine leistungsverbessernden Effekte.

Ursprünglich wurde die Self-Affirmation-Intervention genutzt, um Leistungseinbußen durch Stereotype Threat vor allem bei Frauen und Minderheiten abzumildern (Steele & Aronson, 1995). Bisher liegen jedoch keine Studien vor, die eine Self-Affirmation-Intervention bei Kindern von Alleinerziehenden und aus Stieffamilien im schulischen Kontext untersuchten. Dies könnte darauf zurückzuführen sein, dass es keine Studien gibt, die Stereotype Threat und deren Folgen bei Kindern aus NTF untersuchten.

Da sich gezeigt hat, dass Self-Affirmation-Interventionen bei Stereotype Threat den betroffenen Personen helfen können, ihr vorhandenes Potenzial auszuschöpfen und die Performanz zu verbessern, soll untersucht werden, inwiefern eine Self-Affirmation-Intervention bei Kindern aus NTF dazu beiträgt, kurzfristig die Performanz in einem kognitiven Fähigkeitstest zu steigern.

3 Aktuelle Studie

Die Studie untersuchte an einer Stichprobe von *N* = 614 Schülerinnen und Schülern der Klasse 7 bis 9 aus drei Gymnasien in Baden-Baden welche kurzfristigen Effekte eine Self-Affirmation-Intervention auf die Leistung von Kindern aus NTF hat. Um Rückschlüsse auf die Effekte der Intervention zu ermöglichen, wurde ein randomisiertes 3 x 2 Kontrollgruppen-Design genutzt. Die Schülerinnen und Schüler wurden zufällig einem der Treatments, einer Self-Affirmation und einer Non-Affirmation-Intervention sowie einer Kontrollgruppe, die eine Labyrinthaufgabe bearbeitete, zugewiesen. Dabei gingen wir davon aus, dass sich Kinder aus NTF und TF per Zufall gleichermaßen auf die drei Bedingungen verteilen, was cum grano salis der Fall war.

Auf Basis der dargestellten Befunde lautet die Hypothese, dass eine Self-Affirmation-Intervention bei Kindern aus NTF Effekte in Richtung Leistungsverbesserung zeigt. Es wird erwartet, dass Kinder aus NTF nach der Self-Affirmation-Intervention eine bessere Leistung in einem kognitiven Fähigkeitstest zeigen als Kinder aus NTF ohne Self-Affirmation-Intervention. Diese Kinder sollten nach der Self-Affirmation annähernd die gleiche Leistung zeigen wie die Kinder aus den TF.

4 Methode

4.1 Stichprobe

An der Untersuchung nahmen *N* = 614 Schülerinnen und Schüler der Klassen 7 bis 9 aus drei Gymnasien teil (57 % weiblich, durchschnittliches Alter *M* = 13.42 Jahre, *SD* = 0.95). Insgesamt 127 Kinder stammten aus NTF, davon lebten 74 mit einem Elternteil zusammen, 52 in Stieffamilien. Dies entspricht einem Anteil von 20.1 Prozent, was damit in etwa dem Anteil von Kindern aus NTF in der Gesamtbevölkerung entspricht (24 %).

4.2 Design

Die Fragebögen wurden innerhalb der Klassen randomisiert und zu gleichen Teilen an die Schülerinnen und Schüler verteilt. Es wurde ein 3 x 2 Design umgesetzt: Der Faktor „Bedingung" umfasste die Ausprägungen Self-Affirmation und, in Anlehnung an einschlägige Studien, Non-Affirmation. Zusätzlich wurde eine echte Kontrollgruppe verwendet. Der Faktor Familienstatus bestand aus den Bedingungen NTF (nichttraditionelle Familien) und TF (traditionelle Familien). In der NTF-Gruppe bearbeiteten 51 Schülerinnen und Schüler die Instruktion unter der Self-Affirmation-Bedingung, 34 Schülerinnen und Schüler die Instruktion der Non-Affirmation-Bedingung und 42 Schülerinnen und Schüler die Labyrinthaufgabe der Kontrollbedingung. In der TF-Gruppe erhielten 189 Kinder die Instruktion der Self-Affirmation-Bedingung, 170 die Instruktion der Non-Affirmation und 126 die Aufgabe der Kontrollversion. Erwartungsgemäß gab es deutlich weniger Kinder aus NTF als Kinder aus TF, so dass die Aufteilung der Schülerinnen und Schüler auf die Zellen unausgeglichen war.

4.3 Vorgehen und Variablen

Die Untersuchung fand innerhalb einer regulären Schulstunde statt und wurde von zwei geschulten Versuchsleiterinnen durchgeführt. Um zu vermeiden, dass die Kinder einen bewussten Zusammenhang zwischen ihrem Familienstatus und dem anschließenden Leistungstest herstellen, begann die Untersuchung mit dem Hinweis, dass sich die Studie aus zwei unabhängigen Untersuchungen zusammensetze. Der erste Teil des Fragebogens erfasse die Werte von Kindern und Jugendlichen und der zweite Teil bestehe aus einem Leistungstest.

Unabhängige Variable 1

Zu Beginn der Studie sollten die Teilnehmerinnen und Teilnehmer der Experimentalgruppen der Standardinstruktion der Self- bzw. Non-Affirmation-Intervention folgen (z.B. Cohen, Aronson & Steele, 2000; Sherman, Nelson & Steele, 2000). Alle Teilnehmerinnen und Teilnehmer dieser Bedingungen bekamen eine deutsche Übersetzung einer Liste von 14 Werten (siehe Tabelle 1) auf Basis der amerikanischen Werteliste (Cohen et al., 2006; Sherman & Cohen, 2006). Die Probandinnen und Probanden der Self-Affirmation-Bedingung sollten daraus die zwei oder drei Werte aussuchen, die ihnen am wichtigsten sind. Über die ausgewählten Werte sollten die Personen in wenigen Sätzen beschreiben, warum ihnen diese Werte besonders wichtig sind. Die Non-Affirmation-Bedingung bekam die veränderte Instruktion, aus der Werteliste einen oder mehrere Werte auszuwählen, die ihnen am wenigsten wichtig sind. Anschließend sollten sie kurz schriftlich erläutern, warum die von ihnen ausgewählten am wenigsten wichtigen Werte anderen Personen wichtig sein könnten. Anschließend sollten alle Teilnehmerinnen und Teilnehmer vier Items in Bezug auf ihre ausgewählten Werte auf einer 4-Punkte Skala (stimmt nicht bis stimmt genau) hinsichtlich ihrer Zustimmung oder Ablehnung bewerten. In der Self-Affirmation-Bedingung waren die Items z.B. „Diese Werte haben mein Leben beeinflusst", „Mir sind diese Werte sehr wichtig" in der Non-Affirmation-Bedingung „Diese Werte haben das Leben einiger Leute beeinflusst" und „Einigen Leuten sind diese Werte sehr wichtig". Die echte Kontrollgruppe bearbeitete im ersten Teil des Fragebogens eine Labyrinthaufgabe.

Unabhängige Variable 2

Der Familienstatus ging als quasiexperimentelle unabhängige Variable mit den Ausprägungen (1) Kinder von Alleinerziehenden und aus Stieffamilien (NTF) und (2) Kinder aus vollständigen Familien (TF) ein.

Stereotyp-Aktivierung

Im Anschluss an die Self-, Non-Affirmation und Labyrinthaufgabe und vor dem Leistungstest wurde die stereotype Bedrohung aktiviert. Aus ethischen Gründen wurde diese möglichst subtil gehalten. Sie bestand aus der Frage: „Leben deine Eltern zusammen?" sowie anschließenden Fragen, die die Familienverhältnisse näher spezifizierten.

Manipulationscheck

Auf einer fünfstufigen Skala (von stimme gar nicht überein (0) bis stimme sehr überein (4)) sollten die Kinder die folgende Frage direkt im Anschluss an die Fragen zum Familienstand beantworten: „Kinder von alleinerziehenden Eltern und aus Stieffamilien haben es in der Schule schwerer als andere".

Abhängige Variable

Zur Erfassung der kognitiven Leistung der Probandinnen und Probanden wurden die Untertests Wortanalogien (verbaler Bereich) und Figurale Analogien (nonverbaler Bereich) des Kognitiven Fähigkeitstests 5-12, Revision (KFT 5-12, R; Heller & Perleth, 2000) eingesetzt. Die Reliabilität war gut für den nonverbalen Untertest (Cronbachs $\alpha = .82$), allerdings nicht zufriedenstellend für den verbalen Untertest (Cronbachs $\alpha = .51$). Auf weitere Analysen mit dem Untertest Wortanalogien wurde daher verzichtet. Als Indikator für die Testleistung wurden Summenscores gebildet. Für jede richtige Antwort wurde ein Punkt vergeben (maximal 25 Punkte für den Untertest Figurale Analogien), der Mittelwert für den verwendeten Untertest figurale Analogien lag bei $M = 18.6$ ($SD = 4.6$). Im Schnitt wurden die Items zu 77 % gelöst.

Demographische Angaben und Noten

Erst im Anschluss an den Leistungstest wurden Geschlecht und Noten erfasst. Dieses Vorgehen wurde gewählt, um eine Konfundierung mit möglichen vorhandenen Stereotypen wie z. B. „Mädchen sind schlechter in Mathematik als Jungen" zu verhindern. Die Schülerinnen und Schüler sollten ihre Noten in diversen Fächern (Deutsch, Mathematik, Englisch, Erdkunde, Geschichte, Physik, Biologie, Sport) aus dem letzten Halbjahreszeugnis auf einer Skala von 1 bis 6 angeben.

Zum Ende der Intervention bearbeiteten auch die Non-Affirmation-Gruppe und die echte Kontrollgruppe die Self-Affirmation. Damit sollte den Schülerinnen und Schülern der beiden Gruppen ebenfalls der Nutzen der Intervention ermöglicht werden, falls sich erwartungsgemäß Effekte in Richtung der Interventionsgruppe zeigen sollten. Außerdem sollte durch die Bekräftigung der persönlichen Wertvorstellungen die möglicherweise ausgelöste psychische Belastung durch die Stereotype Threat Manipulation vermindert werden.

5 Ergebnisse

Manipulationscheck

Kinder aus NTF lehnten die Aussage tendenziell ab ($M = 0.94$, $SD = 0.79$), wohingegen Kinder aus TF der Aussage teilweise zustimmten ($M = 1.59$, $SD = 0.66$). Überprüft man diese Unterschiede mithilfe einer einfaktoriellen ANOVA, wird diese Analyse signifikant, $F(1, 596) = 82.119$, $p < .05$, $d = 0.93$. In Bezug auf die Kinder Alleinerziehender ($M = 0.95$, $SD = 0.77$) und aus Stieffamilien ($M = 0.93$, $SD = 0.84$)

Tabelle 1. Häufigkeit der Auswahl der Werte in der Self-Affirmation- und der Non-Affirmation-Bedingung

Werte	Self-Affirmation-Bedingung N = 240	Non-Affirmation-Bedingung N = 204
Beziehung zu Freunden und Familie	75%	0.4%
Intelligent sein und gute Noten haben	38%	12%
Athletisch oder sportlich sein	33%	20%
Sinn für Humor	32%	6%
Musik	21%	13%
Unabhängig sein	20%	6%
Für den Moment leben	20%	13%
Kreativ sein	12%	6%
Natur und Umwelt	12%	5%
Online aktiv sein	6%	38%
Zugehörigkeit zu einer Gruppe	5%	15%
Religiöse und spirituelle Werte	5%	35%
Gut in künstlerischen Bereichen sein	4%	48%
Politik	0.8%	36%

ergaben sich wie erwartet keine Unterschiede, $F(1, 116) = 0.014$, *n.s.*, $d = 0.02$. Hinsichtlich der drei experimentellen Versuchsbedingungen ergaben sich keine Unterschiede ($F(2,611) = 2.46$, *n.s.*).

Häufigkeit der Auswahl der Werte. In Tabelle 1 ist die Liste der 14 vorgegebenen Werte und die Häufigkeit ihrer Nennung in der Self-Affirmations- und Non-Affirmation-Bedingung aufgeführt. Es bestand kein Unterschied hinsichtlich der ausgewählten Werte zwischen Kindern mit unterschiedlichem Familienhintergrund. Die Chi²-Werte des Tests auf Gleichheit der Verteilungen von den fünf als am wichtigsten beurteilten Werte wurden allesamt nicht signifikant mit Ausnahme des Wertes „Beziehung zu Freunden und Familie" (χ^2 (1, $N = 240$) = 4.376, $p < .05$, $\phi = .135$). 79 % der Kinder aus TF gaben an, dass ihnen der Wert wichtig sei, wohingegen nur 65 % der Kinder aus NTF diesen Wert als wichtig angaben. Nimmt man eine Yates-Korrektur vor, wird der Unterschied jedoch nicht-signifikant χ^2 (1, $N = 240$) = 3.639, *n.s.*). In der Non-Affirmation-Bedingung zeigten sich ebenfalls keine signifikanten Unterschiede in der Beurteilung der am wenigsten wichtigen Werte zwischen den Kindern unterschiedlichen Familienhintergrunds. Ein Beispiel für eine Aussage in der Affirmationsbedingung war: „Mir ist eine Beziehung zu meinen Freunden und meiner Familie sehr wichtig, da sie immer für mich da sind und mich unterstützen soweit sie können. Sie helfen mir immer und geben mir Motivation" (Familie und Freunde). Ein Beispiel für eine Aussage in der Non-Affirmation-Bedingung lautete: „Musik kann für andere sehr wichtig sein, da sie sich dabei entspannen können und es ihnen Spaß macht z. B. vor anderen am Klavier zu spielen" (Musik).

Noten

Wie erwartet, gaben Kinder aus NTF (im Durchschnitt aller Fächer: $M = 2.7$, $SD = 0.5$) signifikant schlechtere Noten an als Kinder aus TF (im Durchschnitt über alle Fächer: $M = 2.5$, $SD = 0.6$), $F(1, 610) = 11.968$, $p < .05$, $d = 0.278$. Keinen Unterschied in der schulischen Leistung konnte wie erwartet zwischen Kindern von Alleinerziehenden ($M = 2.7$, $SD = 0.5$) und Kindern aus Stieffamilien ($M = 2.6$, $SD = 0.5$) festgestellt werden, $F(1, 124) = 1.592$, *n.s.*. Betrachtet man die einzelnen Fächer konnte man Unterschiede in Mathematik ($F(1, 609) = 4.872$, $p < .05$, $d = 0.22$), Geschichte ($F(1, 604) = 4.933$, $p < .05$, $d = 0.22$), Physik ($F(1, 599) = 11.027$, $p < .05$, $d = 0.33$) und Sport ($F(1, 605) = 10.054$, $p < .05$, $d = 0.31$) zwischen den Kindern aus NTF und TF feststellen. Geringe, nicht signifikante Unterschiede, gab es in den Fächern Deutsch ($F(1, 597) = 3.105$, *n.s.*), Englisch ($F(1, 603) = 2.979$, *n.s.*) und Erdkunde ($F(1, 548) = 3.084$, *n.s.*). Damit kann die Annahme, dass Kinder aus NTF insgesamt schlechtere Leistungen in der Schule erbringen, in dieser Stichprobe bestätigt werden. Hinsichtlich der drei experimentellen Versuchsbedingungen konnten keine signifikanten Unterschiede hinsichtlich der durchschnittlichen Note festgestellt werden ($F(2,611) = 1.63$, *n.s.*).

Steigert die Self-Affirmation-Intervention die Leistung von Kindern aus NTF? Zur Prüfung der zentralen Hypothese wurde eine 3 (Bedingung: Self-Affirmation vs. Non-Affirmation vs. Kontrollgruppe) x 2 (Familienhintergrund: Kinder aus NTF vs. Kinder aus TF) ANOVA mit der Leistung im Untertest Figurale Analogien des KFT 5-12, R (Heller & Perleth, 2000) als abhängiger Variable gerechnet. Es zeigten sich Haupteffekte in Bezug auf Unterschiede zwischen den Gruppen, $F(2, 605) = 8.38$, $p < .001$ und zwischen Kindern mit unterschiedlichem Familienhintergrund, $F(1,605) = 14.30$, $p < .001$, aber kein Interaktionseffekt ($F(2, 605) = 0.94$, *n.s.*). Wurde in den Analysen der Notendurchschnitt als Kovariate berücksichtigt, hatte er lediglich einen erwarteten Haupteffekt auf den erreichten Wert im Leistungstest, d.h., Schülerinnen und Schüler mit einem besseren Notendurchschnitt erreichten über alle Versuchsbedingungen hinweg einen höheren Wert im Leistungstest ($F(1, 605) = 26.32$, $p < .05$).

Die anschließende Berechnung der Kontraste ergab folgendes Bild, welches in Abbildung 1 veranschaulicht ist: In der Gruppe der NTF schnitten Kinder in der Self-Affirmation-Bedingung signifikant besser ab als die Kinder in der Non-Affirmation-Bedingung ($ts(606) > 2.000$, $ps < .05$, $d = 0.484$) und der Kontrollbedingung ($ts(606) < -2.700$, $ps < .05$, $d = 0.551$). Zwischen Kindern der Non-Affirmation und der Kontrollgruppe konnten keine Unterschiede festgestellt werden ($ts(606) < -0.190$, $ps > .05$, $d = 0.042$).

Für Kinder aus TF ergab sich ein ähnliches Bild (Affirmation vs. Non-Affirmation: $ts(606) > 2.500$, $ps < .05$, $d = 0.323$; Affirmation vs. Kontrollgruppe: $ts(606) < -2.280$, $ps < .05$, $d = 0.27$).

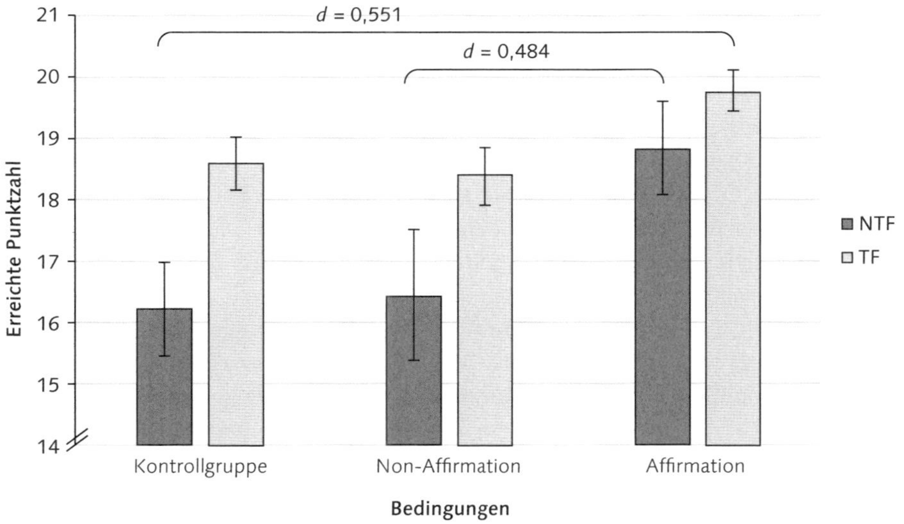

Abbildung 1. Testleistung in Figurale Analogien der Kinder (*M* ±SEM) aus NTF und TF in Abhängigkeit von der Bedingung.

Verglich man die Kinder mit unterschiedlichem Familienhintergrund in der Affirmationsbedingung, so ergaben sich keine Leistungsunterschiede ($ts(606) < -1.280$, $ps > .05$, $d = 0.21$). In der Non-Affirmation und Kontrollbedingung blieben die Unterschiede zwischen den Kindern aus NTF und TF weiterhin bestehen (Non-Affirmation $ts(606) < -2.200$, $ps < .05$, $d = 0.42$; Kontrollgruppe $ts(606) < -2.500$, $ps < .05$, $d = 0.47$).

Zusammengefasst zeigen die Ergebnisse, dass Kinder aus NTF von der Self-Affirmation-Intervention profitieren. Die Kinder schnitten im Untertest Figurale Analogien des KFT 5-12 R unter der Affirmation-Bedingung etwa eine halbe Standardabweichung besser ab als unter der Non-Affirmations- und der Kontrollbedingung. Allerdings zeigte sich, dass auch Kinder aus TF von der Self-Affirmation-Bedingung profitierten, hier betrug der Leistungsunterschied etwa eine Drittel (im Vergleich zur Non-Affirmation-Bedingung) bzw. ein Fünftel Standardabweichung (im Vergleich zur Kontrollgruppe). Somit konnte die zentrale Hypothese eines Interaktionseffektes zwar nicht bestätigt werden, jedoch zeigte sich eine leistungssteigernde Wirkung der Self-Affirmation-Intervention.

6 Diskussion

Die Studie untersuchte die Effekte einer Self-Affirmation-Intervention bei Kindern nichttraditioneller Familien (NTF), d.h. Kindern Alleinerziehender und aus Stieffamilien. Es zeigte sich, dass diese Kinder nach einer Self-Affirmation-Intervention eine bessere Leistung in einem kognitiven Fähigkeitstest, hier Figurale Analogien, aufwiesen als die Kinder desselben Familienhintergrunds in einer Non-Affirmations- und einer Kontrollbedingung. Zudem lag die Leistung dieser Kinder nach der Intervention mit der Leistung der Kinder aus traditionellen Familien (TF) nahezu gleichauf. Damit konnten einerseits ähnliche Effekte der Self-Affirmation-Intervention bei Kindern aus NTF gefunden werden wie z. B. bei Frauen in Mathematik (Martens et al., 2006) und afroamerikanischen und lateinamerikanischen Schülerinnen und Schülern (Cohen et al., 2006; Sherman et al., 2013). Entgegen der Hypothese, wonach die Self-Affirmation ausschließlich Kindern aus NTF zu einer Performanzsteigerung verhelfen sollte, profitierten jedoch auch Kinder aus TF, wenn auch nicht im gleichen Ausmaß.

Zunächst sind die Befunde im Hinblick auf den Manipulationscheck erklärungsbedürftig. Kinder aus NTF lehnten die Aussage „Kinder von alleinerziehenden Eltern und aus Stieffamilien haben es in der Schule schwerer als andere“ (stark) ab, während Kinder aus TF eher zustimmten. Aus unserer Sicht wären drei unterschiedliche Erklärungen für die geringe Zustimmung der Kinder aus NTF möglich. Erstens könnten entgegen der ursprünglichen Erwartung die Kinder aus NTF mit Abwehr auf die Aussage reagieren. Wie bereits erläutert, können Menschen auf Bedrohungen ihrer Selbstintegrität mit Verzerrungen der Realität z. B. in Form einer Leugnung oder Ablehnung der bedrohlichen Information reagieren (Cohen & Sherman, 2014).

Zweitens könnte das Stereotyp „NTF" stärker ein „threat in the air" sein, der durch die Formulierung der Aussage nicht aktualisiert wurde. Folgt man diesem Gedanken, müsste sich bei anderen Formulierungen bzw. Stereotypaktivierungen eine stärkere Reaktion zeigen. Drittens könnte das Stereotyp bei der heutigen Generation nicht so stark ausgeprägt sein, wie von uns ursprünglich angenommen, d. h., das Stereotyp „NTF" existiert nicht in der Form und wurde demnach nicht als Bedrohung wahrgenommen.

Das führt zur Frage, warum sowohl Kinder aus NTF und Kinder aus TF von der Self-Affirmation-Intervention profitieren. Unter der Annahme, dass die Abfrage der Familiensituation eine Bedrohung ausgelöst hat, könnte dies in beiden Gruppen (NTF und TF) aufgetreten sein, denn auch bei Kindern aus TF sind zerstrittene, konfliktreiche Familiensituationen denkbar. Unterstützt wird diese Annahme durch Musick und Meier (2011), die Schulleistungen und Wohlbefinden von Jugendlichen aus NTF und TF verglichen. Letztere unterteilten sie in Familien mit vielen und wenigen Konflikten. In vielen Ergebnisvariablen gab es keine Unterschiede zwischen der Leistung und dem Wohlbefinden der Jugendlichen aus NTF und TF mit vielen Konflikten.

Das heißt für zukünftige Forschungsarbeiten, dass die stereotype Bedrohung durch den Familienstatus genauer untersucht werden sollte, denn der Befund der schlechteren Noten bei den Kindern aus NTF bleibt ja bestehen. Mögliche stereotype Bedrohungen müssten vermutlich nuancierter erfasst werden, was auch der differenzierten gesellschaftlichen Situation stärker Rechnung tragen sollte. Denkbar wäre z. B. nicht die getrenntlebenden Eltern an sich zu thematisieren, sondern das Familienleben insgesamt („Kinder, die kein Pausenbrot bekommen", desolate Familienverhältnisse). Dies könnte u. U. stigmatisierender wirken als getrenntlebende Eltern. In zukünftigen Studien wäre es sinnvoll, zusätzlich Stereotype-Threat-Kontrollbedingungen aufzunehmen, um festzustellen, ob ein Unterschied zwischen den stereotypisierten und den nicht-stereotypisierten Probandinnen und Probanden in demselben Maße auftritt, wenn das Stereotyp nicht aktiviert wird.

Entgegen neueren Erkenntnissen von Hanselman, Rozek, Grigg und Borman (2016), die in einer Replikationsstudie keinerlei Effekte einer Self-Affirmation-Intervention nachweisen konnten, führte diese Intervention bei den von uns untersuchten Kindern zu einer deutlichen Performanzsteigerung in einem Leistungstest. Da jedoch entgegen unserer Forschungshypothese nicht nur Kinder aus NTF profitierten, unterstützen wir die Aufforderung der Forschergruppe um Hanselman, die auf die Fragilität von Self-Affirmation in Bildungskontexten verweisen und "the need for new theory, measures, and evidence about the necessary conditions for self-affirmation success" (S. 2) betonen. Nichtsdestotrotz lässt sich auf Basis dieser Studie das Fazit ziehen, dass Self-Affirmation eine Intervention mit geringem Aufwand ist, welche in diesem Fall vielen Schülerinnen und Schülern kurzfristige Vorteile und keinen Nachteil hinsichtlich der Leistungsperformanz gebracht hat.

Literatur

Amato, P. R. (2001). Children of divorce in the 1990s: An update of the Amato and Keith (1991) meta-analysis. *Journal of Family Psychology, 15*, 355–370.

Amato, P. R. & Keith, B. (1991). Parental divorce and the well-being of children: A meta-analysis. *Psychological Bulletin, 110*, 26–46.

Arkes, J. (2015). The temporal effects of divorces and separations on children's academic achievement and problem behavior. *Journal of Divorce & Remarriage, 56*, 25–42.

Aronson, J., Fried, C. B. & Good, C. (2002). Reducing the effects of stereotype threat on African American college students by shaping theories of intelligence. *Journal of Experimental Social Psychology, 38*, 113–125.

Babalis, T., Tsoli, K., Nikolopoulos, V. & Maniatis, P. (2014). The effect of divorce on school performance and behavior in preschool children in Greece: An empirical study of teachers' views. *Psychology, 5*, 20–26.

Carlson, M. J. & Corcoran, M. E. (2001). Family structure and children's behavioral and cognitive outcomes. *Journal of Marriage and Family, 63*, 779–792.

Cohen, G. L., Aronson, J. & Steele, C. M. (2000). When beliefs yield to evidence: Reducing biased evaluation by affirming the self. *Personality and Social Psychology Bulletin, 26*, 1151–1164.

Cohen, G. L., Garcia, J., Apfel, N. & Master, A. (2006). Reducing the racial achievement gap: A social-psychological intervention. *Science, 313* (5791), 1307–1310.

Cohen, G. L. & Sherman, D. K. (2014). The psychology of change: Self-affirmation and social psychological intervention. *Annual Review of Psychology, 65*, 333–371.

Doyle, R. A. & Voyer, D. (2016). Stereotype manipulation effects on math and spatial test performance: A meta-analysis. *Learning and Individual Differences, 47*, 103–116.

Fein, S. & Spencer, S. J. (1997). Prejudice as self-image maintenance: Affirming the self through derogating others. *Journal of Personality and Social Psychology, 73*, 31–44.

Ghysens, L. (2009). *Parents', teachers' and children's perception of parental involvement in relation with pupils' learning achievement and wellbeing*. Poster presented at the 7th International Conference of the European Research Network about Parents in Education, Malmö, Sweden.

Hanselman, P., Rozek, C. S., Grigg, J. & Borman, G. D. (2016). New evidence on self-affirmation effects and theorized sources of heterogeneity from large-scale replications. *Journal of Educational Psychology, 109*, 405–424.

Harackiewicz, J. M., Canning, E. A., Tibbetts, Y., Giffen, C. J., Blair, S. S., Rouse, D. I. & Hyde, J. S. (2014). Closing the social class achievement gap for first-generation students in undergraduate biology. *Journal of Educational Psychology, 106*, 375–389.

Heller, K. A. & Perleth, Ch. (2000). *Kognitiver Fähigkeitstest für 4. bis 12. Klassen.* Revision (KFT 4-12+ R). Göttingen: Beltz.

Ihme, T. A. & Möller, J. (2015). "He who can, does; he who cannot, teaches?": Stereotype threat and preservice teachers. *Journal of Educational Psychology, 107*, 300–308.

Legault, L., Al-Khindi, T. & Inzlicht, M. (2012). Preserving integrity in the face of performance threat: Self-affirmation enhances neurophysiological responsiveness to errors. *Psychological science, 23*, 1455–1460.

Lillard, D. & Gerner, J. (1999). Getting to the Ivy League: How family composition affects college choice. *Journal of Higher Education, 70*, 706–730.

Mandara, J. & Murray, C. B. (2006). Father's absence and African American adolescent drug use. *Journal of Divorce & Remarriage, 46*, 1–12.

Manning, W. D. & Lamb, K. A. (2003). Adolescent well-being in cohabiting, married, and single-parent families. *Journal of Marriage and Family, 65*, 876–893.

Martens, A., Johns, M., Greenberg, J. & Schimel, J. (2006). Combating stereotype threat: The effect of self-affirmation on women's intellectual performance. *Journal of Experimental Social Psychology, 42*, 236–243.

Musick, K. & Meier, A. (2011). Are both parents always better than one? Parental conflict and young adult well-being. *Social Science Research, 39*, 814–830.

Painter, G., & Levine, D. I. (2000). Family structure and youths' outcomes: Which correlations are causal? *The Journal of Human Resources, 35*, 524–549.

Sander, E., Endepohls-Ulpe, M. & Gollia, A. (2005). Scheidungskinder im Urteil von Lehrerinnen und Lehrern: Ein Vergleich von Lehrerurteilen über Kinder aus Scheidungsfamilien und Zwei-Eltern-Familien im Grundschulalter. *Psychologie in Erziehung und Unterricht, 52*, 272–280.

Schneider, B., Atteberry, A. & Owens, A. (2006). Auf die Familie kommt es an: Familienstruktur und Entwicklung des Kindes. *Bulletin DIJG, 11*, 32–54.

Sherman, D. K. & Cohen, G. L. (2002). Accepting threatening information: Self-affirmation and the reduction of defensive biases. *Current Directions in Psychological Science, 11*, 119–123.

Sherman, D. K. & Cohen, G. L. (2006). The psychology of self-defense: Self-affirmation theory. *Advances in Experimental Social Psychology, 38*, 183–242.

Sherman, D. K. & Hartson, K. A. (2011). Reconciling self-defense with self-criticism: Self-affirmation theory. In M. D. Alicke & C. Sedikides (Eds.), *Handbook of self-enhancement and self-protection* (pp. 128–151). New York, NY: Guilford Press.

Sherman, D. K., Hartson, K. A., Binning, K. R., Purdie-Vaughns, V., Garcia, J., Taborsky-Barba, S., Tomassetti, S., Nussbaum, A. D. & Cohen, G. L. (2013). Deflecting the trajectory and changing the narrative: How self-affirmation affects academic performance and motivation under identity threat. *Journal of Personality and Social Psychology, 104*, 591–618.

Sherman, D. K., Nelson, L. D. & Steele, C. M. (2000). Do messages about health risks threaten the self? Increasing the acceptance of threatening health messages via self-affirmation. *Personality and Social Psychology Bulletin, 26*, 1046–1058.

Sigle-Rushton, W. & McLanahan, S. (2004). Father absence and child well-being: A critical review. In D. Moynihan, T. Smeeding & L. Rainwater (Eds.), *The future of the family* (pp. 116–155). New York, NY: Russell Sage Foundation.

Silverman, A., Logel, C. & Cohen, G. L. (2013). Self-affirmation as a deliberate coping strategy: The moderating role of choice. *Journal of Experimental Social Psychology, 49*, 93–98.

Statistisches Bundesamt (2011). *Wie leben Kinder in Deutschland?: Begleitmaterial zur Pressekonferenz am 3. August 2011 in Berlin*. Wiesbaden: Statistisches Bundesamt.

Steele, C. M. (1988). The psychology of self-affirmation: Sustaining the integrity of the self. In L. Berkowitz (Ed.), *Advances in experimental social psychology* (pp. 261–302). San Diego, CA: Academic Press.

Steele, C. M. (1997). A threat in the air: How stereotypes shape intellectual identity and performance. *American Psychologist, 52*, 613–629.

Steele, C. M. & Aronson, J. (1995). Stereotype threat and the intellectual test performance of African Americans. *Journal of Personality and Social Psychology, 69*, 797–811.

Steele, C. M. & Liu, T. J. (1983). Dissonance processes as self-affirmation. *Journal of Personality and Social Psychology, 45*, 5–19.

Stone, J., Lynch, C. I., Sjomeling, M. & Darley, J. M. (1999). Stereotype threat effects on Black and White athletic performance. *Journal of Personality and Social Psychology, 77*, 1213–1227.

Stone, J. & McWhinnie, C. (2008). Evidence that blatant versus subtle stereotype threat cues impact performance through dual processes. *Journal of Experimental Social Psychology, 44*, 445–452.

Valiquette-Tessier, S.-C., Vandette, M.-P. & Gosselin, J. (2016). Is family structure a cue for stereotyping?: A systematic review of stereotypes and parenthood. *Journal of Family Studies, 22*, 162–181.

Van Laar, C. & Sidanius, J. (2001). Social status and the academic achievement gap: A social dominance perspective. *Social Psychology of Education, 4*, 235–258.

Autorinnen

DR. MICHAELA KÖLLER

Institut für pädagogisch-psychologische Lehr- und Lernforschung, Christian-Albrechts-Universität zu Kiel.

DR. NICOLE NAGY

Institut für pädagogisch-psychologische Lehr- und Lernforschung, Christian-Albrechts-Universität zu Kiel.

KONTAKT

Michaela Köller, Institut für pädagogisch-psychologische Lehr- und Lernforschung, Christian-Albrechts-Universität zu Kiel, Olshausenstr. 75, 24118 Kiel.
E-Mail: *mkoeller@ipl.uni-kiel.de*

Dieser Artikel entstand unter Mitarbeit von Dipl.-Psych. Daria Buttermilch.

Effekte elterlichen Vorleseverhaltens auf die Lesemotivation und das Leseverstehen von Grundschülerinnen und Grundschülern – Eine längsschnittliche Betrachtung

FRANZISKA STUTZ UND ULRICH SCHIEFELE

ZUSAMMENFASSUNG: Zusätzlich zu den kognitiven Grundfähigkeiten, die ein Kind mitbringt, spielt auch die Lesemotivation eine wichtige Rolle in der Entwicklung der Lesekompetenz. Das Vorlesen hat sich dabei als wichtige familiäre Bedingung sowohl der Lesekompetenz als auch der Lesemotivation erwiesen. In diesem Zusammenhang wurde oft die Bedeutung des dialogischen Vorlesens hervorgehoben, bei dem das Kind nicht passiv zuhört, sondern Geschichten miterzählt und mit dem Vorlesenden interagiert. Der/die Vorlesende nimmt dabei die Rolle eines aktiven Zuhörers/einer aktiven Zuhörerin ein. Unklar ist bislang, ob Vorlesehäufigkeit und -qualität langanhaltende Effekte auf die Lesemotivation und die Lesekompetenz haben. Diesen Fragestellungen sind wir im Rahmen einer Längsschnittstudie nachgegangen. Es nahmen N = 1079 Kinder teil, die sich zum ersten von zwei Messzeitpunkten (t1, t2) in der zweiten bzw. dritten Klasse befanden. Strukturgleichungsanalysen belegen signifikante Effekte von Häufigkeit und Qualität des Vorlesens (in Anlehnung an das dialogische Vorlesen wird hier unterschieden nach interaktivem vs. kontrollierendem Vorleseverhalten der Eltern) auf die Lesemotivation und das Leseverständnis der Schülerinnen und Schüler zu t1. Die Häufigkeit und Qualität des Vorlesens zeigten darüber hinaus signifikante indirekte Effekte auf die Lesemotivation und -kompetenz zu t2, die weitgehend durch die t1-Lesekompetenz vermittelt wurden.

Schlüsselwörter: Vorlesen, Lesemotivation, Lesekompetenz, Entwicklung, Grundschule

The effects of reading aloud by parents on the reading motivation and reading comprehension of elementary school students – A longitudinal investigation

ABSTRACT: In addition to basic cognitive abilities, reading motivation plays an important role in the development of reading competence. In this regard, reading aloud to children has emerged as an important family activity contributing to both children's reading comprehension and motivation. Researchers often have emphasized the importance of dialogic reading which requires the child to participate in the telling of the story instead of being a passive listener. The adult's role here is that of an active listener. It is still unclear to what extent reading frequency and reading quality have long-lasting effects on reading motivation and reading comprehension. In the current study, these issues were examined in the context of a longitudinal investigation. One-thousand and seventy-nine children who were in second or third grade at the first point of measurement (t1) participated in the study. Structural equation analyses demonstrated significant effects of the frequency and quality of reading aloud (measured here as interactive vs. controlling parental reading behavior) to students' reading motivation and comprehension at t1. Moreover, the frequency and quality of reading aloud showed significant indirect effects on reading motivation and comprehension at t2 that were mostly mediated by t1 reading comprehension.

Keywords: reading aloud, reading motivation, reading comprehension, development, elementary school

Einleitung

Lesen stellt in der heutigen Gesellschaft eine wichtige Schlüsselfertigkeit dar (Morrow & Gambrell, 2011). Die Entwicklung der Lesekompetenz beginnt nicht erst zum Schuleintritt, sondern wird schon vorher durch mehrere Faktoren maßgeblich beeinflusst (Whitehurst & Lonigan, 1998). Je größer z. B. der Wortschatz eines Kindes ist und je mehr das Kind über Syntax, narrative Strukturen, metasprachliche Aspekte der Sprache und Buchstaben weiß, desto leichter fällt es ihm, lesen zu lernen. Über diese Faktoren hinaus und zusätzlich zu den kognitiven Grundkompetenzen, die ein Kind mitbringt (z. B. Arbeitsgedächtnis), spielt auch die Lesemotivation eine wichtige Rolle für den Werdegang eines Kindes als Leser (z. B. Guthrie, Wigfield, Metsala & Cox, 1999; Retelsdorf, Köller & Möller, 2011; s. Übersicht von Schiefele, Schaffner, Möller & Wigfield, 2012). In der Regel wird Lesemotivation als relativ stabile Bereitschaft zum Lesen beschrieben und sie wird über die Gründe definiert, die eine Person für das Lesen hat (Schiefele et al., 2012). Die Lesemotivation wird somit in intrinsische und extrinsische Gründe für das Lesen unterteilt. Ein intrinsisch motivierter Leser liest demnach, weil der Leseprozess als Tätigkeit an sich als belohnend empfunden wird, während ein extrinsisch motivierter Leser liest, um Ziele zu erreichen, die über den eigentlichen Prozess des Lesens hinausgehen (z. B. lesen, um schlechte Noten zu vermeiden). Diese Formen der Lesemotivation schließen sich nicht aus und können durchaus gleichzeitig auftreten. In einigen Studien konnten sogar sehr deutliche positive Korrelationen zwischen intrinsischer und extrinsischer Lesemotivation festgestellt werden (z. B. Schaffner, Schiefele & Ulferts, 2013).

In bisherigen Studien wurden meist positive Zusammenhänge zwischen intrinsischer Lesemotivation und Lesekompetenz gefunden, während die extrinsische Lesemotivation eine negative oder eine nicht signifikante Beziehung mit der Lesekompetenz zeigte (Schiefele et al., 2012). Es wird davon ausgegangen, dass Kinder, die aus intrinsischen Gründen lesen, ein günstigeres Leseverhalten zeigen als Kinder, die aus extrinsischen Gründen lesen. Insbesondere lesen intrinsisch motivierte Kinder häufiger in ihrer Freizeit aus eigenem Antrieb und haben somit mehr Lesepraxis als Kinder, die dies nicht tun (Guthrie et al., 1999). Die vermehrte Lesepraxis wiederum begünstigt Prozesse (z. B. Dekodiergeschwindigkeit), die die Lesekompetenz erhöhen.

Ein entgegengesetzter Effekt kann für die negative oder neutrale Beziehung zwischen extrinsischer Lesemotivation und Lesekompetenz vermutet werden. Vermutlich lesen extrinsisch motivierte Kinder nur dann, wenn es notwendig ist, um bestimmte Ziele zu erreichen, z. B. um in einer Leistungssituation vergleichsweise besser dazustehen als andere Kinder (Beispielitem: „Liest du, weil es dir wichtig ist, im Lesen immer der/die Beste zu sein?"). Wenn sie (mehr oder weniger) erfolgreich am Ziel angelangt sind, lesen diese Kinder nicht aus eigenem Antrieb weiter. Das bedeutet, dass die Lesepraxis eines extrinsisch motivierten Kindes in der Freizeit vergleichsweise geringer ist als die Lesepraxis eines intrinsisch motivierten Kindes und folglich auch zu einer geringeren Lesekompetenz führt (Schaffner et al., 2013; Wang & Guthrie, 2004).

Betrachtet man den Ursprung der Wirkkette zwischen Motivation und Leseleistung in der frühen Kindheit, so wird deutlich, dass eine Reihe von Prozessen in der Familie die Einstellung der Kinder zum Lesen und ihre Lesekompetenz potenziell beeinflussen (Hurrelmann, 2004; Retelsdorf & Möller, 2008). Familiäre Interaktionsmuster und die Gestaltung einer alltäglichen Lesekultur in der Familie sind für den Erfolg der kindlichen Lesesozialisation mitverantwortlich. Dabei spielt die Ausprägung verschiedener Struktur- (z. B. sozioökonomischer Status) und Prozessmerkmale (z. B. kulturelle Ressourcen, Leseeinstellung der Eltern) in der Familie eine wichtige Rolle (McElvany, Becker & Lüdtke, 2009). Insbesondere prä- und paraliterarische Kommunikationsformen (z. B. Sprachspiele, Kinderlieder) scheinen von großer Bedeutung für die Entwicklung von Sprache und Leseverstehen zu sein (Hurrelmann, 2004). Eine sehr einflussreiche familiäre Aktivität stellt dabei das gemeinsame Vorlesen von Büchern dar (Bus, van Ijzendorn & Pellegrini, 1995). Beim gemeinsamen Vorlesen wird typischerweise eine Situation geschaffen, in der ein geübter Leser (meistens ein Elternteil) einem weniger kompetenten Leser (dem Kind) vorliest (Muratović, 2016).

1 Gemeinsames Vorlesen und Lesemotivation

Bereits 1994 berichteten Scarborough und Dobrich in einer Metaanalyse kleine bis mittlere Zusammenhänge zwischen Qualität und Quantität von gemeinsamem Vorlesen und lesebezogenen Fähigkeiten. Diese Zusammenhänge wurden seither in Quer- und Längsschnittstudien wiederholt bestätigt (z. B. Bus et al., 1995; Mol, Bus, de Jong & Smeets, 2008). Auch für die intrinsische Lesemotivation wurde eine bedeutsame Rolle des Vorlesens sowohl theoretisch (z. B. Muratović, 2016) als auch empirisch begründet (Baker & Scher, 2002; Gottfried, Schlackman, Gottfried & Boutin-Martinez, 2015; Lam, Chow-Yeung, Wong, Lau & Tse, 2013; McElvany & Artelt, 2009; Sonnenschein & Munstermann, 2002). Die Ergebnisse der Längsschnittstudie von Gottfried et al. (2015) zeigen, dass die Vorlesehäufigkeit im Alter von 15, 39, und 60 Monaten nicht nur die Leseleistung, sondern auch die intrinsische Lesemotivation der Kinder im Alter von neun Jahren positiv vorhersagen konnte. Damit werden auch die Befunde der Stiftung Lesen (2011) gestützt, die aufgrund einer retrospektiven Befragung von 10- bis 19-Jährigen positive Zusammenhänge zwischen Vorlesehäufigkeit und Lesefreude belegen konnten.

Allerdings gibt es auch abweichende Befunde. So entwarfen McElvany und Artelt (2009) ein mehrere Wochen dauerndes Interventionsprogramm, in welchem Viertklässler und ihre Eltern sich gegenseitig abwechselnd Texte vorlesen und dann strategieorientierte Aktivitäten dazu ausüben sollten (z. B. Fragen beantworten oder Bilder malen). Hier fanden sich zwar signifikante Verbesserungen der Experimentalgruppe hinsichtlich des Wortschatzes, jedoch gab es weder einen Programmeffekt noch irgendeine Veränderung der Lesemotivation. Baker und Scher (2002) fanden ebenfalls keine Zusammenhänge zwischen den Vorleseerfahrungen von Erstklässlern und deren Lesefreude. Zusammenfassend ergibt sich somit eine unzureichende Befundlage zum Zusammenhang von Vorlesen und Lesemotivation. Ausgehend von der methodisch besten Studie in diesem Bereich, nämlich der von Gottfried et al. (2015), ist jedoch eine signifikante Rolle des Vorlesens für die Lesemotivation anzunehmen.

Mittlerweile hat sich eine Reihe von Studien auch mit der Rolle der Vorlesequalität für den späteren Lese- bzw. Schulerfolg beschäftigt (z. B. Mol et al., 2008). Es wurden dabei insbesondere zwei Qualitätsmerkmale des Vorlesens näher untersucht: der dialogische Charakter und die affektive Qualität des Vorlesens. Der Ansatz des dialogischen Vorlesens (Arnold & Whitehurst, 1994) erweitert das traditionelle Vorlesen, bei welchem das Kind passiv zuhört, durch ein höheres Maß an Interaktion zwischen dem Erwachsenen und dem Kind. Dabei stehen drei Prinzipien im Vordergrund: (1) Interaktive Techniken, um auf Äußerungen des Kindes einzugehen oder gezielt Fragen zu stellen, (2) Rückmeldungen im Sinne von Erweiterung, Korrektur oder Lob der Äußerungen des Kindes und (3) Anpassen des Lesestoffs an die stetig wachsenden Kompetenzen des Kindes. Insgesamt finden sich in der bisherigen Forschung überzeugende Befunde für eine positive Beeinflussung der Sprachentwicklung, wenn sich das Vorlesen an dialogischen oder ähnlichen, kindzentrierten Prinzipien orientiert (z. B. Mol et al., 2008; Mol, Bus & de Jong, 2009).

Neben dem dialogischen Vorlesen haben einige Forscher die zusätzliche Bedeutung der affektiven Qualität der Vorlesesituation für die Sprachentwicklung des Kindes betont (z. B. Bergin, 2001). So wurde eine positive Wirkung des Vorlesens durch unterstützende und freudvolle Vorleseinteraktionen vermutet, während das Vorlesen in einer forcierten, lernzielfokussierten Situation als eher ineffizient eingeschätzt wurde (Muratović, 2016; Snow, 1994). Die Bedeutung der affektiven Vorlesequalität wurde jedoch bislang nur in wenigen Studien geprüft. So konnten Sonnenschein und Munstermann (2002) für fünfjährige Kinder positive Zusammenhänge zwischen der affektiven Qualität des Vorlesens und einem Motivationsmaß feststellen (s.a. Bergin, 2001). Lam et al. (2013) berichteten für ein Programm zur Förderung der affektiven Vorlesequalität signifikante Effekte auf die intrinsische Lesemotivation von Vorschülerinnen und Vorschülern.

Bei der Betrachtung der Zusammenhänge zwischen den oben beschriebenen Aspekten der Vorlesequalität und der intrinsischen Lesemotivation ergibt sich ein deutlicher Bezug zur Selbstbestimmungstheorie (z.B. Ryan & Deci, 2000). Die Selbstbestimmungstheorie stellt für die Entwicklung und Aufrechterhaltung der intrinsischen Motivation drei Bedürfnisse in den Vordergrund, nämlich das Streben nach Autonomie, Kompetenz und sozialer Bezogenheit. Die ersten beiden dieser Bedürfnisse werden offensichtlich durch die Vorgaben des dialogischen Vorlesens angesprochen. Eine Vorlesesituation, in der die kindlichen Interessen wahrgenommen werden und in der das Kind angeregt wird, Fragen zu stellen und Eindrücke zu äußern, unterstützt vermutlich das Autonomiegefühl. Kontinuierliche Rückmeldungen und die Anpassung des Lesestoffs an das Fähigkeitsniveau des Kindes sind wiederum für das Kompetenzerleben förderlich. Demgegenüber vermuten wir, dass das Bedürfnis nach sozialer Bezogenheit eher durch die affektive Qualität der Vorlesesituation beeinflusst wird.

2 Fragestellungen und Hypothesen

Auf der Grundlage der bisherigen Erwägungen wurde die vorliegende Studie von zwei Hauptzielen geleitet. Zum einen sollte die Vorlesehäufigkeit im Vorschulalter in einen längsschnittlichen Bezug zur Lesemotivation und zur Lesekompetenz gebracht werden. Zu diesem Zweck erhoben wir bei einer großen Stichprobe von Zweit- und Drittklässlern zunächst retrospektiv das vorschulische Vorleseverhalten (quantitativ und qualitativ) aus Elternsicht und die gegenwärtige Lesemotivation sowie Lesekompetenz. Ein Jahr später wurden die Messungen von Lesemotivation und Lesekompetenz wiederholt. Vor dem Hintergrund vorliegender Forschungsbefunde vermuteten wir, dass die Vorlesehäufigkeit nicht nur mit der Lesekompetenz einen positiven Zusammenhang zeigt, sondern auch die intrinsische Lesemotivation positiv und die extrinsische Lesemotivation negativ vorhersagt.

Das zweite Hauptziel bezieht sich auf die Berücksichtigung der Vorlesequalität. Hier unterscheiden wir zwischen interaktivem und kontrollierendem Vorleseverhalten. Das interaktive Vorlesen ist dabei in Anlehnung an das Konzept des dialogischen Vorlesens zu verstehen. Allerdings haben wir nicht alle Aspekte des dialogischen Vorlesens erfasst, sondern vor allem auf den interaktiven Austausch zwischen Eltern und Kind fokussiert. Unser Verständnis des kontrollierenden Vorlesens orientiert sich an der Selbstbestimmungstheorie und meint vor allem ein Verhalten, das direktiv und bestimmend ist und wenig Autonomie zulässt. Folglich erwarteten wir hinsichtlich intrinsischer Lesemotivation und Lesekompetenz positive Effekte für das interaktive Vorlesen und negative Effekte für das kontrollierende Vorlesen. Dagegen sollte die extrinsische Lesemotivation positiv mit dem kontrollierenden Vorlesen und negativ mit dem interaktiven Vorlesen assoziiert sein. Aufgrund der zeitlich weit auseinanderliegenden bzw. retrospektiven Messungen erwarteten wir generell eher kleine Effekte des Vorlesens.

3 Methode

3.1 Stichprobe und Untersuchungsablauf

Die folgenden Analysen basieren auf den Daten eines längsschnittlichen Forschungsprojekts zu Risikofaktoren im Kindes- und Jugendalter (vgl. Stutz, Schaffner, & Schiefele, in Druck). Es wurden zwei Messzeitpunkte (t1: 2012; t2: 2013) einbezogen.

Die Stichprobe der Studie stammt aus 125 Klassen von 32 Schulen im Nordosten Deutschlands, die sich sowohl auf ländliche als auch städtische Gebiete mit verschiedenen sozioökonomischen Verhältnissen verteilen. Von den Rückantworten angefragter Familien waren etwa 75 % positiv. Über 97 % aller Kinder nahmen an der Datenerhebung zu beiden Messzeitpunkten teil. Dies resultierte in einer Stichprobe von 549 Zweitklässlern ($M_{Alter} = 8.22$, $SD = 0.49$; 52.1 % weiblich) und 526 Drittklässlern ($M_{Alter} = 9.13$, $SD = 0.49$; 52,5 % weiblich). Zusätzlich wurde von ca. 80 % der teilnehmenden Familien auch ein Elternfragebogen (u.a. zum Vorleseverhalten) ausgefüllt.

Zu beiden Messzeitpunkten wurden die Probanden individuell von geschulten Studierenden oder Doktoranden getestet. Die Sitzungen dauerten jeweils eine Stunde. Alle Erhebungen fanden während der zweiten Hälfte des Schuljahres einschließlich der Sommerferien statt. Das Zeitintervall zwischen t1 und t2 betrug ca. neun Monate.

3.2 Messinstrumente

3.2.1 Vorlesehäufigkeit

Die Vorlesehäufigkeit wurde anhand des Elternfragebogens mit zwei Items erfasst. Die Items wurden eingeleitet mit dem Hinweis, dass viele Eltern ihren Kindern in ihrer Freizeit etwas vorlesen oder gemeinsam mit ihren Kindern lesen. Daraufhin wurden die Eltern befragt, wie häufig sie und/oder der/die Partner/in dem Kind im Alter von 1–3 Jahren (Item 1) und im Alter von 4–6 Jahren (Item 2) vorgelesen haben. Die Antworten wurden jeweils aus einer fünfstufigen Skala ausgewählt, die von „einmal im Monat oder seltener" bis „jeden Tag mehrmals" reichte. Im Zusammenspiel bilden diese beiden Items das latente Konstrukt Vorlesehäufigkeit in der Kindheit (t0). Die Reliabilität der Skala kann mit $\alpha = .83$ als gut eingestuft werden.

3.2.2 Vorlesequalität

Die Vorlesequalität wurde durch einen eigens entwickelten Fragebogen erhoben. Die Eltern wurden gebeten, auf einer Skala von 1 = *nie* bis 5 = *immer* für verschiedene Vorleseaktivitäten anzugeben, wie häufig sie diese in der Vergangenheit gezeigt hatten. Die Skala zum interaktiven Vorleseverhalten umfasste vier Items („Ich frage mein Kind, was ihm an einer Geschichte gefällt oder nicht gefällt", „Ich ermuntere mein Kind, Fragen zu einem Buch oder einer Geschichte zu stellen", „Ich hinterfrage die Bedeutung von Wörtern und Sätzen", „Ich rege dazu an, zusätzliche Informationen in die Geschichte einzubauen"; $\alpha = .80$) und die Skala zum kontrollierenden Vorleseverhalten nur zwei Items („Ich lobe mein Kind, wenn es mich beim Lesen nicht unterbricht", „Ich wähle zum Vorlesen bevorzugt Geschichten aus, in denen neue und schwierige Wörter vorkommen"; $\alpha = .68$). Die Auswahl der Items aus einem größeren Itempool von insgesamt 9 Items erfolgte mittels exploratorischer Faktoranalysen. Anschließend wurde die Zweifaktorenstruktur mit einer konfirmatorischen Faktorenanalyse bestätigt ($\chi^2 = 34.361$, $df = 8$, $p < .01$, CFI = .991, TLI = .984, WRMR = .682).

3.2.3 Lesemotivation

Die intrinsische und die extrinsische Lesemotivation wurden mit Hilfe eines Lesemotivationsfragebogens für Grundschülerinnen und Grundschüler erfasst (RMQ-E = *Reading Motivation Questionnaire for Elementary Students*; Stutz et al., in Druck). Die intrinsische Lesemotivation wird hier durch die Skala *Erleben* abgebildet (3 Items: „Liest du, weil Bücher und Geschichten oft spannend sind?", „Liest du, weil es Spaß macht?", „Liest du, weil es aufregend ist zu sehen, was den Personen in einer Geschichte so passiert?"), während die extrinsische Lesemotivation durch die Skala *Wettbewerb* repräsentiert wird (2 Items: „Liest du, weil es dir wichtig ist, im Lesen immer der/die Beste zu sein?", „Liest du, weil du in der Schule besser sein möchtest als die anderen in deiner Klasse?").

Der RMQ-E enthält eine kurze Einführung, in welcher das Kind instruiert wird, bei der Beantwortung der Fragen an Situationen zu denken, in denen es in der Freizeit alleine in einem Buch liest. Der Testleiter liest alle Instruktionen und Fragen laut vor und das Kind antwortet auf jede Frage mit Hilfe einer vierstufigen Antwortskala („nein", „eher nein", „eher ja", „ja"). Die Reliabilität der beiden Lesemotivationskalen wurde mit Hilfe des ordinalen α-Koeffizienten bestimmt. Nach Zumbo, Gadermann, and Zeisser (2007) führt dieser Koeffizient bei Items mit geringer Zahl von Antwortkategorien und schiefer Verteilung zu einer weniger verzerrten Schätzung. Die festgestellten ordinalen α-Koeffizienten waren zufriedenstellend (Erleben: $\alpha = .75$ [t1] und .78 [t2]; Wettbewerb: $\alpha = .85$ [t1] und .86 [t2]).

3.2.4 Leseverständnis

Das Leseverständnis wurde mit einer verkürzten Version des ELFE-Tests von Lenhard und Schneider (2006) gemessen. Der ELFE-Test umfasst drei Subtests: Wortverständnis, Satzverständnis und Textverständnis. Im Subtest Wortverständnis sollen die Teilnehmer von vier vorgegebenen ähnlich lautenden Wörtern (z. B. Bote / Hose / Dose / Rose) dasjenige auswählen, das mit einem vorgegebenen Bild übereinstimmt.

Im Untertest Satzverständnis muss ein fehlendes Wort durch die Auswahl des inhaltlich passenden Wortes aus einer Reihe von fünf Alternativen ersetzt werden (z. B. „Wenn es [rechnet, regnet, riecht, redet, rennt] und die Sonne scheint, gibt es einen Regenbogen."). Die Zielwörter sind entweder Substantive, Verben, Adjektive, Konjunktionen oder Präpositionen.

Der Test für das Textverständnis sieht vor, dass die Teilnehmer kurze Absätze lesen, die zwischen zwei und sieben Sätzen lang sind (z. B. „Wale leben im Meer. Zum Atmen schwimmen sie zur Wasseroberfläche. Dort holen sie tief Luft und können dann lange unter Wasser tauchen"). Mit Hilfe des vorliegenden Textabschnittes haben die Teilnehmer die Aufgabe, ein oder zwei Multiple-Choice-Fragen zu beantworten. Um diese Fragen erfolgreich zu beantworten, müssen die Kinder spezifische Informationen identifizieren, anaphorische Beziehungen verstehen oder Interferenzen bilden.

Aufgrund von Zeitknappheit wurde jeder der ursprünglichen ELFE-Untertests in zwei Hälften geteilt. Die Aufteilung der Tests in jeweils gleichwertige Hälften wurde anhand der Angaben aus dem ELFE-Manual (Schwierigkeitsgrad und Art der Aufgabenanforderung) vorgenommen. So entstanden jeweils äquivalente Testhälften, von denen eine zu t1 und die andere zu t2 eingesetzt wurden. Trotz ihrer reduzierten Länge erwiesen sich die ELFE-Untertests als sehr reliabel (Wort: α = 0,93 [t1] und 0,94 [t2]; Satz: α = 0,87 [t1] und .85 [t2]; Text: α = 0,82 [t1] und .80 [t2]).

3.2.5 Sozioökonomischer Status

In allen Analysen wurde neben dem Geschlecht und der Klassenstufe auch der sozioökonomische Status (SÖS) der Probanden kontrolliert. Die Angaben zum SÖS wurden von den Eltern in Form von Fragen über den derzeitigen und den erlernten Beruf erhoben und dann nach dem Klassifikationsschema von Blossfeld (1987) näher bestimmt. Das genannte Schema klassifiziert die berufliche Qualifikation jedes Elternteils von 0 (= z. B. Arbeitslosigkeit) bis 5 (= höchster qualifizierter Beruf). Der ranghöchste Beruf jedes Elternpaares wurde als Indikator für den SÖS des jeweiligen Kindes verwendet.

3.3 Datenanalyse

3.3.1 Fehlende Werte

Bei 32 Kinderfragebögen fehlten die Angaben zur Lesemotivation entweder zu t1 (n = 12) oder zu t2 (n = 20). Darüber hinaus wurde bei 10 Teilnehmern Satz- und

Textverständnis nicht erfasst. Da 20.3 % der Elternfragebögen fehlten oder nicht vollständig ausgefüllt waren, lagen uns in diesen Fällen die Angaben zur Vorlesehäufigkeit und/oder zur Vorlesequalität nicht vor.

Für die deskriptiven Analysen (z. B. bivariate Korrelationen) verwendeten wir den EM-Algorithmus, um fehlende Werte zu ersetzen (Graham, 2009). Bei den Strukturgleichungsmodellen wurde der WLSMV-Schätzer verwendet; somit wurden fehlende Daten in Abhängigkeit von den beobachteten Kovariaten modelliert (Muthén & Muthén, 1998–2012).

3.3.2 Strukturgleichungsanalysen

Da sich unsere Hypothesen auf die längsschnittlichen Beziehungen zwischen Vorleseverhalten der Eltern im Vorschulalter (t0) und Lesemotivation bzw. Lesekompetenz der Kinder im Grundschulalter (jeweils t1 und t2) beziehen, haben wir ein Modell mit drei Messzeitpunkten spezifiziert. Die Daten wurden mit Hilfe des statistischen Programms *Mplus* 7.31 (Muthén & Muthén, 1998–2012) analysiert.

Die Variablen Vorlesehäufigkeit, Vorlesequalität und Lesemotivation wurden als latente Faktoren auf Itemebene modelliert, während Wort-, Satz- und Textverständnis jeweils durch zwei Itemparcels unter Anwendung der odd-even-Methode indikatorisiert wurden. Wegen der kategorialen Natur der verwendeten Items wurden die Modelle mit dem mittelwerts- und varianzbereinigten WLSMV-Schätzer berechnet (vgl. Carifio & Perla, 2007). Darüber hinaus wurde die Mehrebenenstruktur unserer Daten durch die Option TYPE=COMPLEX in *Mplus* berücksichtigt. Schließlich kontrollierten wir die Klassenstufe, das Geschlecht und den SÖS in den Modellen, indem wir gerichtete Pfade dieser Faktoren auf alle t1- und t2-Variablen spezifizierten.

Die vorliegenden längsschnittlichen Analysen setzen mindestens schwache Messinvarianz der mehrfach gemessenen Variablen voraus. Die Überprüfung und Bestätigung schwacher Messinvarianz wurde für die Variablen Lesemotivation und Leseverständnis (Wort-, Satz- und Textverständnis) mit der gleichen Stichprobe bereits in einer früheren Publikation dokumentiert (Schiefele, Stutz & Schaffner, 2016).

4 Ergebnisse

4.1 Bivariate Korrelationen

Vor der eigentlichen Hypothesenprüfung analysierten wir zunächst die bivariaten Korrelationen zwischen allen Variablen (siehe Tabelle 1). Dabei konnten wir im Einklang mit unseren Annahmen feststellen, dass die Vorlesehäufigkeit mit dem Wort-, Satz- und Textverständnis und der intrinsischen sowie der extrinsischen Motivation assoziiert ist. Eltern, die häufiger vorlesen, berichten auch eher interaktive als kon-

Tabelle 1. Deskriptive Statistik und bivariate Korrelationen

	Variable	1	2	3	4	5	6	7	8	9	10	11	12	13	14	15	16
1	Geschlecht	-															
2	Schulklasse	.01	-														
3	SÖS	.02	.02	-													
4	t0 VLH	-.01	.05	.30**	-												
5	t0 VLQ interaktiv	.02	.03	-.01	.23**	-											
6	t0 VLQ kontroll.	.02	.01	-.37**	-.16**	.34**	-										
7	t1 intrinsische LM	-.08*	.02	.09**	.12**	.00	-.10**	-									
8	t1 extrinsische LM	.11**	.01	-.18**	-.24**	.01	.15**	.05	-								
9	t1 Wortverständnis	-.03	.45**	.14**	.17**	.06	-.10**	.20**	-.06	-							
10	t1 Satzverständnis	-.04	.40**	.22**	.20**	.04	-.18**	.21**	-.12**	.83**	-						
11	t1 Textverständnis	-.02	.40**	.26**	.26**	.06*	-.17**	.22**	-.16**	.69**	.76**	-					
12	t2 intrinsische LM	-.12**	.03	.11**	.16**	.07*	-.13**	.38**	-.03	.24**	.31**	.29**	-				
13	t2 extrinsische LM	.10**	-.07*	-.25**	-.19**	-.00	.10**	.00	.50**	-.18**	-.23**	-.26**	-.04	-			
14	t2 Wortverständnis	-.06*	.36**	.21**	.20**	.04	-.13**	.20**	-.09**	.82**	.79**	.70**	.26**	-.20**	-		
15	t2 Satzverständnis	-.05	.31**	.28**	.22**	.04	-.17**	.22**	-.14**	.77**	.82**	.75**	.29**	-.25**	.83**	-	
16	t2 Textverständnis	-.03	.26**	.32**	.29**	.03	-.22**	.21**	-.18**	.65**	.74**	.75**	.29**	-.26**	.71**	.78**	-
	M	1.48	2.49	2.82	3.87	2.99	2.10	3.53	2.02	18.03	7.84	5.13	3.54	1.80	20.60	8.85	5.74
	SD	0.50	0.50	1.05	0.77	0.72	0.91	0.64	1.02	6.33	3.17	2.65	0.60	0.86	6.55	2.74	2.58

Anmerkung. $N = 1076$. SÖS = Sozioökonomischer Status. VLH = Vorlesehäufigkeit. VLQ interaktiv = interaktive Vorlesequalität. VLQ kontroll. = kontrollierende Vorlesequalität. LM = Lesemotivation. $^{*}p < .05$, 2-seitig. $^{**}p < .01$, 2-seitig.

trollierende Vorgehensweisen. Der interaktive und der kontrollierende Vorlesestil korrelieren zwar positiv, jedoch sind die Beziehungen der beiden Stile zu allen anderen Variablen eher gegenläufig. Während der interaktive Vorlesestil lediglich niedrige positive Zusammenhänge mit dem Textverständnis zu t1 und intrinsischer Lesemotivation zu t2 zeigt, ist der kontrollierende Vorlesestil positiv mit der extrinsischen Lesemotivation sowie negativ mit der intrinsischen Lesemotivation und allen Leseverständnisvariablen assoziiert.

In Übereinstimmung mit der bisherigen Forschung (vgl. Schiefele et al., 2012) stehen die positiven bzw. negativen Korrelationen zwischen Leseverstehen und intrinsischer extrinsischer Lesemotivation. Darüber hinaus ergab sich erwartungsgemäß, dass Eltern mit höherem SÖS ihren Kindern häufiger vorlesen und dabei kontrollierendes Verhalten vermeiden. Die Kinder mit höherem SÖS waren zudem eher intrinsisch und weniger extrinsisch motiviert und verfügten über eine höhere Lesekompetenz. Ebenfalls theoriegemäß zeigten die Mädchen eine etwas stärkere intrinsische Motivation als die Jungen, während letztere bei der extrinsischen Motivation vorne lagen (vgl. Logan & Johnston, 2009). In Übereinstimmung mit Lenhard (2013) gab es hinsichtlich des Leseverständnisses im ELFE-Test keine bzw. nur geringfügige Geschlechtsunterschiede zugunsten der Mädchen (nur signifikant für t2 Wortverstehen). Schließlich waren für die Zweitklässler schwächere Verstehensleistungen als für die Drittklässler zu verzeichnen.

4.2 Strukturgleichungsanalysen

Es wurden insgesamt drei Modelle berechnet, die sich nur durch die Art der einbezogenen Lesekompetenzdimension unterschieden. In allen drei Modellen wurden die folgenden direkten Pfade angenommen (siehe Tabelle 2): (a) alle t0-Variablen auf alle t1-Variablen und (b) alle t1-Variablen auf alle t2-Variablen mit zwei Ausnahmen (keine direkten Pfade von t1 intrinsische bzw. extrinsische Motivation auf t2 extrinsische bzw. intrinsische Motivation). Zudem wurden die korrelativen Pfade zwischen allen Variablen des jeweils gleichen Messzeitpunkts einbezogen. Schließlich wurden direkte Pfade der Kontrollvariablen auf alle t1- und t2-Variablen spezifiziert. Wir gingen davon aus, dass die Effekte der Vorlesevariablen auf die t2-Variablen nur vermittelt über die t1-Variablen auftreten.

Die getesteten Modelle ergaben in allen Fällen einen guten Modellfit, $\chi^2 = 305.98$, $df = 216$, $p < .01$, CFI = .983, TLI = .976, RMSEA = .020, für das Modell mit Wortverständnis, $\chi^2 = 288.89$, $df = 216$, $p < .01$, CFI = .986, TLI = .981, RMSEA = .018, für das Modell mit Satzverständnis, und $\chi^2 = 289.80$, $df = 216$, $p < .01$, CFI = .986, TLI = .980, RMSEA = .018, für das Modell mit Textverständnis. Die Ergebnisse (vgl. Tabelle 2) bestätigen erwartungsgemäß die Vorlesehäufigkeit als positiven Prädiktor des t1-Leseverstehens, während eine geringere Vorlesehäufigkeit mit einer stärkeren extrinsischen Lesemotivation zu t1 einhergeht. Der angenommene Effekt der Vorlesehäufigkeit auf die intrinsische Motivation zu t1 deutet sich durch marginal signifikante

Tabelle 2. Ergebnisse der Strukturgleichungsanalysen: Darstellung der Effekte

	Wort		Satz		Text	
	Direkt	Indirekt	Direkt	Indirekt	Direkt	Indirekt
			Vorlesehäufigkeit t0 auf Outcome			
Intrinsische LM t1	.10⁺		.10⁺		.09	
Extrinsische LM t1	-.20**		-.20**		-.20**	
Leseverstehen t1	.09*		.10*		.17**	
Intrinsische LM t2		.07*		.07*		.09**
Extrinsische LM t2		-.12**		-.13**		-.14**
Leseverstehen t2		.08*		.09**		.16**
			Vorlesen interaktiv t0 auf Outcome			
Intrinsische LM t1	.10		.09		.08	
Extrinsische LM t1	.02		.01		.01	
Leseverstehen t1	.08⁺		.11*		.11*	
Intrinsische LM t2		.06⁺		.07*		.07*
Extrinsische LM t2		-.00		-.01		-.01
Leseverstehen t2		.07⁺		.10**		.10*
			Vorlesen kontrollierend t0 auf Outcome			
Intrinsische LM t1	-.17*		-.15⁺		-.15⁺	
Extrinsische LM t1	.11		.11		.11	
Leseverstehen t1	-.12*		-.20*		-.20*	
Intrinsische LM t2		-.10*		-.13**		-.13**
Extrinsische LM t2		.08*		.09*		.09*
Leseverstehen t2		-.11*		-.18**		-.19**
			Intrinsische LM t1 auf Outcome			
Intrinsische LM t2	.49**		.46**		.45**	
Leseverstehen t2	.05*		.05⁺		.02	
			Extrinsische LM t1 auf Outcome			
Extrinsische LM t2	.54**		.53**		.52**	
Leseverstehen t2	-.03		-.01		-.03	
			Leseverstehen t1 auf Outcome			
Intrinsische LM t2	.19**		.30**		.32**	
Extrinsische LM t2	-.16**		-.18**		-.19**	
Leseverstehen t2	.81**		.86**		.88**	

Anmerkung. Angezeigt werden standardisierte Pfadkoeffizienten. LM = Lesemotivation.
$+p < .10$. $*p < .05$, $**p < .01$.

Effekte an. Es ergaben sich zudem signifikante indirekte Effekte der Vorlesehäufigkeit auf alle t2-Variablen in der theoretisch zu erwartenden Richtung (vgl. Tabelle 2). Die indirekten Effekte auf die intrinsische Motivation (t2) und das Leseverstehen (t2) wurden dabei nur durch das t1-Leseverstehen vermittelt. Im Falle der extrinsischen Lesemotivation (t2) zeigten sich hingegen sowohl das Leseverstehen als auch die extrinsische Motivation zu t1 als signifikante Mediatoren der Effekte der Vorlesehäufigkeit.

Erwartungsgemäß war der positive Zusammenhang zwischen dem interaktiven Vorlesen und dem Leseverstehen zu t1 signifikant, während der vermutete Effekt auf die intrinsische Motivation (t1) ausblieb. Ebenfalls kein Zusammenhang ergab sich zwischen interaktivem Vorlesen und extrinsischer Lesemotivation. Das interaktive Vorlesen übte jedoch vermittelt über das t1-Leseverstehen indirekte Effekte sowohl auf das Leseverstehen als auch die intrinsische Motivation zu t2 aus.

Weitgehend theoriekonform fielen die Effekte des kontrollierenden Vorlesens aus. Dies betrifft insbesondere die negativen Zusammenhänge mit der intrinsischen Lesemotivation (t1) und dem Leseverstehen (t1) und die positiven Zusammenhänge mit der extrinsischen Lesemotivation (t1). Allerdings konnte der erwartete positive Effekt des kontrollierenden Vorlesens auf die extrinsische Motivation nicht beobachtet werden. Die weiteren Analysen ließen signifikante indirekte Effekte des kontrollierenden Lesens auf alle t2-Variablen erkennen, die durchweg durch das t1-Leseverstehen vermittelt wurden.

Abschließend ist darauf hinzuweisen, dass es nur schwache und teilweise signifikante Beiträge der intrinsischen Lesemotivation zu t1 zur Vorhersage des Leseverstehens zu t2 gab, während die Effekte des t1-Leseverstehens auf die t2-Lesemotivation deutlich und signifikant ausfielen. Diese Befunde stehen jedoch im Einklang mit der bisherigen Forschung (vgl. Schiefele et al., 2016).

5 Diskussion

Das allgemeine Ziel der aktuellen Studie bestand darin, die längsschnittlichen Beziehungen zwischen den Vorleseerfahrungen im Vorschulalter und der Lesemotivation bzw. dem Leseverständnis im Grundschulalter zu analysieren. Angelehnt an frühere Forschungsbefunde vermuteten wir, dass häufiges Vorlesen in der Kindheit positiv mit der späteren intrinsischen Lesemotivation und dem Leseverständnis assoziiert ist (Gottfried et al., 2015). Da sich die Vorlesequalität in der Vergangenheit bereits als signifikanter Prädiktor der Leseentwicklung gezeigt hat (Mol et al., 2008), gingen wir zudem der Frage nach, ob neben der Häufigkeit auch die Qualität des Vorlesens für die Lesemotivation von Bedeutung ist. Wir erwarteten dabei, dass sich ein interaktives Vorleseverhalten positiv auf Leseverständnis und Lesemotivation auswirkt, während ein kontrollierendes Vorleseverhalten negative Effekte zeigen sollte.

Unsere Hypothesen wurden zumindest teilweise gestützt. Bemerkenswert ist insbesondere, dass die Vorlesehäufigkeit und beide Komponenten der Vorlesequalität jeweils unabhängige Beiträge zur Vorhersage des Leseverstehens leisteten. Wie zu erwarten war, ergaben sich dabei für die Vorlesehäufigkeit und das interaktive Vorlesen positive Effekte und für das kontrollierende Vorlesen negative Effekte. Vermittelt über die Verstehensleistungen zu t1 konnten darüber hinaus signifikante indirekte Effekte aller Vorlesensindikatoren auf die Verstehensleistungen zu t2 beobachtet werden.

Bezüglich der Lesemotivation sind die Ergebnisse weniger erwartungskonform. Das gilt insbesondere für die ausgebliebenen Beiträge des interaktiven Vorlesens zur Vorhersage der intrinsischen und extrinsischen Lesemotivation. Dagegen konnten die angenommenen negativen Effekte des kontrollierenden Vorlesens auf die intrinsische Motivation eindeutig bestätigt werden. Allerdings waren keine signifikanten Zusammenhänge zwischen kontrollierendem Vorlesen und extrinsischer Motivation zu beobachten. Die Beiträge der Vorlesehäufigkeit waren wiederum in Übereinstimmung mit unseren Annahmen. Demnach trägt häufiges Vorlesen zur Reduzierung extrinsischer Motivation bei, wohingegen sich zumindest die Tendenz andeutet, dass die intrinsische Motivation durch das Vorlesen gefördert wird.

Schließlich zeigten sich weitgehend hypothesenkonforme indirekte Effekte des Vorleseverhaltens auf die Lesemotivation zu t2. Einschränkend ist anzumerken, dass diese indirekten Effekte fast ausschließlich über das t1-Leseverstehen vermittelt wurden (mit Ausnahme des indirekten Effekts der Vorlesehäufigkeit auf die extrinsische Lesemotivation zu t2). Somit deutet sich an, dass die durch das Vorlesen herbeigeführten Veränderungen der Lesemotivation im Wesentlichen durch Veränderungen der Lesekompetenz vermittelt werden.

Die vorliegende Studie ist mit einigen Mängeln behaftet und daher nur als ein erster Schritt zur Untersuchung der Auswirkungen des vorschulischen Vorlesens zu werten. Eine wichtige Einschränkung der vorliegenden Daten besteht z. B. in der Erfassung der Vorlesequalität in Form eines Elternfragebogens. Es ist nicht ungewöhnlich, dass Eltern in solchen Fragebögen diejenigen Antworten ankreuzen, die sie vermeintlich als gute Eltern erscheinen lassen (Scarborough & Dobrich, 1994). Obwohl wir versucht haben, diesem Problem vorzubeugen, indem wir die Items möglichst neutral formulierten, sind Verzerrungen der Antworten im Sinne sozialer Erwünschtheit nicht auszuschließen.

Eine weitere Einschränkung unserer Studie betrifft die Skala zum kontrollierenden Vorlesen. Diese Skala umfasst nur zwei Items, da es nicht gelungen ist, genügend Items zu generieren, die zusammen einen separaten Faktor bilden. Die verbliebenen zwei Items können das Bedeutungsspektrum des kontrollierenden Vorlesens nicht abdecken. Obwohl die von uns beobachteten Zusammenhänge mit dem Leseverständnis und der Lesemotivation die Validität der Skala zum kontrollierenden Vorlesen stützen, stellt die Weiterentwicklung dieser Skala eine wichtige Aufgabe für die künftige Forschung dar.

Eine dritte Einschränkung unserer Studie liegt darin, dass die Eltern ihr Vorleseverhalten rückblickend einzuschätzen hatten. Da es sich dabei um recht lange Zeiträume handelt, für die Einschätzungen abzugeben waren, kann neben der sozialen Erwünschtheit auch das individuelle Erinnerungsvermögen eine Fehlerquelle darstellen.

Schließlich bleibt in unserer Studie unklar, welche kausale Richtung der Beziehung zwischen dem Vorleseverhalten der Eltern und der Kompetenz bzw. Motivation der Kinder zugrundeliegt (vgl. Baker, Scher & Mackler, 1997). Mit Hilfe einer Längschnittstudie kamen Silinskas, Parrila, Lerkkanen, Poikkeus, Niemi und Nurmi (2010) zu dem Ergebnis, dass die Wortleseleistung von Kindergartenkindern die Vorlesehäufigkeit der Eltern positiv vorhersagte. Diese Erkenntnis wird untermauert durch die Befunde von Farrant und Zubrick (2013), wonach Kinder, die sich beim gemeinsamen Lesen schlecht konzentrieren können, später einen schlechteren Wortschatz haben als ihre Altersgenossen. Es ist zu vermuten, dass ein Kind, dem wenig vorgelesen wird, auch weniger Interesse an Büchern zeigt, aber dass auch das geringe Interesse eines Kindes am Vorlesen dazu führen kann, dass diesem Kind wenig vorgelesen wird. Die Untersuchung dieser komplexen wechselseitigen Prozesse stellt ein wichtiges Forschungsdesiderat dar.

Obwohl die vorliegenden Befunde nicht zu klaren Handlungsvorschlägen für die Praxis taugen, deutet sich zumindest an, worauf Eltern beim Vorlesen achten sollten. Ganz offensichtlich scheint ein Vorleseverhalten förderlich zu sein, das die Interaktion zwischen Eltern und Kind sowie ein Reflektieren des Gehörten fördert und nur in geringem Maß direktiv und überfordernd ist bzw. das Kind nicht in eine passive Rolle drängt. Wie Huebner und Meltzoff (2005) gezeigt haben, kann diese Art förderlichen Vorleseverhaltens sehr ökonomisch und effektiv mit Hilfe von Instruktionsvideos vermittelt werden.

Literatur

Arnold, D. H. & Whitehurst, G. J. (1994). Accelerating language development through picture book reading: A summary of dialogic reading and its effect. In D. K. Dickinson (Ed.), *Bridges to literacy: Children, families, and schools* (pp. 103–128). Malden, MA: Blackwell.

Baker, L. & Scher, D. (2002). Beginning readers' motivation for reading in relation to parental beliefs and home reading experiences. *Reading Psychology, 23*, 239–269.

Baker, L., Scher, D. & Mackler, K. (1997). Home and family influences on motivations for reading. *Educational Psychologist, 32*, 69–82.

Bergin, C. (2001). The parent–child relationship during beginning reading. *Literacy Research, 33*, 681–706.

Blossfeld, H. P. (1987). Labor-market entry and the sexual segregation of careers in the Federal Republic of Germany. *American Journal of Sociology, 93*, 89–118.

Bus, A. G., van Ijzendoorn, M. H. & Pellegrini, A. D. (1995). Joint book reading makes for success in learning to read: A meta-analysis on intergenerational transmission of literacy. *Review of Educational Research, 65*, 1–21.

Carifio, J. & Perla, R. (2007). Ten common misunderstandings, misconceptions, persistent myths and urban legends about Likert scales and Likert response formats and their antidotes. *Journal of Social Sciences, 2*, 106–116.

Farrant, B. M. & Zubrick, S. R. (2013). Parent-child book reading across early childhood and child vocabulary in the early school years: Findings from the Longitudinal Study of Australian Children. *First Language, 33*, 280–293.

Gottfried, A. W., Schlackman, J., Gottfried, A. E. & Boutin-Martinez, A. S. (2015). Parental provision of early literacy environment as related to reading and educational outcomes across the academic lifespan. *Parenting, 15*, 24–38.

Graham, J. W. (2009). Missing data analysis: Making it work in the real world. *Annual Review of Psychology, 60*, 549–76.

Guthrie, J. T., Wigfield, A., Metsala, J. L. & Cox, K. E. (1999). Motivational and cognitive predictors of text comprehension and reading amount. *Scientific Studies of Reading, 3*, 231–256.

Huebner, C. E. & Meltzoff, A. N. (2005). Intervention to change parent-child reading style: A comparison of instructional methods. *Journal of Applied Developmental Psychology, 26*, 296–313.

Hurrelmann, B. (2004). Informelle Sozialisationsinstanz Familie. In N. Groeben & B. Hurrelmann (Hrsg.), *Lesesozialisation in der Mediengesellschaft: Ein Forschungsüberblick* (S. 169–201). Weinheim: Juventa.

Lam, S. F., Chow-Yeung, K., Wong, B. P., Lau, K. K. & Tse, S. I. (2013). Involving parents in paired reading with preschoolers: Results from a randomized controlled trial. *Contemporary Educational Psychology, 38*, 126–135.

Lenhard, W. (2013). *Leseverständnis und Lesekompetenz*. Stuttgart: Kohlhammer.

Lenhard, W. & Schneider, W. (2006). *ELFE 1–6. Ein Leseverständnistest für Erst- bis Sechstklässler.* Göttingen: Hogrefe.

Logan, S. & Johnston, R. (2009). Gender differences in reading ability and attitudes: Examining where these differences lie. *Journal of Research in Reading, 32*, 199–214.

McElvany, N. & Artelt, C. (2009). Systematic reading training in the family: Development, implementation, and initial evaluation of the Berlin Parent–Child Reading Program. *Learning and Instruction, 19*, 79–95.

McElvany, N., Becker, M. & Lüdtke, O. (2009). Die Bedeutung familiärer Merkmale für Lesekompetenz, Wortschatz, Lesemotivation und Leseverhalten. *Zeitschrift für Entwicklungspsychologie und Pädagogische Psychologie, 41*, 121–131.

Mol, S. E., Bus, A. G. & de Jong, M. T. (2009). Interactive book reading in early education: A tool to stimulate print knowledge as well as oral language. *Review of Educational Research, 79*, 979–1007.

Mol, S. E., Bus, A. G., de Jong, M. T. & Smeets, D. J. (2008). Added value of dialogic parent–child book readings: A meta-analysis. *Early Education and Development, 19*, 7–26.

Morrow, L. M. & Gambrell, L. B. (Eds.). (2011). *Best practices in literacy instruction*. New York, NY: Guilford.

Muratović, B. (2016). Lesen und Familie. In U. Rautenberg & U. Schneider (Hrsg). *Lesen: Ein interdisziplinäres Handbuch* (S. 383–400). Berlin: DeGruyter.

Muthén, L. K. & Muthén, B. O. (1998–2012). *Mplus user's guide.* Los Angeles, CA: Muthén & Muthén.

Retelsdorf, J., Köller, O. & Möller, J. (2011). On the effects of motivation on reading performance growth in secondary school. *Learning and Instruction, 21*, 550–559.

Retelsdorf, J. & Möller, J. (2008). Familiäre Bedingungen und individuelle Prädiktoren der Lesekompetenz von

Schülerinnen und Schülern. *Psychologie in Erziehung und Unterricht, 55*, 227–237.

Ryan, R. M. & Deci, E. L. (2000). Intrinsic and extrinsic motivations: Classic definitions and new directions. *Contemporary Educational Psychology, 25*, 54–67.

Scarborough, H. S. & Dobrich, W. (1994). On the efficacy of reading to preschoolers. *Developmental Review, 14*, 245–302.

Schaffner, E., Schiefele, U. & Ulferts, H. (2013). Reading amount as a mediator of the effects of intrinsic and extrinsic reading motivation on reading comprehension. *Reading Research Quarterly, 48*, 369–385.

Schiefele, U., Schaffner, E., Möller, J. & Wigfield, A. (2012). Dimensions of reading motivation and their relation to reading behavior and competence. *Reading Research Quarterly, 47*, 427–463.

Schiefele, U., Stutz, F. & Schaffner, E. (2016). Longitudinal relations between reading motivation and reading comprehension in the early elementary grades. *Learning and Individual Differences, 51*, 49–58.

Silinskas, G., Parrila, R., Lerkkanen, M. K., Poikkeus, A. M., Niemi, P. & Nurmi, J. E. (2010). Mothers' reading-related activities at home and learning to read during kindergarten. *European Journal of Psychology of Education, 25*, 243–264.

Snow, C. E. (1994). Enhancing literacy development: Programs and research perspectives. In D. Dickinson (Ed.), *Bridges to literacy: Children, families and schools* (pp. 267–272). Cambridge, MA: Blackwell.

Sonnenschein, S. & Munsterman, K. (2002). The influence of home-based reading interactions on 5-year-olds' reading motivations and early literacy development. *Early Childhood Research Quarterly, 17*, 318–337.

Stiftung Lesen (2011). *Vorlesestudie 2011: Die Bedeutung des Vorlesens für die Entwicklung von Kindern. Repräsentative Befragung von 10-bis 19-Jährigen* [11.09.2016].

Stutz, F., Schaffner, E. & Schiefele, U. (in Druck). Measurement invariance and validity of a brief questionnaire on reading motivation in elementary students. *Journal of Research in Reading.*

Wang, J. H. & Guthrie, J. (2004). Modeling the effects of intrinsic motivation, extrinsic motivation, amount of reading, and past reading achievement on text comprehension between US and Chinese. *Reading Research Quarterly, 39*, 162–186.

Whitehurst, G. J. & Lonigan, C. J. (1998). Child development and emergent literacy. *Child Development, 69*, 848–872.

Zumbo, B. D., Gadermann, A. M. & Zeisser, C. (2007). Ordinal versions of coefficients alpha and theta for Likert rating scales. *Journal of Modern Applied Statistical Methods, 6*, 21–29.

Diese Studie wurde durch die Deutsche Forschungsgemeinschaft gefördert (GRK 1668/1).

Autorin und Autor

DR. FRANZISKA STUTZ
Department Grundschulpädagogik Deutsch, Universität Potsdam.

PROF. DR. ULRICH SCHIEFELE
Department Psychologie, Universität Potsdam.

KONTAKT
Franziska Stutz, Department Grundschulpädagogik Deutsch, Universität Potsdam, Karl-Liebknecht-Str. 24–25, 14476 Potsdam.
E-Mail: *stutz@uni-potsdam.de*

Gewohnheit macht den Meister: Lesegewohnheit als vermittelnde Variable des Zusammenhangs von Leseselbstkonzept und Leseleistung

JAN RETELSDORF UND FABIAN T. C. SCHMIDT

ZUSAMMENFASSUNG: Der Zusammenhang zwischen Leseselbstkonzept und Leseleistung wird häufig damit erklärt, dass Personen mit einem hohen Leseselbstkonzept eher gewohnheitsmäßig lesen. Das daraus erwachsende größere Ausmaß an Übung soll dann zu einer höheren Lesefähigkeit führen. Empirisch wurde dieser Wirkmechanismus bisher allerdings für das Leseselbstkonzept kaum untersucht. Zudem mangelte es bisher an einer elaborierten Konzeption von Lesegewohnheit, die über eine reine Lesehäufigkeit hinaus geht. In der vorliegenden Untersuchung wurde dieser indirekte Effekt von Leseselbstkonzept über Lesegewohnheit – gemessen mit einem theoretisch fundierten Instrument, das mehr als Lesehäufigkeit berücksichtigt – auf die Veränderung der Leseleistung von der 11. bis zur 13. Klasse überprüft. Dazu wurde anhand einer Stichprobe von $N = 522$ Schülerinnen und Schülern ein latenter Differenzwert der Leseleistung aus Leseselbstkonzept und Lesegewohnheit vorhergesagt sowie der postulierte indirekte Effekt auf Signifikanz getestet. Es zeigte sich wie erwartet, dass das Leseselbstkonzept positiv mit der Lesegewohnheit assoziiert ist, welche wiederum positiv mit der Leistungsveränderung zusammenhing. Auch der postulierte indirekte Effekt war signifikant.

Schlüsselwörter: Lesegewohnheit, Leseselbstkonzept, Leseleistung

Habit makes perfect: Reading habit as a mediator of the relation between reading self-concept and reading achievement

ABSTRACT: The relation between reading self-concept and reading achievement is often explained by the assumption that persons with a high reading self-concept tend to higher amounts of habitual reading. The resulting amount of practice in turn is supposed to lead to higher levels of reading achievement. This chain reaction, however, has only rarely been investigated as regards reading self-concept. Moreover, an elaborated conceptualization of reading habit that moves beyond behavioral frequency has been missing so far. In the present research we investigated the indirect effect of reading self-concept via reading habit on reading achievement growth from grade 11 to grade 13 using an elaborated habit measure. Drawing on a sample of $N = 522$ students we predicted a latent difference score for reading by reading self-concept and reading habit, also testing the postulated indirect effect. As expected, reading self-concept was positively related to reading habit, which in turn was positively related to reading achievement growth. Moreover, the indirect effect yielded significance.

Keywords: reading habit; reading self-concept; reading achievement

Einleitung

Das Leseselbstkonzept gilt als eine zentrale Determinante der Leseleistung von Schülerinnen und Schülern (z. B. Möller & Schiefele, 2004; Morgan & Fuchs, 2007; Retelsdorf, Köller & Möller, 2014). Dabei wird als zugrunde liegender Mechanismus häufig vermutet, dass Schülerinnen und Schüler mit einem höheren Leseselbstkonzept eher gewohnheitsmäßig lesen und dass dies zu einer höheren Leseleistung führt. Während dieser vermittelte Zusammenhang für Lesemotivation als recht gut gesichert gilt (im Überblick z. B. Schiefele, Schaffner, Möller & Wigfield, 2012), liegen bis dato kaum Studien vor, die diesen indirekten Effekt für das Leseselbstkonzept überprüfen. Zudem wurde die vermittelnde Variable in der Vergangenheit ganz verschiedentlich als Lesehäufigkeit, Lesemenge, Leseaktivität oder Lesegewohnheit beschrieben und operationalisiert. Schmidt und Retelsdorf (2016) haben vorgeschlagen, dieses Konstrukt einheitlich und auf einer theoretisch elaborierteren Basis als Lesegewohnheit zu verstehen und zu messen. Im vorliegenden Beitrag nutzen wir diese Konzeptualisierung der Lesegewohnheit, um der Frage nach dem indirekten Effekt von Leseselbstkonzept über Lesegewohnheit auf Leseleistung nachzugehen. Dabei geht unsere Arbeit durch die Nutzung des elaborierten Gewohnheitskonzepts über bisherige Arbeiten hinaus. Zudem stellt die Studie eine der ersten Arbeiten dar, die diesen indirekten Effekt für das Leseselbstkonzept untersuchen.

1 Zusammenhänge zwischen Leseselbstkonzept und Leseleistung

Das Leseselbstkonzept kann als die subjektive Wahrnehmung der Fähigkeit zu lesen definiert werden (Retelsdorf, Köller & Möller, 2011) und gilt als wichtige Determinante tatsächlicher Leseleistung (Möller & Schiefele, 2004; Morgan & Fuchs, 2007). Die empirische Evidenz für diesen Zusammenhang ist allerdings uneindeutig. So zeigten sich vor allem querschnittlich substanzielle Zusammenhänge des Leseselbstkonzepts mit der Leseleistung (Aunola, Leskinen, Onatsu-Arvilommi & Nurmi, 2002; Chapman & Tunmer, 1995, 1997; Chapman, Tunmer & Prochnow, 2000; Marsh, Smith & Barnes, 1985). Dieser Zusammenhang scheint mit höherem Alter der Kinder stärker zu werden (Chapman & Tunmer, 1995, 1997) und bleibt auch unter Kontrolle von Kovariaten wie dem sozialen oder demografischen Hintergrund, der Lesemotivation, verbalen oder allgemeinen kognitiven Fähigkeiten bestehen (Katzir, Lesaux & Kim, 2009; Retelsdorf et al., 2011; Retelsdorf & Möller, 2008). Längsschnittlich zeigten sich bisher allerdings weniger konsistente Befunde. So ergaben sich in einigen Studien überhaupt keine Effekte des Leseselbstkonzepts auf die spätere Leseleistung (Aunola et al., 2002; Chapman & Tunmer, 1997; Retelsdorf et al., 2011), während dieser Zusammenhang in anderen Studien zumindest teilweise, vor allem aber bei jüngeren Kindern, gefunden wurde (Chapman & Tunmer, 1995; Chapman et al., 2000; Retelsdorf et al., 2014).

2 Lesegewohnheiten als vermittelndes Merkmal

Der beschriebene Zusammenhang zwischen Leseselbstkonzept und Leseleistung wurde zwar meist als direkter Zusammenhang untersucht. Theoretisch liegen dem aber vermittelnde Prozesse zugrunde, die etwa im Erwartungs-Wert-Modell der Lesemotivation von Möller und Schiefele (2004) beschrieben sind. Dort wird argumentiert, dass die Wahrnehmung eigener hoher Lesefähigkeiten zu einer höheren Wahrscheinlichkeit gewohnheitsmäßigen Lesens führt, während für Personen mit geringem Leseselbstkonzept eher eine geringe Lesegewohnheit angenommen wird (siehe auch Morgan & Fuchs, 2007; Stanovich, 1986; Wigfield & Guthrie, 1997). Gewohnheiten entwickeln sich nämlich aus wiederholt gezeigtem Verhalten in bestimmten Situationen (Lally, van Jaarsveld, Potts & Wardle, 2010; Wood, Quinn & Kashy, 2002). Damit ein Verhalten aber überhaupt initialisiert wird, muss klassischen Annahmen von Erwartungs-Wert-Theorien zufolge neben dem Wert einer Handlung auch die Erfolgserwartung hoch sein, dass eine Handlung durchgeführt werden kann (Atkinson, 1957; Wigfield & Eccles, 2000). Bezogen auf die Lesegewohnheit bedeutet dies, dass ein hohes Leseselbstkonzept im Sinne einer Erfolgserwartung dazu führt, dass Lesehandlungen mit einer höheren Wahrscheinlichkeit initialisiert werden und dass diese bei wiederholtem Auftreten habitualisert werden können.

Eine höhere Lesegewohnheit wiederum führt dann über die hieraus resultierende Beschäftigung mit Texten zu verbesserten Lesefähigkeiten (Becker, McElvany & Kortenbruck, 2010; Mol & Bus, 2011). Guthrie, Wigfield, Metsala und Cox (1999) erklären dies unter anderem über Übungseffekte und eine damit einhergehende höhere Lesegeschwindigkeit. Durch zunehmende Automatisierung des Lesens werden dann kognitive Ressourcen frei, die für das Verstehen der Textinhalte genutzt werden können (vgl. Juel, 1988). Eine weitere Erklärung dieses Zusammenhangs sehen Guthrie et al. (1999) darin, dass geübte Leserinnen und Leser eher in der Lage sind, ihre kognitiven und motivationalen Leseziele besser aufeinander abzustimmen, so dass der Einsatz von Lesestrategien zur tieferen Verarbeitung der Textinhalte erleichtert wird.

Der indirekte Effekt über die Lesegewohnheiten auf die Leseleistung konnte für die Lesemotivation, für die der Prozess ähnlich postuliert wird, bereits wiederholt gezeigt werden (z.B. Becker et al., 2010; McElvany, Kortenbruck & Becker, 2008; Schiefele et al., 2012; Stutz, Schaffner & Schiefele, 2016; Wang & Guthrie, 2004). Für das Leseselbstkonzept wurde der indirekte Effekt über Lesegewohnheit auf die Leseleistung bisher aber kaum untersucht. In einer der wenigen Ausnahmen fanden Retelsdorf und Möller (2008) zudem inkonsistente Befunde zwischen den zwei Teilstudien ihrer Arbeit. So zeigte sich zwar jeweils ein signifikanter positiver Effekt der Leseaktivität als Proxy für Lesegewohnheit auf das Leseverständnis, der Zusammenhang zwischen Leseselbstkonzept auf die Lesegewohnheit wurde jedoch nur in einer der beiden Teilstudien signifikant. Insgesamt erscheint die Annahme dennoch gerechtfertigt, dass der Zusammenhang zwischen Leseselbstkonzept und Leseleistung über die Lesegewohnheit erklärt werden kann. Dabei muss jedoch nicht zwangsläufig von einem direkten Zusammenhang von Leseselbstkonzept und Leseleistung ausgegangen werden. Vielmehr scheint es plausibel, die beschriebene Wirkkette eher als indirekten Effekt und nicht im Sinne einer klassischen Mediation zu untersuchen (vgl. Collins, Graham & Flaherty, 1998; MacKinnon, Fairchild & Fritz, 2007).

3 Konzeptualisierung und Messung von Lesegewohnheiten

Eine Einschränkung bisheriger Studien – unabhängig davon, ob indirekte Effekte der Lesemotivation oder des Leseselbstkonzepts auf die Leseleistung untersucht wurden – liegt in der Messung und Konzeptualisierung der vermittelnden Variable. Diese wird im Allgemeinen ganz unterschiedlich als Lesehäufigkeit, Leseverhalten, Lesevolumen, Lesemenge, Leseaktivität oder Lesegewohnheit beschrieben und operationalisiert. Die Messung reicht dabei von Ein-Item-Messungen (OECD, 2010) über Kurzfragebögen (McElvany et al., 2008) und Tagebücher (Allen, Cipielewski & Stanovich, 1992) bis zur Erfassung der Kenntnis von Buchtiteln (Schroeder, Segbers & Schröter, 2016). Gemein ist diesen sehr verschiedenen Herangehensweisen, dass ihnen zumindest implizit ein Verständnis von Lesegewohnheit zugrunde liegen, sie sich dabei aber in erster Linie auf die Menge des Gelesenen bzw. die Häufigkeit des Lesens oder gar die Vertrautheit mit Populärliteratur beschränken. Gewohnheit umfasst aber mehr als nur das Ausmaß oder die Frequenz eines Verhaltens (z. B. Verplanken, 2006).

Entsprechend haben Schmidt und Retelsdorf (2016) aufbauend auf gesundheitspsychologischen Arbeiten aus der Arbeitsgruppe um Verplanken (z. B. Verplanken, 2006; Verplanken, Myrbakk & Rudi, 2005; Verplanken & Orbell, 2003) eine theoretisch elaboriertere Konzeptualisierung von Lesegewohnheit und deren Erfassung mittels Fragebogen vorgeschlagen. In den zugrunde liegenden Arbeiten werden Gewohnheiten allgemein definiert als „learned sequences of acts that have become automatic responses to specific cues, and are functional in obtaining certain goals or end states" (Verplanken & Aarts, 1999, S. 104). Lesegewohnheit wird nach Schmidt und Retelsdorf (2016) weiterhin eindimensional beschrieben, umfasst aber neben früheren Leseerfahrungen, die relevant sind, um eine Gewohnheit erst zu entwickeln und anschließend zu erhalten, auch die Aspekte Automatisiertheit und Ausdruck der eigenen Identität. Letzteres gilt als wichtiges Element von Gewohnheiten, da diese das Verhaltensrepertoire substanziell beeinflussen und damit persönliche Identität widerspiegeln. Schließlich hängen Gewohnheiten eng damit zusammen, wie wir unseren Alltag verbringen. Die Automatizität von habitualisiertem Verhalten stellt den Kern der Konzeption dar (Verplanken, 2006). Sie kann in mentale Effizienz, eine reduzierte Bewusstheit der Verhaltensinitiierung und ein Maß von fehlender Kontrolle unterteilt werden (Bargh, 1994). Der Ansatz von Schmidt und Retelsdorf (2016) zeigte zum einen gute psychometrische Kennwerte und zum anderen ergaben sich erste Hinweise auf die Validität des Verfahrens, etwa bei der Vorhersage der Leseleistung in Konkurrenz zur Lesehäufigkeit.

4 Die vorliegende Studie

In der vorliegenden Arbeit sollen in einem prospektiven Design von der 11. bis zur 13. Klasse insgesamt drei Forschungsfragen untersucht werden. In Forschungsfrage 1 haben wir zunächst untersucht, ob es überhaupt noch zu einem substanziellen mittleren Leistungszuwachs im Lesen in dieser Altersgruppe kommt. Bisherige Forschung hat gezeigt, dass Zuwächse im Lesen vor allem in der Primar- und zu Beginn der Sekundarstufe zu verzeichnen sind, während im weiteren Verlauf der Sekundarstufe kaum noch Zuwächse zu verzeichnen sind (z. B. Bloom, Hill, Black & Lipsey, 2008; Cameron, Grimm, Steele, Castro-Schilo & Grissmer, 2015; Nagy, Retelsdorf, Schiepe-Tiska, Goldhammer & Lüdtke, in Druck). Entsprechend haben wir eher ein stabiles Niveau der mittleren Leseleistung erwartet. Selbst wenn die Leseleistung im Mittel stagniert, ist dennoch mit einer substanziellen Variabilität der Veränderung der Leseleistung zu rechnen. Diese sollte in der vorliegenden Arbeit durch Leseselbstkonzept und Lesegewohnheit erklärt werden. In Forschungsfrage 2 haben wir dafür zunächst den direkten Effekt des Leseselbstkonzepts auf den Leistungszuwachs untersucht. Wie eingangs beschrieben ist die Befundlage zu diesem Zusammenhang in längsschnittlichen Designs inkonsistent. Wenn überhaupt, zeigten sich entsprechende Zusammenhänge bei jüngeren Kindern (Chapman et al., 2000; Retelsdorf et al., 2014), so dass wir maximal einen kleinen direkten Effekt des Leseselbstkonzepts erwarteten. Als zentrale Annahme des vorliegenden Beitrags haben wir in Forschungsfrage 3 schließlich den erwarteten indirekten Effekt des Leseselbstkonzepts über die Lesegewohnheit auf die Veränderung in der Leseleistung getestet.

5 Methode

5.1 Stichprobe

Die Daten der vorliegenden Studie stammen aus dem Projekt „Lesen in der Sekundarstufe" (LISA). LISA war eine längsschnittlich angelegte Studie in Schleswig-Holstein mit insgesamt sechs Messzeitpunkten vom Beginn der 5. Klasse bis zum Abitur, die ursprünglich von Jens Möller ins Leben gerufen wurde (für eine ausführlichere Darstellung des Projekts siehe Leucht & Köller, 2016; Retelsdorf & Möller, 2013). Für die hier präsentierten Analysen wurden Daten des fünften (Mitte Klasse 11) und sechsten (Ende Klasse 13) Messzeitpunkts (MZP) genutzt. Da sich die Ausrichtung der LISA-Studie in der 13. Klasse zu einem breiten Assessment mathematischer, naturwissenschaftlicher und fremdsprachlicher Kompetenzen im Fach Englisch zum Vergleich allgemeinbildender und beruflicher Gymnasien in Schleswig-Holstein gewandelt hat (Leucht & Köller, 2016; Leucht, Nagy & Köller, 2016), hat nur eine Teilgruppe der Schülerinnen und Schüler in dieser Jahrgangsstufe an den allgemeinbildenden Gymnasien einen Testblock zur Erfassung der Leseleitung bearbeitet. Die entsprechende Stichprobe umfasste N = 522 Schülerinnen und Schüler (55 % weiblich, Alter zu MZP1: $M = 17.10$, $SD = 0.53$). Für diese Gruppe lagen zusätzlich zu den Leistungsdaten aus der 13. Klasse (hier MZP2) Selbstbericht- und bzw. oder Leistungsdaten aus der 11. Klasse (hier MZP1) vor. Alle Schülerinnen und Schüler besuchten die gymnasiale Oberstufe (91 % Gymnasium, 9 % Gesamtschule).

5.2 Instrumente

5.2.1 Lesegewohnheit

Die Lesegewohnheit der Schülerinnen und Schüler wurde zu MZP1 mit dem zehn Items umfassenden Self-Report Habit Index for Reading (SRHI-R) von Schmidt und Retelsdorf (2016) erfasst. Dieser Fragebogen basiert auf den eingangs genannten inhaltlichen Aspekten der Lesegewohnheit – früheren Leseerfahrungen, Automatisiertheit und Ausdruck der eigenen Identität – und erfasst die Lesegewohnheit als eindimensionales Konstrukt. Den Items war das Präfix „Lesen zum Vergnügen ..." vorangestellt. Die einzelnen Items bestanden dann aus Vervollständigungen der Aussage (z. B. „... ist unverzichtbar für mich."). Die Schülerinnen und Schüler beantworteten die Items auf einer fünfstufigen Skala mit den Ankern „stimmt gar nicht" und „stimmt genau". Die modellbasierte Reliabilität der Skala nach McDonald (1999) war hervorragend ($\omega = .96$).

5.2.2 Leseselbstkonzept

Das Leseselbstkonzept zu MZP1 wurde mit der entsprechenden Skala des Fragebogens zur habituellen Lesemotivation (Möller & Bonerad, 2007) erfasst. Die Skala umfasst vier Items (z. B.: „Ich kann Texte sehr gut und schnell verstehen"), die auf einer vierstufigen Skala von „stimmt gar nicht" bis „stimmt genau" zu beantworten waren. Die modellbasierte Reliabilität war zufriedenstellend ($\omega = .75$).

5.2.3 Leseleistung

Die Leseleistung wurde zu beiden Messzeitpunkten mit demselben Subtest zum Leseverständnis aus dem Ländervergleich des Instituts zur Qualitätsentwicklung im Bildungswesen gemessen (Köller, Knigge & Tesch, 2010). Den Schülerinnen und Schülern wurde ein Stimulustext präsentiert, zu dem sie insgesamt 25 Fragen in verschiedenen Formaten (Multiple-Choice-Items, Zuordnungsaufgaben, offene Antwortformate) bearbeiten sollten. Alle Antworten wurden dichotom kodiert. Die Reliabilität der weighted likelihood estimates (WLEs) war zu beiden Messzeitpunkten zufriedenstellend (MZP1: .68, MZP2: .77).

5.3 Statistische Analysen

Zur Prüfung der Leistungsentwicklung haben wir in der Software *Mplus* 7.4 ein latentes Differenzwertmodell geschätzt (siehe im Überblick McArdle, 2009). Bei dieser Methode werden interindividuelle Unterschiede in der Veränderung in einer Variablen durch eine messfehlerfreie latente Variable repräsentiert. In der vorliegenden Studie wurde die Veränderung der Leseleistung von der 11. zur 13. Klasse in einem entsprechenden Modell geschätzt. Dafür wurden mit der Software ConQuest zunächst WLEs als Fähigkeitsparameter geschätzt, wobei die Itemparameter zu MZP2 auf die Werte der Schätzung zu MZP1 fixiert waren. Der Mittelwert der Fähigkeiten zu MZP1 wurde auf den Wert Null fixiert, während zu MZP2 keine weiteren Restriktionen mehr eingeführt wurden, so dass die Werte zu MZP2 direkt als Leistungszuwachs interpretierbar sind. Die WLEs wurden dann als single indicator genutzt, um im latenten Differenzwertmodell latente Variablen der Leistung zu beiden Messzeitpunkten zu spezifizieren. Bei diesem Vorgehen muss der Wert der Residualvarianz des manifesten Indikators fixiert werden, damit das Modell identifiziert ist. Wir haben diese auf den Mittelwert der quadrierten Standardfehler der individuellen WLEs aus der Schätzung in ConQuest fixiert. Das resultierende Modell ist mit Null Freiheitsgraden genau identifiziert und liefert als interessierende Parameter Schätzungen der latenten Mittelwerte (θ) und Varianzen (φ^2) der Ausgangsleistung (θ_{MZP1}, $\varphi_{MZP1}{}^2$) sowie des Differenzwerts (θ_Δ, $\varphi_\Delta{}^2$).

Zur Prüfung des indirekten Effekts von Leseselbstkonzept über Lesegewohnheit auf die Veränderung der Leseleistung wurden das Leseselbstkonzept und die Lesegewohnheit als zusätzliche Kovariaten in das Modell aufgenommen. Beide wurden jeweils als latente Variable mit den zugehörigen Items als Indikatoren spezifiziert. Wie schon in der Studie von Schmidt und Retelsdorf (2016) wurden dabei für die Lesegewohnheit Korrelationen zwischen zwei Paaren von Residuen ähnlicher Items zugelassen. Lesegewohnheit und Leseselbstkonzept wurden als Prädiktoren des latenten Differenzwerts in das Modell aufgenommen. Zudem wurde die Lesegewohnheit durch das Leseselbstkonzept vorhergesagt und Korrelationen beider Variablen mit der Leseleistung zu MZP1 zugelassen. Der indirekte Effekt von Leseselbstkonzept über Lesegewohnheit auf die Differenz der Leseleistung wurde mittels der in *Mplus* implementieren Delta-Methode (MacKinnon, 2008) auf statistische Signifikanz getestet. Dabei waren wir in erster Linie an einer Wirkkette der drei Variablen interessiert, bei der das Leseselbstkonzept als unabhängige Variable die Lesegewohnheit als Mediator beeinflusst, die wiederum mit der Veränderung der Leseleistung als Outcome zusammenhängt. Bei der Prüfung dieser Art von indirekten Effekten ist eine signifikante Korrelation zwischen unabhängiger Variable und Outcome nicht zwingend erforderlich (Collins et al., 1998; MacKinnon et al., 2007).

Zur Beurteilung der Anpassungsgüte des Modells haben wir in dieser Studie in erster Linie den Root Mean Square Error of Approximation (RMSEA), den Tucker-Lewis Index (TLI), den Comparative Fit Index (CFI) und das Standardized Root Mean Square Residual (SRMR) verwendet. Zudem berichten wir die robuste χ^2-Statistik, der aber aufgrund ihrer Sensitivität gegenüber großen Stichproben keine allzu große Bedeutung bei der Beurteilung der Modellgüte zugemessen werden sollte (z. B. Marsh, 2007). Für TLI und CFI gelten Werte über .90 oder .95, für den RMSEA Werte unter .08 oder .05 und für den SRMR Werte unter .05 oder .10 als Zeichen für eine gute oder akzeptable Modelanpassung (Kline, 2010; Marsh, 2007).

Knapp 12 % der Daten fehlten durchschnittlich pro Variable. Daher wurden mittels multipler Imputation (für eine Einführung siehe z. B. Graham, 2009; Lüdtke, Robitzsch, Trautwein & Köller, 2007) $m = 20$ vollständige Datensätze erstellt. Alle folgenden Analysen wurden dann entsprechend der Regeln von Rubin (1987) zwanzigfach durchgeführt und die Ergebnisse automatisch in *Mplus* kombiniert.

Zur Berücksichtigung der hierarchischen Datenstruktur (Schülerinnen und Schüler in Schulen) wurden in allen Analysen robuste Standardfehler geschätzt (in *Mplus*: Type = complex, Estimator = MLR).

6 Ergebnisse

6.1 Deskriptive Statistiken und Korrelationen

In Tabelle 1 sind die deskriptiven Statistiken sowie die Korrelationen der verwendeten Variablen dargestellt. Zunächst sieht man, dass das Leseselbstkonzept über dem theoretischen Skalenmittelwert liegt, während die Lesegewohnheit sich etwa auf dem Niveau des theoretischen Skalenmittelwerts befindet. Für die Leseleistung zeigte sich in den WLEs deskriptiv ein leichter Zuwachs von MZP1 zu MZP2.[1] Zudem waren alle Variablen signifikant und positiv miteinander korreliert.

Tabelle 1. Deskriptive Statistiken und manifeste Korrelationen der verwendeten Variablen ($N = 522$)

	M	*SD*	1	2	3
1 Leseselbstkonzept	3.10	0.52			
2 Lesegewohnheit	3.11	1.16	.23***		
3 Leseleistung MZP1	-0.01	1.01	.28***	.26***	
4 Leseleistung MZP2	0.14	1.16	.19***	.31***	.35***

*** $p < .001$.

1 Die Summenwerte der Leistungstests lagen bei einem theoretischen Maximum von 25 Punkten bei $M_{MZP1} = 16.84$ ($SD_{MZP1} = 3.50$) bzw. $M_{MZP2} = 17.26$ ($SD_{MZP2} = 4.16$).

6.2 Leistungsentwicklung und Zusammenhänge mit Leseselbstkonzept und Lesegewohnheit

In dem latenten Differenzwertmodell ohne Kovariaten (saturiert) ergaben sich zur Beantwortung von Forschungsfrage 1 entsprechend der Schätzung der Fähigkeitsparameter ein Ausgangsniveau von $\theta_{MZP1} = -0.01$ ($\varphi_{MZP1}{}^2 = 0.69$) sowie ein positiver Differenzwert von $\theta_{\Delta} = 0.15$ ($\varphi_{\Delta}{}^2 = 0.99$), der aber nur tendenziell von Null abwich ($p = .065$). Allerdings zeigte sich eine substanzielle und signifikante Varianz für den Differenzwert ($p < .001$), die in einem weiteren Schritt durch Leseselbstkonzept und Lesegewohnheit erklärt werden sollte.

Das latente Differenzwertmodell mit Kovariaten zeigte eine akzeptable Passung zu den Daten, $\chi^2(98) = 340.47$, CFI = .95, TLI = .94, RMSEA = .07, SRMR = .04. Es ergaben sich wie erwartet signifikante positive Pfade von Leseselbstkonzept auf Lesegewohnheit und von Lesegewohnheit auf den Differenzwert der Leseleistung (siehe Tabelle 2). Der direkte Pfad von Leseselbstkonzept auf den Differenzwert (Forschungsfrage 2) wurde nicht signifikant. Dies zeigte sich übrigens auch in einem Modell ohne Lesegewohnheit ($\beta = -.03$, $SE = 0.09$, $p = .761$). Zudem zeigte sich für die Beantwortung von Forschungsfrage 3 ein signifikanter indirekter Effekt von Leseselbstkonzept über Lesegewohnheit auf den Differenzwert der Leseleitung ($\beta = .04$, $SE = 0.02$, $p = .035$).

Tabelle 2. Zusammenhänge zwischen Leseleistung zu MZP1 und ihrer Veränderung mit Leseselbstkonzept und Lesegewohnheit aus dem latenten Differenzwertmodell (*N* = 522)

	r/β^a	*SE*	z^b	*p*
UNGERICHTETE ZUSAMMENHÄNGE				
Leseleistung MZP1 ↔ Leseselbstkonzept	.37	0.07	5.42	.000
Leseleistung MZP1 ↔ Lesegewohnheit	.24	0.04	5.38	.000
GERICHTETE ZUSAMMENHÄNGE				
Leseselbstkonzept → Lesegewohnheit	.24	0.05	4.50	.000
Leseselbstkonzept → Leseleistung (θ_{Δ})	-.06	0.09	-0.72	.471
Lesegewohnheit → Leseleistung (θ_{Δ})	.15	0.06	2.54	.011

Anmerkung. [a] Dargestellt sind standardisierte Parameter (bei ungerichteten Zusammenhängen Korrelationen, bei gerichteten Zusammenhängen Regressionsgewichte). [b] Die Teststatistik in *Mplus* ist approximativ *z*-verteilt (Muthén & Muthén, 2015).

7 Diskussion

Der häufig postulierte indirekte Zusammenhang zwischen Leseselbstkonzept, Lesegewohnheit und Leseleistung war bislang kaum Gegenstand empirischer Untersuchungen. In der vorliegenden Arbeit wurde diese Forschungslücke adressiert, wobei die Lesegewohnheit anders als in bisherigen Studien breiter als lediglich durch Lesehäufigkeit definiert und erfasst wurde. Zudem konnte durch das prospektive Design der Studie auch die Veränderung der Leseleistung in der gymnasialen Oberstufe untersucht werden. Passend zu aktuelleren Befunden zur Entwicklung der Leseleistung bei älteren Kindern (Cameron et al., 2015; Nagy et al., in Druck) zeigte sich bei der Beantwortung von Forschungsfrage 1 kein substanzieller mittlerer Zuwachs. Auch wenn wir Deckeneffekte ausschließen können (siehe Fußnote 1), könnte der ausbleibende Zuwachs ein Effekt des verwendeten Leistungstests sein. Dieser ist ursprünglich für eine etwas jüngere Zielgruppe entwickelt worden, so dass möglicherweise nicht die Aspekte der Leseleistung erfasst werden, die in der hier untersuchten Population im Kern relevant sind. Andererseits spiegelt unser Ergebnis einen typischen Befund zur Entwicklung der Leseleistung bei älteren Kindern bzw. Jugendlichen wider. Demnach scheint sich das Niveau der Leseleistung etwa ab Mitte bis Ende der Sekundarstufe I zu stabilisieren.

Der in Forschungsfrage 2 untersuchte direkte Effekt des Leseselbstkonzepts auf die Veränderung der Leseleistung zeigte sich wie in anderen längsschnittlichen Studien nicht (vgl. Aunola et al., 2002; Retelsdorf et al., 2011). Bezüglich der Kernfragestellung (Forschungsfrage 3) des vorliegenden Beitrags zeigte sich aber wie erwartet, dass Variabilität in der Leistungsentwicklung durch die Lesegewohnheit vorhersagbar war, die ihrerseits vom Leseselbstkonzept abhing. Der entsprechende indirekte Effekt dieser Wirkkette war ebenfalls wie erwartet signifikant.

Der signifikante indirekte Effekt stützt die theoretische Annahme, die unter anderem im Erwartungs-Wert-Modell der Lesemotivation (Möller & Schiefele, 2004) postuliert wird. In dem Modell führt ein gesteigertes Leseselbstkonzept zu einem höheren Ausmaß an Textexposition, so dass letztlich ein höheres Maß an Übung zu einer besseren Leistung führt. Berücksichtigt man zudem die deutliche Evidenz, dass das Leseselbstkonzept wiederum von der Leseleistung der Schülerinnen und Schüler abhängt (Morgan & Fuchs, 2007; Retelsdorf et al., 2014), zeigt sich hierin auch eine Bestätigung des Prozesses, der schon früh mit dem so genannten Matthäuseffekt in Verbindung gebracht wurde (Stanovich, 1986). Demnach öffnet sich die Leistungsschere zwischen guten und schlechten Leserinnen und Lesern immer weiter.

Neben dem Befund zu indirekten Effekten von Leseselbstkonzept über Lesegewohnheit auf die Leseleistung liefert unser Beitrag auch weitere Evidenz für die Validität der kürzlich entwickelten Skala zu Erfassung der Lesegewohnheit von Schmidt und Retelsdorf (2016). So zeigte sich, dass die postulierten Zusammenhänge mit der Skala gefunden wurden und dass diese sogar in einem Alter, in dem Leseleistung bereits recht stabil ist, noch ausreichend prädiktive Kraft hat, um Variabilität in der Veränderung der Leseleistung zu erklären.

Zusammenfassend konnten wir in dem vorliegenden Beitrag einmal mehr zeigen, dass für die Leseleistung in fortgeschrittenem Alter nur noch geringe Zuwächse zu verzeichnen waren (s.a. Cameron et al., 2015; Nagy et al., in Druck). Zudem liefert unsere Studie Hinweise darauf, dass der Zusammenhang zwischen dem Leseselbstkonzept und der Leseleistung wie postuliert (z.B. Möller & Schiefele, 2004;

Retelsdorf et al., 2014) über die Lesegewohnheiten vermittelt wird. Abschließend sei angemerkt, dass in der vorliegenden Arbeit mit der gymnasialen Oberstufe eine eher untypische Alters- und Leistungsgruppe für die untersuchten Zusammenhänge herangezogen wurde. Zukünftige Forschung sollte die Befunde bei jüngeren Kindern mit einer größeren Leistungsheterogenität replizieren – auch um die Arbeiten von Jens Möller (Möller & Bonerad, 2007; Möller & Schiefele, 2004; Retelsdorf et al., 2011, 2014; Retelsdorf & Möller, 2013; Schiefele et al., 2012) zum Zusammenspiel von Lesemotivation, Leseselbstkonzept und Leseleistung künftig weiter zu würdigen und fortzuführen.

Literatur

Allen, L., Cipielewski, J. & Stanovich, K. E. (1992). Multiple indicators of children's reading habits and attitudes: Construct validity and cognitive correlates. *Journal of Educational Psychology, 84*, 489–503.

Atkinson, J. W. (1957). Motivational determinants of risktaking behavior. *Psychological Review, 64*, 359–372.

Aunola, K., Leskinen, E., Onatsu-Arvilommi, T. & Nurmi, J.-E. (2002). Three methods for studying developmental change: A case of reading skills and self-concept. *British Journal of Educational Psychology, 72*, 343–364.

Bargh, J. A. (1994). The four horsemen of automaticity: Awareness, intention, efficiency, and control in social cognition. In R. S. Wyer & T. K. Srull (Eds.), *Handbook of social cognition* (pp. 1–40). Hillsdale, NJ: Lawrence Erlbaum Associates, Inc.

Becker, M., McElvany, N. & Kortenbruck, M. (2010). Intrinsic and extrinsic reading motivation as predictors of reading literacy: A longitudinal study. *Journal of Educational Psychology, 102*, 773–785.

Bloom, H. S., Hill, C. J., Black, A. R. & Lipsey, M. W. (2008). Performance trajectories and performance gaps as achievement effect-size benchmarks for educational interventions. *Journal of Research on Educational Effectiveness, 1*, 289–328.

Cameron, C. E., Grimm, K. J., Steele, J. S., Castro-Schilo, L. & Grissmer, D. W. (2015). Nonlinear Gompertz curve models of achievement gaps in mathematics and reading. *Journal of Educational Psychology, 107*, 789–804.

Chapman, J. W. & Tunmer, W. E. (1995). Development of young children's reading self-concepts: An examination of emerging subcomponents and their relationship with reading achievement. *Journal of Educational Psychology, 87*, 154–167.

Chapman, J. W. & Tunmer, W. E. (1997). A longitudinal study of beginning reading achievement and reading self-concept. *British Journal of Educational Psychology, 67*, 279–291.

Chapman, J. W., Tunmer, W. E. & Prochnow, J. E. (2000). Early reading related skills and performance, reading self-concept, and the development of academic self-concept: A longitudinal study. *Journal of Educational Psychology, 92*, 703–708.

Collins, L. M., Graham, J. W. & Flaherty, B. P. (1998). An alternative framework for defining mediation. *Multivariate Behavioral Research, 33*, 295–312.

Graham, J. W. (2009). Missing data analysis: Making it work in the real world. *Annual Review of Psychology, 60*, 549–576.

Guthrie, J. T., Wigfield, A., Metsala, J. L. & Cox, K. E. (1999). Motivational and cognitive predictors of text comprehension and reading amount. *Scientific Studies of Reading, 3*, 231–256.

Juel, C. (1988). Learning to read and write: A longitudinal study of 54 children from first through fourth grades. *Journal of Educational Psychology, 80*, 437–447.

Katzir, T., Lesaux, N. K. & Kim, Y.-S. (2009). The role of reading self-concept and home literacy practices in fourth grade reading comprehension. *Reading and Writing, 22*, 261–276.

Kline, R. B. (2010). *Principles and practice of structural equation modeling*. New York, NY: Guilford Press.

Köller, O., Knigge, M. & Tesch, B. (Hrsg.). (2010). *Sprachliche Kompetenzen im Ländervergleich*. Münster: Waxmann.

Lally, P., van Jaarsveld, C. H. M., Potts, H. W. W. & Wardle, J. (2010). How are habits formed: Modelling habit formation in the real world. *European Journal of Social Psychology, 40*, 998–1009.

Leucht, M. & Köller, O. (2016). Anlage und Durchführung der Studie. In M. Leucht, N. Kampa & O. Köller (Hrsg.), *Fachleistungen beim Abitur. Vergleich allgemeinbildender und beruflicher Gymnasien in Schleswig-Holstein* (S. 79–98). Münster: Waxmann.

Leucht, M., Nagy, G. & Köller, O. (2016). LISA-6: Eine Studie zur Öffnung von Wegen zur Hochschulreife in Schleswig-Holstein. In M. Leucht, N. Kampa & O. Köller (Hrsg.), *Fachleistungen beim Abitur. Vergleich allgemeinbildender und beruflicher Gymnasien in Schleswig-Holstein* (S. 11–32). Münster: Waxmann.

Lüdtke, O., Robitzsch, A., Trautwein, U. & Köller, O. (2007). Umgang mit fehlenden Werten in der psychologischen Forschung. *Psychologische Rundschau, 58*, 103–117.

MacKinnon, D. P. (2008). *Introduction to statistical mediation analysis*. New York, NY: Lawrence Erlbaum Associates, Inc.

MacKinnon, D. P., Fairchild, A. J. & Fritz, M. S. (2007). Mediation analysis. *Annual Review of Psychology, 58*, 593–614.

Marsh, H. W. (2007). Application of confirmatory factor analysis and structural equation modeling in sport/exercise psychology. In G. Tenenbaum & R. C. Eklund (Eds.), *Handbook of sport psychology* (pp. 774–798). Hoboken, NJ: Wiley.

Marsh, H. W., Smith, I. D. & Barnes, J. (1985). Multidimensional self-concepts: Relations with sex and academic achievement. *Journal of Educational Psychology, 77*, 581–596.

McArdle, J. J. (2009). Latent variable modeling of differences and changes with longitudinal data. *Annual Review of Psychology, 60*, 577–605.

McDonald, R. P. (1999). *Test theory: A unified treatment*. Mahwah, NJ: Lawrence Erlbaum Associates, Inc.

McElvany, N., Kortenbruck, M. & Becker, M. (2008). Lesekompetenz und Lesemotivation. Entwicklung und Mediation des Zusammenhangs durch Leseverhalten. *Zeitschrift für Pädagogische Psychologie, 22*, 207–219.

Mol, S. E. & Bus, A. G. (2011). To read or not to read: A meta-analysis of print exposure from infancy to early adulthood. *Psychological Bulletin, 137*, 267–296.

Möller, J. & Bonerad, E.-M. (2007). Fragebogen zur habituellen Lesemotivation. *Psychologie in Erziehung und Unterricht, 54*, 259–267.

Möller, J. & Schiefele, U. (2004). Motivationale Grundlagen der Lesekompetenz. In U. Schiefele, C. Artelt, W. Schneider & P. Stanat (Hrsg.), *Struktur, Entwicklung und Förderung von Lesekompetenz. Vertiefende Analysen im Rahmen von PISA 2000* (S. 101–124). Wiesbaden: Verlag für Sozialwissenschaften.

Morgan, P. L. & Fuchs, D. (2007). Is there a bidirectional relationship between children's reading skills and reading motivation? *Exceptional Children, 73*, 165–183.

Muthén, L. K. & Muthén, B. O. (2015). *Mplus User's Guide* (7th ed.). Los Angeles, CA: Autoren.

Nagy, G., Retelsdorf, J., Schiepe-Tiska, A., Goldhammer, F. & Lüdtke, O. (in Druck). Veränderungen der Lesekompetenz von der 9. zur 10. Klasse: Differenzielle Entwicklungen in Abhängigkeit der Schulform und des soziodemografischen Hintergrunds? *Zeitschrift für Erziehungswissenschaft*.

OECD. (2010). *PISA 2009 results: Learning trends. Changes in student performance since 2000*. Paris: OECD.

Retelsdorf, J., Köller, O. & Möller, J. (2011). On the effects of motivation on reading performance growth in secondary school. *Learning and Instruction, 21*, 550–559.

Retelsdorf, J., Köller, O. & Möller, J. (2014). Reading achievement and reading self-concept – testing the reciprocal effects model. *Learning and Instruction, 29*, 21–30.

Retelsdorf, J. & Möller, J. (2008). Familiäre Bedingungen und individuelle Prädiktoren der Lesekompetenz von Schülerinnen und Schülern. *Psychologie in Erziehung und Unterricht, 55*, 227–237.

Retelsdorf, J. & Möller, J. (2013). Lesemotivation und Lesekompetenz in der Sekundarstufe I: Zentrale Ergebnisse der LISA-Studie. In C. Rosebrock & A. Bertschi-Kaufmann (Hrsg.), *Literalität erfassen: Bildungspolitisch, kulturell, individuell* (S. 219–230). Weinheim: Beltz Juventa.

Rubin, D. B. (1987). *Multiple imputation for nonresponse in surveys*. New York, NY: J. Wiley & Sons.

Schiefele, U., Schaffner, E., Möller, J. & Wigfield, A. (2012). Dimensions of reading motivation and their relation to reading behavior and competence. *Reading Research Quarterly, 47*, 427–463.

Schmidt, F. T. C. & Retelsdorf, J. (2016). A new measure of reading habit: Going beyond behavioral frequency. *Frontiers in Psychology, 7:1364*.

Schroeder, S., Segbers, J. & Schröter, P. (2016). Der Kinder-Titelrekognitionstest (K-TRT): Ein Instrument zur Erfassung des Lesevolumens von Kindern im Deutschen. *Diagnostica, 62*, 16–30.

Stanovich, K. E. (1986). Matthew effects in reading: Some consequences of individual differences in the acquisition of literacy. *Reading Research Quarterly, 21*, 360–406.

Stutz, F., Schaffner, E. & Schiefele, U. (2016). Relations among reading motivation, reading amount, and reading comprehension in the early elementary grades. *Learning and Individual Differences, 45*, 101–113.

Verplanken, B. (2006). Beyond frequency: Habit as mental construct. *British Journal of Social Psychology, 45*, 639–656.

Verplanken, B. & Aarts, H. (1999). Habit, attitude, and planned behaviour: Is habit an empty construct or an interesting case of goal-directed automaticity? *European Review of Social Psychology, 10*, 101–134.

Verplanken, B., Myrbakk, V. & Rudi, E. (2005). The measurement of habit. In T. Betsch & S. Haberstroh (Eds.), *The routines of decision making* (pp. 231–247). Mahwah, NJ: Lawrence Erlbaum Associates, Inc.

Verplanken, B. & Orbell, S. (2003). Reflections on past behavior: A self-report index of habit strength. *Journal of Applied Social Psychology, 33*, 1313–1330.

Wang, J. H.-Y. & Guthrie, J. T. (2004). Modeling the effects of intrinsic motivation, extrinsic motivation, amount of reading, and past reading achievement on text comprehension between U.S. and Chinese students. *Reading Research Quarterly, 39*, 162–186.

Wigfield, A. & Eccles, J. S. (2000). Expectancy-value theory of achievement motivation. *Contemporary Educational Psychology, 25*, 68–91.

Wigfield, A. & Guthrie, J. T. (1997). Relations of children's motivation for reading to the amount and breadth of their reading. *Journal of Educational Psychology, 89*, 420–432.

Wood, W., Quinn, J. M. & Kashy, D. A. (2002). Habits in everyday life: Thought, emotion, and action. *Journal of Personality and Social Psychology, 83*, 1281–1297.

Autoren

PROF. DR. JAN RETELSDORF
Fakultät für Erziehungswissenschaft, Universität Hamburg.

FABIAN T. C. SCHMIDT
Erziehungswissenschaft, IPN · Leibniz-Institut für die Pädagogik der Naturwissenschaften und Mathematik (IPN).

KONTAKT
Jan Retelsdorf, Universität Hamburg, Von-Melle-Park 8, 20146 Hamburg.
E-Mail: *jan.retelsdorf@uni-hamburg.de*

Zwischensprachlicher Transfer im immersiven Unterricht: Haben bilinguale Kinder Vorteile bei der Beherrschung von Rechtschreibstrategien?

JOHANNA FLECKENSTEIN, RAJA REBLE UND FRIEDERIKE HOHENSTEIN

ZUSAMMENFASSUNG: Vorteile immersiv unterrichteter Schülerinnen und Schüler bei erstsprachlichen Leistungen werden auf Transfereffekte zurückgeführt, die aufgrund von sprachunabhängigen sowie sprachabhängigen Fähigkeiten bei bilingualen Individuen zwischen Erst- und Zweitsprache auftreten. Während Orthographie im Allgemeinen als sprachspezifisches Oberflächenmerkmal gilt und somit nicht notwendigerweise von Transfereffekten betroffen ist, wird für immersiv unterrichtete Schülerinnen und Schüler ein Vorteil bei der Beherrschung grundlegender, sprachübergreifender Rechtschreibstrategien erwartet. In dem vorliegenden Beitrag wurde die Beherrschung von drei Rechtschreibstrategien mit der Hamburger Schreibprobe an n = 162 monolingual sowie n = 188 immersiv unterrichteten Schülerinnen und Schülern der dritten Klasse untersucht. Die Ergebnisse einer multiplen Regressionsanalyse zeigten erwartungsgemäß, dass immersiv unterrichtete Schülerinnen und Schüler auch unter Kontrolle sozioökonomischer und kognitiver Variablen – einschließlich der allgemeinen Rechtschreibleistung – die alphabetische und die morphematische Rechtschreibstrategie besser beherrschen als monolinguale Schülerinnen und Schüler. Die Ergebnisse werden im Hinblick auf ihre Implikationen für den Schriftspracherwerb im immersiven Unterricht diskutiert.

Schlüsselwörter: Immersiver Unterricht, Transfereffekte, Bilingualität, Rechtschreibung, Schriftspracherwerb

Interlanguage transfer in immersion education: Are there advantages for bilingual children concerning the mastery of orthographic strategies?

ABSTRACT: Advantages in first language skills of students in immersion education are attributed to transfer effects between the first and second language that are due to both language-independent and language-dependent skills. Orthography is generally viewed as a language-specific surface feature and is therefore not necessarily subject to transfer effects. However, common underlying orthographic strategies can be expected to be transferable across different languages. In the present study the mastery of three orthographic strategies was assessed by the *Hamburger Schreibprobe* on n = 162 monolingual and n = 188 immersion students in third grade. According to expectations the results of a multiple regression analysis showed that students in the immersion program outperformed monolingual students on the alphabetic and the morphematic strategy. Results are discussed with respect to their implication for literacy development in the immersion classroom.

Keywords: immersion education, transfer effects, bilingualism, orthography, literacy

Einleitung

Im immersiven Unterricht werden Schülerinnen und Schüler primär in einer Zweit- bzw. Fremdsprache (L2) unterrichtet. Neben deutlichen Vorteilen beim Erwerb der L2, erbringen immersiv unterrichtete Kinder häufig auch in ihrer Erstsprache (L1) vergleichbare bis bessere Lernleistungen (Genesee, 2004; Knell et al., 2007). Diese Vorteile lassen sich mit einem zwischensprachlichen Transfer erklären, der nach Cummins Interdependenzhypothese (1979) von bilingualen Individuen, aufgrund eines gemeinsamen Sprachenspeichers zwischen L1 und L2, geleistet wird. Die Transfereffekte beziehen sich laut Geva und Siegel (2000) entweder auf sprachunabhängige kognitive Fähigkeiten oder sprachabhängige Fähigkeiten, wobei letztere eine Ähnlichkeit struktureller Merkmale beider Sprachen voraussetzen (Ringbom, 2007). Einzelsprachspezifische Fähigkeiten hingegen, die sich für beide Sprachen unterscheiden (z. B. explizites Regel- und Formenwissen), sind nicht von Transfereffekten betroffen.

Der vorliegende Beitrag widmet sich einer differenzierteren Betrachtung von orthographischen Teilkompetenzen. Auch wenn Teile der Rechtschreibung oder die Rechtschreibung im Allgemeinen eher als sprachspezifische Oberflächenmerkmale bewertet werden, liegen der Rechtschreibleistung durchaus sprachübergreifende Fähigkeiten zugrunde (Goodrich & Lonigan, 2017). So baut die Orthographie auf verschiedenen komplexen und anspruchsvollen Konstruktionsprinzipien auf, die sich operationalisierbaren Rechtschreibstrategien zuordnen lassen (Frith, 1991; May, 2002; Nerius, 2007). Zu diesen zählen die alphabetische, die orthographische und die morphematische Rechtschreibstrategie, die im Laufe der Grundschulzeit erworben werden sollen (vgl. Abschnitt 1.3). Aufgrund dieser sprachübergreifenden Konstruktionsprinzipien sollte ein Transfer bei einzelnen Rechtschreibstrategien von der L2 in die L1 stattfinden können. Neben einem sprachunabhängigen Transfer sollte die relative Ähnlichkeit im Schriftsystem der beiden untersuchten Sprachen (Deutsch und Englisch) zudem einen sprachabhängigen Transfer von Strukturen ermöglichen und deren Erwerb unterstützen. Demnach wird erwartet, dass immersiv unterrichtete Schülerinnen und Schüler in ihrer L1 besser in der Lage sind, bestimmte Rechtschreibstrategien anzuwenden als monolingual unterrichtete Schülerinnen und Schüler, auch wenn die allgemeine Rechtschreibleistung und weitere Hintergrundmerkmale konstant gehalten werden.

1 Theoretischer Hintergrund

1.1 Immersiver Unterricht und die Interdependenzhypothese

Immersiver Unterricht (*French immersion*) ist eine Methode des Fremdsprachenunterrichts, bei der die L2 nicht wie im herkömmlichen Unterricht als Lehrgegenstand, sondern als Unterrichtssprache in diversen bzw. allen Schulfächern eingesetzt wird. Ziel immersiven Unterrichts ist es, L2-Kompetenzen gleichzeitig mit den anderen schulischen Leistungen zu fördern, ohne dabei die L1 zu verlieren (Baker & Wright, 2017). Neben den zu erwartenden Leistungszuwächsen in der L2, zeigen immersiv unterrichtete Schülerinnen und Schüler teilweise auch bessere Leistungen in der L1 als monolingual unterrichtete Altersgleiche (Gebauer, Zaunbauer & Möller, 2013). Diese werden auf zwischensprachliche Transferprozesse zurückgeführt.

Um einen theoretischen Rahmen für die Abhängigkeit der Sprach- und Denkprozesse in bilingualen Individuen zu geben, entwickelte Cummins (1979) die Interdependenzhypothese, die eine gegenseitige Abhängigkeit zwischen den Fähigkeiten in der L1 und der L2 und deren positive Auswirkungen für das Sprachenlernen erklären soll. Bestimmte grundlegende Kompetenzen werden zwischen den Sprachen übertragen und können so bei der Entwicklung entsprechender Fähigkeiten in der jeweils anderen Sprache helfen. Transferprozesse zwischen beiden Sprachen können so einen positiven Einfluss auf allgemeine kognitive sowie sprachbezogene Prozesse in beiden Sprachen haben (Cummins, 1981).

Die Interdependenzhypothese basiert auf der Annahme, dass es einen für alle Sprachen gemeinsamen Sprachenspeicher (*common underlying proficiency*; CUP; Cummins, 1984) gibt. Dieser wurde von Cummins anhand des dualen Eisbergmodells visualisiert, bei dem sich über der Wasseroberfläche zwei Sprachen als die Spitzen zweier Eisberge darstellen (Oberflächenaspekte), während sie unter der Wasseroberfläche zu einem einzelnen Eisberg verschmelzen (CUP). Während sich sprachgebundene Oberflächenerscheinungen demnach nicht einfach auf andere Sprachen übertragen lassen, können der Schriftsprache zugrunde liegende Prozesse auch in andere Sprachen transferiert werden (Cummins, 1981). Diese Transfereffekte können entweder auf sprachunabhängigen kognitiven Fähigkeiten basieren (*central processing hypothesis*) oder auf Fähigkeiten, die aufgrund einer strukturellen Ähnlichkeit der Sprachen resultierenden (*script dependent hypothesis*). Empirische Studien stützen diese Annahmen: Neben sprachunabhängigem Transfer spielt auch die strukturelle Ähnlichkeit eine Rolle für die Übertragbarkeit erworbener Fähigkeiten von einer in die andere Sprache (Deventer, Machts, Gebauer & Möller, 2017; Edele & Stanat, 2016; Ringbom, 2007).

Somit erhalten auch sprachliche Fähigkeiten, die sich zunächst auf sprachspezifische Oberflächenmerkmale beziehen, transferierbare Aspekte (Cummins, 1981; Geva & Siegel, 2000; Goodrich & Lonigan, 2017). Während beispielsweise zur Verschriftlichung von Sprache bestimmte sprachspezifische Regeln und Formen gelernt werden müssen (z. B. die Groß- und Kleinschreibung in der deutschen Schriftsprache), sind andere Aspekte durchaus von einer in die andere Sprache übertragbar. Zu diesen zählt die grundlegende sprachunabhängige Fähigkeit, die Lautstruktur von gesprochener Sprache zu erfassen und in kleinere Einheiten (z. B. Wörter in Silben oder Laute) zu zerlegen. Diese elementare Voraussetzung für den Schriftspracherwerb wird als phonologische Bewusstheit bezeichnet und mit Vorteilen von Mehrsprachigkeit in Verbindung gebracht (Durgunoglu, Nagy & Hancin-Bhatt, 1993; Gnutzmann, 2003; Reese, Garnier, Gallimore & Goldenberg, 2000; Verhoeven, 2007). Die phonologische Bewusstheit ist mit der alphabetischen Rechtschreibstrategie assoziiert, da es hier noch nicht um eine orthographisch korrekte Schreibweise geht, sondern um ein grundlegendes Verständnis für die Strukturiertheit von Sprache.

Ein weiteres wesentliches Prinzip von Alphabetschriften ist das Wissen über Wortbausteine (Morpheme). So bleibt bei Wortableitungen die Schreibung eines Wortstammes gleich, auch wenn sich die lautliche Gestaltung der Umwelt ändert (z. B. *Bäcker* und nicht „Becker" als Ableitung von *backen*). Eine eindeutige Graphem-Phonem-Korrespondenz ist hier nicht immer gegeben, so dass die Einsicht in abweichende Schreibungen für den Erwerb der morphematischen Rechtschreibstrategie hochrelevant ist. Demnach sind Vorteile immersiv unterrichteter Schülerinnen und Schüler beim Erwerb der alphabetischen und der morphematischen Strategie zu erwarten. Um einen Eindruck davon zu bekommen, inwiefern sprachabhängige Transfereffekte bestehen können, erscheint eine detaillierte Analyse schriftsprachlicher Eigenschaften von L1 und L2 lohnenswert.

1.2 Orthographische Eigenschaften von L1 und L2

Die Ähnlichkeit der verwendeten Sprachen kann einen Einfluss darauf haben, wie gut die Vorteile von Mehrsprachigkeit genutzt werden (Reder, Marec-Breton, Gombert & Demont, 2013; Chen, Ku, Koyama, Anderson & Li, 2008; Bialystok, Luk & Kwan, 2005). Neben dem Transfer grundlegender sprachlicher Fähigkeiten sind demnach auch Interdependenzen zu erwarten, die sich aus der spezifischen Beziehung zwischen L1 und L2 ergeben.

Sowohl in der englischen als auch in der deutschen Schriftsprache ist die Übertragung von Lauten in Buchstaben und das Wissen um Korrespondenzregeln eine grundsätzliche Voraussetzung für die Rechtschreibung. Ein Unterschied findet sich allerdings, wenn man die Buchstaben-Laut-Beziehung der Schriften genauer betrachtet, da diese im Englischen weniger regelmäßig ist als im Deutschen (Frisch, 2013). Dementsprechend gibt es im Englischen eine größere Anzahl von Wörtern, die nicht ausschließlich mithilfe von Graphem-Phonem-Zuordnungen korrekt geschrieben werden können. Frost, Katz und Bentin (1987) entwickelten hierzu die Hypothese der orthographischen Tiefe, die einen Vergleich der Konsistenz der Buchstaben-Laut-Beziehung verschiedener Schriftsysteme ermöglicht. Eine Orthographie, in der viele dieser Unregelmäßigkeiten existieren, wird als tiefe Orthographie bezeichnet. Eine Orthographie, die hingegen eine relativ gleichmäßige Graphem-Phonem-Korrespondenz aufweist, nennt man flache Orthographie (Katz & Frost, 1992).

Das deutsche Schriftsystem ist durch eine relativ regelmäßige Graphem-Phonem-Korrespondenz gekennzeichnet, da es vergleichsweise wenige Fälle gibt, bei denen ein Graphem mehreren Phonemen oder ein Phonem mehreren Graphemen entspricht. Dagegen verfügt das englische Schriftsystem über eine der intransparentesten Graphem-Phonem-Korrespondenzen der europäischen Sprachen (Seymour, Aro & Erskine, 2003). Dies lässt sich historisch begründen: Im Englischen hat seit dem 15. Jahrhundert keine Rechtschreibreform mehr stattgefunden, obwohl sich die Aussprache (z. B. Vokalverschiebung) weiter entwickelt hat (König & Gast, 2009). Der Buchstabe <a> kann im Englischen beispielsweise durch acht verschiedene Phoneme realisiert werden: /æ/ in *rat*, /a:/ in *giraffe*, /eì/ in *snake*, /ə/ in *elephant*, /ɔ:/ in *tall*, /ɪ/ in *percentage*, /e/ in *many*, /ɒ/ in *was*.

Die unterschiedlichen orthographischen Eigenschaften, bei grundsätzlicher Ähnlichkeit beider Schriftssprachen, lassen einen interlingualen Transfer bei der Rechtschreibleistung bilingualer Schülerinnen und Schüler vermuten. So dürfte insbesondere die tiefe Orthographie der englischen Sprache einen Einfluss auf die weniger komplexe deutsche Schriftsprache haben: Durch die häufig nicht vorhandene Phonem-Graphem-Korrespondenz im Englischen lernen die Kinder früh, dass eine direkte Übertragung von Lauten in Buchstaben nicht immer zielführend ist. Neben dem Regelwissen werden hier auch komplexe Konstruktionsprinzipien der Rechtschreibung häufiger notwendig, um eine korrekte Schreibweise zu erreichen. Werden diese Konstruktionsprinzipien von immersiv unterrichteten Schülerinnen und Schülern in ihre Erstsprache übertragen, ist von Transfereffekten insbesondere bei der morphematischen Strategie auszugehen. Wir erwarten demnach für die immersiv unterrichteten Schülerinnen und Schüler einen Vorteil bei der Beherrschung der alphabetischen Strategie aufgrund der grundsätzlich durch Zweisprachigkeit gesteigerten phonologischen Bewusstheit und bei der morphematischen Strategie durch die spezifische Beziehung zwischen den beiden untersuchten Sprachen.

1.3 Modelle des Schriftspracherwerbs und Rechtschreibstrategien

Die in dieser Studie eingesetzte Hamburger Schreibprobe (HSP) orientiert sich mit der Hervorhebung der vorwiegend nacheinander erworbenen Rechtschreibstrategien an gängigen Modellen des Schreibenlernens, welche von einem chronologischen, stufenweisen Erwerb der Schriftsprache ausgehen (Günther, 1986; Frith, 1991; Valtin, 1993; Thomé, 2003). Es gibt verschiedene theoretische Modelle, die zum Teil unterschiedlich viele Entwicklungsstufen vorgeben und unterschiedliche Termini hierfür verwenden. Sie alle teilen allerdings die Anschauung, dass diverse Rechtschreibstrategien existieren, die in verschiedenen Entwicklungsstufen unterschiedlich stark dominieren. Die Strategien sollten dabei nach Scheerer-Neumann (1998) nicht als rein linear aufeinanderfolgend, sondern – trotz der Stufen – auch als miteinander verwoben angesehen werden.

May (2002) orientiert sich bei den Rechtschreibstrategien, die die HSP misst, an dem weiterentwickelten Modell von Frith (1991). So kommt er zu fünf Hauptstrategien, an denen sich ein Schreiblerner orientiert, wenn er die Prinzipien des deutschen Schriftsystems rekonstruiert: Das *logographemische Schreiben*, die *alphabetische Strategie*, die *orthographische Strategie*, die *morphematische Strategie* und die *wortübergreifende Strategie* (May, 2002). In der vorliegenden Studie wurden Schülerinnen und Schüler der dritten Klassenstufe untersucht. Deshalb sind ausschließlich die alphabetische, die orthographische und die morphematische Strategie von Relevanz: Das logographemische Schreiben findet in einer voralphabetisierten Phase statt und die wortübergreifende Strategie wird erst ab der vierten Klasse von den Schreiblernern erschlossen (May, 2002). Im Folgenden sollen die drei relevanten Strategien kurz erläutert werden:

Spätestens in der ersten Klasse erkennen Schülerinnen und Schüler, dass Schrift nicht nur Gegenstände abbildet, sondern auch lautsprachliche Informationen aufweist. Die *alphabetische Strategie* befähigt die Schreiberinnen und Schreiber, den Lauten Buchstaben oder Buchstabencluster zuzuordnen. Die auf diese Weise geschriebenen Wörter sind zwar noch nicht notwendigerweise orthographisch richtig (im Folgenden durch ein Asterisk angezeigt), dennoch lässt sich – spätestens durch lautes Vorlesen – ihre Bedeutung erkennen (z. B. „*meuse*" für *Mäuse* oder „*farat*" für *Fahrrad*).

Ab der zweiten Klasse und bis zum Ende der Grundschulzeit erwerben Schreiblernerinnen und -lerner die wichtigsten orthographischen Merk- und Regelelemente. Zu den Merkelementen der *orthographischen Strategie* gehören vor allem Längezeichen in manchen Vokalen, Fremdwortschreibungen oder Ausnahmegrapheme (z. B. <V> statt /f/ in Vater), deren Schreibweise wortspezifisch gemerkt werden muss. Zu den Regelelementen zählen zum Beispiel die Umlautung, die Schreibung von <st>/<sp> am Silbenanfang und die Bezeichnung kurzer Vokale mithilfe doppelter Konsonanten. Die Lerner können sich nun also von der Lautung abweichende Schreibung an bestimmten Wortstellen merken und kennen Regeln, die sie für die Schreibung anwenden können.

Ende der zweiten Klasse, wenn die Schreiblernerinnen und -lerner realisieren, dass Wörter aus Morphemen (also Spracheinheiten, denen eine Bedeutung oder grammatische Funktion zugeordnet wird) bestehen, können sie Wörter gliedern, den Wortgliedern Wortstämme zuordnen und so die Rechtschreibung für einzelne Wortstellen ableiten. Zur *morphematischen Strategie* gehören demnach Wörter mit Umlautableitung (Hand – Hände) und Wörter mit Verhärtung des Auslautes (<d> statt /t/ bei z. B. Mund). Auch bei Wortgebilden, wie Derivaten oder längeren Komposita, kann diese Strategie bei der richtigen Schreibung helfen.

2 Die vorliegende Studie

Gebauer, Zaunbauer und Möller (2012) konnten keine Vorteile bei der allgemeinen Rechtschreibleistung immersiv unterrichteter Schülerinnen und Schüler finden. Ähnliche Befunde zeigten sich auch in anderen Studien (Gottardo, Yan, Siegel & Wade-Woolley, 2001). In der vorliegenden Studie hingegen stehen statt der absoluten

Rechtschreibleistung drei konkrete, auf verschiedenen grundlegenden Prinzipien beruhende, Rechtschreibstrategien im Fokus. Angenommen es handelt sich bei den Rechtschreibstrategien nicht, wie bei der allgemeinen Rechtschreibleistung, um sprachspezifische Oberflächenmerkmale, sondern um grundlegende sprachunabhängige oder sprachabhängige Konzepte, müsste ein Strategietransfer stattfinden können. Da die englische Orthographie kontraintuitiver und somit komplexer ist als die deutsche, müssten in Englisch alphabetisierte Schülerinnen und Schülern ihre hier erworbenen orthographischen Kompetenzen auf die der deutschen Orthographie ebenfalls zugrundeliegenden verschiedenen Prinzipien der Rechtschreibung übertragen können.

Die alphabetische und die morphematische Strategie stellen wichtige Konstruktionsprinzipien der deutschen und englischen Rechtschreibung dar. Für die alphabetische Strategie müssen Schülerinnen und Schüler die Zusammenhänge zwischen Lauten und Buchstaben verstehen; für die morphematische Strategie müssen sie grammatische oder bedeutungstragende Spracheinheiten erkennen können. Für die orthographische Strategie hingegen müssen Schülerinnen und Schüler sprachspezifische orthographische Regeln und Ausnahmen lernen. Wir erwarten demnach, das der Erwerb der alphabetischen und der morphematischen Strategie bei bilinugal Lernenden weiter fortgeschritten sein sollte, während die orthographische Strategie ähnlich weit entwickelt ist wie bei monolingual unterrichteten Kindern.

Abbildung 1 dient der Visualisierung dieser Hypothese. In Anlehnung an das allgemeine duale Eisbergmodell der bilingualen Kompetenz (Cummins, 1984) zeigt

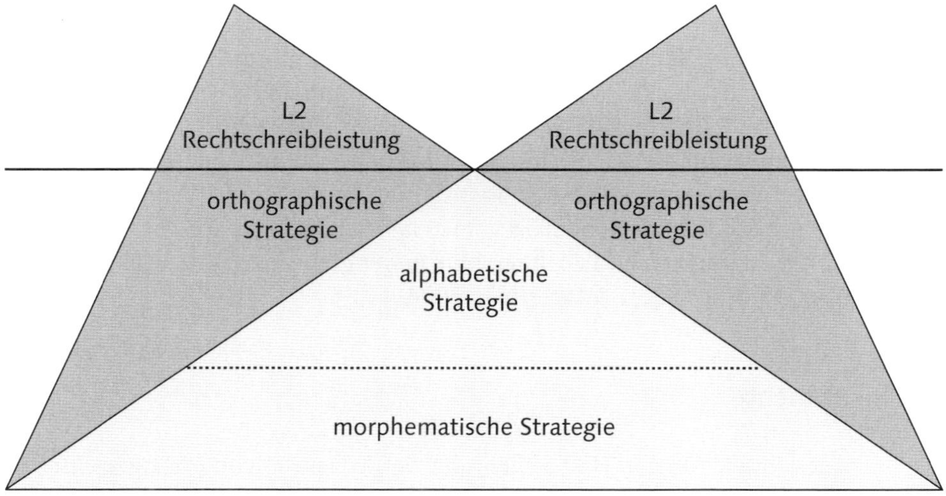

Abbildung 1. Erweitertes duales Eisbergmodell der bilingualen orthographischen Kompetenz; ergänzt um die allgemeinen Rechtschreibleistungen und Rechtschreibstrategien (in Anlehnung an Cummins, 1984).

Abbildung 1 die orthographische Kompetenz von bilingual Lernenden: Die allgemeine Rechtschreibleistung ist als Oberflächenmerkmal in den Spitzen der Eisberge abgebildet. Die ihr zugrunde liegenden Kompetenzen, die drei Rechtschreibstrategien, liegen unter dem Meeresspiegel. Die orthographische Strategie ist aufgrund von sprachspezifischen Merk- und Regelelementen nicht Teil der CUP. Die alphabetische und die morphematische Strategie liegen im Bereich der CUP, da sie zwischensprachlich übertragbar sein sollten.

Bilinguale Schülerinnen und Schüler sollten demnach in der Lage sein, das in der L2 Englisch erworbene alphabetische und morphematische Strategiewissen in die L1 Deutsch zu übertragen. Solche Transfereffekte sollten bei immersiv unterrichteten Kindern unter Konstanthaltung der allgemeinen Rechtschreibleistung und weiterer Kontrollvariablen zu einer besseren Beherrschung der alphabetischen und morphematischen Strategie führen als herkömmlicher, monolingualer Unterricht. Für die orthographische Strategie sind hingegen keine Vorteile zu erwarten.

3 Methoden

3.1 Stichprobe

Die Gesamtstichprobe des Querschnittsdesigns besteht aus zwei Kohorten von Grundschülerinnen und -schülern dritter Klassen (ca. 8 Wochen vor Schuljahresende) an Schulen in Schleswig-Holstein und Hamburg. Sie umfasst N = 350 Schülerinnen und Schüler mit zwei Teilstichproben: Den monolingual unterrichteten Schülerinnen und Schülern (n = 162; 42.0 % weiblich; M = 9.37 Jahre alt) sowie immersiv unterrichteten Schülerinnen und Schülern (n = 188; 48.9 % weiblich; M = 9.16 Jahre alt).

Während die monolingual unterrichteten Schülerinnen und Schüler ausschließlich in ihrer L1 Deutsch unterrichtet wurden, war die Unterrichtssprache der immersiv unterrichteten Teilstichprobe seit Schulbeginn in allen Fächern mit Ausnahme des Deutschunterrichts die L2 Englisch. Es handelt sich also um eine frühe englischsprachige Teilimmersion. Die Alphabetisierung fand in der L1 Deutsch statt; das englische Schriftbild war aber ebenfalls vom ersten Schuljahr an präsent. Die formale Einführung der Grammatik und Orthographie in der L2 Englisch setzte ab dem zweiten Schuljahr ein (Burmeister & Pasternak, 2004).

3.2 Instrumente

Die hier verwendete Version HSP 3 dient der der Erfassung von orthographischem Strukturwissen und grundlegenden Rechtschreibstrategien von Schülerinnen und Schülern am Ende der dritten Klasse (May, 1997). Mit der HSP können verschiedene Indikatoren orthographischer Kompetenz erhoben werden: Für die vorliegende Studie wurde zum einen die Zahl aller richtig geschriebener Grapheme (*Graphemtreffer*) erhoben, um die allgemeine Rechtschreibleistung zu ermitteln. Zum anderen wurden die Werte für die sogenannten *Lupenstellen* erhoben, die den Grad der Herausbildung der verschiedenen Rechtschreibstrategien bestimmen. Die HSP 3 testet mit den Lupenstellen folgende drei Rechtschreibstrategien: Die alphabetische Strategie (20 Lupenstellen; $\alpha = .73$), die orthographische Strategie (15 Lupenstellen; $\alpha = .81$) und die morphematische Strategie (10 Lupenstellen; $\alpha = .74$). Die Coloured Progressive Matrices (CPM; Raven, Raven & Court, 2001) wurden zur sprachfreien Erfassung der kognitiven Grundfähigkeiten verwendet. Der sozioökonomische Hintergrund der Schülerinnen und Schüler wurde durch den höchsten Bildungsabschluss eines Elternteils operationalisiert (ISCED-97).

Statistisches Vorgehen

Die Hypothesen wurden mittels einer multiplen Regressionsanalyse in *Mplus 7* untersucht. Die Mittelwerte der drei Rechtschreibstrategien bildeten dabei die abhängigen Variablen. Als manifester Prädiktor wurde der Einfluss der Unterrichtsform mit den beiden Ausprägungen immersiver Unterricht (1) und monolingualer Unterricht (0) untersucht. Zur Kontrolle von systematischen Gruppenunterschieden wurden Geschlecht, HISCED, CPM und die allgemeine Rechtschreibleistung (Graphemtreffer) als Kovariaten in die Analyse einbezogen. Die Prädiktoren waren untereinander korreliert. Die fehlenden Werte wurden unter Zuhilfenahme der *full information maximum likelihood* (FIML)-Methode geschätzt. Diese Analyse bildet auch die Grundlage der Berechnung von Effektstärken, wobei der y-standardisierte Regressionskoeffizient der 0/1-kodierten Gruppenvariable herangezogen wurde. So konnte für die Größe des Gruppenunterschieds auch unter Konstanthaltung der Kovariaten ein Wert angegeben werden, der mit Cohens *d* vergleichbar ist (d. h., die Größe der Mittelwertdifferenz in Einheiten der Standardabweichung wiedergibt). Dies ermöglicht eine praktisch bedeutsame Verortung der aus der Regressionsanalyse berechneten Effekte. Im HSP-Manual (May, 2002) werden Mittelwertunterschiede zwischen Testergebnissen zur Mitte und zum Ende der dritten Klasse berichtet. Diese bieten einen Maßstab für den Leistungszuwachs im Laufe eines halben Schuljahrs in Bezug auf den Erwerb der Rechtschreibstrategien.

4 Ergebnisse

Für die Lupenstellen zeigten sich insgesamt hohe Lösungshäufigkeiten (63 % – 99 %), was aufgrund der Anlage der HSP als Instrument zur Diagnose spezifischer Rechtschreibschwächen zu erwarten war. Die Trennschärfen einiger Items lagen unterhalb von $r_{it} = .30$, was möglicherweise auf die hohen Lösungshäufigkeiten zurückzuführen ist. Da das Entfernen dieser Items nicht zu einer Verbesserung der internen Konsistenz der Skalen beitrug, wurden alle Items in den weiteren Analysen beibehalten. Die Korrelationen zwischen den Rechtschreibstrategien lagen erwartungsgemäß hoch: $r = .59$ für die alphabetische und die morphematische Strategie, $r = .64$ für die alphabetische und orthographische und $r = .74$ für die orthographische und die morphematische Strategie. Wie Tabelle 1 zu entnehmen ist, erreichten die immersiv unterrichteten Schülerinnen und Schüler bei allen Rechtschreibstrategien höhere Werte als die monolingual unterrichtete Vergleichsgruppe. Beide Gruppen erreichten höhere Werte als die Normstichprobe der HSP 3, was eine Positivselektion der Gesamtstichprobe vermuten lässt.

Tabelle 1. Mittelwerte (Standardabweichung) der Lösungshäufigkeiten in der Gesamtstichprobe, getrennt nach Gruppen (monolingual/immersiv) sowie in der Normierungsstichprobe der HSP 3 (May, 2002)

Rechtschreibstrategie	*M (SD)*				
	gesamt	monolingual	immersiv	Norm, Mitte Klasse 3	Norm, Ende Klasse 3
Alphabetische Strategie	.93 (.10)	.91 (.12)	.95 (.08)	.92 (.12)	.94 (.09)
Orthographische Strategie	.86 (.18)	.84 (.19)	.87 (.16)	.73 (.25)	.80 (.23)
Morphematische Strategie	.78 (.22)	.74 (.23)	.81 (.21)	.66 (.26)	.72 (.24)

Zur Überprüfung der Mittelwertunterschiede zwischen den immersiv und den monolingual unterrichteten Kindern auf statistische Signifikanz wurde eine multiple Regressionsanalyse mit der dummy-kodierten Gruppenvariable und den Kovariaten Geschlecht, HISCED, CPM und Graphemtreffern gerechnet. Wie in Tabelle 2 dargestellt, fanden sich signifikante Regressionskoeffizienten für die Gruppe bei der alphabetischen und bei der morphematischen Strategie zugunsten der immersiv unterrichteten Schülerinnen und Schüler. Diese blieben auch bei Konstanthaltung der sozioökonomischen Hintergrundvariablen (Modell 2) und der kognitiven Hintergrundvariablen (Modell 3) bestehen, wobei die allgemeine Rechtschreibleistung den mit Abstand größten Anteil der Varianz aufklärte. Bei der orthographischen Strategie zeigte sich in keinem der Modelle ein signifikanter Effekt.

Für die alphabetische und die morphematische Strategie zeigte sich der erwartete Befund, dass die immersiv unterrichteten Schülerinnen und Schüler die entsprechenden Rechtschreibstrategien besser beherrschen als die monolingual unterrichteten. Die y-standardisierten Regressionskoeffizienten wurden als Indikatoren für die Effektstärke herangezogen und der Entwicklung der Strategiebeherrschung der HSP 3-Normstichprobe im Laufe eines Schulhalbjahres gegenübergestellt ($d = 0.24$ für die alphabetische, $d = .28$ für die orthographische und $d = .24$ für die morphematische Strategie). Demnach liegt der absolute Vorsprung der immersiv unterrichteten im Vergleich zu konventionell unterrichteten Schülerinnen und Schülern in der Größenordnung von über einem halben Schuljahr (*d* = .34 für die alphabetische und *d* = .36 für die morphematische Strategie). Nach der Kontrolle verschiedener Hintergrundvariablen reduziert sich der Effekt bei beiden Strategien auf *d* = .10, was dem Lernzuwachs von etwa einem Vierteljahr entspricht.

Tabelle 2. Ergebnisse der multiplen Regressionsanalyse (standardisierte Regressionskoeffizienten)

Ordinatenabschnitt, Prädiktoren und Varianzaufklärung	Modell 1			Modell 2			Modell 3		
	A	O	M	A	O	M	A	O	M
Intercept	9.13 (.37)	4.89 (.21)	3.35 (.16)	9.00 (.51)	5.03 (.40)	3.43 (.36)	9.01 (.36)	4.83 (.20)	3.40 (.15)
Unterrichtsform[a]	.34 (.10)**	.20 (.11)	.36 (.10)**	.16 (.06)**	.11 (.06)	.19 (.06)**	.10 (.05)*	.04 (.04)	.10 (.04)*
Geschlecht[a]				.14 (.05)**	.13 (.05)*	.07 (.05)	.02 (.04)	.00 (.04)	-.05 (.04)
Sozioökonomischer Hintergrund[b]				.01 (.10)	-.07 (.09)	-.04 (.09)	.03 (.07)	-.03 (.07)	.00 (.06)
Kognitive Grundfähigkeiten[b]							.05 (.06)	.05 (.06)	.09 (.05)
Allgemeine Rechtschreibleistung[b]							.71 (.03)**	.77 (.02)**	.75 (.03)**
R^2	.03 (.02)	.01 (.01)	.03 (.02)	.05 (.02)	.03 (.02)	.04 (.02)	.54 (.04)	.62 (.03)	.60 (.03)

Anmerkungen. A = Alphabetische Strategie; O = Orthographische Strategie; M = Morphematische Strategie
[a]Dummy-kodiert (0 = monolingual/männlich; 1 = immersiv/weiblich)
[b]*z*-standardisiert (*M* = 0; *SD* = 1)
*$p < .05$; **$p < .01$

5 Diskussion

5.1 Theoretische Implikationen

Die immersiv unterrichteten Schülerinnen und Schüler zeigen bei der alphabetischen und morphematischen Strategie Vorteile gegenüber den monolingual unterrichteten Schülerinnen und Schülern, während sich bei der orthographischen Strategie kein signifikanter Unterschied zeigt. Bei Rechtschreibstrategien scheint es sich – im Gegensatz zur allgemeinen Rechtschreibleistung – um Fähigkeiten zu handeln, bei denen Transferprozesse zwischen den Sprachen zu positiven Effekten führen. Dies kann sowohl auf sprachunabhängige als auch auf sprachabhängige Fähigkeiten zurückzuführen sein (Geva & Siegel, 2000). Ein solcher Transfereffekt ist allerdings bei Sprachen mit unterschiedlichen Schriftsystemen nicht zu erwarten (Ringbom, 2007). Die Tatsache, dass der deutschen und der englischen Schriftsprache ähnliche

Konstruktionsprinzipien zugrundeliegen (siehe Abschnitt 1.2), legt einen auf linguistischen Ähnlichkeiten basierten Transfer nahe. Erwartungskonform zeigte sich kein signifikanter Effekt bei der orthographischen Strategie. Sie stellt zu einem großen Teil sprachspezifische und damit nicht transferierbare Merkmale der verschiedenen Sprachen dar.

Aufgrund der vorliegenden Daten kann folgende, der Hypothese zugrunde liegende, Theorie gestützt werden: Es existieren Transfereffekte bei bilingualen Kindern in Hinblick auf grundlegende Kompetenzen und Strategien. Einzelsprachliche Fähigkeiten müssen hingegen sprachspezifisch erlernt werden. Somit entsprechen die Befunde dieser Studie dem für die Rechtschreibleistung adaptierten dualen Eisberg-Modell (Cummins, 1981; siehe Abbildung 1).

5.2 Praktische Implikationen

Für den immersiven Unterricht kann es von Vorteil sein, zu wissen, dass bestimmte Prinzipien der Rechtschreibung von einem Sprachtransfer profitieren können. Grundlegende Rechtschreibstrategien müssen bilinguale Schülerinnen und Schüler so nicht gänzlich zweimal erlernen. Konkret heißt das, den Schülerinnen und Schülern im englischen und deutschen Sprachunterricht während der Alphabetisierungsprozesse zu verdeutlichen, welche der unterschiedlichen Rechtschreibprinzipien sprachspezifisch und welche Prinzipen in beiden Sprachen gleich sind und somit übertragen werden können. Einerseits können Lehrkräfte grundlegende Gemeinsamkeiten in beiden Schriftsprachen, wie die Zerlegung von Wörtern in kleinere Einheiten (alphabetische Strategie) oder die Gliederung von Wörtern (morphematische Strategie), hervorheben. Andererseits muss darauf geachtet werden, dass die einzelsprachlichen Regel- und Merkelemente (orthographische Strategie) in jeder Sprache spezifisch erlernt werden. Ein kontrastiver Unterricht, der den Gemeinsamkeiten und Unterschieden beider Schriftsprachen mehr Beachtung schenkt und damit auch die metalinguistische Bewusstheit der Schülerinnen und Schüler fördert, könnte die positiven Effekte noch verstärken, die immersiver Unterricht auf den Lernerfolg der Schülerinnen und Schüler hat (Kuo, Uchikoshi, Kim & Yang, 2016; Reder et al., 2013).

5.3 Limitationen und Ausblick

Einschränkend sollte erwähnt werden, dass die Lösungshäufigkeiten vieler Items sehr hoch waren. Vor allem bei der alphabetischen Strategie wurden von beiden Gruppen nur sehr wenige Fehler gemacht. Dies begründet sich in der Anlage der HSP als individualdiagnostisches Instrument, das mögliche grundlegende Störungen im Schriftspracherwerb aufzudecken sucht. Die zum Teil eher geringen Trennschärfen lassen sich möglicherweise auf Deckeneffekte durch ebendiese hohen Lösungshäufigkeiten zurückführen. Zudem war aus diesem Grund eine empirische Prüfung der faktoriellen Struktur nicht möglich. Es wurde also a priori angenommen, dass es sich bei den drei Rechtschreibstrategien um drei voneinander verschiedene Faktoren handelt. Konfirmatorische Faktorenanalysen könnten zeigen, ob es sich tatsächlich um drei verschiedenartige Strategien handelt oder vielmehr um ein allgemeines Strategiekonstrukt, welches sich nicht weiter differenzieren lässt.

Darüber hinaus wären tiefergehende Analysen beteiligter Prozesse von Interesse, welche den Vorteilen immersiv unterrichteter Schülerinnen und Schüler bei der Verwendung von Rechtschreibstrategien zugrundeliegen. Nach wie vor gilt es zu klären, ob interlinguale Transfereffekte tatsächlich für diese Vorteile verantwortlich sind und ob es sich in dem Fall tatsächlich um sprachunabhängige oder sprachabhängige Effekte handelt. Hierfür wären zum einen Längsschnittstudien notwendig, die Zusammenhänge mit externen Kriterien untersuchen, sowie Interventionsstudien, die eine explizite Thematisierung sprachlicher Gemeinsamkeiten und Unterschiede einschließen. Weiterführende kontrastiv-linguistische Analysen auf Itemebene könnten zusätzlich Aufschluss darüber geben, ob und inwiefern sich interlingualer Transfer in der Übertragung sprachspezifischer Eigenheiten zeigen lässt.

Literatur

Baker, C. & Wright, W. E. (2017). *Foundations of bilingual education and bilingualism.* Bristol: Multilingual Matters.

Bialystok, E., Luk, G. & Kwan, E. (2005). Bilingualism, biliteracy, and learning to read: Interactions among languages and writing systems. *Scientific Studies of Reading, 9*, 43–61.

Burmeister, P. & Pasternak, R. (2004). Früh und intensiv: Englische Immersion in der Grundschule am Beispiel der Claus-Rixen-Grundschule in Altenholz. *FMF-Landesverband Schleswig-Holstein. Mitteilungsblatt*, 24–30.

Chen, X., Ku, Y. M., Koyama, E., Anderson, R. C. & Li, W. (2008). Development of phonological awareness in bilingual Chinese children. *Journal of Psycholinguistic Research, 37*, 405–418.

Cummins, J. (1979). Linguistic interdependence and the educational development of bilingual children. *Review of Educational Research, 49*, 222–251.

Cummins, J. (1981). The role of primary language development in promoting educational success for language minority students. In California State Department of Education (Hrsg.), *Schooling and language minority students: A theoretical framework* (S. 3–49). Los Angeles: California State University.

Cummins, J. (1984). *Bilingualism and special education: Issues in assessment and pedagogy* (Bd. 6). Clevedon: Multilingual Matters.

Deventer, J., Machts, N., Gebauer, S.K. & Möller, J. (2017). One-way immersion and school achievement: A three-level meta-analysis. *Manuscript submitted for publication.*

Durgunoglu, A. Y., Nagy, W. E. & Hancin-Bhatt, B. J. (1993). Crosslanguage transfer of phonological awareness. *Journal of Educational Psychology, 85*, 453–465.

Edele A. & Stanat, P. (2016). The role of first-language listening comprehension in second-language reading comprehension. *Journal of Educational Psychology, 108*, 163–180.

Frisch, S. (2013). *Lesen im Englischunterricht der Grundschule.* Tübingen: Narr.

Frith, U. (1991). Dyslexia as a developmental disorder of language. In Bundesverband Legasthenie (Hrsg.), *Legasthenie: Bericht über den Europäischen Fachkongreß 1990* (S. 26–34). Emden: Ostfriesische Beschützende Werkstätten.

Frost, R., Katz, L. & Bentin, S. (1987). Strategies for visual word recognition and orthographical depth: Amultilingual comparison. *Journal of Experimental Psychology: Human Perception and Performance, 13*, 104–115.

Gebauer, S. K., Zaunbauer, A. C. M. & Möller, J. (2012). Erstsprachliche Leistungsentwicklung im Immersionsunterricht: Vorteile trotz Unterrichts in einer Fremdsprache? *Zeitschrift für Pädagogische Psychologie, 3*, 183–196.

Gebauer, S. K., Zaunbauer, A. C. M. & Möller, J. (2013). Cross-language transfer in English immersion programs: Reading comprehension and reading fluency. *Contemporary Educational Psychology, 38*, 64–74.

Genesee, F. (2004). What do we know about bilingual education for majority language students. In T. K. Bhatia & W. C. Ritchie (Hrsg.), *The Handbook of Bilingualism and Multiculturalism* (S. 547–576). Malden, MA. [u. a.]: Blackwell.

Geva, E. & Siegel, L. S. (2000). Orthographic and cognitive factors in the concurrent development of basic reading skills in two languages. *Reading and Writing, 12*, 1–30.

Gnutzmann, C. (2003). Language awareness, Sprachbewusstheit, Sprachbewusstsein. In K.-R. Bausch, H. Christ & H.-J. Krumm (Hrsg.), *Handbuch Fremdsprachenunterricht* (S. 335–339). Tübingen: Franke.

Goodrich, J. M. & Lonigan, C. J. (2017). Language-independent and language-specific aspects of early literacy: An evaluation of the Common Underlying Proficiency model. *Journal of Educational Psychology.* Advance online publication.

Gottardo, A., Yan, B., Siegel, L. S. & Wade-Woolley, L. (2001). Factors related to English reading performance in children with Chinese as a first language: More evidence of cross-language transfer of phonological processing. *Journal of Educational Psychology, 93*, 530–542.

Günther, K.-B. (1986). Ein Stufenmodell der Entwicklung kindlicher Lese- und Schreibstrategien. In H. Brügelmann (Hrsg.), *ABC und Schriftsprache: Rätsel für Kinder, Lehrer und Forscher* (S. 32–54). Konstanz: Faude.

Katz, L. & Frost, R. (1992). The reading process is different for Different Orthographies: The orthographic depth hypothesis. *Haskins Laboratories Status Report on Speech Research* (SR-111/112), 147–160.

Knell, E., Qiang, H., Pei, M., Chi, Y., Siegel, L. S., Zhao, L. & Zhao, W. (2007). Early English immersion and literacy in Xi'an, China. *Modern Language Journal, 3*(91), 395–417.

König, E. & Gast, V. (2009). *Understanding English-German contrasts* (2. Ausg.). Berlin: Schmidt.

Kuo, L.-J., Uchikoshi, Y., Kim, T.-J. & Yang (2016). Bilingualism and phonological awareness: Re-examining theories of cross-language transfer and structural sensitivity. *Contemporary Educational Psychology, 46*, 1–9.

May, P. (1997). *HSP 3. Hinweise zur Durchführung und Auswertung.* Hamburg: vpm.

May, P. (2002). *Hamburger Schreibprobe. HSP 1–9. Diagnose orthographischer Kompetenz zur Erfassung der grundlegenden Rechtschreibstrategien.* Hamburg: vpm.

Nerius, D. (2007). *Deutsche Orthographie* (4 Ausg.). Hildesheim: Olms.

Raven, J., Raven, J. C. & Court, J. H. (2001). *Manual for Raven's progressive matrices and vocabulary scales.* Oxford: Oxford Psychologists Press.

Reder, F., Marec-Breton, N., Gombert, J.-E. & Demont, E. (2013). Second-language learners' advantage in metalinguistic awareness: A question of languages' characteristics. *British Journal of Educational Psychology*, 83, 686–702.

Reese, L., Garnier, H., Gallimore, R. & Goldenberg, C. (2000). Longitudinal analysis of the antecedents of emergent Spanish literacy and middle-school English reading achievement of Spanish-speaking students. *American Educational Research Journal, 37*, 633–662.

Ringbom, H. (2007). *Cross-linguistic similarity in foreign language learning.* Clevedon: Multilingual Matters Ltd.

Scheerer-Neumann, G. (1998). Schriftspracherwerb: "The State of the Art" aus psychologischer Sicht. In L. Huber, G. Kegel, A. Speck-Hamdan (Hrsg.), *Einblicke in den Schriftspracherwerb* (S. 31–46). Braunschweig: Westermann.

Seymour, P. H., Aro, M. & Erskine, J. M. (2003). Foundation literacy acquisition in European orthographies. *British Journal of Psychology, 94*, 143–174.

Thomé, G. (2003). Entwicklung der basalen Rechtschreibkenntnisse. In U. Bredel, H. Günther, P. Klotz, J. Ossner & G. Siebert-Ott (Hrsg.), *Didaktik der deutschen Sprache – Ein Handbuch.* (Bd. 2, S. 369–379). Paderborn: Schöningh.

Valtin, R. (1993). Stufen des Lesen- und Schreibenlernens. Schriftspracherwerb als Entwicklungsprozess. In D. Haarmann (Hrsg.), *Handbuch Grundschule* (S. 68–80). Weinheim: Beltz.

Verhoeven, L. (2007). Early bilingualism, language transfer and phonological awareness. *Applied Psycholinguistics, 28*, 425–429.

Autorinnen

DR. JOHANNA FLECKENSTEIN
Erziehungswissenschaft, IPN · Leibniz-Institut für die Pädagogik der Naturwissenschaften und Mathematik.

RAJA REBLE
Germanistisches Seminar, Christian-Albrechts-Universität zu Kiel.

DR. FRIEDERIKE HOHENSTEIN
Institut für Pädagogisch-Psychologische Lehr- und Lernforschung, Christian-Albrechts-Universität zu Kiel.

KONTAKT
Johanna Fleckenstein, IPN · Leibniz-Institut für die Pädagogik der Naturwissenschaften und Mathematik (IPN), Olshausenstr. 62, 24118 Kiel.
E-Mail: *fleckenstein@ipn.uni-kiel.de*

Inhaltliche und didaktische Aspekte des Englischunterrichts an der gymnasialen Oberstufe aus Sicht der Lernenden – Eine Analyse auf der Basis der LISA-6-Studie

STEFAN KELLER, MALEIKA KRÜGER, MICHAEL LEUCHT UND OLAF KÖLLER

ZUSAMMENFASSUNG: Anhand von Daten aus der LISA-6-Studie untersucht dieser Beitrag, wie Lernende (N = 3 639) in Schleswig-Holstein im 13. Schuljahr ihren Englischunterricht wahrnehmen. Dabei wurden Skalen zu folgenden Kerndimensionen einer kompetenzorientierten Unterrichtsgestaltung gebildet: Gebrauch der Fremdsprache durch Lehrpersonen und Lernende, Kontakt mit Muttersprachlern, Verwendung vielfältiger Texte und Medien sowie Förderung der rezeptiven Kompetenzen Hören und Lesen.

Die Resultate zeigen, dass die Verwendung der englischen Sprache durch Lehrpersonen und Lernende nicht durchgängig zum Repertoire der befragten Klassen zu gehören scheint und dass kaum Kontakte mit Muttersprachlern vorhanden sind. Neben Schulbüchern scheinen vielfältige Inputmaterialien eingesetzt und ein didaktischer Schwerpunkt auf das Leseverstehen gelegt zu werden. Die Förderung von Hörverstehen wird von den Lernenden als deutlich geringer wahrgenommen.

Als fachdidaktische Entwicklungsempfehlungen im Rahmen der laufenden Umstellung von Englischunterricht auf die Bildungsstandards der Kultusministerkonferenz (KMK, 2012) ergeben sich, im Abschlussjahr Englisch konsequent als Medium der Interaktion einzusetzen, dem Hörverstehen mehr Platz einzuräumen sowie dazu passende Verstehensstrategien konsequent zu fördern.

Schlüsselwörter: Englischunterricht, Gymnasium, Kompetenzorientierung, Bildungsstandards

Content and methodology of English teaching at upper secondary level from the learners' perspective – An analysis on the basis of the LISA-6-study

ABSTRACT: This study uses data from the LISA-6 study to describe English teaching in Schleswig-Holstein in year 13 from the learners' perspective (n = 3 639). Scales were constructed for the following key components of competence-oriented language teaching: use of the foreign language by teachers and learners, contact with native speakers, use of varied texts and media as input materials and fostering of reading and listening competences.

Results show that teachers and learners do not seem to use the English language consistently in their interactions, and that there is little contact with native speakers. Learners report that a variety of texts and media are used besides course-books and that much attention is given to the fostering of reading competencies. They report less emphasis being placed on listening competencies, however.

In the context of the on-going process of aligning teaching in English with the educational standards by the Standing Conference of the Ministers of Education and Cultural Affairs (KMK, 2012), the following recommendations could be given: The English language should be used consistently by teachers and learners in all interactions in the final year and more room should be given to the fostering of listening competences, which should include the training of suitable comprehension strategies.

Keywords: English teaching, upper-secondary education (gymnasium), competence-oriented teaching, educational standards

Einleitung

Die 2012 für alle Bundesländer flächendeckend eingeführten Bildungsstandards für die allgemeine Hochschulreife haben den Anspruch, Unterrichtsprozesse und -outcomes auf unterschiedliche Weise zu steuern und messbar zu machen. Sie sollen erstens die Transparenz schulischer Anforderungen sicherstellen, zweitens die Entwicklung eines kompetenzorientierten Unterrichts fördern und drittens eine Grundlage für die Überprüfung der erreichten Ergebnisse schaffen (KMK, 2012). Mit der Einführung der Standards war nicht nur die Idee einer empirischen Erfassung des *Outputs* von Bildungsprozessen, sondern auch einer Weiterentwicklung des Unterrichts verbunden. Die Bildungsstandards zielen auf kumulatives Lernen in dem Sinne, dass Inhalte und Prozesse des Unterrichts aufeinander bezogen und systematisch vernetzt werden (Klieme et al., 2003). Für die Umsetzung in der Praxis bedeutet dies eine wechselseitige Orientierung („alignment") von Lernformen bzw. Unterrichtsgestaltung auf der einen, und Leistungsmessung auf der anderen Seite (Pellegrino, Chudowski & Glaser, 2001).

Der hier vorgelegte Beitrag untersucht anhand von Daten aus der LISA-6-Studie (Leucht, Kampa & Köller, 2016) die Wahrnehmung der Schülerinnen und Schüler in gymnasialen Abschlussklassen (13. Schuljahr; 2012/13) in Schleswig-Holstein mit Hinblick auf ausgewählte Qualitätsmerkmale des Englischunterrichts. Der Beitrag liefert damit eine Art Innensicht auf den Englischunterricht und ist dabei im Bereich einer Forschungslücke angesiedelt, da die Unterrichtsgestaltung in der Oberstufe – nach Einführung der Bildungsstandards – bisher kaum Gegenstand von empirischen Studien war. Bestehende Arbeiten beziehen sich primär auf den Unterricht bis zum 9. Schuljahr, wobei die detailliertesten Informationen zur Gestaltung des Englischunterrichts aus der DESI-Studie stammen (DESI-Konsortium, 2008; Helmke et al., 2008). Dabei wurden im Rahmen von Schüler- und Lehrerbefragungen sowie Videostudien auch Bedingungen des Lernerfolgs in Englisch untersucht, wobei z. B. Organisationsformen des Unterrichts, verwendete Lern- und Unterrichtsmaterialien, Verwendung der Zielsprache durch die Lernenden oder Rede- und Frageverhalten der Lehrkräfte im Detail betrachtet wurden (DESI-Konsortium, 2008). Entsprechende Studien für die Oberstufe liegen jedoch nicht vor.

Die Studie von Lenski, Richter und Pant (2015) bezog sich auf den Deutschunterricht in der 9. Jahrgangsstufe, wobei die kompetenzorientierten Unterrichtsaktivitäten „Sprechen und Zuhören", „Schreiben", „Lesen" sowie „Sprache und Sprachgebrauch" untersucht wurden. Eine empirische Erprobung entsprechender Skalen für den Englischunterricht steht bisher allerdings aus.

In der folgenden Darstellung des Englischunterrichts aus Sicht der Schülerinnen und Schüler werden zunächst die Bildungsstandards für die erste bzw. fortgeführte Fremdsprache Englisch beim Erwerb der allgemeinen Hochschulreife (im Folgenden: Abitur) beschrieben und in Bezug zu zentralen Qualitätsfaktoren des schulischen Fremdsprachenlernens gesetzt. Anschließend werden die betrachteten Gymnasialtypen beschrieben, wobei auch untersucht wird, ob in den inhaltlichen Profilen des allgemeinbildenden sowie den zwei Anforderungsniveaus des beruflichen Gymnasialtyps unterschiedliche Unterrichtswahrnehmungen der Schülerinnen und Schüler existieren. Am Ende diskutieren wir die Resultate dieser Schülerwahrnehmungen im Lichte moderner Konzeptionen von kompetenzorientiertem Unterricht und zeigen mögliche Konsequenzen aus fachdidaktischer Perspektive auf.

1 Theoretischer Hintergrund

1.1 Die Bildungsstandards für das Fach Englisch beim Erwerb des Abiturs

Das Fremdsprachenlernen hat mit Blick auf Europa als Kultur- und Wirtschaftsraum sowie auf die zunehmende Globalisierung, zunehmend an Bedeutung gewonnen (Keller, 2013a; Romaine, 2009). Der Fremdsprachenunterricht soll deshalb gemäß der KMK-Standards einen grundlegenden Beitrag zu den Bildungszielen der gymnasialen Oberstufe leisten und sprachlich-kommunikative Fähigkeiten vermitteln, die für das Studium, die Berufsausbildung und erfolgreiches Handeln im Beruf erforderlich sind. Spezifisch für die Oberstufe ist dabei die „Diskursfähigkeit" als zentrales Bildungsziel genannt, d. h. „Verstehens- und Mitteilungsfähigkeit, die inhaltlich zielführend, sprachlich sensibel und differenziert, adressatengerecht und pragmatisch angemessen ist" (KMK, 2012, S. 12). Diskursfähigkeit umfasst neben formal-sprachlichen auch ästhetische und interkulturelle Fähigkeiten, die im Rahmen der Auseinandersetzung der Lernenden mit Themen, Texten und Medien integriert erworben werden sollen.

1.2 Zentrale Qualitätsfaktoren des schulischen Fremdsprachlernens

Die didaktischen Anforderungen, welche sich aus den Bildungsstandards für den Englischunterricht ergeben, betreffen sowohl die inhaltliche Ebene (z. B. Materialien und Themen), wie auch dessen methodische Gestaltung (z. B. Arbeits- und Interaktionsformen). Diese Anforderungen beziehen sich auf allgemeine Qualitätsfaktoren von Unterricht, welche Voraussetzung für effiziente Lernprozesse darstellen, beispielsweise kognitive Aktivierung der Lernenden, Angebotsvariation oder die Herstellung eines lernförderlichen Klimas (Helmke, 2015; Seidel & Shavelson, 2007). Fachliche Spezifizierungen dieser Faktoren ergeben sich aus der empirischen Forschungsliteratur zum schulischen Fremdsprachenerwerb (DESI-Konsortium, 2008; Ellis, 2008; Möller, Zaunbauer & Leucht, 2010) sowie zur Methodik des kompetenzorientierten Fremdsprachenunterrichts (Keller, 2013b).

1.2.1 Gebrauch der englischen Sprache durch Lehrkräfte und Lernende

Grundvoraussetzung für die Erreichung einer komplexen und hoch ausgeprägten Diskursfähigkeit in der Fremdsprache, wie sie von Lernenden beim Abitur erwartet wird, sind ein reichhaltiger und verständlicher Input sowie eine kognitiv herausfordernde Interaktion unter den Lernenden selbst und mit den Lehrpersonen (Ellis, 2008). Durch das gemeinsame Lösen anspruchsvoller kommunikativer Aufgaben können die Lernenden an die Grenzen ihrer momentanen sprachlichen Handlungsfähigkeit geführt und so der Aufbau neuer, leistungsfähigerer Strukturen in der Lernersprache („interlanguage") ausgelöst werden (Gass, Mackey & Pica, 1998). Solche kommunikativen Interaktionen unter *Peers* wirken lernfördernd, da sie die Produktion neuer Sprachformen im Dialog anregen („collaborative dialoguing"), welche die Lernenden internalisieren und nachher eigenständig wieder anwenden können (Ellis, 2008).

Auch beim Gebrauch der Zielsprache durch die Lehrkraft zeigen eine Reihe empirischer Studien einen direkten Zusammenhang mit dem Kompetenzerwerb der Lernenden (Turnball & Arnett, 2002). Besonders zuträglich ist es dem Lernerfolg, wenn Lehrpersonen die strikte Kontrolle über Diskursmuster abgeben und so eine Kommunikation in L2 mit den Lernenden ermöglichen, welche sich an natürlichen Interaktionsmustern orientiert (Ellis, 2008). Die Ergebnisse der DESI-Videostudie im 9. Schuljahr wiesen einen entsprechenden Zusammenhang nach: Klassen, in denen häufig Englisch gesprochen wurde und in denen die Interaktion über einfache Frage-Antwort-Sequenzen hinausging, zeigten höhere Kompetenzzuwächse (Helmke et al., 2008).

Neben der Unterrichtssprache von Lehrpersonen und Lernenden stellt auch der Kontakt zu Muttersprachlern einen signifikanten Aspekt der Interaktionsqualität des Fremdsprachenunterrichts dar: Dieser kann darin bestehen, dass Lernende Brief- oder E-Mail-Kontakte zu englischsprachigen Personen pflegen oder an einer Schule Austausch mit englischsprachigen Klassen besteht. In beiden Fällen würde der Austausch auf Individual- oder auf Klassenebene gehaltvolle zielsprachliche Interaktionen auslösen und damit dem Aufbau kommunikativer Handlungskompetenzen dienlich sein (Ellis, 2008).

1.2.2 Verwendung vielfältiger Texte und Medien als Lernmaterialien

Fremdsprachliche Handlungskompetenz wächst immer im Kontakt mit zielsprachlichen Äußerungen, Medien und Artefakten heran. Dazu zählen im Unterricht alle Arten von Texten in unterschiedlichsten medialen Ausdrucksformen. Die Auseinandersetzung mit vielfältigen und komplexen Materialien ist Voraussetzung für den Aufbau höherwertiger „Medien- oder Textkompetenz", verstanden als Fähigkeit zur Rezeption und Produktion mündlicher, schriftlicher und medial vermittelter Texte (KMK, 2012). Um dies zu erreichen, sollten besonders in der Oberstufe Materialien verwendet werden, welche über Lehrbücher hinausgehen (Hallet, 2011). An Hand von vielfältigen, teilweise unvereinfachten und authentischen Materialien lernen fortgeschrittene Schülerinnen und Schüler, für die Zielkultur gesellschaftlich und sprachlich typische Handlungs- und Verhaltensweisen adäquat zu verwenden (Candlin, Edelhoff & Grewer, 1996).

1.2.3 Förderung rezeptiver Kompetenzen: Hören und Lesen

Im Bereich des englischen Hörverstehens sollen die Jugendlichen beim Abitur in der Lage sein, komplexen Hör- bzw. Hörsehtexten Einzelinformationen zu entnehmen, implizite Einstellungen und Stimmungen von Sprechenden zu erfassen und dabei angemessene Strategien zur Lösung von Verständnisproblemen einzusetzen (KMK, 2012). Aus der Perspektive des Kompetenzaufbaus ist dafür der regelmäßige Umgang mit geeigneten Medien zentral, welche die aktive Verwendung höherwertiger Verstehens- und Interpretationsstrategien einzufordern (White, 2012). Auf der Oberstufe gehören dazu z. B. authentische Videos oder Podcasts.

Beim Lesen auf der gymnasialen Oberstufe ist – zusätzlich zur Auseinandersetzung mit Sachtexten – besonders der Umgang mit Literatur bedeutsam. Dazu treten neben der Fähigkeit des sinnentnehmenden Lesens auch Fähigkeiten wie ästhetisches Lesen oder literarische Interpretation (KMK, 2012). Literarische Texte bieten Jugendlichen die Gelegenheit, soziale und kulturelle Prozesse in verschiedenen gesellschaftlichen Kontexten und Epochen zu reflektieren, an ihnen Problemlösungsfähigkeit zu entwickeln und diese auch nachzuweisen (Hallet, 2011). Darüber hinaus fordern sie die jungen Menschen zum Mitdenken und Mitfühlen auf, fördern ihre Empathie und Sympathiefähigkeit, motivieren sie zum Einnehmen unterschiedlicher Perspektiven und tragen dadurch zum interkulturellen Verstehen bei (Bredella, 2007).

1.3 Gymnasialtypen und Kompetenzprofile English in Schleswig-Holstein

In der Oberstufe können an den allgemeinbildenden und beruflichen Gymnasien Schleswig-Holsteins je fünf Profile unterschieden werden. An den allgemeinbildenden Gymnasien sind diese Profile Resultat der im Rahmen der Husumer Beschlüsse der KMK vorgenommenen Gymnasialreform; am beruflichen Gymnasium ergeben sich die Profilzugehörigkeiten von Schülerinnen und Schülern durch die zu Beginn der 11. Jahrgangsstufe gewählten berufsbezogenen Schwerpunktfächer (s. Schmidt, Broux & Leucht, 2016).

In allen Profilen des allgemeinbildenden Gymnasiums umfasste der Englischunterricht in der Jahrgangsstufe 11 einheitlich drei, und in den Jahrgangsstufen 12 und 13 einheitlich vier Wochenstunden und erfolgte damit formal auf erhöhtem Anforderungsniveau. Allerdings belegten Leucht, Retelsdorf, Pant, Möller und Köller im Rahmen der LISA-6-Studie (2015), dass Schülerinnen und Schüler im sprachlichen Profil des allgemeinbildenden Gymnasiums bereits in der 11. Jahrgangsstufe ein mittleres Niveau im englischsprachigen Leseverstehen erreichten, das die anderen vier Profile sogar am Ende der 13. Jahrgangsstufe noch verfehlten. Ausgehend von diesen Leistungsunterschieden zu Beginn der Sekundarstufe II wäre zu vermuten, dass die Englischlehrkräfte im sprachlichen Profil auf das höhere Leistungsniveau ihrer Schülerinnen und Schüler reagieren und im Verlauf der gymnasialen Oberstufe einen qualitativ höherwertigen Englischunterricht realisieren können. Denkbar wäre darüber hinausgehend auch, dass zwischen den Englischlehrkräften an den sprachlichen und den nicht-sprachlichen Profilen systematische Unterschiede bestehen, etwa dahingehend, dass Schulleiterinnen und Schulleiter ihre besonders gut ausgebildeten bzw. fortbildungsbereiten Englischlehrkräfte eher dem sprachlichen Profil ihrer Schule zuordnen (Leucht et al., 2015). Der Besuch eines sprachlichen gegenüber eines nicht-sprachlichen Profils sollte somit am allgemeinbildenden Gymnasium ausschlaggebend mitbestimmen, wie Lernende den Englischunterricht wahrnehmen.

Die am *beruflichen* Gymnasium infolge der berufsbezogenen Schwerpunktfächer resultierenden Zweigzugehörigkeiten erscheinen demgegenüber für eventuelle Unterschiede in der Schülerwahrnehmung von Englischunterricht nachrangig, da keiner der dortigen Zweige genuin sprachenbezogen ist. Die Beschulung an den in LISA-6 untersuchten beruflichen Gymnasien vollzog sich in weiten Teilen noch auf Basis der diesbezüglichen KMK-Vereinbarungen von 1972 (Schmidt et al., 2016). Demnach waren in den Zweigen des beruflichen Gymnasiums je zwei Schülergruppen zu unterscheiden, deren Englischunterricht entweder dreistündig und damit auf grundlegendem oder fünfstündig und damit auf erhöhtem Anforderungsniveau erfolgte. Bei der konkreten Planung und Durchführung von Unterricht waren die Anforderungsniveaus von den Englischlehrkräften zu berücksichtigen. Beispielsweise sah der Unterricht auf grundlegendem Niveau bis zum Ende der gymnasialen Oberstufe die Auseinandersetzung mit nur einer, auf erhöhtem Anforderungsniveau dagegen mit zwei literarischen Ganzschriften vor (Ministerium für Bildung und Frauen des Landes Schleswig-Holstein (MBF), 2008). Ähnlich wie die Unterscheidung von sprachlichen und nicht-sprachlichen Profilen am allgemeinbildenden Gymnasium sollte auch das Anforderungsniveau des Unterrichts am beruflichen Gymnasium die Wahrnehmungen der Schülerinnen und Schüler zu ihrem Englischunterricht prägen.

2 Die vorliegende Studie

2.1 Fragestellungen

Ausgehend vom Soll-Zustand des Englischunterrichts, welcher durch die Bildungsstandards und zugehörige Curricula vorgegeben ist, stellt sich zunächst Frage, inwieweit dieser aus der Perspektive der Lernenden bereits einem Ist-Zustand entspricht. Für die oben dargestellten Bereiche würde dies einen Unterricht nahelegen, in welchem (1) Lehrkräfte und Lernende gleichermaßen darum bemüht sind, die englische Sprache durchgängig und konsequent als Umgangssprache im Klassenzimmer einzusetzen, um anspruchsvolle Kommunikations- und Interaktionsszenarien zu schaffen; (2) individuelle und klassenbasierte Kontakte zu Muttersprachlern vorhanden sind; (3) die Medien- oder Textkompetenz sowie Rezeptionsstrategien anhand vielfältiger Materialien gezielt ausgebildet werden; und (4) die Lese- und Hörkompetenzen der Lernenden durch geeignete Aufgaben und Szenarien gefördert werden. Diese vier Annahmen werden im Folgenden anhand der Angaben der Schülerinnen und Schüler zu ihrem Englischunterricht untersucht.

Daneben stellt sich die Frage, ob sich die Wahrnehmungen der Lernenden zu ihrem Englischunterricht aufgrund der unterschiedlichen Ausrichtung und Zielsetzung der einzelnen Gymnasialtypen und -profile unterscheiden. Entsprechende Anhaltspunkte lieferte die DESI-Studie, wo die einzelnen Bildungsgänge der 9. Jahrgangsstufe bezüglich zentraler Faktoren von Unterrichtsqualität aus Sicht der Lernenden different wahrgenommen wurden: So lieferten Lernende an Gymnasien deutlich höhere Einschätzungen zur Prozessqualität und Anspruchsniveau des Unterrichts, sowie tiefere zur Verwendung von Deutsch als Unterrichtssprache, als Lernende an integrierten Gesamtschulen, Real- oder Hauptschulen (Helmke et al., 2008). Für die vorliegende Untersuchung wollten wir deshalb überprüfen, ob sich ähnliche Unterschiede – bezogen auf die von uns beobachteten Unterrichtsaspekte – auch zwischen den Gymnasialtypen und -profilen des Landes Schleswig-Holstein finden lassen.

2.2 Stichprobe

Die Stichprobe der LISA-6-Studie setzt sich aus Lernenden der allgemeinen und beruflichen Gymnasien im 13. Schuljahr (Abiturabschlussklasse) Schleswig-Holsteins im Schuljahr 2012/2013 zusammen. Dabei wurde der Datensatz nach dem Vorbild der Hauptuntersuchung auf Lernende reduziert, die Englisch im 13. Jahrgang noch belegt hatten, für die es die erste schulisch erlernte Fremdsprache war und (für die Teilstichprobe des allgemeinbildenden Gymnasiums) welche ausschließlich vier Wochenstunden Unterricht im Fach Englisch erhalten hatten (s. Leucht, Fleckenstein & Köller, 2016). Um eine Repräsentativität der Daten zu gewährleisten, wurde in der folgenden Analyse mit Fallgewichten gearbeitet. Daraus resultiert eine Teilstichprobe von n = 3 639 für die vorliegende Untersuchung, wobei n = 223 ($n_{\text{gewichtet}}$ = 1 157)

Lernende das sprachliche und $n = 726$ ($n_{gewichtet} = 3812$) nichtsprachliche Profile am allgemeinbildenden Gymnasium besuchten. Auf dem beruflichen Gymnasium wurden $n = 1\,467$ ($n_{gewichtet} = 1467$) Lernende des grundlegenden Niveaus und $n = 855$ ($n_{gewichtet} = 855$) des erhöhten Niveaus untersucht (zur Gewichtung vgl. Leucht & Köller, 2016). Eine dritte Gruppe der allgemeinbildenden Gymnasien wird in der folgenden Analyse dagegen nicht mit einbezogen, da es sich hierbei um Kurse handelt, in denen sowohl Lernende des sprachlichen Profils als auch Lernende aus nicht-sprachlichen Profilen gemeinsam unterrichtet wurden.

2.3 Verwendete Untersuchungsinstrumente und Umgang mit fehlenden Werten

Die in LISA-6 verwendeten Items und Skalen zur Unterrichtswahrnehmung in Englisch entstammen zum einen der Studie TOSCA-Repeat (Trautwein et al., 2007, siehe S. 182f. für entsprechende Kennwerte). Dabei sollten die Lernenden einschätzen, welche Rolle bestimmte Unterrichtsfaktoren ihrer Einschätzung nach im Englischunterricht spielen (4-stufige Skala von *stimmt genau* bis *stimmt gar nicht*). Diese Items umfassen Fragen nach der gesprochenen Unterrichtssprache der Lernenden (bspw. *„Im Unterricht meines Englischkurses achtet die Lehrkraft darauf, dass wir, wenn wir in Gruppen arbeiten, Englisch miteinander sprechen"*; 5 Items; $\alpha = .77$; ICC(1) = . 0.27, ICC(2) = .88)[1]; Sprache der Lehrkraft (bspw. *„... spricht die Lehrkraft im Unterricht meistens Englisch."*; 2 Items; $\alpha = .61$; ICC(1) = .20, ICC(2) = .82)[2]; Kontakte zu Muttersprachlern (bspw. *„... haben wir englischsprachige Klassen besucht oder sie haben uns gesucht"*; 2 Items; $\alpha = .74$; ICC(1) = .20, ICC(2) = .83); und nach der Verwendung von Unterrichtsmaterialen (bspw. *„... verwendet die Lehrkraft vielfältige Materialien"*; 2 Items; $\alpha = .72$; ICC(1) = .13, ICC(2) = .73).

Zum anderen wurden Fragen zur Ausrichtung des Englischunterrichts in den letzten 6 Monaten an den Bildungsstandards gestellt und in einer Häufigkeitsabfrage auf einer fünfstufigen Skala erfasst (*Nie – 1 Mal – 2–5 Mal – 6–10 Mal – >10 Mal*). Für unsere Analyse herangezogen wurden Items zu Unterrichtsmethoden im Bereich Lesen (bspw. *„Wir haben uns im Unterricht mit literarischen Texten (z.B. Kurzgeschichten) beschäftigt"*; 5 Items; $\alpha = .45$; ICC(10. = (1, ICC(67. = (2) sowie im Bereich Hören (bspw. *„Ich habe geübt englischsprachige Wegbeschreibungen zu verstehen und nachzuvollziehen"*; 4 Items; $\alpha = .72$; ICC(1) = .22, ICC(2) = .84). Diese Items sind Teil eines

---

1 ICC(1): Intraklassen-Korrelationskoeffizient. ICC(2): Reliabilität des Gruppenmittelwertes (Bliese, 2000). Formel für ICC(2) nach Lüdtke, Trautwein, Kunter & Baumert (2006); mittlere Gruppengröße k=19

2 Man beachte den Unterschied in der Skalierung zu jener in Trautwein et al. (2007). Die hier verwendete Zuteilung der Items auf die einzelnen Skalen unterstreicht die Unterscheidung Englischgebrauch Lehrkraft im Gegensatz zum Englischgebrauch der Lernenden.

größeren Fragenkataloges zum Englischunterricht und entstammen der ersten Ländervergleichsstudie des IQB (zur Skalendokumentation s. Sachse, Kretschmann & Kocaj, 2012, S. 143f.).

Da die Teilnahme am Fragebogen der LISA-6-Studie für die Teilnehmenden freiwillig war, ergab sich für die Angaben der Schülerinnen und Schüler zum Englischunterricht eine hohe Anzahl an fehlenden Werten (42.1 %; Leucht & Köller, 2016). Für die Analysen wurden daher mit Hilfe der *Multiple Chained Imputation-Methode* $m = 40$ komplette Datensätze in Stata 13 erstellt.[3] Alle berichteten Koeffizienten wurden gemäß Rubin (1987) in Stata über die 40 Datensätze gemittelt.

Da sich die zentralen Forschungsfragen des vorliegenden Beitrags auf die tatsächliche Unterrichtsausgestaltung in den verschiedenen Gymnasialtypen der Schleswig-Holsteiner Oberstufe richten, sind für die Analyse vor allem die auf Klassenebene aggregierten Werte der Schüleraussagen interessant. Für die Analysen werden daher die Klassenmittelwerte der Schülerangaben herangezogen.

3 Ergebnisse

Wie Tabelle 1 zeigt, wird in den befragten Klassen Englisch nicht immer konsequent als Unterrichtssprache eingesetzt, weder durch die Lehrpersonen noch durch die Lernenden selbst. Zudem wird der Kontakt zu Muttersprachlern in allen befragten Klassen nur selten gepflegt.

Im Bereich der Materialauswahl legen die Schülerantworten nahe, dass vielfältigen Texten und Medien (neben Schulbüchern) im gymnasialen Unterricht Schleswig-Holsteins ein vergleichsweise hoher Stellenwert zukommt. Insbesondere das (literarische) Lesen scheint in dem erfragten Schuljahr einen bedeutsamen Teil der Unterrichtskultur auszumachen. Im Gegensatz dazu wurden Aufgaben, welche explizit die Förderung des Hörverstehens im Zentrum stellen, von den Lernenden im Befragungszeitraum viel weniger stark wahrgenommen.

---

3 Siehe White, Royston & Wood (2009) zur Empfehlung bezüglich Anzahl der Imputationen bei fehlenden Werten. Die fehlenden Werte wurden auf Ebene der Einzelitems imputiert und anschließend die jeweiligen Skalen als passive Variablen erstellt (StataCorp, 2013). Für die Imputationen verwendete Angaben: Gruppenzugehörigkeit, Englischnotenpunkte auf dem 13/2 Zeugnis (0–15), die Abiturgesamtnote (1–4), der jeweils erste Plausible Value im englischsprachigen Lese- und Hörverstehen und der erste Plausible Value in den kognitiven Grundfähigkeiten (zu deren Schätzung s. Leucht & Köller, 2016).

Tabelle 1. Unterrichtsskalenmittelwerte nach Gruppenzugehörigkeit auf Kursebene

	Gesamt		(1) SP-AG		(2) NSP-AG		(3) GK-BG		(4) LK-BG	
	M	*SD*	*M*	*SD*	*M*	*SD*	*M*	*SD*	*M*	*SD*
Unterrichts-sprache Schüler	2.79	.61	2.86	.48	2.83[3]	.44	2.63[2,4]	.43	2.79[3]	.36
Unterrichts-sprache Lehrkraft	2.95	.71	2.90	.53	2.95	.53	2.91[4]	.43	3.13[3]	.34
Materialien	2.96	.53	2.96	.39	2.97	.38	2.93	.39	3.02	.36
Kontakte zu Muttersprachlern	1.74	.70	1.96	.61	1.73	.44	1.65	.50	1.63	.44
Leseverstehen	3.11	.48	3.20[3]	.20	3.07[4]	.37	3.04[1,4]	.34	3.22[2,3]	.28
Hörverstehen	2.20	.64	2.36	.48	2.19	.45	2.10	.55	2.16	.47

Anmerkung. SP-AG / NSP-AG = sprachliches / nichtsprachliches Profil allgemeinbildendes Gymnasium, GK-BG/LK-BG = grundlegendes/erhöhtes Anforderungsniveau berufliches Gymnasium. Hochgestellte Ziffern zeigen an, mit Blick auf welche der anderen drei Gruppen signifikante Mittelwertunterschiede bestehen ($p < .05$); Auf Grund von fehlender Unterstützung des ANOVA-Befehls für imputierte Datensätze wurden Gruppenvergleiche als Regressionsgleichungen ausgeführt (StataCorp, 2013).

Betrachtet man die vier Gymnasialprofile im Vergleich, fällt auf, dass sich nur für drei Bereiche kleine bis mittlere Effekte finden lassen. Da sich die gefundenen Mittelwertunterschiede vor allem im Nachkommastellenbereich bewegen, scheint es angemessen, diese eher als Tendenzen oder Trends bei der Unterrichtsgestaltung zu sehen. Da die gefundenen Mittelwertunterschiede fast alle die Differenzen zwischen dem grundlegenden Zug des beruflichen Gymnasiums und einem oder allen anderen betreffen, kann man annehmen, dass die grundlegenden Kurse unter den hier untersuchten Schultypen eine gesonderte Position einnehmen.

Der auffälligste Unterschied betrifft die verwendete Unterrichtssprache der Lernenden untereinander, wobei die Lernenden im grundlegenden beruflichen Zweig eine geringere Bedeutung der Fremdsprachennutzung wahrnehmen als die Lernenden des fünfstündigen beruflichen Zweiges und des allgemeinen nicht-sprachlichen Zweiges. Überraschenderweise zeigt sich jedoch kein Unterschied zu den Lernenden des sprachlichen Zweiges auf allgemeinbildenden Gymnasien. Im Bereich der Sprache der Lehrkraft unterscheidet sich das grundlegende berufliche Gymnasium nur vom erhöhten Anforderungsniveau am beruflichen Gymnasium.

Was die Förderung der beiden Teilkompetenzen Lesen und Hören angeht, so lassen sich für das Lesen Unterschiede zwischen dem grundlegenden Profil am beruflichen Gymnasium und dem sprachlichen Profil am allgemeinen Gymnasium finden. Auch die beiden Profile am beruflichen Gymnasium unterscheiden sich untereinander. Das erhöhte Profil am beruflichen Gymnasium unterscheidet sich darüber hinaus vom allgemeinbildenden nicht-sprachlichen Profil. Diese Unterschiede sind jedoch insgesamt sehr klein. Für den Bereich Hören ließen sich keine Unterschiede zwischen den verschiedenen Schultypen finden.

Tabelle 2. Korrelation der Unterrichtskalen

	Unterrichtssprache Schüler	Unterrichtssprache Lehrkraft	Materialien	Kontakte zu Muttersprachlern	Leseverstehen
Unterrichtssprache Lehrkraft	.77*				
Materialien	.64*	.64*			
Kontakte zu Muttersprachlern	-.12	-.30*	-.23*		
Leseverstehen	.44*	.37*	.47*	.07	
Hörverstehen	-.09	-.27*	-.18	.82*	.04

Anmerkung. Korrelationskoeffizienten und Signifikanzangaben (* $p < .05$) resultieren aus Regressionsgleichungen zwischen den einzelnen Variablenpaaren (zum Zusammenhang von standardisierten Regressionskoeffizienten und Korrelationskoeffizienten in bivariaten linearen Regressionen siehe Urban & Mayerl, 2011: 70f.). Die Aggregation über die Imputationen erfolgte mit Hilfe der Fisher Z-Transformation (Marshall, Altman, Holder & Royston, 2009; White et al., 2009) in Stata 13 mit dem Add-On *mibeta*.

In Tabelle 2 sind die Korrelationen der Unterrichtsskalen untereinander dargestellt. Ein starker Zusammenhang zeigt sich erwartungsgemäß bei der Unterrichtsprache von Lernenden und Lehrkraft, da beide als Aspekte der Sprachkultur im Klassenzimmer angesehen werden können. Einen signifikanten Zusammenhang gibt es auch zwischen den Unterrichtsprachen und den verwendeten Unterrichtsmaterialien: Je stärker Englisch verwendet wird, desto mehr geben die Schülerinnen und Schüler auch an, sich mit vielfältigen Materialien auseinanderzusetzen.

Auffällig ist, dass es keinen signifikanten Zusammenhang gibt zwischen der Förderung von Hör- und Leseverstehen: Die Lernenden nehmen die Ausrichtung des Englischunterrichts auf die Förderung des Leseverstehens im letzten halben Jahr vor der Befragung als komplett unabhängig wahr von der Ausrichtung desselben Unterrichts auf die Förderung des Hörverstehens. Außerordentlich stark ist hingegen der Zusammenhang von Hörverstehen mit den Kontakten der Lernenden bzw. Klassen zu Muttersprachlern: Sind solche vorhanden, wird verstärkt auch eine Förderung des Hörverstehens wahrgenommen, und vice versa. Allerdings kann auf Basis der Itemwortlaute nicht eindeutig bestimmt werden, ob entsprechende Kontakte tatsächlich über den auditiven Kanal (z. B. Telefon oder Skype) gepflegt wurden.

4 Diskussion

Die hier vorgelegten Einschätzungen der Lernenden erlauben erstmals eine Innensicht auf den Englischunterricht an der gymnasialen Oberstufe in Schleswig-Holstein. Sie können Hinweise auf den Ist-Zustand des Unterrichts geben und anschließend mit dem Soll-Zustand von kompetenzorientiertem Unterricht abgeglichen werden, welcher durch die Bildungsstandards sowie die curricularen Vorgaben vorgegeben ist. Da der Unterricht und die Prüfungsaufgaben beim Abitur in Schleswig-Holstein erst sukzessive auf die Bildungsstandards von 2012 umgestellt werden, kann man nicht erwarten, dass dieser Prozess zum Zeitpunkt der hier vorgelegten Befragung (2012/13) schon abgeschlossen war.[4] Aus den Wahrnehmungen der Jugendlichen ergeben sich jedoch Hinweise auf didaktische Entwicklungen, die in diesem Prozess möglicherweise noch erfolgen sollten.

Im Bereich der verwendeten Unterrichtsprache dürfte eigentlich angenommen werden, dass im gymnasialen Fremdsprachenunterricht alle Interaktionen durchgängig in der Zielsprache stattfinden. Gerade im letzten Schuljahr gälte es, die englische Sprache noch stärker zum prägenden Kommunikationsmedium des Unterrichts zu machen. Aus fachdidaktischer Perspektive kann man annehmen, dass die konsequente Verwendung der englischen Sprache in Zusammenhang mit der Arbeit an vielfältigen, authentischen Materialien besonders günstige Voraussetzungen für den Erwerb hochwertiger Diskursfähigkeit schaffen. Verstärkend dazu sollte versucht werden, den Lernenden den aktiven Kontakt und Austausch mit Gleichaltrigen im englischsprachigen Ausland zu ermöglichen. Besonders im grundlegenden Niveau des beruflichen Gymnasiums wären in diesen Bereichen Anstrengungen zu unternehmen, um den Erwerb hochwertiger Englischkompetenzen auch in diesem Schultyp sicherzustellen, da diese als Schlüsselkompetenzen für die spätere Studierfähigkeit und „employability" angesehen werden können (Keller, 2013a).

Aus didaktischer Sicht günstig ist die praktisch durchgängig wahrgenommene hohe Bedeutung des Leseverstehens in allen befragten Klassen – literarisches Lesen und Interpretieren scheinen auch im Zeitalter der Output-Orientierung fest zum didaktischen Kanon des Gymnasiums zu gehören, und entsprechende Anforderungen in den Bildungsstandards bereits zum Zeitpunkt der Befragung gut umgesetzt zu werden.

Die durchgängig niedrigeren Mittelwerte im Bereich des Hörverstehens können vielleicht dem Umstand zugeschrieben werden, dass im letzten Gymnasialjahr (d. h. zum Zeitpunkt der Befragung) die Erarbeitung literarischer Inhalte stärker im Zentrum stehen. Auch die aus Sicht der Lernenden fehlenden Zusammenhänge bei der Förderung von Lese- und Hörverstehen (siehe Tabelle 2) lassen sich unter Umständen so erklären. Stimmt diese Annahme, so ergäbe sich angesichts der Anforderungen beim Abitur ein erheblicher didaktischer Entwicklungsbedarf: In der Auseinander-

4 Zu den Prüfungsvorgaben in Schleswig-Holstein, siehe http://za.lernnetz2.de/content/zentralabitur.php?group=11&ugroup=1 [21.06.2017]

setzung mit authentischen Materialien und Medien (Videos, Podcasts, usw.) sollte der Förderung des Hörverstehens gerade im letzten Schuljahr ein hoher Stellenwert zukommen und dabei Sprachlernstrategien vermittelt werden, welche das Dekodieren und Memorieren des sprachlichen Inputs unterstützen (Vorwissen aktivieren, intelligentes Raten, Schlüsselwörter erkennen, usw.; s. Oxford, 1990). Damit wäre eine wichtige Forderung der Bildungsstandards umgesetzt, nämlich dass Lernende auch in Hörsituationen in Abhängigkeit der jeweiligen Verstehensabsicht gezielt Rezeptionsstrategien anwenden können (KMK, 2012).

Die divergierenden Wahrnehmungen der Lernenden in Bezug auf Hören und Lesen sind auch im Lichte empirischer Studien zur Kompetenzentwicklung in der Oberstufe relevant. Diese zeigen beim Leseverstehen an den allgemeinbildenden Gymnasien eine merkliche Dezeleration der Leistungsentwicklung von der 9. über das 11. bis zum 13. Schuljahr (Leucht et al., 2015; Köller, Knigge und Tesch, 2010). Beim Hörverstehen bleiben die Leistungszuwächse im selben Zeitraum jedoch weitgehend stabil (Leucht et al., 2015). Dies scheint dem oben festgestellten Trend zu widersprechen, dass die Lernenden die Förderung des Leseverstehens im letzten Schuljahr stärker wahrnehmen als jene des Hörverstehens.

Da die Operationalisierung in der LISA-6-Studie jedoch ausschließlich auf Hörverstehensaufgaben im Unterrichtskontext abzielte, steht eine geringere Wahrnehmung solcher Aufgaben im letzten Schuljahr nicht unbedingt im Widerspruch mit den Leistungszuwächsen in diesem Bereich. Hörverstehen entwickelt sich besonders auf höheren Lernniveaus über die Interaktion mit Peers und Lehrkräften (White, 2012). Neben den schulischen Interaktionen dürften dabei auch außerschulische Lerngelegenheiten einen Einfluss haben (vgl. auch Leucht et al., 2015). Das Aufkommen neuer technischer Möglichkeiten über das Internet sowie die mediale Ausstattung der meisten Haushalte ermöglichen es den Jugendlichen, zahlreiche informelle, außerschulische englische Freizeitkontakte zu knüpfen sowie vielfältige Medienangebote (Video-on-demand, interaktive Online-Games, etc.) selbständig zu nutzen. Diesen Aspekt des inkrementellen Fremdspracherwerbs gilt es in Zukunft genauer ins Auge zu fassen, auch mit Blick auf differentielle Lerneffekte unterschiedlicher Mediennutzungen durch die Jugendlichen in ihrer Freizeit.

Bei der Interpretation der Ergebnisse dürfen die Limitationen des vorliegenden Datenmaterials nicht außer Acht gelassen werden. Zentrale Kompetenzbereiche des gymnasialen Unterrichts auf der Oberstufe, wie etwa das englische Schreiben, konnten damit nicht erfasst werden, da im Unterrichtsfragebogen der LISA-6 Studie keine entsprechenden Items zur Verfügung standen. Hier sei auf die laufende MEWS-Studie verwiesen (*Measuring Englisch Writing at Secondary Level*), welche sich insbesondere der Messung sachlicher und argumentativer Schreibfähigkeiten im 12. Schuljahr des Gymnasiums widmet (Keller, 2016). Dabei wird neben schulischen Faktoren auch die außerschulische Mediennutzung von Jugendlichen in Englisch detailliert erfasst.

Die hier auf Basis der LISA-6-Studie gebildeten Skalen stellen eher rudimentäre Operationalisierungen der zugrundeliegenden Unterrichtsstrukturen dar. So bestehen die Skalen zum Kontakt zu Muttersprachlern und zum Einsatz von Materialien nur aus jeweils zwei Einzelitems und bilden nur einen relativ schmalen Ausschnitt dieser beiden Themenbereiche ab. Bei den geschilderten Angaben handelt es sich zudem um Aussagen von Lernenden, welche in der Forschung zwar häufig angewendet, aber selbst nicht vollkommen unproblematisch zu sehen sind (Clausen, 2002). So tendieren Schülerinnen und Schüler unter anderem zu Übergeneralisierungen, die einer differenzierenden Betrachtung des Unterrichtsgeschehens zuwiderlaufen (Helmke, 2003). Daneben kommt es unter Umständen zu Verzerrungen der Darstellung auf Seiten der Lernenden ausgelöst durch persönliche Eigenschaften. Studien zeigen, dass Jugendliche mit guten Leistungen den Unterricht häufig anders wahrnehmen und von der Lehrperson anders behandelt werden, als solche mit weniger guten Leistungen (Ulich, 2001). Zwar gibt es Befunde, die darauf hindeuten, dass die subjektive Wahrnehmung der Lernenden eher einen Zusammenhang zu Kennwerten wie Leistung oder Motivation zeigen, als durch Lehrerbefragung oder Beobachtungen generierte Aussagen über den Unterricht (Clausen, 2002). Dieser positive Effekt kann in einer Analyse wie der vorliegenden, welche auf eine Bestandsaufnahme des Unterrichtsgeschehens abzielt, allerdings nicht zum Tragen kommen.

Auf der Basis der vorliegenden Daten lassen sich deshalb kaum gesicherte Aussagen über die Qualität der englischen Didaktik oder über Lernprozessverläufe in den befragten Klassen treffen. Um ein genaueres Bild des Unterrichtsgeschehens zu gewinnen, sollten zukünftige Studien bemüht sein, die inhaltlichen Teilbereiche des (Englisch-)Unterrichts stabiler zu erfassen und facettenreicher zu operationalisieren. Die tiefergehende Erforschung von Lernprozessmerkmalen sollte in Zukunft einen wichtigen Fokuspunkt empirischer Untersuchungen darstellen, besonders im Rahmen der Erforschung von kompetenzorientiertem Unterricht. Dies nicht nur in Bezug auf die vielbeschworene Rückbesinnung auf Unterricht als Kerngeschäft der Schule (Helmke, 2003), sondern aus dem Gedanken heraus, dass sich die Qualität der gemessenen Handlungskompetenzen in einem Fachgebiet nicht sinnvoll trennen lässt von der Qualität der Situationen oder Gelegenheiten, in denen diese erworben wurden (Keller, 2013a). Umgekehrt erhöhen valide Erfassungen von Prozessmerkmalen die fachdidaktische Relevanz empirischer Lernstandsmessungen in dem Sinne, dass Angebots- und Nutzungsstrukturen des Lernens systematisch aufeinander bezogen werden können.

Literatur

Bliese, P. D. (2000). Within-Group Agreement, Non-Independence, and Reliability. Implication for Data Aggregation and Analysis. In K. J. Klein & S. W.J. Kozlowski (Hrsg.), *Multilevel Theory, Research, and Methods in Organizations. Foundation, Extensions, and New Directions* (S. 349–381). San Francisco: Jossey- Bass.

Bredella, L. (2007). Die welterzeugende und die welterschließende Kraft literarischer Texte. In L. Bredella & W. Hallet (Hrsg.), *Literaturunterricht, Kompetenzen und Bildung* (S. 65–86). Trier: WVT.

Candlin, C., Edelhoff C. & Grewer, U. (1996). *Kommunikativer Englischunterricht – Prinzipien und Übungstypologie.* Berlin: Langenscheidt.

Clausen, M. (2002). *Unterrichtsqualität: Eine Frage der Perspektive? Empirische Analysen zur* Übereinstimungs-, *Konstrukt- und Kriteriumsvalidität.* Münster: Waxmann.

DESI-Konsortium (Hrsg.) (2008): *Unterricht und Kompetenzerwerb in Deutsch und Englisch. Ergebnisse der DESI-Studie.* Weinheim: Beltz.

Ellis, R. (2008). *The Study of Second Language Acquisition.* Oxford, Oxford University Press.

Gass, S. M., Mackey, A. & Pica, T. (1998). The Role of Input and Interaction in Second Language Acquisition: Introduction to the Special Issue. *The Modern Language Journal,* 82, 299–305.

Hallet, W. (2011). *Lernen fördern: Englisch. Kompetenzorientierter Unterricht in der Sekundarstufe.* Seelze: Klett-Kallmeyer.

Helmke, A. (2003). Rezension von Clausen, Unterrichtsqualität – Eine Frage der Perspektive? *Zeitschrift für Pädagogik* 49, 443–447.

Helmke, T., Helmke, A., Schrader, F.-W., Wagner, W., Nold, G. & Schröder, K. (2008). Die Videostudie des Englischunterrichts. In DESI-Konsortium (Hrsg.), *Unterricht und Kompetenzerwerb zu Deutsch und Englisch. DESI-Studie: Die Ergebnisse, Leistungsverteilungen und Bedingungsfaktoren* (S. 345–363). Weinheim: Beltz.

Helmke, A. (2015). *Unterrichtsqualität und Lehrerprofessionalität. Diagnose, Evaluation und Verbesserung des Unterrichts.* 6. überarbeitete Auflage. Seelze: Klett-Kallmeyer.

Keller, S. (2016). Measuring English Writing at Secondary Level (MEWS). Eine binationale Studie. *Babylonia, 3/2016,* 46–47

Keller, S. (2013a). *Integrative Schreibdidaktik Englisch für die Sekundarstufe. Theorie, Prozessgestaltung, Empirie. Giessener Beiträge zur Fremdsprachendidaktik.* Tübingen: Narr.

Keller, S. (2013b). *Kompetenzorientierter Englischunterricht.* Berlin: Cornelsen.

Klieme, E., Avernarius, H., Blum, W., Döbrich, P., Gruber, H., Prenzel, M., (...) & Vollmer, H. (2003). *Expertise. Zur Entwicklung nationaler Bildungsstandards.* Bonn: Bundesministerium für Bildung und Forschung.

KMK [Sekretariat der ständigen Konferenz der Kultusminister der Länder der Bundesrepublik Deutschland] (2012). *Bildungsstandards für die fortgeführte Fremdsprache (Englisch / Französisch) für die Allgemeine Hochschulreife.* Beschluss der Kultusministerkonferenz vom 18.10.2012. Köln: Wolters.

Köller, O., Knigge M. & Tesch, B. (Hrsg.) (2010). *Sprachliche Kompetenzen im Ländervergleich.* Münster: Waxmann.

Lenski, A. E., Richter, D., & Pant, H. A. (2015). Competence orientation in teaching from the perspective of teachers and students. *Zeitschrift für Pädagogik*, 61, 712–737.

Leucht, M., Fleckenstein, J. & Köller, O. (2016). Erreichen kriterialer Leistungsstandards in der ersten Fremdsprache Englisch. In M. Leucht, N. Kampa & O. Köller (Hrsg.). *Fachleistungen beim Abitur. Vergleich allgemeinbildender und beruflicher Gymnasien in Schleswig-Holstein* (S. 171–199). Münster: Waxmann.

Leucht, M., Kampa, N. & Köller, O. (Hrsg.) (2016). *Fachleistungen beim Abitur. Vergleich allgemeinbildender und beruflicher Gymnasien in Schleswig-Holstein.* Münster: Waxmann.

Leucht, M. & Köller, O. (2016). Anlage und Durchführung der Studie. In M. Leucht, N. Kampa & O. Köller (Hrsg.). *Fachleistungen beim Abitur. Vergleich allgemeinbildender und beruflicher Gymnasien in Schleswig-Holstein* (S. 79–98). Münster: Waxmann.

Leucht, M., Retelsdorf, J., Pant, H. A., Möller, J. & Köller, O. (2015). Effekte der Gymnasialprofilzugehörigkeit auf Leistungsentwicklungen im Fach Englisch. *Zeitschrift für Pädagogische Psychologie*, 29, 77–88.

Lüdtke, O., Trautwein, U., Kunter, M., & Baumert, J. (2006). Reliability and agreement of student ratings of the classroom environment – A reanalysis of TIMSS data. *Learning Environments Research*, 9, 215–230.

Marshall, A., Altman, D.G., Holder, R. L. & Royston, P. (2009). Combining estimates of interest in prognostic modelling studies after multiple imputation: current practice and guidelines. *Medical Research Methodology*, 9, o.S.

MBF [Ministerium für Bildung und Frauen des Landes Schleswig-Holstein] (2008). *Lehrplan für die Sekundarstufe II. Berufliches Gymnasium.* Kiel: MBF.

Möller, J., Zaunbauer, A. & Leucht, M. (2010). Fremdsprachenlernen. In D. H. Rost (Hrsg.), *Handwörterbuch Pädagogische Psychologie* (4. Auflage) (S. 219–225). Weinheim: Beltz.

Oxford, R. (1990). *Language Learning Strategies*. London: Heinle.

Pellegrino, J.W., Chudowsky, N. & Glaser, R. (2001). *Knowing What Students Know. Washington*, DC: National Academy Press.

Romaine, S. (2009). Global English: From island tongue to world language. In A. van Kemenade & B. Los (Hrsg.), *The handbook of the history of English* (S. 589–608). Malden: Blackwell.

Rubin, D. B. (1987). *Multiple imputation for nonresponse in surveys*. New York: Wiley.

Sachse, K., Kretschmann, J. & Kocaj, A. (2012). *Sprachliche Kompetenzen im Ländervergleich. Skalenhandbuch* (Stand 29. 11. 2012). IQB: Berlin.

Seidel T. & Shavelson R. J. (2007). Teaching effectiveness research in the last decade: Role of theory and research design in disentangling meta-analysis results. *Review of Educational Research, 77*, 454–499.

Schmidt, F. T. C., Broux, A. & Leucht, M. (2016). Allgemeinbildende und berufliche Gymnasien in Schleswig-Holstein. In M. Leucht, N. Kampa & O. Köller (Hrsg.), *Fachleistungen beim Abitur. Vergleich allgemeinbildender und beruflicher Gymnasien in Schleswig-Holstein* (S. 55–77). Münster: Waxmann.

StataCorp. 2013. *Stata: Release 13. Statistical Software & Reference Manual*. College Station, TX: StataCorp LP

Trautwein, U., Jonkmann, K, Gresch, C., Lüdtke, O., Neumann, M., Klusmann, U. & Baumert, J. (2007). *TOSCA-Repeat: Dokumentation der Items und Skalen* (Stand 15. 09. 2007). MPIB: Berlin.

Turnball, M. & Arnett, K (2002). Teachers' use of the target and first languages in second and foreign language classrooms. *Annual Review of Applied Linguistics, 22* 204–218.

Ulich, K. (2001). *Einführung in die Sozialpsychologie der Schule*. Weinheim: Beltz.

Urban, D. und Mayerl, J. (2011). *Regressionsanalyse: Theorie, Technik und Anwendung* (4. überarbeitete Auflage). Wiesbaden: VS Verlag für Sozialwissenschaften

White, G. (2012). Teaching Listening: Time for a Change in Methodology. In E. Usó-Juan & A. Martínez (Hrsg.). *Current Trends in the Development and Teaching of the four Language Skills* (S. 111–138). Berlin: de Gruyter.

White, I.R., Royston, P. und Wood, A.M. (2009). Multiple imputation using chained equations: Isssues and guidance for practice. *Statistics in Medicine*, 30, 377–399.

Autorin und Autoren

PROF. DR. STEFAN KELLER
Institut für Bildungswissenschaften, gemeinsam getragen von der Pädagogischen Hochschule FHNW und der Universität Basel.

MALEIKA KRÜGER
Pädagogische Hochschule, Fachhochschule Nordwestschweiz, Basel.

DR. MICHAEL LEUCHT
Erziehungswissenschaft, IPN · Leibniz-Institut für die Pädagogik der Naturwissenschaften und Mathematik, Kiel.

PROF. DR. OLAF KÖLLER
Erziehungswissenschaft, IPN · Leibniz-Institut für die Pädagogik der Naturwissenschaften und Mathematik, Kiel.

KONTAKT
Institut für Bildungswissenschaften, PH FHNW und Universität Basel, Riehenstr. 154, CH-4058 Basel.
E-Mail: *ste.keller@unibas.ch*

Ziele der gymnasialen Oberstufe im Fremdsprachenunterricht: Wunsch oder Wirklichkeit?

OLAF KÖLLER, MICHAEL LEUCHT, JOHANNA FLECKENSTEIN UND JÜRGEN BAUMERT

ZUSAMMENFASSUNG: Mit ihren Beschlüssen von 2012 hat die Kultusministerkonferenz (KMK) Bildungsstandards für die fortgeführte Fremdsprache für die Allgemeine Hochschulreife verabschiedet. Im Bereich der funktionalen kommunikativen Kompetenzen wird als Zielniveau B2 (Selbstständige Sprachverwendung) des Gemeinsamen Europäischen Referenzrahmens für Sprachen (GER), in den rezeptiven Teilkompetenzen auch das Niveau C1 (kompetente Sprachverwendung) erwartet. Es stellt sich die Frage, welche Anteile der Schülerinnen und Schüler diese Ziele am Ende der gymnasialen Oberstufe erreichen. Anhand der LISA-6-Studie ($N = 3.639$), in der eine Stichprobe von Abiturientinnen und Abiturienten aus Schleswig-Holstein hinsichtlich der rezeptiven Englischleistungen untersucht wurde, gehen wir der Frage nach, ob die Zielerreichung durch das Profil der allgemeinbildenden Gymnasien, die Schulform (berufliches vs. allgemeinbildendes Gymnasium), das Kursniveau (Grund- vs. Leistungskurs in beruflichen Gymnasien) und die verwendeten Leistungsmaße (Test vs. Lehrkrafturteil) moderiert wird. Die Analysen zeigen, dass erhebliche Anteile der Schülerinnen und Schüler das Zielniveau C1 verfehlen. Die Befunde werden vor dem Hintergrund einer Kluft zwischen einer Ideallogik der Standards und der Reallogik, wie sie sich in den Klassenräumen abspielt, diskutiert.

Schlüsselwörter: Large-scale Assessment, Bildungsstandards, Fremdsprachen, Unterrichtsziele

Goals of foreign language learning in upper secondary schools: Dream or reality?

ABSTRACT: The Standing Conference of Ministers of Education and Cultural Affairs of the Länder in the Federal Republic of Germany has decided in 2012 on educational standards for foreign languages (English and French) at the end of upper secondary school. According to communicative competencies students are expected to reach the level B2 (Independent User; Vantage) of the Common European Framework of Reference for Languages (CEF), with respect to receptive skills (listening and reading) the standards formulate even higher competencies (CEF level C; Proficient User). The question, however, is whether students really reach these expectations at the end of upper secondary school. We thus carried out a large empirical study (LISA-Project; $N = 3.639$) with graduates at the end of grade 13 in high schools (in German: Gymnasien) of the federal state Schleswig-Holstein. Based on their test results students from different profiles (language profile vs. other profiles in high school), school types (traditional "Gymnasium" vs. vocation "Gymnasium") and course levels (basic vs. advanced) were assigned to the different CEF-levels. Furthermore, we were interested whether different tests moderated these student assignments to CEF-levels. Findings suggest that large proportions of students do not reach C1 at the end of upper secondary school. Based on these results we discuss the gap between real findings and ideal expectations defined in the standards.

Keywords: large-scale assessment, educational standards, foreign languages, learning goals

Einleitung

Hinreichende Englischkenntnisse gehören zu den zentralen Basisqualifikationen für die berufliche und gesellschaftliche Teilhabe in einer globalisierten Welt (vgl. KMK-Expertenkommission, 1995; Tenorth, 2001). Als globale Verkehrssprache (*lingua franca*) wird Englisch von etwa einem Drittel der Weltbevölkerung gesprochen (Crystal, 2003). Englisch ist für viele Menschen nicht die Erst- bzw. Muttersprache, sondern wird als Zweitsprache erworben oder als Fremdsprache in einem institutionellen Kontext (d.h. der Schule) gelernt. Innerhalb der Europäischen Union ist Englisch die am häufigsten erlernte Fremdsprache (Eurobarometer, 2012). Im Bereich des voruniversitären Lernens kommt den Englischkenntnissen eine besondere Relevanz zu, da sich Englisch weltweit als Wissenschaftssprache etabliert hat und mehr und mehr Studiengänge und akademische Berufe den sicheren Umgang mit der englischen Sprache verlangen.

Die hohe Bedeutung des Englischen findet bildungspolitisch darin Ausdruck, dass alle Bundesländer den Fremdsprachenunterricht spätestens in der 3. Jahrgangsstufe der Grundschule beginnen, in der Regel ist dies Englisch. In der Oberstufe ist ebenfalls Englisch die dominierende Fremdsprache; im Schuljahr 2015/2016 wurden in gymnasialen Oberstufen an Gymnasien und integrierten Gesamtschulen deutlich über 90 % aller Schülerinnen und Schüler im Fach Englisch unterrichtet (siehe ebd.). Folgerichtig hat die KMK im Jahr 2012 Bildungsstandards für die fortgeführte Fremdsprache (Englisch/Französisch) für die Allgemeine Hochschulreife verabschiedet. Diese Standards schließen an die Bildungsstandards für den Mittleren Schulabschluss (KMK, 2004) an und basieren auf dem GER (Europarat, 2001), der aufsteigende Niveaus (A1, A2, B1, B2, C1, C2) des Sprachgebrauchs in der Fremdsprache definiert. Für den Englischunterricht insgesamt liegen die normativen Zielerwartungen der KMK im Sinne von Regelstandards für das Ende der Sekundarstufe II bei B2, für die rezeptiven Kompetenzen Hören und Lesen beim Niveau C1. Inwieweit Schülerinnen und Schüler diese Ziele tatsächlich erreichen, ist eine empirische Frage. Der vorliegende Beitrag nimmt sich dieser Frage an. Zusätzlich prüfen wir, ob unterschiedliche Instrumente zur Erfassung von GER-Niveaus zu verschiedenen Befunden führen.

1 Bildungsstandards für die Fremdsprachen Englisch und Französisch

Im Jahr 2004 hat die KMK begonnen, Bildungsstandards im Sinne bundesweit verbindlicher Zielvorgaben für die zu bestimmten Zeitpunkten in Bildungskarrieren zu erreichenden Kompetenzen zu verabschieden. Für die erste Fremdsprache (Englisch/Französisch) wurde zunächst das Erreichen des Mittleren (MSA; KMK, 2004) und des Hauptschulabschlusses (HSA; KMK, 2005) adressiert.[1] Eine erste standardbasierte Testung der Schülerinnen und Schüler im Fach Englisch fand 2009 statt (vgl. Köller, Knigge & Tesch, 2010) und hat sich im Jahr 2015 wiederholt (vgl. Stanat, Böhme, Schipolowski & Haag, 2016). Seit 2012 existiert ein gleichlautender politischer Beschluss für die in der fortgeführten Fremdsprache (Englisch/Französisch) zu erreichenden Kompetenzen beim Erwerb der Allgemeinen Hochschulreife (nachfolgend: Abitur; s. KMK, 2012). Eine Operationalisierung dieser Abitur-Standards steht bislang aus und ist unserem Wissen nach auch nicht geplant.

In ihrer Anlage sind Bildungsstandards *abschlussbezogene Regelstandards* (z. B. Köller, 2010), da sie *unabhängig* vom jeweiligen Bildungsgang *im Mittel* zu erreichende Lernstandniveaus beschreiben. *Mindest-* bzw. *Maximalstandards* für das Erreichen des MSA wurden nachträglich operational definiert, im Jahr 2009 verbindlich beschlossen (Köller, 2009) und von Köller et al. (2010) empirisch quantifiziert. Da Abitur-Bildungsstandards bislang nicht operationalisiert wurden, liegt hier nur der politische Beschluss für den Regelstandard, d. h. für *im Mittel* zu erreichende Leistungen, vor (KMK, 2012). Die konkret erwartbaren fremdsprachlichen Leistungen werden im GER anhand von sechs Niveaus graduiert. Die Niveaus A1 und A2 kennzeichnen dabei eine elementare, die Niveaus B1 und B2 eine selbstständige und die Niveaus C1 und C2 eine kompetente Fremdsprachenverwendung. Tabelle 1 illustriert dies anhand der Globalskala des GER (siehe Europarat, 2001, S. 35).

---

1 Bildungsstandards für den Hauptschulabschluss sind für alle nachfolgenden Ausführungen unerheblich.

Tabelle 1. Globalskala des GER

Kompetente Sprachverwendung	C2	Kann praktisch alles, was er/sie liest oder hört, mühelos verstehen. Kann Informationen aus verschiedenen schriftlichen und mündlichen Quellen zusammenfassen und dabei Begründungen und Erklärungen in einer zusammenhängenden Darstellung wiedergeben. Kann sich spontan, sehr flüssig und genau ausdrücken und auch bei komplexeren Sachverhalten feinere Bedeutungsnuancen deutlich machen.
	C1	Kann ein breites Spektrum anspruchsvoller, längerer Texte verstehen und auch implizite Bedeutung erfassen. Kann sich spontan und fließend ausdrücken, ohne öfter deutlich erkennbar nach Worten suchen zu müssen. Kann die Sprache im gesellschaftlichen und beruflichen Leben oder in Ausbildung und Studium wirksam und flexibel gebrauchen. Kann sich klar, strukturiert und ausführlich zu komplexen Sachverhalten äußern und dabei verschiedene Mittel zu Textverknüpfung angemessen verwenden.
Selbstständige Sprachverwendung	B2	Kann die Hauptinhalte komplexer Texte zu konkreten und abstrakten Themen verstehen. Versteht im eigenen Fachgebiet auch Fachdiskussionen. Kann sich so spontan und fließend verständigen, dass ein normales Gespräch mit Muttersprachlern ohne größere Anstrengung auf beiden Seiten möglich ist. Kann sich zu einem breiten Themenspektrum klar und detailliert ausdrücken, einen Standpunkt zu einer aktuellen Frage erläutern und die Vor- und Nachteile verschiedener Möglichkeiten angeben.
	B1	Kann die Hauptpunkte verstehen, wenn klare Standardsprache verwendet wird und wenn es um vertraute Dinge aus Arbeit, Schule, Freizeit usw. geht. Kann die meisten Situationen bewältigen, denen man auf Reisen im Sprachgebiet begegnet. Kann sich einfach und zusammenhängend über vertraute Themen und persönliche Interessengebiete äußern. Kann über Erfahrungen und Ereignisse berichten, Träume, Hoffnungen und Ziele beschreiben und zu Plänen und Ansichten kurze Begründungen oder Erklärungen geben.
Elementare Sprachverwendung	A2	Kann Sätze und häufig gebrauchte Ausdrücke verstehen, die mit Bereichen von ganz unmittelbarer Bedeutung zusammenhängen (z. B. Informationen zur Person und zur Familie, Einkaufen, Arbeit, nähere Umgebung). Kann sich in einfachen, routinemäßigen Situationen verständigen, in denen es um einen einfachen und direkten Austausch von Informationen über vertraute und geläufige Dinge geht. Kann mit einfachen Mitteln die eigene Herkunft und Ausbildung, die direkte Umgebung und Dinge im Zusammenhang mit unmittelbaren Bedürfnissen beschreiben.
	A1	Kann vertraute, alltägliche Ausdrücke und ganz einfache Sätze verstehen und verwenden, die auf die Befriedigung konkreter Bedürfnisse zielen. Kann sich und andere vorstellen und anderen Leuten Fragen zu ihrer Person stellen – z. B. wo sie wohnen, was für Leute sie kennen oder was für Dinge sie haben – und kann auf diese Fragen Antworten geben. Kann sich auf einfache Art verständigen, wenn die Gesprächspartner langsam und deutlich sprechen und bereit sind zu helfen.

Tabelle 2 zeigt die Zuordnung der Regel- (MSA und Abitur), Mindest- und Maximalstandards (lediglich MSA) zu diesen GER-Teilniveaus.

Tabelle 2. Mindest-, Regel- und Maximalstandards für Englischleistungen beim Erreichen des Mittleren Schulabschlusses und des Abiturs

GER-Niveau	BILDUNGSZERTIFIKAT: Mittlerer Schulabschluss	BILDUNGSZERTIFIKAT: Abitur
A1.1	Unterhalb des Mindeststandards	
A1.2	Unterhalb des Mindeststandards	
A2.1	Unterhalb des Mindeststandards	
A2.2	Mindeststandard	
B1.1	Mindeststandard	
B1.2	Regelstandard	
B2.1	Regelstandard plus	Regelstandard für Englisch als Fach insgesamt
B2.2	Maximalstandard	Regelstandard für Englisch als Fach insgesamt
C1.1	Maximalstandard	Regelstandard für rezeptive Kompetenzen
C1.2	Maximalstandard	Regelstandard für rezeptive Kompetenzen

Demnach wurde als Regelstandard für das Abitur für kommunikative Fertigkeiten im Fach Englisch insgesamt das GER-Niveau B2 beschlossen (siehe KMK, 2012). Dies steht im Einklang mit den Festlegungen in anderen europäischen Ländern (Lim, 2013) sowie mit den Zulassungsbestimmungen vieler europäischer Hochschulen (Deygers, Zeidler, Vilcu & Hamnes Carlsen, in press). Im *rezeptiven* Lese- und Hörverstehen wird dagegen das Niveau C1 als Regelstandard erwartet. Weiterhin unterscheiden die Bildungsstandards für das Abitur ein *grundlegendes* und ein *erhöhtes* Niveau, um Unterschieden in der Unterrichtsgestaltung sowie den im Fach Englisch unterrichteten Wochenstunden Rechnung tragen zu können.

2 Erfassung von Englischkompetenzen und Feststellung von GER-Niveaus

Mittlerweile existieren sehr viele Verfahren zur Testung von Schülerinnen und Schülern mit Englisch als Zweit- oder Fremdsprache hinsichtlich ihrer kommunikativen Fähigkeiten sowie zur Klassifikation derselben Schülerinnen und Schüler bzgl. der Niveaustufen des GER. In deutschen Schulen sind vor allem die Zertifikatstests des *Cambridge English Language Assessment* populär.[2] In Deutschland selbst bietet *The European Language Certificates (TELC)* in Frankfurt Zertifikatstests auf allen Stufen an. Das besondere an diesen Zertifikatstests ist, dass sie lediglich die Diagnose zulassen,

2 Bis 2013 sprach man von den *University of Cambridge ESOL Examinations*, wobei ESOL für *English for Speakers of Other Languages* stand.

ob eine Person, die den Test bearbeitet hat, auf der jeweiligen Stufe liegt oder darunter. Somit wird diagnostiziert, ob eine Person Niveau B1 erreicht oder nicht. Erreicht sie nicht B1, ist offen, ob sie auf A1 oder A2 liegt; erreicht sie B1, so schließt dies nicht aus, dass sie auch noch höher, beispielsweise auf B2, liegt.

Auch US-amerikanische Tests lassen es zunehmend zu, Personen mit ihren Leistungen auf den GER-Niveaus abzubilden. Im Gegensatz zu den Zertifikatstests erlauben sie Personenklassifikationen auf allen Stufen. In Deutschland weit verbreitet ist hierbei der *Test of English as a Foreign Language* (TOEFL), der auch in der vorliegenden Untersuchung in einer Kurzersion verwendet wurde. Der TOEFL wurde vom *Educational Testing Service* (ETS) in Princeton entwickelt, um die Sprachfertigkeiten von internationalen Studienplatzbewerberinnen und -bewerbern in den USA und Kanada zu überprüfen, deren Muttersprache nicht Englisch ist. Bei dem ursprünglichen Testverfahren handelt es sich um einen *Paper-and-Pencil*-Test mit Aufgaben im *Multiple-Choice*-Format. Seit 1998 wird eine Computerversion (*Computer-Based Test*) des TOEFL eingesetzt. Seit 2005 hat in vielen Ländern eine Internet-basierte Version (*Internet-Based Test*) des TOEFL die beiden älteren Formate weitgehend abgelöst; sie ermöglicht nun auch eine Überprüfung der Fähigkeiten beim Sprechen.

Anders als bei den Zertifikatstests bestimmen beim TOEFL die Mindestanforderungen der jeweiligen Institution, bei der sich eine Kandidatin oder ein Kandidat bewirbt, ob Eignung gemäß des TOEFL vorliegt. Amerikanische Universitäten und Colleges definieren üblicherweise Testwerte, die internationale Bewerberinnen und Bewerber erreichen müssen, um dort studieren zu können. Auch für die Aufnahme eines Englischstudiums (Bachelor Anglistik/Amerikanistik) in Deutschland wird an vielen Universitäten mittlerweile das Erreichen bestimmter TOEFL-Werte verlangt.

Jenseits dieses offiziellen Testprogramms gibt es aber auch die TOEFL-Versionen des so genannten *Institutional Testing Program* (ITP). Es handelt sich hierbei um Versionen, die zu Trainings-, Evaluations- und Selektionszwecken verwendet werden können. Die ITP-Versionen werden an Institutionen für deren interne Zwecke geschickt, die Auswertungen können allerdings nur durch ETS autorisierte Institute vornehmen. Der ITP-TOEFL-Wert wird zwar nicht von nordamerikanischen und kanadischen Universitäten anerkannt, aber auf der üblichen TOEFL-Metrik abgebildet. Um diese TOEFL-Leistungen nun auf den Stufen des GER zu verorten, wurden wiederholt so genannte *Standard-Settings* durchgeführt (Cizek, 2006, S. 226). Tannenbaum und Baron (2011) berichten, wie ITP-TOEFL-Testwerte post-hoc via Standard-Setting mit den GER-Stufen A1 bis C1 verknüpft wurden.

In Deutschland hat das Institut zur Qualitätsentwicklung im Bildungswesen (IQB) auf Basis der Bildungsstandards für den MSA Tests zum Hören, Lesen und Schreiben erarbeitet (vgl. Rupp, Vock, Harsch & Köller, 2008). Dabei wurde ein Vorgehen gewählt, bei dem für die jeweiligen Kompetenzen getrennt Aufgaben ganz unterschiedlicher Schwierigkeit konstruiert wurden, um später die Leistungen der Schülerinnen und Schüler auf den Stufen A1 bis C1 abbilden zu können. Das entsprechende Standard-Setting ist ausführlich bei Harsch, Pant und Köller (2010) beschrieben. Die Leistungen wurden auf einer nationalen Skala mit M = 500 und SD = 100 in der Gruppe der Neuntklässlerinnen und Neuntklässler abgetragen und anschließend wurden in einem Expertenworkshop vier Cut Scores bestimmt, um zu fünf Stufen zu kommen (vgl. hierzu auch Köller et al., 2010). Details zur Überführung der kontinuierlichen Bildungsstandards-Metrik in die GER-Teilniveaus finden sich bei Tesch et al. (2010).

Die auf der Basis der Bildungsstandards entwickelten Testinstrumente werden zum Bildungsmonitoring eingesetzt, bei dem die 16 Länder der Bundesrepublik Deutschland stichprobenbasiert dahingehend verglichen werden, wie hoch die Anteile der Schülerinnen und Schüler am Ende der Sekundarstufe I sind, die die vorgegebenen Standards erreichen.

Für schulische Klausuren oder zentrale Abschlussprüfungen spielen diese Tests keine Rolle. Vielmehr basieren die Ergebnisse – egal ob bei zentralen oder dezentralen Prüfungen – auf den Urteilen von Lehrkräften, die sich auch nicht an den GER-Niveaus, sondern an der Notenskala (1 bis 6 bzw. 0 bis 15 Punkte in der gymnasialen Oberstufe) orientieren. Ob Lehrkräfte ihre Schülerinnen und Schüler entsprechend den GER-Stufen einschätzen können, ist daher eine interessante Forschungsfrage, die im Rahmen der diagnostischen Kompetenz von Fremdsprachenlehrkräften (Zhu & Urhahne, 2015) bisher wenig adressiert wurde, aber zentral ist, da Lehrkräfte letztendlich mit dem GER verbundene Ziele erreichen sollen. Eine Ausnahme bilden die Studien von Leucht, Tiffin-Richards, Vock, Pant und Köller (2012) sowie Fleckenstein, Leucht und Köller (in press), in denen Schülerinnen und Schüler auf der Basis eines Tests den GER-Stufen zugewiesen wurden und parallel dazu die Lehrkräfte eine Zuordnung auf dem GER vornahmen. Die Übereinstimmung zwischen Lehrkrafturteil und Test lag bei lediglich $r = .27$ bzw. $r = .41$. Beide Werte liegen unterhalb des in einer Metaanalyse zur Beurteilungsgenauigkeit von Lehrkräften gefunden durchschnittlichen Wertes von $r = .63$ (Südkamp, Kaiser & Möller, 2012). In der Studie von Leucht et al. (2012; $N = 1.363$) unterschätzten die Lehrkräfte eher das mittlere GER-Niveau ihrer Schülerinnen und Schüler und überschätzten die Streuung. Fleckenstein et al. (in press; $N = 1.315$) zeigten eine starke Überschätzung des mittleren Niveaus und eine leichte Überschätzung der Streuung. Auch North und Jones (2009) fanden, dass Lehrkräfte in ihren GER-Einschätzungen die Varianz der Schülerinnen und Schüler überschätzen. Zudem fand Runnels (2013), dass die GER-Urteile unterschiedlicher Lehrkräfte für dieselben Schülerinnen und Schüler erheblich variierten. Die Befunde lassen insgesamt den Schluss zu, dass Lehrkrafturteile mit Bezug zum GER mit erheblicher Unsicherheit verbunden sein können.

3 Ausgewählte Befunde zu GER-basierten Englischleistungen

Mittlerweile existieren einige Studien in Deutschland, die sich mit den Englischleistungen am Ende der gymnasialen Oberstufe beschäftigen (vgl. im Überblick Köller, 2016). In diesen Studien wurde in der Regel ein ITP-TOEFL eingesetzt, dessen Testleistungen sich den Stufen A, B und C des GER zuordnen ließen.

Köller und Trautwein (2004) haben in Baden-Württemberg die Englischleistungen in der gymnasialen Oberstufe systematisch untersucht. Berücksichtigt wurden am Ende des Schuljahres 2001/2002 die Leistungen von $N = 2.854$ Schülerinnen und Schülern allgemeinbildender und $N = 1.876$ Schülerinnen und Schülern beruflicher Gymnasien in der 13. Jahrgangsstufe. Im Fach Englisch wurde der oben beschriebene TOEFL in einer *Paper-Pencil*-Version eingesetzt. Die Zuordnung der TOEFL-Leistungen zu Stufen des GER erfolgte mit einem Standard-Setting für den papierbasierten TOEFL (vgl. Tannenbaum & Wiley, 2004), da bis zu dem Zeitpunkt kein Standard-Setting für ITP-TOEFL (Tannenbaum & Baron, 2011) vorlag. Die Analysen der TOSCA-Daten ergaben folgende Befunde: Schülerinnen und Schüler der Grundkurse kamen in der Regel nicht über die Niveaus B1/B hinaus, in Leistungskursen erreichten zumindest die Schülerinnen und Schüler an allgemeinbildenden Gymnasien zu substanziellen Anteilen das Niveau C1. Erhebliche Problemlagen ergaben sich an beruflichen Gymnasien, wo beispielsweise über 40 % der Grundkursschülerinnen und -schüler nicht auf das Nivau B1 kamen.

Der im vorherigen Abschnitt beschriebene ITP-TOEFL wurde auch in der Lernausgangslagenuntersuchung LAU-13 eingesetzt. In LAU-13 wurde der gesamte Hamburger Abiturjahrgang am Ende der 13. Jahrgangsstufe im Schuljahr 2004/2005 in verschiedenen Fächern hinsichtlich der erreichten Fachleistungen untersucht (siehe hierzu ausführlich Trautwein, Köller, Lehmann & Lüdtke, 2007). Die LAU-13-Ergebnisse lassen sich so direkt mit den TOSCA-Ergebnissen vergleichen. An allgemeinbildenden Gymnasien ergaben sich in den Leistungskursen Vorteile zugunsten der Schülerinnen und Schüler in Hamburg (50 % vs. 40 %). In den Grundkursen und bei den Schülerinnen und Schülern, welche Englisch in der gymnasialen Oberstufe abgewählt haben, zeigen sich Vorteile zugunsten Baden-Württembergs. Insgesamt sehr schwache Leistungen zeigten die Schülerinnen und Schüler, die Englisch abgewählt haben.

Von besonderem Interesse sind weiterhin die in Schleswig-Holstein gewonnenen GER-Befunde, die sich auf die Sekundarstufe II beziehen (Leucht, Fleckenstein & Köller, 2016). Dort lässt sich direkt der Bezug von Oberstufenleistungen zu Leistungen von Gymnasiastinnen und Gymnasiasten der Sekundarstufe I herstellen. Die von Köller et al. (2010) und Stanat et al. (2016) durchgeführten Ländervergleiche erlauben Aussagen darüber, wo auf der Bildungsstandardmetrik Neuntklässlerinnen und Neuntklässler des allgemeinbildenden Gymnasiums in Schleswig-Holstein zu verorten sind. Gleichzeitig gestattet die LISA-6-Studie (Lernergebnisse an allgemeinbildenden und beruflichen Gymnasien in Schleswig-Holstein) die Abbildung von Abiturientinnen und Abiturienten auf derselben Metrik. Die Tabelle 3 zeigt die entsprechenden Befunde. Erkennbar ist, dass die Leistungen der Schülerinnen und Schüler der 9. Jahrgangsstufe in den letzten sechs Jahren deutlich gestiegen sind.

Akzeptiert man Leistungen auf B2.2 und darüber als Erreichen der Regelstandards am Ende der gymnasialen Oberstufe (Maximalstandard am Ende der Sekundarstufe I), so erreichten im Jahr 2015 bereits rund 28 % (Lesen) bzw. 21 % (Hören) der Jugendlichen am Ende der 9. Jahrgangsstufe die Leistungserwartungen, die mit dem Abitur verknüpft sind. Am Ende der gymnasialen Oberstufe liegen die Leistungen dann noch einmal deutlich höher und weisen darauf hin, dass viele Schülerinnen und Schüler an allgemeinbildenden Gymnasien Ziele des Englischunterrichts in der Sekundarstufe II erreichen. Inwieweit dies Folge von schulischen oder außerschulischen Lerngelegenheiten ist, diskutieren Leucht, Retelsdorf, Pant, Möller und Köller (2015). Beide Lernumwelten scheinen danach bedeutsam für den Leistungsanstieg zu sein.

Tabelle 3. Prozentuale Verteilung auf GER-Niveaus im englischsprachigen Lese- und Hörverstehen am Ende der 9. Jahrgangsstufe (IQB-Ländervergleiche 2009 und 2015) und am Ende der 13. Jahrgangsstufe (LISA-6-Studie) für das allgemeinbildende Gymnasium in Schleswig-Holstein

	LESEVERSTEHEN			HÖRVERSTEHEN		
	9. Jg. 2009	9. Jg. 2015	13. Jg. 2013	9. Jg. 2009	9. Jg. 2015	13. Jg. 2013
Unter Mindeststandard MSA	3.3	2.6	0.1	1.2	0.3	0
Mindeststandard MSA	29.7	20.5	5.2	25.4	12.1	0.4
Regelstandard MSA	28.4	23.9	14.5	39.7	29.7	3.2
Regelstandard plus MSA	24.9	25.0	27.9	26.0	36.5	19.4
Maximalstandard MSA	13.8	27.9	52.3	7.7	21.4	77.1

Anmerkung. Spaltenweise Summierung zu 100 %. Abweichungen von 100.0 durch Rundungsfehler sind möglich. MSA = Mittlerer Schulabschluss. Quellen: Werte für 2009 und 2015: Stanat et al. (2016; S. 318); Werte für 2013: Berechnungen auf Basis der LISA-6-Studie (gewichtete Daten).

Fasst man die Ergebnisse zusammen, so wird deutlich, dass zumindest an allgemeinbildenden Gymnasien vergleichsweise hohe Englischleistungen gezeigt werden und diese für erhebliche Anteile der Schülerinnen und Schüler auch kompatibel zu den Erwartungen der Bildungsstandards für die Abiturprüfung sind. Die Leistungen der Abiturientinnen und Abiturienten in Schleswig-Holstein scheinen höher zu sein als die der Abiturientinnen und Abiturienten in Baden-Württemberg und Hamburg. Da in Schleswig-Holstein aber ein anderer Test verwendet wurde, ist auch denkbar, dass unterschiedliche Tests einfach zu unterschiedlichen Einschätzungen der GER-Niveaus von Schülerinnen und Schülern führen. Diese Annahme wird, neben anderen Fragestellungen, in dem vorliegenden Beitrag untersucht.

4 Fragestellungen

Drei wesentliche Ziele lagen der vorliegenden Untersuchung zugrunde: Zum einen interessierte uns, wie hoch die Anteile von Schülerinnen und Schülern sind, welche die in den Bildungsstandards Englisch für die Abiturprüfung beschriebenen Leistungserwartungen erfüllen. Dazu nutzten wir eine Stichprobe von Schülerinnen und Schülern unterschiedlicher Gymnasialformen in Schleswig-Holstein. Schleswig-Holstein scheint für solch eine Frage besonders geeignet zu sein, da die Leistungen der Schülerinnen und Schüler in der Sekundarstufe I an Gymnasien in etwa dem nationalen Mittelwert entsprechen. Geht man davon aus, dass dies auch für die Sekundarstufe II gilt, so lassen sich die in Schleswig-Holstein gefundenen Ergebnisse mit Vorsicht auf Deutschland generalisieren.

Zum zweiten interessierten uns Schulformunterschiede (allgemeinbildende vs. berufliche Gymnasien) hinsichtlich der Erreichung von Standards. Dass in beruflichen Gymnasien die Leistungen niedriger ausfallen als an allgemeinbildenden, ist nicht neu (vgl. Köller & Trautwein, 2004; Trautwein et al., 2007). Daher interessierte uns auch, ob die Standards voruniversitären Englischunterrichts an den beruflichen Gymnasien dennoch erreicht werden.

Zum dritten sollte der Frage nachgegangen werden, inwieweit die Einschätzung des GER-Niveaus durch das verwendete diagnostische Instrument moderiert wird. Wir wollen damit deutlich machen, dass die Zuweisung von Englischlernenden zu Niveaustufen und die daran gebundenen Zertifikate erheblich vom verwendeten Verfahren abhängen und sich hier Unschärfen ergeben, vor allem, wenn das erreichte Niveau Voraussetzung für die Vergabe von Studienplätzen ist. In diesem Sinne sollten einerseits Lehrkräfte ihre Schülerinnen und Schüler auf dem GER einschätzen, andererseits wurden zwei unterschiedliche Testverfahren zur Feststellung der Englischleistungen verwendet, die beide mittels Standard-Setting mit dem GER verlinkt wurden. Wir berücksichtigen die unterschiedlichen Maße, da sie alle in der Praxis verwendet werden, um Schülerinnen und Schüler auf dem GER zu verorten, gleichzeitig aber zu erwarten ist, dass sich Unterschiede zwischen ihnen in der Zuordnung zu den Niveaus ergeben.

5 Methode

Die Datengrundlage für die vorliegende Untersuchung stellt die LISA-6-Studie dar, in der Fachleistungen am Ende der gymnasialen Oberstufe in Schleswig-Holstein erfasst wurden. Die Anlage und Durchführung der Studie ist detailliert in Leucht, Kampa und Köller (2016; siehe dort Kapitel 4) beschrieben.

In Schleswig-Holstein ist die Oberstufe an allgemeinbildenden Gymnasien seit dem Schuljahr 2008/09 als Profilsystem strukturiert. Schülerinnen und Schüler der gymnasialen Oberstufe müssen die Fächer Deutsch, Mathematik und eine Fremdsprache auf erhöhten Anforderungsniveau mit vier Wochenstunden besuchen. Darüber hinaus müssen sie eines von fünf Profilen wählen (sprachlich vs. naturwissenschaftlich vs. ästhetisch s. sportwissenschaftlich vs. gesellschaftswissenschaftlich). Für das sprachliche Profil bedeutet dies beispielsweise, dass die Schülerinnen und Schüler eine weitere Fremdsprache auf erhöhtem Anforderungsniveau (vierstündig) und eine dritte Fremdsprache dreistündig auf grundlegendem Niveau belegen. In den anderen Profilen wird in der Einführungsphase typischerweise eine weitere Fremdsprache auf grundlegendem Niveau gewählt, in der Qualifizierungsphase entfällt diese dann.

In beruflichen Gymnasien wird weiterhin in Grund- und Leistungskursen unterrichtet, wobei einer der Leistungskurse die inhaltliche Schwerpunktsetzung des jeweiligen Zweiges abbildet (vgl. Schmidt, Broux & Leucht, 2016).

5.1 Stichprobe

An der LISA-6-Studie nahmen im Frühjahr 2013 Abiturientinnen und Abiturienten der 13. Jahrgangsstufe aus allen Profilen und Zweigen ($N = 3.639$) teil. An den allgemeinbildenden Gymnasien wurde eine Stichprobe gezogen, während für die beruflichen Gymnasien eine annähernde Vollerhebung stattfand (vgl. Leucht & Köller, 2016). Die Testungen fanden an einem Schultag statt und dauerten fünf Zeitstunden. Die Test- und Fragebogenadministration erfolgte durch geschulte Testleiterinnen und -leiter des IEA *Data Processing and Research Center* (DPC) in Hamburg. Lehrerinnen und Lehrer schätzten zudem ihre Schülerinnen und Schüler auf der Schülerteilnahmeliste hinsichtlich des GER-Niveaus (Globalskala; Stufen A1 bis C2) ein. Zur Familiarisierung mit dem GER erhielten sie die Beschreibung der sechs Stufen der Globalskala (vgl. Tabelle 1).

5.2 Instrumente

Englischtests: Zwei unterschiedliche Englischtests kamen zum Einsatz, ein ITP-TOEFL von ETS und ein auf den Bildungsstandards für den MSA in Deutschland basierendes Testverfahren, das auch im Rahmen der IQB-Ländervergleiche (Köller et al., 2010; Stanat et al., 2016) eingesetzt wurde. Der hier verwendete ITP-TOEFL enthält drei Untertests, (1) Hörverständnis *(Listening Comprehension)*, (2) Grammatik und Orthographie *(Structure and Written Expression)* und (3) Leseverständnis *(Vocabulary and Reading Comprehension)*. Die jeweilige Anzahl richtig gelöster Aufgaben (Rohwerte) dient als Basis der Testwerte in den drei Untertests und des Gesamtwerts. Die genauen Testinhalte der drei Untertests sowie beispielhafte Testaufgaben können den Darstellungen von Köller und Trautwein (2004), Jonkmann, Trautwein und Köller (2007) sowie Jonkmann, Trautwein, Nagy und Köller (2010) entnommen werden. Wiewohl der TOEFL nicht den Anspruch erhebt, die Ziele des Englischunterrichts in der Oberstufe in toto zu erfassen, zeigen die Ergebnisse von Köller und Trautwein (2004), dass die Testergebnisse substanziell ($r > .50$) mit der Englischzeugnisnote korrelieren, was für die Validität des Tests spricht.

Zur Erfassung des Lese- und Hörverstehens wurde eine Teilmenge der Aufgaben des Ländervergleichs von Köller et al. (2010) eingesetzt. Die ihnen zugrunde liegenden Bildungsstandards für der erste Fremdsprache Englisch (MSA) sowie die konkret operationalisierten Konstrukte wurden von Rupp et al. (2008) beschrieben, ihre Anbindung an die Niveaus des GER bei Harsch et al. (2010). Es wurden 42 Aufgaben zum Lese- sowie 32 Aufgaben zum Hörverstehen eingesetzt (*Multi-Matrix-*

Design). Die Schätzung von Personenfähigkeiten erfolgte auf Basis einparametriger *Item Response*-Modelle (z. B. Embretson & Reise, 2000) in ConQuest (Version 3.0; Adams, Wu & Wilson, 2012). Als Schätzer für die Personenfähigkeiten wurden fünf *Plausible Values* (PVs) verwendet (im Detail siehe Leucht & Köller, 2016).

5.3 Statistische Analysen

Die Auswertung der Daten erfolgte mit *Mplus* (Version 7.3; Muthen & Muthen, 1998–2012). Da die Leistungstestwerte als PVs vorlagen, wurden alle Analysen fünfmal durchgeführt und die Koeffizienten entsprechend dem Vorgehen bei Rubin (1987) gemittelt. Um bei inferenzstatistischen Analysen zu unverzerrten Standardfehlern zu kommen, wurde die Option *Type* = *Complex* gewählt, wodurch der hierarchische Datencharakter (Schülerinnen und Schüler innerhalb von Kursen bzw. Klassen) berücksichtigt wurde.

6 Ergebnisse

In der Stichprobe an allgemeinbildenden Gymnasien befanden sich 223 (6.1 %) Schülerinnen und Schüler in Englischkursen des sprachlichen Profils (SP-AG); weitere 1.094 (30.1 %) Schülerinnen und Schüler besuchten Englischkurse in einem nicht-sprachlichen Profil (NSP-AG). An beruflichen Gymnasien befanden sich 1.467 Schülerinnen und Schüler im Grundkurs (dreistündig; GK-BG) und 855 Schülerinnen und Schüler (23.5 %) im Leistungskurs (LK-BG). Gegenüber der LISA-6-Gesamtstichprobe (N = 3.775) ergibt sich die minimal reduzierte Teilstichprobe von N = 3.639, da Schülergruppen ausgeschlossen wurden: Schülerinnen und Schüler, a) die Englisch abgewählt hatten (n = 7), b) für die Englisch nicht die erste schulisch erlernte Fremdsprache war (n = 61) sowie c) die am allgemeinbildenden Gymnasium mit weniger als vier Wochenstunden im Fach Englisch unterrichtet worden waren (n = 68; s. Leucht, Fleckenstein & Köller, 2016). Um die Repräsentativität der Ergebnisse gewährleisten zu können, wurden die Daten unter Zuhilfenahme von Fallgewichten analysiert.

Die Tabelle 4 zeigt die Korrelationen zwischen den eingesetzten Maßen zur Feststellung der Englischkompetenzen in der Gesamtstichprobe. Die Korrelationen sind durchgängig signifikant und substanziell. Koeffizienten zwischen Tests sind messfehlerkorrigiert, da PVs verwendet werden, im Falle der Korrelationen mit dem Lehrkrafturteil sind die Koeffizienten nicht um Messfehler des Lehrkrafturteils korrigiert, da sich hierfür keine Reliabilität bestimmen ließ.

Tabelle 4. Korrelationen zwischen den verschiedenen Maßen zur Feststellung der Englischkompetenzen

	(2)	(3)	(4)	(5)	(6)	Lehrkrafturteil
IQB Lesen (1)	.80	.66	.63	.64	.69	.44
IQB Hören (2)		.67	.66	.68	.72	.47
TOEFL Lesen (3)			.84	.80	.96	.44
TOEFL SWE (4)				.74	.93	.44
TOEFL Hören (5)					.90	.39
TOEFL Gesamt (6)						.45

Anmerkung. SWE Structure and Written Expression; alle Korrelationen sind signifikant ($p < .001$); Lehrkrafturteil auf den sechs Stufen des GER.

Es zeigen sich Methodeneffekte dahingehend, dass Subskalen desselben Tests höher miteinander korrelieren als zwischen den Tests, selbst, wenn es sich um dasselbe Konstrukt (beispielsweise Hörverstehen) handelt. Die Korrelationen der TOEFL-Subskalen mit dem TOEFL-Gesamtwert fallen so hoch aus, weil die Teilskalen in den Summenwert einfließen. Die deutlich geringeren, aber immer noch substanziellen Korrelationen mit dem Lehrkrafturteil rühren auch daher, dass die Lehrkräfte die Schülerinnen und Schüler ja direkt auf den sechs GER-Stufen einschätzen sollten, während es sich bei den Tests um kontinuierliche Leistungsskalen handelt. Die niedrigeren Korrelationen, die auch unter dem bei Südkamp et al. (2012) berichteten mittleren Wert von $r = .63$ liegen, mögen aber auch Grenzen der diagnostischen Kompetenz auf Seiten der Lehrkräfte abbilden. Insgesamt kann aufgrund des Korrelationsmusters davon ausgegangen werden, dass je nach verwendetem Instrument durchaus Differenzen in der Klassifikation der Schülerinnen und Schüler auf dem GER auftreten können, zumal Tiffin-Richards, Pant und Köller (2013) zeigen, dass selbst bei perfekter Reliabilität mit steigender Zahl von Kompetenzniveaus die Zahl der Fehlklassifikationen deutlich steigt.

Die Tabelle 5 gibt Auskunft über die erreichten Leistungen in den vier untersuchten Schülergruppen. Neben Mittelwert und Standardabweichung (1. Zeile pro Zelle) sind die Prozentzahlen der Schülerinnen und Schüler angegeben, die die GER-Niveaus B2 oder C1 und höher erreichen (2. Zeile pro Zelle). Damit kann festgestellt werden, wie hoch die Anteile der Schülerinnen und Schüler sind, welche die Vorgaben der KMK-Standards für die Abiturprüfung erreichen. Hinsichtlich der Mittelwertunterschiede ergeben sich erwartungskonforme Ergebnisse. Die höchsten Leistungen werden im sprachlichen Profil am allgemeinbildenden Gymnasium erreicht, gefolgt vom nicht-sprachlichen Profil, dann dem Leistungskurs an beruflichen Gymnasien. Die schwächsten Leistungen werden im beruflichen Gymnasium im Grundkurs erreicht. Die Differenzen sind dabei erheblich (siehe Effektstärken Eta^2), die stärksten Unterschiede zwischen den Gruppen treten im Hörverstehen auf, die geringsten beim globalen Lehrkrafturteil.

Tabelle 5. Englischleistungen nach Erhebungsinstrument und Untersuchungsgruppe

	Sprachl. Profil allg. Gymn.	Anderes Profil allg. Gymn.	Grundkurs berufl. Gymn.	Leistungskurs berufl. Gymn.	Eta²
IQB Lesen	682 (54) 55.3/38.4	647 (62) 58.3/19.3	597 (60) 42.9/4.3	631 (59) 58.6/11.5	.13
IQB Hören	745 (52) 47.0/52.7	714 (60) 62.4/33.5	642 (59) 66.9/4.6	688 (58) 72.0/18.6	.21
TOEFL Lesen	176 (18) 26.0/2.7	164 (21) 14.0/1.0	147 (20) 3.1/0.3	158 (20) 6.8/0.4	.13
TOEFL SWE	180 (17) 53.1/3.0	169 (19) 34.9/1.0	149 (18) 7.4/-	160 (18) 18.3/0.3	.18
TOEFL Hören	187 (13) 68.9/2.6	182 (15) 53.7/1.7	162 (16) 12.6/0.1	175 (15) 34.1/0.6	.21
TOEFL Gesamt	542 (43) 46.1/2.6	516 (51) 28.4/1.0	459 (50) 5.5/0.2	493 (48) 14.9/0.3	.19
Lehrkrafturteil	4.73 (0.80) 35.7/60.5	4.18 (1.09) 35.3/36.4	3.65 (0.75) 54.0/8.6	4.25 (0.83) 49.2/35.9	.08

Anmerkung. 1. Zeile Mittelwert und in Klammern Standardabweichung; 2. Zeile: Prozent Schülerinnen und Schüler auf Niveau B2/Prozent Schülerinnen und Schüler auf Niveau C1/C2; SWE: Untertest *Structure und Written Expression*.

Die paarweisen Unterschiede sind durchgängig signifikant ($p < .05$ nach Bonferroni-Korrektur). Bei den drei Gruppen, die auf erhöhtem Anforderungsniveau unterrichtet werden (sprachliches Profil an allgemeinbildenden Gymnasien; anderes Profil an allgemeinbildenden Gymnasien; Leistungskurs an beruflichen Gymnasien), grenzen sich die Schülerinnen und Schüler des sprachlichen Profils deutlich ab. Hinsichtlich aller Maße entspricht ihr Leistungsvorsprung gegenüber den nicht-sprachlichen Profilen und den Leistungskursen in den beruflichen Gymnasien Effektstärken von $d > 0.50$. Damit haben sie bei zielgleichem Unterricht in der gymnasialen Oberstufe einen Leistungsvorsprung, der dem Wissenszuwachs von ca. 1.5 Schuljahren entspricht.[3] Noch deutlich niedriger liegen die Leistungen in den Grundkursen in den beruflichen Gymnasien. Hier entsprechen die Mittelwertdifferenzen durchgängig Effektstärken über $d = 1.0$, was Wissenszuwächsen in der Größenordnung von drei Schuljahren entspricht.

3 Gemäß Köller und Baumert (2012) entspricht ein Schuljahr am Ende der Sekundarstufe I in etwa dem Leistungsunterschied von 30 Punkten auf einer 500/100-Skala, d.h. $d = 0.30$. In Deutschland zeigen sich vergleichbare Zuwächse auch noch in der Oberstufe (z.B. für das Fach Englisch Leucht et al., 2015).

Mit Blick auf die eigentlichen Fragestellungen sind die Befunde zur Standarderreichung bedeutsamer. Oben wurde argumentiert, dass Schülerinnen und Schüler am Ende der gymnasialen Oberstufe das Niveau B2 des GER, im Falle der rezeptiven Kompetenzen das Niveau C1 erreichen sollten. Tabelle 5 macht deutlich, dass die prozentualen Anteile der Schülerinnen und Schüler, die B2 oder C1 erreichen, erheblich nach Gruppenzugehörigkeit, aber auch nach verwendetem Instrument oder verwendeter Subskala variieren. Der TOEFL-Gesamtwert und das Lehrkrafturteil erlauben Einschätzungen auf der Globalskala des GER. Dabei zeigen sich erhebliche Differenzen. Folgt man dem Argument, dass B2 global das erwartete Niveau für das Abitur ist, so ergibt sich aufgrund des Lehrkrafturteils ein optimistisches Bild. Die prozentualen Anteile, die mindestens B2 erreichen, liegen zwischen 62.6 % (Grundkurs berufliches Gymnasien) und 96.2 % (sprachliches Profil, allgemeinbildende Gymnasien). Ein dramatisch ungünstigeres Bild ergibt sich auf der Basis des TOEFL-Gesamtwertes. Hier liegen die entsprechenden Zahlen zwischen 5.7 % und 48.7 %. Hinsichtlich der Dimensionen Hören und Lesen zeigen sich auch je nach Instrument erhebliche Diskrepanzen. Für rezeptive Kompetenzen wird das Niveau C1 in den TOEFL-Instrumenten quasi nicht erreicht, bei den IQB-Tests liegen die Quoten zwischen 4.3 % (Lesen im Grundkurs, berufliches Gymnasium) und 52.7 % (Hören im sprachlichen Profil, allgemeinbildendes Gymnasium).

7 Zusammenfassung und Diskussion

Mit der Verabschiedung der Bildungsstandards für die Abiturprüfung im Jahr 2012 hat die KMK verbindliche Leistungserwartungen für die fortgeführte Fremdsprache am Ende der gymnasialen Oberstufe formuliert. Gleichzeitig sieht die Gesamtstrategie der KMK zur Qualitätssicherung im Bildungssystem nicht vor, die Erreichung der in den Standards formulierten Erwartungen zu überprüfen. Dies impliziert auch, dass keine Aufgabenpools generiert werden, mit denen analog zur Sekundarstufe I Ländervergleiche durchgeführt werden können. Mit der vorliegenden Untersuchung wurde davon losgelöst der Versuch unternommen, sich den Standards für die Fremdsprache Englisch empirisch zu nähern. Die genutzten Instrumente erheben dabei nicht den Anspruch, passgenau für die Überprüfung der Abiturstandards entwickelt worden zu sein, gleichwohl orientieren sie sich am GER und wurden in Standard-Settings zu den Stufen des GER verlinkt. Die Korrelationen mit dem Lehrkrafturteil in einer Größenordnung von $r = .40$ können dabei durchaus als Validitätshinweise für die eingesetzten Tests interpretiert werden, gleichzeitig weisen aber die unterschiedlichen prozentualen Anteile auf den GER-Stufen je nach Instrument darauf hin, wie schwierig es ist, am GER orientierte normativ festgelegte Leistungserwartungen valide zu überprüfen. Im Folgenden diskutieren wir die Befunde entlang von zwei Linien. Im ersten Schritt werden die Mittelwertsdifferenzen zwischen den vier Gruppen reflektiert, es folgen dann Ausführungen zur Passung der Leistungen zu den normativen Vorgaben der Standards.

7.1 Unterschiede zwischen den vier Gruppen

Zwischen den Schulformen (allgemeinbildende vs. berufliche Gymnasien) und innerhalb der Schulformen (sprachliches Profil vs. anderes Profil; Leistungskurs vs. Grundkurs) finden sich sehr große Mittelwertdifferenzen in den Testleistungen, die mit Effektstärken (Eta^2) zwischen .13 und .21 einhergehen und Differenzen aufdecken, die dem Lernfortschritt von bis zu drei Schuljahren entsprechen. Dementsprechend variieren auch deutlich die Anteile der Schülerinnen und Schüler, welche die Niveaus B2 und C1 des GER erreichen. Beispielsweise liegen die kumulierten Anteile im Hörverstehentest des TOEFL im sprachlichen Profil bei gut 70 %, im Grundkurs des beruflichen Gymnasiums erreichen in diesem Test lediglich 12.7 % B2 oder C1. Je nach Untertest fallen die Ergebnisse besser oder schlechter aus, ein in allen Gruppen günstiges Bild ergibt sich nur bei den Lehrkrafturteilen, aber auch hier hinken die Grundkursschülerinnen und -schüler an beruflichen Gymnasien hinterher. Die Gründe für die großen Leistungsunterschiede zwischen den Gruppen wurden bereits andernorts ausführlich diskutiert (Leucht, Fleckenstein et al., 2016). So spielen Unterschiede in den Leistungen beim Übertritt in die Sekundarstufe II eine erhebliche Rolle, zudem mag es im sprachlichen Profil Transfereffekte aus den anderen Fremdsprachen auf die englischsprachigen Leistungen geben. Gleichzeitig bleibt aber die Frage im Raum, ob es mit Blick auf die große Bedeutung der Fremdsprache Englisch zielführend ist, dass sich die Schülerinnen und Schüler, die mit vergleichsweise geringen Leistungen in die Sekundarstufe II übertreten, selbst in den Grundkurs wählen, um dort immer weiter in ihren Leistungen zurückzufallen. Hier existiert ein dauerhaftes Spannungsverhältnis zwischen normativen Zielen des voruniversitären Unterrichts (Standards) und den Freiheitsgraden im Wahlverhalten der Schülerinnen und Schüler.

7.2 Passung der Leistungen zu den normativen Vorgaben der Standards

Normative Vorgaben wie die Bildungsstandards der KMK ergeben sich aus politischen und gesellschaftlichen Erwartungen in Bezug auf bestimmte Kompetenzen von Individuen. Solche Vorgaben können nicht vollkommen isoliert von empirischen Befunden betrachtet werden. Ein Mindeststandard, den kaum jemand erreicht, ist von geringem Nutzen, weil er die Realität ignoriert und die pädagogische und didaktische Arbeit in den Schulen erschwert. Unerreichbare Ziele und die Konfrontation mit dem Scheitern an diesen Zielen unterlaufen die Lern- und Leistungsmotivation sowohl der Lehrkräfte als auch der Schülerinnen und Schüler. Die Berücksichtigung empirisch ermittelter Kompetenzstände muss daher bei der Festlegung und Bewertung von Bildungsstandards auch eine Rolle spielen. Der vorliegende Beitrag ermöglicht eine Bewährungsprobe der normativ gesetzten Standards (KMK, 2012) an den empirisch ermittelten Leistungsständen. Aus Sicht der Lehrkräfte scheinen dabei die Niveaus B2 und C1 angemessene Zielgrößen zu sein, die mit Ausnahme der Grundkurse an beruflichen Gymnasien von der großen Mehrheit der Schülerinnen und Schüler erreicht werden. Die IQB-Testergebnisse zeichnen ein etwas kritischeres Bild. Danach scheint das GER-Niveau B2 als Regelstandard für voruniversitäre Englischleistungen adäquat zu sein, da dieses Niveau in allen Gruppen über die Hälfte der Schülerinnen und Schüler im IQB-Test erreichen. Niveau C1 hingegen scheint aus einer rein empirischen Perspektive eine Art Maximalstandard abzubilden, den nur die sprachlich leistungsstärksten Schülerinnen und Schüler erreichen (die insbesondere im sprachlichen Profil am allgemeinbildenden Gymnasium zu finden sind). Insgesamt entsteht so der Eindruck, dass die durch die KMK a priori festgelegten Bildungsstandards etwas zu optimistisch sind.

Ein Blick auf den TOEFL legt dagegen nahe, dass B2 von deutlich weniger Schülerinnen und Schülern erreicht wird; C1 wird hier von so gut wie niemandem erreicht. Im Vergleich zu früheren Berichten über die Leistungen von Abiturientinnen und Abiturienten (z. B. Köller & Trautwein, 2004) fallen diese Ergebnisse deutlich schlechter aus. Der Hauptgrund für diese Diskrepanz ist ein methodischer. Die *Cut Scores* des hier verwendeten ITP-TOEFL basieren auf dem Standard-Setting von Tannenbaum und Baron (2011), das explizit für ITP-TOEFL gemacht wurde. Frühere Publikationen mit dem von uns verwendeten Test bezogen sich dagegen auf Standard-Settings, die nicht explizit für diesen ITP-TOEFL durchgeführt worden waren (zu den Details Köller & Trautwein, 2004). Insofern scheinen unsere aktuellen Befunde hier ein realistischeres Bild zu zeichnen. Losgelöst von diesen methodischen Problemen sind die TOEFL-Ergebnisse ernüchternd, schwanken doch beispielsweise die Anteile derer, die im TOEFL-Gesamtwert mindestens B2 erreichen, zwischen 5.7 % (Grundkurs berufliches Gymnasium) und 48.7 % (sprachliches Profil am allgemeinbildenden Gymnasium). In der Gesamtschau der Befunde über alle Maße hinweg ergibt sich ein Bild, das keine klaren Aussagen über die Anteile der Schülerinnen und Schüler zulässt, welche die Erwartungen der Standards erfüllen. Die Anteile der Schülerinnen und Schüler auf den GER-Niveaus wird sehr stark durch die Art des Tests moderiert. Die Heterogenität der Befunde weist darauf hin, dass valide Aussagen über die Leistungsfähigkeit der gymnasialen Oberstufe im Fremdsprachenunterricht am ehesten getroffen werden könnten, wenn Tests explizit für das Monitoring in diesem Bildungsabschnitt entwickelt würden. Dies ist aber aktuell politisch nicht gewünscht.

Literatur

Adams, R. J., Wu, M., & Wilson, M. (2012). *ACER ConQuest. Version 3.0. Generalised item response modeling software* [Computer software & manual]. Hawthorn, Australia: ACER.

Cizek, G. J. (2006). Standard Setting. In S. M. Downing & T. M. Haladyna (Eds.), *Handbook of Test Development* (S. 225–258). Mahwah, NJ: Earlbaum.

Crystal, D. (2003). *English as a Global Language* (2nd ed.). Cambridge: Cambridge University Press.

Deygers, B., Zeidler, B., Vilcu, D. & Hamnes Carlsen, C. (in press). Deep impact: the CEFR's influence on L2 university entrance policies across Europe. *Language Assessment Quarterly*.

Embretson, S. E., & Reise, S. P. (2000). *Item response theory for psychologists*. Mahwah, NJ: Erlbaum

Eurobarometer (2012). *Europeans and their languages: Special Eurobarometer 386*. Retrieved from http://ec.europa.eu/public_opinion/index_en.htm

Europarat (2001). *Gemeinsamer europäischer Referenzrahmen für Sprachen: lernen, lehren, beurteilen*. München: Langenscheidt.

Fleckenstein, J., Leucht, M. & Köller, O. (in press). Teachers' judgment accuracy concerning CEFR levels of prospective university students. *Language Assessment Quarterly*.

Harsch, C., Pant, H. A. & Köller, O. (Eds.) (2010). *Calibrating Standards-based Assessment Tasks for English as a First Foreign Language. Standard-setting Procedures in Germany*. Münster: Waxmann.

Jonkmann, K., Köller, O. & Trautwein, U. (2007). Englischleistungen am Ende der Sekundarstufe II. In U. Trautwein, O. Köller, R. Lehmann & O. Lüdtke (Hrsg.), *Schulleistungen von Abiturienten. Regionale, schulformbezogene und soziale Disparitäten*. Waxmann: Münster.

Jonkmann, K., Trautwein, U., Nagy, G. & Köller, O. (2010). Fremdsprachenkenntnisse in Englisch vor und nach der Neuordnung der gymnasialen Oberstufe in Baden-Württemberg. In U. Trautwein, M. Neumann, G. Nagy, O. Lüdtke & K. Maaz (Hrsg.), *Schulleistungen von Abiturienten. Die neu geordnete gymnasiale Oberstufe auf dem Prüfstand*. Verlag für Sozialwissenschaften: Wiesbaden.

KMK (2004). *Beschlüsse der Kultusministerkonferenz. Bildungsstandards für die erste Fremdsprache (Englisch/Französisch) für den Mittleren Schulabschluss. Beschluss vom 04.12.2003*. München: Luchterhand.

KMK (2005). *Beschlüsse der Kultusministerkonferenz. Bildungsstandards für die erste Fremdsprache (Englisch/Französisch) für den Hauptschulabschluss. Beschluss vom 15.10.2004*. München: Luchterhand.

KMK (2012). *Bildungsstandards für die fortgeführte Fremdsprache (Englisch/Französisch) für die Allgemeine Hochschulreife (Beschluss der Kultusministerkonferenz vom 18.10.2012)*. Berlin: Sekretariat der KMK.

KMK-Expertenkommission (1995). *Weiterentwicklung der Prinzipien der gymnasialen Oberstufe und des Abiturs: Abschlussbericht der von der Kultusministerkonferenz eingesetzten Expertenkommission*. Bonn: Sekretariat der Ständigen Konferenz der Kultusminister der Länder in der Bundesrepublik Deutschland.

Köller, O. (2009). *Kompetenzstufenmodell zu den Bildungsstandards im Fach Englisch für den Mittleren Schulabschluss*. Zugriff am 09. Dezember 2013 unter www.iqb.hu-berlin.de/bista/ksm/KSM_SekI_MSA_Eng.pdf.

Köller, O. (2010). Bildungsstandards. In R. Tippelt & B. Schmidt (Hrsg.), *Handbuch Bildungsforschung* (S. 529–550). Verlag für Sozialwissenschaften: Wiesbaden.

Köller, O. (2016). Schulleistungsuntersuchungen und Bildungsmonitoring. In J. Möller, M. Köller, & T. Riecke-Baulecke (Hrsg.), *Basiswissen Lehrerbildung: Schule und Unterricht – Lehren und Lernen* (S. 189–204). Seelze: Klett Kallmeyer.

Köller, O., Knigge, M. & Tesch, B. (Hrsg.) (2010). *Sprachliche Kompetenzen im Ländervergleich. Überprüfung der Erreichung der Bildungsstandards für den Mittleren Schulabschluss für Deutsch und die erste Fremdsprache in der neunten Jahrgangsstufe*. Münster: Waxmann.

Köller, O. & Trautwein, U. (2004). Englischleistungen von Schülerinnen und Schülern an allgemein bildenden und beruflichen Gymnasien. In O. Köller, R. Watermann, U. Trautwein & O. Lüdtke (Hrsg.), *Wege zur Hochschulreife in Baden-Württemberg. TOSCA – Eine Untersuchung an allgemein bildenden und beruflichen Gymnasien* (S. 285–326). Opladen: Leske + Budrich.

Leucht, M. (2010). *Diagnostik rezeptiver Kompetenzen in der ersten Fremdsprache Englisch auf Basis des Gemeinsamen Europäischen Referenzrahmens für Sprachen*. Dissertation, Freie Universität Berlin.

Leucht, M., Fleckenstein, J. & Köller, O. (2016). Erreichen kriterialer Leistungsstandards in der ersten Fremdsprache Englisch. In M. Leucht, N. Kampa & O. Köller (Hrsg.). *Fachleistungen beim Abitur. Vergleich allgemeinbildender und beruflicher Gymnasien in Schleswig-Holstein* (S. 171–199). Münster: Waxmann.

Leucht, M., Kampa, N. & Köller, O. (Hrsg.) (2016). *Fachleistungen beim Abitur. Vergleich allgemeinbildender und beruflicher Gymnasien in Schleswig-Holstein*. Münster: Waxmann.

Leucht, M. & Köller, O. (2016). Anlage und Durchführung der Studie. In M. Leucht, N. Kampa & O. Köller (Hrsg.), *Fachleistungen beim Abitur. Vergleich allgemeinbildender und beruflicher Gymnasien in Schleswig-Holstein* (S. 79–98). Münster: Waxmann.

Leucht, M., Retelsdorf, J., Pant, H. A., Möller, J. & Köller, O. (2015). Effekte der Gymnasialprofilzugehörigkeit auf Leistungsentwicklungen im Fach Englisch. *Zeitschrift für Pädagogische Psychologie, 29*, 77–88.

Leucht, M., Tiffin-Richards, S. P., Vock, M., Pant, H. A. & Köller, O. (2012). Diagnostische Kompetenz von Englischlehrkräften bei der Bewertung von Schülerleistungen mit Hilfe des Gemeinsamen Europäischen Referenzrahmens für Sprachen. *Zeitschrift für Entwicklungspsychologie und Pädagogische Psychologie, 44*, 163–177.

Lim, G. S. (2013). Assessing English in Europe. *The Companion to Language Assessment. IV*: 13: 104: 1700–1708.

Muthén, L.K. & Muthén, B.O. (1998–2012). *Mplus user's guide. Seventh edition*. Los Angeles, CA: Muthén & Muthén.

North, B. & Jones, N. (2009). *Further material on maintaining standards across languages, contexts and administrations by exploiting teacher judgment and IRT scaling*. Strasbourg: Language Policy Division.

Rubin, D. B. (1987). *Multiple imputation for nonresponse in surveys*. New York: Wiley.

Runnels, J. (2013). Student ability, self-assessment, and teacher assessment on the CEFR-J's can-do statements. *The Language Teacher Online, 37*, 3–7.

Rupp, A. A., Vock, M., Harsch, C. & Köller, O. (2008). *Developing standards-based assessment tasks for English as a first foreign language – Context, processes, and outcomes in Germany*. Münster: Waxmann.

Schmidt, F. T. C., Broux, A. & Leucht, M. (2016). Allgemeinbildende und berufliche Gymnasien in Schleswig-Holstein. In M. Leucht, N. Kampa & O. Köller (Hrsg.). *Fachleistungen beim Abitur. Vergleich allgemeinbildender und beruflicher Gymnasien in Schleswig-Holstein* (S. 55–77). Münster: Waxmann.

Stanat, P., Böhme, K., Schipolowski, S., & Haag, N. (Hrsg.) (2016). *IQB-Bildungstrend 2015 – Sprachliche Kompetenzen am Ende der 9. Jahrgangsstufe im zweiten Ländervergleich*. Münster: Waxmann.

Südkamp, A., Kaiser, J., & Möller, J. (2012). Accuracy of teachers' judgments of students' academic achievement: A meta-analysis. *Journal of Educational Psychology*, *104*, 743–762.

Tannenbaum, R. J., & Baron, P. A. (2011). *Mapping TOEFL ITP scores onto the Common European Framework of Reference*. Princeton, NJ: Educational Testing Service.

Tenorth, H.-E. (2001). Englisch: Ein Kerncurriculum, seine Notwendigkeit und seine Gestalt – Zusammenfassung. In H.-E. Tenorth (Hrsg.), *Kerncurriculum Oberstufe: Mathematik – Deutsch – Englisch: Expertisen im Auftrag der Ständigen Konferenz der Kultusminister* (S. 156–161). Weinheim: Beltz.

Tesch, B., Porsch, R., Leupold, E., Grotjahn, R., Kleppin, K., Frenzel, J., Harsch, C., Leucht, M., Pant, H. A., Rupp, A. A., Tiffin-Richards, S. P. & Köller, O. (2010). Kompetenzstufenmodelle für Lese- und Hörverstehen in der ersten Fremdsprache. In O. Köller, M. Knigge & B. Tesch (Hrsg.), *Sprachliche Kompetenzen im Ländervergleich. Überprüfung der Erreichung der Bildungsstandards für den Mittleren Schulabschluss für Deutsch und die erste Fremdsprache in der neunten Jahrgangsstufe* (S. 50–64). Münster: Waxmann.

Tiffin-Richards, S. P., Pant, H. A. & Köller, O. (2013). Setting Standards for English Foreign Language Assessment: Methodology, Validation and a Degree of Arbitrariness. *Educational Measurement: Issues and Practice, 32*, 15–25.

Trautwein, U., Köller, O., Lehmann, R. & Lüdtke, O. (Hrsg.) (2007). *Schulleistungen von Abiturienten: Regionale, schulformbezogene und soziale Disparitäten*. Münster: Waxmann.

Zhu, M., & Urhahne, D. (2015). Teachers' judgements of students' foreign-language achievement. *European Journal of Psychology of Education, 30*, 21–39.

Autorin und Autoren

PROF. DR. OLAF KÖLLER
Erziehungswissenschaft, IPN · Leibniz-Institut für die Pädagogik der Naturwissenschaften und Mathematik.

DR. MICHAEL LEUCHT
Erziehungswissenschaft, IPN · Leibniz-Institut für die Pädagogik der Naturwissenschaften und Mathematik.

DR. JOHANNA FLECKENSTEIN
Erziehungswissenschaft, IPN · Leibniz-Institut für die Pädagogik der Naturwissenschaften und Mathematik.

PROF. DR. JÜRGEN BAUMERT
Max-Planck-Institut für Bildungsforschung, Berlin.

KONTAKT
Olaf Köller, IPN · Leibniz-Institut für die Pädagogik der Naturwissenschaften und Mathematik, Olshausenstr. 62, 24118 Kiel.
E-Mail: *koeller@ipn.uni-kiel.de*

Studienwahlmotive, berufsbezogene Interessen und Selbstkonzepte angehender Lehrerinnen und Lehrer

LILIAN STREBLOW UND BRITTA POHLMANN

ZUSAMMENFASSUNG: Ziel der vorliegenden Studie ist, verschiedene Typen von Lehramtsstudierenden auf Basis ihrer Studienwahlmotive zu differenzieren und deren Entwicklung im weiteren Studienverlauf (Studienbeginn bis Beginn Master of Education (i.d.R. 7. Studiensemester) zu betrachten.

Mittels Clusteranalyse konnten drei Typen identifiziert werden: die „Berufenen“ (N = 160, 20.3 %), die „Pragmatikerinnen“ und „Pragmatiker“ (N = 161, 20.5 %) und der Typus „indifferent“ (N = 466, 59.2 %). Bei den „Berufenen“ waren ausgeprägte pädagogische und fachbezogene Interessen sowie ein positives berufsbezogenes Selbstkonzept dominierende Studienwahlmotive, die eher extrinsischen Aspekte der Nützlichkeit, geringen antizipierten Schwierigkeit sowie der sozialen Einflüsse spielten eine geringe Rolle. Für die „Pragmatikerinnen“ und „Pragmatiker“ waren intrinsische und extrinsische Motive bedeutsam, es dominierten allerdings deutlich die extrinsischen Motive. Bei dem Typus „indifferent“ waren alle genannten Motive geringer ausgeprägt. Es zeigte sich u.a., dass die „Berufenen“ im weiteren Studienverlauf erwartungsgemäß höhere pädagogische Interessen, ein positiveres Selbstkonzept und mehr Einsatz von Elaborationsstrategien schilderten. Die Befunde werden vor dem Hintergrund aktueller Reformen der Lehrerbildung diskutiert.

Schlüsselwörter: Lehrerbildung, Studienwahlmotive, berufsbezogenes Selbstkonzept, berufsbezogenes Interesse

Career choice motivation, work-related self-concept and interest of teacher students

ABSTRACT: The present study aims at identifying different types of teacher students on the basis of their career choice motivations and at analyzing their development in the course of their studies (from their first term to the beginning of their Master's studies, usually in their 7th term).

A cluster analysis rendered three different types of students: The "called ones" (N = 160, 20.3 %), the "pragmatic ones" (N = 161, 20.5 %) and the "indifferent ones" (N = 466, 59.2 %). Students of the "called type" chose their studies because of a high educational and subject-specific interest and a positive work-related self-concept. The extrinsic factors of utility, low anticipated difficulties, and social influences only play a minor role. With the "pragmatic ones", however, both intrinsic and extrinsic motives are significant, the extrinsic motives being the most dominant. All of these motives are less pronounced with the "indifferent ones". The study also shows that the "called ones" maintain a higher educational interest throughout their studies.

They also show a more positive self-concept and a more frequent use of elaboration strategies. The results are discussed in the light of current teacher education reforms.

Keywords: teacher education, career choice motivation, work-related self-concept, work-related interest

Einleitung

Dem Modell professioneller Handlungskompetenz von Baumert und Kunter (2006) zufolge zählen „Motivationale Orientierungen" zu den Professionsmerkmalen, die zur unterschiedlichen Nutzung von Lerngelegenheiten und damit zu unterschiedlichen Studienverläufen von Lehramtsstudierenden beitragen. Umfangreiche, längsschnittlich angelegte Studien berücksichtigen motivationale Merkmale, wie die PaLea-Studie (Panel zum Lehramtsstudium, z.B. Bauer et al., 2010; Gröschner et al., 2015), die LEK-Studie (Längsschnittliche Erhebung pädagogischer Kompetenzen von Lehramtsstudierenden, König & Seifert, 2012), die EMW-Studie (Entwicklung von berufsspezifischer Motivation und pädagogischem Wissen in der Lehrerbildung, König & Rothland, 2013) oder – speziell für die Ausbildung von Mathematiklehrerinnen und Mathematiklehrern – die Studie TEDS-M (Teacher Education and Development Study in Mathematics, Blömeke, Kaiser & Lehmann, 2010a; b).

Die vorliegende Untersuchung ist Teil einer umfangreicheren formativen Evaluationsstudie, die aktuell auch in die wissenschaftliche Begleitung des in der Qualitätsoffensive Lehrerbildung verorteten Projektes eingebunden ist.[1] Die Studie soll u.a. dazu dienen, genauere Erkenntnisse über die Bedeutung und Entwicklung motivationaler Merkmale von Lehramtsstudierenden zu gewinnen. Im Verlauf des Studiums werden die Studierenden zu fünf verschiedenen Zeitpunkten befragt, wobei die Zeitpunkte abhängig von dem Durchlaufen der Praxisphasen sind, und nicht von der absolvierten Semesterzahl. Dies ist sowohl dem politischen als auch dem wissenschaftlichen Stellenwert der Praxisphasen geschuldet. Zudem ist die Notwendigkeit gegeben, im Rahmen der formativen Evaluation zeitnah Probleme der Praxisphasen zu identifizieren, zu kommunizieren und letztendlich bearbeiten zu können. Die formative Evaluationsstudie versteht sich somit nicht als Grundlagenforschung, sondern als Instrument zur Qualitätssicherung und -entwicklung. In der Panelstudie werden Themen aufgegriffen, die – neben den unstrittig wichtigen fachwissenschaftlichen und fachdidaktischen Ausbildungszielen – aktuelle Desiderate der Lehrerbildung aufgreifen und dazu beitragen sollen genauer zu verstehen, unter welchen Bedingungen die Praxiselemente für die Lehramtsstudierenden einen Mehrwert für die Entwicklung professionsbezogener Kompetenzen darstellen.

---

1 Bi[professional] wird im Rahmen der gemeinsamen Qualitätsoffensive Lehrerbildung von Bund und Ländern aus Mitteln des Bundesministeriums für Bildung und Forschung gefördert (Förderkennzeichen: 01JA1608).

Motivationalen Merkmalen könnten dabei gerade in diesen Phasen, in denen schulische Praxisanteile sinnvoll in das Studium integriert werden müssen, eine besondere Bedeutung zukommen. So beschreibt Hascher (2012, S. 124) die Lehramtsstudierenden in den Praxisphasen als „besonders vulnerabel" und fordert, „motivationale und emotionale Aspekte" und ihre wechselseitigen Einflüssen mit kognitiven Merkmalen zukünftig mehr zu berücksichtigen.

In dem vorliegenden Beitrag liegt der Fokus auf den Motiven, die für die Aufnahme des Lehramtsstudiums von den Studierenden als besonders bedeutsam erlebt werden. Ziel dieser Untersuchung ist, auf Basis der Studienwahlmotive verschiedene Typen von Lehramtsstudierenden zu identifizieren und zu untersuchen, ob sich in Abhängigkeit von den zugrunde liegenden Motiven im Studienverlauf Unterschiede im berufsbezogenen Selbstkonzept, in den berufsbezogenen Interessen sowie in der Nutzung von Elaborationsstrategien zeigen lassen.

1 Studienwahlmotive und ihre Bedeutung für die Aufnahme des Lehramtsstudiums

Angehende Lehrkräfte aller Schulformen müssen sich in ihrer professionellen Entwicklung intensiver mit der zunehmenden sozialen und kulturellen Vielfalt in der Schule, dem schnellen gesellschaftlichen Wandel und zum Teil sehr unterschiedlichen Bedürfnissen von Schülerinnen und Schülern an Schule und Unterricht auseinandersetzen. Im Studium müssen sie darauf vorbereitet werden, ihren angestrebten Beruf später in einem inklusiven Schulsystem auszuüben (vgl. Forlin, 2010; Heinrich, Urban & Werning, 2013). Zentral sind insbesondere adaptive Kompetenzen, die die Studierenden auf Veränderungen vorbereiten und es ihnen ermöglichen, den mit Heterogenität verbundenen Herausforderungen in Bildung und Erziehung zukünftig besser gerecht zu werden (Heinrich et al., 2013). Somit scheinen insbesondere die Studierenden auf die mit ihrem zukünftigen Beruf verbundenen Anforderungen gut vorbereitet zu sein, die selbstgesteuert lernen können (vgl. Hauser, 2009). Die Praxisphasen könnten dabei eine Schlüsselrolle einnehmen (vgl. HRK & KMK, 2015). Mit den Praxisphasen sind in der Regel hohe Erwartungen der Studierenden verknüpft (Hascher & Zordo, 2015) und auch bildungspolitisch wird immer wieder eine praxisnahe Ausbildung und intensive Nutzung der Lerngelegenheiten im Praktikum gefordert. Dies kann beispielsweise der Bund-Länder-Vereinbarung über die im Rahmen der Qualitätsoffensive Lehrerbildung ausgelobten zusätzlichen Mittel für Maßnahmen in der Lehrerbildung entnommen werden (BMBF, 2013). In vielen Bundesländern wurden und werden aktuell Praxisphasen ausgeweitet und Langzeitpraktika wie das Praxissemester in das Studium integriert. Hoffnungsträger und Sorgenkinder zugleich sind in diesem Zusammenhang das „Forschende Lernen" und die „theoriegeleitete und reflexive Portfolioarbeit", da mit beiden hohe Erwartungen verknüpft sind, diese aber in der Umsetzung keine Selbstläufer sind (Barsch & Glutsch, 2016) und sehr hohe Anforderungen an die Selbststeuerung der Studierenden stellen (vgl. Werfel, Streblow & Schüssler, 2016). In der Lehrerbildung wird zudem immer wieder die Frage gestellt, ob der Zugang zum Lehramtsstudium an eine Form der Eignungsprüfung gebunden sein sollte und darüber diskutiert, ob der Anteil der vermeintlich nicht für den Lehrerberuf geeigneten Studierenden zu hoch sei. Doch bisher liegen keine überzeugenden Belege für eine prognostisch-valide Eignungsprüfung vor Aufnahme des Studiums vor (vgl. Klusmann, Köller & Kunter, 2011; Rothland & Terhart, 2011) und auch die Annahme, eine Gruppe von Lehramtsstudierenden würden über ungünstigere Voraussetzungen für das Studium verfügen, bedarf erst der genauen Prüfung. So untersuchte Neugebauer (2013) in einer umfangreichen Studie die These der Negativselektion und fragte, ob Lehramtsstudierende ungünstigere kognitive und motivationale Merkmale aufweisen als andere Studierende. Für die Gruppe der angehenden Gymnasiallehrkräfte zeigten sich mit Blick auf die Abiturleistung und die fachlichen Studienwahlmotive keine bedeutsamen Unterschiede zu den Nicht-Lehramtsstudierenden. Lehramtsstudierende anderer Schulformen wiesen hingegen schlechtere Abiturnoten sowie geringer ausgeprägte fachliche und wissenschaftliche Studienwahlmotive auf. Besonders ausgeprägt sind bei den Lehramtsstudierenden aller Schulformen hingegen – verglichen mit Studierenden ohne Lehramtsbezug – soziale Interessen. Dies deckt sich zum Teil mit den Befunden von Klusmann, Trautwein, Lüdtke, Kunter und Baumert (2009), die ebenfalls Lehramtsstudierende mit Studierenden anderer Bereiche verglichen. Sie fanden bedeutsame Unterschiede mit Blick auf die beruflichen Interessen und konnten ebenfalls zeigen, dass die Wahl eines Lehramtsstudiums insbesondere durch eine ausgeprägte soziale Orientierung vorhergesagt werden konnte. Klusmann et al. konnten keine stützenden Belege für eine ausgeprägte Negativselektion ins Lehramtsstudium finden. Pohlmann und Möller (2010) haben diese Studie als einen Ausgangspunkt für ihre Studien gewählt und verfolgten das Ziel, zunächst auf Basis des Erwartungs-Wert-Modells einen Fragebogen für die differenzierte Erfassung lehramtsspezifischer Berufswahlmotive zu entwickeln und diesen in mehreren Studien zu validieren. Es ist ihnen dabei gelungen, mit *Pädagogischem Interesse*, *Fachlichem Interesse* sowie der *Nützlichkeit* drei Aspekte der Wertkomponente zu ermitteln und mit *Fähigkeitsüberzeugung* und *Geringe Schwierigkeit des Studiums* die Erwartungskomponente abzubilden. Zudem wurden *Soziale Einflüsse* als eine weitere bedeutsame Dimension identifiziert, was auch im Einklang mit den bereits berichteten Befunden von Neugebauer (2013) sowie Klusmann et al. (2009) steht.

2 Ableitung der Fragestellung

Studien haben gezeigt, dass sich Lehramtsstudierende in ihren Studienwahlmotiven unterscheiden (z. B. Mayr, 2011; Retelsdorf & Möller, 2012; Rothland, 2011). Pohlmann und Möller (2010) haben mit dem Fragebogen zur Erfassung der Motivation für die Wahl des Lehramtsstudiums (FEMOLA) ein Instrument entwickelt, welches die differenzierte Erfassung unterschiedlicher Studienwahlmotive Lehramtsstudierender ermöglicht.

Mit der vorliegenden Studie wird ein Desiderat aus der Untersuchung von Pohlmann und Möller (2010) aufgegriffen, die schreiben: „Ungeklärt bleibt aktuell die prognostische Validität der FEMOLA-Skalen. In Folgestudien soll erfragt werden, welchen Einfluss die unterschiedlichen Motivationen auf die Motivations- und Kompetenzentwicklung von Lehramtsstudierenden haben. [...] Um derartige Zusammenhänge analysieren zu können, sind jedoch weitere insbesondere längsschnittlich angelegte Untersuchungen erforderlich, die die kontinuierliche Entwicklung motivationaler und leistungsbezogener Merkmale während des Studiums abbilden (S. 83)". In der vorliegenden Studie werden zunächst Faktoren betrachtet, die als mögliche wichtige motivationale Voraussetzungen für ein gewinnbringendes Studium betrachtet werden können und nicht Leistung oder Studienerfolg.

Die erste Fragestellung lautet, ob sich auf Basis ihrer zu Studienbeginn angegebenen Studienwahlmotive verschiedene Studierendengruppen identifizieren lassen. Falls sich die Annahme bestätigt und sich zwei oder mehr interpretierbare und theoretisch begründbare Untergruppen bilden lassen, soll in einem nächsten Schritt geprüft werden, ob die unterschiedlichen Gruppen in vergleichbarer Weise in den unterschiedlichen Lehramtsstudiengängen repräsentiert sind oder ob sich in dieser Studie Hinweise auf Unterschiede zwischen unterschiedlichen Schulformen wie in der Studie von Neugebauer (2013) zeigen. Dann wird die Frage der prognostischen Validität verfolgt und geprüft, ob sich im weiteren Verlauf des Studiums Unterschiede zwischen den Gruppen in den Ausprägungen der beruflichen Interessen, des berufsbezogenen Selbstkonzepts sowie im Einsatz von Elaborationsstrategien beobachten lassen. Es wurden mit den berufsbezogenen Interessen sowie dem berufsbezogenen Selbstkonzept für die Befragungen im Studienverlauf Konstrukte gewählt, die einen engen Bezug zu den zum ersten Messzeitpunkt erfassten Studienwahlmotiven erwarten lassen. Überdies haben wir mit *Elaboration* noch eine ausgewählte Lernstrategie berücksichtigt, für die in besonderem Maße ein Unterschied zu Gunsten von Studierenden erwartet wird, die aus eher intrinsischen Motiven ein Lehramtsstudium aufgenommen haben (vgl. Pintrich & Garcia, 1994). Auch mit Blick auf die eingangs beschriebenen besonderen Anforderungen an die Selbststeuerung des Lernens, handelt es sich bei *Elaboration* um ein zentrales Merkmal (vgl. Friedrich, 2008).

2.1 Hypothesen

Die erste zu prüfende Fragestellung lautet, ob sich auf Basis von Studienwahlmotiven unterschiedliche Typen von Lehramtsstudierenden identifizieren lassen. Es wird ausgehend von den vorliegenden Befunden von Pohlmann und Möller (2010) vermutet, dass sich mindestens zwei Gruppen unterscheiden lassen: Studierende, die eher intrinsisch motiviert sind, ein Lehramtsstudium aufzunehmen und bei denen somit das pädagogische und das fachliche Interesse stark ausgeprägt sind, sowie Studierende, die sich aus eher extrinsischen Motiven, wie *Nützlichkeit*, *geringe antizipierte Schwierigkeit* oder aufgrund von *sozialen Einflüssen* für dieses Studium entschieden haben. Auf diese Zweiteilung deuten die entsprechenden beiden Sekundärfaktoren *intrinsisch* und *extrinsisch* in den Analysen von Pohlmann und Möller (2010) hin.

Die anschließend zu prüfende Annahme ist, dass Studierende, die aus eher intrinsischen Motiven ein Lehramtsstudium aufnehmen, im weiteren Studienverlauf verglichen mit anderen, weniger intrinsisch motivierten Studierenden bzw. insgesamt weniger motivierten Studierenden ein positiveres berufsbezogenes Selbstkonzept sowie ausgeprägter pädagogisches, didaktisches und fachliches Interesse zeigen und sie zudem angeben, eher Elaborationsstrategien einzusetzen.

2.2 Forschungsmethodisches Vorgehen

Durch neue gesetzliche Vorgaben und Rahmenbedingungen sind die lehramtsbezogenen Studiengänge in Nordrhein-Westfalen erheblich verändert worden. Mit der Umsetzung der neuen Studienstruktur zum Wintersemester (WS) 2011/12 wurde damit begonnen, zentrale Elemente des Studiums formativ zu evaluieren. Ein zentrales Anliegen dieser Evaluationsstudien ist zu prüfen, wie die Studierenden die Einbindung der Praxisphasen in den Studienablauf bewerten. Die Teilnahme ist freiwillig und anonym. Die Befragungen werden als Paper-Pencil-Befragungen im Rahmen von Lehrveranstaltungen durchgeführt. Die Messzeitpunkte sind aufgrund der inhaltlichen Schwerpunktsetzung an die Praxisphasen und nicht an die Studiensemester gekoppelt. Vor Aufnahme des Studiums sollen die Studierenden ein Eignungspraktikum (20 Praktikumstage) absolviert haben. Nach dem ersten oder zweiten Semester absolvieren die Studierenden ein vierwöchiges Blockpraktikum, das Orientierungspraktikum. Am Ende des Bachelors wird ein Berufsfeldpraktikum absolviert und an dem Praxissemester, welches einen fünfmonatigen schulpraktischen Teil umfasst, nehmen die Studierenden nicht vor dem zweiten Fachsemester im Masterstudium teil. Angaben zu den Messzeitpunkten und zu den Stichproben der vorliegenden Studie sind Tabelle 1 zu entnehmen.

2.3 Stichprobe

Für die vorliegenden Analysen konnten Daten von Studierenden berücksichtigt werden, die ein Lehramtsstudium in der Zeitspanne WS 2011/12 bis WS 2015/16 an einer mittelgroßen Universität in Nordrhein-Westfalen aufgenommen haben. Die nachfolgend berichteten Analysen und Befunde basieren mit 796 Fällen auf denjenigen Studierenden der Kohorten WS 2011/12 bis WS 2013/14, die den Fragebogen zu T1 (Beginn des Studiums) absolviert haben. Die Differenz zu der Gesamtzahl an 1.683 Fällen im aktuellen Längsschnittdatensatz (Stand: Juli 2016) ist sowohl darauf zurückzuführen, dass die Studienwahlmotive, die mit dem FEMOLA (Pohlmann & Möller, 2010) erfasst wurden, nur in den Befragungen WS 2011/12 bis WS 2013/14 mit erhoben wurden, als auch darauf, dass durch die Freiwilligkeit der Befragung

Tabelle 1. Messzeitpunkte, Erläuterungen und Angaben zu den Stichproben

Messzeitpunkt	Erläuterung	Kohorten	Stichprobe	Grundgesamtheit	Rücklauf
t1	Studienbeginn	WS 11/12–WS 13/14	824	2025	0.41
t2	nach den Orientierenden Praxisstudien (nach dem 1. oder 2. Semester)	WS 11/12–SoSe 14	1529	1869	0.82
t3	Anfang Master of Education (7. Semester)	WS 14/15–SoSe 16	359	665	0.54
t4	nach dem Praxissemester (8. Semester)	SoSe 15–WS 15/16	182	232	0.78
t5	Absolventen Master of Education (10. Semester)	im Aufbau	im Aufbau	im Aufbau	im Aufbau

eine Teilnahme der Studierenden an jedem Messzeitpunkt nicht gewährleistet werden konnte und insbesondere im ersten Messzeitpunkt (T1) der Rücklauf vergleichsweise schwach ausfiel (siehe Tabelle 1: Messzeitpunkte/Rücklauf).[2] Somit sind die folgenden Analysen so zu interpretieren: Auf Basis der 796 Studierenden zu T1 (Studienbeginn) wurden Cluster anhand 6 verschiedener Subskalen des FEMOLA gebildet, wobei drei Subskalen als intrinsische Studienwahlmotivation und drei Subskalen als extrinsische Studienwahlmotivation verstanden wurden.[3] Für die anschließenden Varianzanalysen wurden nun die Fälle in späteren Messzeitpunkten mit den nach FEMOLA „geclusterten") Fälle des T1 zusammengefügt. Da die Erreichbarkeit der Studierenden problematisch und die Teilnahme der Studierenden freiwillig ist, reduziert sich diese Stichprobe von 796 Studierenden auf diejenigen, die zu einem späteren Messzeitpunkt befragt werden konnten. Es ist somit nicht auszuschließen, dass die Nicht-Erreichbarkeit von Studierenden zu späteren Messzeitpunkten durch verschiedene Ursachen (Studienabbruch, sehr langsame Studiergeschwindigkeit, geringe Präsenz in Veranstaltungen, in denen erhoben wird etc.) bedingt ist, die mit der Studienwahlmotivation korrelieren.

2 Weitere, geringere Ausfälle erklären sich dadurch, dass wenige Studierende einen selbst zu generierenden Code nicht erstellten und somit in einem fehlertoleranten, distanzbasierten Matching-Verfahren nicht zu den anderen Messzeitpunkten in Beziehung gesetzt werden konnten.

3 Die siebte Subskala „Eigene Lehrer" wurde nicht genutzt, da die beiden Items in dieser Stichprobe etwas gänzlich anderes zu messen scheinen (zwei faktorielle Lösung bei einer explorativen Faktorenanalyse, negatives Cronbachs Alpha beim Test auf Reliabilität) und damit eine Zusammenfassung zu einer Skala nicht zu rechtfertigen war.

Von dieser Teilstichprobe der 796 Studierenden haben sich 320 Personen für das Lehramt Gymnasium/Gesamtschule (GymGe) eingeschrieben (40.5 %), 119 für das Lehramt HRGe (Haupt-, Real-, Gesamtschule, 14.9 %), 231 für das Grundschullehramt (26.8 %) und 139 Studierende gaben an, die Variante Grundschullehramt mit integrierter Sonderpädagogik zu studieren (GISP, 17.5 %). Vor den Teilnehmenden haben 514 Frauen (65.9 %) und 266 Männer (34.1 %) Angaben zum Geschlecht gemacht. In den hier vorgestellten Analysen sind die Stichproben unterschiedlich groß, was darauf zurückzuführen ist, dass nur ein Teil der Studierenden bereits so weit im Studium fortgeschritten ist und von vielen Studierenden zu den Messzeitpunkten T3 und T4 noch keine Daten erhoben wurden. Hinzu kommt, dass die sehr umfangreichen Instrumente FEMOLA (Pohlmann & Möller, 2010) und ERBSE-L (Erfassung berufsbezogener Selbstkonzepte von angehenden Lehrkräften, Retelsdorf, Bauer, Gebauer, Kauper & Möller, 2014) nicht in allen Kohorten eingesetzt werden konnten, da zum Teil andere inhaltliche Schwerpunkte gesetzt worden sind.

Alle Analysen wurden mit SPSS 24.0 gerechnet. Obgleich es keinen Hinweis auf systematisch fehlende Werte gibt und die Anzahl der fehlenden Werte sich im Bereich von 5–10 % bewegte, wurden zur Vergrößerung der sich noch im Aufbau befindlichen Datenbasis fehlende Werte mittels Multipler Datenimputation (MI) ersetzt (vgl. Lüdtke, Robitzsch, Trautwein & Köller, 2015).[4]

2.4 Instrumente

Die statistischen Kennwerte zu den verwendeten Instrumenten sind Tabelle 2 zu entnehmen (Reliabilitäten, Mittelwerte, Standardabweichungen).

Tabelle 2. Deskriptive Statistik. Die Merkmale wurden mittels einer vierstufigen Ratingskala von 1 („trifft nicht zu") bis 4 („trifft zu") erfasst. Alle Items sind so kodiert, dass ein hoher Wert eine positive Ausprägung des jeweils betrachteten Konstruktes widerspiegelt

Studienwahlmotive (t1)	*N*	Items	*M*	*SD*	α
Nützlichkeit	796	9	2.88	0.55	.833
Pädagogisches Interesse	796	6	3.62	0.41	.837
Selbstkonzept	796	5	3.26	0.44	.717
Soziale Einflüsse	796	5	2.19	0.71	.813
Geringe Schwierigkeit	796	4	1.52	0.50	.795
Fachliches Interesse	796	5	3.30	0.54	.852

4 Beim verwendeten Verfahren handelt es sich um Predictive Mean Matching (PMM). Es wurden 20 Imputationen vorgenommen.

Elaboration (t1)	796	8	3.12	0.45	.757
Berufsbezogenes Selbstkonzept (t2)					
Fach	141	3	3.04	0.56	.774
Erziehung	141	4	3.39	0.45	.694
Diagnostik	141	4	3.19	0.47	.651
Innovation	141	3	2.95	0.54	.638
Medien	141	3	3.14	0.56	.778
Beratung	141	3	3.28	0.48	.676
Interesse (t3)					
Fachlich	180	8	3.06	0.42	.669
Didaktisch	180	5	3.30	0.39	.624
Pädagogisch	180	5	3.40	0.38	.687

Studienwahlmotive

Die Studierenden wurden zu Studienbeginn mit dem FEMOLA von Pohlmann und Möller (2010) zu ihren Studienwahlmotiven befragt. Folgende Dimensionen werden mit den Subskalen erfasst: Nützlichkeit (z. B. „Ich habe das Lehramtsstudium gewählt[5], weil ich als Lehrer/in gut verdiene."), Pädagogisches Interesse (z. B. „ ..., weil ich gern mit Kindern und Jugendlichen arbeite."), Fähigkeitsüberzeugungen (z. B.: „..., weil ich denke, dass ich eine gute Lehrerin/ ein guter Lehrer sein werde."), Soziale Einflüsse (z. B. „..., weil mir von Freunden und Bekannten zum Lehramtsstudium geraten wurde."), Geringe Schwierigkeit des Lehramtsstudiums (z. B. „..., weil es leichter ist als andere Studiengänge.") sowie Fachliches Interesse (z. B.: „..., weil ich mich gern mit den Inhalten meiner Fächer beschäftige.")

Elaboration

Als ein im Zusammenhang mit motivationalen Merkmalen besonders wichtiger Aspekt des Lernverhaltens, insbesondere mit Blick auf das selbstgesteuerte Lernen, wird *Elaboration* mit einer modifizierten Subskala aus dem LIST erfragt (Lernstrategien im Studium, Wild & Schiefele, 1994; z. B.: „Ich beziehe das, was ich lerne, auf meine eigenen Erfahrungen.").

5 Jedes Item beginnt mit diesem Satzteil.

Berufsbezogene Selbstkonzepte (SK)

Das professionsbezogene Selbstbild der Studierenden wird mit der Skala zur ERBSE-L (Retelsdorf et al., 2014) erfasst. Das Instrument setzt sich aus den folgenden Subskalen zusammen: SK Fach (z. B.: „Ich denke, meine Studienfächer liegen mir besonders."), SK Erziehung (z. B.: „Ich finde auch zu „schwierigen" Kindern und Jugendlichen einen guten Zugang."), SK Diagnostik (z. B.: „Ich merke schnell, wenn andere Probleme haben."), SK Innovation (z. B.: „Es liegt mir, neue Projekte zu planen und umzusetzen."), SK Medien (z. B. „Der Umgang mit neuen Medien fällt mir leicht.") und SK Beratung (z. B.: „Andern bei Problemen weiterzuhelfen ist etwas, das ich gut kann.").

Berufliches Interesse

Im weiteren Studium werden berufsbezogene Interessen mit der Skala von Schiefele, Streblow und Retelsdorf (2013) erfasst. Dieser Fragebogen basiert auf der Personen-Gegenstandstheorie des Interesses und einer früheren Version eines Fragebogens zur Erfassung des Studieninteresses (vgl. Schiefele, 2009; Schiefele, Krapp, Wild & Winteler, 1993). Es werden mit fachlichem (z. B.: „Ich habe mein Fach vor allem wegen seiner interessanten Inhalte gewählt."), didaktischem (z. B.: „Die Beschäftigung mit Unterrichtsmethoden hat für mich persönlich einen hohen Wert.") und pädagogischem Interesse (z. B.: „Ich interessiere mich besonders für die erzieherische Seite des Lehrerberufs.") Aspekte erfasst, die sich aus den Arbeiten von Shulman (1986, 1987) ableiten lassen, auf die sich auch Baumert und Kunter (2006) beziehen.

Zusätzlich wurden noch soziodemographische Daten wie Alter und Geschlecht, bisherige Stationen der schulischen und gegebenenfalls einer beruflichen Ausbildung sowie die Durchschnittsnote des Abschlusses, mit dem die Hochschulzugangsberechtigung erworben wurde, erfragt. Diese Angaben werden von dem Arbeitsbereich vor allem für statistische Zwecke benötigt. Für die hier vorgestellten Analysen sind sie nur insofern von Bedeutung, als dass sie bei Uneindeutigkeiten der Codes im Matching der verschiedenen Messzeitpunkte als Heuristik hinzugezogen wurden.

2.5 Ergebnisse

Studierendentypologie – Ergebnisse der Clusteranalyse

Zur Identifizierung verschiedener Typen wurde mit den sechs z-standardisierten Skalen des FEMOLA in zwei Stufen hierarchische Clusteranalysen gerechnet. Bei den sogenannten hierarchisch-agglomerativen Verfahren werden „aus n Objekten zunächst n Cluster gebildet, aus den n Clustern durch Zusammenfassung der beiden ähnlichen Cluster dann n-1 Cluster, aus diesen wiederum n-2 Clustern usw." (Bacher, 2010). Zunächst wurden dabei Ausreißer schrittweise ausgeschlossen (Distanzmaß: Quadrierte Euklidische Distanz, Nearest Neighbour-Verfahren) und in einem zweiten Schritt dann die Cluster gebildet (Distanzmaß: Quadrierte Euklidische Distanz, Ward-Verfahren). Die Interpretation des Dendrogramms – der optischen Abbildung des hierarchischen Clusterprozesses – fällt zufrieden stellend aus. Es konnten drei Gruppen differenziert werden (vgl. Abbildung 1). Die erste Gruppe, die „Berufenen" ($N = 160$, 20.3 %), benennen insbesondere ein ausgeprägtes pädagogisches Interesse sowie ein großes inhaltliches Interesse als dominierende Motive für ihre Studienwahl. Das berufsbezogene Selbstkonzept ist ebenfalls positiv ausgeprägt und die eher extrinsischen Motive Nützlichkeit und geringe wahrgenommene Schwierigkeit sind hingegen nur in geringem Maße beschrieben worden. Bei den „Pragmatikerinnen" und „Pragmatikern", der zweiten Gruppe ($N = 161$, 20.5 %), ist hingegen die geringe wahrgenommene Schwierigkeit das dominierende Motiv, gefolgt von sozialen Einflüssen und Nützlichkeit. Das fachliche Interesse sowie das pädagogische Interesse sind nur in geringem Maße bedeutsam und das berufsbezogene Selbstkonzept ist weniger positiv. Somit werden von dieser Gruppe insbesondere die eher extrinsischen Motive als entscheidend für ihre

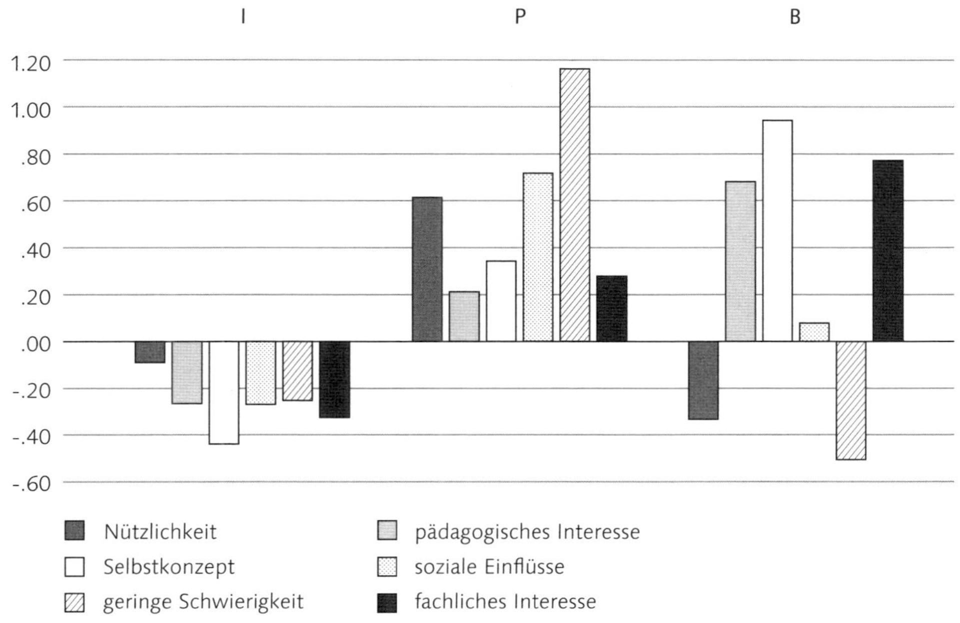

Abbildung 1. Clustermittelwerte (z-standardisiert, $N = 780$) der drei Typen „Studienwahlmotive" (FEMOLA, Pohlmann & Möller, 2010). I (indifferent), P (Pragmatikerinnen und Pragmatiker), B (Berufene).

Studienwahl genannt. Bei der dritten und größten Gruppe, dem Typus „indifferent" ($N = 466$, 59.2 %), dominieren weder die eher intrinsischen noch die eher extrinsischen Motive, sondern alle genannten möglichen Motive werden in geringem Maße als bedeutsam für die Studienwahl charakterisiert. Eine Validierung erfuhr das Cluster-Verfahren mittels einer Diskriminanzanalyse: Die beiden mittleren Werte der Diskriminanzfunktion in allen drei Gruppen unterscheiden sich höchst signifikant untereinander (Wilks-Lambda < .000) Der hohe Eigenwert von 1.131 deutet auf eine gut schätzende Diskriminationsfunktion hin.

Die „Berufenen" und die Gruppe „indifferent" wiesen leicht bessere Abiturnoten auf als die „Pragmatikerinnen" und „Pragmatiker" (vgl. Tabelle 3). Bezogen auf die Wahl der Schulform zeigten sich bedeutsame Unterschiede ($F = 7,190$, $p < .001$), aber kein klares Bild. Die Gruppe „indifferent" wählte insbesondere das Lehramt Gymnasium / Gesamtschule sowie das Grundschullehramt, während die anderen beiden Gruppen keine so ausgeprägte Präferenz zeigten und sich gleichmäßiger verteilten. Da die Zulassung jedoch an Bedingungen geknüpft ist und über einen Numerus Clausus in den Bildungswissenschaften gesteuert wird, ist diese Analyse ohnehin nur sehr eingeschränkt interpretierbar.

Im Einklang mit Befunden der Lernstrategieforschung (vgl. Friedrich, 2008) geben die eher intrinsisch motivierten Lehramtsstudierenden an, im Studium mehr tiefenverarbeitende Lernstrategien einzusetzen, was der signifikante Unterschied von mittlerer Stärke bei „Elaboration" zu Gunsten der „Berufenen" widerspiegelt (vgl. Tabelle 3). Darüber hinaus wurde zu T2 geprüft, ob sich etwa ein Jahr nach Aufnahme des Studiums, Unterschiede zwischen den Gruppen in der Ausprägung der berufsbezogenen Selbstkonzeptfacetten zeigen lassen. Für alle sechs Dimensionen konnten bedeutsame Unterschiede zu Gunsten der „Berufenen" gefunden werden. Anschließend durchgeführte Post-hoc-Tests bestätigen die positiveren Selbstbilder verglichen mit den „indifferent" und auch im Unterschied zu den „Pragmatikerinnen" und „Pragmatikern". Allein für die Dimension „Diagnostik" konnte kein Unterschied zwischen den Berufenen und den „Pragmatikerinnen" und „Pragmatikern" festgestellt werden.

Auch zu T3, wiesen die „Berufenen" noch positivere motivationale Merkmale auf, bedeutsame – wenn auch kleine – Unterschiede zeigten sich zu diesem Zeitpunkt allerdings nur für das pädagogische und nicht für das fachbezogene und das (fach-)didaktische Interesse und nur verglichen mit der Gruppe „indifferent" (vgl. Tabelle 3).

Tabelle 3. Ergebnisse der ANOVA

	I *M (SD)*	P *M (SD)*	B *M (SD)*	ANOVA F(df1,df2)	eta²	post-hoc
Abiturnote	2.29 (.58)	2.46 (.58)	2.23 (.55)	*F*(2,777)=7.190**	.018	B, I > P
Studienwahlmotive (t1)						
Nützlichkeit	2.83 (.51)	3.22 (.41)	2.69 (.62)	*F*(2,784)=47.317**	.108	P > I > B
Pädagogisches Interesse	3.51 (.42)	3.71 (.35)	3.91 (.13)	*F*(2,784)=73.919**	.159	B > P > I
Selbstkonzept	3.07 (.40)	3.41 (.33)	3.68 (.27)	*F*(2,784)=24.899**	.324	B > P > I
Soziale Einflüsse	1.99 (.67)	2.70 (.57)	2.25 (.70)	*F*(2,784)=70.625**	.153	P > B > I
Geringe Schwierigkeit	1.39 (.40)	2.11 (.39)	1.26 (.28)	*F*(2,784)=259.538**	.398	P > I > B
Fachliches Interesse	3.12 (.52)	3.45 (.42)	3.72 (.30)	*F*(2,784)=109.772**	.219	B > P > I
Elaboration (t1)	3.01 (.42)	3.22 (.44)	3.34 (.42)	*F*(2,784)=42.455**	.098	B > P > I
Berufsbezogenes Selbstkonzept (t2)						
Fach	2.96 (.53)	3.07 (.49)	3.32 (.66)	*F*(2,138)=4.229*	.058	B > I
Erziehung	3.29 (.45)	3.44 (.46)	3.72 (.31)	*F*(2,138)=9.828**	.125	B>I
Diagnostik	3.07 (.46)	3.35 (.43)	3.43 (.43)	*F*(2,138)=8.359**	.108	P, B>I
Innovation	2.83 (.54)	2.99 (.50)	3.35 (.39)	*F*(2,138)=9.726**	.124	B>I, P
Medien	3.01 (.57)	3.19 (.44)	3.53 (.50)	*F*(2,138)=8.852**	.114	B>I
Beratung	3.18 (.47)	3.39 (.50)	3.50 (.39)	*F*(2,138)=5.721**	.077	B>I
Interesse (t3)						
Fachlich	3.02 (.04)	3.06 (.08)	3.16 (.06)	*F*(2,177)=1.975 ns.	.022	
Didaktisch	3.27 (.37)	3.25 (.38)	3.4 (.42)	*F*(2,177)=2.453 ns.		
Pädagogisch	3.36 (.39)	3.31 (.38)	3.53 (.33)	*F*(2,177)=4.037*	.044	B>I

Anmerkungen. Die Codierung der Abiturnoten entspricht der gewohnten Handhabung, ein niedriger Wert spiegelt eine bessere Leistung wider; $p < .05$. $^{**}p < .01$. I (indifferent), P (Pragmatikerinnen und Pragmtiker), B (Berufene).

3 Diskussion und Ausblick

Die Lehrerbildung steht, insbesondere im Zusammenhang mit dem Abschneiden von Schülerinnen und Schülern an deutschen Schulen in internationalen Vergleichsstudien, chronisch in der Kritik (Baumert et al., 2001). Hinzu kommen Erkenntnisse aus der Forschung zu Lehrerbelastung (z.B. Klusmann, Kunter, Trautwein & Baumert, 2006; Schaarschmidt, Kieschke & Fischer, 1999) und – aktuell im Zuge der Umsetzung der UN-Behindertenrechtskonvention seit 2009 – neue Anforderungen mit Blick auf die Umsetzung eines inklusiven Schulsystems (z.B. Amrhein, Veber & Fischer, 2014).

Insbesondere über Praxiselemente und ihre Ausgestaltung wird immer wieder kontrovers diskutiert. Ausgehend von Theorien und Forschungsbefunden zum selbstgesteuerten Lernen und unter Berücksichtigung bildungspolitischer Vorgaben ist es nachvollziehbar, warum Praxiselemente ausgebaut worden sind und mit dem Portfolio an vielen lehrerbildenden Universitäten auf hochschuldidaktische Instrumente gesetzt wird, die die theoriegeleitete, kritisch-reflexive Begleitung der schulischen Praktika unterstützen sollen.

Mit den vorliegenden Analysen sollte geprüft werden, ob sich ausgehend von den Studienwahlmotiven unterschiedliche Studierendengruppen differenzieren lassen und sich die verschiedenen zu Grunde liegenden Motive im weiteren Studienverlauf auch in unterschiedlichen Ausprägungen berufsbezogener Selbstkonzepte und Interessen wiederspiegeln. Überdies wurde geprüft, ob eher intrinsisch motivierte Lehramtsstudierende auch eher tieferverarbeitende Elaborationsstrategien im Studium einsetzen. Die Annahmen zu der Bedeutung der Studienwahlmotive für das berufsbezogene Selbstkonzept, das berufliche Interesse sowie für Elaboration konnte anhand der vorliegenden Analysen im Wesentlichen bestätigt werden.

Die vorliegenden Befunde basieren allerdings auf Daten aus nur einer Universität und weitere Studien sind erforderlich, um die identifizierten Typen zu validieren. Zudem wurde – mit Blick auf die von Pohlmann und Möller (2010) formulierten Desiderate bezüglich der prognostischen Validität der FEMOLA-Skalen, hier zunächst mit Motivation nur ein kleiner Teilbereich im Studienverlauf näher betrachtet. In zukünftigen umfangreicheren Studien sollten kognitive Merkmale und idealerweise auch die Leistungsentwicklung der unterschiedlichen Studierendtypen im Studienverlauf mit betrachtet werden.

Mit der Einführung neuer Langzeitpraktika sowie der Forderung, hochschuldidaktische Prinzipien wie das Forschende Lernen und die Entwicklung einer forschenden Grundhaltung sowie Elemente selbstgesteuerten Lernens mit einem Portfolio im Studium zu integrieren muss der Anspruch verbunden sein, die bisherigen Forschungserkenntnisse bezüglich der notwendigen Voraussetzungen für intrinsisch motiviertes, selbstgesteuertes Lernen zu berücksichtigen. Befunde aus großen Studien weisen darauf hin, dass an dieser Stelle dringender Handlungsbedarf besteht. So konnten König und Seifert (2012) in der LEK-Studie zeigen, dass Lehramtsstudierende zwar große Lernfortschritte bei Testaufgaben zeigen, die auf Faktenwissen ausgerichtet sind. Sie fanden allerdings auch, dass der Lernfortschritt bei Aufgaben, die die Anwendung von Wissen auf typische berufliche Problemstellungen verlangt, deutlich geringer ausfiel. Dies gilt auch, obwohl die Studierenden ja durchaus an den fachlichen, didaktischen und pädagogischen Inhalten ihres Studiums interessiert sind. Rheinberg und Vollmeyer (2000) argumentieren zum Verhältnis von Sachinteresse und leistungsthematischen Herausforderungen, dass „das bekundete Sachinteresse im Lernprozess erst dann nachhaltig genug wirksam wird, wenn die Person die Situation überhaupt als Gelegenheit zur Kompetenzsteigerung auffasst und deshalb in eine enge Interaktion mit dem Lernmaterial eintritt" (S. 158).

Mit Blick auf die bildungspolitischen Vorgaben und ihre Konkretisierungen im Rahmen der Lehrerbildung wird zu prüfen sein, ob es gelingt, den neuen Herausforderungen der Lehrerbildung besser gerecht zu werden. Dafür benötigen wir Erkenntnisse, unter welchen Bedingungen die Integration dieser Elemente ins Studium gelingt und unter welchen Bedingungen wer in welcher Hinsicht von neuen Studienelementen profitiert. Aus der bisherigen Forschung zum selbstgesteuerten Lernen kann resümiert werden, dass intrinsische Motivation und Interesse wichtige Voraussetzungen sein können. Mit der vorliegenden Studie konnte gezeigt werden, dass sich unterschiedliche Studierendengruppen differenzieren lassen und diese sich auch im weiteren Studienverlauf unterscheiden. Langfristig muss geprüft werden, wie sich diese Merkmale auf die Nutzung von Lerngelegenheiten und auf die Kompetenzentwicklung der Studierenden auswirkt. Allerdings sei hier auf Schiefele (2000) verwiesen, der in Frage stellt, „ob denn Motivationen lediglich Mittel zum Zweck sind" (S. 239), und die „Forderung nach Interessenentwicklung als Bildungsziel formuliert" (S. 240).

Mit der aktuellen intensiven Forschung zur Lehrerbildung, zum Beispiel im Rahmen der eingangs erwähnten großen längsschnittlichen Studien, aber auch im Kontext der Qualitätsoffensive Lehrerbildung, ist die Hoffnung verknüpft, genauer zu verstehen, wie kognitive, affektive und motivationale Prozesse zusammenwirken und welche Bedeutung strukturellen Merkmalen zukommt, um die dringend erforderliche Theoriebildung in diesem Bereich zu fördern.

Literatur

Amrhein, B., Veber, M. & Fischer, C. (2014). Potenzialentwicklung in der inklusiven Bildung. *Journal für Begabtenförderung, 2*, 7–19.

Bacher, J. (2010). *Clusteranalyse* (3., erg., vollst. überarb. und neu gestaltete Aufl.). München: Oldenbourg.

Barsch, S. & Glutsch, N. (2016). Der reflektierte Blick auf Praxis. Empirische Befunde zum Kölner Portfoliomodell. In M. Boos, A. Krämer & M. Kricke (Hrsg.), *Portfolioarbeit phasenübergreifend gestalten. Konzepte, Ideen und Anregungen aus der LehrerInnenbildung* (S. 54–65). Münster: Waxmann.

Bauer, J., Drechsel, B., Retelsdorf, J., Sporer, T., Rösler, L., Prenzel, M. & Möller, J. (2010). Panel zum Lehramtsstudium – PaLea: Entwicklungsverläufe zukünftiger

Lehrkräfte im Kontext der Reform der Lehrerbildung. *Beiträge zur Hochschulforschung, 32,* 34–55.

Baumert, J., Klieme, E., Neubrand, M., Prenzel, M., Schiefele, U., Schneider, W., Stanat, P., Tillmann, K.-J. & Weiß, M. (Hrsg.). (2001). *PISA 2000 – Basiskompetenzen von Schülerinnen und Schülern im internationalen Vergleich.* Opladen: Leske und Budrich.

Baumert, J. & Kunter, M. (2006). Stichwort: Professionelle Kompetenz von Lehrkräften. *Zeitschrift für Erziehungswissenschaft, 9,* 469–520.

Blömeke, S., Kaiser, G. & Lehmann, R. (Hrsg.). (2010a). *TEDS-M 2008 – Professionelle Kompetenz und Lerngelegenheiten angehender Primarstufenlehrkräfte im internationalen Vergleich.* Münster: Waxmann.

Blömeke, S., Kaiser, G. & Lehmann, R. (Hrsg.). (2010b). *TEDS-M 2008. Professionelle Kompetenz und Lerngelegenheiten angehender Mathematiklehrkräfte für die Sekundarstufe I im internationalen Vergleich.* Münster: Waxmann.

BMBF (2013). *Bund-Länder-Vereinbarung über ein gemeinsames Programm „Qualitätsoffensive Lehrerbildung"* gemäß Artikel 91 b des Grundgesetzes. 12. April 2013. Verfügbar unter: https://www.bmbf.de/files/bund_laender_vereinbarung_qualitaetsoffesive_lehrerbildung.pdf [03.10.2016].

Forlin, C. (2010). Reframing teacher education for inclusion. In C. Forlin (Hrsg.), *Teacher Education for Inclusion. Changing paradigms and innovative approaches* (S. 3–12). London: Routledge.

Friedrich, H. F. (2008). Selbstreguliertes Lernen in der Hochschule. In J. Zumbach & H. Mandl (Hrsg.), *Pädagogische Psychologie in Theorie und Praxis. Ein fallbasiertes Lehrbuch* (S. 61–68). Göttingen: Hogrefe.

Gröschner, A., Müller, K., Bauer, J., Seidel, T., Prenzel, M., Kauper, T. & Möller, J. (2015). Praxisphasen in der Lehrerausbildung – Eine Strukturanalyse am Beispiel des gymnasialen Lehramtsstudiums in Deutschland. *Zeitschrift für Erziehungswissenschaft, 18,* 639–665.

Hascher, T. (2012). Lernfeld Praktikum: Evidenzbasierte Entwicklungen in der Lehrer/innenbildung. *Zeitschrift für Bildungsforschung, 2,* 109–129.

Hascher, T. & Zordo, L. de (2015). Praktika und Inklusion. In T. Häcker & M. Walm (Hrsg.), *Inklusion als Entwicklung* (S. 165–184). Bad Heilbrunn: Klinkhardt.

Hauser, B. (2009). Den Lehrerberuf selbstgesteuert erlernen. *Journal für LehrerInnenbildung, 2,* 8–15.

Heinrich, M., Urban, M. & Werning, R. (2013). Grundlagen, Handlungsstrategien und Forschungsperspektiven für die Ausbildung und Professionalisierung von Fachkräften für inklusive Schulen. In H. Döbert & H. Weishaupt (Hrsg.), *Inklusive Schulbildung professionell gestalten – Situationsanalyse und Handlungsempfehlungen* (S. 69–133). Münster: Waxmann.

HRK & KMK (2015). *Lehrerbildung für eine Schule der Vielfalt.* Verfügbar unter: http://www.hrk.de/uploads/media/HRK-KMKEmpfehlung_Inklusion_in_LB_032015.pdf. [01.10.2016].

Klusmann, U., Köller, M. & Kunter, M. (2011). Anmerkungen zur Validität eignungsdiagnostischer Verfahren bei angehenden Lehrkräften. *Zeitschrift für Pädagogik, 57* (5), 711–721.

Klusmann, U., Kunter, M., Trautwein, U. & Baumert, J. (2006). Lehrerbelastung und Unterrichtsqualität aus der Perspektive von Lehrenden und Lernenden. *Zeitschrift für Pädagogische Psychologie, 20* (3), 161–173.

Klusmann, U., Trautwein, U., Lüdtke, O., Kunter, M. & Baumert, J. (2009). Eingangsvoraussetzungen beim Studienbeginn – Werden die Lehramtskandidaten unterschätzt? *Zeitschrift für Pädagogische Psychologie, 23*, 265–278.

König, J. & Rothland, M. (2013). Motivationale Bedingungen der Kompetenzentwicklung in der Lehrerbildung. In A. Gehrmann, B. Kranz, S. Pelzmann & A. Reinartz (Hrsg.), *Formation und Transformation der Lehrerbildung. Entwicklungstrends und Forschungsbefunde* (S. 88–103). Bad Heilbrunn: Klinkhardt.

König, J. & Seifert, A. (2012). Der Erwerb von pädagogischem Professionswissen: Ziele, Design und zentrale Ergebnisse der LEK-Studie. In J. König & A. Seifert (Hrsg.), *Lehramtsstudierende erwerben pädagogisches Professionswissen. Ergebnisse der Längsschnittstudie LEK zur Wirksamkeit der erziehungswissenschaftlichen Lehrerausbildung* (S. 7–31). Münster: Waxmann.

Lüdtke, O., Robitzsch, A., Trautwein, U. & Köller, O. (2007). Umgang mit fehlenden Werten in der psychologischen Forschung. *Psychologische Rundschau, 58*, 103–117.

Mayr, J. (2011). Der Persönlichkeitsansatz in der Lehrerforschung. Konzepte, Befunde und Folgerungen. In E. Terhart, H. Bennewitz & M. Rothland (Hrsg.), *Handbuch der Forschung zum Lehrerberuf* (S. 125–148). Münster: Waxmann.

Neugebauer, M. (2013). Wer entscheidet sich für ein Lehramtsstudium – und warum? Eine empirische Überprüfung der These von der Negativselektion in den Lehrerberuf. *Zeitschrift für Erziehungswissenschaft, 16*, 157–184.

Pintrich, P. R. & Garcia, T. (1994). Self-regulated learning in college students: Knowledge, strategies, and motivation. In P. R. Pintrich, D. R. Brown & C. E. Weinstein (Eds.), *Student motivation, cognition, and learning* (pp. 113–133). Hillsdale, NJ: Erlbaum.

Pohlmann, B. & Möller, J. (2010). Fragebogen zur Erfassung der Motivation für die Wahl des Lehramtsstudiums (FEMOLA). *Zeitschrift für Pädagogische Psychologie, 24*, 73–84.

Retelsdorf, J., Bauer, J., Gebauer, S. K., Kauper, T. & Möller, J. (2014). Erfassung berufsbezogener Selbstkonzepte von angehenden Lehrkräften (ERBSE-L). *Diagnostica, 60*, 98–110.

Retelsdorf, J. & Möller, J. (2012). Grundschule oder Gymnasium? Zur Motivation ein Lehramt zu studieren. *Zeitschrift für Pädagogische Psychologie, 26*, 5–17.

Rheinberg, F. & Vollmeyer, R. (2000). Sachinteresse und leistungsthematische Herausforderungen – zwei verschiedenartige Motivationskomponenten und ihr Zusammenwirken beim Lernen. In U. Schiefele & K.-P. Wild (Hrsg.), *Interesse und Lernmotivation* (S. 145–161). Münster: Waxmann.

Rothland, M. (2011). Wer entscheidet sich für den Lehrerberuf? Forschung zum soziodemographischen Profil sowie zu Persönlichkeits- und Leistungsmerkmalen angehender Lehrkräfte. In E. Terhart, H. Bennewitz & M. Rothland (Hrsg.), *Handbuch der Forschung zum Lehrerberuf* (S. 243–267). Münster: Waxmann.

Rothland, M. & Terhart, M. (2011). Eignungsabklärung angehender Lehrkräfte. Einführung in den Thementeil. *Zeitschrift für Pädagogik, 57* (5), 635–638.

Schaarschmidt, U., Kieschke, U. & Fischer, A. (1999). Beanspruchungsmuster im Lehrerberuf. *Psychologie in Erziehung und Unterricht*, 46, 244–268.

Schiefele, H. (2000). Befunde – Fortschritte – neue Fragen. In U. Schiefele & K.-P. Wild (Hrsg.), *Interesse und Lernmotivation* (S. 227–241). Münster: Waxmann.

Schiefele, U. (2009). Situational and individual interest. In A. Wigfield & K. Wentzel (Hrsg.), *Handbook on motivation at school* (S. 197–222). New York, NY: Routledge.

Schiefele, U., Krapp, A., Wild, K.-P. & Winteler, A. (1993). Der „Fragebogen zum Studieninteresse" (FSI). *Diagnostica*, 39, 335–351.

Schiefele, U., Streblow, L. & Retelsdorf, J. (2013). Dimensions of teacher interest and their relations to occupational well-being and instructional practices. *Journal of Educational Research Online*, 5, 7–37.

Shulman, L. S. (1986). Those who understand: Knowledge growth in teaching. *Educational Researcher, 15*, 4–14.

Shulman, L. S. (1987). Knowledge and teaching: Foundations of the New Reform. *Harvard Educational Review*, 57, 1–23.

Werfel, A., Streblow, L. & Schüssler, R. (2016). Das Portfolio im Praxissemester als Instrument zur Unterstützung Forschenden Lernens. In Ministerium für Schule und Weiterbildung (Hrsg.), *Schule NRW. Das Praxissemester auf dem Prüfstand. Zur Evaluation des Praxissemesters in Nordrhein-Westfalen*, Beilage Schule NRW, 11, 18–19.

Wild, K.-P. & Schiefele, U. (1994). Lernstrategien im Studium: Ergebnisse zur Faktorenstruktur und Reliabilität eines neuen Fragebogens. *Zeitschrift für Differentielle und Diagnostische Psychologie*, 15, 185–200.

Autorinnen

DR. LILIAN STREBLOW
Bielefeld School of Education, Universität Bielefeld.

DR. BRITTA POHLMANN
Institut für Bildungsmonitoring und Qualitätsentwicklung, Hamburg.

KONTAKT
Lilian Streblow, Bielefeld School of Education,
Universität Bielefeld, Postfach 100 131, 33615 Bielefeld.
E-Mail: *lilian.streblow@uni-bielefeld.de*

„Nur Lehramt"? – Lehramtsstudierende und Stereotype Threat

TONI ALEXANDER IHME

ZUSAMMENFASSUNG: Stereotype Threat bezeichnet eine Bedrohung ausgehend von einem negativen Stereotyp über die eigene soziale Gruppe, die zu Leistungseinbußen in und zum Rückzug von der bedrohten Domäne führen kann. Ein für die Ausbildung von Lehrkräften hoch relevantes und häufig wiedergegebenes negatives Stereotyp ist das der geringeren kognitiven Leistungsfähigkeit Lehramtsstudierender im Vergleich zu Fachstudierenden. Die hier vorgestellten Studien untersuchen verschiedene Ausprägungen des Stereotyps und die Wahrnehmung von Stereotype Threat durch Lehramtsstudierende.

Eine Online-Befragung (Studie 1, N = 134) auf Basis des Stereotype Content Model (Fiske, Xu, Cuddy & Glick, 1999) stellte studiengangspezifische Unterschiede in der Ausprägung des Stereotyps zu Lehramtsstudierenden fest. Eine zweite Online-Befragung Studierender verschiedener Lehramtsstudiengänge (Studie 2, N = 104) zeigte, dass soziale Vergleiche mit Fachstudierenden mit einem höheren Erleben von Stereotype Threat assoziiert waren. Ein ebenfalls festgestellter Zusammenhang zwischen Stereotype Threat und Studienzufriedenheit war negativ. Es werden mögliche Konsequenzen für die Ausbildung Lehramtsstudierender diskutiert.

Schlüsselwörter: Stereotype Threat, Lehramtsstudierende, Stereotype, Studienzufriedenheit

"Only a teaching degree?": Prospective teachers and stereotype threat

ABSTRACT: Stereotype threat is defined as a threat that diminishes performance and domain identification, originating from a negative stereotype about one's own social group. One negative stereotype often found in research literature and highly relevant for teacher training is the stereotype of prospective teachers appearing less competent than other students. The studies outlined in this chapter investigate different forms of this stereotype and the perception of stereotype threat by prospective teachers.

An online survey (Study 1, N = 134) based on the Stereotype Content Model (Fiske, Xu, Cuddy & Glick, 1999) identified differences in stereotypes linked to individual courses of study in teaching. A second online survey (Study 2, N = 104) showed that social comparisons with members of the outgroup (i.e., students majoring in the respective subjects) were associated with experiences of stereotype threat. A further correlation between stereotype threat and overall student satisfaction was negative. Possible consequences for the education of prospective teachers are discussed.

Keywords: stereotype threat, prospective teachers, stereotypes, student satisfaction

Einleitung

Im Mai 2016 erschien in Spiegel Online der Artikel „Lehramtsstudenten werden für doof gehalten". In diesem beschrieb eine Lehramtsstudierende das mit ihrem Studium einhergehende Stereotyp und die daraus resultierende Erfahrung, eine Studierende zweiter Klasse zu sein: „[...] In den ersten Monaten an der Uni habe ich es noch als ungeschickte Formulierung abgetan, wenn mich Kommilitonen fragten: „Studierst du Deutsch auf Lehramt oder richtig Germanistik?" Doch nach Gesprächen mit zahlreichen Lehramtsmitstreitern wurde mir irgendwann klar, dass sich die Ansicht, wir würden gar nicht „richtig" studieren, in beinahe allen Studienfächern manifestiert hatte [...]" (Sarand, 2016).

Wie wirken sich derartige Stereotype aus? Motivieren sie Lehramtsstudierende, sich umso mehr anzustrengen, um das Gegenteil zu beweisen? Zumindest für die Autorin des Artikels ist das nicht der Fall. Sie beschreibt stattdessen Unzufriedenheit, Motivationsverlust und Rückzug vom Studium und zeigt damit einen möglichen Faktor für die Distanzierung von Lehramtsstudierenden von ihrem Studium und ihrem zukünftigen Beruf auf. In der HIS[1]-Exmatrikuliertenbefragung 2008 gaben 18 % der befragten ehemaligen Lehramtsstudierenden Motivationsverlust als ausschlaggebenden Grund für ihren Studienabbruch an (Heublin, Hutzsch, Schreiber, Sommer & Besuch, 2009).

Im folgenden Abschnitt wird aufgezeigt, dass ein negatives leistungsbezogenes Stereotyp gegenüber Lehramtsstudierenden besteht und dass dieses Stereotyp die Leistungen dieser Studierenden einzuschränken vermag. Die Existenz negativer Stereotype und daraus resultierendem Stereotype Threat sind für die Ausbildung von Lehrkräften ein hoch relevantes Problem, da Stereotype negative Auswirkungen nicht nur auf Lernen und Leistung (Rydell, Rydell & Boucher, 2010; Taylor & Walton, 2011), sondern auch auf die Identifikation mit dem Lehramtsstudium (und letztendlich dem Lehrerberuf) haben können (Milner & Woolfolk Hoy, 2003). In den darauf folgenden Abschnitten betrachten zwei Studien zwei verschiedene Aspekte der negativen Stereotypisierung Lehramtsstudierender. Studie I untersucht, ob verschiedene Lehramtsstudiengänge unterschiedlich stereotypisiert werden. Studie II untersucht die Zusammenhänge zwischen sozialen Vergleichen, Stereotype Threat und Studienzufriedenheit.

1 Theorie

Lehrkräfte und – wie das Eingangsbeispiel demonstriert – Lehramtsstudierende sind soziale Gruppen, die einer negativen Stereotypisierung unterliegen (Blömeke, 2005; Rauin, 2007; Spinath, van Ophuysen & Heise, 2005). Laut dem Stereotyp unterscheiden sich Lehramtsstudierende in solchen Merkmalen, die eine Voraussetzung für

1 HIS – Hochschul-Informations-System GmbH

ein wissenschaftliches Studium darstellen (Intelligenz, Leistungsmotivation etc.) von anderen Studierenden (Spinath et al., 2005). Carlsson und Björklund (2010) konnten zeigen, dass sich Lehramtsstudierende selbst als weniger kompetent einschätzen als Studierende der Rechtswissenschaften. Spinath et al. (2005) zeigten jedoch, dass sich Lehramtsstudierende im Hinblick auf Intelligenz, Leistungsmotivation und Lesekompetenz nicht von anderen Studierenden unterscheiden. Die einzige Ausnahme hinsichtlich der Intelligenz der Teilnehmenden ergab sich für Diplomstudierende der Mathematik sowie der Ingenieurswissenschaften, die bessere Ergebnisse erzielten als Lehramtsstudierende. Vergleichbare Ergebnisse konnten in verschiedenen anderen Studien gefunden werden (Gold & Giesen, 1993; Roloff Henoch, Klusman, Lüdtke & Trautwein, 2015).

Wir untersuchten die Existenz der hier skizzierten Stereotype in zwei Online-Befragungen (Ihme & Möller, 2015). Die Teilnehmenden wurden zu ihren Stereotypen bezüglich Lehramtsstudierenden befragt. Die theoretische Basis für die Befragung war das Stereotype Content Model (Fiske et al., 1999). Nach diesem Modell werden Stereotype anhand der Dimensionen *competence* (Kompetenz) und *warmth* (Wärme; gemeint ist, als wie sympathisch und sozial kompetent die Gruppe wahrgenommen wird) kategorisiert. In Übereinstimmung mit der Darstellung Lehramtsstudierender in den oben genannten Forschungsarbeiten und medialen Darstellungen wurden Lehramtsstudierende (von sich und anderen) als wenig kompetent, aber warm eingeschätzt.

Die Studien von Carlsson und Björklund (2010) sowie Ihme und Möller (2015) sind meines Wissens die einzigen Studien, die bisher Stereotype zu Lehramtsstudierenden untersucht haben. So ist bislang nicht erforscht, ob es Unterschiede zwischen der Stereotypisierung verschiedener Gruppen Lehramtsstudierender (z. B. Grundschule, Haupt- und Realschule etc.) gibt. Untersuchungen zu den Stereotypen über verschiedene soziale Gruppen konnten in der Vergangenheit abweichende Substereotype für Gruppen nachweisen, selbst wenn für diese stark ausgeprägte und gesellschaftlich hoch saliente Stereotype bestanden (z. B. schwarze Politiker, Geschäftsleute und andere Gruppen als Subgruppen der Afroamerikaner: Czopp & Monteith, 2006; Walzer & Czopp, 2011). Das Auftreten von Substereotypen ist insofern relevant, als dass sich aus einer unterschiedlichen Stereotypisierung auch unterschiedliche Auswirkungen von Stereotype Threat auf Studierende verschiedener Lehramtsstudiengänge ergeben können. Daher soll eine der in diesem Kapitel dargestellten Studien die Frage beantworten, ob verschiedene Lehramtsstudiengänge im Vergleich untereinander unterschiedlich stereotypisiert werden.

1.1 Stereotype Threat und dessen Auswirkungen auf Lehramtsstudierende

Wie im vorigen Abschnitt ausgeführt, liegen Befunde vor, die auf eine negative Stereotypisierung von Lehramtsstudierenden hindeuten. Daher liegt die Vermutung nahe, dass Lehramtsstudierende von Stereotype Threat betroffen sind.

Stereotype Threat bezeichnet eine Bedrohung, die von einem negativen Stereotyp über die eigene soziale Gruppe ausgeht (Steele, 1997, 2010; Steele & Aronson, 1995). Wird ein negatives Stereotyp über die eigene Gruppe aktiviert oder tritt eine Situation ein, in der das Stereotyp salient wird, so setzt ein situationaler Druck ein. Dieser Druck resultiert aus der Befürchtung, dem negativen Stereotyp zu entsprechen beziehungsweise nach ihm bewertet zu werden. Es kommt zu einer emotionalen Reaktion, die die kognitiven Ressourcen der betroffenen Person reduziert und die Leistungen der Person beeinträchtigt (Schmader, Johns & Forbes, 2008). So erzielen Schülerinnen, deren weibliche Identität vor einem Mathematiktest salient gemacht wird, eine schlechtere Leistung in diesem Test als Schülerinnen, deren weibliche Identität nicht salient gemacht wird (z. B. Ihme & Mauch, 2007; Nguyen & Ryan, 2008).

Um die Wirkung negativer Stereotype auf Lehramtsstudierende zu untersuchen, wurden in einer von uns durchgeführten Studie (Ihme & Möller, 2015) Lehramtsstudierende des gymnasialen Lehramts durch das Stereotyp geringerer Kompetenz bedroht. Zu diesem Zweck wurde ihnen in der Stereotype-Threat-Bedingung mitgeteilt, dass in dieser Studie die kognitiven Fähigkeiten Studierender verschiedener Studiengänge verglichen würden. In der Kontrollbedingung wurde nicht von kognitiven Fähigkeiten und dem Vergleich mit anderen Studierenden gesprochen. Lehramtsstudierende, die durch das Stereotyp bedroht wurden, zeigten signifikant geringere Leistungen in einem kognitiven Fähigkeitstest als nicht bedrohte Kommilitonen und Studierende der Psychologie, die die Kontrollgruppe bildeten.

Neben den Auswirkungen auf Leistungen hat Stereotype Threat weitere negative Effekte. Sich wiederholende Erfahrungen von Stereotype Threat beeinträchtigen die Identifikation mit der bedrohten Leistungsdomäne oder der negativ stereotypisierten Gruppe (Woodcock, Hernandez, Estrada & Schultz, 2012). Weiterhin beeinträchtigt das Erleben von Stereotype Threat die Zufriedenheit mit der Arbeit (Von Hippel, Issa, Ma & Stokes, 2011; Von Hippel, Kalokerinos & Henry, 2013) oder dem Studium (Fassiotto et al., 2016). Die Unzufriedenheit mit Studium oder Beruf und die Desidentifikation mit der bedrohten Domäne werden als eine der Ursachen für die geringere Repräsentation verschiedener Gruppen in solchen Leistungsbereichen angesehen, die jeweils vom Stereotyp bedroht sind (Steele, 1997). Außerdem ist Studienzufriedenheit eine motivationale Studienerfolgsvariable, die unter anderem mit geringerer Studienabbruchswahrscheinlichkeit und höheren Studienleistungen assoziiert ist (z. B. Oja, 2011; Sembiring, 2015; Sockalingam, 2012). Daher soll die zweite der in diesem Kapitel dargestellten Studien die Frage beantworten, ob Stereotype Threat die Studienzufriedenheit von Lehramtsstudierenden beeinträchtigt.

1.2 Die moderierende Rolle der Gruppenidentifikation und die Rolle sozialer Vergleiche in der Aktivierung von Stereotype Threat

Der Identifikation mit der Leistungsdomäne und der bedrohten Gruppe kommen – neben ihren Rollen als von Stereotype Threat beeinträchtigten Variablen – auch moderierende Rollen in der Wirkung von Stereotype Threat zu. So sind hoch mit ihrer Gruppe identifizierte Personen stärker von Stereotype Threat betroffen als niedrig identifizierte (Schmader, 2002). Für Lehramtsstudierende liegen derzeit keine Befunde zu den Effekten der Gruppenidentifikation auf Stereotype Threat vor. Diese Variable ist insofern von Interesse, als dass Lehramtsstudierende Teil einer Gruppe sind, die sie selbst durch Wahl ihres Studiengangs ausgewählt haben. Inwiefern die Identifikation mit selbstgewählten Gruppen eine moderierende Wirkung auf Stereotype Threat haben kann, ist bislang nicht untersucht, da sich die bestehenden Forschungen ausschließlich auf Gruppen richten, zu denen der Zugang nicht oder nur sehr beschränkt auf eigener Auswahl beruht.

Im Gegensatz zur Manipulation in einem experimentellen Setting wird Stereotype Threat im Alltag auf wesentlich subtilere Weise ausgelöst. Ein möglicher Auslöser sind soziale Vergleiche (Van Loo, Boucher, Rydell & Rydell, 2013; Von Hippel et al., 2011). Laut Van Loo et al. (2013) wird Stereotype Threat durch soziale Vergleiche mit Personen einer Fremdgruppe aktiviert, die als kompetenter wahrgenommen werden. Vergleiche mit Personen der Eigengruppe hingegen aktivieren die negativ stereotypisierte Identität, was ebenfalls Stereotype Threat auslösen kann (Van Loo et al., 2013). Umgekehrt könnten soziale Vergleiche mit Mitgliedern der Eigengruppe aber auch helfen, Stereotype als irrelevant oder unzutreffend zu erkennen und damit Stereotype Threat entgegenzuwirken (Hoyt & Simon, 2011).

In ihrer Studie zum Erleben von Stereotype Threat und seinen Auswirkungen auf Frauen am Arbeitsplatz fanden von Hippel et al. (2011) die erwartete Wirkung von sozialen Vergleichen mit der Fremdgruppe (in diesem Falle Männer). Frauen am Arbeitsplatz erlebten umso mehr Stereotype Threat, je häufiger sie sich mit männlichen Kollegen verglichen. Die Häufigkeit ihrer Vergleiche mit Kolleginnen hatte keine Auswirkungen auf das Erleben von Stereotype Threat. Dementsprechend könnten soziale Vergleiche mit der Fremdgruppe der Fachstudierenden bei Lehramtsstudierenden zu Stereotype Threat führen. Derzeit liegen keine Befunde zur Auslösung und zum Auftreten von Stereotype Threat bei Lehramtsstudierenden im Universitätskontext vor.

1.3 Fragestellungen und durchzuführende Studien

Aus den bisherigen Ausführungen wurden mehrere Fragestellungen abgeleitet, die in zwei Studien untersucht wurden. Die Studien betrachteten ihre jeweiligen Fragestellungen separat voneinander.

Während Unterschiede in der wahrgenommenen Kompetenz und Wärme zwischen Lehramtsstudierenden und Fachstudierenden festgestellt wurden, waren mögliche Substereotype zwischen Studierenden verschiedener Lehramtsstudiengänge bislang nicht untersucht worden. Daraus ergab sich folgende Fragestellung:

1. Welche Unterschiede bestehen zwischen der Kompetenz und Wärme, die den Studierenden verschiedener Lehramtsstudiengänge zugeschrieben werden?

Diese Fragestellung wurde in Studie I nach dem Vorbild bereits vorgenommener Befragungen zur Stereotypisierung sozialer Gruppen untersucht. Psychologie-Studierende schätzten die Eigenschaften der Angehörigen verschiedener Lehramtsstudiengänge ein.

Ebenso wie die Forschung zur Stereotypisierung von Lehramtsstudierenden lässt auch die Forschung zu Lehramtsstudierenden und Stereotype Threat derzeit noch viele Fragen offen. Weder die Auslösung und das Auftreten von Stereotype Threat an Universitäten, noch dessen Auswirkungen auf Studienzufriedenheit waren – außerhalb von experimentellen Manipulationen – bislang untersucht worden. Darüber hinaus hatte die vorhandene experimentelle Studie mögliche Moderatorvariablen außer Acht gelassen (Ihme & Möller, 2015). Daraus ergaben sich mehrere zu untersuchende Fragestellungen:

2. Erleben Lehramtsstudierende an Universitäten Stereotype Threat?
3. Tragen soziale Vergleiche mit Fachstudierenden oder anderen Lehramtsstudierenden zum Stereotype Threat von Lehramtsstudierenden bei?
4. Beeinträchtigt Stereotype Threat die Studienzufriedenheit Lehramtsstudierender?
5. Wird ein möglicher Effekt von Stereotype Threat auf die Studienzufriedenheit durch die Identifikation mit der Gruppe der Lehramtsstudierenden moderiert?

Diese Fragestellungen wurden in Studie II nach dem Vorbild bestehender Forschung zu Stereotype Threat am Arbeitsplatz (Von Hippel et al., 2011; 2013) untersucht. Lehramtsstudierende wurden zu ihrem Erleben von Stereotype Threat, ihren sozialen Vergleichen mit Lehramts- und Fachstudierenden, ihrer Identifikation mit der Eigengruppe und ihrer Studienzufriedenheit befragt.

2 Studie I

Das Ziel der ersten Studie war die Prüfung möglicher Unterschiede in den Ausprägungen des Stereotyps zwischen verschiedenen Gruppen von Lehramtsstudierenden (Grundschule, Haupt- und Realschule, Gymnasium). Es sollte geprüft werden, ob das Stereotyp geringer Kompetenz und hoher Wärme gegenüber Lehramtsstudierenden nicht-gymnasialer Studiengänge stärker ausgeprägt ist als gegenüber Lehramtsstudierenden gymnasialer Studiengänge. Diese Erwartung beruht auf der Annahme, dass die Vermittlung komplexer Fachinhalte (z. B. im Rahmen der Ausbildung von Gymnasiasten) stereotyp auch eine höhere kognitive Fähigkeit auf Seiten der Lehrkräfte bedingt als die Vermittlung von Fachinhalten auf nicht-gymnasialem Niveau.

2.1 Stichprobe

Als Teilnehmende wurden *N* = 134 Psychologie-Studierende der FernUniversität in Hagen rekrutiert (*M* = 32.10 Jahre, *SD* = 9.16; 67.4 % weiblich).

2.2 Vorgehen

Die Befragung fand in einer passwortgeschützten Online-Umgebung statt. Angehörige drei verschiedener Lehramtsstudiengänge (Grundschule, Haupt- und Realschule, Gymnasium) sollten anhand der Dimensionen Kompetenz und Wärme eingeschätzt werden. Dafür wurde die vollständige Eigenschaftsliste aus der Untersuchung von Fiske et al. (1999) übersetzt und angewandt. Den Teilnehmenden wurde eine Liste mit 27 Eigenschaften vorgelegt (arrogant, entschlossen, unabhängig etc.).

Die Teilnehmenden bearbeiteten die Eigenschaftslisten für die drei Studiengänge in zufälliger Reihenfolge; die Eigenschaften auf jeder Liste wurden ebenfalls in randomisierter Reihenfolge präsentiert. Für jede Eigenschaft gaben sie auf einer fünfstufigen Skala (1 – „überhaupt nicht" bis 5 – „außerordentlich") an, inwieweit sie ihrer Einschätzung nach auf die gegebene Gruppe zutraf. Dadurch ergab sich für jeden der drei Studiengänge eine Einschätzung für die Ausprägung jeder der 27 Eigenschaften.

2.3 Ergebnisse

Die ersten Auswertungsschritte entsprachen denen von Fiske et al. (1999). Für jede einzelne beurteilte Gruppe wurde je eine Faktorenanalyse (PCA, Varimax-Rotation) mit den 27 Eigenschaftsitems durchgeführt. Die weiteren Analysen basierten auf zwei Faktoren, auf denen die Items „kompetent" (im englischen Original: competent) und „sympathisch" (likable) luden (Faktorladungen $a_{ij} > |.40|$). Darauf aufbauend wurden die Eigenschaften ermittelt, die konsistent für alle Studierendengruppen entweder zusammen mit „kompetent" oder zusammen mit „sympathisch" auf ein und demselben Faktor luden (wiederum Faktorladungen über $|.40|$). Analog zu den Ergebnissen von Fiske et al. (1999) ergaben sich zwei Skalen mit vier beziehungsweise fünf Eigenschaften. Die Items „kompetent", „fleißig", „intelligent" und „entschlossen" luden für alle Studierendengruppen auf dem Faktor Kompetenz. Die Items „sympathisch",„hilfsbereit", „aufrichtig", „warm" und „freundlich" luden auf dem Faktor Wärme. Alle Skalen wiesen zufriedenstellende Reliabilitäten ($.79 \leq \alpha \leq .88$) auf.

Tabelle 1 fasst die Mittelwerte und Standardabweichungen der untersuchten Gruppen zusammen. Zwei ANOVAs mit dem Messwiederholungsfaktor Studiengang ergaben sowohl für die Variable Kompetenz ($F(2,266) = 49.25$, $p < .001$, $\eta^2 = .27$) als auch für die Variable Wärme ($F(2,266) = 83.42$, $p < .001$, $\eta^2 = .39$) einen signifikanten Effekt. Paarweise Vergleiche für die Variable Kompetenz wiesen die Gymnasiallehramtsstudierenden als die Gruppe aus, die am kompetentesten wahrgenommen wurde (alle p-Werte < .001). Lehramtsstudierende für Grund- sowie Haupt- und Realschule unterschieden sich nicht in ihrer zugeschriebenen Kompetenz. Die Vergleiche für die Variable Wärme wiesen die Grundschullehramtsstudierenden (alle p-Werte < .001) als die soziabelste Gruppe aus, während Gymnasiallehramtsstudierende als am wenigsten soziabel eingeschätzt wurden (alle p-Werte < .001).

Tabelle 1. Mittelwerte (Standardabweichungen) der Dimensionen Kompetenz und Wärme in den untersuchten Gruppen

		M (SD)
Kompetenz	Grundschule	3.23 (.75)
	Haupt- & Realschule	3.34 (.73)
	Gymnasium	3.81 (.65)
Wärme	Grundschule	3.99 (.67)
	Haupt- & Realschule	3.45 (.61)
	Gymnasium	3.25 (.66)

Die den Studierendengruppen zugeschriebene Kompetenz wurde mit der ihnen zugeschriebenen Wärme verglichen. Für Grundschullehramtsstudierende war die zugeschriebene Kompetenz signifikant geringer als die zugeschriebene Wärme ($t = -11.11$, $df = 133$, $p < .001$). Für Studierende des Haupt- und Realschullehramts war dieser Unterschied marginal signifikant ($t = -1.91$, $df = 134$, $p = .058$). Für Gymnasiallehramtsstudierende zeigte sich das umgekehrte Muster: Die ihnen zugeschriebene Kompetenz war signifikant größer als die ihnen zugeschriebene Wärme ($t = 10.15$, $df = 134$, $p < .001$).

Die Ergebnisse dieser ersten Studie sprechen für die Existenz von Substereotypen für spezifische Gruppen von Lehramtsstudierenden.

3 Studie II

Studie II verfolgte vier Ziele. Erstens wurde untersucht, ob Lehramtsstudierende außerhalb von Experimenten Stereotype Threat erleben. Zweitens wurde untersucht, inwieweit dieser Stereotype Threat von sozialen Vergleichen mit Mitgliedern der Eigengruppe (Lehramtsstudierende) oder der Fremdgruppe (Fachstudierende) abhängt. Drittens sollten die Auswirkungen von Stereotype Threat auf Studienzufriedenheit untersucht werden. Viertens wurde die Identifikation mit der Gruppe der Lehramtsstudierenden als ein möglicher Moderator eines Stereotype-Threat-Effekts geprüft.

3.1 Stichprobe

Als Teilnehmende wurden N = 104 Lehramtsstudierende der Technischen Universität Dortmund rekrutiert (M = 24.96 Jahre, SD = 6.01; 68.3 % weiblich). Die Teilnehmenden studierten Lehramt für Gymnasium und Gesamtschule (n = 38), Grundschule (n = 19), Haupt- und Realschule (n = 11), Sonderpädagogische Förderung (n = 20) und das Berufskolleg (n = 12). Die potenziellen Teilnehmenden wurden über einen E-Mail-Verteiler der Universität zur Online-Befragung eingeladen.

3.2 Variablen

3.2.1 Unabhängige Variablen und Moderatoren

Soziale Vergleiche (Eigengruppe/Fremdgruppe). Die Häufigkeit sozialer Vergleiche mit anderen Lehramtsstudierenden oder Fachstudierenden wurde mit jeweils vier Fragen erfasst, die aus Von Hippel et al. (2011) adaptiert wurden (z. B. „Wenn Sie an Ihre Fortschritte im Studium denken, wie häufig vergleichen Sie sich mit anderen Lehramtsstudierenden?"). Die Teilnehmenden gaben auf einer fünfstufigen Skala an, wie oft sie derartige Vergleiche vornahmen (1 – „überhaupt nicht häufig"; 5 – „sehr häufig"; α (Eigengruppe) = .83 / α (Fremdgruppe) = .91).

Stereotype Threat. Der Stereotype Threat wurde über ein Instrument erfasst, das aus Von Hippel et al. (2011, 2013) adaptiert wurde. Die aus acht Items bestehende Skala erfasste, inwiefern die befragten Personen in ihrem Studium negative stereotype Bewertungen durch andere erwarteten oder sich durch solche Bewertungen bedroht fühlten (z. B. „Einige meiner Kommilitonen glauben, ich wäre weniger fähig, weil ich Lehramtsstudierende/r bin."). Die Teilnehmenden gaben auf einer siebenstufigen Skala an, wie sehr die getroffenen Aussagen auf sie zutrafen (1 – „trifft überhaupt nicht zu"; 7 – „trifft völlig zu"; α = .91).

Eigengruppen-Identifikation. Die Identifikation mit der Gruppe der Lehramtsstudierenden wurde mit einer inhaltlich angepassten Kurzskala erfasst, die sich an Skalen orientiert, wie sie für derartige Untersuchungen typisch sind (z. B. Simon & Stürmer, 2005). Die Skala umfasste vier Items (z. B. „Ich fühle mich anderen Lehramtsstudierenden verbunden."; 1 – „trifft überhaupt nicht zu"; 7 – „trifft völlig zu"; α = .85).

3.2.2 Abhängige Variablen

Studienzufriedenheit. Die Zufriedenheit mit dem Studium wurde über sechs Items erfasst (z. B. „Mein Studium macht mir wirklich Spaß.", „Mein Studium ist interessant."), die zum Teil vorhandenen Instrumenten entlehnt (Westermann, Heise, Spies & Trautwein, 1996) und zum Teil selbst entwickelt waren. Die Teilnehmenden gaben auf einer siebenstufigen Skala an, wie sehr die getroffenen Aussagen auf sie zutrafen (1 – „trifft überhaupt nicht zu"; 7 – „trifft völlig zu"; α = .84).

3.3 Ergebnisse

Tabelle 2 fasst die Mittelwerte und Interkorrelationen der gemessenen Variablen zusammen. Entsprechend den Ergebnissen von Von Hippel et al. (2011) wurden positive Korrelationen zwischen der Häufigkeit sozialer Vergleiche mit der Eigengruppe der Lehramtsstudierenden und der Fremdgruppe der Fachstudierenden erwartet sowie zwischen den sozialen Vergleichen und Stereotype Threat. Des Weiteren wurde entsprechend den Ergebnissen von Fassiotto et al. (2016) eine negative Korrelation zwischen Stereotype Threat und Studienzufriedenheit erwartet.

Es gab eine signifikante positive Korrelation zwischen den Häufigkeiten sozialer Vergleiche mit der Eigengruppe der Lehramtsstudierenden und solchen mit der Fremdgruppe der Fachstudierenden. Lehramtsstudierende, die sich häufiger mit anderen Lehramtsstudierenden verglichen, tendierten dazu, sich auch häufiger mit Fachstudierenden zu vergleichen (und umgekehrt). Die beiden Kategorien sozialer Vergleiche korrelierten positiv mit Stereotype Threat; je häufiger sich die Teilnehmenden mit anderen Studierenden verglichen, desto mehr Stereotype Threat erlebten sie. Stereotype Threat korrelierte negativ mit der Studienzufriedenheit. Die Identifikation mit der Eigengruppe der Lehramtsstudierenden korrelierte mit keiner anderen Variablen als der Studienzufriedenheit: je höher die Identifikation mit der Gruppe der Lehramtsstudierenden, desto höher die Studienzufriedenheit.

Tabelle 2. Mittelwerte (Standardabweichungen) und Interkorrelationen der in Studie II erfassten Variablen

Variable		M (SD)	1	2	3	4	5
1	soziale Vergleiche (Lehramtsstudierende)	3.47 (.88)		.30**	.24*	.15	.06
2	soziale Vergleiche (Hauptfachstudierende)	2.18 (1.18)			.31**	-.04	<.01
3	Stereotype Threat	2.49 (1.36)				.01	-.26**
4	Eigengruppenidentifikation (Lehramtsstudierende)	4.95 (1.43)					.36***
5	Studienzufriedenheit (Lehramtsstudium)	4.92 (1.31)					

* $p < .05$, ** $p < .01$, *** $p < .001$

Angelehnt an die Analysen bei Von Hippel et al. (2011, 2013) wurden die in Studie II erfassten Variablen in das in Abbildung 1 dargestellte Strukturmodell eingeordnet. Die sozialen Vergleiche wurden als Prädiktoren für Stereotype Threat angenommen.

Dieser wiederum, moderiert durch die Identifikation mit der Gruppe der Lehramtsstudierenden, fungierte als Prädiktor für die Zufriedenheit mit dem Studium.

Das dargestellte Modell wies einen guten Fit auf; $\chi^2(8) = 7.87$, $p = .45$, RMSEA < .001, CFI = 1.00, TLI = 1.00[2]; alternative Modelle boten keine Verbesserung des Modell-Fits. Soziale Vergleiche mit der Fremdgruppe beeinflussten das Erleben von Stereotype Threat; je mehr sie sich mit Fachstudierenden verglichen, desto stärker fühlten sich Lehramtsstudierende von Stereotypen bedroht. Die sozialen Vergleiche mit der Eigengruppe standen in einen vernachlässigbaren Zusammenhang mit Stereotype Threat. Das Erleben von Stereotype Threat und die Studienzufriedenheit hingen negativ zusammen. Der indirekte Effekt von sozialen Vergleichen mit der Fremdgruppe war klein, aber signifikant (indirekter Effekt $\beta = -.07$, $p = .03$), wohingegen der indirekte Effekt von sozialen Vergleichen mit der Eigengruppe nicht signifikant war (indirekter Effekt $\beta = -.04$, $p = .11$). Es gab keine signifikante Interaktion zwischen Stereotype Threat und der Identifikation mit der Gruppe der Lehramtsstudierenden; der angenommene moderierende Effekt der Gruppenidentifikation konnte nicht aufgezeigt werden. Die Identifikation mit der Gruppe der Lehramtsstudierenden hatte einen positiven Effekt auf die Studienzufriedenheit; je mehr sich die Studierenden mit ihrer Eigengruppe identifizierten, desto zufriedener waren sie mit ihrem Studium.

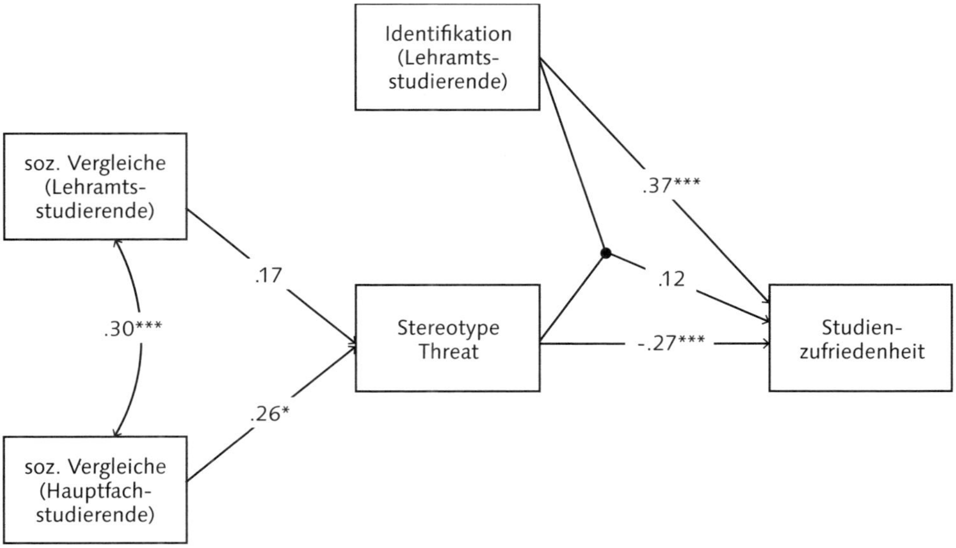

Abbildung 1. Modell der Beziehungen zwischen sozialen Vergleichen, wahrgenommenem Stereotype Threat und Studienzufriedenheit.
* $p < .05$, *** $p < .001$

2 Die Analysen wurden mit MPlus 7.3 vorgenommen.

4 Diskussion

Der vorliegende Beitrag stellte zwei verschiedene Studien vor. Die erste Studie untersuchte das Auftreten des Stereotyps niedriger Kompetenz und hoher Wärme von Lehramtsstudierenden im Vergleich zu Fachstudierenden für verschiedene Lehramtsstudiengänge. Die Studie konnte eine Substereotypisierung der Lehramtsstudiengänge aufzeigen. Lehramtsstudierende für Grund-, Haupt- und Realschule wurden als weniger kompetent eingeschätzt als Studierende des Gymnasiallehramts. Ob und inwiefern diese Substereotypisierung auch eine unterschiedliche Verwundbarkeit gegenüber Stereotype Threat mit sich bringt, muss noch erforscht werden.

Die zweite Studie stellte einen positiven Zusammenhang zwischen sozialen Vergleichen mit der Gruppe der Fachstudierenden und dem Erleben von Stereotype Threat fest: Je häufiger sich Lehramtsstudierende mit Fachstudierenden hinsichtlich ihres Studiums vergleichen, desto mehr fühlen sie sich von Stereotypen bedroht. Alternativerklärungen, die beispielsweise die Richtung und die generelle Häufigkeit sozialer Vergleiche berücksichtigen (siehe z. B. Mussweiler & Strack, 2000; Suls, Martin & Wheeler, 2002), konnten mit dem vorliegenden Design nicht erforscht werden.

Stereotype Threat erwies sich als signifikant negativer Prädiktor der Studienzufriedenheit. Je stärker die Teilnehmenden Stereotype Threat erlebten, desto weniger beschrieben sie ihr Studium als interessant oder befriedigend. Dies impliziert, dass Stereotype Threat langfristig Leistung und Motivation von Lehramtsstudierenden untergraben kann. Im schlimmsten Falle könnten Studierende ihr Studium abbrechen oder sich zunehmend von ihrem späteren Beruf distanzieren, was wiederum negative Konsequenzen für ihre Motivation und Leistung als Lehrkräfte hätte.

Der Effekt von Stereotype Threat in Studie II wurde nicht durch die Identifikation mit der Gruppe der Lehramtsstudierenden moderiert. Dieser Befund lässt verschiedene Interpretationen zu. Die meisten der Teilnehmenden waren Studierende im Bachelorstudium (n = 93). Es besteht die Möglichkeit, dass zu Studienbeginn, wenn ein Verlassen des Lehramtsstudiums noch mit vergleichsweise geringen Kosten möglich ist, die Identifikation mit der Gruppe der Lehramtsstudierenden nur einen vernachlässigbaren Effekt auf die Wirkung von Stereotype Threat hat. Eine weitere Möglichkeit ist, dass die Identifikation mit der übergeordneten Kategorie der Lehramtsstudierenden irrelevant ist und stattdessen der Domänenidentifikation (Mathematik, Deutsch etc.) eine stärkere Bedeutung zukommt. Zum gegenwärtigen Zeitpunkt sind diese und andere Möglichkeiten jedoch rein spekulativ und können lediglich Ansätze für spätere Forschungen bieten.

Die vorgestellten Studien weisen verschiedene Einschränkungen auf. Beide Studien stützten sich auf kleine Stichproben aus stark eingegrenzten Gruppen (Studie I: Psychologiestudierende der FernUniversität in Hagen, Studie II: Lehramtsstudierende der Technischen Universität Dortmund). Dies schränkt generell die Übertragbarkeit und Aussagekraft der Befunde ein. Des Weiteren sind durch die geringe Anzahl der Teilnehmenden in Studie II keine Vergleiche zwischen verschiedenen Gruppen (z. B. Lehramtsstudiengängen) möglich. Darüber hinaus beschränkte sich Studie II auf eine

Querschnittsuntersuchung, die weder sichere Aussagen zu kausalen noch zu langfristigen Effekten von Stereotype Threat ermöglicht. Auch wurden keine weiteren studienrelevanten Variablen zum Studienerfolg (z. B. Prüfungsleistungen) berücksichtigt.

Die vorliegenden Ergebnisse bestärken die Annahme, dass Lehramtsstudierende im Studium durch Stereotype Threat Beeinträchtigungen erleben. Eine Quelle möglichen Bedrohungserlebens stellt die Begegnung mit Fachstudierenden dar, die Lehramtsstudierende unter Umständen nicht als „richtige" Studierende wahrnehmen. Eine Möglichkeit dem zu begegnen wäre, Lehramtsstudierende in spezifischen Lehrveranstaltungen in ihren Fachinhalten zu unterweisen. Dies hätte – über die mögliche Verringerung von Stereotype Threat hinaus – zwei Vorteile: Erstens könnten die Inhalte der Veranstaltungen an die Anforderungen des späteren Berufs der Studierenden angepasst werden. Zweitens könnten diese Lehrveranstaltungen Lehrenden die Gelegenheit bieten, in einer Umgebung mit geringerer Bedrohung mit Lehramtsstudierenden in Kontakt zu treten. Dies wiederum könnte langfristig zum Abbau von Stereotypen auf Seiten der Lehrenden und so zum Wandel des stereotypen Bildes der Lehramtsstudierenden als „doofe" Studierende beitragen.

Literatur

Blömeke, S. (2005). Das Lehrerbild in Printmedien. Inhaltsanalyse von „Spiegel"- und „Focus"-Berichten seit 1990. *Die Deutsche Schule, 97*, 24–39.

Carlsson, R. & Björklund, F. (2010). Implicit stereotype content: Mixed stereotypes can be measured with the implicit association test. *Social Psychology, 41*, 213–222.

Czopp, A. M. & Monteith, M. J. (2006). Thinking well of African Americans: Measuring complimentary stereotypes and negative prejudice. *Basic & Applied Social Psychology, 28*, 233–250.

Fassiotto, M., Hamel, E. O., Ku, M., Correll, S., Grewal, D., Lavori, P. & Valantine, H. (2016). Women in academic medicine: Measuring stereotype threat among junior faculty. *Journal of Women's Health, 25*, 292–298.

Fiske, S. T., Xu, J., Cuddy, A. J. C. & Glick, P. (1999). (Dis)respecting versus (dis)liking: Status and interdependence predict ambivalent stereotypes of competence and warmth. *Journal of Social Issues, 55*, 473–489.

Gold, A. & Giesen, H. (1993). Leistungsvoraussetzungen und Studienbedingungen bei Studierenden verschiedener Lehrämter. *Psychologie in Erziehung und Unterricht, 40*, 111–124.

Heublin, U., Hutzsch, C., Schreiber, J., Sommer, D. & Besuch, G. (2009). *Ursachen des Studienabbruchs in Bachelor- und in herkömmlichen Studiengängen: Ergebnisse einer bundesweiten Befragung von Exmatrikulierten des Studienjahres 2007/08.* Verfügbar unter: http://www.dzhw.eu/pdf/21/studien abbruch_ursachen.pdf [28.07.2016].

Hoyt, C. L. & Simon, S. (2011). Female leaders: Injurious or inspiring role models for women? *Psychology of Women Quarterly*, *35*, 143–157.

Ihme, T. A. & Mauch, M. (2007). Werbung als implizite Aktivierungsquelle von Geschlechterstereotypen und ihr Einfluss auf Mathematikleistungen sowie auf das Computerwissen bei Mädchen und Jungen. *Empirische Pädagogik, 21*, 291–305.

Ihme, T. A. & Möller, J. (2015). 'He who can, does; he who cannot, teaches?': Stereotype threat and preservice teachers. *Journal of Educational Psychology*, *107*, 300–308.

Milner, H. R. & Woolfolk Hoy, A. (2003). A case study of an African American teacher's self-efficacy, stereotype threat, and persistence. *Teaching and Teacher Education, 19*, 263–276.

Mussweiler, T. & Strack, F. (2000). Consequences of social comparison: Selective accessibility, assimilation, and contrast. In J. Suls & L. Wheeler (Eds.), *Handbook of social comparison. Theory and research* (pp. 253–270). New York, NY: Kluwer Academic/Plenum Publishers.

Nguyen, H.-H. D. & Ryan, A. M. (2008). Does stereotype threat affect test performance of minorities and women? A meta-analysis of experimental evidence. *Journal of Applied Psychology, 93*, 1314–1334.

Oja, M. (2011). Student satisfaction and student performance. *Journal of Applied Research in the Community College, 19*, 50–57.

Rauin, U. (2007). *Im Studium wenig engagiert – im Beruf schnell überfordert. Studierverhalten und Karrieren im Lehrerberuf – Kann man Risiken schon im Studium prognostizieren?* Verfügbar unter: http://www.uni-frankfurt.de/fb/fb04/download/Rauin_Studierverhalten.pdf [08.01.2008].

Roloff Henoch, J., Klusmann, U., Lüdtke, O. & Trautwein, U. (2015). Die Entwicklung beruflicher Selbstregulation: Ein Vergleich zwischen angehenden Lehrkräften und anderen Studierenden. *Zeitschrift für Pädagogische Psychologie*, *29*, 151–162.

Rydell, R. J., Rydell, M. T. & Boucher, K. L. (2010). The effect of negative performance stereotypes on learning. *Journal of Personality and Social Psychology, 99*, 883–896.

Sarand, L. (2016). Lehramtsstudierende werden für doof gehalten. *Spiegel Online.* Verfügbar unter: http://www.spiegel.de/unispiegel/studium/lehramtsstudenten-in-pruefungen-wir-werden-fuer-doof-gehaltena-1092900.html [24.05.2016].

Schmader, T. (2002). Gender identification moderates stereotype threat effects on women's math performance. *Journal of Experimental Social Psychology*, *38*, 194–201.

Schmader, T., Johns, M. & Forbes, C. (2008). An integrated process model of stereotype threat effects on performance. *Psychological Review, 115*, 336–356.

Sembiring, M. G. (2015). Validating student satisfaction related to persistence, academic performance, retention and career advancement within ODL perspectives. *Open Praxis*, *7*, 325–337.

Simon, B. & Stürmer, S. (2005). In search of the active ingredient of respect: A closer look at the role of acceptance. *European Journal of Social Psychology*, *35*, 809–818.

Sockalingam, N. (2012). The relation between student satisfaction and student performance in blended learning curricula. *International Journal of Learning*, *18*, 121–134.

Spinath, B., van Ophuysen, S. & Heise, E. (2005). Individuelle Voraussetzungen von Studierenden zu Studienbeginn: Sind Lehramtsstudierende so schlecht wie ihr Ruf? *Psychologie in Erziehung und Unterricht, 52*, 186–197.

Steele, C. M. (1997). A threat in the air. How stereotypes shape intellectual identity and performance. *American Psychologist, 52*, 613–629.

Steele, C. M. (2010). *Whistling Vivaldi and other clues to how stereotypes affect us*. New York, NY: W. W. Norton & Company.

Steele, C. M. & Aronson, J. (1995). Stereotype threat and the intellectual test performance of African Americans. *Journal of Personality and Social Psychology, 69*, 797–811.

Suls, J., Martin, R. & Wheeler, L. (2002). Social comparison: Why, with whom, and with what effect? *Current Directions in Psychological Science, 11*, 159–163.

Taylor, V. J. & Walton, G. M. (2011). Stereotype threat undermines academic learning. *Personality & Social Psychology Bulletin, 37*, 1055–1067.

Von Hippel, C., Issa, M., Ma, R. & Stokes, A. (2011). Stereotype threat: Antecedents and consequences for working women. *European Journal of Social Psychology, 41*, 151–161.

Von Hippel, C., Kalokerinos, E. K. & Henry, J. D. (2013). Stereotype threat among older employees: Relationship with job attitudes and turnover intentions. *Psychology and Aging, 28*, 17–27.

Van Loo, K. J., Boucher, K. L., Rydell, R. J. & Rydell, M. T. (2013). Competition in stereotyped domains: Competition, social comparison, and stereotype threat. *European Journal of Social Psychology, 43*, 648–660.

Walzer, A. S. & Czopp, A. M. (2011). Able but unintelligent: Including positively stereotyped black subgroups in the Stereotype Content Model. *Journal of Social Psychology, 151*, 527–530.

Westermann, R., Heise, E., Spies, K. & Trautwein, U. (1996). Identifikation und Erfassung von Komponenten der Studienzufriedenheit. *Psychologie in Erziehung und Unterricht, 43*, 1–22.

Woodcock, A., Hernandez, P. R., Estrada, M. & Schultz, P. W. (2012). The consequences of chronic stereotype threat: Domain disidentification and abandonment. *Journal of Personality and Social Psychology, 103*, 635–646.

Autor

DR. TONI ALEXANDER IHME

Dezernat 1.1 – Lehre und Qualitätsmanagement, FernUniversität in Hagen.

KONTAKT

Toni Alexander Ihme, Dezernat 1.1 – Lehre und Qualitätsmanagement,
FernUniversität in Hagen, Universitätsstraße 47, 58097 Hagen.
E-Mail: *toni-alexander.ihme@fernuni-hagen.de*

Get the picture – Eine Response-Surface-Analyse des Zusammenhangs zwischen Urteilssicherheit und Urteilsakkuratheit

JOHANNA KAISER UND ANNA SÜDKAMP

ZUSAMMENFASSUNG: Die Fähigkeit zur akkuraten Beurteilung der Leistungen ihrer Schülerinnen und Schüler gilt als ein Aspekt professioneller Kompetenz von Lehrkräften. In dieser Studie wurde der Zusammenhang zwischen der Urteilsakkuratheit und der Sicherheit bezüglich des Urteils bei Lehramtsstudierenden untersucht. In zwei experimentellen Studien (Studie 1: $N = 182$, Studie 2: $N = 92$) beurteilten Lehramtsstudierende die individuelle schulische Leistung von am Computer simulierten Schülerinnen und Schülern und gaben ihre subjektive Sicherheit bezüglich jedes Urteils an. Die Daten wurden mithilfe der Response-Surface-Analyse ausgewertet, die es erlaubt, den Zusammenhang zwischen der Leistung der Schülerinnen und Schüler, der Leistungsbeurteilung und Urteilssicherheit differenziert zu betrachten. Die Analysen zeigten, dass die Lehramtsstudierenden sich bei der Einschätzung objektiv leistungsschwacher und leistungsstarker Schülerinnen und Schüler sicherer waren als bei der Einschätzung von Schülerinnen und Schülern im mittleren Leistungsbereich. Im mittleren, nicht aber im hohen und niedrigen Leistungsbereich, sank die Urteilssicherheit mit abnehmender Urteilsakkuratheit. Aus den Ergebnissen kann z. B. abgeleitet werden, dass die Unsicherheiten in Zusammenhang mit schulischer Leistungsbeurteilung im Rahmen der Aus- und Fortbildung von Lehrkräften thematisiert werden sollten.

Schlüsselwörter: Urteilsakkuratheit, Urteilssicherheit, Response-Surface-Analyse, Simulierter Klassenraum

Get the picture – A response surface analysis on the relationship between judgment confidence and judgment accuracy

ABSTRACT: The ability to accurately assess students' academic achievement is considered to be an important aspect of teachers' professional competence. In this paper, we studied the relationship between pre-service teachers' judgment accuracy and self-reported judgment confidence. In two experimental studies (Study 1: $N = 182$, Study 2: $N = 92$) pre-service teachers judged students' academic achievement in a computer simulation of a classroom situation individually and reported their confidence concerning each judgment. Data were analyzed by means of response surface analysis which allows considering the relationship between students' academic achievement, achievement judgment and judgment confidence. The analyses showed that pre-service teachers were more confident in their judgments of objectively low-achieving and high-achieving students than in their judgments of average-achieving students. When judging average-achieving, but not low or high-achieving students, lower judgment confidence went along with lower judgment accuracy. From the results may be inferred that uncertainties of judging students' academic achievement should be made a subject of discussion in teacher education and professional training.

Keywords: judgment accuracy, judgment confidence, response surface analysis, simulated classroom

Einleitung

Lehrkrafteinschätzungen sind neben standardisierten Testverfahren (Pellegrino, Chudowsky & Glaser, 2001) und Schülerinnen- und Schülerselbsteinschätzungen (Panadero, Brown & Strijbos, 2015) eine der wichtigsten Informationsquellen über die schulischen Leistungen von Schülerinnen und Schülern (Baker, Tichovolsky, Kupersmidt, Voegler-Lee & Arnold, 2015). Sie stehen daher wiederkehrend im Blickpunkt pädagogisch-psychologischer Forschung.

Lehrkrafteinschätzungen wurden bisher vor allem im Hinblick auf ihre Akkuratheit untersucht (*teacher judgment accuracy*, z. B. Furnari, Whittaker, Kinzie & DeCoster, 2017), die im Mittel als zufriedenstellend beurteilt werden kann (Südkamp, Kaiser & Möller, 2012). Andere Aspekte von Lehrkrafteinschätzungen, wie die Sicherheit, mit der Lehrkräfte Schülerinnen- und Schülerleistungen einschätzen, wurden bisher selten untersucht (Gabriele, Joram & Park, 2016; Praetorius, Berner, Zeinz, Scheunpflug & Dresel, 2013). Auch liegen bisher nur vereinzelte Befunde zum Zusammenhang von Urteilsakkuratheit und Urteilssicherheit vor (Gabriele et al., 2016; Praetorius et al., 2013). In dieser Studie untersuchen wir den Zusammenhang zwischen den Leistungen von Schülerinnen und Schülern und Lehrkrafteinschätzungen schulischer Leistungen (Urteilsakkuratheit) sowie der Urteilssicherheit mit der Methode der Response-Surface-Analyse (Schönbrodt, 2016b), die eine differenzierte Betrachtung des Zusammenhangs der drei Variablen erlaubt.

1 Theoretischer Hintergrund

1.1 Akkuratheit der Einschätzung von Schülerinnen- und Schülerleistungen durch Lehrkräfte

Die Fähigkeit, die schulischen Leistungen von Schülerinnen und Schülern akkurat einschätzen zu können, gilt als ein bedeutender Aspekt der professionellen Kompetenz von Lehrkräften (Ready & Wright, 2011). Nur wenn Lehrkräfte die Lernvoraussetzungen ihrer Schülerinnen und Schüler kennen, können sie gute pädagogische Entscheidungen treffen (Herppich et al., 2017) und ihren Unterricht optimal an diese Voraussetzungen anpassen (Baker et al., 2015). Die Akkuratheit der Einschätzungen der Leistungen von Schülerinnen und Schülern durch Lehrkräfte wird in der Regel über den Zusammenhang zwischen den Lehrkrafteinschätzungen und den objektiv gemessenen Schülerinnen- und Schülerleistungen operationalisiert. In einer Metaanalyse auf der Basis von 75 Studien ermittelten Südkamp et al. (2012) eine mittlere Effektstärke von $r = .63$ für diesen Zusammenhang. Den Lehrkräften gelingt es demnach im Mittel recht gut, eine Rangfolge der Schülerleistungen innerhalb ihrer Klasse zu erstellen. Die Spannweite zwischen den in den einzelnen Studien ermittelten Korrelationen erwies sich jedoch als sehr groß ($r = -.03$ bis $r = .84$). Studien zur Urteilsakkuratheit von Lehrkräften sprechen außerdem für eine Tendenz von Lehrkräften, leistungsschwache Schülerinnen und Schüler zu überschätzen und leistungsstarke Schülerinnen und Schüler zu unterschätzen (Coladarci, 1986; Demaray & Elliott, 1998). Auch gibt es Hinweise darauf, dass leistungsschwache Schülerinnen und Schüler weniger akkurat beurteilt werden als leistungsstarke Schülerinnen und Schüler (z. B. Begeny, Eckert, Montarello & Storie, 2008). Bisher gibt es in diesem Bereich nur wenige experimentelle Studien, die jedoch seit der Nutzung des Simulierten Klassenraums (SKR; Südkamp, Möller & Pohlmann, 2008) für solche Fragestellungen zahlreicher geworden sind. Der SKR ist eine Methode zur experimentellen Untersuchung der Urteilsakkuratheit von Lehrkräften. In Studien mit dem SKR wurden leistungsschwache Schülerinnen und Schüler ebenfalls überschätzt und leistungsstarke Schülerinnen und Schüler unterschätzt, während Lehrkrafteinschätzungen im mittleren Leistungsbereich am genauesten waren (z. B. Kaiser, Retelsdorf, Südkamp & Möller, 2013).

1.2 Sicherheit von Lehrkräften bei der Einschätzung von Schülerinnen- und Schülerleistungen

Lehrkrafteinschätzungen sollten zum einen akkurat sein (Baker et al., 2015), zum anderen sollte es von Vorteil für das unterrichtliche Handeln von Lehrkräften sein, wenn sie sich ihrer Einschätzung sicher sind (Praetorius et al., 2013). Gabriele et al. (2016) unterscheiden eine motivationale und eine metakognitive Dimension von Urteilssicherheit. Aus motivationaler Perspektive spiegelt die Sicherheit bezüglich der eigenen Einschätzung die Bereitschaft von Personen wieder, auf Basis ihres selbst wahrgenommenen Kenntnisstands zu handeln. Demnach treffen Lehrkräfte vermutlich nur dann pädagogische Entscheidungen auf Basis ihrer eigenen Einschätzung, wenn sie sich bezüglich der Einschätzung sicher sind (Praetorius et al., 2013). Sowohl die Urteilsakkuratheit als auch die Urteilssicherheit sind somit Voraussetzungen dafür, dass Lehrkräfte gute pädagogische Entscheidungen treffen, die förderlich für die schulischen Leistungen von Schülerinnen und Schülern sind. Ist eine Lehrkraft sich bezüglich einer inakkuraten Einschätzung sicher, so trifft sie vermutlich weniger gute pädagogische Entscheidungen, die die schulische Entwicklung von Schülerinnen und Schülern negativ beeinflussen könnten (Praetorius et al., 2013). Für den Fall, dass Lehrkräfte sich bezüglich ihrer Einschätzung unsicher sind, nehmen Praetorius et al.

(2013) an, dass Lehrkräfte vermutlich keine pädagogischen Entscheidungen auf Basis dieser Einschätzungen treffen.

Aus metakognitiver Perspektive (z.B. Dunlosky & Metcalfe, 2009) kann angenommen werden, dass Lehrkräfte, die sich entweder sicher sind, wenn sie Schülerinnen und Schüler akkurat beurteilen (d.h., die wissen, dass sie etwas wissen) oder die sich unsicher sind, wenn sie Schülerinnen und Schüler inakkurat beurteilen (d.h., die wissen, dass sie etwas nicht wissen), ihre eigene Urteilsakkuratheit effizient selbst überwachen (Gabriele et al., 2016). Gariele et al. (2016) sprechen in diesem Zusammenhang von kalibrierten Einschätzungen (*calibrated judgments*). Sie nehmen an, dass Lehrkräfte, die kalibrierte Einschätzungen abgeben, ihr unterrichtliches Handeln gut regulieren und anpassen können – entweder indem sie gute pädagogische Entscheidungen auf Basis ihrer akkuraten und sicheren Einschätzungen treffen oder indem sie mehr Informationen über Schülerinnen und Schüler sammeln, bezüglich derer die Einschätzung noch inakkurat und unsicher ist.

Bisher gibt es nur wenige Studien, die sich mit der Sicherheit von Lehrkräften bezüglich der Einschätzung ihrer Schülerinnen und Schüler beschäftigen (Gariele et al., 2016; Praetorius et al., 2013). Praetorius et al. (2013) baten Lehrkräfte die Fähigkeitsselbstkonzepte von Schülerinnen und Schülern im Fach Mathematik einzuschätzen und gleichzeitig anzugeben, wie sicher sie sich ihrer Urteile waren. Es zeigte sich ein „*overconfidence*"-Effekt (DePaulo, Charlton, Cooper, Lindsay & Muhlenbruck, 1997; Fischhoff, Slovic & Lichtenstein, 1977), d.h., die Lehrkräfte waren sich in ihren Einschätzungen sicherer, als dies auf Basis der Urteilsakkuratheit angemessen wäre. In der Studie von Gabriele et al. (2016) schätzten Lehrkräfte die Fähigkeit ihrer Schülerinnen und Schüler im Rechnen ein und gaben ihre Sicherheit bezüglich der Einschätzung an. Die Urteilsakkuratheit – gemessen als „*hit rate*" (Artelt & Rausch, 2014) – lag in einem hohen Bereich und ihre Urteilssicherheit schätzten die Lehrkräfte ebenfalls hoch ein.

1.3 Zusammenhänge zwischen Urteilsakkuratheit und Urteilssicherheit

Die Urteilssicherheit wird theoretisch (Gabriele et al., 2016; Praetorius et al., 2013) in einen Zusammenhang mit der Urteilsakkuratheit gestellt. Sozialpsychologische Studien haben den Zusammenhang zwischen Urteilsakkuratheit und Urteilssicherheit in verschiedenen, nicht-schulischen Kontexten untersucht. In der Studie von Ames, Kammrath, Suppes und Bolger (2010) hatten Personen beispielsweise die Aufgabe, Persönlichkeitsmerkmale von Fremden anhand von Video- und Bildmaterial einzuschätzen. Die Urteilsakkuratheit der Teilnehmerinnen und Teilnehmer korrelierte nicht signifikant mit der Urteilssicherheit. Patterson, Foster und Bellmer (2001) ließen die Teilnehmerinnen und Teilnehmer an ihrer Studie das Verhalten von Personen in Videos beurteilen und ihren Status einschätzen (z.B. „Wer von beiden Personen ist der Chef, wer der Arbeitnehmer?") und fanden ebenfalls keinen signifikanten Zusammenhang zwischen Urteilsakkuratheit und Urteilssicherheit. In Studien von Smith

Archer und Costanzo (1991) und Vallone, Griffin, Lind und Ross (1990) ergaben sich geringe positive Korrelationen ($r = .08$. bis $r = .24$) zwischen den beiden Personenmerkmalen. Insgesamt lassen diese Studien auf einen nicht vorhandenen bzw. geringen linearen Zusammenhang zwischen Urteilssicherheit und Urteilsakkuratheit schließen. In der Studie von Praetorius et al. (2013) im schulischen Kontext wurde der Zusammenhang zwischen den Lehrkrafteinschätzungen und den selbstberichteten Fähigkeitsselbstkonzepten der Schülerinnen und Schüler im Fach Mathematik durch die Urteilssicherheit moderiert ($\beta = .17$): Eine höhere Urteilssicherheit ging mit einer höheren Urteilsakkuratheit einher. Die Lehrkräfte waren sich außerdem sicherer in ihren Einschätzungen, wenn sie extreme Einschätzungen abgaben, d.h., wenn sie die Fähigkeitsselbstkonzepte der Schülerinnen und Schüler besonders hoch oder niedrig einschätzten, als wenn sie Einschätzungen im mittleren Skalenbereich abgaben. Im Einklang damit zeigten Studien zu Urteilsverzerrungen in Ratingverfahren (Myford & Wolfe, 2003), dass Personen sich ihrer Einschätzungen unsicherer waren, wenn sie Urteile im mittleren Bereich einer Skala abgaben. Gabriele et al. (2016) fanden in ihrer Studie eine Korrelation von $r = .41$ zwischen der Urteilsakkuratheit und der Urteilssicherheit. Aus der Darstellung der bisherigen Befunde zum Zusammenhang von Urteilsakkuratheit und Urteilssicherheit wird deutlich, dass es bisher nur wenige Studien im schulischen Kontext gibt. Außerdem erscheint es uns auf Basis der bisherigen Ergebnisse sinnvoll, das Leistungsniveau der Schülerinnen und Schüler in der Analyse dieses Zusammenhangs mit zu berücksichtigen.

2 Fragestellungen und Hypothesen

In diesem Beitrag wird der Zusammenhang zwischen der Urteilsakkuratheit und der Sicherheit bezüglich der Einschätzung von Schülerinnen- und Schülerleistungen mithilfe der Response-Surface-Analyse (RSA, z.B. beschrieben bei Schönbrodt, 2016b) untersucht. Die Urteilsakkuratheit wird dabei als Übereinstimmung zwischen Lehrkrafteinschätzungen der schulischen Leistungen von Schülerinnen und Schülern und den objektiv gemessenen Leistungen der Schülerinnen und Schüler operationalisiert (Südkamp et al., 2012). Hinsichtlich des Zusammenhangs der Urteilsakkuratheit mit der Urteilsicherheit nehmen wir theoretisch zwei Modelle an, die im Rahmen der RSA geprüft werden sollen. Auf Basis bisheriger empirischer Befunde (Gabriele et al., 2016, Praetorius et al., 2013) gehen wir zunächst von einem geringen, positiven linearen Zusammenhang zwischen der Urteilsakkuratheit und der Urteilssicherheit aus: Je akkurater Lehrkräfte Schülerinnen- und Schülerleistungen beurteilen, desto sicherer sollten sie sich sein. Zur Überprüfung dieser Hypothese wird das sogenannte *Squared Difference* (SQD) Model berechnet und in einem Modellvergleich berücksichtigt (Hypothese 1: Gültigkeit des SQD Models). Auf der anderen Seite sind komplexere Zusammenhänge zwischen Urteilsakkuratheit und Urteilssicherheit vorstellbar. Unter Berücksichtigung der Ergebnisse von Studien zur Urteilsakkuratheit im Feld (Demaray & Elliot, 1998) und im SKR (Kaiser et al., 2013; Südkamp et al., 2008) ist einerseits davon auszugehen, dass Lehrkräfte in Abhängigkeit vom Leistungsniveau der Schülerinnen und Schüler zu unterschiedlich akkuraten Urteilen kommen. Andererseits ist zu berücksichtigen, dass Personen sich bei der Beurteilung anderer Personen im Extrembereich eines Merkmals sicherer sind als bei Personen, deren Merkmalsausprägung im mittleren Bereich liegt (Myford & Wolfe, 2003; Praetorius et al., 2013). Auf Basis dieser Ergebnisse gehen wir davon aus, dass die Urteilsakkuratheit von Lehrkräften bei der Einschätzung von Schülerinnen und Schülern im mittleren Leistungsbereich höher ausfällt als von Schülerinnen und Schülern im hohen Leistungsbereich, sich die Lehrkräfte bei der Einschätzung von Schülerinnen und Schülern im niedrigen und hohen Leistungsbereich jedoch sicherer sind als bei der Einschätzung von Schülerinnen und Schülern im mittleren Leistungsbereich. Zur Überprüfung dieser Hypothese wird das Full Model berechnet und in den Modellvergleich einbezogen (Hypothese 2: Gültigkeit des Full Model). Die Hypothesen wurden in zwei experimentellen Studien überprüft.

3 Methode

Als Untersuchungssetting wurde der Simulierte Klassenraum (SKR) gewählt. Dabei handelt es sich um eine am Computer simulierte Unterrichtssituation, in der die Anwenderin oder der Anwender die Rolle einer Lehrkraft übernimmt, mit Schülerinnen und Schülern interagiert und deren Leistung beurteilt (Kaiser et al., 2013; Südkamp et al., 2008). Die Teilnehmerinnen und Teilnehmer an der Studie waren Lehramtsstudierende. Insgesamt wurden zwei experimentelle Studien durchgeführt. Studie 2 erfolgte im Anschluss an Studie 1 und diente der Replikation der Ergebnisse. Das Design beider Studien war identisch.

3.1 Der Simulierte Klassenraum

Ursprünglich stammt die Idee des SKR von der Arbeitsgruppe um Klaus Fiedler, die diesen nutzte, um sozialpsychologischen Fragestellungen nachzugehen (z. B. Fiedler, Walther, Freytag & Plessner, 2002). Für die Untersuchung von Fragestellungen zur Urteilsakkuratheit bietet das Instrument einen vielversprechenden Ansatz, da einzelne Faktoren des Unterrichtsgeschehens und des Kontextes gezielt variiert bzw. konstant gehalten werden können (Schrader, 2010). Eine ausführliche Beschreibung der für diese Untersuchung verwendeten Version des SKR findet sich bei Kaiser, Südkamp und Möller (2016).

Für die Leistung der simulierten Schülerinnen und Schüler wurden die Fähigkeitsparameter .20, .40, .60 und .80 für die Wahrscheinlichkeit einer richtigen Antwort gewählt. Beispielsweise gaben Schülerinnen bzw. Schüler mit einem Fähigkeitsparameter von .20 auf ca. 20 % der Fragen, die ihnen gestellt wurden, eine korrekte Antwort. Die Fähigkeitsparameter wurden zu gleichen Anteilen auf die 16 Schülerinnen und Schüler (mit ausschließlich deutschen Vornamen) der Klasse verteilt und pro Teilnehmerin oder Teilnehmer randomisiert zugewiesen. Pro Schülerin bzw. Schüler wurde im Anschluss an die Untersuchung die tatsächlich gezeigte Leistung registriert, die leicht vom festgelegten Fähigkeitsparameter abweichen konnte.

Im Anschluss an eine 17-minütige „Unterrichtsstunde" wurden die Anwenderinnen und Anwender aufgefordert, den Anteil korrekter Antworten der einzelnen Schülerinnen und Schüler auf einer Skala von 1 bis 100 % einzuschätzen (Leistungsbeurteilung). Zum Schluss sollten die Teilnehmerinnen und Teilnehmer auf einer Skala von 1 (sehr unsicher) bis 6 (sehr sicher) für jede Leistungsbeurteilung angeben, wie sicher sie sich bezüglich ihres Urteils waren (Urteilssicherheit).

3.2 Stichprobe

Die Stichprobe für Studie 1 setzte sich aus $N = 182$ Studierenden (64.8 % weiblich) des Lehramts der Christian-Albrechts-Universität zu Kiel zusammen. Die Studierenden studierten im Durchschnitt $M = 4.3$ Semester ($SD = 3.9$). Für Studie 2 bestand die Stichprobe aus $N = 92$ Lehramtsstudierenden (63.0 % weiblich). Sie studierten zum Zeitpunkt der Erhebung im Mittel $M = 5.3$ ($SD = 3.4$) Semester.

3.3 Analysen

In der Forschung werden verschiedene statistische Methoden zur Analyse der Urteilsakkuratheit von Lehrkräften eingesetzt (Karst, Hartig, Kaiser & Lipowsky, 2017). In dieser Studie wurde eine Response-Surface-Analyse (RSA; Schönbrodt, 2016b) der Urteilsakkuratheit und Urteilssicherheit von Lehrkräften mit dem R-Paket *RSA* (Schönbrodt, 2016a) durchgeführt (Humberg, Förster, Kaiser & Schönbrodt, 2017). Mithilfe der RSA wurde der Zusammenhang zwischen den Lehrkrafteinschätzungen, den objektiv gemessenen Leistungen der Schülerinnen und Schülern sowie der Urteilssicherheit überprüft. Der Zusammenhang der drei Variablen wurde über die Berechnung mehrerer, anzunehmender Modelle untersucht. Das *Full Model* entsprach dabei einem polynomialen Regressionsmodell mit den Lehrkrafteinschätzungen und den objektiv gemessenen Schülerinnen- und Schülerleistungen als Prädiktoren (X und Y) und der Urteilssicherheit (Z) als Kriterium, bei dem keine ungetesteten Einschränkungen der Koeffizienten gemacht wurden, wie sie z. B. in Regressionsmodellen mit Differenzwerten vorkommen. Im Full Model der RSA waren in der polynomialen Regression zweiter Ordnung die beiden Prädiktoren X und Y, die Interaktion der beiden Prädiktoren ($X * Y$) und die quadrierten Terme der beiden Prädiktoren (X^2 und Y^2) enthalten. Es resultierte die folgende Regressionsgleichung: $Z = b_0 + b_1X + b_2Y + b_3X^2 + b_4XY + b_5Y^2 + \varepsilon$. Dem *SQD Model* lag hingegen die Annahme eines positiv linearen Zusammenhangs zwischen Urteilsakkuratheit und Urteilsicherheit zugrunde. Im SQD Model wurden die Koeffizienten der zugrunde liegenden Regression im

Vergleich zum Full Model entsprechend beschränkt. Anhand von Modellvergleichen wurde geprüft, welches der Modelle am besten auf die vorliegenden Daten passte. Das SDQ Model und das Full Model wurden dabei auch gegen ein Nullmodell getestet, welches keinen Zusammenhang zwischen der Kriteriumsvariable und den Prädiktoren annimmt. Als zentraler Output der RSA wurde eine dreidimensionale grafische Darstellung des Zusammenhangs der drei Variablen generiert und zur Interpretation der Analyse genutzt.

4 Ergebnisse

In Tabelle 1 sind die Mittelwerte und Standardabweichungen der tatsächlichen Leistung der simulierten Schülerinnen und Schüler, der Leistungsbeurteilung und der Urteilssicherheit pro Gruppe von Schülerinnen und Schülern nach voreingestelltem Fähigkeitsparameter aufgeführt. Da im Versuchsablauf nur fortgefahren werden konnte, wenn alle Beurteilungen vollständig abgegeben wurden, lagen keine fehlenden Werte vor.

Tabelle 1. Mittelwerte (und Standardabweichungen) der tatsächlichen Leistung, der Leistungsbeurteilung und der Urteilssicherheit aufgeteilt nach den verschiedenen Fähigkeitsparametern der simulierten Schülerinnen und Schüler

Studie 1				
Fähigkeitsparameter	0.20	0.40	0.60	0.80
Anzahl beurteilter Schüler	728	728	728	728
Tatsächliche Leistung *M* (*SD*)	0.19 (0.10)	0.42 (0.13)	0.64 (0.12)	0.86 (0.11)
Leistungsbeurteilung *M* (*SD*)	0.42 (0.20)	0.52 (0.18)	0.62 (0.17)	0.70 (0.19)
Urteilssicherheit *M* (*SD*)	3.82 (1.35)	3.66 (1.18)	3.68 (1.27)	4.12 (1.45)
Studie 2				
Fähigkeitsparameter	0.20	0.40	0.60	0.80
Anzahl beurteilter Schüler	368	368	368	368
Tatsächliche Leistung *M* (*SD*)	0.19 (0.09)	0.41 (0.11)	0.62 (0.11)	0.86 (0.10)
Leistungsbeurteilung *M* (*SD*)	0.40 (0.21)	0.50 (0.19)	0.62 (0.19)	0.74 (0.18)
Urteilssicherheit *M* (*SD*)	3.88 (1.39)	3.69 (1.29)	3.82 (1.29)	4.12 (1.50)

Die Ergebnisse der Response-Surface-Analyse sind in Tabelle 2 dargestellt. Im oberen Teil der Tabelle 2 sind die Modellfitparameter der χ^2-Statistik für das Nullmodell, das SDQ Model und das Full Model aufgeführt. Der R^2-Wert zeigt den Anteil der durch das Modell aufgeklärten Varianz an.

Tabelle 2. Modellfitparameter und Modellvergleiche für das Null-, SQD- und Full Model der Response-Surface-Analyse

	Studie 1				**Studie 2**			
Modell	*df*	χ^2		R^2	*df*	χ^2		R^2
Null	5	956.054		.000	5	461.642		.000
SQD	4	911.126		.015	4	413.412		.032
Full	0	0.000		.280	0	0.000		.269
Modellvergleich	Δdf	$\Delta\chi^2$	*p*	ΔR^2	Δdf	$\Delta\chi^2$	*p*	ΔR^2
Null – SQD	1	36.492	.000	.015	1	37.154	.000	.032
SQD – Full	4	808.572	.000	.265	4	381.248	.000	.237
Null – Full	5	833.015	.000	.280	5	409.579	.000	.269

Der Modellvergleich (Tabelle 2, unterer Teil) zeigt, dass das *Full Model* die Daten am besten repräsentiert (Hypothese 2). Der signifikante χ^2-Modellvergleichstest bedeutet, dass die Einschränkung der Freiheitsgrade gerechtfertigt ist. Der Unterschied in der Varianzaufklärung ist ein Hinweis darauf, dass mit dem Full Model ein deutlicher Zuwachs der Erklärungskraft erreicht werden kann. Die grafische Veranschaulichung des Zusammenhangs von Urteilssicherheit und Urteilsakkuratheit anhand des Full Model befindet sich in Abbildung 1 für Studie 1 und in Abbildung 2 für Studie 2. Die resultierenden Grafiken sind jeweils aus drei Blickwinkeln abgebildet, um die Interpretation zu erleichtern. Die Leistungsbeurteilung und die tatsächliche Leistung der simulierten Schülerinnen und Schüler sind auf den horizontalen Achsen und die Urteilssicherheit auf der vertikalen Achse abgetragen. Die Linie, die auf der Fläche eingezeichnet ist, kennzeichnet die perfekte Übereinstimmung zwischen Leistungsbeurteilung und tatsächlicher Leistung (*Line of Congruence, LOC*). Zur besseren Orientierung ist die LOC auch auf den Boden der Grafiken projiziert.

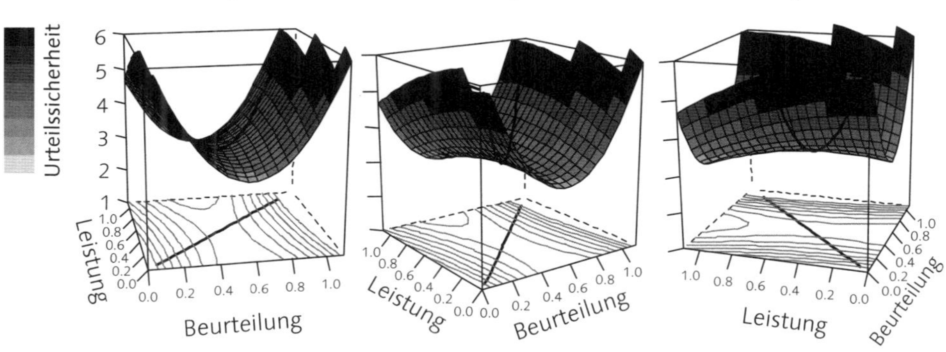

Abbildung 1. Veranschaulichung des Full Models der RSA zum Zusammenhang von Urteilsakkuratheit und Urteilssicherheit in Studie 1.

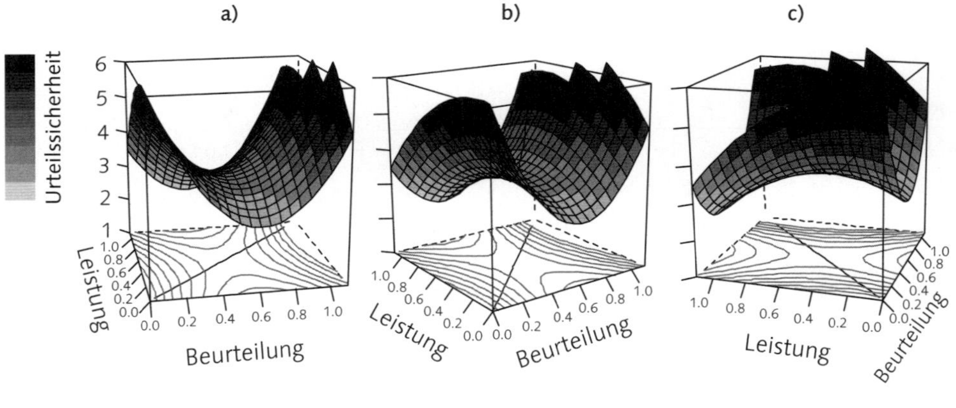

Abbildung 2. Veranschaulichung des Full Models der RSA zum Zusammenhang von Urteilsakkuratheit und Urteilssicherheit in Studie 2.

Aus den Grafiken wird deutlich, dass ein komplexer Zusammenhang zwischen den drei Variablen besteht. Entlang der LOC zeigte sich, dass die Lehramtsstudierenden sich bei der Einschätzung besonders leistungsschwacher und besonders leistungsstarker Schülerinnen und Schüler sicherer waren als bei der Einschätzung von Schülerinnen und Schülern im mittleren Leistungsbereich. Ausgehend vom tiefsten Punkt der LOC sinkt im mittleren Leistungsbereich die Urteilssicherheit mit abnehmender Urteilsakkuratheit, je weiter sich also von der LOC fortbewegt wird. Betrachtet man das „hintere Ende" der LOC und geht von dort aus nach rechts am Rand der Fläche entlang, ist erkennbar, dass die Versuchspersonen bei Schülerinnen und Schülern, die sie als leistungsstark beurteilten, auch bei fallender Urteilsakkuratheit noch eine recht hohe Urteilssicherheit angaben. Für eine akkurate Beurteilung im mittleren Leistungsbereich wurde eine geringere Sicherheit angegeben als für eine Überschätzung im hohen Leistungsbereich.

5 Diskussion

In diesem Beitrag wurde der Zusammenhang zwischen der Urteilsakkuratheit und der Sicherheit bezüglich der Einschätzung von Schülerinnen- und Schülerleistungen analysiert. Zur Auswertung ist mit der Response Surface Analyse eine – gerade in Bezug auf die Forschung zur Urteilsakkuratheit – innovative Methode zur Anwendung gekommen, die im Vergleich zu bisherigen Auswertungsstrategien ein detailliertes Bild der Zusammenhänge liefert (Humberg et al., 2017).

Es zeigte sich, dass ein komplexer Zusammenhang zwischen Urteilsakkuratheit und Urteilssicherheit besteht. Aus der grafischen Veranschaulichung des Zusammenhangs lässt sich ableiten, dass sich angehende Lehrkräfte bei der Einschätzung von Schülerinnen und Schülern am oberen und unteren Rand des Leistungsspektrums sicherer sind als bei mittleren Leistungen. Ein ähnliches Ergebnis zeigte sich in der Studie von Praetorius et al. (2013), in der Lehrkräfte sich bei der Einschätzungen von Schülerinnen und Schülern mit hohen und niedrigen Selbstkonzepten sicherer waren als bei mittlerer Ausprägung des Selbstkonzepts. Darüber hinaus zeigte sich in dieser Studie, dass im mittleren Leistungsbereich eine umso geringere Urteilsicherheit angegeben wurde, je geringer die Urteilsakkuratheit ausfiel. Dieses Ergebnis deutet darauf hin, dass die Teilnehmerinnen und Teilnehmer ihre eigene Urteilsakkuratheit im mittleren Leistungsbereich effizient selbst überwachten (Gabriele et al., 2016). In zukünftigen Studien mit dem SKR sollte die Informationssuche der Teilnehmerinnen und Teilnehmer (z. B. das Aufrufverhalten, Kaiser et al., 2016) gezielt analysiert werden, um zu überprüfen, ob sie die Informationssuche gezielt regulieren, d. h. mehr Informationen über Schülerinnen und Schüler sammeln, bezüglich derer sie sich unsicher sind. Ein weiteres Ergebnis unserer Studie ist, dass leistungsstarke Schülerinnen und Schüler unterschätzt und leistungsschwache Schülerinnen und Schüler überschätzt wurden. Dieses Ergebnis steht im Einklang mit den Ergebnissen früherer Studien zur Urteilsakkuratheit von Lehrkräften (Coladarci, 1986; Demaray & Elliott, 1998, Kaiser et al., 2013). Dieser Befund könnte u. a. darauf zurückzuführen sein, dass die teilnehmenden Studierenden bei der Leistungsbeurteilung berücksichtigt haben, dass die objektiv erbrachte Leistung nicht immer ein guter Indikator für die schulische Leistungsfähigkeit ist, sondern dass schwache schulische Leistungen neben mangelnder Fähigkeit auch auf andere Faktoren (z. B. Leistungsängstlichkeit, mangelnde Motivation) zurückgeführt werden können.

Unsere Befunde können durch die ähnlichen Ergebnisse in Studie 1 und 2 insgesamt als robust angesehen werden. Bei ihrer Interpretation sollte berücksichtigt werden, dass hier variablen-zentriert und nicht personen-zentriert vorgegangen wurde (vgl. Asendorpf & van Aken, 1991, für die Unterscheidung zwischen variablen-zentrierten und personen-zentrierten Ansätzen in der Forschung zu Persönlichkeitseinschätzungen). In zukünftigen Studien sollte auch die Personenebene (d. h. der intraindividuelle Zusammenhang zwischen Urteilsakkuratheit und Urteilssicherheit) Berücksichtigung finden. Da es sich bei der RSA um eine innovative Methode zur Untersuchung der Urteilsakkuratheit im Zusammenhang mit weiteren Variablen handelt, muss hier der explorative Charakter unserer Ergebnisse betont werden.

Mit dem experimentellen Ansatz zur Untersuchung des Zusammenhangs von Urteilsakkuratheit und -sicherheit haben wir eine Methode mit hoher interner Validität gewählt. Die ökologische Validität hingegen ist in verschiedener Hinsicht eingeschränkt. So wurde beispielsweise die Schwierigkeit der verwendeten Mathematikaufgaben in beiden Studien konstant gehalten, obwohl die Schwierigkeit des Aufgabenmaterials in der schulischen Praxis (z. B. die Schwierigkeit von Fragen in mündlichen Prüfungen) einen bedeutsamen Einfluss auf die Leistungsbeurteilung durch Lehrkräfte hat. Insgesamt eignet sich die hier verwendete Version des SKR eher dazu, allgemeine Urteilsphänomene zu untersuchen, da fachliche und fachdidaktische Aspekte im Hintergrund stehen. Darüber hinaus besteht die Aufgabe von Lehrkräften in der Realität eher darin, die Fähigkeit von Schülerinnen und Schülern zu beurteilen, die deren schulischer Leistung zugrundeliegt. Im SKR hingegen soll die gezeigte Leistung beurteilt werden. Obgleich die Generalisierbarkeit unserer Befunde auf die Unterrichtsrealität durch diese und weitere Aspekte eingeschränkt ist, sehen wir in diesem Vorgehen eine Stärke. Wang, Treat und Brownell (2008) betonen die Wichtigkeit solcher Studien, in denen für viele Variablen kontrolliert werden und somit die Interpretierbarkeit der Ergebnisse erhöht werden kann.

Aus motivationaler und metakognitver Perspektive (Gabriele et al., 2016) kann angenommen werden, dass sich die Urteilssicherheit in Zusammenhang mit der Urteilsakkuratheit von Lehrkräften auf ihre pädagogischen Entscheidungen und das unterrichtliche Handeln auswirkt. Pädagogische Entscheidungen, die von Lehrkräften aufgrund einer falschen Einschätzung getroffen werden, können den Lernprozess von Schülerinnen und Schülern behindern. Noch problematischer wird es, wenn die Lehrkräfte ihre pädagogischen Maßnahmen nicht reflektieren, da sie überzeugt von fehlerhaften Einschätzungen sind. Die vorgestellten Studien sind eine Grundlage (angehenden) Lehrkräften den Zusammenhang zwischen ihrer Urteilsakkuratheit und ihrer eingeschätzten Sicherheit rückzumelden. Sie veranschaulichen, dass deutliche Diskrepanzen zwischen Lehrkrafteinschätzungen und den Leistungen von Schülerinnen und Schüler bestehen können und dass die Sicherheit bezüglich des Urteils „trügerisch" sein kann. Im Rahmen der Aus- und Weiterbildung von Lehrkräften sollte das Thema schulischer Leistungsbeurteilung und damit einhergehende Unsicherheiten gezielt in den Blick genommen werden (Kaiser & Möller, 2017). Anhand praktischer Beispiele und dem Austausch über Erfahrungen mit der Leistungsbeurteilung sollten dabei Strategien im Umgang mit Unsicherheit (z. B. Suche nach Quellen der Unsicherheit, Suche nach weiteren Informationen) erarbeitet werden.

Literatur

Ames, D. R., Kammrath, L. K., Suppes, A. & Bolger, N. (2010). Not so fast: The (not-quite-complete) dissociation between accuracy and confidence in thin-slice impressions. *Personality and Social Psychology Bulletin, 36*, 264–277.

Artelt, C. & Rausch, T. (2014). Accuracy of teacher judgments: When and for what reasons? In S. Krolak-Schwerdt, S. Glock & M. Böhmer (Eds.), *Teachers' professional development: Assessment, training, and learning* (pp. 229–248). Rotterdam: Sense Publishers.

Asendorpf, J. B. & van Aken, M. A. G. (1991). Correlates of the temporal consistency of personality patterns in childhood. *Journal of Personality, 59*, 689–703.

Baker, C. N., Tichovolsky, M. H., Kupersmidt, J. B., Voegler-Lee, M. E. & Arnold, D. H. (2015). Teacher (mis)perceptions of preschoolers' academic skills: Predictors and associations with longitudinal outcomes. *Journal of Educational Psychology, 107*, 805–820.

Begeny, J. C., Eckert, T. L., Montarello, S. A. & Storie, M. S. (2008). Teachers' perceptions of students' reading abilities: An examination of the relationship between teachers' judgments and students' performance across a continuum of rating methods. *School Psychology Quarterly, 23*, 43–55.

Coladarci, T. (1986). Accuracy of teacher judgments of student responses to standardized test items. *Journal of Educational Psychology, 78*, 141–146.

Demaray, M. K. & Elliott, S. N. (1998). Teachers' judgments of students academic functioning: A comparison of actual and predicted performances. *School Psychology Quarterly, 13*, 8–24.

DePaulo, B. M., Charlton, K., Cooper, H., Lindsay, J. M. & Muhlenbruck, L. (1997). The accuracy-confidence correlation in the detection of deception. *Personality and Social Psychology Review, 1*, 346–357.

Dunlosky, J. & Metcalfe, J. (2009). *Metacognition.* Thousand Oaks, CA: Sage Publications.

Fiedler, K., Walther, E., Freytag, P. & Plessner, H. (2002). Judgment biases in a simulated classroom: A cognitive–environmental approach. *Organizational Behavior and Human Decision Processes, 88*, 527–561.

Fischhoff, B., Slovic, P. & Lichtenstein, S. (1977). Knowing with certainty: The appropriateness of extreme confidence. *Journal of Experimental Psychology: Human Perception and Performance, 3*, 552–564.

Furnari, E. C., Whittaker, J., Kinzie, M. & DeCoster, J. (2017). Factors associated with accuracy in Prekinderkarten teachers' ratings of students' mathematics skills. *Journal of Psychoeducational Assessment, 35*, 410–423.

Gabriele, A. J., Joram, E. & Park, H. K. (2016). Elementary mathematics teachers' judgment accuracy and calibration accuracy: Do they predict students' mathematics achievement outcomes? *Learning and Instruction, 45*, 49–60.

Herppich, S., Praetorius, A.-K., Hetmanek, A., Glogger, I., Ufer, S., Leutner, D., Behrmann, L., Böhmer, I., Förster, N., Kaiser, J., Karing, C., Karst, K., Klug, J., Ohle, A. & Südkamp, A. (2017). Ein Arbeitsmodell für die empirische Erforschung der diagnostischen Kompetenz von Lehrkräften. In A. Südkamp & A.-K. Praetorius (Hrsg.), *Diagnostische Kompetenz von Lehrkräften: Theoretische und methodische Weiterentwicklungen* (S. 75–93). Münster: Waxmann.

Humberg, S., Förster, N., Kaiser, J. & Schönbrodt, F. D. (2017). Konsequenzen akkurater Lehrerurteile: Response-Surface-Analyse als statistisches Verfahren zur Untersuchung von Übereinstimmungshypothesen. In A. Südkamp & A.-K. Praetorius (Hrsg.), *Diagnostische Kompetenz von Lehrkräften: Theoretische und methodische Weiterentwicklungen* (S. 174–200). Münster: Waxmann.

Kaiser, J. & Möller, J. (2017). Diagnostische Kompetenz von Lehramtsstudierenden. In C. Gräsel & K. Trempler (Hrsg.), *Entwicklung von Professionalität pädagogischen Personals* (S. 55–74). Wiesbaden: Springer.

Kaiser, J., Retelsdorf, J., Südkamp, A. & Möller, J. (2013). Achievement and engagement: How student characteristics influence teacher judgments. *Learning and Instruction, 28*, 73–84.

Kaiser, J., Südkamp, A. & Möller, J. (2016). The effects of student characteristics on teachers' judgment accuracy: Disentangling ethnicity, minority status, and achievement. *Journal of Educational Psychology.* Advance online publication.

Karst, K., Hartig, J., Kaiser, J. & Lipowsky, F. (2017). Mehrebenenmodelle als Werkzeuge zur Analyse diagnostischer Kompetenz von Lehrkräften – ein lineares

Mischmodell (LMM) und seine Anwendung in R. In A. Südkamp & A.-K. Praetorius (Hrsg.), *Diagnostische Kompetenz von Lehrkräften: Theoretische und methodische Weiterentwicklungen* (S. 153–174). Münster: Waxmann.

Myford, C. M. & Wolfe, E. W. (2003). Detecting and measuring rater effects using many-facet Rasch measurement: Part I. *Journal of Applied Measurement, 4*, 386–422.

Panadero, E., Brown, G. T. L. & Strijbos, J. W. (2016). The future of student self-assessment: A review of known unknowns and potential directions. *Educational Psychology Review*, 1–28.

Patterson, M. L., Foster, J. L. & Bellmer, C. G. (2001). Another look at accuracy and confidence in social judgments. *Journal of Nonverbal Behavior, 25*, 207–219.

Pellegrino, J., Chudowsky, N. & Glaser, R. (2001). *Knowing what students know: The science and design of educational assessment.* Washington, DC: National Academy Press.

Praetorius, A.-K., Berner, V.-D., Zeinz, H., Scheunpflug, A. & Dresel, M. (2013). Judgment confidence and judgment accuracy of teachers in judging self-concepts of students. *The Journal of Educational Research, 106*, 64–76.

Ready, D. D. & Wright, D. L. (2011). Accuracy and inaccuracy in teachers' perceptions of young children's cognitive abilities: The role of child background and classroom context. *American Educational Research Journal, 48*, 335–360.

Schönbrodt, F. D. (2016a). *RSA: An R package for response surface analysis 0.9.9 (Shareware):* Zugriff am 18.08.2016 https://cran.r-project.org/package=RSA

Schönbrodt, F. D. (2016b). Testing fit patterns with polynomial regression models. Retrieved from osf.io/3889z [16.01.2017]

Schrader, F.-W. (2010). Diagnostische Kompetenz von Eltern und Lehrern. In D. H. Rost (Hrsg.), *Handwörterbuch Pädagogische Psychologie* (S. 102–108). Weinheim: Beltz.

Smith, H. J., Archer, D. & Costanzo, M. (1991). "Just a hunch": Accuracy and awareness in person perception. *Journal of Nonverbal Behavior, 15*, 3–18.

Südkamp, A., Kaiser, J. & Möller, J. (2012). Accuracy of teachers' judgments of students' academic achievement: A meta-analysis. *Journal of Educational Psychology, 104*, 743–762.

Südkamp, A., Möller, J. & Pohlmann, B. (2008). Der Simulierte Klassenraum: Eine experimentelle Untersuchung zur diagnostischen Kompetenz. *Zeitschrift für Pädagogische Psychologie, 22*, 261–276.

Vallone, R. P., Griffin, D. W., Lind, S. L. & Ross, L. (1990). Overconfident prediction of futures actions and outcomes by self and others. *Journal of Personality and Social Psychology, 58*, 582–592.

Wang, S. S., Treat, T. A. & Brownell, K. D. (2008). Cognitive processing about classroom-relevant contexts: Teachers' attention to and utilization of girls' body size, ethnicity, attractiveness, and facial affect. *Journal of Educational Psychology, 100*, 473–489.

Autorinnen

DR. JOHANNA KAISER
Institut für pädagogisch-psychologische Lehr- und Lernforschung,
Christian-Albrechts-Universität zu Kiel.

DR. ANNA SÜDKAMP
Rehabilitationspsychologie – Psychologische Diagnostik,
Technische Universität Dortmund.

KONTAKT
Johanna Kaiser, Institut für pädagogisch-psychologische Lehr- und Lernforschung,
Christian-Albrechts-Universität zu Kiel, Olshausenstr. 75, 24118 Kiel.
E-Mail: *johannakaiser@gmx.de*

Können Persönlichkeitsmerkmale das Wohlbefinden von Lehrkräften in Studium und Beruf vorhersagen? – Ergebnisse einer Längsschnittstudie

JANINA ROLOFF, UTA KLUSMANN, OLIVER LÜDTKE UND ULRICH TRAUTWEIN

ZUSAMMENFASSUNG: Ursachen von geringem Wohlbefinden im Lehrerberuf stehen vor dem Hintergrund negativer Konsequenzen für Lehrergesundheit und Schülerergebnisse im Mittelpunkt aktueller Forschung. In diesem Zusammenhang wird unter anderem die Bedeutung globaler Persönlichkeitsmerkmale diskutiert, welche die angehenden Lehrkräfte bereits vor Antritt der Lehrerausbildung charakterisieren. Die vorliegende Arbeit untersucht erstmalig im Längsschnitt den Zusammenhang von Persönlichkeitsmerkmalen (Big Five) mit dem Wohlbefinden in Studium und Beruf bei Lehrkräften. Als Datenbasis diente die TOSCA-Studie, in welcher Schülerinnen und Schüler beginnend mit dem letzten Schuljahr längsschnittlich begleitet wurden. Die Analysestichprobe bildeten 184 Lehrkräfte, für die bis zu acht Jahre nach erfolgtem Schulabschluss Informationen zum Wohlbefinden in Studium und Beruf vorlagen. Die Ergebnisse von Regressionsanalysen zeigten, dass das Wohlbefinden von Lehrkräften in Studium und Beruf insbesondere durch Neurotizismus vorhergesagt werden konnte. Damit stehen die Befunde im Einklang mit berufsübergreifenden Zusammenhängen in der bisherigen Literatur und zeigen keine differentiellen Befunde für die Vorhersage des beruflichen Wohlbefindens angehender Lehrkräfte.

Schlüsselwörter: Wohlbefinden, Lehrkräfte, Persönlichkeit, Lehrerausbildung

Do personality traits predict teacher well-being in teacher education and their later career? – A longitudinal study

ABSTRACT: Current research focuses on causes of low well-being in the teaching profession because of their negative consequences for teachers' health and student outcomes. In this context, the role of teachers' personality characteristics, which exist prior to teacher education, is discussed. This has not yet been investigated longitudinally. The present study examines the relation between personality characteristics (Big Five) and well-being in teacher education and the teaching profession over a period of up to eight years. Data from 184 teachers who took part in the longitudinal study TOSCA were used. Results from multiple regression analyses showed that neuroticism was the best predictor of well-being in teacher education and the teaching profession. This is in line with cross-occupational findings in the literature indicating that there are no differential effects of personality characteristics for future teachers.

Keywords: well-being, teachers, personality, teacher education

Einleitung

Das berufliche Wohlbefinden von Lehrkräften ist von entscheidender Bedeutung: Beruflicher Stress und Burnout-Symptome sowie Unzufriedenheit im Beruf sind nicht nur negativ mit der allgemeinen körperlichen und mentalen Gesundheit der Lehrkräfte korreliert (Beer & Beer, 1992; Melamed, Shirom, Toker, Berliner & Shapira, 2006), sie sind auch mit der Unterrichtsqualität sowie der Leistung der Schülerinnen und Schüler assoziiert (Arens & Morin, 2016; Klusmann, Richter & Lüdtke, 2016; McLean & McDonald Connor, 2015; Shen et al., 2015). Die negativen Konsequenzen von Stress, Burnout und Unzufriedenheit im Beruf bei Lehrkräften sind besonders relevant, da der Berufsgruppe der Lehrkräfte immer wieder ein geringes berufliches Wohlbefinden zugeschrieben wird (Kieschke & Schaarschmidt, 2008; Lehr, 2014), welches sich in Dienstunfähigkeit und Frühpensionierung mit hohen volkswirtschaftlichen Kosten niederschlagen kann (Schmitz & Jehle, 2013).

Dementsprechend hat sich eine große Anzahl von Forschungsarbeiten der Frage nach den Ursachen von Stress, Beanspruchung und Zufriedenheit im Lehrerberuf gewidmet. Dabei lassen sich zwei Perspektiven unterscheiden: Zum ersten gibt es eine Reihe von Arbeiten, die sich bei der Suche nach Bedingungsfaktoren auf spezifische Merkmale des Lehrerberufs wie bspw. seine soziale Natur, Unterrichtsstörungen oder Lärmbelästigung konzentrieren (vgl. Krause, Dorsemagen & Baeriswyl, 2013; Rieg, Paquette & Chen, 2007). Zum zweiten wurde in empirischen Arbeiten immer wieder die Bedeutung von persönlichen Merkmalen der Lehrkräfte selbst bestätigt (Kyriacou, 2001; Schaufeli & Enzmann, 1998; Semmer, 1996). Die bisherige Forschung untersucht als personale Einflussgrößen überwiegend situationsübergreifende Persönlichkeitseigenschaften wie den Neurotizismus oder Kontrollüberzeugungen (Caprara, Barbaranelli, Borgogni & Steca, 2003; Rothland & Klusmann, 2012). Dabei kann argumentiert werden, dass schon die Persönlichkeitsmerkmale, die Lehrkräfte mit in die Lehrerausbildung bringen, bedeutsam für das Wohlbefinden im Studium und späteren Beruf sind (vgl. Mayr, 2014) und sich spätere Lehrkräfte bereits in der Ausbildung im Vergleich zu anderen Studierendengruppen durch ein geringes Wohlbefinden kennzeichnen lassen (Römer, Drews, Rauin & Fabricius, 2013). Bislang haben die wenigsten Studien tatsächlich die längsschnittliche Perspektive im Blick und betrachten sowohl das Wohlbefinden im Studium als auch im beruflichen Alltag. Basierend auf einer 8-Jahres-Längsschnittstudie untersucht die aktuelle Arbeit, inwieweit das Wohlbefinden von Lehrkräften in Studium und Beruf durch Persönlichkeitsmerkmale, mit denen die angehenden Lehrkräfte die Lehrerausbildung antreten, vorhergesagt werden kann.

1 Theoretischer Hintergrund

1.1 Wohlbefinden in Studium und Beruf

Lehrkräfte werden in Bezug auf ihr berufliches Wohlbefinden häufig als Risikogruppe beschrieben (Johnson et al., 2005; OECD, 2005; Schaarschmidt, 2005). Berufliches Wohlbefinden von Lehrkräften beschreibt das optimale psychische Erleben und Verhalten in ihrer Arbeit als Lehrkraft (Ryan & Deci, 2001) und umfasst dabei einerseits positives Erleben, wie Berufszufriedenheit und Arbeitsmotivation, und andererseits die Abwesenheit negativer Erfahrungen, bspw. Stress und Burnout (Diener, Suh, Lucas & Smith, 1999; Watson, Clark & Tellegen, 1988). In der vorliegenden Arbeit werden emotionale Erschöpfung und Berufszufriedenheit als Indikatoren für das berufliche Wohlbefinden herangezogen (vgl. Bakker & Oerlmans, 2011). *Emotionale Erschöpfung* bezeichnet ein Gefühl emotionaler Leere und Überlastung und stellt ein Kernsymptom von Burnout dar (Dicke, Holzberger, Kunina-Habenicht, Linninger & Schulze-Stocker, 2016; Klusmann, Kunter, Trautwein, Lüdtke & Baumert, 2008; Maslach, Jackson & Leiter, 1996). *Berufszufriedenheit* beschreibt eine kognitiv-evaluierende Beurteilung der eigenen Arbeitssituation in Form einer positiven (oder negativen) Bewertung bezüglich des Berufs oder der beruflichen Situation (Weiss, 2002). Ein hohes Ausmaß an emotionaler Erschöpfung und geringe Berufszufriedenheit sind nicht nur negativ mit der individuellen Gesundheit assoziiert (Melamed et al., 2006), sondern auch mit geringerer Leistung und stärkerer Fluktuation im Beruf (Judge, Thoresen, Bono & Patton, 2001; Swider & Zimmermann, 2010). Bei Lehrkräften finden sich entsprechend negative Zusammenhänge mit dem Unterrichtsverhalten sowie Schülerleistungen und -motivation (Arens & Morin, 2016; Klusmann et al., 2016; Shen et al., 2015). Individuelle Unterschiede im beruflichen Wohlbefinden bei Lehrkräften zeigen sich bereits kurz nach dem Übergang in den Beruf. Neben der Rolle berufsbezogener Faktoren (z. B. Störungen im Unterricht, Zeitdruck) wird häufig die Bedeutung von Persönlichkeitsmerkmalen diskutiert (Goddard, O'Brien & Goddard, 2006; Kokkinos, 2007; Kyriacou, 2001; Zimmermann, Kaiser, Bernholt, Bauer & Rösler, 2016).

1.2 Die Rolle von Persönlichkeitsmerkmalen für das Wohlbefinden in Studium und Beruf

Zur Erklärung der Bedeutung von Persönlichkeitsmerkmalen für das Wohlbefinden in Studium und Beruf können unter anderem zwei theoretische Perspektiven herangezogen werden: die Perspektive der Passung von Individuum und Arbeitsplatz sowie das transaktionale Stressmodell. Die meisten Theorien zur Berufswahl gehen davon aus, dass die Studien- bzw. Berufswahl nach dem Kriterium der maximalen Passung zwischen Persönlichkeitsmerkmalen und wahrgenommenen beruflichen Bedingungen und Anforderungen erfolgt (Dawis, 1996; Holland, 1997; Parson,

1909). Dabei geht es zum einen um die Passung zwischen persönlichen Interessen und der Möglichkeit ihrer Realisierung und zum anderen um die individuellen Fähigkeiten und deren Passung zu den umweltseitigen Anforderungen. Das Ausmaß der Passung sollte sich demnach auf die Zufriedenheit mit der Studien- und Berufswahl auswirken. Die zweite Perspektive bezieht sich auf das transaktionale Stressmodell (Lazarus & Folkman, 1984; Maslach, Schaufeli & Leiter, 2001). Hier wird postuliert, dass individuelle Merkmale einer Person wie die Persönlichkeit, Einstellungen, Überzeugungen und Kompetenzen als Ressourcen fungieren können, die einen entscheidenden Einfluss darauf haben, ob es angesichts umweltseitiger Anforderungen bzw. Stressoren zu negativen Beanspruchungsreaktionen kommt (Lazarus & Folkman, 1984; Maslach et al., 2001). Beiden theoretischen Perspektiven zufolge beeinflussen Persönlichkeitsmerkmale das berufliche Wohlbefinden, indem sie sich auf die Zufriedenheit und das Beanspruchungserleben in Studium und Beruf auswirken.

Berufsübergreifende Untersuchungen zum Zusammenhang von Persönlichkeitsmerkmalen und dem Wohlbefinden in Studium und Beruf untersuchen klassischerweise Persönlichkeitsmerkmale in Form der *Big Five* (Bruk-Lee, Khoury, Nixon, Goh & Spector, 2009; vgl. McCrae & Costa, 2008; Swider & Zimmermann, 2010; Trapmann, Hell, Hirn & Schuler, 2007). Bei Lehrkräften ist es ein konsistenter Befund, dass Neurotizismus positiv mit dem Erleben beruflicher Beanspruchung und geringer Berufszufriedenheit assoziiert ist. Lehrkräfte, die über sich sagen, dass sie in unterschiedlichen Situationen dazu tendieren, ängstlich oder nervös zu werden, reizbar sind und negative Gefühle entwickeln, berichten signifikant mehr beruflichen Stress und ein geringeres Ausmaß an Berufszufriedenheit (vgl. Cramer & Binder, 2015; Foley & Murphy, 2015; Klusmann, Kunter, Voss & Baumert, 2012; Kokkinos, 2007; Schult, Münzer-Schrobildgen & Sparfeldt, 2014). Foley und Murphy (2015) berichteten einen positiven Zusammenhang zwischen Neurotizismus und emotionaler Erschöpfung ($r = .50$, $p < .01$) bei irischen Lehrkräften. Bei Klusmann et al. (2012) zeigte sich bei deutschen Lehrkräften zwischen Neurotizismus und emotionaler Erschöpfung ein positiver Zusammenhang ($r = .50$, $p < .05$) sowie zwischen Neurotizismus und Berufszufriedenheit ein negativer Zusammenhang ($r = -.40$, $p < .05$). Befunde zu den anderen Persönlichkeitsmerkmalen waren bislang uneinheitlich. Während einerseits positive Zusammenhänge zwischen Extraversion, Offenheit für Erfahrungen, Verträglichkeit und Gewissenhaftigkeit mit dem beruflichen Wohlbefinden berichtet wurden, wiesen andere Befunde auf Nullkorrelationen oder negative Zusammenhänge hin (Cramer & Binder, 2015; Klusmann et al., 2012; Kokkinos, 2007; Schult et al., 2014).

Nur wenige Studien untersuchten bislang Prädiktoren des beruflichen Wohlbefindens von Lehrkräften im Längsschnitt (vgl. Zimmermann et al., 2016). Eine Ausnahme bildet eine längsschnittliche Untersuchung von Klusmann et al. (2012). In dieser lag ein Schuljahr zwischen der Erfassung der Big Five Persönlichkeitsmerkmale und der Erhebung des beruflichen Wohlbefindens der Lehrkräfte und es wurde für das Wohlbefinden des ersten Messzeitpunktes kontrolliert. Unter anderem erwies sich dabei Neurotizismus als prädiktiv valide für die emotionale Erschöpfung ($\beta = .21$, $p < .05$) und die Berufszufriedenheit ($\beta = -.16$, $p < .05$) der Lehrkräfte (für eine weitere Ausnahme siehe Schult et al., 2014). Dabei untersuchte keine der bisherigen Studien den Zusammenhang zwischen Persönlichkeitsmerkmalen, mit denen die angehenden Lehrkräfte das Studium antreten, und ihrem späteren Wohlbefinden in Studium und Beruf.

1.3 Zielsetzung und Fragestellungen

Das Ziel der vorliegenden Studie ist die Untersuchung des Zusammenhangs von Persönlichkeitsmerkmalen mit dem Wohlbefinden in Studium und Beruf bei Lehrkräften. In der vorliegenden Arbeit werden das Erleben von emotionaler Erschöpfung und die Zufriedenheit in Studium und Beruf als Indikatoren für das berufliche Wohlbefinden herangezogen. Dabei werden zwei Fragestellungen verfolgt:

1. Kann das Wohlbefinden im Studium durch Persönlichkeitsmerkmale, mit denen die angehenden Lehrkräfte das Studium antreten, vorhergesagt werden? Es wird angenommen, dass Neurotizismus positiv mit der emotionalen Erschöpfung und negativ mit der Zufriedenheit im Studium assoziiert ist.
2. Kann das Wohlbefinden im Beruf durch Persönlichkeitsmerkmale und das Wohlbefinden im Studium vorhergesagt werden? Es wird angenommen, dass Neurotizismus prädiktive Validität für das Wohlbefinden im Beruf hat, indem Personen mit höheren Werten im Neurotizismus eine höhere emotionale Erschöpfung und eine geringere Berufszufriedenheit berichten. Zudem wird angenommen, dass Personen, die im Studium eine höhere Zufriedenheit berichten, auch im Beruf zufriedener sind sowie Personen, die im Studium ein höheres Ausmaß an emotionaler Erschöpfung erleben, auch im Beruf stärker emotional erschöpft sind.

2 Methode

2.1 Stichprobe

Die vorliegende Arbeit basiert auf Daten der längsschnittlich angelegten Studie „Transformation des Sekundarschulsystems und akademische Karrieren" (TOSCA; Köller, Watermann, Trautwein & Lüdtke, 2004; Trautwein, Neumann, Nagy, Lüdtke & Maaz, 2010). In dieser Studie wird der Lebensweg von Schülerinnen und Schülern beruflicher und allgemeinbildender Gymnasien in Baden-Württemberg seit ihrem Abschlussjahr begleitet. An der ersten Erhebung der Untersuchungskohorte (TOSCA-2002), die im Jahr 2002 an 149 Gymnasien stattfand, nahmen 4.730 Schülerinnen und Schüler teil. Seitdem wurden alle zwei Jahre postalische Nacherhebungen durchgeführt. In die vorliegende Untersuchung gingen Daten zu Persönlichkeitsmerkmalen des ersten Messzeitpunktes (Jahr: 2002; im Folgenden T1) und Informationen zum Wohlbefinden in Studium und Beruf bis einschließlich dem Jahr 2010 ein. 2.174 Personen gaben in den Jahren 2004 bis 2010 an, in ein Hochschulstudium eingeschrieben zu sein oder nach abgeschlossenem Studium im Beruf tätig zu sein. Für 858 von diesen Personen (39.5 %) lagen vollständige Angaben zu den Persönlichkeitsmerkmalen und dem Wohlbefinden im Studium sowie zu mindestens einem Indikator des Wohlbefindens im Beruf vor. Von diesen gaben 184 Personen an, ein Lehramtsstudium absolviert und im Lehrerberuf tätig zu sein. Diese 184 Lehrkräfte bilden die Untersuchungsstichprobe der vorliegenden Arbeit. Zu T1 waren die Teilnehmenden ca. 19 Jahre alt und 83.7 % weiblich. In der vorliegenden Untersuchung wurden jeweils personenspezifisch die letzten verfügbaren Angaben zum Wohlbefinden im Studium genutzt sowie die ersten verfügbaren Angaben zum Wohlbefinden im Beruf, so dass die Zeitabstände zwischen dem jeweiligen Abitur und der Erfassung des Wohlbefindens in Studium und Beruf interindividuell variieren.

2.2 Instrumente

Persönlichkeitsmerkmale

Die *Big-Five-Persönlichkeitsmerkmale* wurden mittels des NEO-FFI (Borkenau & Ostendorf, 1991) erhoben, das die folgenden fünf Dimensionen umfasst: (a) Neurotizismus (Beispielitem: „Ich fühle mich oft angespannt und nervös"); (b) Extraversion („Ich habe gern viele Leute um mich herum"); (c) Offenheit für Erfahrungen („Ich habe oft Spaß daran, mit Theorien oder abstrakten Ideen zu spielen"); (d) Verträglichkeit („Ich versuche zu jedem, dem ich begegne, freundlich zu sein"); (e) Gewissenhaftigkeit („Wenn ich eine Verpflichtung eingehe, so kann man sich auf mich bestimmt verlassen"). In der TOSCA-Studie wurde eine vierstufige Antwortskala (1 = *trifft überhaupt nicht zu*, 4 = *trifft völlig zu*) eingesetzt (Lüdtke, Trautwein, Nagy & Köller, 2004). Die interne Konsistenz der Skalen war zufriedenstellend ($.70 \leq \alpha \leq .82$).

Wohlbefinden im Studium

Es wurden Studienzufriedenheit und emotionale Erschöpfung im Studium als Indikatoren berücksichtigt. Im Mittel wurden diese Merkmale bei den späteren Lehrkräften $M = 4.63$ Jahre ($SD = 0.93$, Min = 4.00, Max = 6.00) nach T1 erfasst. Die *Studienzufriedenheit* wurde mit drei Items von Westermann, Heise, Spies und Trautwein (1996) erfasst. Mittels einer vierstufigen Antwortskala (1 = *trifft überhaupt nicht zu*, 4 = *trifft völlig zu*) sollte eingeschätzt werden, inwieweit die jeweiligen Items auf die Teilnehmenden persönlich zutreffen (z. B.: „Insgesamt bin ich mit meinem jetzigen Studium/meiner jetzigen Ausbildung zufrieden."). Die *emotionale Erschöpfung im Studium* wurde mit vier Items des Maslach Burnout Inventory (Maslach et al., 1996) erfasst (z. B.: „Ich fühle mich bei der Arbeit oft erschöpft."). Mit dem Begriff Arbeit sollte sich hier auf die berufliche bzw. ausbildungsbezogene Tätigkeit, bspw. das Studium, bezogen werden. Dabei wurde eine vier-stufige Antwortskala eingesetzt (1 = *trifft überhaupt nicht zu*, 4 = *trifft völlig zu*). Die interne Konsistenz der Skalen war gut (Studienzufriedenheit: $\alpha = .83$; Emotionale Erschöpfung: $\alpha = .80$).

Wohlbefinden im Beruf

Es wurden Berufszufriedenheit und emotionale Erschöpfung im Beruf als Indikatoren berücksichtigt. Im Mittel wurden diese Merkmale bei den Lehrkräften 6.84 Jahre ($SD = 0.99$, Min = 6.00, Max = 8.00) nach T1 erfasst. Die *Berufszufriedenheit* wurde in Anlehnung an den Job Diagnostic Survey (Hackman & Oldham, 1975) mit 13 Items erfasst. Mittels einer vier-stufigen Antwortskala (1 = *sehr unzufrieden*, 4 = *sehr zufrieden*) sollte die Zufriedenheit mit dem Beruf bezüglich verschiedener Aspekte (z. B. Tätigkeitsinhalte, Arbeitsklima) eingeschätzt werden. Die *emotionale Erschöpfung im Beruf* wurde mit denselben vier Items des Maslach Burnout Inventory (Maslach et al., 1996) erfasst, die zur Erfassung der emotionalen Erschöpfung im Studium herangezogen wurden. Dabei wurde eine vier-stufige Antwortskala eingesetzt (1 = *trifft überhaupt nicht zu*, 4 = *trifft völlig zu*). Die interne Konsistenz der Skalen war akzeptabel (Berufszufriedenheit: $\alpha = .74$; Emotionale Erschöpfung: $\alpha = .70$).

Kontrollvariablen

Als Kontrollvariablen wurden das Geschlecht, die Durchschnittsnote der Hochschulzugangsberechtigung (im Folgenden Abiturnote) basierend auf Angaben der Schulen – als Indikator für eine generelle Lernfähigkeit – sowie das allgemeine Wohlbefinden zu T1 (Skala nach Pavot, Diener & Suh, 1998; Beispielitem: „Das Leben, das ich derzeit führe, ist genau das richtige für mich.") einbezogen.

3 Ergebnisse

Die Analysen wurden mit MPlus Version 7.11 durchgeführt (Muthén & Muthén, 1998–2012). Um einen adäquaten Umgang mit fehlenden Werten zu gewährleisten, wurde das Full-Information-Maximum-Likelihood-Verfahren gewählt (Schafer & Graham, 2002), das bei der Schätzung der Modellparameter auch Personen mit nicht vollständigen Daten berücksichtigt. Der Anteil fehlender Werte lag für die einzelnen Variablen zwischen 0.0 % und 11.6 %. Tabelle 1 gibt einen Überblick über die deskriptiven Statistiken und die Interkorrelationen der untersuchten Variablen.

Das erste Forschungsanliegen bestand darin, zu untersuchen, inwiefern Persönlichkeitsmerkmale, mit denen die angehenden Lehrkräfte das Studium antreten, das Wohlbefinden im Studium vorhersagen können. Zu diesem Zweck wurden multiple lineare Regressionen mit der Studienzufriedenheit und der emotionalen Erschöpfung im Studium als Kriterien gerechnet. Die Ergebnisse sind in Tabelle 2 in Form von standardisierten Regressionskoeffizienten dargestellt (Modelle 1a und 2a). Entsprechend unserer Annahmen zeigte sich ein signifikanter Zusammenhang zwischen Neurotizismus und der emotionalen Erschöpfung im Studium ($\beta = .35$, $p < .05$). Spätere Lehrkräfte, die sich zum Zeitpunkt ihres Abiturs eher als ängstlich, nervös und reizbar beschrieben, berichteten demnach mindestens vier Jahre später im Studium von einer höheren emotionalen Erschöpfung. Des Weiteren zeigten sich positive Zusammenhänge zwischen Verträglichkeit ($\beta = .19$, $p <.05$) und Offenheit für Erfahrungen ($\beta = .14$, $p < .05$) mit der Studienzufriedenheit. Es zeigte sich keine signifikante Vorhersagekraft von Extraversion und Gewissenhaftigkeit für das Wohlbefinden im Studium ($-.09 \leq \beta \leq .09$, *ns*). Insgesamt ist die Effektstärke des Zusammenhangs der Persönlichkeitsmerkmale mit der Studienzufriedenheit als eher klein zu bewerten ($R^2 = .10$), während sich für den Zusammenhang mit der emotionalen Erschöpfung im Studium eine mittlere Effektstärke ($R^2 = .16$) zeigte, die vornehmlich auf die Bedeutung von Neurotizismus zurückzuführen war. Die statistische Signifikanz der berichteten Zusammenhänge blieb auch nach Kontrolle für Geschlecht, die Abiturnote und das allgemeine Wohlbefinden zu T1 bestehen (siehe Modell 1b und 2b in Tabelle 2).

Tabelle 1. Deskriptive Statistiken und Interkorrelationen für Lehrkräfte ($N = 184$)

	M	*SD*	1	2	3	4	5	6	7	8
1 Neurotizismus	2.32	0.17								
2 Extraversion	2.94	0.13	–.39**							
3 Offenheit	2.76	0.18	.16*	–.04						
4 Verträglichkeit	3.01	0.10	–.26**	.39**	.02					
5 Gewissenhaftigkeit	2.94	0.18	–.24**	.01	–.08	.13				
6 Studienzufriedenheit	3.12	0.32	–.18*	.13	.12	.24**	.13			
7 Emotionale Erschöpfung im Studium	2.13	0.27	.38**	–.18*	–.01	–.15*	–.18*	–.38**		
8 Berufszufriedenheit	3.10	0.16	–.13	.09	.00	.15	.18*	.29**	–.17*	
9 Emotionale Erschöpfung im Beruf	1.99	0.23	.28**	–.07	.13	–.15*	–.32**	–.21**	.34**	–.43**

Anmerkungen. ** $p < .01$; * $p < .05$.

Tabelle 2. Persönlichkeitsmerkmale, Wohlbefinden im Studium und Wohlbefinden im Beruf: Standardisierte Regressionskoeffizienten (β) und Standardfehler (*SE*) in Klammern aus multiplen Regressionsanalysen (*N = 184)*

		Studium				Beruf					
		Zufriedenheit		Emotionale Erschöpfung		Zufriedenheit			Emotionale Erschöpfung		
		M1a	M1b	M2a	M2b	M3a	M3b	M3c	M4a	M4b	M4c
PERSÖNLICHKEITSMERKMALE	Neurotizismus	–.12 (.08)	–.04 (.09)	.35** (.07)	.33** (.08)	–.05 (.09)	–.02 (.09)	.04 (.10)	.21** (.08)	.12 (.08)	.11 (.09)
	Extraversion	.02 (.08)	.02 (.08)	–.03 (.08)	–.02 (.08)	.03 (.09)	.02 (.09)	.04 (.09)	.05 (.08)	.06 (.08)	.04 (.08)
	Offenheit	.14* (.07)	.14* (.07)	–.07 (.07)	–.09 (.07)	.01 (.08)	–.02 (.08)	–.05 (.08)	.08 (.07)	.11 (.07)	.14* (.07)
	Verträglichkeit	.19* (.08)	.19* (.08)	–.03 (.07)	–.01 (.08)	.09 (.08)	.05 (.08)	.07 (.08)	-.08 (.08)	-.06 (.07)	–.08 (.07)
	Gewissenhaftigkeit	.09 (.07)	.04 (.08)	–.09 (.07)	–.08 (.07)	.15 (.08)	.13 (.08)	.09 (.08)	–.25** (.07)	–.22** (.07)	–.20** (.07)
WOHL-BEFINDEN IM STUDIUM	Studienzufriedenheit						.25** (.08)	.23** (.08)		–.08 (.07)	–.08 (.07)
	Emotionale Erschöpfung im Studium						–.03 (.08)	–.04 (.08)		.23** (.07)	.24** (.07)
KONTROLL-VARIABLEN	Geschlecht		–.03 (.07)		.01 (.07)			–.04 (.08)			.04 (.07)
	Abiturnote		–.02 (.08)		–.07 (.07)			–.09 (.08)			.12 (.07)
	Wohlbefinden zu T1		.18* (.08)		–.07 (.08)			.10 (.09)			.02 (.08)
	R^2	.10	.12	.16	.17	.05	.11	.13	.16	.21	.23

Anmerkungen. ** $p < .01$; * $p < .05$; *M* = Modell.

Zur Untersuchung des zweiten Forschungsanliegens, der Vorhersage des Wohlbefindens im Beruf durch Persönlichkeitsmerkmale und das Wohlbefinden im Studium, wurden ebenfalls multiple lineare Regressionen gerechnet. Dabei wurden die Berufszufriedenheit und die emotionale Erschöpfung im Beruf als Kriterien betrachtet. In einem ersten Schritt wurden die Persönlichkeitsmerkmale als Prädiktoren in die Analysen einbezogen (Modelle 3a und 4a in Tabelle 2). Im Einklang mit unseren Annahmen zeigte sich ein signifikanter Zusammenhang von Neurotizismus und der emotionalen Erschöpfung im Beruf ($\beta = .21$, $p < .01$). Des Weiteren zeigte sich ein signifikant negativer Zusammenhang zwischen Gewissenhaftigkeit und der emotionalen Erschöpfung im Beruf ($\beta = -.25$, $p < .01$). Personen, die sich zum Zeitpunkt ihres Abiturs als neurotischer und weniger gewissenhaft beschrieben, erlebten demnach im Beruf ein höheres Ausmaß an emotionaler Erschöpfung. Es zeigten sich keine signifikanten Zusammenhänge zwischen Extraversion, Offenheit und Verträglichkeit mit der emotionalen Erschöpfung im Beruf ($-.08 \leq \beta \leq .08$, *ns*) sowie keine signifikanten Zusammenhänge zwischen den Persönlichkeitsmerkmalen und der Berufszufriedenheit ($-.05 \leq \beta \leq .15$, *ns*). Die Effektstärken für den Zusammenhang der Persönlichkeitsmerkmale mit der Berufszufriedenheit ($R^2 = .05$) bzw. der emotionalen Erschöpfung im Beruf ($R^2 = .16$) können dabei als klein bzw. moderat bewertet werden.

Im zweiten Schritt wurden Studienzufriedenheit und emotionale Erschöpfung im Studium als zusätzliche Prädiktoren in die Untersuchung aufgenommen (Modelle 3b und 4b in Tabelle 2). Entsprechend der Annahmen zeigte sich ein signifikanter Zusammenhang der Studienzufriedenheit mit der Berufszufriedenheit ($\beta = .25$, $p < .01$) und ein signifikanter Zusammenhang der emotionalen Erschöpfung im Studium mit der emotionalen Erschöpfung im Beruf ($\beta = .23$, $p < .01$). Lehrkräfte, die bereits im Studium eine höhere Zufriedenheit erlebten, zeigten somit auch eine höhere Berufszufriedenheit, während Lehrkräfte, die bereits im Studium eher emotional erschöpft waren, auch im Beruf ein höheres Ausmaß an emotionaler Erschöpfung beschrieben. Dabei konnte das Wohlbefinden im Studium zusätzlich zu den Persönlichkeitsmerkmalen 6 % der interindividuellen Unterschiede in der Berufszufriedenheit bzw. 5 % in der emotionalen Erschöpfung im Beruf aufklären. Des Weiteren zeigte sich, dass Gewissenhaftigkeit auch nach Kontrolle der emotionalen Erschöpfung im Studium ein signifikanter Prädiktor für die emotionale Erschöpfung im Beruf war ($\beta = -.22$, $p < .01$). Neurotizismus hingegen war nach Kontrolle der emotionalen Erschöpfung im Studium nicht mehr signifikant prädiktiv valide für die emotionale Erschöpfung im Beruf ($\beta = .12$, *ns*). Die berichteten Zusammenhänge erweisen sich auch unter Einbezug der Kontrollvariablen (siehe Modelle 3c und 4c in Tabelle 2) als statistisch signifikant.

4 Diskussion

Das Hauptanliegen der vorliegenden Studie war die Untersuchung des Zusammenhangs zwischen Persönlichkeitsmerkmalen, mit denen angehende Lehrkräfte das

Studium antreten, und dem Wohlbefinden in Studium und Beruf bei Lehrkräften. Basierend auf längsschnittlichen Daten der TOSCA-Studie zeigte sich, dass besonders das Persönlichkeitsmerkmal Neurotizismus, aber auch Merkmale wie Offenheit, Verträglichkeit und Gewissenhaftigkeit eine bedeutsame Rolle für das Wohlbefinden in Studium und Beruf spielen. Dabei wurden die emotionale Erschöpfung und die Zufriedenheit in Studium und Beruf als Indikatoren des Wohlbefindens betrachtet.

Erwartungsgemäß berichteten Lehrkräfte, die zum Zeitpunkt ihres Abiturs tendenziell eher ängstlich, nervös und reizbar waren, sowohl im Studium als auch im Beruf ein höheres Ausmaß an emotionaler Erschöpfung. Die Richtung der Zusammenhänge steht dabei im Einklang sowohl mit lehrerspezifischen als auch berufsübergreifenden Befunden (Goddard et al., 2006; Klusmann et al., 2012; Kokkinos, 2007; Trapmann et al., 2007). Wenngleich Ergebnisse basierend auf querschnittlichen Daten stärkere Zusammenhänge zeigten (Klusmann et al., 2012; Trapmann et al., 2007), weisen längsschnittliche Daten auf ein vergleichbares Befundmuster hin (Goddard et al., 2006; Klusmann et al., 2012). Die emotionale Erschöpfung im Studium wiederum war positiv mit der emotionalen Erschöpfung im Beruf assoziiert. Lehrkräfte, die sich im Studium als lustlos, erschöpft und überlastet beschrieben, empfanden demnach auch im Beruf ähnlich. Entsprechend erscheint es vielversprechend, Interventionen, die auf eine Verringerung der emotionalen Erschöpfung von Lehrkräften ausgerichtet sind, bereits frühzeitig im Rahmen der Lehrerausbildung einzubinden (vgl. Dicke, Elling, Schmeck & Leutner, 2015).

Des Weiteren zeigte sich ein negativer Zusammenhang zwischen der emotionalen Erschöpfung im Beruf und dem Persönlichkeitsmerkmal Gewissenhaftigkeit. Demnach erlebten Lehrkräfte, die sich selbst zum Zeitpunkt ihres Abiturs als organisiert, zuverlässig und planvoll handelnd beschrieben, im Beruf ein geringeres Ausmaß an emotionaler Erschöpfung verglichen mit jenen Lehrkräften, die sich als weniger gewissenhaft beschrieben. Das Persönlichkeitsmerkmal Gewissenhaftigkeit könnte demnach, entsprechend dem transaktionalen Stressmodell (Lazarus & Folkman, 1984; Maslach et al., 2001), als eine Ressource verstanden werden, die womöglich beeinflusst, ob es angesichts umweltseitiger Anforderungen zu negativen Beanspruchungsreaktionen kommt. Eine Erklärung könnte sein, dass gewissenhaftere Lehrkräfte den Anforderungen des Lehrerberufs strukturierter begegnen, bspw. indem sie sich rechtzeitig und in ausreichendem Maße auf den Unterricht vorbereiten und dadurch den Unterricht als weniger belastend erleben. Dies scheint sich allerdings nicht auf die berufliche Leistung auszuwirken. So fanden zumindest Emmerich, Rock und Trapani (2006) keine Zusammenhänge zwischen Gewissenhaftigkeit und dem durch Experten eingeschätzten erfolgreichen Lehrerverhalten. Zudem erwies sich Gewissenhaftigkeit als nicht prädiktiv valide für die von Schülerinnen und Schülern eingeschätzte Unterrichtsqualität von Lehrkräften (Roloff, Klusmann, Lüdtke & Trautwein, 2017). Jedoch könnten gewissenhaftere Lehrkräfte im Studium ein höheres Ausmaß an professioneller Kompetenz erwerben, indem sie bspw. zusätzliche Kurse an der Universität belegen. Ein höheres Ausmaß an professioneller Kompetenz sollte Lehrkräften helfen, die beruflichen Anforderungen erfolgreich zu meistern und sich dadurch positiv auf das berufliche Wohlbefinden auswirken (Kunter, Kleickmann, Klusmann & Richter, 2011). Allerdings zeigten die Befunde von Tok und Morali (2009) und Roloff et al. (2017) keinen positiven Zusammenhang zwischen Gewissenhaftigkeit und Studiennoten als Indikatoren für den Erwerb professioneller Kompetenz. Weiterführende Forschung sollte hier anschließen und die Bedeutung von Persönlichkeitsmerkmalen für den Erwerb professioneller Kompetenz und dessen Bedeutung für das berufliche Wohlbefinden von Lehrkräften noch näher beleuchten, bspw. unter Verwendung von Testverfahren als proximale Maße für professionelle Kompetenz.

Neben der emotionalen Erschöpfung wurde Zufriedenheit als Indikator für das Wohlbefinden in Studium und Beruf untersucht. Es zeigten sich positive Zusammenhänge zwischen der Offenheit für Erfahrungen und Verträglichkeit mit der Studienzufriedenheit der angehenden Lehrkräfte. Lehramtsstudierende, die sich vor Antritt ihres Studiums durch ihr Vertrauen, Entgegenkommen und ihre Gutherzigkeit auszeichneten sowie offen für Fantasie, Ideen und Werte waren, waren demnach in ihrem Studium zufriedener. Einige Theorien zur Berufswahl gehen davon aus, dass eine Passung zwischen persönlichen Merkmalen und den umweltseitigen Bedingungen ursächlich für Studien- und Berufszufriedenheit ist (Dawis, 1996; Holland, 1997; Parson, 1909). Es kann spekuliert werden, dass spezifische Aspekte der universitären Curricula die Zusammenhänge zwischen Verträglichkeit und Offenheit mit der Studienzufriedenheit erklären können. So könnten insbesondere der Umgang mit neuen Studieninhalten sowie mit den Kommilitoninnen und Kommilitonen (bspw. im Rahmen von gemeinsamen Referaten) von Lehramtsstudierenden mit einer ausgeprägten Offenheit für Erfahrungen und Verträglichkeit als angenehm und befriedigend erlebt werden. Ob diese Zusammenhänge zwischen Persönlichkeitsmerkmalen, mit denen Studierende das Studium antreten, und der Studienzufriedenheit auch in anderen Studiengruppen zutreffen, gilt es in künftiger Forschung zu untersuchen.

Entgegen der Erwartungen und bisheriger Befunde (Klusmann et al., 2012) zeigte sich kein signifikanter Zusammenhang zwischen den Persönlichkeitsmerkmalen und der Berufszufriedenheit. Im Unterschied zu den aktuellen Befunden waren in der Arbeit von Klusmann et al. (2012) Gewissenhaftigkeit positiv und Neurotizismus sowie Offenheit für Erfahrungen negativ mit der Berufszufriedenheit von Lehrkräften assoziiert. Eine mögliche Erklärung könnte sein, dass in der Arbeit von Klusmann et al. (2012) eine kognitiv-evaluative Komponente der eigenen Berufstätigkeit erfasst wurde (Beispielitem globaler Berufszufriedenheit: „Wenn ich noch einmal wählen könnte, würde ich sofort wieder Lehrkraft werden"), während der Fokus in der vorliegenden Arbeit auf der Zufriedenheit mit spezifischen, eher objektiven Aspekten der Berufstätigkeit (bspw. Tätigkeitsinhalte, Fort- und Weiterbildungsmöglichkeiten) lag. Während die Persönlichkeitsmerkmale keinen signifikanten Beitrag zur Erklärung der Berufszufriedenheit leisteten, stand die Studienzufriedenheit in einem positiven Zusammenhang mit der Berufszufriedenheit: Lehrkräfte, die bereits im Studium eine höhere Zufriedenheit berichteten, waren demnach auch eher mit ihrer Berufstätigkeit zufrieden. Offen bleibt die Frage, inwieweit die Zufriedenheit von angehenden Lehrkräften bereits im Studium gesteigert werden kann. Zudem sollte in zukünftiger Forschung neben den Big-Five-Persönlichkeitsmerkmalen die Bedeutung anderer personaler Lehrermerkmale für die Berufszufriedenheit von Lehrkräften untersucht werden. Beispielsweise könnten motivationale Aspekte, wie sie unter anderem mit Hilfe des „Fragebogens zur Erfassung der Motivation für die Wahl eines Lehramtsstudiums" (FEMOLA; Pohlmann & Möller, 2010) erfasst werden, im Zusammenhang mit der Berufszufriedenheit von Lehrkräften stehen. So könnten Lehrkräfte mit einem hohen pädagogischen Interesse durch die Interaktion mit den Schülerinnen und Schülern eine höhere Zufriedenheit im Beruf empfinden.

Als Einschränkungen der vorliegenden Arbeit muss zum einen darauf hingewiesen werden, dass die Stichprobe eher klein und keineswegs repräsentativ für die Lehrerpopulation in Deutschland ist. Wenngleich erstmalig längsschnittliche Befunde zu der Bedeutung von Persönlichkeitsmerkmalen für das Wohlbefinden in Studium und Beruf vorliegen, bleibt offen, welche Rolle weitere Merkmale der Lehrkraft oder ihrer Ausbildungs- und Berufsumwelt in diesem Kontext spielen. Wenngleich uns die Verwendung der subjektiven Methode der Fragebogenerhebung zur Erfassung des subjektiven Wohlbefindens angemessen erscheint, wäre es interessant, auch objektive Maße zur Erfassung der Belastung zu verwenden, bspw. Kortisolmessungen (siehe z. B. Staufenbiel, Penninx, Spijker, Elzinga & van Rossum, 2013). Zudem wäre es wünschenswert, die Informationen aus dem Selbstbericht zu den Big-Five-Persönlichkeitsmerkmalen durch Fremdeinschätzungen (bspw. Peer-Ratings) zu ergänzen. Bei der Interpretation der vorliegenden Ergebnisse sollte berücksichtigt werden, dass der Zeitabstand zwischen dem Abitur und der Erfassung des Wohlbefindens in Studium und Beruf zwischen den Studienteilnehmenden variierte.

Zusammenfassend lässt sich feststellen, dass die Relevanz von Persönlichkeitsmerkmalen für Lehrerausbildung und -beruf teilweise gezeigt werden konnte. Es kann spekuliert werden, dass es entsprechend der Persönlichkeitsmerkmale einen gewissen stabilen Teil im Beanspruchungserleben gibt, welcher möglicherweise durch situationsübergreifende Bewertungsmuster und Bewältigungsstile erklärt werden kann. Dabei entsprechen die vorliegenden Ergebnisse zu Lehrkräften überwiegend auch bisherigen berufsübergreifenden Befunden. Es zeigt sich demnach in der aktuellen Arbeit kein lehrerspezifisches Muster der Wirkung von Persönlichkeitsmerkmalen auf das berufliche Wohlbefinden. Allerdings konnte ein substanzieller Anteil der interindividuellen Unterschiede im Wohlbefinden nicht durch die untersuchten Persönlichkeitsmerkmale erklärt werden. Inwieweit hier lehrerspezifische Umweltmerkmale und ihre Interaktion mit Persönlichkeitsmerkmalen für die Entwicklung des beruflichen Wohlbefindens von Lehrkräften eine Rolle spielen, sollte in zukünftiger Forschung fokussiert werden.

Literatur

Arens, A. K. & Morin, A. J. S. (2016). Relations between teachers' emotional exhaustion and students' educational outcomes. *Journal of Educational Psychology*, *108*, 800–813.

Bakker, A. B. & Oerlmans, W. G. (2011). Subjective well-being in organizations. In K. S. Cameron & G. M. Spreitzer (Eds.), *Handbook of positive organizational scholarship* (pp. 178–189). New York, NY: Oxford University.

Beer, J. & Beer, J. (1992). Burnout and stress, depression and self-esteem of teachers. *Psychological Reports*, *71*, 1331–1336.

Borkenau, P. & Ostendorf, F. (1991). Ein Fragebogen zur Erfassung fünf robuster Persönlichkeitsfaktoren. *Diagnostica*, *37*, 29–41.

Bruk-Lee, V., Khoury, H. A., Nixon, A. E., Goh, A. & Spector, P. E. (2009). Replicating and extending past personality/job satisfaction meta-analyses. *Human Performance*, *22*, 156–189.

Caprara, G. V., Barbaranelli, C., Borgogni, L. & Steca, P. (2003). Efficacy beliefs as determinants of teachers' job satisfaction. *Journal of Educational Psychology*, *95*, 821–832.

Cramer, C. & Binder, K. (2015). Zusammenhänge von Persönlichkeitsmerkmalen und Beanspruchungserleben im Lehramt. Ein internationales systematisches Review. *Zeitschrift für Erziehungswissenschaft*, *18*, 101–123.

Dawis, R. V. (1996). The theory of work adjustment and person-environment-correspondence counseling. In D. Brown & L. Brooks (Eds.), *Career choice and development* (3rd ed., pp. 75–115). San Francisco, CA: Jossey-Bass.

Dicke, T., Elling, J., Schmeck, A. & Leutner, D. (2015). Reducing reality shock: The effects of classroom management skills training on beginning teachers. *Teaching and Teacher Education*, *48*, 1–12.

Dicke, T., Holzberger, D., Kunina-Habenicht, O., Linninger, C. & Schulze-Stocker, F. (2016). „Doppelter Praxisschock" auf dem Weg ins Lehramt? Verlauf und potenzielle Einflussfaktoren emotionaler Erschöpfung während des Vorbereitungsdienstes und nach dem Berufseintritt. *Psychologie in Erziehung und Unterricht*, *63*, 244–257.

Diener, E., Suh, E. M., Lucas, R. E. & Smith, H. L. (1999). Subjective well-being: Three decades of progress. *Psychological Bulletin*, *125*, 276–302.

Emmerich, W., Rock, D. A. & Trapani, C. S. (2006). Personality in relation to occupational outcomes among established teachers. *Journal of Research in Personality*, *40*, 501–528.

Foley, C. & Murphy, M. (2015). Burnout in Irish teachers: Investigating the role of individual differences, work environment and coping factors. *Teaching and Teacher Education*, *50*, 46–55.

Goddard, R., O'Brien, P. & Goddard, M. (2006). Work environment predictors of beginning teacher burnout. *British Educational Research Journal*, *32*, 857–874.

Hackman, J. R. & Oldham, G. R. (1975). Development of the Job Diagnostic Survey. *Journal of Applied Psychology*, *60*, 159–170.

Holland, J. L. (1997). *Making vocational choices: A theory of vocational personalities and work environments* (3rd ed.). Odessa, FL: Psychological Assessment Resources.

Johnson, S., Cooper, C., Cartwright, S., Donald, I., Taylor, P. & Millet, C. (2005). The experience of work-related stress across occupations. *Journal of Managerial Psychology*, *20*, 178–187.

Judge, T. A., Thoresen, C. J., Bono, J. E. & Patton, G. K. (2001). The job satisfaction-job performance relationship: A qualitative and quantitative review. *Psychological Bulletin*, *127*, 376–407.

Kieschke, U. & Schaarschmidt, U. (2008). Professional commitment and health among teachers in Germany: A typological approach. *Learning and Instruction*, *18*, 429–437.

Klusmann, U., Kunter, M., Trautwein, U., Lüdtke, O. & Baumert, J. (2008). Engagement and emotional exhaustion in teachers: Does the school context make a difference? *Applied Psychology: An International Review*, *57*, 127–151.

Klusmann, U., Kunter, M., Voss, T. & Baumert, J. (2012). Berufliche Beanspruchung angehender Lehrkräfte: Die Effekte von Persönlichkeit, pädagogischer Vorerfahrung und professioneller Kompetenz. *Zeitschrift für Pädagogische Psychologie*, *26*, 275–290.

Klusmann, U., Richter, D. & Lüdtke, O. (2016). Teachers' emotional exhaustion is negatively related to students' achievement: Evidence from a large-scale assessment study. *Journal of Educational Psychology*, *108*, 1193–1203

Kokkinos, C. M. (2007). Job stressors, personality and burnout in primary school teachers. *British Journal of Educational Psychology*, *77*, 229–243.

Köller, O., Watermann, R., Trautwein, U. & Lüdtke, O. (2004). *Wege zur Hochschulreife in Baden-Württemberg. TOSCA – Eine Untersuchung an allgemein bildenden und beruflichen Gymnasien*. Opladen: Leske + Budrich.

Krause, A., Dorsemagen, C. & Baeriswyl, S. (2013). Zur Arbeitssituation von Lehrerinnen und Lehrern: Ein Einstieg in die Lehrerbelastungs- und -gesundheitsforschung. In M. Rothland (Hrsg.), *Belastung und Beanspruchung im Lehrerberuf. Modelle, Befunde, Interventionen* (2. Aufl., S. 61–80). Wiesbaden: Springer VS.

Kunter, M., Kleickmann, T., Klusmann, U. & Richter, D. (2011). Die Entwicklung professioneller Kompetenz von Lehrkräften. In M. Kunter, J. Baumert, W. Blum, U. Klusmann, S. Krauss & M. Neubrand (Hrsg.), *Professionelle Kompetenz von Lehrkräften. Ergebnisse des Forschungsprogramms COACTIV* (S. 55–68). Münster: Waxmann.

Kyriacou, C. (2001). Teacher stress: Directions for future research. *Educational Review*, *53*, 27–35.

Lazarus, R. S. & Folkman, S. (1984). *Stress, appraisal, and coping*. New York, NY: Springer Publishing.

Lehr, D. (2014). Belastung und Beanspruchung im Lehrerberuf – Gesundheitliche Situation und Evidenz für Risikofaktoren. In E. Terhart, H. Bennewitz & M. Rothland (Hrsg.), *Handbuch der Forschung zum Lehrerberuf* (2. Aufl., S. 947–967). Münster: Waxmann.

Lüdtke, O., Trautwein, U., Nagy, G. & Köller, O. (2004). Eine Validierungsstudie zum NEO-FFI in einer Stichprobe junger Erwachsener. *Diagnostica*, *50*, 134–144.

Maslach, C., Jackson, S. E. & Leiter, M. P. (1996). *Maslach Burnout Inventory manual*. Mountain View, CA: CPP.

Maslach, C., Schaufeli, W. B. & Leiter, M. P. (2001). Job burnout. *Annual Review of Psychology*, *52*, 397–422.

Mayr, J. (2014). Der Persönlichkeitsansatz in der Forschung zum Lehrerberuf. In E. Terhart, H. Bennewitz & M. Rothland (Hrsg.), *Handbuch der Forschung zum Lehrerberuf* (2. Aufl., S. 189–215). Münster: Waxmann.

McCrae, R. R. & Costa, P. T. (2008). The Five-Factor theory of personality. In O. P. John, R. W. Robins & L. A. Pervin (Eds.), *Handbook of personality. Theory and research* (3rd ed., pp. 159–181). New York, NY: Guilford Press.

McLean, L. & McDonald Connor, C. (2015). Depressive symptoms in third-grade teachers: Relations to classroom quality and student achievement. *Child Development, 86*, 945–954.

Melamed, S., Shirom, A., Toker, S., Berliner, S. & Shapira, I. (2006). Burnout and risk of cardiovascular disease: Evidence, possible causal paths, and promising research directions. *Psychological Bulletin, 132*, 327–353.

Muthén, L. K. & Muthén, B. O. (1998–2012). *MPlus user's guide (7th ed.)*. Los Angeles, CA.

OECD. (2005). *Attracting, developing and retaining effective teachers – Final report: Teachers matter*. Paris: OECD.

Parson, F. (1909). *Choosing a vocation*. Boston, MA:: Houghton-Mifflin.

Pavot, W., Diener, E. & Suh, E. (1998). The temporal satisfaction with life scale. *Journal of Personality Assessment, 70*, 340–354.

Pohlmann, B. & Möller, J. (2010). Fragebogen zur Erfassung der Motivation für die Wahl des Lehramtsstudiums (FEMOLA). *Zeitschrift für Pädagogische Psychologie, 24*, 73–84.

Rieg, S. A., Paquette, K. R. & Chen, Y. (2007). Coping with stress: An investigation of novice teachers' stressors in the elementary classroom. *Education, 128*, 211–226.

Roloff, J., Klusmann, U., Lüdtke, O. & Trautwein, U. (2017). *Born teachers? Investigating the role of high school leavers' personality characteristics in predicting teachers' instructional quality a decade later. Manuscript submitted for publication.*

Römer, J., Drews, F., Rauin, U. & Fabricius, D. (2013). Riskante Studien- und berufsrelevante Merkmale von Studierenden: Ein Vergleich von Lehramts- und Jurastudierenden. *Zeitschrift für Bildungsforschung, 3*, 153–173.

Rothland, M. & Klusmann, U. (2012). Belastung und Beanspruchung im Lehrerberuf. In S. Rahm & C. Nerowski (Hrsg.), *Enzyklopädie Erziehungswissenschaft Online (EEO), Fachgebiet Schulpädagogik.* Weinheim: Juventa.

Ryan, R. M. & Deci, E. L. (2001). Self-determination theory and the facilitation of intrinsic motivation, social development, and well-being. *American Psychologist, 55*, 68–78.

Schaarschmidt, U. (Hrsg.). (2005). *Halbtagsjobber: Psychische Gesundheit im Lehrerberuf.* Analyse eines veränderungsbedürftigen Zustandes (2. Aufl.). Weinheim: Beltz.

Schafer, J. L. & Graham, J. W. (2002). Missing data: Our view of the state of the art. *Psychological Methods, 7*, 147–176.

Schaufeli, W. B. & Enzmann, D. (1998). *The burnout companion to study and practice: A critical analysis*. London: Taylor & Francis.

Schmitz, E. & Jehle, P. (2013). Innere Kündigung und vorzeitige Pensionierung bei Lehrkräften. In M. Rothland (Hrsg.), *Belastung und Beanspruchung im Lehrerberuf. Modelle, Befunde, Interventionen* (2. Aufl., S. 155–174). Wiesbaden: Springer VS.

Schult, J., Münzer-Schrobildgen, M. & Sparfeldt, J. R. (2014). Belastet, aber hochzufrieden? Arbeitsbelastung von Lehrkräften im Quer- und Längsschnitt. *Zeitschrift für Gesundheitspsychologie, 22*, 61–67.

Semmer, N. (1996). Individual differences, work stress and health. In M. J. Schabracq, J. A. M. Winnubst & C. L. Cooper (Eds.), *Handbook of work and health psychology* (pp. 53–86). Chichester: Wiley.

Shen, B., McCaughtry, N., Martin, J., Garn, A., Kulik, N. & Fahlman, M. (2015). The relationship between teacher burnout and student motivation. *The British Journal of Educational Psychology, 85*, 519–532.

Staufenbiel, S. M., Penninx, B. W. J. H., Spijker, A. T., Elzinga, B. M. & van Rossum, E. F. C. (2013). Hair cortisol, stress exposure, and mental health in humans: A systematic review. *Psychoneuroendocrinology, 38*, 1220–1235.

Swider, B. W. & Zimmermann, R. D. (2010). Born to burnout: A meta-analytic path model of personality, job burnout and work outcomes. *Journal of Vocational Behavior, 76*, 487–506.

Tok, S. & Morali, S. (2009). Trait emotional intelligence, the Big Five personality dimensions and academic success in physical education teacher candidates. *Social Behavior and Personality: An International Journal, 37*, 921–931.

Trapmann, S., Hell, B., Hirn, J.-O. W. & Schuler, H. (2007). Meta-analysis of the relationship between the Big Five and academic success at university. *Journal of Psychology, 215*, 132–151.

Trautwein, U., Neumann, M., Nagy, G., Lüdtke, O. & Maaz, K. (2010). *Schulleistungen von Abiturienten: Die neugeordnete gymnasiale Oberstufe auf dem Prüfstand.* Wiesbaden: VS Verlag für Sozialwissenschaften.

Watson, D., Clark, L. A. & Tellegen, A. (1988). Development and validation of brief measures of positive and negative affect: The PANAS scales. *Journal of Personality and Social Psychology, 54*, 1063–1070.

Weiss, H. M. (2002). Deconstructing job satisfaction: Separating evaluations, beliefs and affective experiences. *Human Resource Management Review, 12*, 173–194.

Westermann, R., Heise, E., Spies, K. & Trautwein, U. (1996). Identifikation und Erfassung von Komponenten der Studienzufriedenheit. *Psychologie in Erziehung und Unterricht, 43*, 1–22.

Zimmermann, F., Kaiser, J., Bernholt, A., Bauer, J. & Rösler, L. (2016). Veränderungsverläufe in Burnout-Dimensionen. Die Bedeutung personaler und sozialer Faktoren angehender Lehrkräfte im Vorbereitungsdienst. *Psychologie in Erziehung und Unterricht, 63*, 258–277.

Autorinnen und Autoren

DR. JANINA ROLOFF
Erziehungswissenschaft, IPN · Leibniz-Institut für die Pädagogik der Naturwissenschaften und Mathematik.

PROF. DR. UTA KLUSMANN
Erziehungswissenschaft, IPN · Leibniz-Institut für die Pädagogik der Naturwissenschaften und Mathematik.

PROF. DR. OLIVER LÜDTKE
Pädagogisch-Psychologische Methodenlehre, IPN · Leibniz-Institut für die Pädagogik der Naturwissenschaften und Mathematik.
Zentrum für internationale Bildungsvergleichsstudien.

PROF. DR. ULRICH TRAUTWEIN
Hector-Institut für Empirische Bildungsforschung,
Eberhard Karls Universität Tübingen.

KONTAKT
Janina Roloff, IPN · Leibniz-Institut für die Pädagogik der Naturwissenschaften und Mathematik, Olshausenstr. 62, 24118 Kiel
E-Mail: *jroloff@ipn.uni-kiel.de*

Gibt es einen Zusammenhang zwischen fachdidaktischem Wissen von Lehrkräften über Schülervorstellungen und dem naturwissenschaftlichen Wissen von Grundschulkindern?

THILO KLEICKMANN, MIRJAM STEFFENSKY UND HEIKE WENDT

ZUSAMMENFASSUNG: Fachdidaktisches Wissen von Lehrkräften ist ein zentraler Bereich der professionellen Kompetenz von Lehrkräften. Eine Facette dieses Wissens stellt das Wissen über Schülervorstellungen in einem konkreten Inhaltsgebiet dar. Die vorliegende Studie untersuchte anhand von Daten aus TIMSS 2015 die Frage, inwieweit dieses fachdidaktische Wissen bei Grundschullehrkräften in Deutschland mit dem naturwissenschaftlichen Wissen von Schülerinnen und Schülern in Beziehung steht. Die hier untersuchte Stichprobe setzte sich aus Daten von 154 Lehrkräften und 2857 Grundschulkindern zusammen. Die Lehrkräfte schätzten bei einer Auswahl von Multiple-Choice-Aufgaben aus dem TIMSS-Test ein, wie viele Schülerinnen und Schüler (in Prozent) einer fiktiven, leistungsmäßig durchschnittlichen vierten Klasse in Deutschland die einzelnen Antwortalternativen wählen würden. Die Abweichung der Einschätzungen der Lehrkräfte von den objektiven empirischen Daten (relative Antworthäufigkeiten) aus TIMSS wurde als Maß für das Wissen über Schülervorstellungen genutzt (niedrige Abweichung in Prozentpunkten als Indikator für hohes Wissen). In Mehrebenenanalysen zeigte sich, dass mit diesem Maß das naturwissenschaftliche Wissen der Schülerinnen und Schüler vorhergesagt werden konnte. Die Ergebnisse unterstreichen die Bedeutung des fachdidaktischen Wissens von Lehrkräften für den Lernerfolg von Schülerinnen und Schülern.

Schlüsselwörter: Fachdidaktisches Wissen, Schülervorstellungen, Naturwissenschaften, Schülerleistung, Mehrebenenanalyse, TIMSS 2015, Grundschule

Is Teachers' pedagogical content knowledge of student conceptions related to elementary school children's scientific knowledge?

ABSTRACT: Pedagogical content knowledge is a core component of teacher competence. Knowledge of content-specific student conceptions is a facet of that knowledge. Using data from TIMSS 2015, the present study investigated whether elementary school teachers' knowledge of student conceptions was related to students' scientific knowledge. In all, 154 teachers and 2,857 students participated in the present study. Based on a selection of multiple choice items from the TIMSS test, teachers judged the proportion of students in a class with average science achievement choosing the respective answers. The deviation of teachers' judgements from the objective empirical data from TIMSS was used as a measure of teacher knowledge of student conceptions (low values indicating high knowledge). Multilevel analyses revealed that teacher knowledge was related to students' scientific knowledge. The results highlight the role of teachers' pedagogical content knowledge for student achievement.

Keywords: pedagogical content knowledge, student conceptions, science, student achievement, multilevel analysis, TIMSS 2015, elementary school

Einleitung

Nicht erst seit den Arbeiten von Shulman (1986–1987) zum fachdidaktischen Wissen von Lehrkräften wird davon ausgegangen, dass Lehrkräfte Wissen darüber benötigen, welche Vorstellungen Schülerinnen und Schüler in den einzelnen Inhaltsgebieten eines Faches haben. Dieses Wissen sei erforderlich, um Lernschwierigkeiten zu identifizieren, den Unterricht an die Lernvoraussetzungen anpassen und verständnisvolles Lernen der Schülerinnen und Schüler unterstützen zu können (Ausubel, Novak & Hanesian, 1978; Morrison & Lederman, 2003; Shulman, 1987). In den auf Shulmans Arbeiten aufbauenden Konzeptionen zum fachdidaktischen Wissen von Lehrkräften spiegelt sich diese Annahme deutlich wider. Das Wissen über inhaltsspezifische Schülervorstellungen stellt neben dem Wissen über inhaltsspezifische Lehrstrategien und Darstellungsformen eine der beiden zentralen Komponenten des fachdidaktischen Wissens dar (Depaepe, Verschaffel & Kelchtermans, 2013; Gess-Newsome, 2015).

Sadler, Sonnert, Coyle, Cook-Smith und Miller (2013) haben ein Verfahren zur Erfassung des Wissens über Schülervorstellungen vorgestellt, bei dem Lehrkräfte sowie Schülerinnen und Schüler dieselben Multiple-Choice-Aufgaben zum Fachwissen in Physik vorgelegt werden. Die Lehrkräfte müssen einschätzen, welche der vorgegebenen falschen Antworten (Distraktoren) von den Schülerinnen und Schülern am häufigsten gewählt wird. Auf diese Weise kann ermittelt werden, inwieweit die Einschätzungen der Lehrkräfte mit den empirisch gefundenen relativen Antworthäufigkeiten der Schülerinnen und Schüler übereinstimmen. Dieses Verfahren basiert analog zu den Verfahren zur Erfassung der diagnostischen Kompetenz von Lehrkräften (Machts, Kaiser, Schmidt & Möller, 2016; Südkamp, Kaiser & Möller, 2012) auf einer objektiven Referenz (hier die empirischen relativen Antworthäufigkeiten) zur Beurteilung des Wissens über Schülervorstellungen. Im vorliegenden Beitrag wird dieser Ansatz für die Erfassung des fachdidaktischen Wissens von Grundschullehrkräften über Schülervorstellungen in den Naturwissenschaften genutzt. Naturwissenschaften werden in Deutschland im Grundschulbereich im Rahmen des Faches Sachunterricht behandelt. Anhand von Daten der *Trends in Mathematics and Science Study* (TIMSS) 2015 wird untersucht, inwieweit das Wissen der Lehrkräfte über Schülervorstellungen mit dem naturwissenschaftlichen Wissen der Schülerinnen und Schüler in Beziehung steht.

1 Theoretischer Hintergrund

1.1 Wissen von Lehrkräften über Schülervorstellungen in den Naturwissenschaften

Forschung zu Schülervorstellungen in den Naturwissenschaften hat gezeigt, dass Schülerinnen und Schüler Vorstellungen zu Naturphänomenen haben, die häufig nicht mit den naturwissenschaftlichen Sichtweisen übereinstimmen. Diese Schülervorstellungen resultieren u.a. aus früheren Erfahrungen mit dem Phänomen, aus der Alltagssprache oder sie werden spontan generiert. Schülervorstellungen umfassen sowohl theorieartige und kohärente Vorstellungen als auch fragmentierte Vorstellungen, die von Schülerinnen und Schülern ad hoc konstruiert werden, wenn ein Naturphänomen erklärt werden soll (diSessa, 2013; Driver, 2007; Duit & Treagust, 2003; Murphy & Mason, 2006; Wandersee, Novak & Mintzes, 1994). Konfligieren Schülervorstellungen mit fachlichen Konzepten, erfordert naturwissenschaftliches Lernen eine Veränderung der ursprünglichen Vorstellungen. Die zugrunde liegenden Lernprozesse werden als Conceptual Change bezeichnet. Sie umfassen Wissenserweiterungen und -differenzierungen sowie im Falle theorieartiger Vorstellungen auch eine Reorganisation des Wissens (Murphy & Mason, 2006; Vosniadou, 2013a). Schülervorstellungen werden vor diesem Hintergrund als zentraler Ausgangspunkt für die Gestaltung naturwissenschaftlichen Unterrichts angesehen (Duit & Treagust, 2003; Vosniadou, 2013b).

Theoretische Konzeptionen zum fachdidaktischen Wissen von Lehrkräften greifen diese Theorien zum naturwissenschaftlichen Lernen auf und heben die Bedeutung des Wissens von Lehrkräften über Schülervorstellungen hervor (z. B. Gess-Newsome, 2015, Shulman, 1987). Dabei können zwei Aspekte dieses Wissens unterschieden werden. Einige Studien untersuchen das Wissen von Lehrkräften über allgemeine, nicht inhaltsspezifische Eigenschaften von Schülervorstellungen in den Naturwissenschaften und über Verfahren zur Diagnose der Vorstellungen im Unterricht (z. B. Gomez-Zwiep, 2008; Larkin, 2012; Morrison & Lederman, 2003). Andere Studien untersuchen das Wissen von Lehrkräften über Schülervorstellungen inhaltsspezifisch, d. h. in konkreten naturwissenschaftlichen Inhaltsbereichen (z. B. zu Bewegung und Kräften oder zu Materie). Diese Studien zeigen, dass es deutliche Wissensunterschiede zwischen Lehrkräften gibt (z. B. Lucero, Petrosino & Delgado 2017; Otero & Nathan, 2008; Sadler et al., 2013).

Weitgehend unklar ist, inwiefern das Wissen über Schülervorstellungen bereits im Rahmen formaler Lerngelegenheiten in der Ausbildung entsteht und welche Bedeutung der Unterrichtserfahrung als informellen Lerngelegenheit zukommt. Bisherige Studien zum fachdidaktischen Wissen geben Hinweise darauf, dass formale Lerngelegenheiten im Rahmen der Erstausbildung eine wichtige Rolle zu spielen scheinen, während die Lehrerfahrung nicht mit den Wissensständen der Lehrkräfte in Beziehung zu stehen scheint (Friedrichsen et al., 2009; Kleickmann et al., 2013; Schneider & Plasman, 2011).

1.2 Bedeutung für den Lernerfolg von Schülerinnen und Schülern

Das Wissen von Lehrkräften über Schülervorstellungen wird als wichtige Ressource angesehen, um Unterricht an die Voraussetzungen der Schülerinnen und Schüler anpassen und fachbezogenes Lernen unterstützen zu können (Ausubel et al., 1978; Gess-Newsome, 2015; Morrison & Lederman, 2003; Shulman, 1986). Inhaltsspezifische Vorstellungen von Lernenden antizipieren zu können sollte bspw. eine wichtige Ressource darstellen, um Lernschwierigkeiten identifizieren und schließlich Lerngelegenheiten gestalten zu können, die Schülervorstellungen gezielt herausfordern und eine Differenzierung oder Restrukturierung des Wissens unterstützen (Larkin, 2012; Morrison & Lederman, 2003).

Bislang gibt es nur wenige Studien, die diese Annahmen empirisch überprüft haben. Zwar gibt es insbesondere aus dem Bereich Mathematik Befunde, die die Bedeutung des fachdidaktischen Wissens von Lehrkräften für fachliche Lernerfolge der Schülerinnen und Schüler zeigen (Baumert et al., 2010; Hill, Rowan & Ball, 2005). Allerdings untersuchen diese Studien nicht die prädiktive Kraft einzelner Facetten des fachdidaktischen Wissens. Unklar ist daher, welche spezifische Bedeutung dem Wissen über Schülervorstellungen zukommt. Erste Befunde zu dieser Frage liefert die Studie von Sadler et al. (2013), die das Wissen von Lehrkräften über Schülervorstellungen im Bereich der Mittelstufen-Physik untersucht. Hier zeigt sich, dass es deutliche interindividuelle Unterschiede im Wissen über Schülervorstellungen zwischen Lehrkräften gibt und dass mit diesem Wissen der Lehrkräfte die Lernfortschritte der Schülerinnen und Schüler vorhergesagt werden können (Sadler et al., 2013). Beim fachdidaktischen Wissen von Lehrkräften über Schülervorstellungen handelt es sich somit um einen potenziell zentralen Bereich der Kompetenz von Lehrkräften, der allerdings bislang noch unzureichend empirisch untersucht ist.

2 Die vorliegende Studie

Die vorliegende Studie verfolgt das Ziel, das fachdidaktische Wissen von Lehrkräften über Schülervorstellungen zu erfassen und dessen Relevanz für den fachbezogenen Lernerfolg von Grundschulkindern im Bereich Naturwissenschaften zu untersuchen. Zwar liegen Studien vor, die das Wissen von Lehrkräften über Schülervorstellungen beschrieben haben (Lucero et al., 2017; Otero & Nathan, 2008; Sadler et al., 2013), Evidenz zur Relevanz dieses Wissens der Lehrkräfte für das Lernen von Schülerinnen und Schülern ist allerdings bislang rar. Die unseres Wissens einzige Studie, die spezifisch die Relevanz des Wissens über Schülervorstellungen untersucht hat, ist die Studie von Sadler et al. (2013). In der vorliegenden Studie nutzen wir in Anlehnung an diese Studie (Sadler et al., 2013) ein Maß für das fachdidaktische Wissen über Schülervorstellungen (siehe Abschnitt 3.2.1), bei dem ebenfalls objektive empirische Daten als Referenz zur Beurteilung des Wissens herangezogen werden. Zunächst interessiert uns (Fragestellung 1), wie das Wissen der Grundschullehrkräfte über

Schülervorstellungen ausgeprägt ist, d.h., wie genau Lehrkräfte das Vorkommen inhaltsspezifischer Schülervorstellungen bei Viertklässlerinnen und Viertklässlern im Bereich Naturwissenschaften einschätzen können. Außerdem beschäftigen wir uns mit der Frage (Fragestellung 2), inwiefern sich Lehrkräfte mit und ohne formale Ausbildung im Fach Sachunterricht im Wissen über Schülervorstellungen unterscheiden und wie das Wissen mit der Lehrerfahrung der Lehrkräfte korreliert. Im Zentrum der vorliegenden Studie steht die Frage (Fragestellung 3), inwiefern das Wissen der Lehrkräfte über Schülervorstellungen in Zusammenhang mit dem im Rahmen von TIMSS 2015 erfassten naturwissenschaftlichen Wissen der Schülerinnen und Schüler steht (prädiktive Validität des Wissens).

3 Methode

3.1 Untersuchungsanlage und Stichproben

Für die vorliegende Studie nutzten wir Daten der für Deutschland vorliegenden Teilstichprobe aus TIMSS 2015 Grundschule (Wendt, Bos, Kasper, Walzebug, Goy & Jusufi, 2016). Im Rahmen von TIMSS 2015 Grundschule wurden in einem zweistufigen auf stratifizierten Zufallsziehungen beruhenden Verfahren zunächst Schulen und dann je Schule eine Klasse des vierten Jahrgangs gezogen, die an der Studie teilnahm. Die Schülerinnen und Schüler dieser Klassen bearbeiteten u.a. den TIMSS-Test zum naturwissenschaftlichen Wissen. Die Lehrkräfte, die in den ausgewählten Klassen das Fach Sachunterricht unterrichteten, bearbeiteten einen Fragebogen (Wendt et al., 2016). Dieser Fragebogen beinhaltete u.a. den Test zum fachdidaktischen Wissen über Schülervorstellungen. Insgesamt bearbeiteten 203 Sachunterrichtslehrkräfte den Lehrerfragebogen (90 % der Zielstichprobe). Von diesen Lehrkräften bearbeiteten 154 Lehrkräfte den Test zum Wissen über Schülervorstellungen (68 % der Zielstichprobe). An der vorliegenden Studie nahmen somit 154 Grundschullehrkräfte und die von ihnen im Fach Sachunterricht unterrichteten Schülerinnen und Schüler (n = 2,857) der jeweiligen TIMSS-Klasse teil.

Die Lehrkräfte waren im Durchschnitt M = 46.2 Jahre alt (SD = 12.2; Spannweite = 25 bis 64 Jahre) und unterrichteten im Durchschnitt seit M = 20.0 Jahren als Lehrkraft (SD = 12.6; Spannweite = 1 bis 43 Jahre). 90.8 % waren weiblich. Die Schülerinnen und Schüler waren im Durchschnitt M = 10.3 Jahre alt (SD = 0.5) und 47.8 % waren weiblich. Bei 22.0 % der Schülerinnen und Schüler sind beide Elternteile nicht in Deutschland geboren. Ein sonderpädagogischer Förderbedarf wurde bei 5.3 % der Schülerinnen und Schüler diagnostiziert.

3.2 Instrumente

3.2.1 Erfassung des Wissens der Lehrkräfte über Schülervorstellungen

Den Lehrkräften wurden 10 veröffentlichte Multiple-Choice-Aufgaben vorgelegt, die bei TIMSS 2011 Grundschule (Bos, Wendt, Köller & Selter, 2012) zur Erfassung des naturwissenschaftlichen Wissens der Schülerinnen und Schüler eingesetzt wurden. Drei Aufgaben stammten aus dem Bereich Geografie (naturgeografische Perspektive), drei Aufgaben aus dem Bereich Biologie und vier Aufgaben aus dem Bereich Physik/Chemie. Jede der 10 Aufgaben hatte vier Antwortalternativen: Eine korrekte Antwort (Attraktor) und drei falsche Antworten (Distraktoren). Die Lehrkräfte sollten für jede der vier Antwortalternativen angeben, welcher Anteil (in Prozent) der Schülerinnen und Schüler einer durchschnittlich leistungsfähigen vierten Klasse in Deutschland die jeweilige Antwortalternative wählen würde (Abbildung 1). Da aus den empirischen Daten aus TIMSS 2011 Grundschule für jede Antwortalternative bekannt war, welcher Anteil der Schülerinnen und Schüler in Deutschland die jeweilige Antwortalternative gewählt hatte, konnten jeweils die Abweichungen der Einschätzungen der Lehrkräfte von den empirisch gefundenen Werten errechnet werden. Je größer der Betrag dieser Differenz war, desto schlechter konnte die Lehrkraft den Anteil der Schülerinnen und Schüler einschätzen, die einen Distraktor als plausibel bzw. korrekt erachten.

Aufgabe 8 **Welche der zwei Gegenstände erzeugen ihr eigenes Licht?**	**Antwortmöglichkeiten**	**Anteil der Schülerinnen und Schüler in Prozent** (Durchschnittliche Klasse in Deutschland)
	A. Kerze und Mond	
	B. Mond und Spiegel	
	C. Sonne und Kerze	
	D. Spiegel und Sonne	
	Gesamt	**100 %**

Abbildung 1. Beispielaufgabe zum fachdidaktischen Wissen über Schülervorstellungen im Bereich Physik/Chemie.

In Anlehnung an das bei Sadler et al. (2013) gewählte Verfahren nutzten wir in der vorliegenden Studie pro Aufgabe jene Distraktoren, die von den Schülerinnen und Schülern am häufigsten gewählt wurden. Diese Distraktoren beinhalteten also eine naturwissenschaftlich inkorrekte Antwort, die aber vielen Schülerinnen und Schülern als plausible, korrekte Antwort erschien (in Abbildung 1: Antwort D). Gleichzeitig wurde darauf geachtet, dass die drei Inhaltsbereiche Geografie, Biologie und Physik/Chemie im Test zum Wissen über Schülervorstellungen ähnlich stark repräsentiert waren wie im TIMSS-Test zur Erfassung des naturwissenschaftlichen Wissens der

Schülerinnen und Schüler (siehe folgender Abschnitt). Dazu wurden drei weitere häufig gewählte Distraktoren aus den Bereichen Geografie und Biologie ergänzt. Die so gebildete Skala basierte auf 13 Distraktoren (Cronbachs Alpha = .61).

3.2.2 Erfassung des naturwissenschaftlichen Wissens der Schülerinnen und Schüler

Zur Erfassung des naturwissenschaftlichen Wissens der Schülerinnen und Schüler wurde der in TIMSS 2015 für die Jahrgangsstufe 4 eingesetzte Test verwendet. Der Test umfasste 168 Aufgaben aus den Inhaltsbereichen Geografie (33 Aufgaben), Biologie (74 Aufgaben) und Physik/Chemie (61 Aufgaben). Etwa die Hälfte der Aufgaben (82) waren Multiple-Choice-Aufgaben. Die übrigen 86 Aufgaben erforderten eine kurze schriftliche Antwort von den Schülerinnen und Schüler oder die Zuordnung verschiedener Begriffe (Steffensky, Kleickmann, Kasper & Köller, 2016).

Da jeder Schülerin bzw. jedem Schüler nur ein Teil der Aufgaben vorgelegt wurde (Multi-Matrix-Design), wurden mit Verfahren der Item-Response-Theory für jede Schülerin bzw. jeden Schüler fünf Plausible Values ermittelt. Diese wurden in der vorliegenden Studie verwendet. Der Gesamttest hatte eine Reliabilität von $Rel_{EAP/PV} = .75$. Die Intra-Klassen-Korrelation lag in der Stichprobe der vorliegenden Studie mit 154 Klassen bei $ICC = 0.20$, d.h. 20% der Varianz im naturwissenschaftlichen Wissen lag zwischen den Klassen.

3.3 Analyseverfahren

Fragestellung 1 (Deskription des Wissens) wurde mit deskriptiven Analysen, Fragestellung 2 (Bedeutung der Ausbildung im Fach und der Lehrerfahrung) mit varianzanalytischen und korrelativen Verfahren und Fragestellung 3 (prädiktive Validität des Wissens) mit Mehrebenenanalysen (Random Intercept Models; Maximum-Likelihood-Schätzung mit robusten Standardfehlern; Raudenbush & Bryk, 2002) untersucht. Die zentrale unabhängige Variable war dabei das fachdidaktische Wissen der Lehrkräfte. Als abhängige Variable wurde das in TIMSS 2015 erfasste naturwissenschaftliche Wissen der Schülerinnen und Schüler genutzt. Auf Ebene der Schülerinnen und Schüler (Ebene 1) und auf Klassenebene (Ebene 2) wurde eine Reihe von Kovariaten berücksichtigt, um dafür zu kontrollieren, dass Schülerinnen und Schüler den Klassen bzw. Lehrkräften nicht zufällig zugewiesen wurden. Kovariaten auf Ebene 1 waren das Geschlecht der Schülerinnen und Schüler, der Bildungshintergrund (operationalisiert über die Zahl der zu Hause verfügbaren Bücher), der sozioökonomische Status der Berufstätigkeit der Eltern (HISEI; Ganzeboom, De Graaf, Treiman & De Loeff, 1992), Deutsch als hauptsächlich verwendete Sprache zu Hause, das Vorliegen eines diagnostizierten sonderpädagogischen Förderbedarfs und ein Maß für kognitive Grundfähigkeiten (Subtest Reihenfortsetzen aus dem CFT 20-

R; Weiß, 2006). Auf Ebene 2 wurden das Niveau in Bezug auf kognitive Grundfähigkeiten und sozioökonomischen Status als Kovariaten berücksichtigt (latent covariate approach; Lüdtke et al., 2008).

Während für alle teilnehmenden Schülerinnen und Schüler Daten zum naturwissenschaftlichen Wissen vorlagen (plausible values), gab es im Test zum Wissen über Schülervorstellungen und auf den Kovariaten fehlende Werte mit einem Anteil von durchschnittlich je 9.1 Prozent (SD = 2.4). Fehlende Werte wurden mit dem in *Mplus* implementierten Baysianischen Verfahren imputiert (10 Imputationen). Diese Prozedur wurde auf jeden Datensatz mit je einem plausible value für das naturwissenschaftliche Wissen angewandt, so dass insgesamt 50 Datensätze mit vollständigen Daten resultierten. Die Analysen der 50 Datensätze wurden mit *Mplus* (Muthén & Muthén, 2015) durchgeführt und kombiniert.

4 Ergebnisse

Zur Beschreibung des Wissens der Lehrkräfte über Schülervorstellungen (Fragestellung 1) ermittelten wir zunächst die mittleren absoluten Abweichungen der Einschätzungen der Lehrkräfte von den empirischen relativen Antworthäufigkeiten der Schülerinnen und Schüler aus TIMSS 2011. Über die 13 Aufgaben unseres Maßes für das Wissen über Schülervorstellungen wichen die Lehrkräfte im Durchschnitt M = 13.6 Prozentpunkte (SD = 3.6) von den empirischen Häufigkeiten ab. Da diese Werte auf den Beträgen der Differenzwerte basierten, ermittelten wir zu explorativen Zwecken auch die Differenzwerte pro Aufgabe unter Berücksichtigung von negativen und positiven Abweichungen, um eine Über- bzw. Unterschätzung der Häufigkeiten von Schülervorstellungen analysieren zu können. Hier zeigte sich in fast allen Aufgaben, dass die Lehrkräfte den Anteil der Schülerinnen und Schüler, die die jeweilige Antwortmöglichkeit für korrekt erachteten, unterschätzten. Die Differenzwerte je Aufgabe lagen im Durchschnitt bei M = –8.6 Prozentpunkten (SD = 12.3). Bei den beiden Aufgaben mit den stärksten Abweichungen von Null lagen die mittleren Differenzwerte bei M = –21.6 und M = –15.7 Prozentpunkten. Zu diesen Aufgaben gehörte auch die in Abbildung 1 gezeigte Aufgabe. Bei den beiden Aufgaben mit den geringsten Abweichungen von Null unterschieden sich die Werte mit 0.1 Prozentpunkten und –2.0 Prozentpunkten nur deskriptiv von Null. Die Standardabweichungen der Differenzwerte pro Aufgabe (Spannweite von 8.8 bis 16.3) zeigten, dass es deutliche Unterschiede zwischen Grundschullehrkräften im Wissen über Schülervorstellungen gab.

Im Hinblick auf Fragestellung 2 zeigte sich, dass ein Teil dieser Variation in Beziehung mit formalen Lerngelegenheiten im Rahmen der Ausbildung stand. Bei Lehrkräften, die das Fach Sachunterricht studiert hatten, lag der Mittelwert der absoluten Abweichungen mit M = 13.1 Prozentpunkten (SD = 5.0) signifikant niedriger als bei Lehrkräften, die das Fach nicht studiert hatten (M = 14.7 Prozentpunkte, SD = 2.9), $F(1, 153) = 6.163$, $p = .01$, $\eta^2 = .04$, $d = 0.39$). Die Berufserfahrung hingegen stand nicht mit den Wissensständen der Lehrkräfte in Beziehung ($r = -.01$, $p = .86$).

Schließlich untersuchten wir (Fragestellung 3), inwiefern das Wissen der Lehrkräfte über Schülervorstellungen mit dem naturwissenschaftlichen Wissen der Schülerinnen und Schüler in Beziehung steht. Hier zeigte sich in den Mehrebenenanalysen zunächst (Modell 1, Tabelle 1), dass auf Individualebene alle Kovariaten in signifikantem Zusammenhang mit dem naturwissenschaftlichen Wissen der Schülerinnen und Schülern standen. Die beiden stärksten Prädiktoren waren das verwendete Maß der kognitiven Grundfähigkeit und der sozioökonomische Hintergrund. Diese beiden Merkmale wurden auch auf Klassenebene als Kompositionsmerkmale berücksichtigt. Beide Merkmale der Klassenkomposition standen in signifikantem Zusammenhang mit dem naturwissenschaftlichen Wissen der Schülerinnen und Schüler. Die Varianzaufklärung auf Klassenebene war mit 61 % hoch.

Tabelle 1. Standardisierte Regressionsgewichte aus Mehrebenenanalysen zur Vorhersage des naturwissenschaftlichen Wissens der Schülerinnen und Schüler

	Modell 1		Modell 2		Modell 3	
	B	*SE*	*B*	*SE*	*B*	*SE*
Individualebene						
Geschlecht (0 = weibl.; 1 = männl.)	**.05**	.02	**.05**	.02	**.05**	.02
Kognitive Fähigkeiten	**.30**	.02	**.31**	.02	**.30**	.02
Sozio-ökonom. Hintergrund	**.21**	.02	**.22**	.02	**.21**	.02
Bildungshintergrund	**.15**	.02	**.15**	.02	**.15**	.02
Deutsch zu Hause (0 = nein; 1 = ja)	**.15**	.02	**.15**	.02	**.15**	.02
SPF (0 = nein; 1 = ja)	**–.15**	.02	**–.15**	.02	**–.15**	.02
R^2	.28		.30		.28	
Klassenebene						
Wissen über Schülervorstellungen			**–.25**	.10	**–.23**	.08
Kognitive Fähigkeiten	**.60**	.13			**.60**	.12
Sozio-ökonom. Hintergrund	**.31**	.13			**.33**	.13
R^2	.61		.06		.66	

Anmerkung. Fettgesetzte Koeffizienten sind signifikant ($p < .05$); SPF = Sonderpädagogischer Förderbedarf.

Wurde auf Klassenebene das Wissen der Lehrkräfte über Schülervorstellungen zusätzlich eingefügt (Modell 3), zeigte sich, dass dieses in einem signifikanten und negativen Zusammenhang mit dem in TIMSS 2015 erfassten naturwissenschaftlichen Wissen der Schülerinnen und Schüler stand. Je besser die Lehrkräfte einschätzen konnten, welcher Anteil von Viertklässlerinnen und Viertklässlern die vorgelegten Schülervorstellungen als korrekt annahm, desto besser war das naturwissenschaftliche Wissen der Schülerinnen und Schüler. Das standardisierte Regressionsgewicht für das Wissen der Lehrkräfte betrug $B = -.23$ ($SE = .07$). Die durch das Wissen der

Lehrkräfte zusätzlich erklärte Varianz auf Klassenebene (Vergleich von Modell 1 und 3) betrug 5 %. Unter Ausschluss der Merkmale der Klassenkomposition (Modell 2) war das Regressionsgewicht für das Wissen über Schülervorstellungen etwa so groß wie in Modell 3.

5 Diskussion

5.1 Zusammenfassung und Implikationen

In der vorliegenden Studie untersuchten wir das Wissen von Grundschullehrkräften über inhaltsspezifische Schülervorstellungen in den Naturwissenschaften. In Bezug auf unsere Fragestellung 1 (Deskription des Wissens) zeigte sich, dass Lehrkräfte den Anteil der Schülerinnen und Schüler, die eine bestimmte Schülervorstellung für korrekt erachteten, bei den meisten Aufgaben unterschätzten. Bei einigen Aufgaben zeigte sich eine deutliche Unterschätzung (21.6 und 15.7 Prozentpunkte bei den beiden Aufgaben mit den größten Abweichungen von Null). Im Durchschnitt schätzten die Lehrkräfte den Anteil der Schülerinnen und Schüler, die eine Schülervorstellung wählten, um 8.6 Prozentpunkte zu niedrig ein. Die Unterschiede zwischen den Lehrkräften waren wie auch in den Studien von Lucero et al. (2017) und Sadler et al. (2013) groß. Im Hinblick auf Fragestellung 2 zeigte sich, dass ein Teil dieser Unterschiede durch formale Lerngelegenheiten im Rahmen der Ausbildung aufgeklärt werden konnte. Lehrkräfte, die das Fach Sachunterricht studiert, also fachliche und/oder fachdidaktische Veranstaltungen in diesem Bereich absolviert hatten, konnten das Vorkommen der Schülervorstellungen bei kleiner bis mittlerer Effektgröße ($d = 0.39$) besser einschätzen als Lehrkräfte, die das Fach nicht studiert hatten. Während das Wissen mit diesen formalen Lerngelegenheiten im Studium assoziiert war, zeigte sich kein Zusammenhang mit der Lehrerfahrung der Lehrkräfte. Die Lehrerfahrung (operationalisiert als Dauer der Berufstätigkeit) schien nicht hinreichend zu sein, um das Vorkommen von inhaltsspezifischen Schülervorstellungen einschätzen zu können.

Im Hinblick auf Fragestellung 3 (prädiktive Validität) zeigte sich, dass das Wissen der Lehrkräfte über Schülervorstellungen mit dem in TIMSS 2015 Grundschule erfassten naturwissenschaftlichen Wissen der Schülerinnen und Schüler in Beziehung stand. Je besser Lehrkräfte den Anteil der Schülerinnen und Schüler einschätzen konnten, die eine bestimmte Schülervorstellung für korrekt erachteten, desto besser schnitten die Schülerinnen und Schüler im TIMSS-Test ab.

Insgesamt betrachtet stehen die Ergebnisse der vorliegenden Studie zu Zusammenhängen des Wissens von Lehrkräften über Schülervorstellungen mit formalen und informellen Lerngelegenheiten (hier: Sachunterrichtsstudium bzw. Lehrerfahrung) in Einklang mit bisherigen Befunden zum fachdidaktischen Wissen (Friedrichsen et al., 2009; Kleickmann et al., 2013; Schneider & Plasman, 2011). Der zentrale Befund der vorliegenden Studie zum Zusammenhang des Wissens der Lehrkräfte über Schülervorstellungen mit dem Lernerfolg von Grundschulkindern im Bereich Naturwissenschaften steht in Einklang mit den Befunden von Sadler et al. (2013) aus dem Bereich der Mittelstufen-Physik. Außerdem ergänzt der Befund die bisherigen Befunde zum Einfluss des fachdidaktischen Wissens auf den Lernerfolg von Schülerinnen und Schülern (Baumert et al., 2010; Hill et al., 2005). Die vorliegende Studie beleuchtet jedoch im Unterschied zu diesen Studien eine spezifische Facette des fachdidaktischen Wissens, das Wissen über Schülervorstellungen, konkret das Wissen über das Vorkommen inhaltsspezifischer Schülervorstellungen. Die Ergebnisse der vorliegenden Studie stehen im Einklang mit der theoretischen Annahme, dass dieses Wissen der Lehrkräfte eine wichtige Ressource für eine adäquate Unterstützung verständnisvollen Lernens der Schülerinnen und Schüler darstellt (Sadler et al., 2013; Vosniadou, 2013b).

Die Befunde der vorliegenden Studie zeigen Perspektiven für die Fortbildung von Grundschullehrkräften im Bereich Naturwissenschaften auf. Grundschullehrkräfte unterschätzen offenbar die Verbreitung von Schülervorstellungen in den Naturwissenschaften bei Schülerinnen und Schülern. Gleichzeitig steht dieses Wissen von Lehrkräften über Schülervorstellungen mit dem naturwissenschaftlichen Wissen der Schülerinnen und Schüler in Beziehung. Mit Blick auf die Gestaltung von Lehrerfortbildungen lässt sich also erstens folgern, dass inhaltsspezifische Schülervorstellungen ein wichtiger Fortbildungsinhalt sein sollten. Insbesondere gilt dies für Lehrkräfte, die nicht das Fach Sachunterricht studiert haben, also fachfremd unterrichten. In Übereinstimmung mit dieser Folgerung heben Forschungsübersichten zur Wirksamkeit von Lehrerfortbildungen hervor (Desimone, 2009; Lipowsky, 2011), dass wirksame Fortbildungen einen Schwerpunkt auf fachliche Inhalte sowie inhaltsspezifische Lernschwierigkeiten, Schülervorstellungen und Lehrstrategien setzen (content focus). Zweitens deuten die Befunde von Sadler et al. (2013) und auch die recht geringe interne Konsistenz des in dieser Studie verwendeten Tests darauf hin, dass es über generelle Niveauunterschiede im Wissen über Schülervorstellungen zwischen Lehrkräften auch deutliche interindividuelle Unterschiede im Wissen über Schülervorstellungen in einzelnen Inhaltsgebieten gibt. Daher scheint es sinnvoll, das Wissen der Lehrkräfte über Schülervorstellungen in den entsprechenden Inhaltsgebieten zu diagnostizieren, damit auf dieser Basis entsprechende Lerngelegenheiten geschaffen und individuelle Lücken im Wissen geschlossen werden können (Sadler et al., 2013).

5.2 Stärken und Einschränkungen

In der vorliegenden Studie nutzten wir ein Verfahren, das in Anlehnung an die Studie von Sadler et al. (2013) entwickelt, aber in einigen Punkten modifiziert wurde. Während Sadler et al. (2013) die Lehrkräfte baten, pro Testaufgabe die häufigste Schülervorstellung zu identifizieren, ermittelten wir die Abweichung der Lehrkrafteinschätzungen von den empirisch gefundenen relativen Antworthäufigkeiten, so dass wir kontinuierliche Indikatoren für das Wissen erhielten. Ein weiterer Unterschied zu dem von Sadler et al. (2013) verwendeten Verfahren bestand darin, dass die in der vorliegenden Studie verwendeten Distraktoren des TIMSS-Tests nur zum Teil auf solchen Schülervorstellungen basierten, die in der Literatur als theorieartige, kohärente Schülervorstellungen beschrieben wurden (z.B. Sadler et al., 2013; Wandersee, Mintzes & Novak, 1994). Die weiteren in dieser Studie verwendeten Distraktoren hatten allerdings ebenfalls für viele Schülerinnen und Schüler eine hohe spontane Plausibilität (ad hoc generierte Schülervorstellungen). Die Lehrkräfte mussten bei unserem Verfahren also das Vorkommen typischer kohärenter Schülervorstellungen wie auch solcher Vorstellungen beurteilen, die für viele Schülerinnen und Schüler eine spontane Plausibilität besaßen. Es ist davon auszugehen, dass Lehrkräfte im naturwissenschaftlichen Unterricht mit beiden Arten von Schülervorstellungen konfrontiert werden (diSessa, 2013; Vosniadou, 2013a).

Vorteile des Verfahrens von Sadler et al. (2013) wie auch des in der vorliegenden Studie eingesetzten Verfahrens lagen darin, dass sie von den Lehrkräften in verhältnismäßig kurzer Zeit bearbeitet und verhältnismäßig ökonomisch ausgewertet werden konnten. Außerdem basierten beide Verfahren analog zu den Verfahren zur Erfassung der diagnostischen Kompetenz von Lehrkräften auf einem objektiven, empirisch ermittelten Kriterium zur Beurteilung des Wissens (Machts et al., 2016; Südkamp et al., 2012). Eine Weiterentwicklung des Verfahrens könnte darin bestehen, das Auftreten von Schülervorstellungen für die Klasse beurteilen zu lassen, in der die jeweilige Lehrkraft unterrichtet. Diese Einschätzungen könnten möglicherweise für die Gestaltung herausfordernder und unterstützender Lerngelegenheiten im Unterricht noch bedeutsamer sein.

Eine Einschränkung der vorliegenden Studie waren die nur querschnittlichen, korrelativen Daten. Im Rahmen von TIMSS war keine Vortestleistung der Schülerinnen und Schüler verfügbar. Dafür konnte aber eine Reihe wichtiger Kovariaten in den Analysen berücksichtigt werden, darunter kognitive Grundfähigkeiten und weitere Merkmale auf Individual- und Klassenebene.

Schließlich wäre eine Ergänzung um ein Maß zum Fachwissen der Lehrkräfte wünschenswert gewesen. Möglicherweise konnten Lehrkräfte zwar die Verbreitung von Schülervorstellungen einschätzen, bewerteten aber die fachliche Angemessenheit der Vorstellungen falsch. Bei Sadler et al. (2013) zeigte sich allerdings, dass nur in zwei Prozent aller Einschätzungen der Lehrkräfte eine korrekte Benennung der häufigsten Schülervorstellung innerhalb einer MC-Aufgabe mit einer fachlich inkorrekten Beantwortung der entsprechenden Aufgabe einherging. In der vorliegenden Studie wiesen außerdem Lehrkräfte, die im Rahmen des Studiums fachliche und fachdidaktische Lerngelegenheiten erhalten hatten, ein höheres Wissen über Schülervorstellungen auf. Vermutlich verfügten diese Lehrkräfte auch über ein besseres Fachwissen. Ferner zeigte sich in der vorliegenden Studie auch der vermutete Zusammenhang mit dem Lernerfolg der Schülerinnen und Schüler. Das in dieser Studie erfasste Wissen über die Verbreitung bestimmter Schülervorstellungen stellt offenbar eine relevante Ressource für die Unterstützung verständnisvollen Lernens der Schülerinnen und Schüler dar (Morrison & Lederman, 2003). Dieses Wissen muss im Unterricht vermutlich mit Fachwissen zur fachlichen Bewertung der Schülervorstellungen, aber auch mit weiterem fachdidaktischen Wissen, bspw. über inhaltsspezifische Lehrstrategien, kombiniert werden (Depaepe et al., 2013). Für künftige Studien wäre es interessant zu untersuchen, wie verschiedene Komponenten des fachlichen und fachdidaktischen Wissens der Lehrkräfte zusammenspielen und wie Zusammenhänge des Wissens der Lehrkräfte mit dem naturwissenschaftlichen Wissen der Schülerinnen und Schüler über die Unterrichtsgestaltung vermittelt werden.

5.3 Folgerung

Die vorliegende Studie zeigt mit Hilfe eines relativ ökonomischen Maßes, dass das Wissen von Grundschullehrkräften über die Verbreitung von Schülervorstellungen mit dem naturwissenschaftlichen Wissen der Schülerinnen und Schüler zusammenhängt und dass Grundschullehrkräfte das Auftreten von Schülervorstellungen bei Schülerinnen und Schülern unterschätzen. Es scheint daher wichtig zu sein, Lehrkräfte bspw. im Rahmen von Fortbildungen mit inhaltsspezifischen Schülervorstellungen in den Naturwissenschaften und den daraus resultierenden Lernschwierigkeiten der Schülerinnen und Schüler vertraut zu machen.

Literatur

Ausubel, D. P., Novak, J. D. & Hanesian, H. (1978). *Educational psychology: A cognitive view.* New York, NY: Holt, Rinehart & Winston.

Baumert, J., Kunter, M., Blum, W., Brunner, M., Voss, T., Jordan, A. & Tsai, Y.-M. (2010). Teachers' mathematical knowledge, cognitive activation in the classroom, and student progress. *American Educational Research Journal, 47*, 133–180.

Bos, W., Wendt, H., Köller, O. & Selter, C. (Hrsg.). (2012). *TIMSS 2011. Mathematische und naturwissenschaftliche Kompetenzen von Grundschulkindern in Deutschland im internationalen Vergleich.* Münster: Waxmann.

Depaepe, F., Verschaffel, L. & Kelchtermans, G. (2013). Pedagogical content knowledge: A systematic review of the way in which the concept has pervaded mathematics educational research. *Teaching and Teacher Education, 34*, 12–25.

Desimone, L. M. (2009). Improving impact studies of teachers' professional development: Toward better conceptualizations and measures. *Educational Researcher, 38*, 181–199.

diSessa, A. (2013). A bird's-eye view of the "pieces" vs. "coherence" controversy (from the "pieces" side of the fence). In S. Vosniadou (Ed.), *International handbook of research on conceptual change* (2nd ed., pp. 31–48). New York, NY: Routledge.

Driver, R. (2007). Students' conceptions and the learning of science. *International Journal of Science Education, 11*, 481–490.

Duit, R. & Treagust, D. (2003). Conceptual change: A powerful framework for improving science teaching and learning.

International Journal of Science Education, 25, 671–688.

Friedrichsen, P. J., Abell, S. K., Pareja, E. M., Brown, P. L., Lankford, D. M. & Volkmann, M. J. (2009). Does teaching experience matter? Examining biology teachers' prior knowledge for teaching in an alternative certification program. *Journal of Research in Science Teaching, 46*, 357–383.

Ganzeboom, H. B. G., De Graaf, P. M., Treiman, D. J. & De Leeuw, J. (1992). A standard international socio-economic index of occupational status. *Social Science Research, 21*, 1–56.

Gess-Newsome, J. (2015). A model of teacher professional knowledge and skill including PCK: Results of the thinking from the PCK summit. In A. Berry, P. Friedrichsen & L. Loughran (Eds.), *Re-examining pedagogical content knowledge in science education* (pp. 28–42). New York, NY: Routledge.

Gomez-Zwiep, S. (2008). Elementary teachers' understanding of students' science misconceptions: Implications for practice and teacher education. *Journal of Science Teacher Education, 19*, 437–454.

Hill, H. C., Rowan, B. & Ball, D. (2005). Effects of teachers' mathematical knowledge for teaching on student achievement. *American Educational Research Journal, 42*, 371–406.

Kleickmann, T., Richter, D., Kunter, M., Elsner, J., Besser, M., Krauss, S. & Baumert, J. (2013). Teachers' pedagogical content knowledge and content knowledge: The role of structural differences in teacher education. *Journal of Teacher Education, 64*, 90–106.

Larkin, D. (2012). Misconceptions about "misconceptions": Preservice secondary science teachers' views on the value and role of student ideas. *Science Education, 96*, 927–959.

Lipowsky, F. (2011). Theoretische Perspektiven und empirische Befunde zur Wirksamkeit von Lehrerfort- und -weiterbildung. In E. Terhart, H. Bennewitz & M. Rothland (Hrsg.), *Handbuch der Forschung zum Lehrerberuf* (S. 398–417). Münster: Waxmann.

Lucero, M. M., Petrosino, A. J. & Delgado, C. (2017). Exploring the relationship between secondary science teachers' subject matter knowledge and knowledge of student conceptions while teaching evolution by natural selection. *Journal of Research in Science Teaching, 54*, 219–246.

Lüdtke, O., Marsh, H., Robitzsch, A., Trautwein, U., Asparouhov, T. & Muthén, B. (2008). The multilevel latent covariate model: A new, more reliable approach to group-level effects in contextual studies. *Psychological Methods, 13*, 203–229.

Machts, N., Kaiser, J., Schmidt, F. & Möller, J. (2016). Accuracy of teachers' judgments of students' cognitive abilities: A meta-analysis. *Educational Research Review, 19*, 85–103.

Morrison, J. & Lederman, N. (2003). Science teachers' diagnosis and understanding of students' preconceptions. *Science Education, 87*, 849–867.

Murphy, K. & Mason, L. (2006). Changing knowledge and beliefs. In P. Alexander & P. Winne (Eds.), *Handbook of educational psychology* (2nd ed., pp. 305-326). Mahwah, NJ: Lawrence Erlbaum Associates.

Muthén, L. K. & Muthén, B. O. (2015). *Mplus user's guide* (7th ed.). Los Angeles, CA: Authors.

Otero, V. & Nathan, M. (2008). Preservice elementary teachers' views of their students' prior knowledge of science. *Journal of Research in Science Teaching, 45*, 497–523.

Raudenbush, S. W. & Bryk, A. S. (2002). *Hierarchical linear models* (2nd ed.). Thousand Oaks, CA: Sage.

Sadler, P. M., Sonnert, G., Coyle, H. P., Cook-Smith, N. & Miller, J. L. (2013). The influence of teachers' knowledge on student learning in middle school physical science classrooms. *American Educational Research Journal, 50*, 1020–1049.

Schneider, R. & Plasman, K. (2011). Science teacher learning progressions: A review of science teachers' pedagogical content knowledge development. *Review of Educational Research, 81*, 530–565.

Shulman, L. S. (1986). Those who understand: Knowledge growth in teaching. *Educational Researcher, 15*, 4–14.

Shulman, L. S. (1987). Knowledge and teaching: Foundations of the new reform. *Harvard Educational Review, 57*, 1–22.

Steffensky, M., Kleickmann, T., Kasper, D. & Köller, O. (2016). Naturwissenschaftliche Kompetenzen im internationalen Vergleich. Testkonzeption und Ergebnisse. In H. Wendt, H., W. Bos, O. Köller, C. Selter & D. Kasper (Hrsg.), *TIMSS 2015 – Mathematische und naturwissenschaftliche Kompetenzen von Grundschulkindern in Deutschland im internationalen Vergleich* (S. 133–183). Münster: Waxmann.

Südkamp, A., Kaiser, J. & Möller, J. (2012). Accuracy of teachers' judgments of students' academic achievement: A meta-analysis. *Journal of Educational Psychology, 104*, 743–762.

Vosniadou, S. (2013a). Conceptual change in learning and instruction: The framework theory approach. In S. Vosniadou (Ed.), *International handbook of research on conceptual change* (2nd ed., pp. 11–30). New York, NY: Routledge.

Vosniadou, S. (Ed.). (2013b). *International handbook of research on conceptual change* (2nd ed.). New York, NY: Routledge.

Wandersee, J., Mintzes, J. & Novak, J. (1994). Research on alternative conceptions in science. In D. L. Gabel (Ed.), *Handbook of research on science teaching and learning* (pp. 177–210). New York, NY: Macmillan.

Weiß, R. (2006). *CFT 20-R. Grundintelligenztest Skala 2. Revision.* Göttingen: Hogrefe.

Wendt, H., Bos, W., Kasper, D. Walzebug, A., Goy, M. & Jusufi, D. (2016). Ziele, Anlage und Durchführung der Trends in International Mathematics and Science Study (TIMSS 2011). In H. Wendt, H., W. Bos, O. Köller, C. Selter & D. Kasper (Hrsg.), *TIMSS 2015 – Mathematische und naturwissenschaftliche Kompetenzen von Grundschulkindern in Deutschland im internationalen Vergleich* (S. 29–74). Münster: Waxmann.

Autorinnen und Autoren

PROF. DR. THILO KLEICKMANN
Institut für Pädagogik, Christian-Albrechts-Universität zu Kiel.

PROF. DR. MIRJAM STEFFENSKY
Abteilung Didaktik der Chemie, IPN · Leibniz-Institut für die Pädagogik der Naturwissenschaften und Mathematik, Kiel.

DR. HEIKE WENDT
Institut für Schulentwicklungsforschung, Technische Universität Dortmund.

KONTAKT
Thilo Kleickmann, Institut für Pädagogik, Christian-Albrechts-Universität zu Kiel, Olshausenstraße 75, 24118 Kiel.
E-Mail: *kleickmann@paedagogik.uni-kiel.de*

Verzeichnis der Gutachterinnen und Gutachter

Um die Qualität der Beiträge zu gewährleisten, wurde ein anonymes Begutachtungsverfahren mit insgesamt zwei Gutachten pro Beitrag vorgesehen. Wir möchten uns bei allen nachfolgend genannten Gutachterinnen und Gutachtern für die sorgfältige und zügige Prüfung der Manuskripte herzlich bedanken.

ARENS, A. KATRIN (Frankfurt)

BECHERER, JULIA (Kiel)

BERENDES, KARIN (Tübingen)

BIERMANN, ANTJE (Saarbrücken)

DICKE, THERESA (Strathfield, Australien)

DICKHÄUSER, OLIVER (Mannheim)

EDELE, AILEEN (Berlin)

FLECKENSTEIN, JOHANNA (Kiel)

GASPARD, HANNA (Tübingen)

GNIEWOSZ, BURKHARD (Salzburg, Österreich)

HANNOVER, BETTINA (Berlin)

HARMS, UTE (Kiel)

HELM, FRIEDERIKE (Kiel)

IHME, TONI A. (Hagen)

JANSEN, MALTE (Berlin)

JONKMANN, KATHRIN (Hagen)

KAISER, JOHANNA (Kiel)

KELLER, STEFAN (Basel, Schweiz)

KESSELS, URSULA (Berlin)

KLEICKMANN, THILO (Kiel)

KÖLLER, OLAF (Kiel)

MARTINY, SARAH E. (Tromsø, Norwegen)

MCELVANY, NELE (Dortmund)

NAGY, NICOLE (Kiel)

NIEPEL, CHRISTOPH (Esch-sur-Alzette, Luxemburg)

POHLMANN, BRITTA (Hamburg)

ROLOFF-BRUCHMANN, JANINA (Kiel)

RUMLICH, DOMINIK (Münster)

SCHMIDT, FABIAN T. C. (Kiel)

SCHÜTTE, KERSTIN (Kiel)

SOUVIGNIER, ELMAR (Münster)

STEINMAYR, RICARDA (Dortmund)

STREBLOW, LILIAN (Bielefeld)

STUTZ, FRANZISKA (Potsdam)